GREAT BRITAIN & IRELAND

TOURIST and MOTORING ATLAS / ATLAS ROUTIER et TOURISTIQUE
TOERISTISCHE WEGENATLAS / ATLANTE STRADALE e TURISTICO / ATLAS

GW00707922

Contents

Sommaire / Inhaltsübersicht / Inhoud / Sommario / Sumario

Inside front cover: key to map pages

Intérieur de couverture : tableau d'assemblage / Umschlaginnenseite: Übersicht / Binnenzijde van het omslag: overzichtskaart
-Copertina interna: quadro d'insieme / Portada interior: mapa índice

II - III

Channel Tunnel - Tunnel sous la Manche

Folkestone Terminal - Terminal de Calais (F)

Shipping Services

Liaisons maritimes / Schiffsverbindungen / Scheepvaartverbindingen / Collegamenti marittimi / Líneas marítimas

IV - XXI

Main road map

Grands axes routiers / Durchgangsstraßen / Grote verbindingswegen / Grandi arterie stradali / Carreteras principales
1 inch = 15.8 miles - 1:1 000 000 - 1 cm = 10 km

1 - 119

Key **1**

Légende / Zeichenerklärung / Verklaring van de tekens / Legenda / Signos convencionales

Great Britain & Ireland **2 - 119**

Grande-Bretagne & Irlande / Großbritannien & Irland / Groot-Brittannië & Ierland
Gran Bretagna & Irlanda / Gran Bretaña & Irlanda
1 inch = 4.75 miles - 1: 300 000 - 1 cm = 3 km

120 - 147

Index Great Britain **120 - 138**

Index Grande-Bretagne / Register Großbritannien / Register Groot-Brittannië / Indice Gran Bretagna / Índice Gran Bretaña

Index Ireland **139 - 147**

Index Irlande / Register Irland / Register Ierland / Indice Irlanda / Índice Irlanda

148 - 190

Key **148**

Légende / Zeichenerklärung / Verklaring van de tekens / Legenda / Signos convencionales

Town plans Great Britain **149 - 185**

Plans de ville Grande-Bretagne / Stadtpläne Großbritannien / Stadsplattegronden Groot-Brittannië
Piante di città Gran Bretagna / Planos de ciudades Gran Bretaña

Town plans Ireland **183 - 189**

Plans de ville Irlande / Stadtpläne Irland / Stadsplattegronden Ierland / Piante di città Irlanda / Planos de ciudades Irlanda

Eochair / Allwedd / Comnarthai ar phleanna bailte / Symbolau ar gynlluniau'r trefi **190**

Back of the guide: distances

En fin de volume : distances / Am Ende des Buches: Entfernungen / Achter in het boek: afstanden
Alla fine del volume: distanze / Al final del volumen: distancias

Channel Tunnel
Tunnel sous la Manche

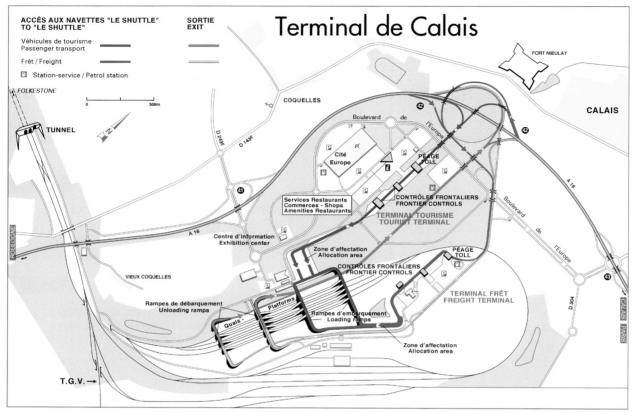

Terminal de Calais

ACCÈS AUX NAVETTES "LE SHUTTLE"
TO "LE SHUTTLE"

SORTIE
EXIT

Véhicules de tourisme
Passenger transport

Frêt / Freight

Station-service / Petrol station

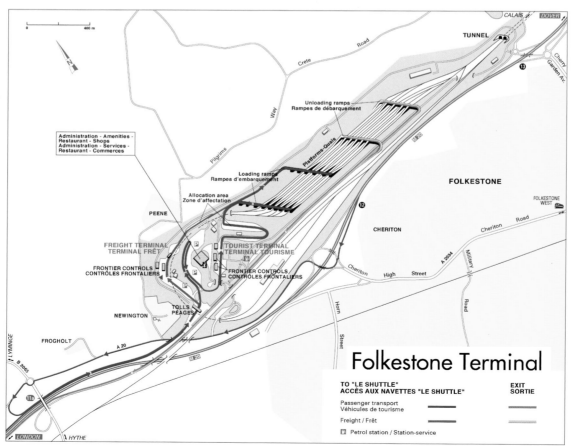

Folkestone Terminal

TO "LE SHUTTLE"
ACCÈS AUX NAVETTES "LE SHUTTLE"

EXIT
SORTIE

Passenger transport
Véhicules de tourisme

Freight / Frêt

Petrol station / Station-service

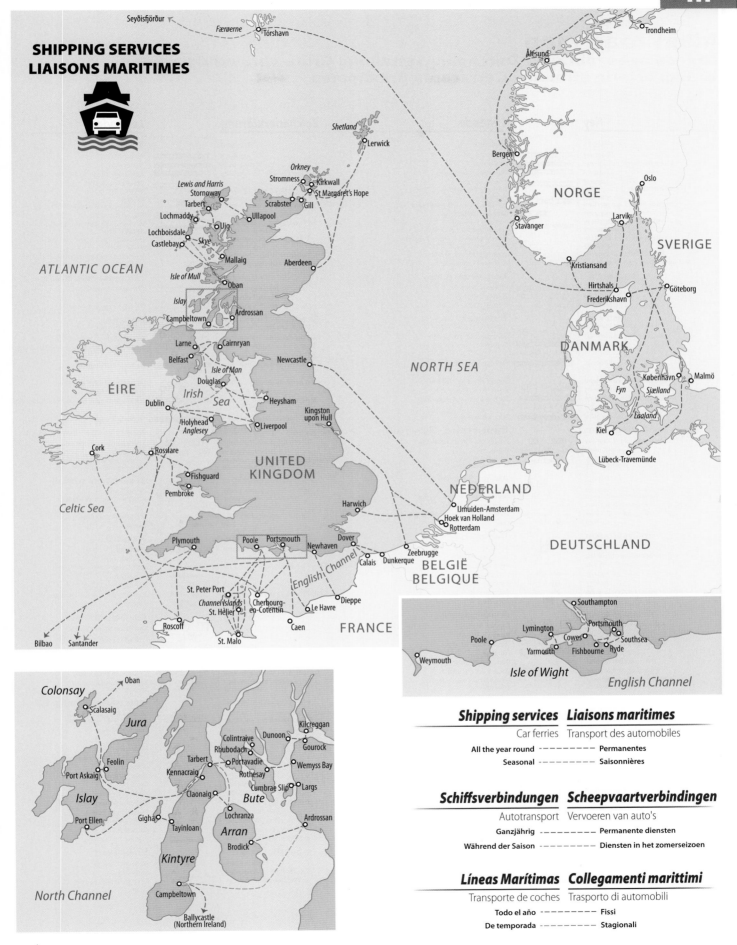

SHIPPING SERVICES
LIAISONS MARITIMES

Seyðisfjörður
Færøerne
Tórshavn
Trondheim
Ålesund
Shetland
Lerwick
Bergen
NORGE
Oslo
Orkney
Stromness
Kirkwall
St Margaret's Hope
Gill
Larvik
Lewis and Harris
Stornoway
Tarbert
Scrabster
Stavanger
SVERIGE
Lochmaddy
Ullapool
Uig
Kristiansand
Lochboisdale
Skye
Castlebay
Mallaig
Hirtshals
Göteborg
ATLANTIC OCEAN
Isle of Mull
Aberdeen
Frederikshavn
Oban
DANMARK
Islay
Ardrossan
Campbeltown
København
Malmö
Larne
Cairnryan
NORTH SEA
Fyn
Sjælland
Belfast
Newcastle
Isle of Man
Douglas
Laaland
ÉIRE
Irish
Heysham
Kiel
Dublin
Sea
Kingston upon Hull
Lübeck-Travemünde
Holyhead
Anglesey
Liverpool
Cork
Rosslare
UNITED
KINGDOM
NEDERLAND
Fishguard
IJmuiden-Amsterdam
Pembroke
Hoek van Holland
Rotterdam
Celtic Sea
Harwich
DEUTSCHLAND
Plymouth
Poole
Portsmouth
Newhaven
Dover
Zeebrugge
English Channel
Calais
Dunkerque
BELGIË
St. Peter Port
BELGIQUE
Channel Islands
Cherbourg-
St. Hélier
en-Cotentin
Le Havre
Dieppe
Roscoff
Caen
FRANCE
Bilbao
Santander
St. Malo

Southampton
Lymington
Portsmouth
Poole
Cowes
Southsea
Yarmouth
Fishbourne
Ryde
Weymouth
Isle of Wight
English Channel

Colonsay
Oban
Scalasaig
Jura
Kilcreggan
Colintraive
Dunoon
Rhubodach
Gourock
Feolin
Tarbert
Portavadie
Wemyss Bay
Port Askaig
Kennacraig
Rothesay
Islay
Claonaig
Cumbrae Slip
Largs
Bute
Port Ellen
Gigha
Lochranza
Ardrossan
Tayinloan
Arran
Brodick
Kintyre
North Channel
Campbeltown
Ballycastle
(Northern Ireland)

Shipping services | Liaisons maritimes
Car ferries | Transport des automobiles
All the year round - - - - - - Permanentes
Seasonal - - - - - - Saisonnières

Schiffsverbindungen | Scheepvaartverbindingen
Autotransport | Vervoeren van auto's
Ganzjährig - - - - - - Permanente diensten
Während der Saison - - - - - - Diensten in het zomerseizoen

Líneas Marítimas | Collegamenti marittimi
Transporte de coches | Trasporto di automobili
Todo el año - - - - - - Fissi
De temporada - - - - - - Stagionali

Main road map
Grands axes routiers / Durchgangsstraßen / Grote verbindingswegen
Grandi arterie stradali / Carreteras principales

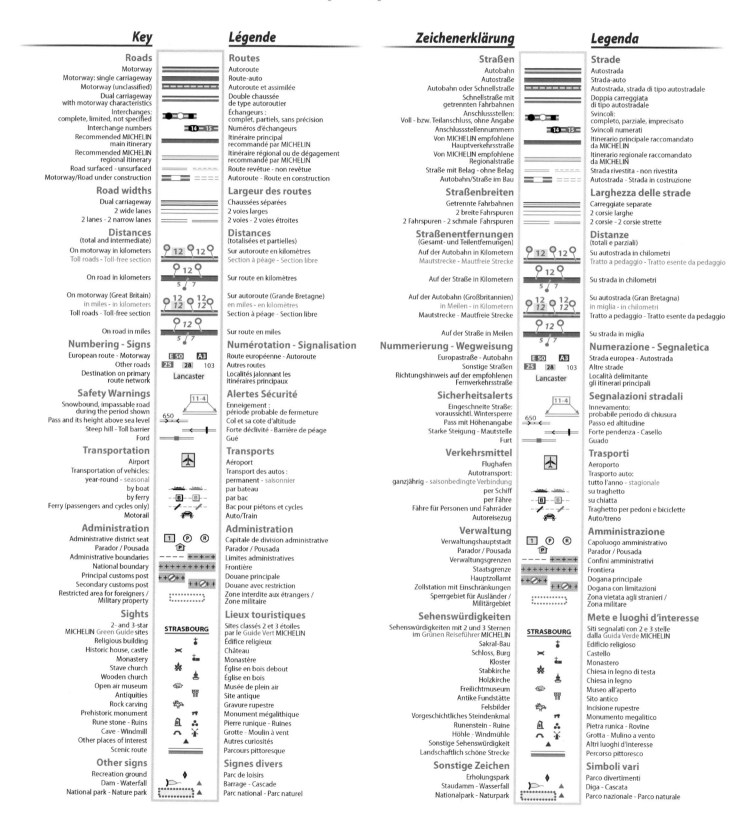

Key / Légende / Zeichenerklärung / Legenda

Roads / Routes / Straßen / Strade

Key	Légende	Zeichenerklärung	Legenda
Motorway	Autoroute	Autobahn	Autostrada
Motorway: single carriageway	Route-auto	Autostraße	Strada-auto
Motorway (unclassified)	Autoroute et assimilée	Autobahn oder Schnellstraße	Autostrada, strada di tipo autostradale
Dual carriageway with motorway characteristics	Double chaussée de type autoroutier	Schnellstraße mit getrennten Fahrbahnen	Doppia carreggiata di tipo autostradale
Interchanges: complete, limited, not specified	Échangeurs : complet, partiels, sans précision	Anschlussstellen: Voll - bzw. Teilanschluss, ohne Angabe	Svincoli: completo, parziale, imprecisato
Interchange numbers	Numéros d'échangeurs	Anschlussstellennummern	Svincoli numerati
Recommended MICHELIN main itinerary	Itinéraire principal recommandé par MICHELIN	Von MICHELIN empfohlene Hauptverkehrsstraße	Itinerario principale raccomandato da MICHELIN
Recommended MICHELIN regional itinerary	Itinéraire régional ou de dégagement recommandé par MICHELIN	Von MICHELIN empfohlene Regionalstraße	Itinerario regionale raccomandato da MICHELIN
Road surfaced - unsurfaced	Route revêtue - non revêtue	Straße mit Belag - ohne Belag	Strada rivestita - non rivestita
Motorway/Road under construction	Autoroute - Route en construction	Autobahn/Straße im Bau	Autostrada - Strada in costruzione

Road widths / Largeur des routes / Straßenbreiten / Larghezza delle strade

Key	Légende	Zeichenerklärung	Legenda
Dual carriageway	Chaussées séparées	Getrennte Fahrbahnen	Carreggiate separate
2 wide lanes	2 voies larges	2 breite Fahrspuren	2 corsie larghe
2 lanes - 2 narrow lanes	2 voies - 2 voies étroites	2 Fahrspuren - 2 schmale Fahrspuren	2 corsie - 2 corsie strette

Distances (total and intermediate) / Distances (totalisées et partielles) / Straßenentfernungen (Gesamt und Teilentfernungen) / Distanze (totali e parziali)

Key	Légende	Zeichenerklärung	Legenda
On motorway in kilometers	Sur autoroute en kilomètres	Auf der Autobahn in Kilometern	Su autostrada in chilometri
Toll roads - Toll-free section	Section à péage - Section libre	Mautstrecke - Mautfreie Strecke	Tratto a pedaggio - Tratto esente da pedaggio
On road in kilometers	Sur route en kilomètres	Auf der Straße in Kilometern	Su strada in chilometri
On motorway (Great Britain) in miles - in kilometers	Sur autoroute (Grande Bretagne) en miles - en kilomètres	Auf der Autobahn (Großbritannien) in Meilen - in Kilometern	Su autostrada (Gran Bretagna) in miglia - in chilometri
Toll roads - Toll-free section	Section à péage - Section libre	Mautstrecke - Mautfreie Strecke	Tratto a pedaggio - Tratto esente da pedaggio
On road in miles	Sur route en miles	Auf der Straße in Meilen	Su strada in miglia

Numbering - Signs / Numérotation - Signalisation / Nummerierung - Wegweisung / Numerazione - Segnaletica

Key	Légende	Zeichenerklärung	Legenda
European route - Motorway	Route européenne - Autoroute	Europastraße - Autobahn	Strada europea - Autostrada
Other roads	Autres routes	Sonstige Straßen	Altre strade
Destination on primary route network	Localités jalonnant les itinéraires principaux	Richtungshinweis auf der empfohlenen Fernverkehrsstraße	Località delimitante gli itinerari principali

E 50   A3   25   28   103   Lancaster

Safety Warnings / Alertes Sécurité / Sicherheitsalerts / Segnalazioni stradali

Key	Légende	Zeichenerklärung	Legenda
Snowbound, impassable road during the period shown	Enneigement : période probable de fermeture	Eingeschneite Straße: voraussichtl. Wintersperre	Innevamento: probabile periodo di chiusura
Pass and its height above sea level	Col et sa cote d'altitude	Pass mit Höhenangabe	Passo ed altitudine
Steep hill - Toll barrier	Forte déclivité - Barrière de péage	Starke Steigung - Mautstelle	Forte pendenza - Casello
Ford	Gué	Furt	Guado

11-4   650

Transportation / Transports / Verkehrsmittel / Trasporti

Key	Légende	Zeichenerklärung	Legenda
Airport	Aéroport	Flughafen	Aeroporto
Transportation of vehicles: year-round - seasonal	Transport des autos : permanent - saisonnier	Autotransport: ganzjährig - saisonbedingte Verbindung	Trasporto auto: tutto l'anno - stagionale
by boat	par bateau	per Schiff	su traghetto
by ferry	par bac	per Fähre	su chiatta
Ferry (passengers and cycles only)	Bac pour piétons et cycles	Fähre für Personen und Fahrräder	Traghetto per pedoni e biciclette
Motorail	Auto/Train	Autoreisezug	Auto/treno

Administration / Administration / Verwaltung / Amministrazione

Key	Légende	Zeichenerklärung	Legenda
Administrative district seat	Capitale de division administrative	Verwaltungshauptstadt	Capoluogo amministrativo
Parador / Pousada	Parador / Pousada	Parador / Pousada	Parador / Pousada
Administrative boundaries	Limites administratives	Verwaltungsgrenzen	Confini amministrativi
National boundary	Frontière	Staatsgrenze	Frontiera
Principal customs post	Douane principale	Hauptzollamt	Dogana principale
Secondary customs post	Douane avec restriction	Zollstation mit Einschränkungen	Dogana con limitazioni
Restricted area for foreigners / Military property	Zone interdite aux étrangers / Zone militaire	Sperrgebiet für Ausländer / Militärgebiet	Zona vietata agli stranieri / Zona militare

1   P   R

Sights / Lieux touristiques / Sehenswürdigkeiten / Mete e luoghi d'interesse

Key	Légende	Zeichenerklärung	Legenda
2- and 3-star MICHELIN Green Guide sites	Sites classés 2 et 3 étoiles par le Guide Vert MICHELIN	Sehenswürdigkeiten mit 2 und 3 Sternen im Grünen Reiseführer MICHELIN	Siti segnalati con 2 e 3 stelle dalla Guida Verde MICHELIN
Religious building	Édifice religieux	Sakral-Bau	Edificio religioso
Historic house, castle	Château	Schloss, Burg	Castello
Monastery	Monastère	Kloster	Monastero
Stave church	Église en bois debout	Stabkirche	Chiesa in legno di testa
Wooden church	Église en bois	Holzkirche	Chiesa in legno
Open air museum	Musée de plein air	Freilichtmuseum	Museo all'aperto
Antiquities	Site antique	Antike Fundstätte	Sito antico
Rock carving	Gravure rupestre	Felsbilder	Incisione rupestre
Prehistoric monument	Monument mégalithique	Vorgeschichtliches Steindenkmal	Monumento megalitico
Rune stone - Ruins	Pierre runique - Ruines	Runenstein - Ruine	Pietra runica - Rovine
Cave - Windmill	Grotte - Moulin à vent	Höhle - Windmühle	Grotta - Mulino a vento
Other places of interest	Autres curiosités	Sonstige Sehenswürdigkeit	Altri luoghi d'interesse
Scenic route	Parcours pittoresque	Landschaftlich schöne Strecke	Percorso pittoresco

STRASBOURG

Other signs / Signes divers / Sonstige Zeichen / Simboli vari

Key	Légende	Zeichenerklärung	Legenda
Recreation ground	Parc de loisirs	Erholungspark	Parco divertimenti
Dam - Waterfall	Barrage - Cascade	Staudamm - Wasserfall	Diga - Cascata
National park - Nature park	Parc national - Parc naturel	Nationalpark - Naturpark	Parco nazionale - Parco naturale

Signos Convencionales

Carreteras
Autopista
Carretera
Autopista, Autovía
Autovía
(otra vía similar a las autopistas)
Accesos:
completo, parcial, sin precisar
Números de los accesos
Itinerario principal
recomendado por MICHELIN
Itinerario regional
recomendado por MICHELIN
Carretera asfaltada - sin asfaltar
Autopista - Carretera en construcción

Ancho de las carreteras
Calzadas separadas
Dos carriles anchos
Dos carriles - Dos carriles estrechos

Distancias
(totales y parciales)
En autopista en kilómetros
Tramo de peaje - Tramo libre

En carretera en kilómetros

En autopista (Gran Bretaña)
en millas - en kilómetros
Tramo de peaje - Tramo libre

En carretera en millas

Numeración - Señalización
Carretera europea - Autopista
Otras carreteras
Localidades situadas en
los principales itinerarios

Lancaster

Alertas Seguridad
Nevada:
Período probable de cierre
Puerto y su altitud
Pendiente Pronunciada - Barrera de peaje
Vado

Transportes
Aeropuerto
Transporte de coches:
todo el año - de temporada
por barco
por barcaza
Barcaza para el paso de peatones y vehículos dos ruedas
Auto-tren

Administración
Capital de división administrativa
Parador / Pousada
Limites administrativos
Frontera
Aduana principal
Aduana con restricciones
Zona prohibida a los extranjeros /
Propiedad militar

Curiosidades
Lugares clasificados con 2 y 3 estrellas
por la Guía Verde MICHELIN

STRASBOURG

Edificio religioso
Castillo
Monasterio
Iglesia de madera
Iglesia de madera
Museo al aire libre
Zona de vestigios antiguos
Grabado rupestre
Monumento megalítico
Piedra rúnica - Ruinas
Cueva - Molino de viento
Otras curiosidades
Recorrido pintoresco

Signos diversos
Zona recreativa
Presa - Cascada
Parque nacional - Parque natural

Verklaring van de tekens

Wegen
Autosnelweg
Autoweg
Autosnelweg of gelijksoortige weg
Gescheiden rijbanen
van het type autosnelweg
Aansluitingen:
volledig, gedeeltelijk, zonder aanduiding
Afritnummers
Michelin
Hoofdweg
Michelin
Regionale weg
Verharde weg - onverharde weg
Autosnelweg - Weg in aanleg

Breedte van de wegen
Gescheiden rijbanen
2 brede rijstroken
2 rijstroken - 2 smalle rijstroken

Afstanden
(totaal en gedeeltelijk)
Op autosnelwegen in kilometers
Gedeelte met tol - Tolvrij gedeelte

Op andere wegen in kilometers

Op autosnelwegen (Groot Brittannië)
in mijlen - in kilometers
Gedeelte met tol - Tolvrij gedeelte

Op andere wegen in mijlen

Wegnummers - Bewegwijzering
Europaweg - Autosnelweg
Andere wegen
Plaatsen langs een hoofdweg
met bewegwijzering

Veiligheidswaarschuwingen
Sneeuw:
vermoedelijke sluitingsperiode
Bergpas en hoogte boven de zeespiegel
Steile helling - Tol
Wad

Vervoer
Luchthaven
Vervoer van auto's:
het hele jaar - tijdens het seizoen
per boot
per veerpont
Veerpont voor voetgangers en fietsers
Autotrein

Administratie
Hoofdplaats van administratief gebied
Parador / Pousada
Administratieve grenzen
Staatsgrens
Hoofddouanekantoor
Douanekantoor met beperkte bevoegdheden
Terrein verboden voor buitenlanders /
Militair gebied

Bezienswaardigheden
Locaties met 2 en 3 sterren volgens
de Groene Gids van MICHELIN
Kerkelijk gebouw
Kasteel
Klooster
Stavkirke (houten kerk)
Houten kerk
Openluchtmuseum
Overblijfsel uit de Oudheid
Rotstekening
Megaliet
Runensteen - Ruïne
Grot - Molen
Andere bezienswaardigheden
Schilderachtig traject

Diverse tekens
Recreatiepark
Stuwdam - Waterval
Nationaal park - Natuurpark

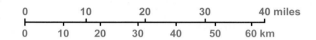

0   10   20   30   40 miles
0   10   20   30   40   50   60 km

**Republic of Ireland: All distances
and speed limits are signed in kilometres.**

**République d'Irlande: Les distances
et les limitations de vitesse sont exprimées en
kilomètres.**

**Irland: Alle Entfernungsangaben und
Geschwindigkeitsbegrenzungen in km.**

**Ierland: Alle afstanden en
maximumsnelheden zijn uitsluitend
in kilometers aangegeven.**

**Repubblica d'Irlanda: Distanze e limiti
di velocità sono espressi soltanto in chilometri.**

**República de Irlanda: Distancias y límites de
velocidad están expresados sólo en kilómetros.**

Key to 1:1 000 000 map pages
Légende des cartes au 1/1 000 000
Zeichenerklärung der Karten 1:1 000 000
Verklaring van de tekens voor kaarten met schaal 1:1 000 000
Legenda carte scala 1:1 000 000
Signos convencionales de los mapas a escala 1:1 000 000

ENGLAND

UNITARY AUTHORITIES

1 Bath and North East Somerset
2 Bedford
3 Blackburn with Darwen
4 Blackpool
5 Bournemouth, Christchurch and Poole
6 Bracknell Forest
7 Brighton and Hove
8 Buckinghamshire
9 Cambridgeshire
10 Central Bedfordshire
11 Cheshire East
12 Cheshire West and Chester
13 City of Bristol
14 City of Leicester
15 Cornwall
16 Cumbria
17 Derby
18 Derbyshire
19 Devon
20 Dorset
21 Durham
22 East Riding of Yorkshire
23 East Sussex
24 Essex
25 Gloucestershire
26 Greater London
27 Greater Manchester
28 Halton
29 Hampshire
30 Hartlepool
31 Herefordshire
32 Hertfordshire
33 Kent
34 Kingston-upon-Hull
35 Lancashire
36 Leicestershire
37 Lincolnshire
38 Luton
39 Medway
40 Merseyside
41 Middlesbrough
42 Milton Keynes
43 Norfolk
44 North East Lincolnshire
45 North Lincolnshire
46 North Northamptonshire
47 North Somerset
48 North Yorkshire
49 Northumberland
50 Nottingham
51 Nottinghamshire
52 Oxfordshire
53 Peterborough
54 Plymouth
55 Portsmouth
56 Reading
57 Redcar and Cleveland
58 Rutland
59 Shropshire
60 Somerset
61 South Gloucestershire
62 South Yorkshire
63 Southend-on-Sea
64 Staffordshire
65 Stockton-on-Tees
66 Stoke-on-Trent
67 Suffolk
68 Surrey
69 Swindon
70 Telford and Wrekin
71 Thurrock
72 Torbay
73 Tyne and Wear
74 Warrington
75 Warwickshire
76 West Berkshire
77 West Midlands
78 West Northamptonshire
79 West Sussex
80 West Yorkshire
81 Wiltshire
82 Windsor and Maidenhead
83 Wokingham
84 Worcestershire
85 York

SCOTLAND

UNITARY AUTHORITIES

1 Aberdeen City
2 Aberdeenshire
3 Angus
4 Argyll and Bute
5 Clackmannanshire
6 City of Edinburgh
7 City of Glasgow
8 Dumfries and Galloway
9 Dundee City
10 East Ayrshire
11 East Dunbartonshire
12 East Lothian
13 East Renfrewshire
14 Falkirk
15 Fife
16 Highland
17 Inverclyde
18 Midlothian
19 Moray
20 North Ayrshire
21 North Lanarkshire
22 Orkney Islands
23 Perthshire and Kinross
24 Renfrewshire
25 Scottish Borders
26 Shetland Islands
27 South Ayrshire
28 South Lanarkshire
29 Stirling
30 West Dunbartonshire
31 West Lothian
32 Western Isles

NORTHERN IRELAND

DISTRICT COUNCILS

1 Antrim and Newtownabbey
2 Ards and North Down
3 Armagh City, Banbridge & Craigavon
4 Belfast
5 Causeway Coast and Glens
6 Derry City and Strabane
7 Fermanagh and Omagh
8 Lisburn and Castlereagh
9 Mid and East Antrim
10 Mid Ulster
11 Newry, Mourne and Down

32 = UNITARY AUTHORITIES

WALES

UNITARY AUTHORITIES

1 Anglesey/Sir Fôn
2 Blaenau Gwent
3 Bridgend/Pen-y-bont ar Ogwr
4 Caerphilly/Caerffili
5 Cardiff/Caerdydd
6 Carmarthenshire/Sir Gaerfyrddin
7 Ceredigion
8 Conwy
9 Denbighshire/Sir Ddinbych
10 Flintshire/Sir y Fflint
11 Gwynedd
12 Merthyr Tydfil/Merthyr Tudful
13 Monmouthshire/Sir Fynwy
14 Neath Port Talbot/Castell-nedd Phort Talbot
15 Newport/Casnewydd
16 Pembrokeshire/Sir Benfro
17 Powys
18 Rhondda Cynon Taff/Rhondda Cynon Taf
19 Swansea/Abertawe
20 Torfaen/Tor-faen
21 Vale of Glamorgan/Bro Morgannwg
22 Wrexham/Wrecsam

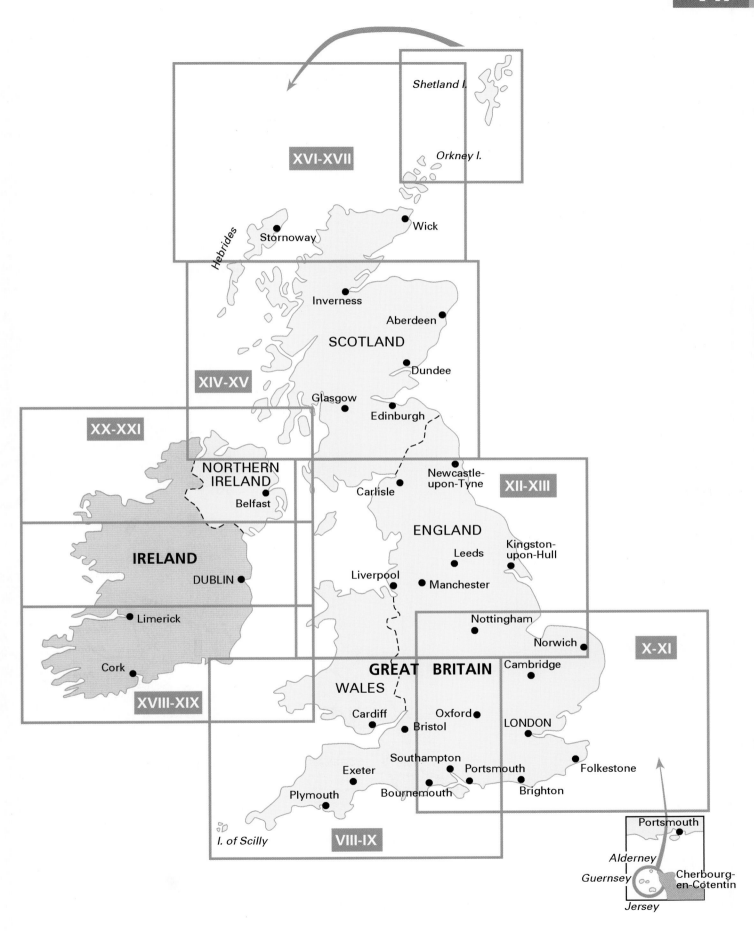

XVI-XVII

Shetland I.

Orkney I.

Hebrides

Stornoway

Wick

Inverness

Aberdeen

SCOTLAND

Dundee

XIV-XV

Glasgow

Edinburgh

XX-XXI

NORTHERN
IRELAND

Belfast

Newcastle-
upon-Tyne

XII-XIII

Carlisle

ENGLAND

IRELAND

Leeds

Kingston-
upon-Hull

DUBLIN

Liverpool

Manchester

Limerick

Nottingham

Norwich

X-XI

Cork

GREAT BRITAIN

Cambridge

XVIII-XIX

WALES

Cardiff

Oxford

LONDON

Bristol

Folkestone

Southampton

Portsmouth

Exeter

Brighton

Plymouth

Bournemouth

I. of Scilly

VIII-IX

Portsmouth

Alderney

Guernsey

Cherbourg-
en-Cotentin

Jersey

ST. GEORGE'S CHANNEL

e Harbour/ Ros Láir
Point
ltee Islands

Aberaeron A 487
New Quay
Synod Inn
58
93
Aberporth
A 486
A 484
Cardigan
Strumble Head
Newport
A 487
Pentre Ifan
Fishguard/ Abergwaun
Crymmych
26
531
National Wool Museum
A 478
16
74
46
21
St. Clears
Carmarthen/ Caerfyrddin
53
A 40
St. David's Head
St. David's
A 487
Narberth
11
Whitland
23
Haverfordwest/Hwlffordd
St. Bride's Bay
Pembrokeshire Coast National Park
30
48
Kidwelly
32
52
Pendine
Saundersfoot
Milford Haven/ Aberdaugleddau
10
Neyland
5
Tenby/ Dinbych-y-pysgod
Pembroke Dock
Pembroke A 4139
St. Govan's Head
Carmarthen Bay

Pembrokeshire Coast National Park

Llanrhystud
Bridge 593
Elan Valley
Teifi
7
Tregaron
11
Lampeter
Llandovery
Llandysul
Llandeilo
85
53
Black Mountain
Brecon National
802
Merthyr
Hirwaun
Cross Hands
Ammanford
Pontardawe
68
42
Aberdare/
Aberdar
Pontarddulais
Llanelli
Neath/ Castell Nedd
Rh
SWANSEA/ ABERTAWE
Port Talbot
Rhossili
The Mumbles
53
33
Worms Head
Gower Peninsula
Port- Eynon
Maesteg
Porthcawl
Bridgend/ Pen-y-bont

BRISTOL CHANNEL

Lundy

Lynton Lynmouth Porlock
Ilfracombe 10 Combe Martin
Mortehoe
Croyde
Dunk Beac
519
Braunton
Simonsbath
Barnstaple
Tarr Steps
493
Northam
South Molton
Dulverton
Hartland Point Clovelly
Bideford
35
56
Cliffs of Morwenstow
Great Torrington
Tiverton
Kilkhampton
Hatherleigh
Stratton
Holsworthy
Winkleigh
19
Bude
22
Crediton
Poundstock
28
Okehampton
EXETER
Boscastle
621
Tintagel
Drogo
Launceston
12
Moretonhampstead
177
109
Lydford Gorge
High Willhays
Dartmoor
Port Isaac
Camelford
420
Brent Tor
National
Padstow
330
Bovey Tracey
Wadebridge
113
182
Tavistock
Princetown
Ashburton
Newton Abbot
Callington
Bodmin
Liskeard
78
126
Buckland
Buckfastleigh
Newquay
Lanhydrock
Saltash
Fraddon
Lostwithiel
Plympton
Saltram
St. Austell
West Looe
St. Germans
Plymstock
Totnes
Trewithen
Fowey
Polperro
Torpoint
Modbury
Truro
Tregony
Mevagissey
PLYMOUTH
Dartmouth
Camborne
Trelissick
Newton Ferrers
Kingsbridge
St. Ives
Hayle
Redruth
Penryn
Salcombe
St. Just
252
Penzance
St. Mawes
Falmouth
Glendurgan
Start Point
Land's End
Sennen
Helston
St. Keverne
St. Michael's Mount
Mount's Bay
Coverack
Subtropical Gardens
Lizard
Tresco St. Martin's
Isles of Scilly
St. Mary's
Lizard Point

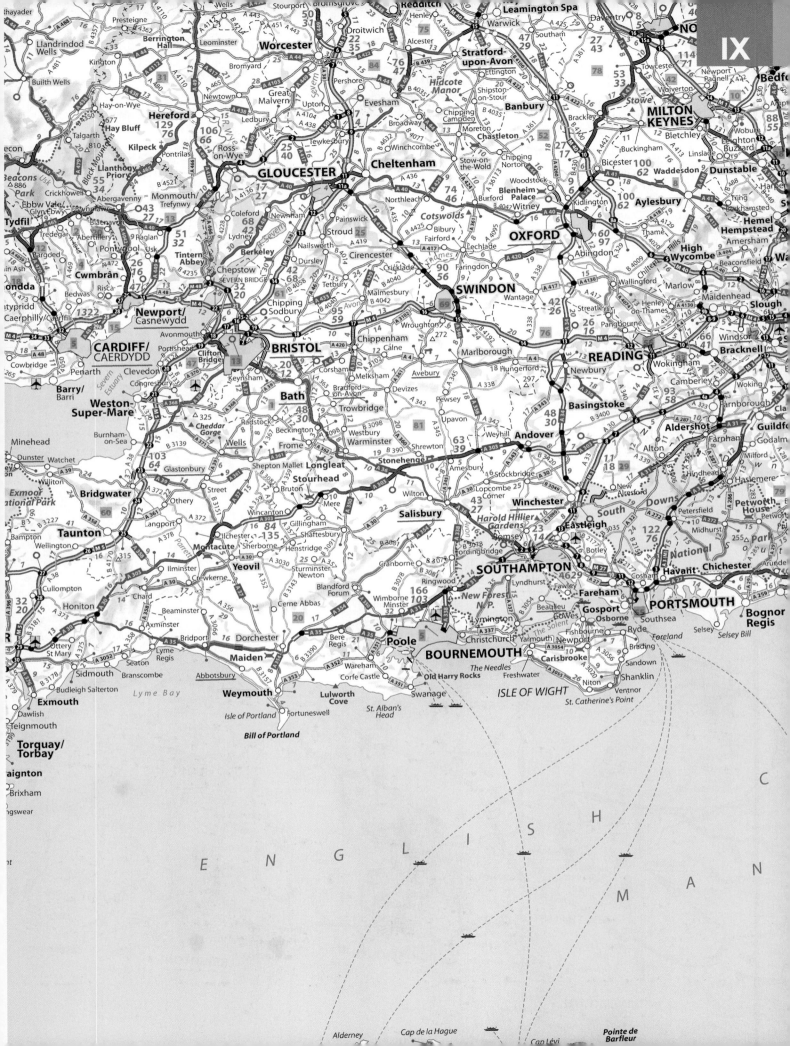

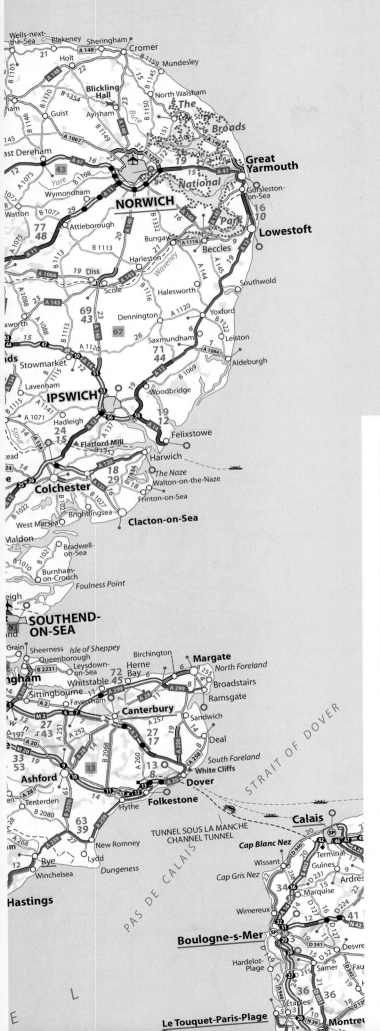
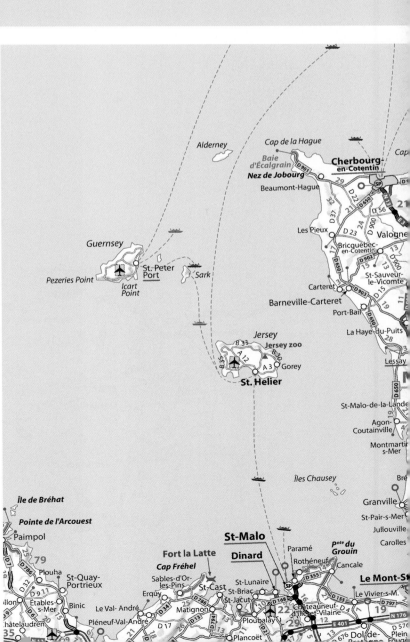

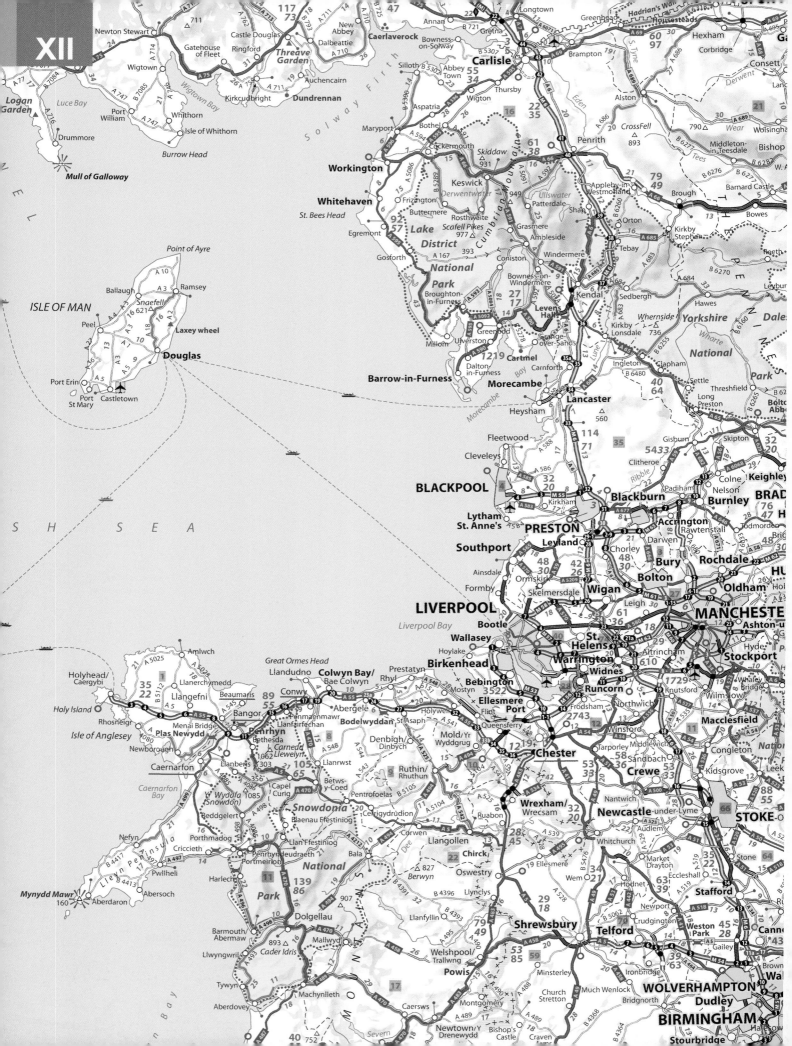

South Shields
SUNDERLAND
Jarrow
Gateshead
Beamish Hall
Washington
Seaham
Chester-le-Street
Houghton-le-Spring
Horden
Durham
Peterlee
Hartlepool
Crook
Spennymoor
Sedgefield
Redcar
Marske-by-the-Sea
Stockton-on-Tees
Saltburn-by-the-Sea
Billingham
Brotton
Darlington
Eaglescliffe
Guisborough
Loftus
Whitby
MIDDLESBROUGH
Richmond
North York Moors National Park
Cleveland Hills
Northallerton
Scalby
Scarborough
Bedale
Rievaulx Abbey
Hutton-le-Hole
Helmsley
Pickering
Filey
Thirsk
Fountains Abbey
Ripon
Malton
Burton Agnes Hall
Flamborough Head
Pateley Bridge
Easingwold
Howard
Norton
Bridlington
Boroughbridge
Knaresborough
Driffield
Beeford
Harrogate
Wetwang
Ilkley
Otley
York
Hornsea
Bingley
Harewood
Wetherby
Tadcaster
Market Weighton
Leven
LEEDS
Beverley
Burton Constable Hall
Bradford
Selby
Barlby
Halifax
Garforth
Castleford
KINGSTON UPON HULL
Withernsea
Howden
Goole
Hedon
Patrington
Dewsbury
Pontefract
Snaith
Kilnsea
HUDDERSFIELD
Wakefield
Thorne
Barton-upon-Humber
Immingham Dock
Spurn Head
Barnsley
Crowle
Scunthorpe
Immingham
Grimsby
Cleethorpes
Doncaster
Brigg
Caistor
Conisbrough
Epworth
SHEFFIELD
Rotherham
Bentley
Market Rasen
Louth
Mablethorpe
Stocksbridge
Bawtry
Gainsborough
Sutton-on-Sea
Maltby
Wragby
Worksop
Retford
Alford
Dronfield
Staveley
Lincoln
Partney
Chesterfield
Tuxford
Horncastle
Spilsby
Skegness
Hardwick Hall
Ollerton
Woodhall Spa
Mansfield
Tattershall
Clay Cross
Southwell
Leadenham
Alfreton
Sutton-in-Ashfield
Newark-on-Trent
Sleaford
Boston
Hunstanton
Wells-next-the-Sea
Blakeney
Holt
Ripley
Heanor
Hucknall
Holkham Hall
Houghton Hall
Belper
NOTTINGHAM
Bingham
Donington
Sandringham House
Fakenham
East Dereham
DERBY
West Bridgford
Grantham
Sutterton
Rising
King's Lynn
Long Eaton
Belvoir
Holbeach
Long Sutton
Spalding
Wisbech
Swaffham
Burton-upon-Trent
Loughborough
Melton Mowbray
Bourne
Outwell
Oxburgh Hall
Watton
Swadlincote
Shepshed
Stamford
Crowland
Downham Market
Ashby de la Zouch
Coalville
Oakham
Burghley
Guyhirn
March
Tamworth
Oadby
Uppingham
Market Harborough
Corby
Eye
Whittlesey
PETERBOROUGH
Mundford
Thetford
Sutton Coldfield
Hinckley
LEICESTER
Weldon
Oundle
Chatteris
Nuneaton
Bedworth
Lutterworth
Boughton House
Kettering
Ramsey
Littleport
Ely

Kinnairds Head
Lossiemouth
Elgin
Buckie
Banff Macduff
Fraserburgh
Loch of Strathbeg
Rattray Head
Cullen
Duff House
Peterhead
Buchan Ness
Inverness
Nairn
Forres
Fochabers
Keith
Huntly
New Deer
Mintlaw
Cruden Bay
Tore
Fortrose
Black Isle
Cromarty
Invergordon
Alness
Sueno's Stone
Rothes
Craigellachie
Dufftown
Rhynie
Mossat
Alford
Oldmeldrum
Inverurie
Kintore
Newburgh
Ellon
Pitmedden Garden
Dava
Grantown-on-Spey
Tomintoul
Colnabaichin
Craigievar Castle
ABERDEEN
Carrbridge
Dulnain Bridge
Aviemore
Glenmore Forest Park
Crathes Castle
Cairn Gorm
Cairngorm Mountains
Ben Macdui
Craigievar Castle
Crathes Castle
Banchory
Kingussie
Newtonmore
Laggan
Cairn Ban
Cairngorms National Park
Balmoral Castle
Braemar
Ballater
Aboyne
Stonehaven
Dunnottar Castle
Dalwhinnie
Pass of Drumochter
Devil's Elbow
Glas Maol
The Pleasance
Laurencekirk
Inverbervie
Blair Castle
Blair Atholl
Kinloch Rannoch
Beinn a' Ghlò
N. Esk
Brechin
Marykirk
Montrose
Loch Rannoch
Schiehallion
Pitlochry
Queen's view
Kirriemuir
Forfar
Arbroath
Aberfeldy
Dunkeld
Glamis
Glamis
Ben Lawers
Loch Tay
Rattray
Blairgowrie
Meigle
Coupar Angus
DUNDEE
Carnoustie
Monifieth
BenChonzie
Perth
Scone Palace
Newburgh
Tayport
Newport-on-Tay
Buddon Ness
Killin
Crieff
Auchtermuchty
Cupar
Leuchars
St. Andrews
Fife Ness
Lochearnhead
Auchterarder
Ochil Hills
Falkland
Crail
Callander
Ben Vorlich
Glenrothes
Leven
Pittenweem
Saint Monans
Doune
Dunblane
Dollar
Kinross
Lochgelly
Methil
Buckhaven
Elie
Firth of Forth
Bridge of Allan
Alva
Stirling
Alloa
Dunfermline
Kincardine
Culross
Cowdenbeath
Burntisland
Kirkcaldy
Kilsyth
Denny
Grangemouth
Bo'ness
Rosyth
Inverkeithing
S. Queensferry
Hopetoun
Leith
North Berwick
Tantallon
Dunbar
Cockburnspath
Cumbernauld
Falkirk
Linlithgow
Musselburgh
Prestonpans
Aberlady
East Linton
Haddington
Siccar Point & Huttons Unconformity
St. Abb's Head
St Abb's Head National Nature Reserve
Kirkintilloch
Clydebank
Armadale
Bathgate
Livingston
Tranent
Eyemouth
Airdrie
Whitburn
Dalkeith
Loanhead
Rosslyn
EDINBURGH
Lammermuir Hills
Manderston
Coatbridge
Motherwell
Penicuik
Pentland Hills
Moorfoot Hills
Lauder
Duns
Berwick-upon-Tweed
Barrhead
Hamilton
Wishaw
Carluke
West Linton
Greenlaw
Holy Island
East Kilbride
Strathaven
Lanark
Carnwath
Peebles
Innerleithen
Earlston
Mellerstein
Coldstream
Farne Islands
Kilmarnock
Galston
New Lanark
Biggar
Galashiels
Tweed Valley
Abbotsford
Melrose
Dryburgh Abbey
Newtown St Boswells
Kelso
Belford
Bamburgh Castle
Mauchline
Douglas
Broad Law
Bowhill
Selkirk
Jedburgh
The Cheviot
Wooler
Dunstanburgh Castle
Cumnock
Muirkirk
Abington
Grey Mare's Tail
Hawick
Carter Bar
Northumberland National Park
Alnwick
Warkworth
New Cumnock
Sanquhar
Elvanfoot
Moffat
Hermitage Castle
Otterburn
Rothbury
Felton
Dalmellington
Thornhill
Drumlanrig
Beattock
Lochmaben
Lockerbie
Langholm
Kielder Resr.
Wallington
Newbiggin-by-the-Sea
Morpeth
Ashington
Blyth
Amble

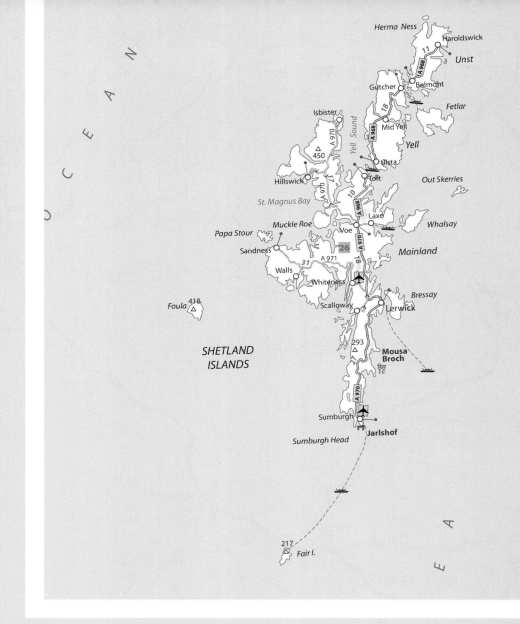

O C E A N

Herma Ness
Haroldswick
11
Unst
A 968
Gutcher
Belmont
18
Fetlar
Isbister
Mid Yell
Ulsta
Yell
A 970
450
Out Skerries
Hillswick
70
Toft
St. Magnus Bay
A 970
A 968
Laxo
Whalsay
Muckle Roe
Voe
A 970
Papa Stour
26
Bressay
Sandness
A 971
31
18
Mainland
Walls
Whiteness
Scalloway
Lerwick
418
Foula
293
SHETLAND
ISLANDS
Mousa
Broch
A 970
Sumburgh
Jarlshof
Sumburgh Head
217
Fair I.

S E A

Cape
Sandwood B
Oldshoremo
Kinlochb
Butt of Lewis
Port of Ness
Scourie
A 857
16
Eddrachillis
Bay
LEWIS
Barvas
Stoer
Peninsula
A 857
THE MINCH
Flannan I.
A 858
Carloway
292
12
Portnaguran
A 83
Broad
Bay
Callanish
Standing
Stones
Stornoway
Tiumpan Head
Lochinver
34
A 858
Eye Peninsula
Garynahine
Rubha Còigeach
574
36
32
A 859
Achiltibuie
C 1047
Hushinish
B 887
Kebock Head
Coigach
572
743
Clisham
NA H-EILEANAN
799
Loch Broom
Gruinard
Tarbert
Bay
SIAR
A 859
24
Rubha Réidh
Laide
29
Toe Head
St. Kilda

B R I D E S

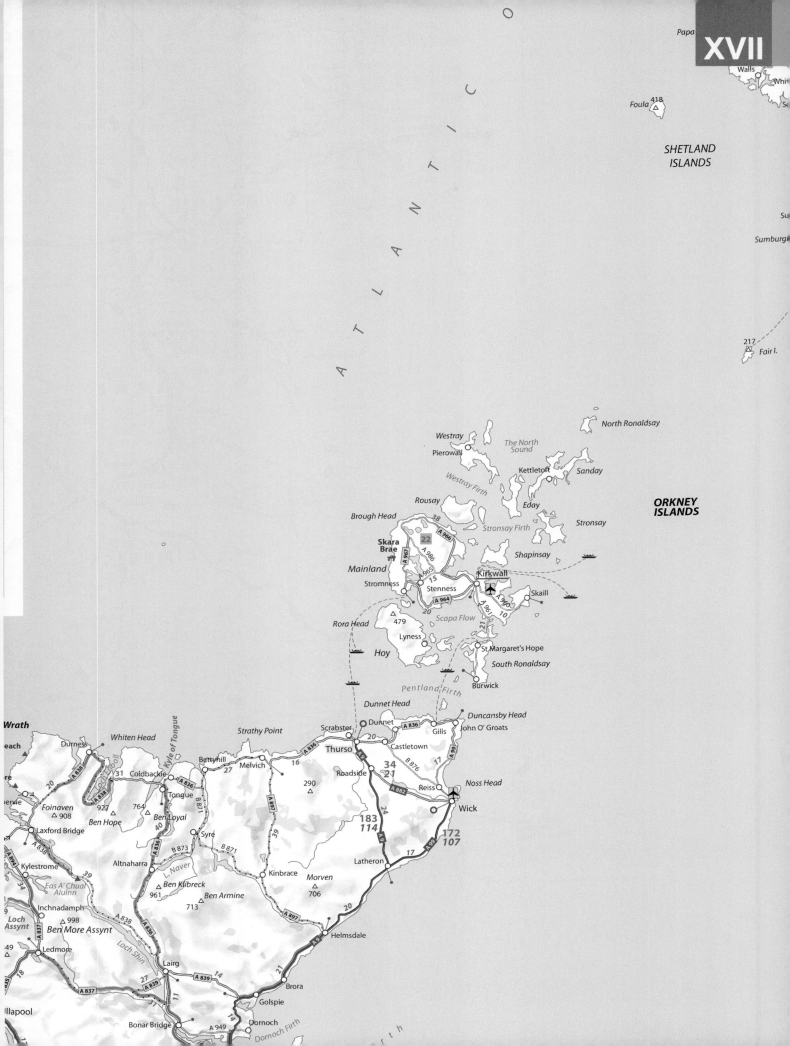

Papa

Walls

Whit

Foula 418

SHETLAND
ISLANDS

Su

Sumburg

Sumburgl

217 Fair I.

A T L A N T I C   O

North Ronaldsay

Westray

Pierowall

The North
Sound

Kettletoft

Sanday

Westray Firth

Rousay

Eday

Stronsay

ORKNEY
ISLANDS

Brough Head

38

A 966

22

Stronsay Firth

Skara
Brae

A 986

Shapinsay

A 967

A 986

965

Mainland

15

Kirkwall

Skaill

Stromness

Stenness

A 964

20

Scapa Flow

A 960

10

479

21

Rora Head

Lyness

St Margaret's Hope

Hoy

South Ronaldsay

Burwick

Pentland Firth

Dunnet Head

Duncansby Head

Scrabster   Dunnet

John O' Groats

Wrath

20

A 836

Gills

each

Durness

Whiten Head

Kyle of Tongue

Strathy Point

Thurso

Castletown

A 99

A 838

Bettyhill

A 836

Melvich

16

Roadside

34
21

B 876

17

Noss Head

ore

31

Coldbackie

A 836

27

290

A 882

Reiss

Foinaven
△ 908

927

764

Tongue

B 871

A 897

24

Wick

Ben Hope

Ben Loyal

39

183
114

Laxford Bridge

40

Syre

B 871

172
107

Kylestrome

A 836

B 873

Altnaharra

L. Naver

Latheron

39

Eas A' Chual
Aluinn

Ben Klibreck

Kinbrace

Morven
△ 706

17

Inchnadamph

961

Ben Armine

△ 998

713

A 897

20

Loch
Assynt

Ben More Assynt

Loch Shin

Helmsdale

49

Ledmore

Lairg

14

Brora

18

A 837

27

A 839

11

21

llapool

Bonar Bridge

A 949

Golspie

Dornoch

Dornoch Firth

th

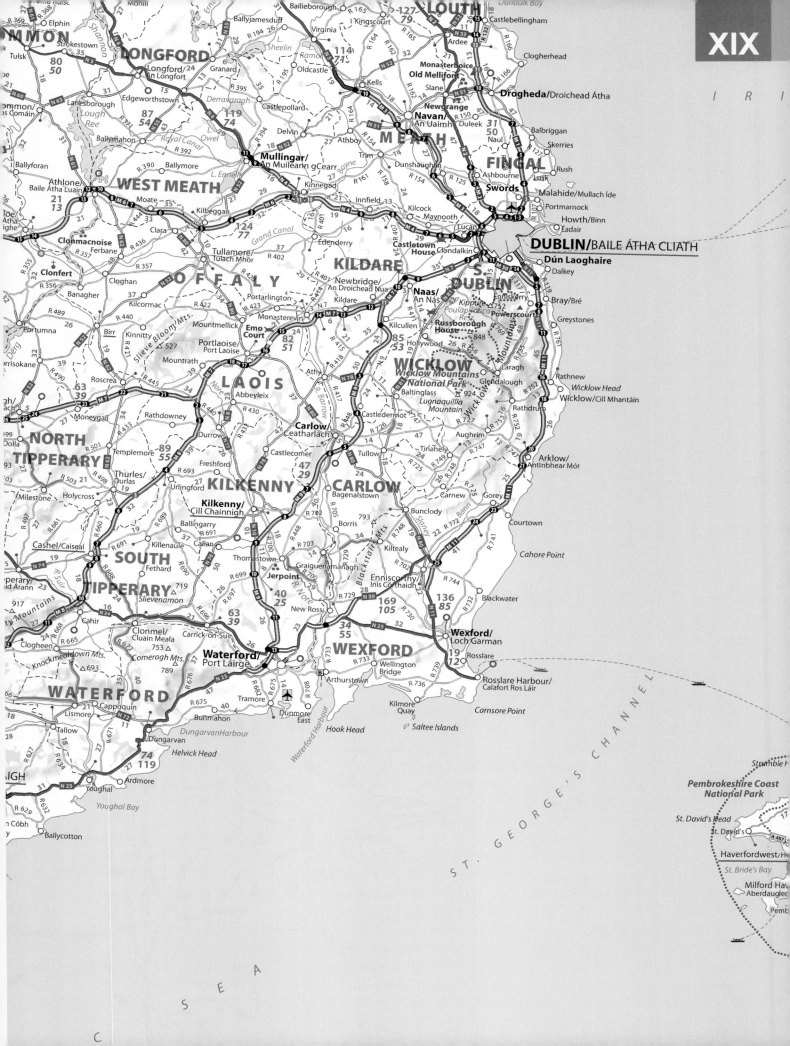

Key   Légende   Zeichenerklärung

Roads — Routes — Straßen

Key	Légende	Zeichenerklärung
Motorway - Service areas	Autoroute - Aires de service	Autobahn - Tankstelle mit Raststätte
Dual carriageway with motorway characteristics	Double chaussée de type autoroutier	Schnellstraße mit getrennten Fahrbahnen
Interchanges: complete, limited	Échangeurs : complet, partiels	Anschlussstellen: Voll - bzw. Teilanschlussstellen
Interchange numbers	Numéros d'échangeurs	Anschlussstellennummern
International and national road network	Route de liaison internationale ou nationale	Internationale bzw. nationale Hauptverkehrsstraße
Interregional and less congested road	Route de liaison interrégionale ou de dégagement	Überregionale Verbindungsstraße oder Umleitungsstrecke
Road surfaced - unsurfaced	Route revêtue - non revêtue	Straße mit Belag - ohne Belag
Footpath - Waymarked footpath / Bridle path	Sentier - Sentier balisé/Allée cavalière	Pfad - Ausgeschilderter Weg / Reitpfad
Motorway / Road under construction (when available: with scheduled opening date)	Autoroute - Route en construction (le cas échéant : date de mise en service prévue)	Autobahn - Straße im Bau (ggf. voraussichtliches Datum der Verkehrsfreigabe)

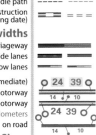

Road widths — Largeur des routes — Straßenbreiten

Key	Légende	Zeichenerklärung
Dual carriageway	Chaussées séparées	Getrennte Fahrbahnen
4 lanes - 2 wide lanes	4 voies - 2 voies larges	4 Fahrspuren - 2 breite Fahrspuren
2 lanes - 2 narrow lanes	2 voies - 2 voies étroites	2 Fahrspuren - 1 Fahrspur

Distances (total and intermediate) — Distances (totalisées et partielles) — Entfernungen (Gesamt- und Teilentfernungen)

Key	Légende	Zeichenerklärung
Toll roads on motorway	Section à péage sur autoroute	Mautstrecke auf der Autobahn
Toll-free section on motorway	Section libre sur autoroute	Mautfreie Strecke auf der Autobahn
in miles - in kilometers	en miles - en kilomètres	in Meilen - in Kilometern
on road	sur route	Auf der Straße

Numbering - Signs — Numérotation - Signalisation — Nummerierung - Wegweisung

Key	Légende	Zeichenerklärung
Motorway - GB: Primary route	Autoroute - GB : itinéraire principal (Primary route)	Autobahn - GB: Empfohlene Fernverkehrsstraße (Primary route)
IRL : National primary and secondary route	IRL : itinéraire principal (National primary et secondary route)	IRL: Empfohlene Fernverkehrsstraße (National primary und secondary route)
Other roads	Autres routes	Sonstige Straßen
Destination on primary route network	Localités jalonnant les itinéraires principaux	Richtungshinweis auf der empfohlenen Fernverkehrsstraße

M5   A 38   **N 20**   N 31   A 190   B 629   R 561   **YORK**

Obstacles — Obstacles — Verkehrshindernisse

Key	Légende	Zeichenerklärung
Roundabout - Pass and its height above sea level (meters)	Rond-point - Col et sa cote d'altitude (en mètres)	Verkehrsinsel - Pass mit Höhenangabe (in Meter)
Steep hill (ascent in direction of the arrow)	Forte déclivité (flèches dans le sens de la montée)	Starke Steigung (Steigung in Pfeilrichtung)
IRL: Difficult or dangerous section of road	IRL : Parcours difficile ou dangereux	IRL: Schwierige oder gefährliche Strecke
In Scotland: narrow road with passing places	En Écosse : route très étroite avec emplacements pour croisement	In Schottland: sehr schmale Straße mit Ausweichstellen (passing places)

Key	Légende	Zeichenerklärung
Level crossing: railway passing, under road, over road	Passages de la route : à niveau, supérieur, inférieur	Bahnübergänge: schienengleich, Unterführung, Überführung
Prohibited road - Road subject to restrictions	Route interdite - Route réglementée	Gesperrte Straße - Straße mit Verkehrsbeschränkungen
Toll barrier - One way road	Barrière de péage - Route à sens unique	Mautstelle - Einbahnstraße
Height limit under 15'6 IRL, 16'6 GB	Hauteur limitée au dessous de 15'6 IRL, 16'6 GB	Beschränkung der Durchfahrtshöhe bis 15'6 IRL, 16'6 GB
Load limit (under 16 t.)	Limites de charge (au-dessous de 16 t.)	Höchstbelastung (angegeben, wenn unter 16 t)

Transportation — Transports — Verkehrsmittel

Key	Légende	Zeichenerklärung
Railway - Passenger station	Voie ferrée - Gare	Bahnlinie - Bahnhof
Airport - Airfield	Aéroport - Aérodrome	Flughafen - Flugplatz
Transportation of vehicles: (seasonal services in red)	Transport des autos: (liaison saisonnière en rouge)	Autotransport: (rotes Zeichen: saisonbedingte Verbindung)
by boat	par bateau	per Schiff
by ferry (load limit in tons)	par bac (charge maximum en tonnes)	per Fähre (Höchstbelastung in t)
Ferry (passengers and cycles only)	Bac pour piétons et cycles	Fähre für Personen und Fahrräder

Accommodation - Administration — Hébergement - Administration — Unterkunft - Verwaltung

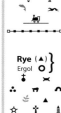

Key	Légende	Zeichenerklärung
Administrative boundaries	Limites administratives	Verwaltungshauptstadt
Scottish and Welsh borders	Limite de l'Écosse et du Pays de Galles	Grenze von Schottland und Wales
National boundary - Customs post	Frontière - Douane	Staatsgrenze - Zoll

Sport & Recreation Facilities — Sports - Loisirs — Sport - Freizeit

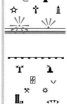

Key	Légende	Zeichenerklärung
Golf course - Horse racetrack	Golf - Hippodrome	Golfplatz - Pferderennbahn
Racing circuit - Pleasure boat harbour	Circuit automobile - Port de plaisance	Rennstrecke - Yachthafen
Caravan and camping sites	Camping, caravaning	Campingplatz
Waymarked footpath - Country park	Sentier balisé - Base ou parc de loisirs	Ausgeschilderter Weg - Freizeitanlage
Safari park, zoo - Bird sanctuary, refuge	Parc animalier, zoo - Réserve d'oiseaux	Tierpark, Zoo - Vogelschutzgebiet
IRL: Fishing - Greyhound track	IRL : Pêche - Cynodrome	IRL: Angeln - Windhundrennen
Tourist train	Train touristique	Museumseisenbahn
Funicular, cable car, chairlift	Funiculaire, téléphérique, télésiège	Standseilbahn, Seilbahn, Sessellift

Sights — Curiosités — Sehenswürdigkeiten

Key	Légende	Zeichenerklärung
Principal sights: see THE GREEN GUIDE	Principales curiosités : voir LE GUIDE VERT	Hauptsehenswürdigkeiten: siehe GRÜNER REISEFÜHRER
Towns or places of interest, Places to stay	Localités ou sites intéressants, lieux de séjour	Sehenswerte Orte, Ferienorte
Religious building - Historic house, castle	Édifice religieux - Château	Sakral-Bau - Schloss, Burg
Ruins - Prehistoric monument - Cave	Ruines - Monument mégalithique - Grotte	Ruine - Vorgeschichtliches Steindenkmal - Höhle
Garden, park - Other places of interest	Jardin, parc - Autres curiosités	Garten, Park - Sonstige Sehenswürdigkeit
IRL: Fort - Celtic cross - Round Tower	IRL : Fort - Croix celte - Tour ronde	IRL: Fort, Festung - Keltisches Kreuz - Rundturm
Panoramic view - Viewpoint	Panorama - Point de vue	Rundblick - Aussichtspunkt
Scenic route	Parcours pittoresque	Landschaftlich schöne Strecke

Rye (▲)   Ergol

Other signs — Signes divers — Sonstige Zeichen

Key	Légende	Zeichenerklärung
Industrial cable way	Transporteur industriel aérien	Industrieschwebebahn
Telecommunications tower or mast - Lighthouse	Tour ou pylône de télécommunications - Phare	Funk-, Sendeturm - Leuchtturm
Power station - Quarry	Centrale électrique - Carrière	Kraftwerk - Steinbruch
Mine - Industrial activity	Mine - Industries	Bergwerk - Industrieanlagen
Refinery - Cliff	Raffinerie - Falaise	Raffinerie - Klippen
National forest park - National park	Parc forestier national - Parc national	Waldschutzgebiet - Nationalpark

1

Verklaring van de tekens

Wegen
Autosnelweg - Serviceplaatsen
Gescheiden rijbanen van het type autosnelweg
Aansluitingen: volledig, gedeeltelijk
Afritnummers
Internationale of nationale verbindingsweg
Interregionale verbindingsweg

Verharde weg - Onverharde weg
Pad - Bewegwijzerd wandelpad / Ruiterpad
Autosnelweg in aanleg - weg in aanleg
(indien bekend: datum openstelling)

Breedte van de wegen
Gescheiden rijbanen
4 rijstroken - 2 brede rijstroken
2 rijstroken - 2 smalle rijstroken

Afstanden (totaal en gedeeltelijk)
Gedeelte met tol op autosnelwegen
Tolvrij gedeelte op autosnelwegen
in mijlen - in kilometers
op andere weg

Wegnummers - Bewegwijzering
Autosnelweg - GB: Hoofdweg
(Primary route)
IRL: Hoofdweg
(National primary en secondary route)
Andere wegen
Plaatsen langs een autosnelweg of Primary route met bewegwijzering

Hindernissen
Rotonde - Bergpas en hoogte boven de zeespiegel (in meters)
Steile helling (pijlen in de richting van de helling)
IRL: Moeilijk of gevaarlijk traject
In Schotland: smalle weg met uitwijkplaatsen

Wegovergangen:
gelijkvloers, overheen, onderdoor
Verboden weg - Beperkt opengestelde weg
Tol - Weg met eenrichtingsverkeer
Vrije hoogte indien lager dan
15'6" IRL, 16'6" GB
Maximum draagvermogen (indien minder dan 16 t)

Vervoer
Spoorweg - Reizigersstation
Luchthaven - Vliegveld
Vervoer van auto's: (tijdens het seizoen: rood teken)
per boot
per veerpont (maximum draagvermogen in t.)
Veerpont voor voetgangers en fietsers

Verblijf - Administratie
Administratieve grenzen
Grens van Schotland en Wales

Staatsgrens - Douanekantoor

Sport - Recreatie
Golfterrein - Renbaan
Autocircuit - Jachthaven
Kampeerterrein (tent, caravan)
Sentiero segnalato - Recreatiepark
Safaripark, dierentuin - Vogelreservaat
IRL: Vissen - Hondenrenbaan
Toeristentreintje
Kabelspoor, kabelbaan, stoeltjeslift

Bezienswaardigheden
Belangrijkste bezienswaardigheden: zie DE GROENE GIDS
Interessante steden of plaatsen, vakantieoorden
Kerkelijk gebouw - Kasteel
Ruïne - Megaliet - Grot
Tuin, park - Andere bezienswaardigheden
IRL: Fort - Keltisch kruis - Ronde toren
Panorama - Uitzichtpunt
Schilderachtig traject

Diverse tekens
Kabelvrachtvervoer
Telecommunicatietoren of -mast - Vuurtoren
Elektriciteitscentrale - Steengroeve
Mijn - Industrie
Raffinaderij - Klif
Staatsbos - Nationaal park

Legenda

Strade
Autostrada - Aree di servizio
Doppia carreggiata di tipo autostradale
Svincoli: completo, parziale
Svincoli numerati
Strada di collegamento internazionale o nazionale
Strada di collegamento interregionale o di disimpegno

Strada rivestita - non rivestita
Sentiero - Sentiero segnalato / Pista per cavalli
Autostrada, strada in costruzione
(data di apertura prevista)

Larghezza delle strade
Carreggiate separate
4 corsie - 2 corsie larghe
2 corsie - 2 corsie strette

Distanze (totali e parziali)
Tratto a pedaggio su autostrada
Tratto esente da pedaggio su autostrada
in miglia - in chilometri
su strada

Numerazione - Segnaletica
Autostrada - GB: itinerario principale
(Strada «Primary»)
IRL: itinerario principale
(Strada «National primary» e «Secondary»)
Altre Strade
Località delimitante gli itinerari principali

Ostacoli
Rotonda - Passo ed altitudine (in metri)
Forte pendenza (salita nel senso della freccia)
IRL: Percorso difficile o pericoloso
In Scozia: Strada molto stretta con incrocio

Passaggi della strada:
a livello, cavalcavia, sottopassaggio
Strada vietata - Strada a circolazione regolamentata
Casello - Strada a senso unico
Limite di altezza inferiore a
15'6" IRL, 16'6"GB
Limite di portata (inferiore a 16 t.)

Trasporti
Ferrovia - Stazione viaggiatori
Aeroporto - Aerodromo
Trasporto auto: (stagionale in rosso)
su traghetto
su chiatta (carico massimo in t.)
Traghetto per pedoni e biciclette

Risorse alberghiere - Amministrazione
Confini amministrativi
Confine di Scozia e Galles

Frontiera - Dogana

Sport - Divertimento
Golf - Ippodromo
Circuito Automobilistico - Porto turistico
Campeggi, caravaning
Sentiero segnalato - Area o parco per attività ricreative
Parco con animali, zoo - Riserva ornitologica
IRL: Pesca - Cinodromo
Trenino turistico
Funicolare, funivia, seggiovia

Mete e luoghi d'interesse
Principali luoghi d'interesse, vedere LA GUIDA VERDE
Località o siti interessanti, luoghi di soggiorno
Edificio religioso - Castello
Rovine - Monumento megalitico - Grotta
Giardino, parco - Altri luoghi d'interesse
IRL: Forte - Croce celtica - Torre rotonda
Panorama - Vista
Percorso pittoresco

Simboli vari
Teleferica industriale
Torre o pilone per telecomunicazioni - Faro
Centrale elettrica - Cava
Miniera - Industrie
Raffineria - Falesia
Parco forestale nazionale - Parco nazionale

Signos convencionales

Carreteras
Autopista - Áreas de servicio
Autovía
Enlaces: completo, parciales
Números de los accesos
Carretera de comunicación internacional o nacional
Carretera de comunicación interregional o alternativo

Carretera asfaltada - sin asfaltar
Sendero - Sendero señalizado / Camino de caballos
Autopista, carretera en construcción
(en su caso: fecha prevista de entrada en servicio)

Ancho de las carreteras
Calzadas separadas
Cuatro carriles - Dos carriles anchos
Dos carriles - Dos carriles estrechos

Distancias (totales y parciales)
Tramo de peaje en autopista
Tramo libre en autopista
en millas - en kilómetros
en carretera

Numeración - Señalización
Autopista - GB: Vía principal
(Primary route)
IRL: Vía principal
(National primary et secondary route)
Otras carreteras
Localidad en itinerario principal

Obstáculos
Rotonda - Puerto y su altitud (en métros)
Pendiente Pronunciada (las flechas indican el sentido del ascenso)
IRL: Recorrido difícil o peligroso
En escocia: carretera muy estrecha con ensanchamientos para poder cruzarse

Pasos de la carretera:
a nivel, superior, inferior
Tramo prohibido - Carretera restringida
Barrera de peaje - Carretera de sentido único
Altura limitada
(15'6" IRL, 16'6"GB)
Limite de carga (inferior a 16 t)

Transportes
Línea férrea - Estación de viajeros
Aeropuerto - Aeródromo
Transporte de coches: (Enlace de temporada: signo rojo)
por barco
por barcaza (carga máxima en toneladas)
Barcaza para el paso de peatones y vehículos dos ruedas

Alojamiento - Administración
Limites administrativos
Limites de Escocia y del País de Gales

Frontera - Puesto de aduanas

Deportes - Ocio
Golf - Hipódromo
Circuito de velocidad - Puerto deportivo
Camping, caravaning
Sendero señalizado - Parque de ocio
Reserva de animales, zoo - Reserva de pájaros
IRL: Pêche - Cynodrome
Tren turístico
Funicular, Teleférico, telesilla

Curiosidades
Principales curiosidades: ver LA GUÍA VERDE
Localidad o lugar interesante, lugar para quedarse
Edificio religioso - Castillo
Ruinas - Monumento megalítico - Cueva
Jardín, parque - Curiosidades diversas
IRL: Fortaleza - Cruz celta - Torre redonda
Vista panorámica - Vista parcial
Recorrido pintoresco

Signos diversos
Transportador industrial aéreo
Emisor de Radiodifusión - Faro
Central eléctrica - Cantera
Mina - Industrias
Refinería - Acantilado
Parque forestal nacional - Parque nacional

KEELE
Rye (▲)
Ergol
M5 A 38
N 20 N 31
A 190 B 629 R 561
YORK

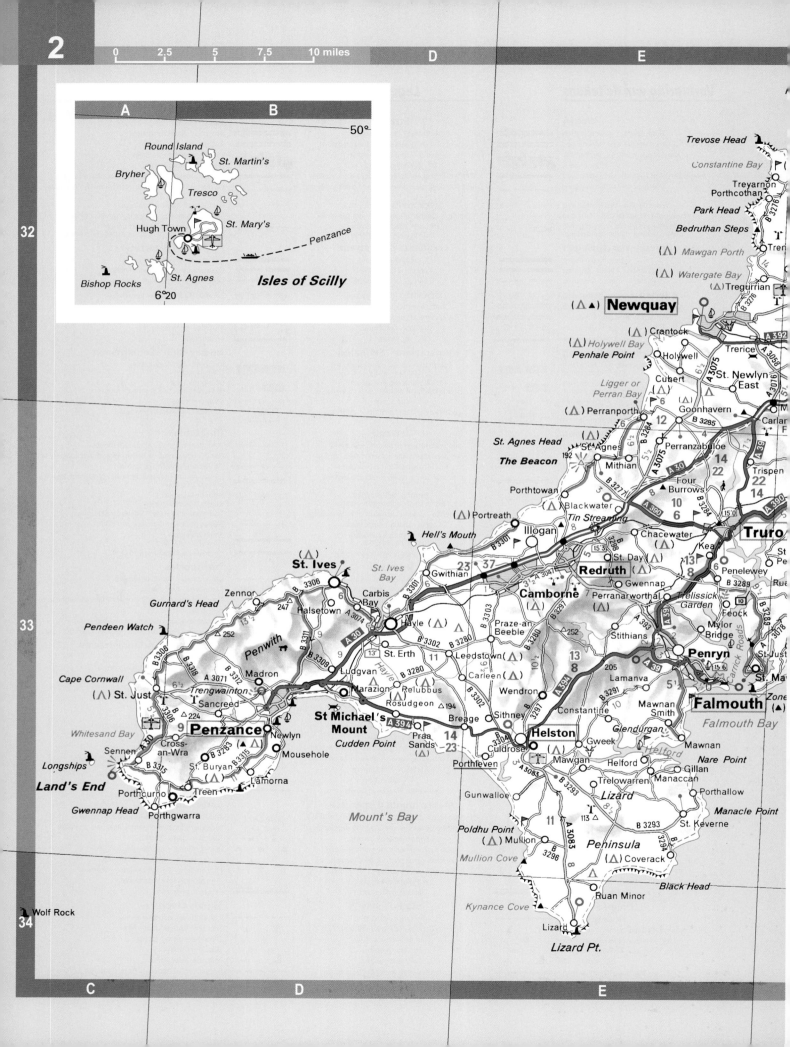

0   2.5   5   7.5   10 miles

D

E

Isles of Scilly

A   B

50°

Round Island

St. Martin's

Bryher

Tresco

Hugh Town

St. Mary's

Penzance

Bishop Rocks

St. Agnes

6°20

Isles of Scilly

32

Trevose Head

Constantine Bay

Treyarnon
Porthcothan

Park Head

Bedruthan Steps

Tren

(Λ) Mawgan Porth

(Λ) Watergate Bay

(Λ) Tregurrian

(Λ ▲) **Newquay**

(Λ) Crantock

(Λ) Holywell Bay
Penhale Point

Holywell

Trerice

A 392

Cubert

A 3075

St. Newlyn
East

Carlar

(Λ) Perranporth

Ligger or
Perran Bay

Goonhavern

B 3285

A 30

A 390

14
22

Trispen

22
14

M

St. Agnes Head

The Beacon

St. Agnes

Perranzabuloe

Mithian

A 3075

Four
Burrows

10
6

B 3284

15.0

A 390

Truro

Porthtowan

Blackwater

Tin Streaming

Chacewater

(Λ)

Kea

St
Pe

(Λ) Portreath

Illogan

St. Day

(Λ)

Redruth

(Λ)

13
8

Penelewey

Rua

B 3289

33

Hell's Mouth

Gwithian

23   37

Camborne

Gwennap

Perranarworthal

*Trelissick
Garden*

Feock

B 3289

B 3078

St. Just

St. Ives
Bay

B 3301

(Λ)

Praze-an
Beeble

Stithians

A 393

A 39

Mylor
Bridge

Carrick Roads

(Λ) **St. Ives**

Zennor

B 3306

Carbis
Bay

A 3074

Hayle (Λ)

B 3302   B 3280

Leedstown (Λ)

252

13
8

Penryn

15 6

St. Ma

Gurnard's Head

247

Halsetown

St. Erth

11

Carleen (Λ)

Wendron

A 394

Lamanva

5½

Pendeen Watch

252

B 3311

9

13'

10½

A 39

Falmouth

Zone

Penwith

B 3309

Ludgvan

B 3280

9½

Mawnan
Smith

Falmouth Bay

(▲)

B 3306

B 3318

A 3071

Madron

Marazion

(Λ)

A 394

Constantine

10

Glendurgan

Mawnan

Helford

Cape Cornwall

6½

Trengwainton

Relubbus

Rosudgeon

194

Sithney

Mawgan

Gweek

Nare Point

(Λ) St. Just

Sancreed

224

St Michael's
Mount

A 394

Breage

14

Helston

Culdrose

(Λ)

Helford

Gillan

Trelowarren

Manaccan

9   **Penzance**

Newlyn

Cudden Point

Praa
Sands

23

Porthleven

Gunwalloe

3
A 3083

Porthallow

Lizard

Sennen

Cross-
an-Wra

B 3283   B 3315

Mousehole

Manacle Point

B 3293

St. Keverne

Longships

St. Buryan

(Λ)

Lamorna

113

B 3293

A 30

Whitesand Bay

Land's End

Porthcurno

Treen

11

A 3083

B 3296

Peninsula

(Λ) Coverack

Gwennap Head

Porthgwarra

Mount's Bay

Poldhu Point

(Λ) Mullion

Mullion Cove

Black Head

Ruan Minor

34

Wolf Rock

Kynance Cove

Lizard

Lizard Pt.

C   D   E

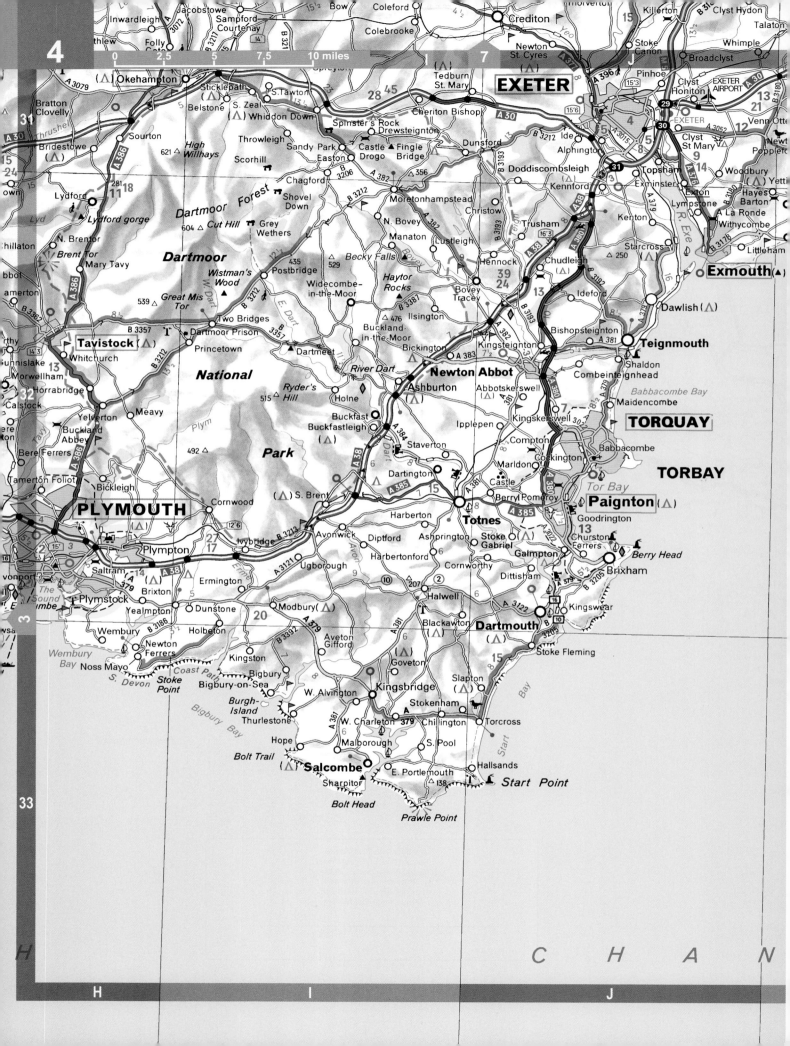

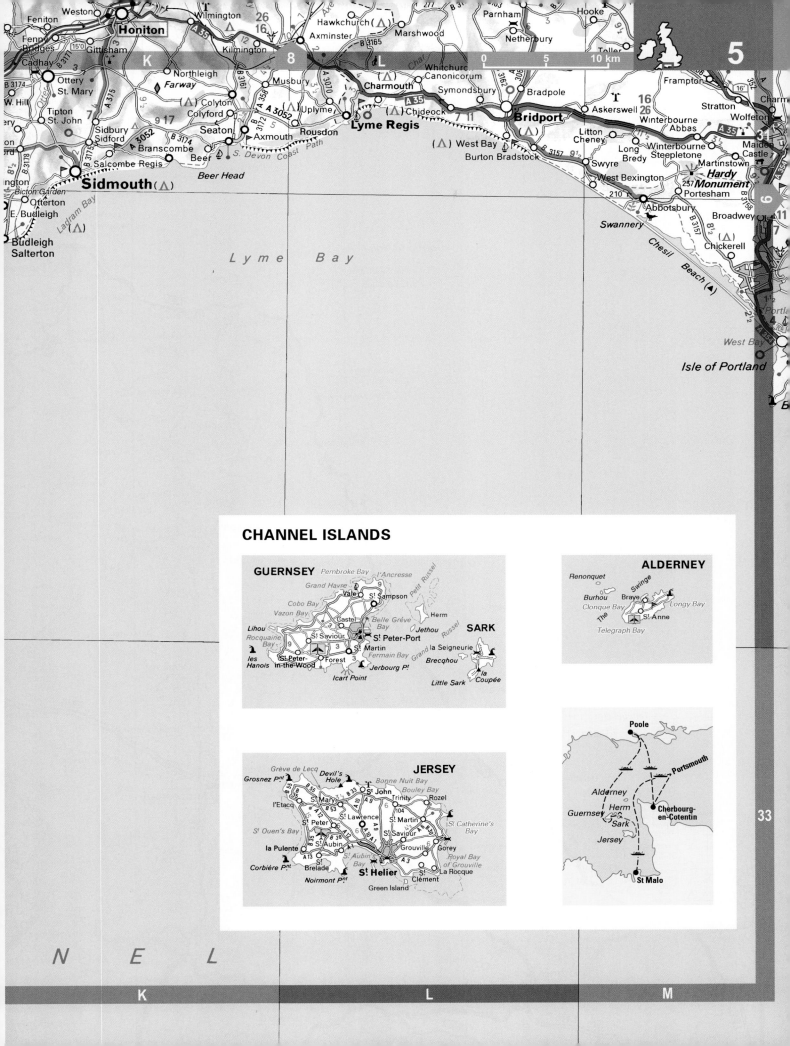

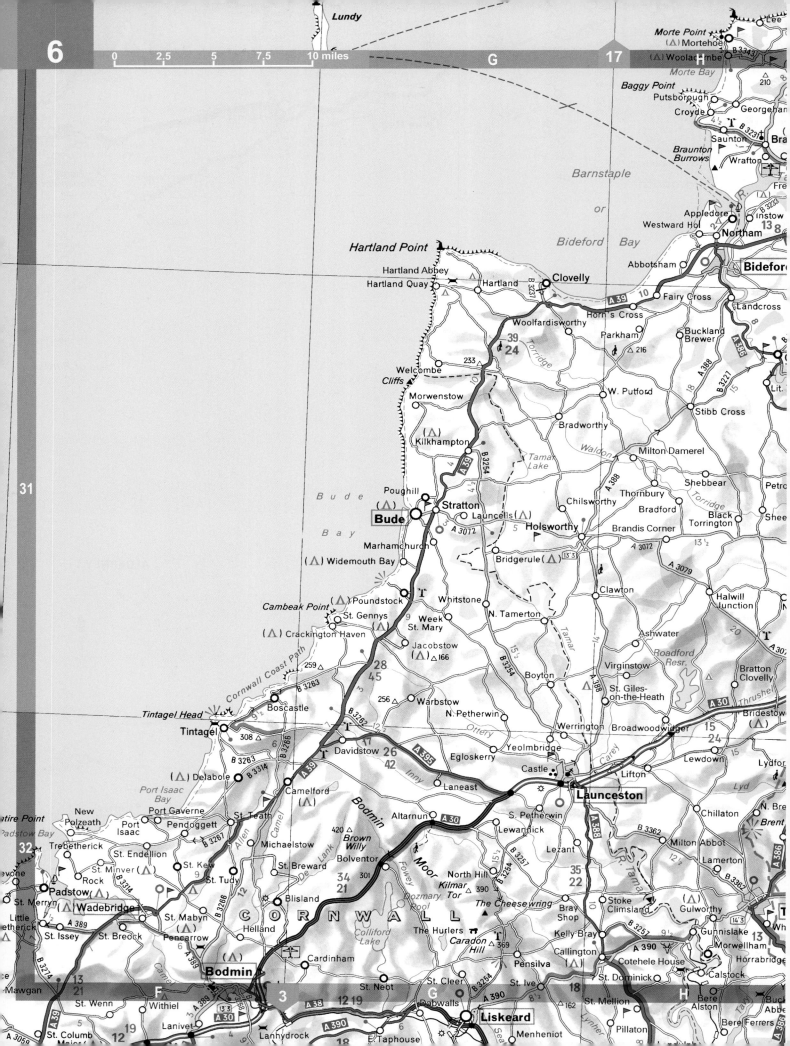

0   2.5   5   7.5   10 miles

27

28

29

Rosslare

Pembrokeshire Coast

Trwyn-y

Dinas
Head

Newpor
Bay

Strumble
Head
(▲)

Fishguard
Bay

Bryn-
Henllan

Goodwick

Dinas

3½

A 487

213

Fishguard

/Abe

10

A 40

Pemb

St Nicholas

Llanychaer

B 43/a

Ynysdeullyn

Abercastle

Trecwn

334

Penclegyr

Mathry

17

Western Cleddau

Letterston

Puncheston

Porthgain

Trevine

Welsh Hook

347

St. David's Head (▲)

Abereiddy

Croes-goch

B

164

B 4331

A 330

△ *Carn Llidi*

181

P E M B R O K E S

15
24

Wolf's Castle

*Whitesand
Bay*

6

Solva

Llandeloy

Hayscastle

Spittal

Walt

Bishop's
Palace

A 487

3½

St. David's
Tyddewi (△)

Solva

A 487

100

Newgale

△

Scolton Man

Camrose

Clarb
Road

Ramsey Sound

*Ramsey
Island*

Bishops and Clerks

Rudbaxton

Wiston

Pembrokeshire Coast Path

16

B 4330

51

Nolton

B 4329

A 487

7½

St. Bride's Bay

Haverfordwest

14'9

Broad Haven
(△)

B 4341

B 4327

13

A 4076

Hwlffordd

Pictor

National Park

Lit. Haven

A 40

The Smalls

*Martin's
Haven*

Johnston

A 477

10

Llangwm

Ma

Skomer Island
(▲)

St-Brides

B 4327

Steynton

Rosemarket

Lawrenny

Grassholme I.

Herbrandston

5½

St.
Ishmael's

Marloes

Milford Haven

Neyland

16   Cas

Broad Sound

Aberdaugleddau

6½

Dale

Milford Haven
Dauddreddau

4½   27

10   1

Skokholm Island (▲)

71

Pembroke Dock

Doc Penfro

15'

A 47

Thorn I.

Angle

St. Ann's Head (▲)

Rhoscrowther

Pembroke
Penfro

4075   Bish

Rosslare

B 4320

*Freshwater
West*

Hundleton

Lamphey   Ja

14'6

B 4319

B 4594

B 4136

Castlemartin

12

B 4319

*Freshwater
East*

*Linney
Head*

National Park

Stackpole

Bosherston

Stackpole H

Stack Rocks

**St. Govan's
Head** (▲)

P e m b r o k e s h i r e

D   **E**   **F**

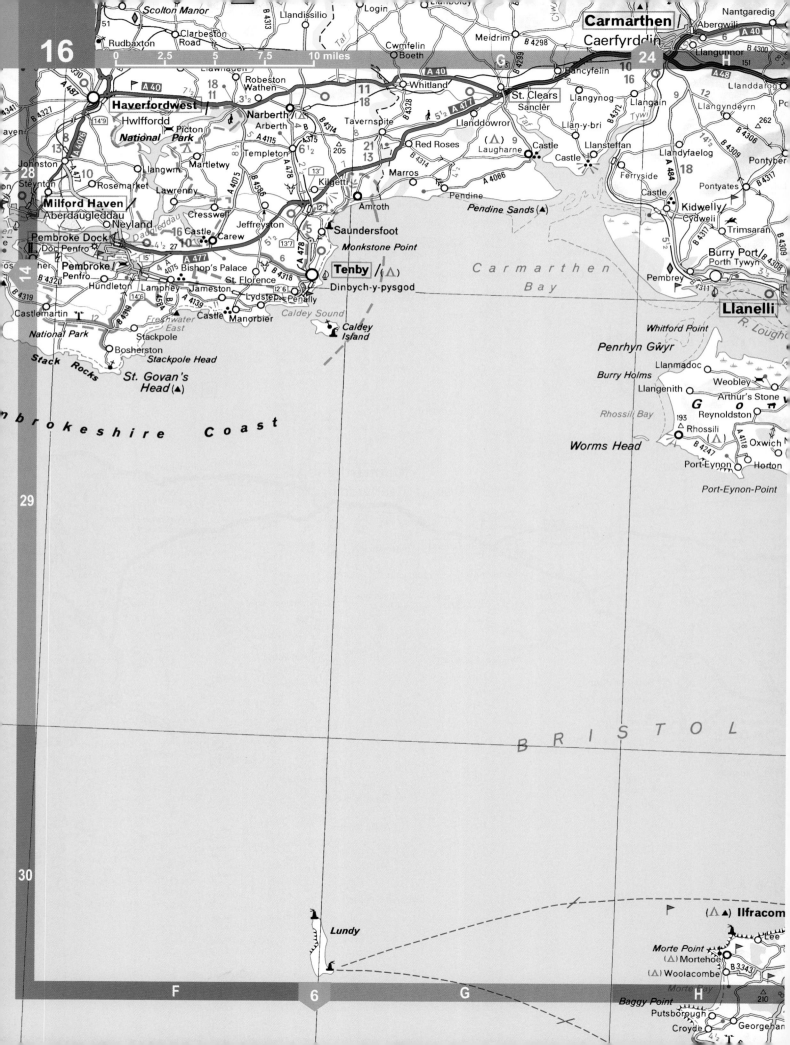

Carmarthen
Caerfyrddin

Nantgaredig
Abergwili

Scolton Manor
Llandissilio
Login
Llanboidy

Rudbaxton
Clarbeston
Road
B 4313
Llawhaden
Cwmfelin
Boeth
Meidrim
B 4298
Bancyfelin
A 40
Llangunnor
6
A 40

Llandafog
B 4300

A 40
Robeston
Wathen
18
11
3½
11
18
Whitland
St. Clears
Sanclêr
Llangynog
Llangain
Llangyndeyrn
151

Haverfordwest
Hwlffordd
Narberth
Arberth
Tavernspite
A 417
Llanddowror
Llan-y-bri
12
Llanddarog
A 48

National Park
Templeton
A 4115
21
13
Red Roses
(Δ) 9
Laugharne
Castle
Llanstefan
Llandyfaelog
A 484
18
Pontyber

Johnston
A 411
10
Rosemarket
Martletwy
A 4075
205
B 4314
Marros
Pendine
Ferryside
Castle
Pontyates
B 4306
B 4309

Milford Haven
Aberdaugleddau
Neyland
Cresswell
Jeffreyston
Amroth
Pendine Sands (Δ)
Kidwelly
Cydweli
Trimsaran
B 4317

Pembroke Dock
Dôc Penfro
16
Castle
Carew
A 478
Saundersfoot
Monkstone Point
Burry Port
Porth Tywyn
B 4308
3½

Pembroke
Penfro
Bishop's Palace
St. Florence
Tenby
Dinbych-y-pysgod
(Δ)
Pembrey
Carmarthen Bay

Hundleton
Lamphey
Jameston
Lydstep
Penally
Whitford Point
Penrhyn Gŵyr
Llanelli

Castlemartin
National Park
Freshwater East
Castle
Manorbier
Caldey Sound
Caldey Island
Burry Holms
Llanmadoc
Weobley
Arthur's Stone
G
O

Stackpole
Bosherston
Stackpole Head
Rhossili Bay
193
Rhossili
(Δ)
Reynoldston
Oxwich
W
E
R

Stack Rocks
St. Govan's Head (Δ)
Worms Head
B 4247
Port-Eynon
Horton

P e m b r o k e s h i r e   C o a s t
Port-Eynon-Point

29

30

B R I S T O L

(Δ ▲) Ilfracom

Lundy
Lee
Morte Point
(Δ) Mortehoe
(Δ) Woolacombe
B 3343

Morte Bay
Baggy Point
Putsborough
Croyde
Georgeham

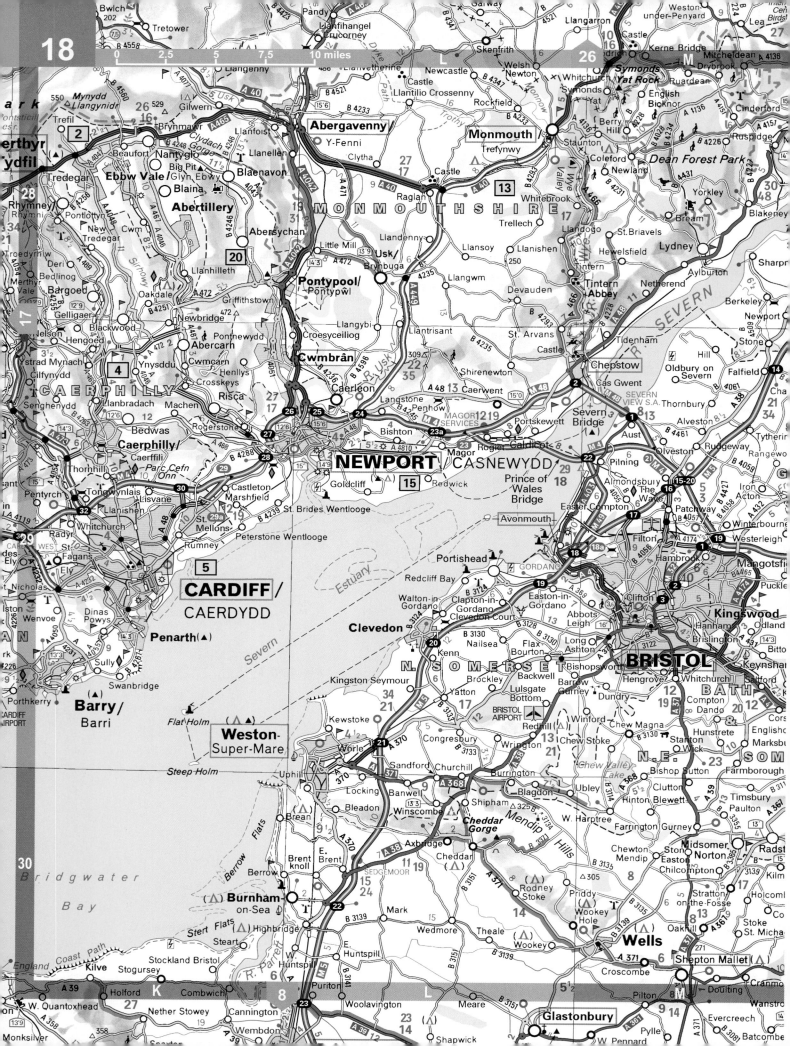

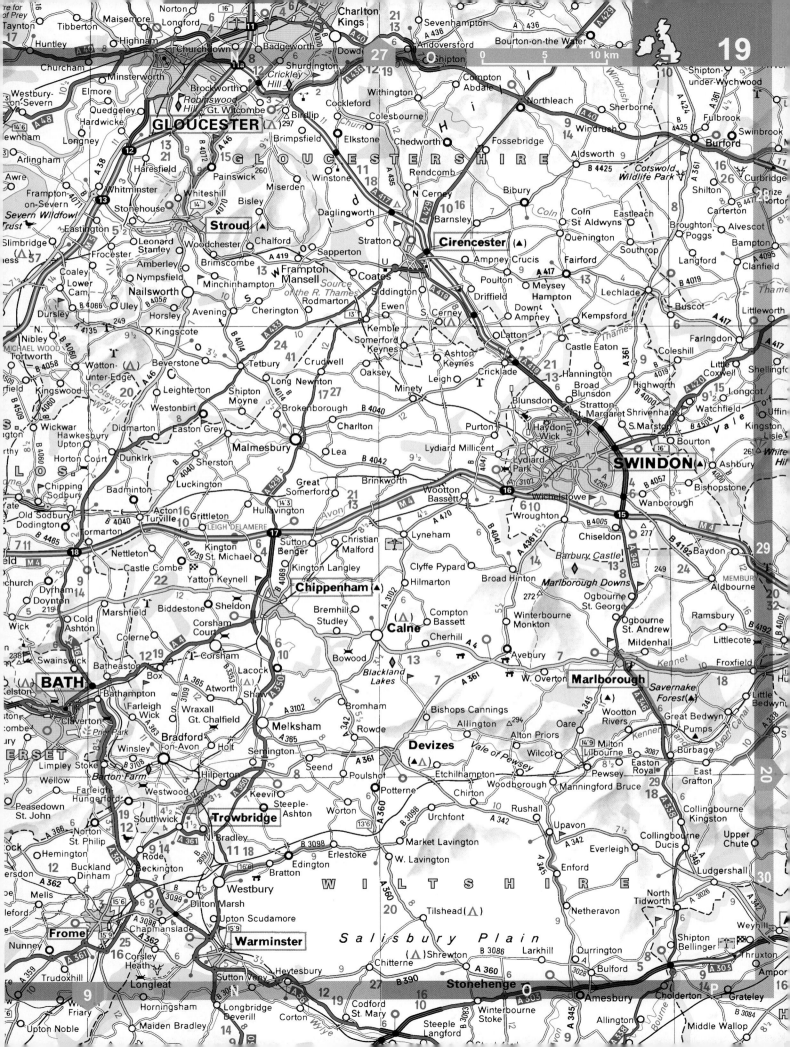

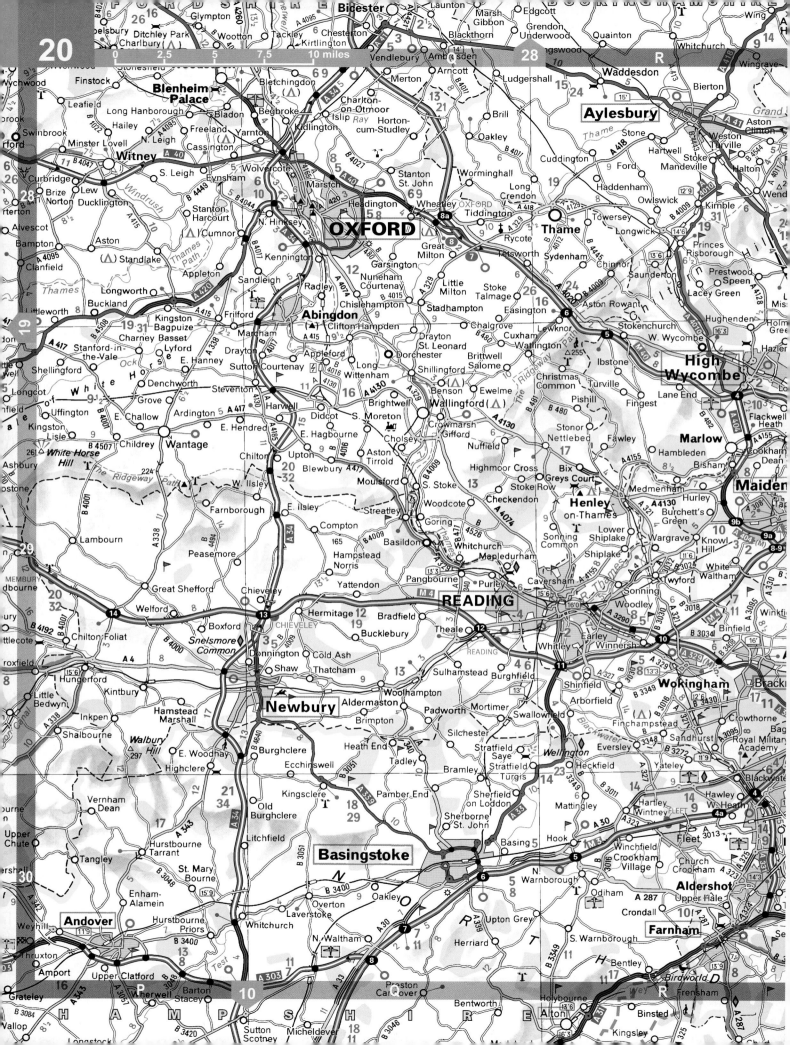

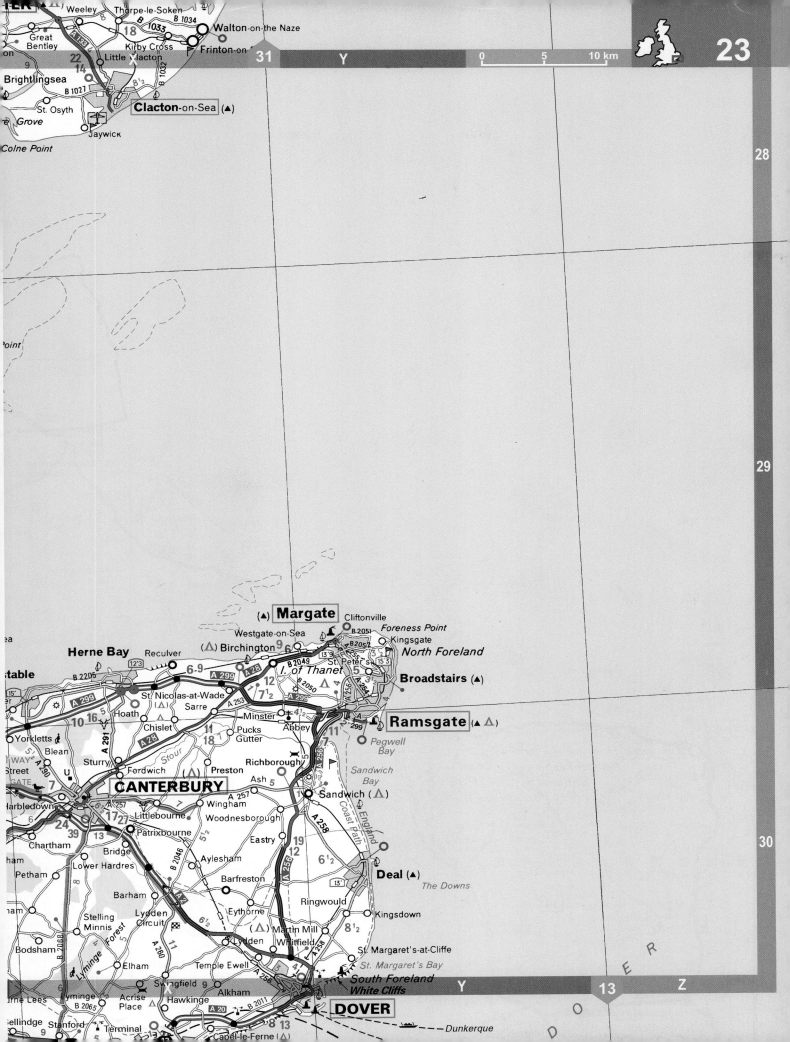

Weeley Thorpe-le-Soken
Great
Bentley
B 1033 B 1034 Walton-on-the Naze
18
Kirby Cross Frinton-on-
22
14 Little Clacton
31
Brightlingsea
B 1027
St. Osyth
Grove Clacton-on-Sea (▲)
Jaywick
Colne Point

29

(▲) **Margate** Cliftonville
Westgate-on-Sea B 2051 Foreness Point
(△) Birchington 9 6 Kingsgate
Herne Bay Reculver B 205 North Foreland
B 2049 St. Peter's
stable B 2205 12'3 6·9 A 299 A 28 I. of Thanet 5
10 16 St. Nicolas-at-Wade 12 B 2050 **Broadstairs** (▲)
Hoath 7½ A 299
Yorkletts Sarre A 253 Minster 4½
Blean A 291 Chislet 11 Pucks Abbey **Ramsgate** (▲ △)
Sturry 18 Gutter 7 Pegwell
Street A 290 Fordwich (△) Preston Richborough Bay
GATE 7 **CANTERBURY** Ash 5 Sandwich
Harbledown A 257 Wingham Bay
24 17 27 Littlebourne Woodnesborough A 258 Sandwich (△)
39 13 Patrixbourne Eastry 19
Chartham Bridge Aylesham 12 6½
Lower Hardres Barfreston Deal (▲)
Petham Barham 13' The Downs
Stelling Ringwould
Minnis Lydden Eythorne Kingsdown
Bodsham Circuit 8½
Lydden (△) Martin Mill
Stanford Elham Whitfield
Lyminge Temple Ewell St. Margaret's-at-Cliffe
Forest St. Margaret's Bay
Acrise Swingfield 9 Alkham South Foreland
Place Hawkinge White Cliffs
B 2065 A 20 B 2011 **DOVER**
ellindge Terminal 8 13
9 Capel-le-Ferne (△) — Dunkerque

0   2.5   5   7.5   10 miles

26

14

27

CARDIGAN BAY

(▲) Ab

Llansa

(▲) Llanon
37
23

Aberaeron

(△) Llanerchaeron
New Quay / Gardens
Ceinewydd
B 4342   Llanarth   174
4   A 4342   Mydroilyn   B 4342

Ynys-Lochtyn   Llwyndafydd
Llangrannog   26   A 487   Synod Inn
16   A 486
B 4334   Talgarreg   B 4338
Clegyr (▲)   9   324
Aberporth   Brynhoffnant   Cwrt-
Cardigan   B 2   Bettws   Rhydlewis   newydd
Island   A 4333   Evan   B 4571   Ffostrasol
Mwnt   Blaenannerch   Beulah   Ceri   Penrhiwpal   Pontshaen
Cemaes Head   Gwbert   A 484   B 4333   27   Rhydowen
St. Dogmaels   Cardigan   Aberteifi   B 4570   Aber-Banc   Horeb   Llanwenog
Llechryd   Teifi   Cwmcoy   B 4476   Llandysul
Moylgrove   Castle   A 484   Llanfihangel
646   Cilgerran   31   Cenarth   Llangeler   ar-Arth
Trwyn-y-bwa   Nevern   A 4582   Newchapel   Newcastle Emlyn /   Drefach
Dinas   Castell   A 487   Boncath   Castell Newydd Emlyn   A 484
Head   Henllys   Eglwyswrw   Moelfre   National   169   Pencader
Newport Bay   B 4332   335   Wool   Llanfihangel
Bryn   Newport   19   Museum   Gwyddgrug
Fishguard Bay   Henllan   Dinas   A 487   31   Felindre   Cilrhedyn   A 485
Goodwick   Pentre Ifan   A 478   Nyfer
213   Fishguard / Abergwaun   Crymych   CARMAR
St. Nicholas   Pembrokeshire Coast   B 4299   314
A 40   Llanychaer   B 4329   National   Park   Cilrhedyn   A 484   355
A 487   Mynydd Preseli   Llanfyrhach   Cwmduad
Trecwn   334   Crymych   Trelech   Llanpumsaint
Mathry   Letterston   Puncheston   536   Glandwr   Trelech a'r   Cynwyl
B 4331   347   Rosebush   Mynachlog-   Betws   Elfed
28   Welsh Hook   ddu   Cwmbach   B 4307
BROKESHIRE   Maenclochog   Pantymenyn   Pontarsais
Hayscastle   15   Wolf's Castle   E. Cleddau   Cefn-y-pant   Llanboidy   291
24   Llys-y-frân   16   Login   Newchurch
Spittal   Resr   Cwmfelin
A 40   Walton E.   21   A 478   Boeth   B 4298   Carmarthen /
Scolton Manor   Llandissilio   B 4333   Meidrim   Caerfyrddin
Camrose   Clarbeston   Taf   A 40   Llangunnor
16   Rudbaxton   Road   Abergwili
B 4329   Wiston   151
B 4330   Llawhaden   A 40   Llanddarog
Haverfordwest   16   Whitland   St. Clears   Bancyfelin   10   A 48
14·9   Hwlffordd   Robeston   A 477   Sanclêr   16   Llangynog   Llangain
Narberth   Wathen   A 40   Llanddowror   Tywi   Llangyndeyrn
Arberth   Tavernspite   Cwmfelin   Llan-y-bri   262
Picton   B 4314   Boeth

Pembrokeshire Coast Path

Coast

CHANNEL

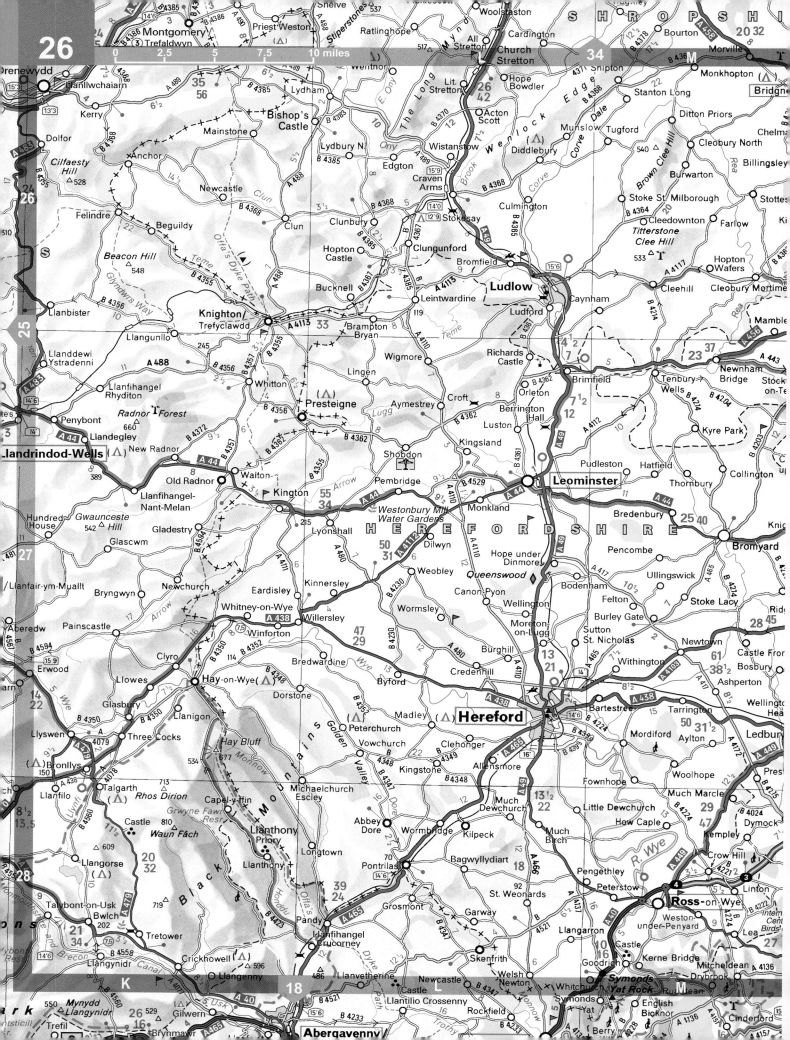

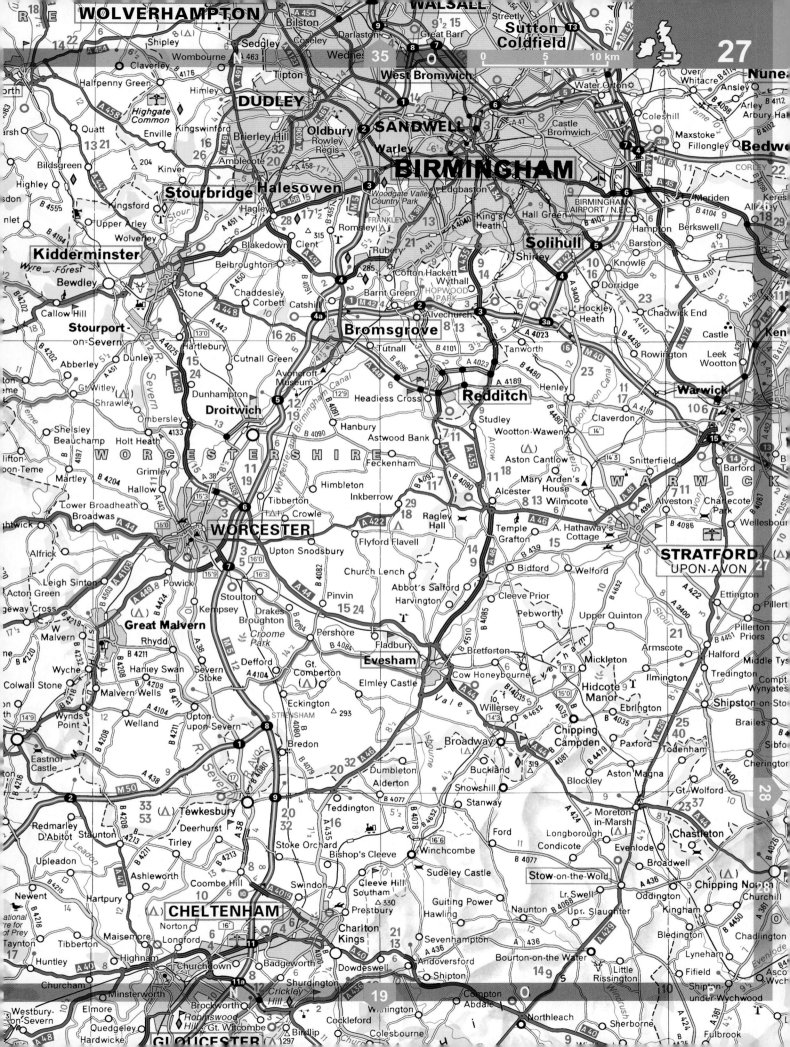

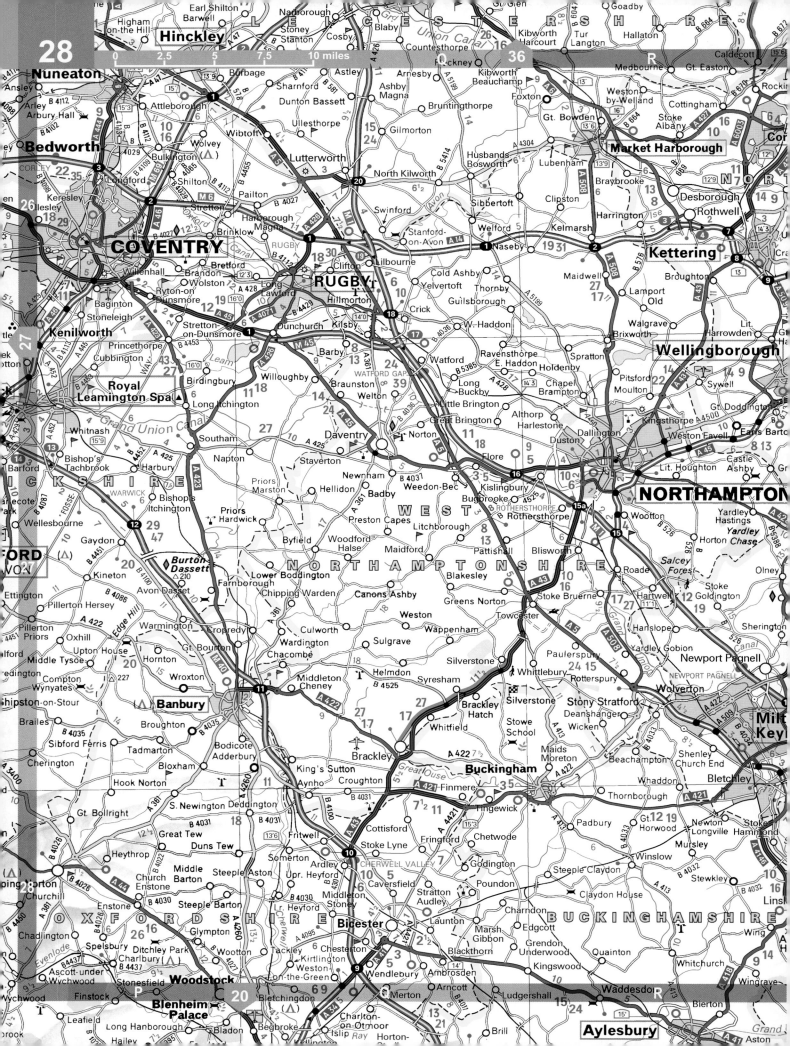

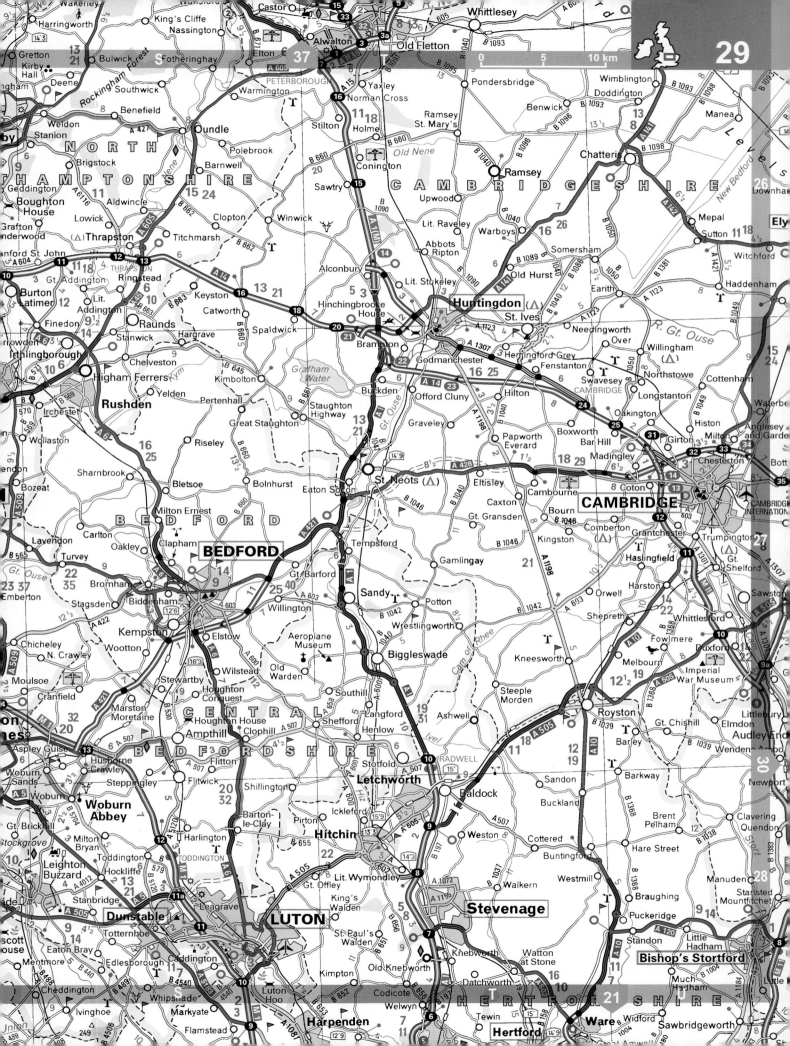

0   2.5   5   7.5   10 miles

F A N 40 ESEY

Cymyran Bay
Rhosneigr
(Λ)
Llanfaelog
34
5
6
Pentre Berw
7
B 4422
A 4080
B 4419
Cefni
Llanfair-Pwl
Bryn-Celli-ddu
Aberffraw
A 4080
10½
6
(Λ)
A 4421
Plas New
Bordogan
A 4080
Brynsiencyn
(Λ)
A 4419
Newborough
Mermaid Inn
B 4366
Menai
Malltraeth Bay
(Λ)
Llanddwyn-Island
Caernarfón
Bontr

24

C a e r n a r f o n

B a y

Llanwnda
(Λ)
Dinas Dinlle
53
Llandwrog
(Λ)
Pen-y-gr
Pontlyfni
(Λ)
A 499
B 4
A 487
13½
9
Llanllyfni
Clynnog-Fawr
21
16
25
Trevor
A 499
522
Yr Eifl
Trwyn y Gorlech
564
Llanaelhaearn
B 4411
Carreg Ddu
Llithfaen
B 4417
6
7½
(Λ)
B 4411
4½
Morfa Nefyn
B 4412
Nefyn
L l e y n
P e n i n s u l a
(Λ)
Llanystumdwy
Y Ffor
A 497
B 4354
A 499
B 4354
Chwilog
14
Porth Ysgaden
7
Efailnewydd
A 497
9½
Criccieth
Tudweiliog
△ 312
B 4415
(Λ)
Pwllheli
(Λ)
B 4417
Llangwnnadl
(Λ)
Sarn Meyllteyrn
13
Tremadd
Penrhyn Mawr
103
Botwnnog
B 4413
Llanbedrog
Bay
8½
A 499
6½
305
4
St. Tudwal's
Road
Mynydd Mawr
Aberdaron
Llanengan
Abersoch
Braich y Pwll
△ 160
Rhiw
Porth Neigwl or
Hell's Mouth
Bwlchtocyn
Bardsey Sound
St. Tudwal's Islands
Trwyn Cilan

Bardsey Island (▲)

C A R D I G A N   B A Y

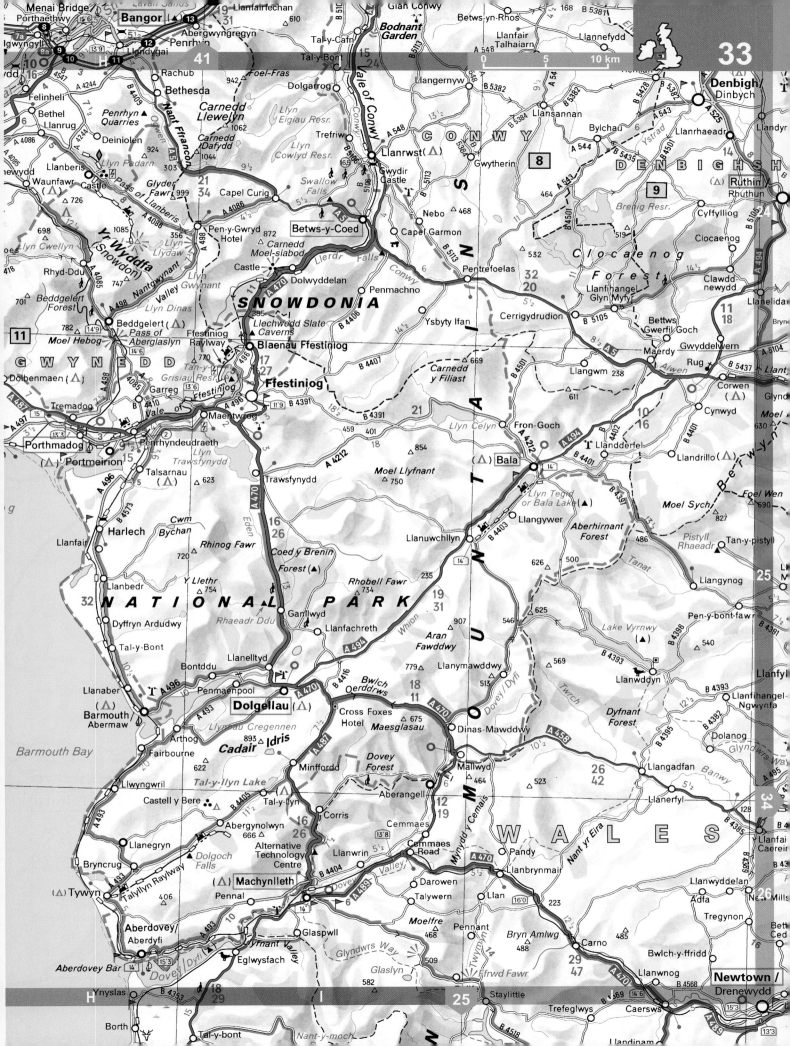

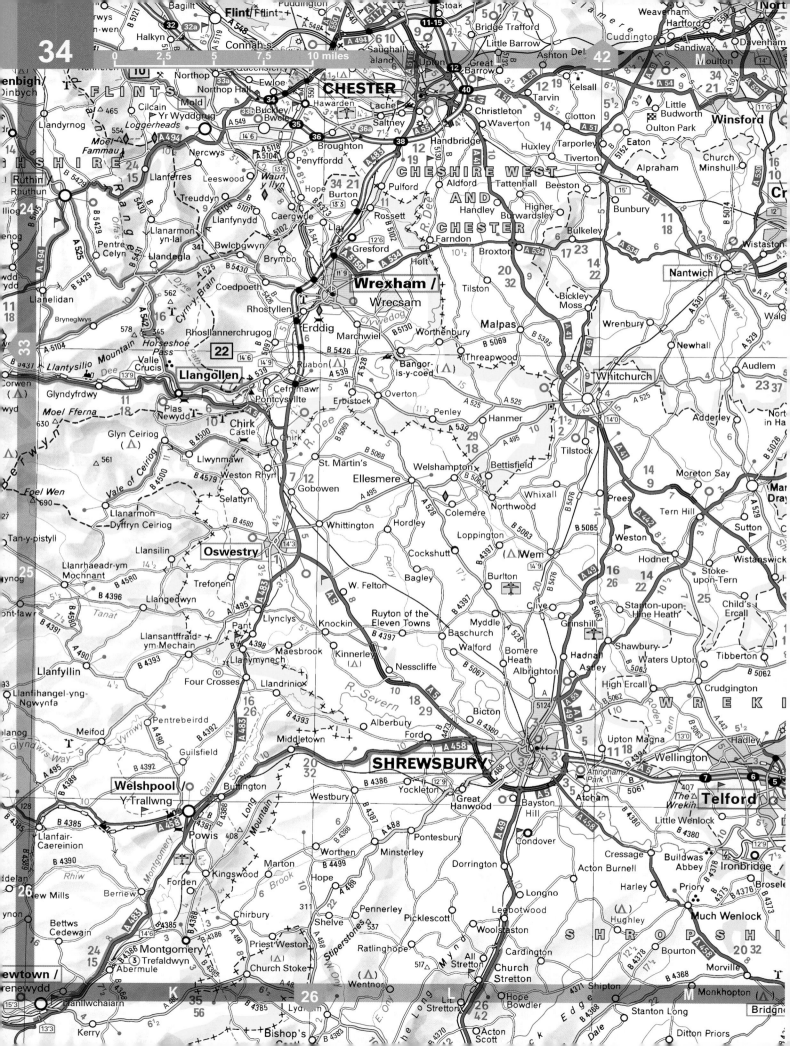

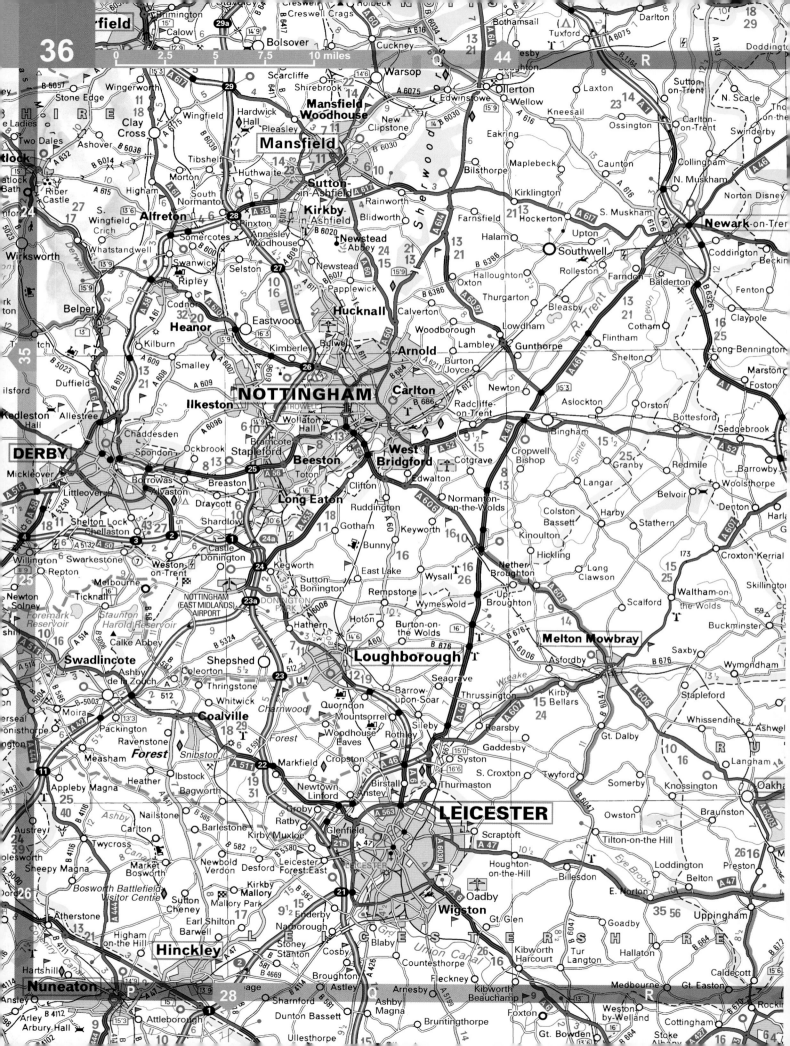

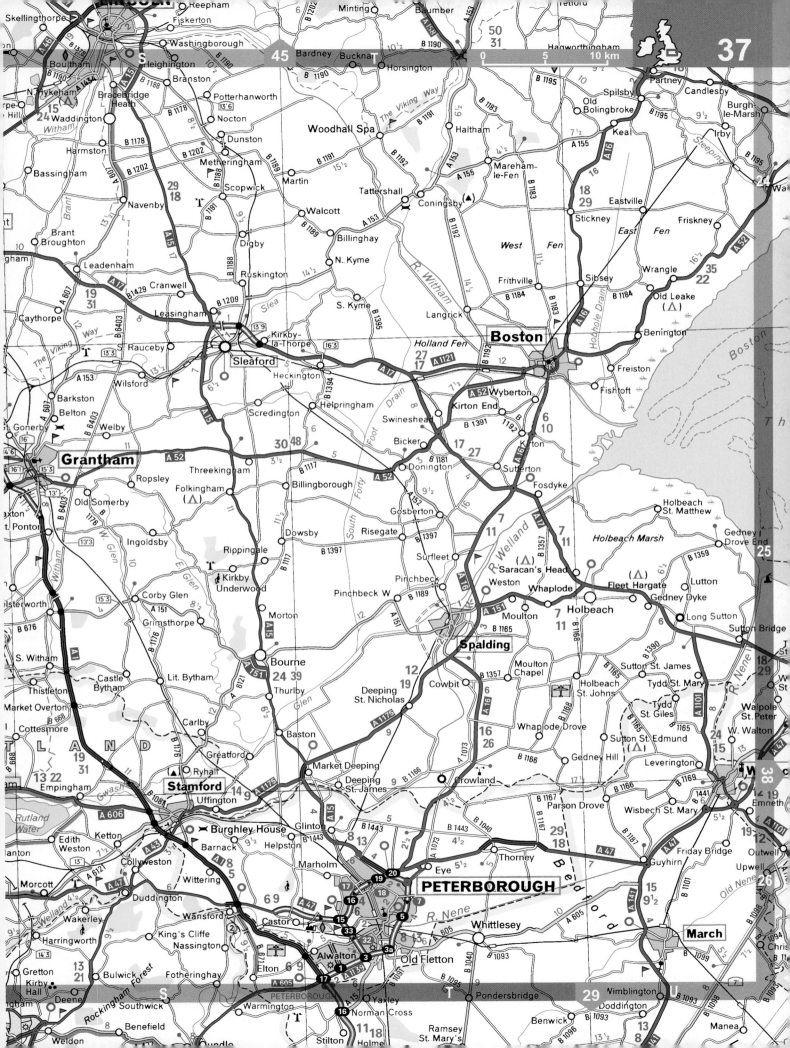

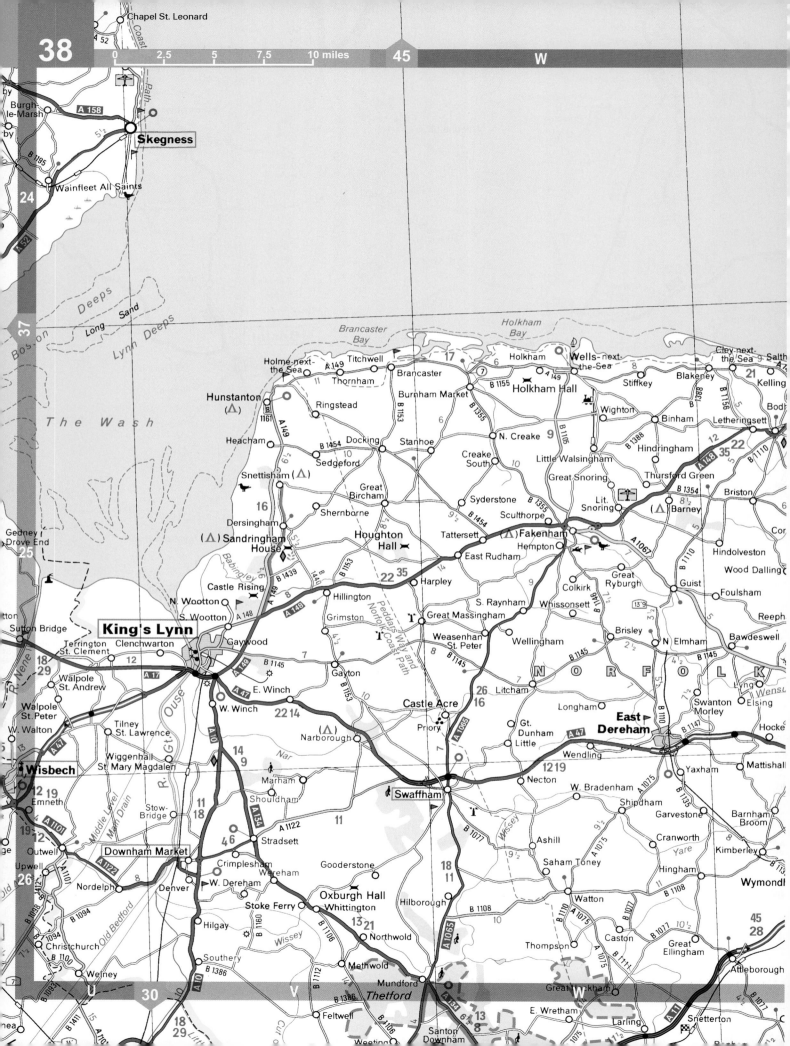

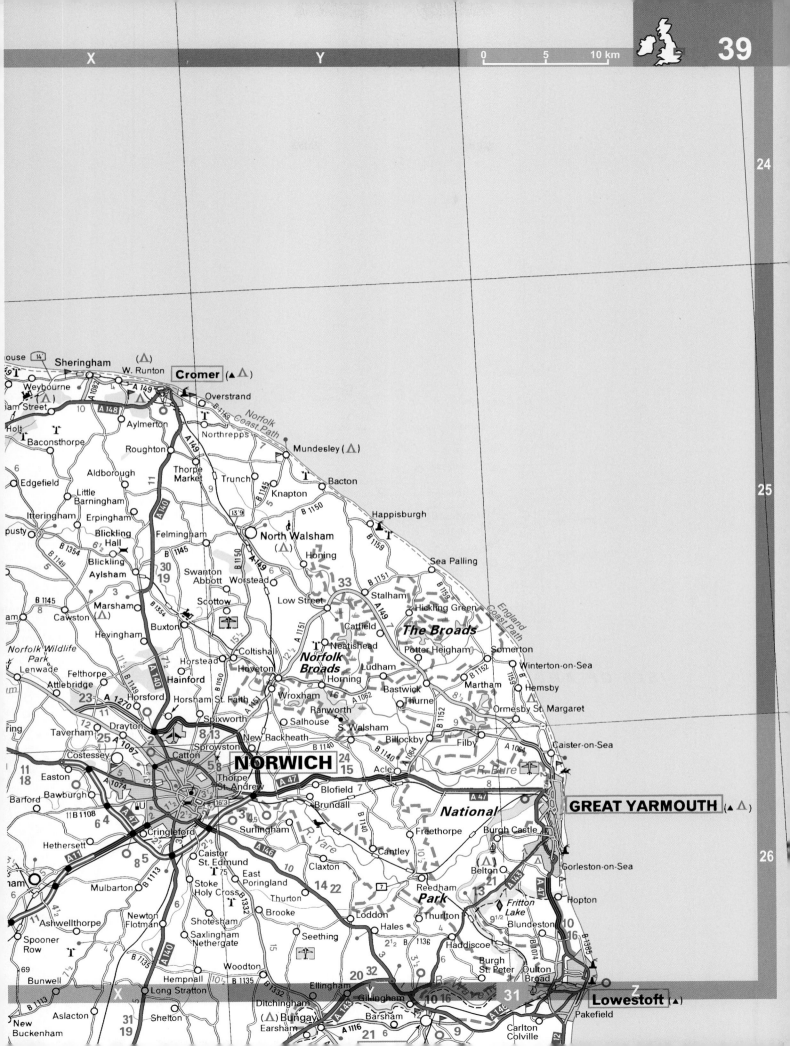

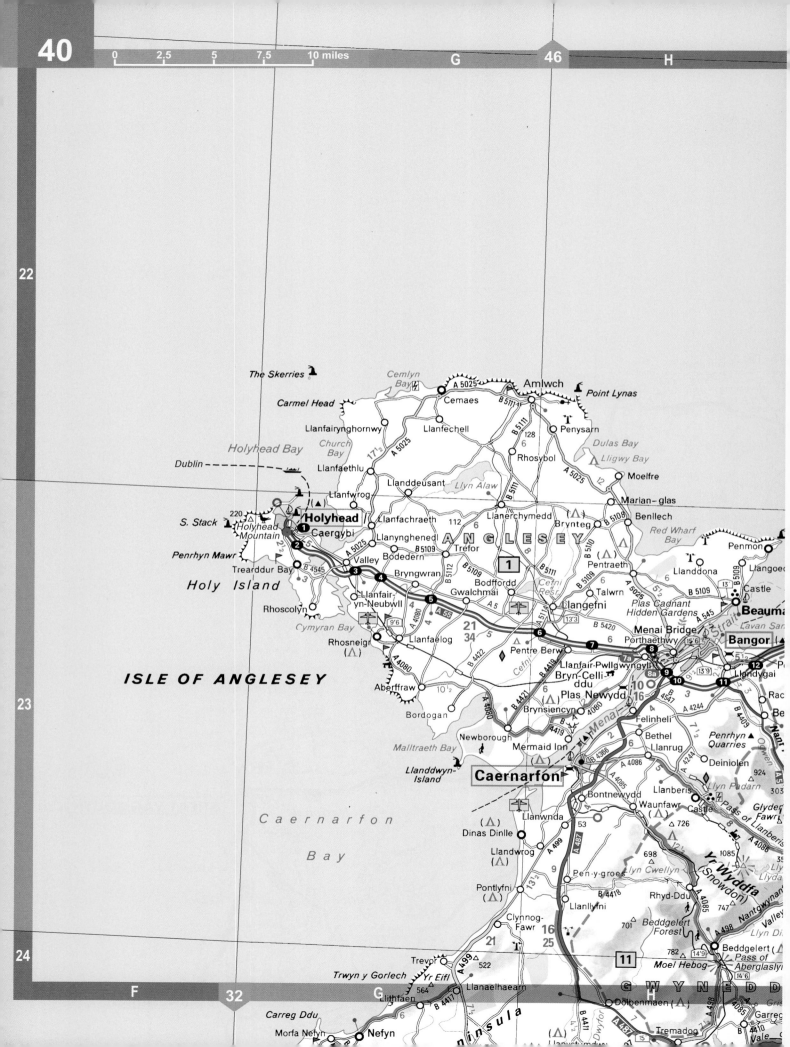

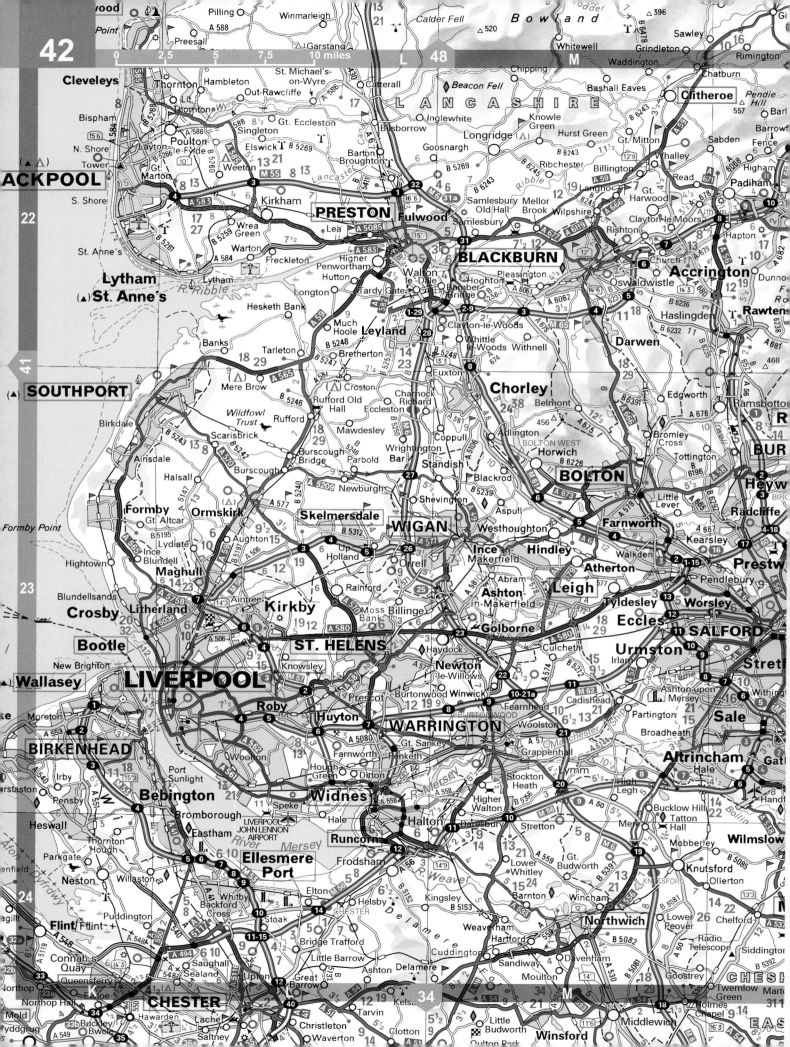

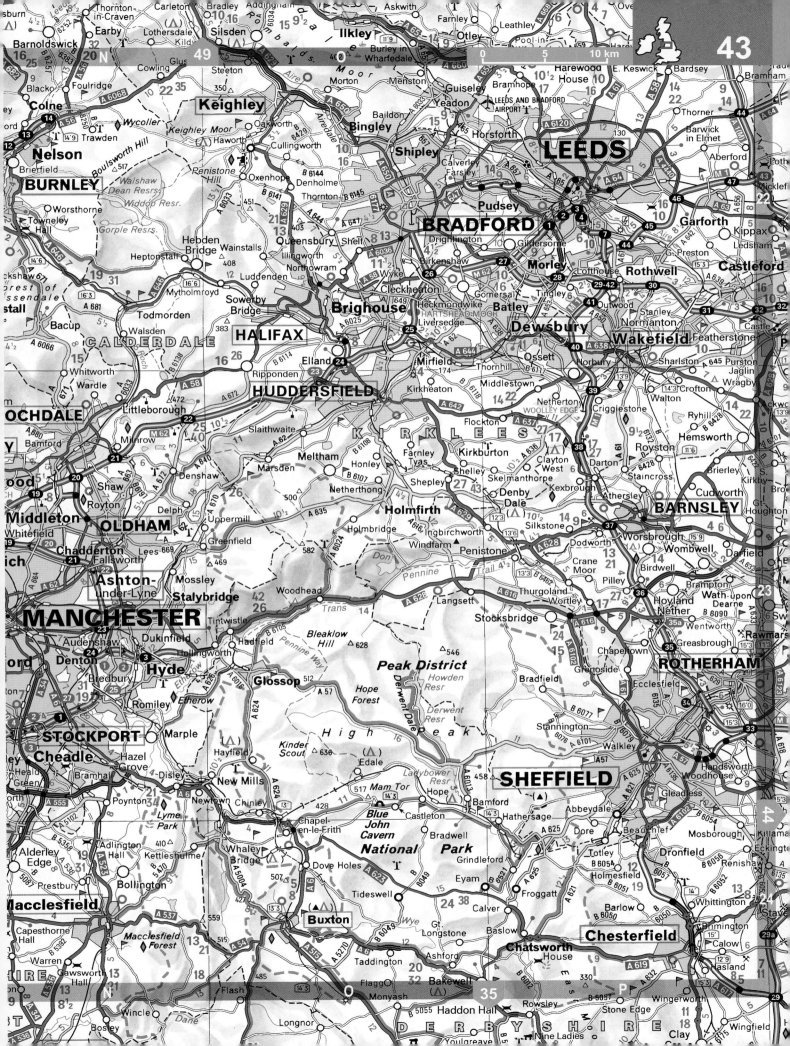

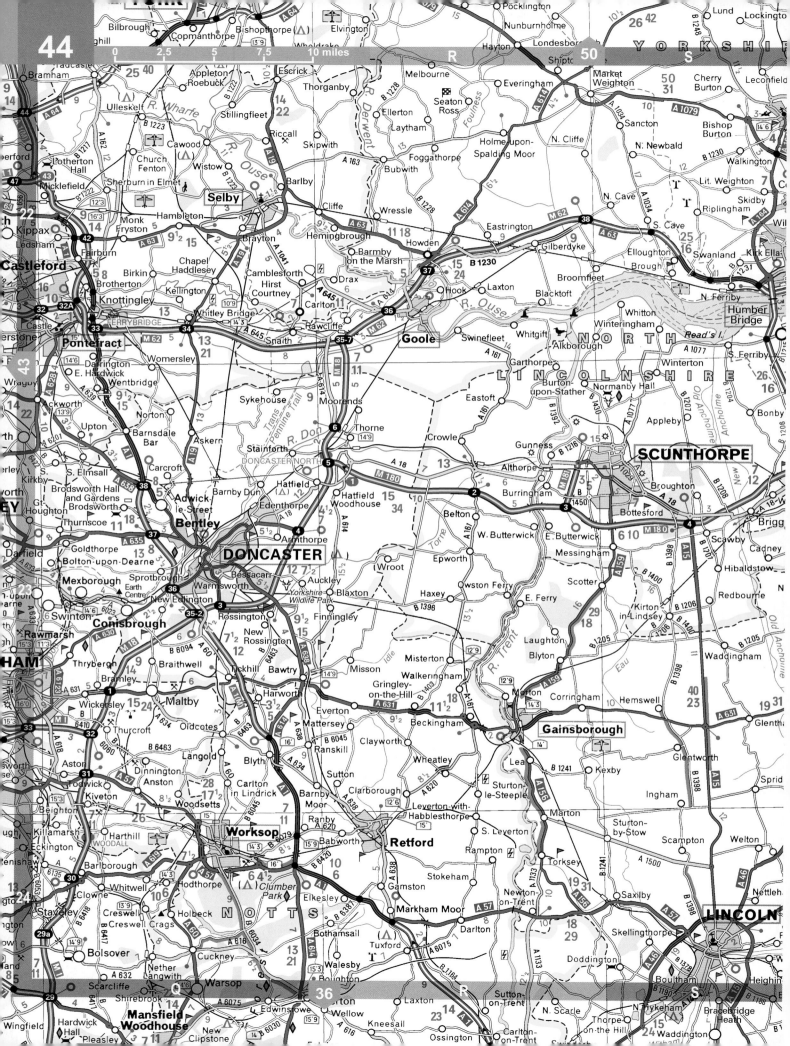

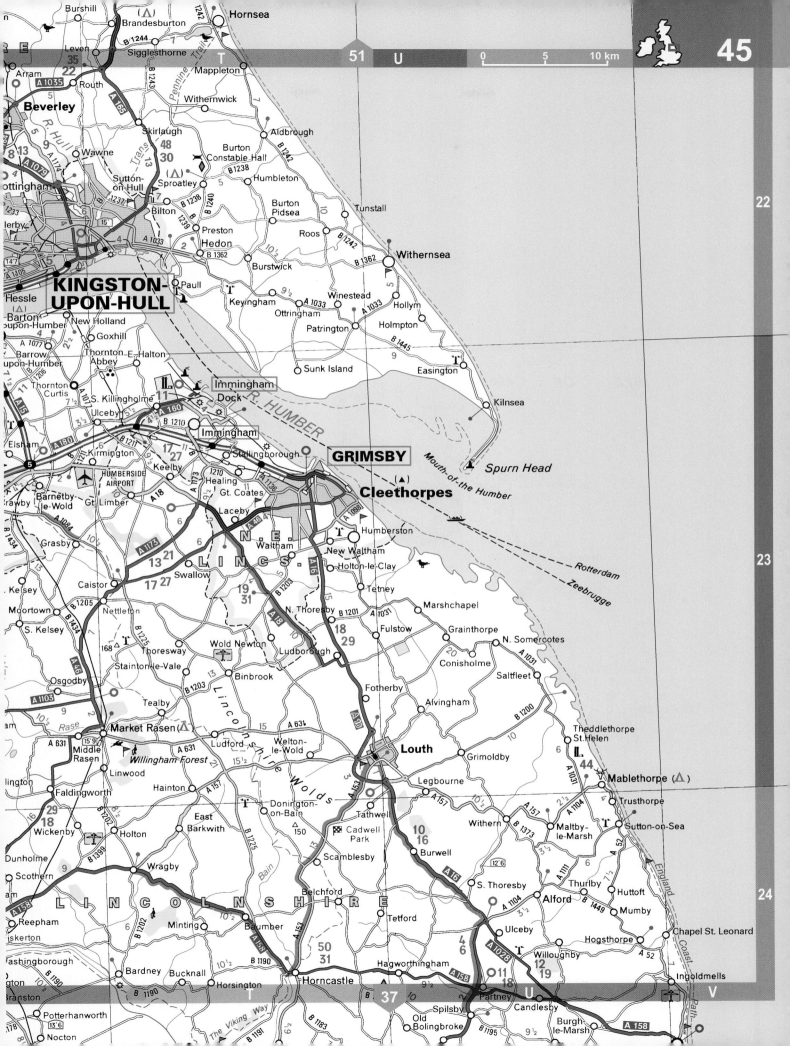

0   2.5   5   7.5   10 miles

G   H

20

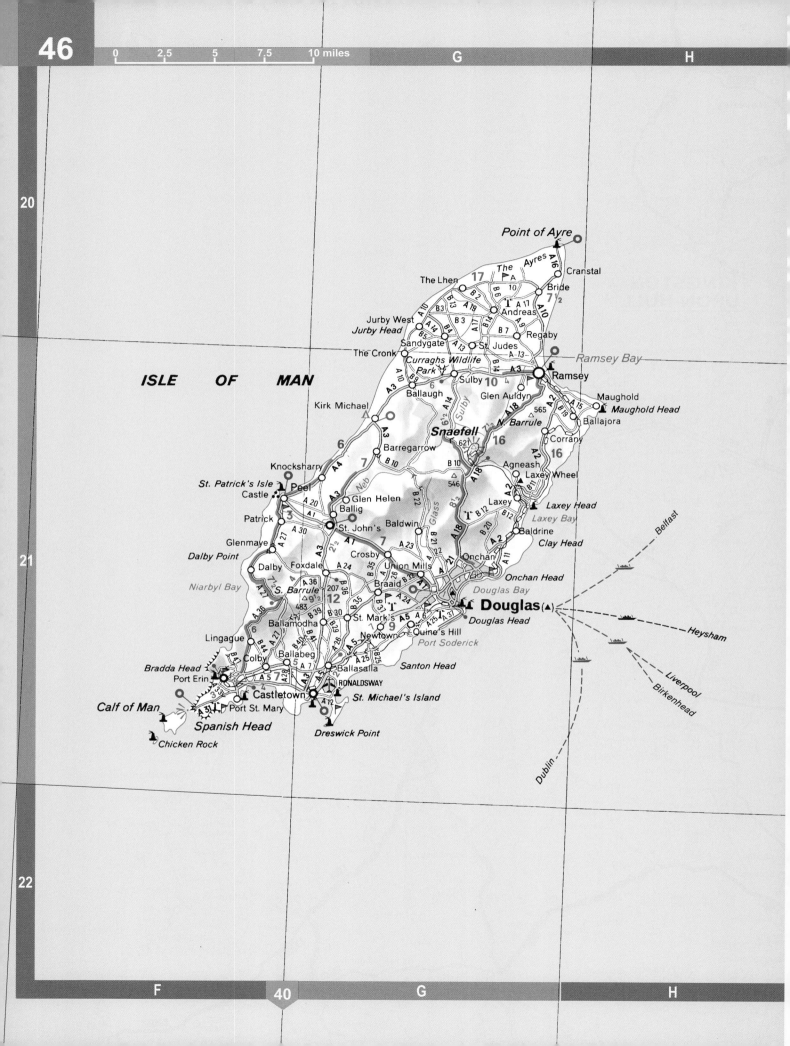

ISLE OF MAN

Point of Ayre

The Ayres

The Lhen   **17**   *A*   A 16   Cranstal

Bride   A 10   **7½**

Andreas   A 17

Jurby West   A 14   B 3   A 17   B 7   Regaby

Jurby Head   B 5   B 4   A 13

Sandygate   St. Judes   A-13

The Cronk   *Curraghs Wildlife Park*   *Ramsey Bay*

B 9   Sulby   **10**   A 3   **Ramsey**

Ballaugh   Glen Auldyn   Maughold

Kirk Michael   A 3   *Sulby*   565   *Maughold Head*

N. Barrule   **16**   Ballajora

A 3   Barregarrow   621   Corrany

6   B 10   A 18   **16**

Knocksharry   **7**   B 10   Agneash

A 4   *Neb*   546   Laxey Wheel

St. Patrick's Isle   **Peel**

Castle   A 20   Glen Helen   Laxey

Patrick   **3**   Ballig   B 12   *Laxey Head*

A 1   Baldwin   *Glass*   *Laxey Bay*

Glenmaye   A 27   St. John's   B 20   Baldrine

Dalby Point   A 30   **7**   A 23   *Clay Head*

Dalby   Foxdale   Crosby   Onchan

Niarbyl Bay   A 36   207   Union Mills   *Onchan Head*

7½   *S. Barrule*   **12**   Braaid   A 24   *Douglas Bay*

483   B 39   B 35   St. Mark's

Ballamodha   A 5   A 6   **Douglas** (▲)

Lingague   **6**   **9**   Quine's Hill   *Douglas Head*

Colby   Newtown   *Port Soderick*

Bradda Head   Ballabeg   A 25   *Santon Head*

Port Erin   **7**   Ballasalla

A 5   **RONALDSWAY**

Calf of Man   Castletown   *St. Michael's Island*

A 31   Port St. Mary   A 12

Spanish Head   *Dreswick Point*

Chicken Rock

Belfast

Heysham

Liverpool

Birkenhead

Dublin

21

22

Distington Ullock

Lowca

Parton

Morc

Whitehaven

0   5   10 km

B 5295 A 5086

B 5294 Frizington

Ennerdale Bridge

Ennerdale Water

Cleator Moor

Ehen

6
10

St. Bees Head

B 5345

(Δ) St. Bees

B 5345 Egremont

A 595

England

Beckermet

Calder Bridge

Gosforth

10°9

B 5344

Seascale

Santon
Bridge

Irt

B 5344

Holmrook

Drigg

Esk

Ravenglass
(Δ)

Muncaster

Coast

Path

A 595

43
69

Selker Bay

Bootle

Black Combe

600 22

Silecroft
(Δ)

Millom

Haverigg

A 5093

7

Duddon Sands

A 595

Askam
in Furness

Ireleth

Dalton-in-Furness

(Δ) **Barrow** -in-Furness

Isle of Walney

14 3

Biggar

Rampsi

England ·Costal· *Path*

Hilpsford Point

Grange

Buttermere

Buttermere

754

B 5289

358 14

Honister Pass

Seathwaite

Great Gable
899

Copeland Forest
692

Wasdale Head

Scafell Pikes

977

20

902

Cumbrian

Nether
Wasdale

*Wast
Water*

Hard Knott
Pass

39

393

17

Eskdale Green

Boot

Eskdale

Furn

The Old Man

Duddon

Seathwaite

Ulpha

(Δ) Tor

Whitfell
572

A 593

Broughton Mills

A 595

Broughton-
in-Furness

Lowick

A 5092

Grizebeck

Sand Side

(Δ) Ulvers

8

21

Urswick

12 19

Furness
Abbey

Gleas

Dougla

48

22

F

Ro

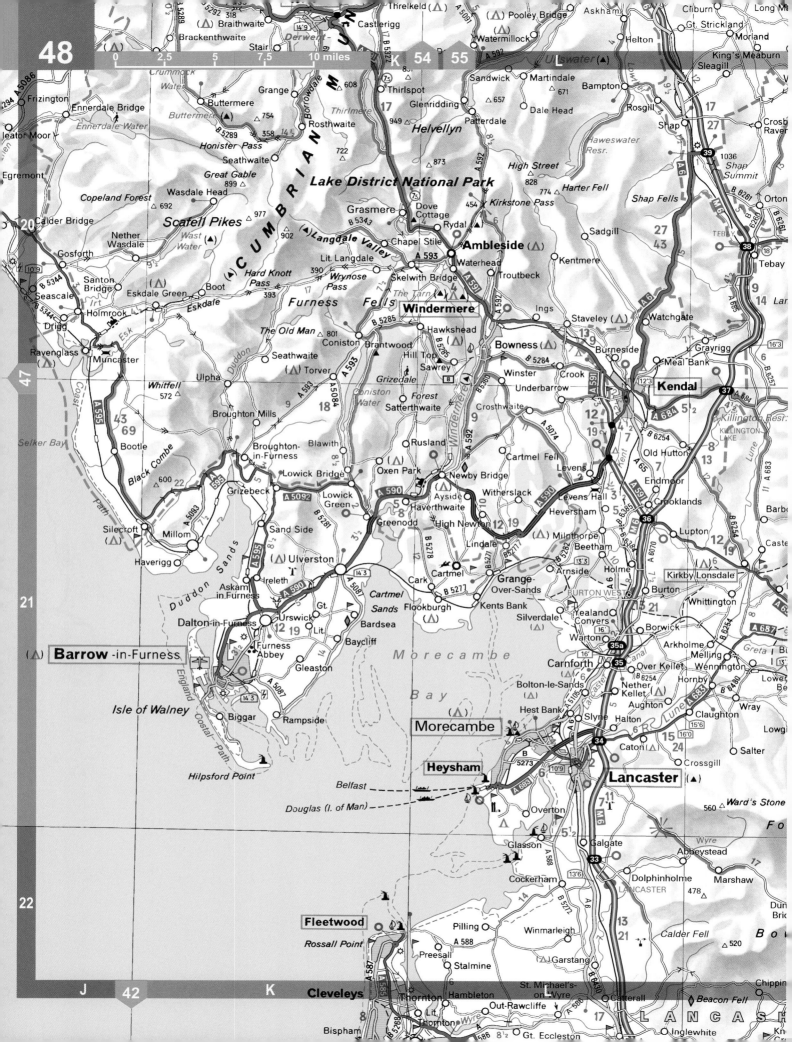

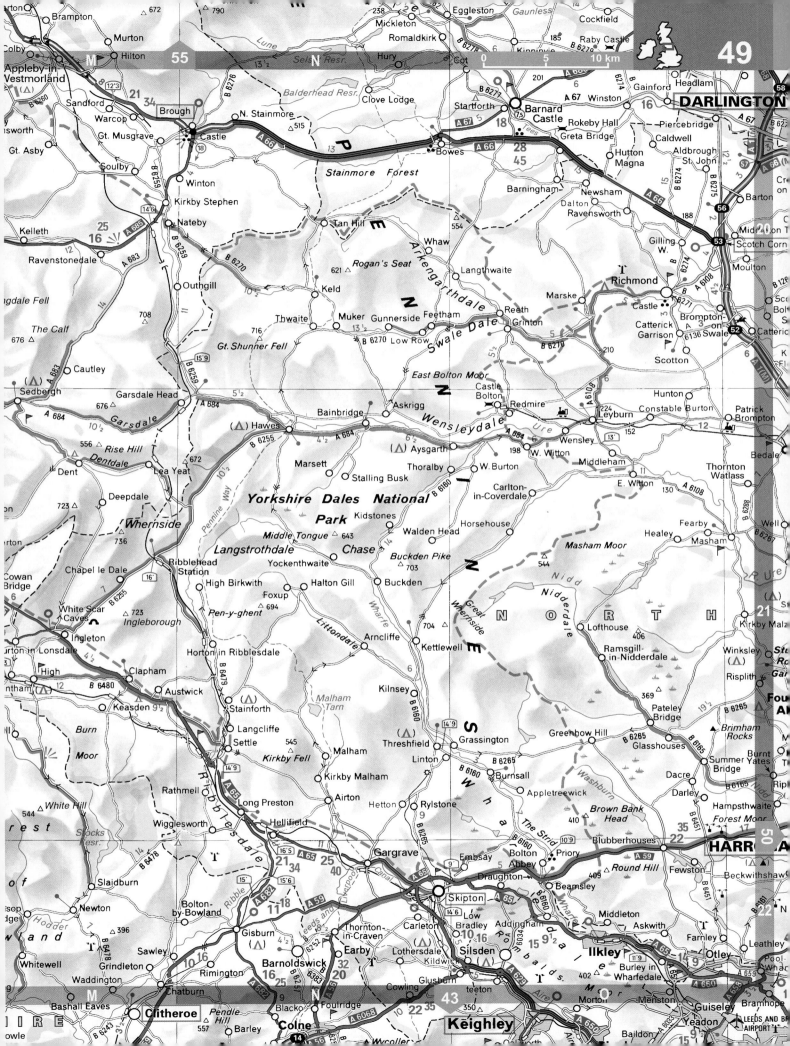

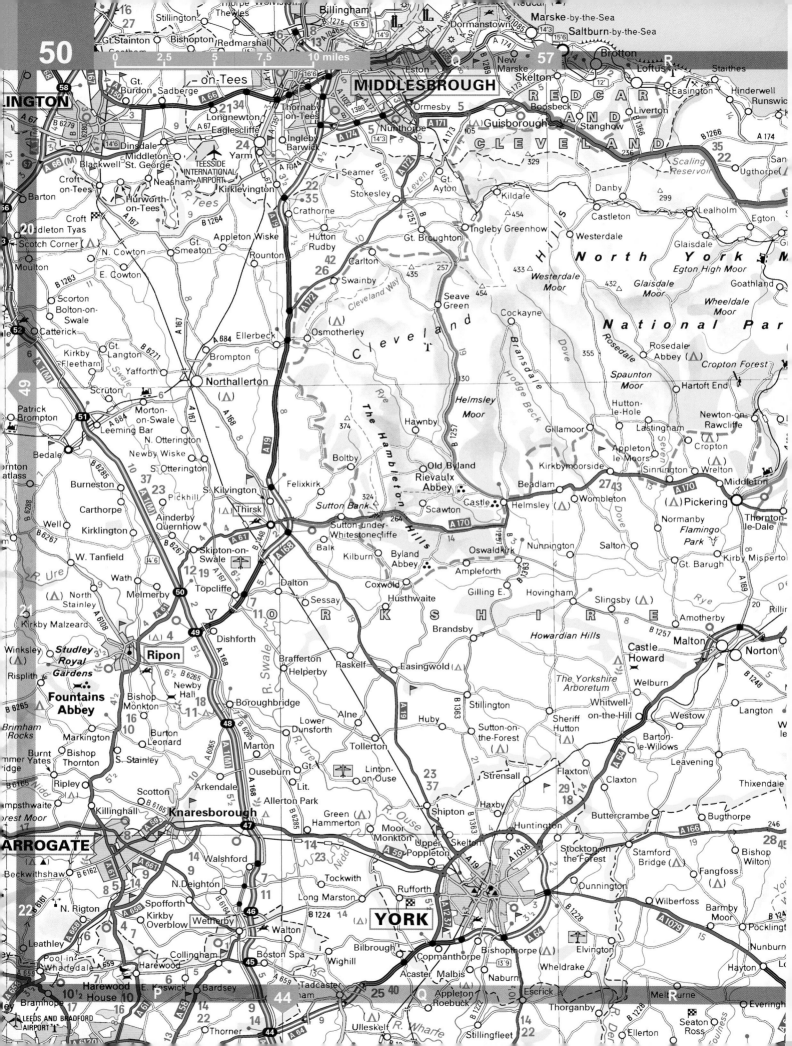

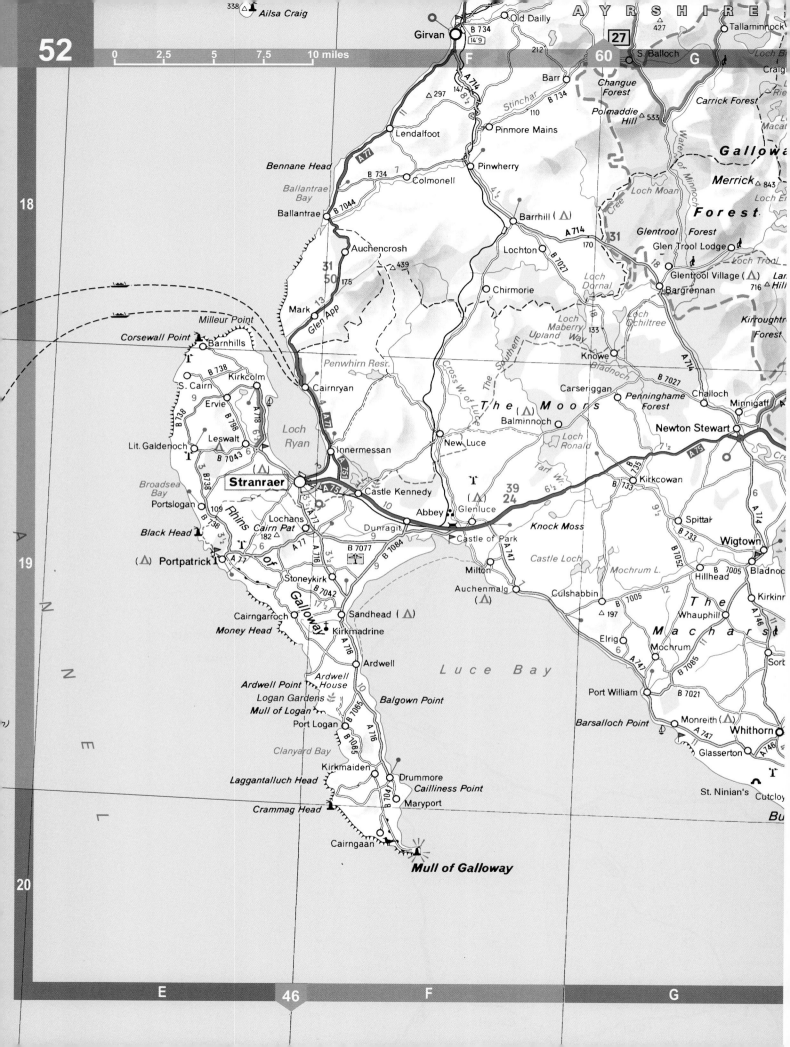

338 △ ▲ **Ailsa Craig**

A Y R S H I R E

0   2.5   5   7.5   10 miles

Old Dailly
Girvan
B 734
14·9
Tallaminnock
427
Barr
212
Changue Forest
60
S. Balloch
27
Carrick Forest
A 714
147
8½
△ 297
Polmaddie Hill △ 533
Galloway
Lendalfoot
Pinmore Mains
Stinchar
110
B 734
18
Bennane Head
A77
7
Colmonell
Pinwherry
Merrick △ 843
Ballantrae Bay
B 734
4½
Barrhill (△)
A 714
F o r e s t
Ballantrae
B 7044
Lochton
Glentrool Forest
Loch Moan
Cree
170
Glen Trool Lodge
31
Loch
Auchencrosh
B 7027
Glentrool Village (△) Lar
△ 439
Chirmorie
Loch Dornal
Bargrennan
716 △ Hill
31
50
175
18
Mark
13
Glen App
Loch Maberry
133
Loch Chiltree
Kirroughtree Forest
Milleur Point
Penwhirn Resr.
Upland Way
Knowe
Bladnoch
Corsewall Point
Barnhills
Cross W. of Luce
The Southern
Carseriggan
A 714
Challoch
B 738
Cairnryan
Penninghame Forest
B 7027
Minnigaff
S. Cairn
Kirkcolm
T h e (△) **M o o r s**
9
A 77
Newton Stewart
Ervie
B 798
A 718
Balminnoch
6½
Loch Ryan
New Luce
Loch Ronald
7½
A 75
Lit. Galdenoch
Leswalt
3
B 738
B 7043
6
Innermessan
Tarf Wr.
6½
Kirkcowan
A 751
39
B 735
Broadsea Bay
Stranraer (△)
Castle Kennedy
B 133
24
Spittal
Portslogan
B 738
109
Rhins
Lochans
10
Abbey
Glenluce
9½
B 733
A 114
Black Head
Cairn Pat
A 77
Dunragit
(△)
Knock Moss
Mochrum L.
B 1052
Wigtown
182 △
B 7077
Castle of Park
of
A 716
B 7084
12
Hillhead
(△) **Portpatrick**
A 77
6
3½
9
Milton
A 741
Castle Loch
B 7005
Bladnoc
Galloway
Stoneykirk
Auchenmalg
△ 197
Whauphill
Kirkinn
B 7042
(△)
Culshabbin
A 146
Cairngarroch
Sandhead (△)
B 7005
T h e
Money Head
Kirkmadrine
Elrig
Mochrum
M a c h a r s
A 718
6
B 7085
Sort
Ardwell
L u c e   B a y
A 747
Ardwell House
Port William
B 7021
Ardwell Point
10
Balgown Point
Logan Gardens
Mull of Logan
A 716
Monreith (△)
Barsalloch Point
Port Logan
B 1065
Whithorn
Clanyard Bay
Glasserton
A 146
Kirkmaiden
A 747
St. Ninian's
Cutcloy
Laggantalluch Head
Drummore
B 7041
Cailliness Point
Bu
Crammag Head
Maryport
Cairngaan
Mull of Galloway

18

19

20

E   46   F   G

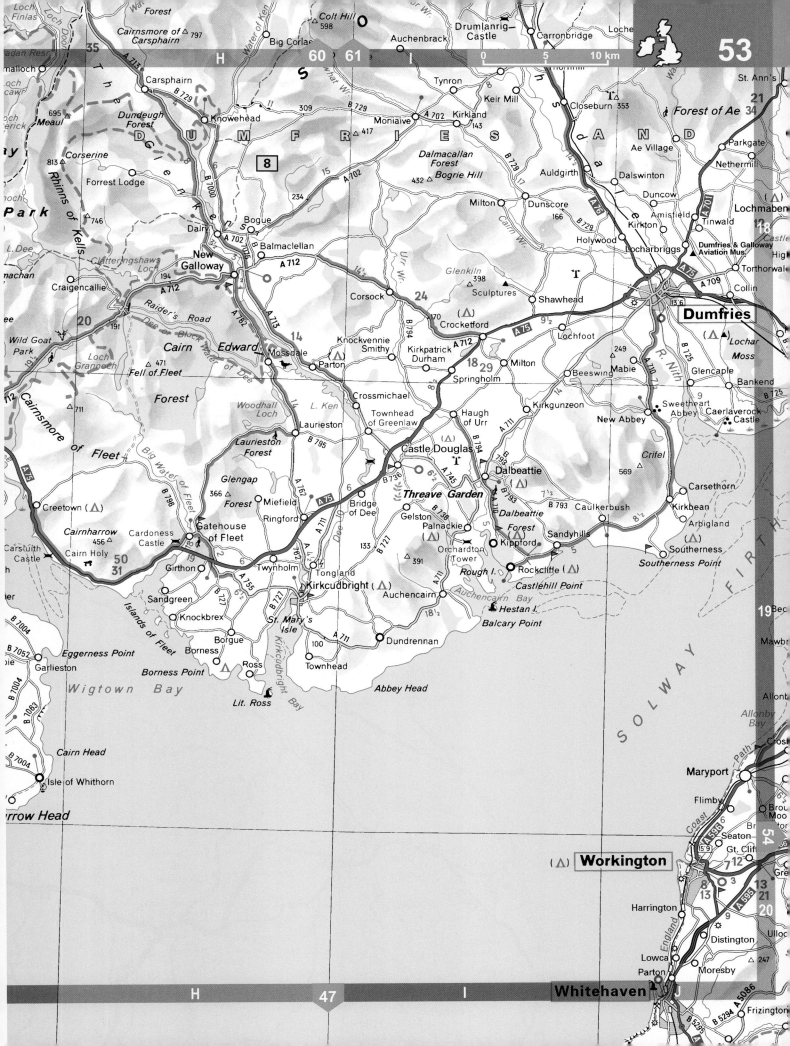

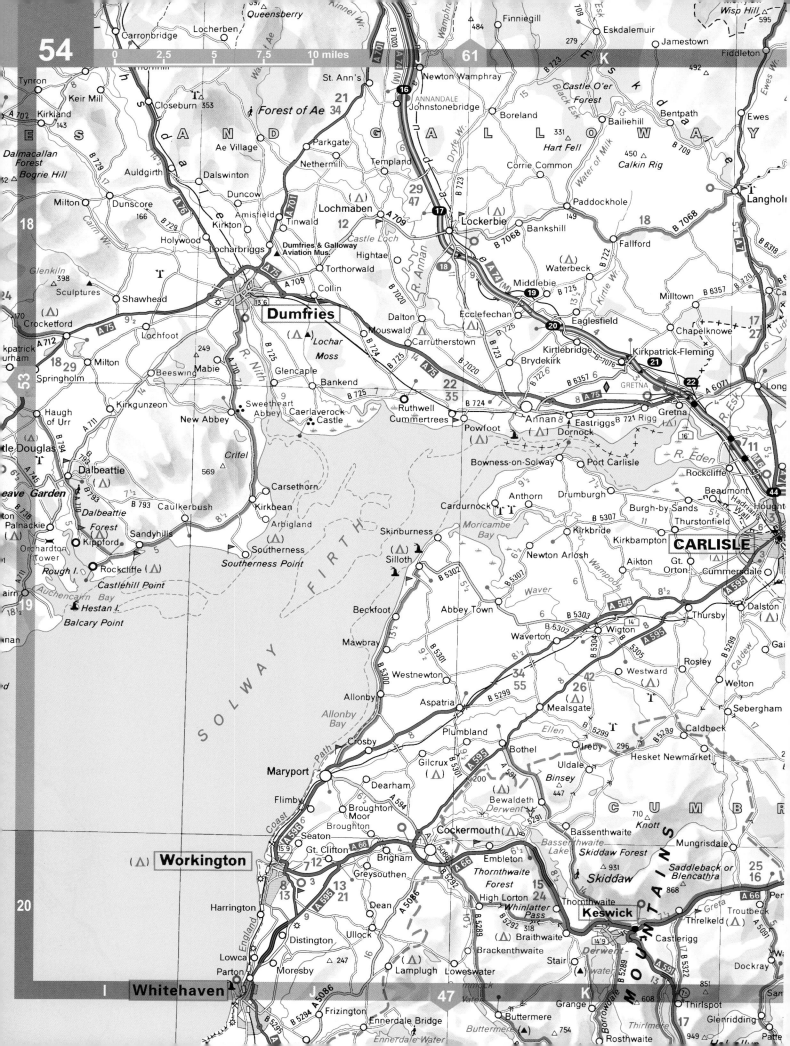

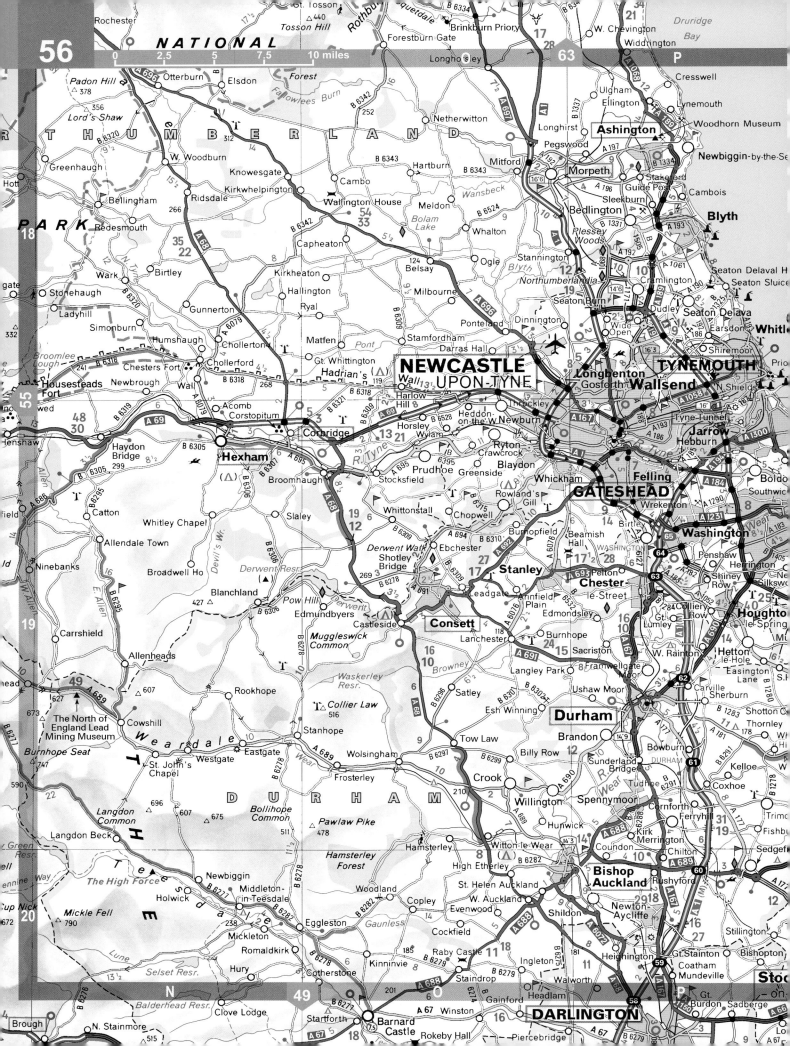

18

SOUTH SHIELDS

Amsterdam

Cleadon
Whitburn

N O R T H   S E A

SUNDERLAND

Ryhope

19

Seaham

England

Hetton
Easington

Horden

Coast

Peterlee
Blackhall
Blackhall Rocks

Hesleden

Path

34
21
Hart
15'9

A 1086

B 1280
A 179
1

HARTLEPOOL

Elwick

-15
9½
A 689
Seaton Carew

Tees Bay

Greatham
A 178
A 1185

20

Thorpe
Wolviston
Redcar (▲)

Billingham
Marske-by-the-Sea

B 1275
Dormanstown
Saltburn-by-the-Sea

Redmarshall
A 1085
Brotton

New
Marske
Loftus
Staithes

kton
Skelton
R
S

MIDDLESBROUGH
Eston
Easington
Hinderwell
50

Ormesby
5
R E D C A R

Thornaby
on-Tees
Boosbeck
Liverton
Runswick Bay

A 171
Guisborough
Stanghow
Kettleness

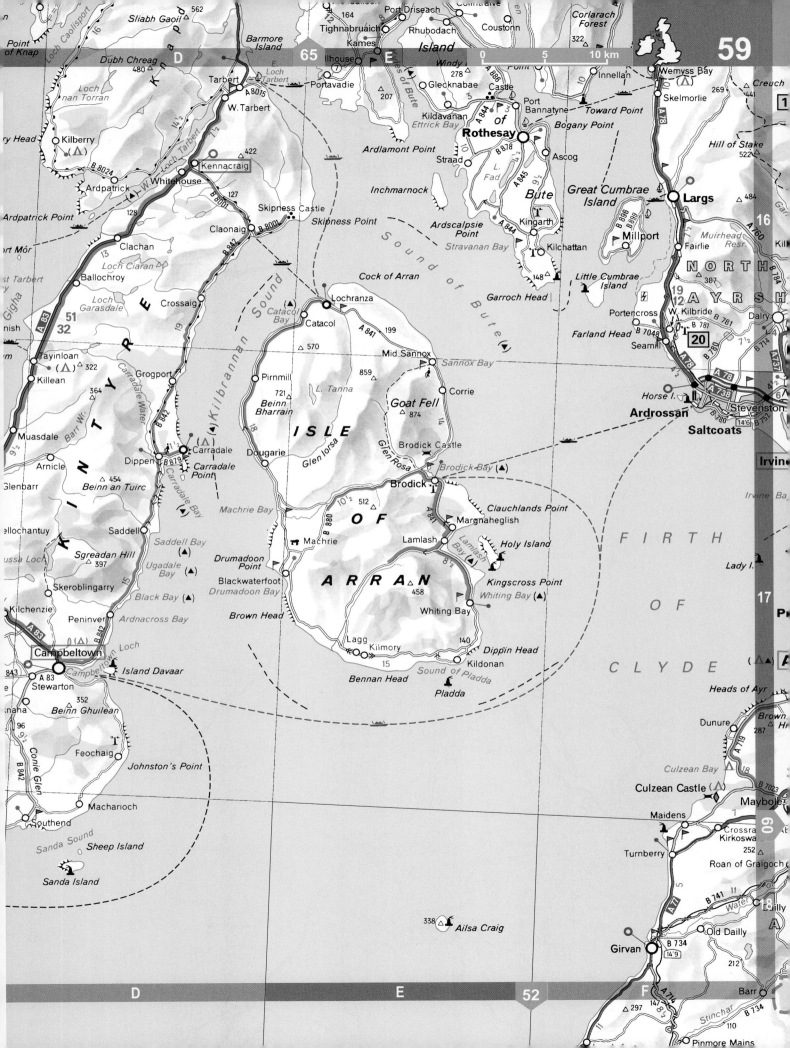

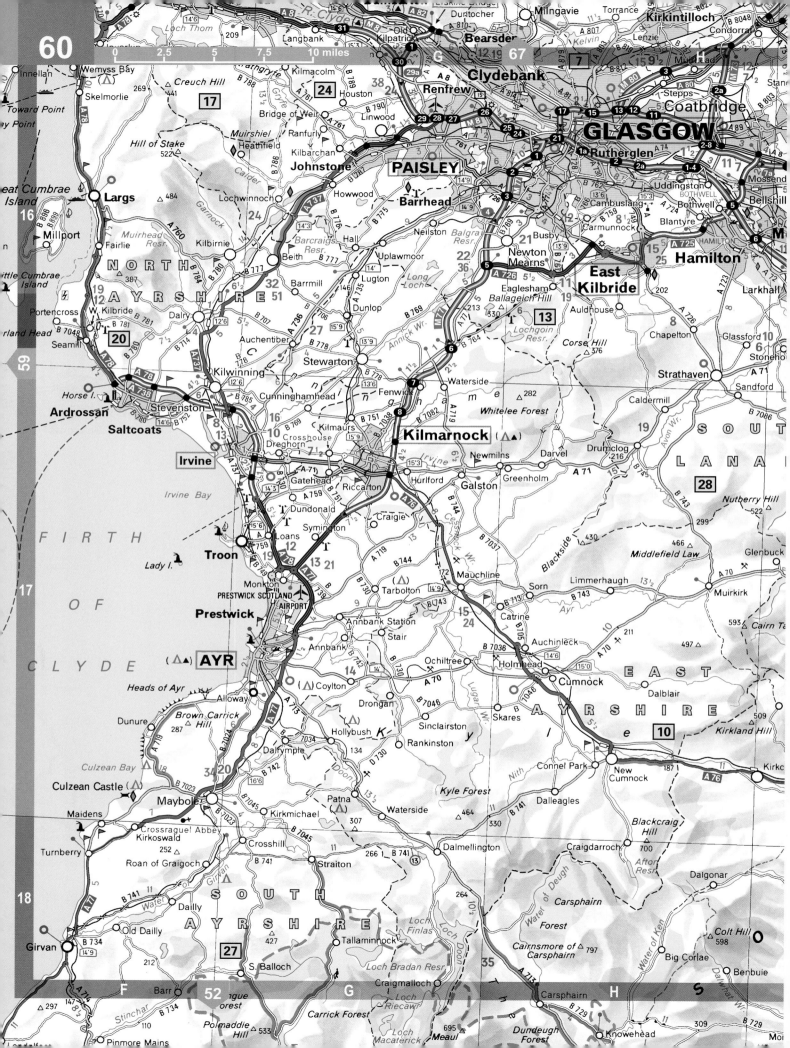

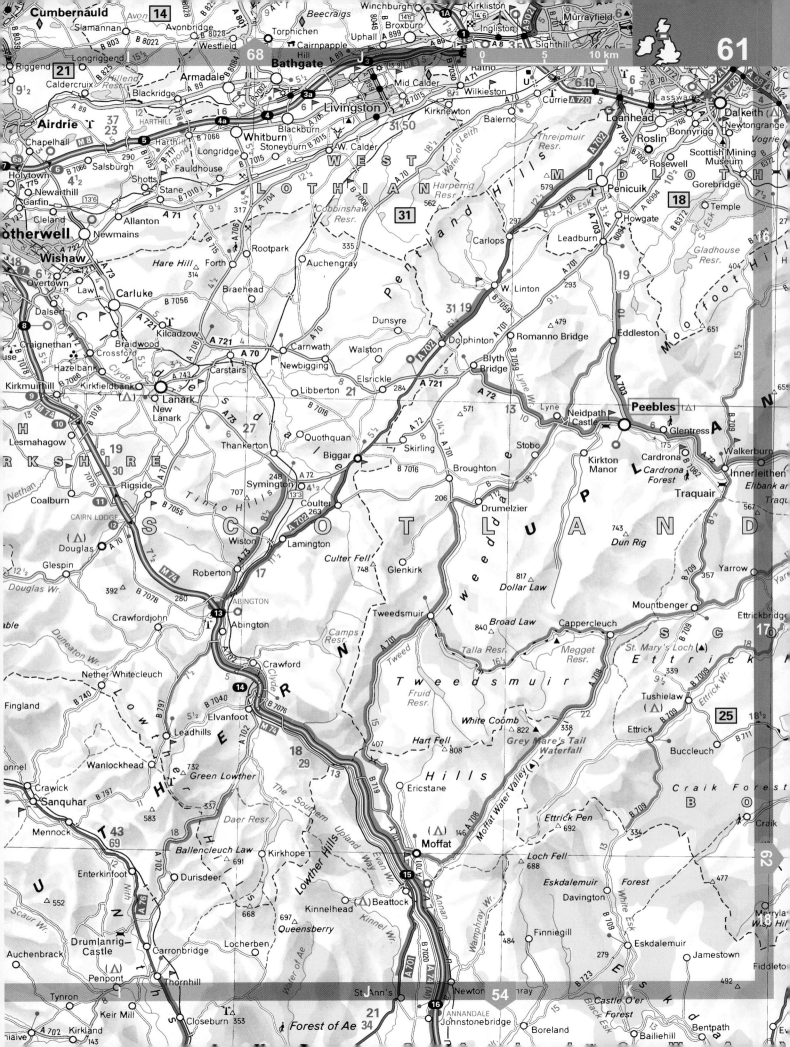

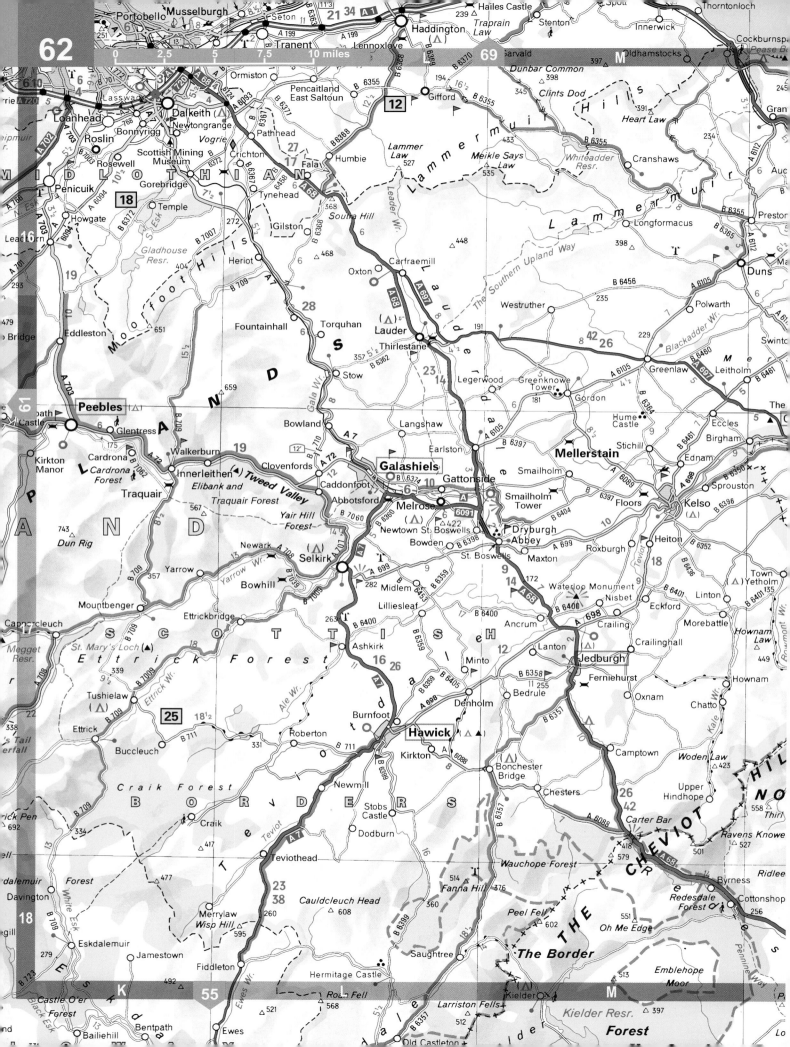

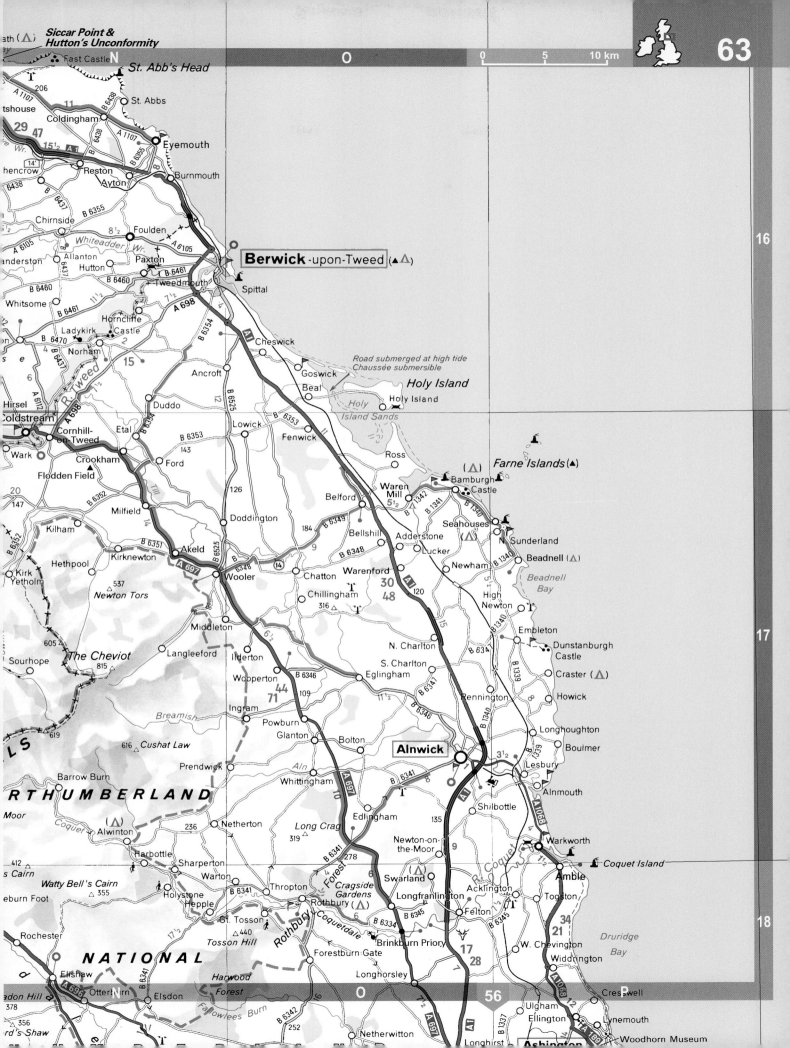

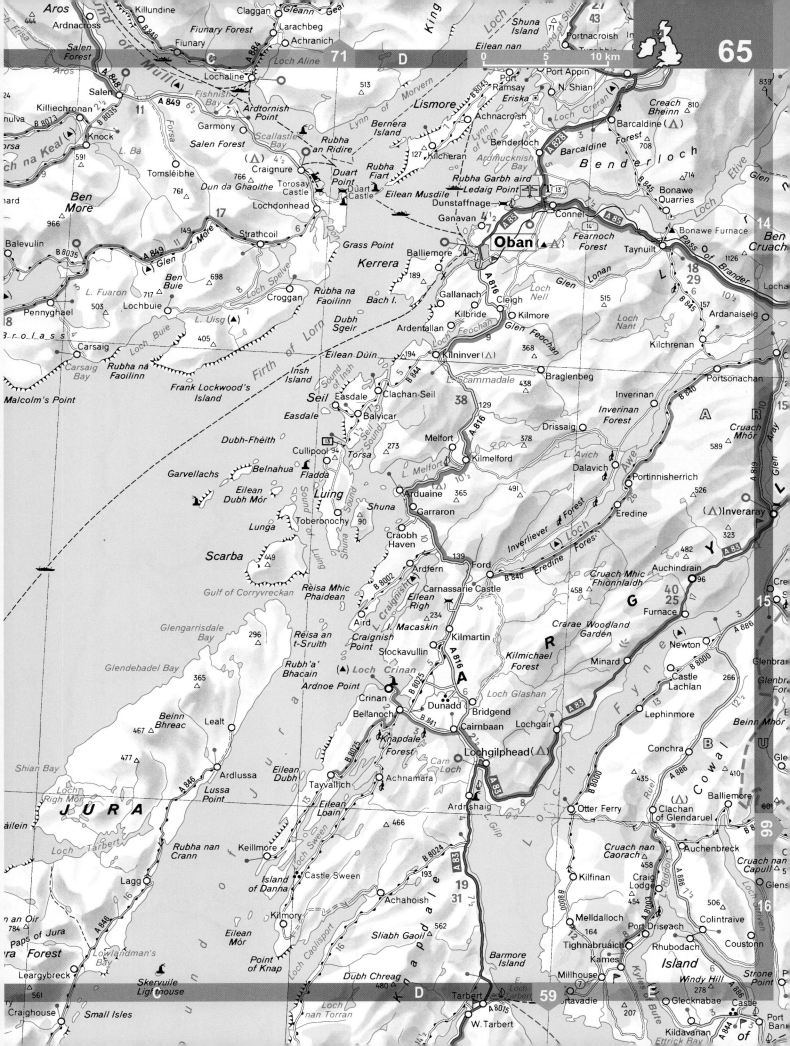

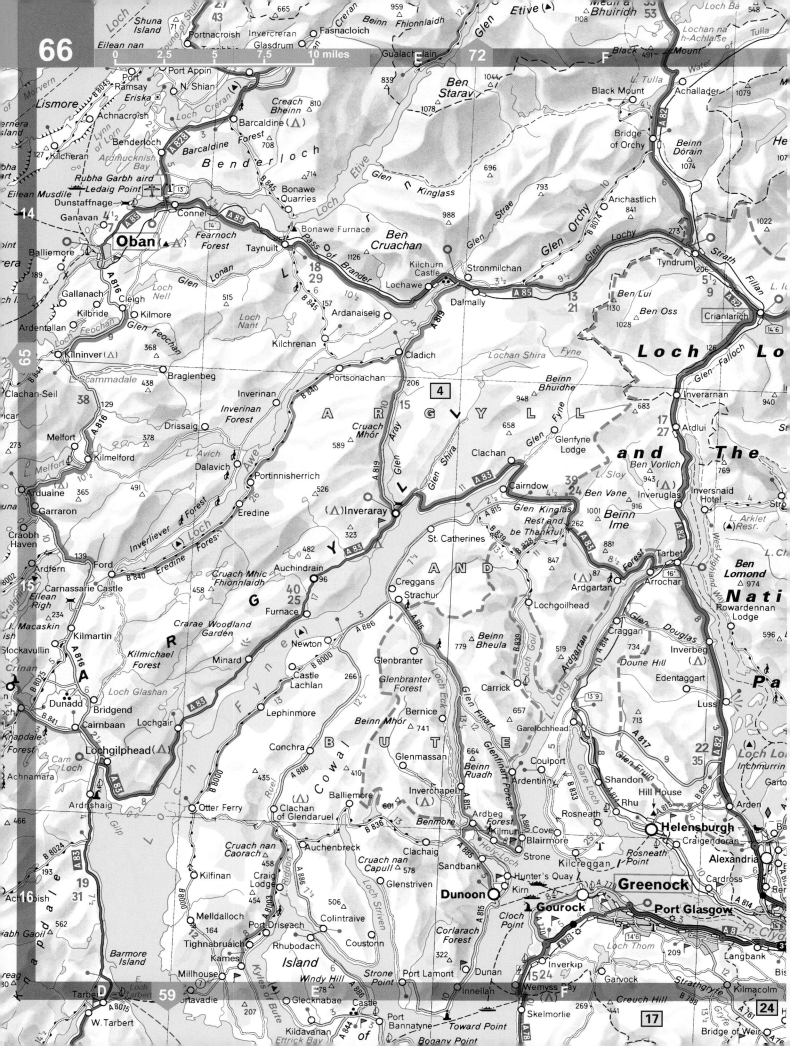

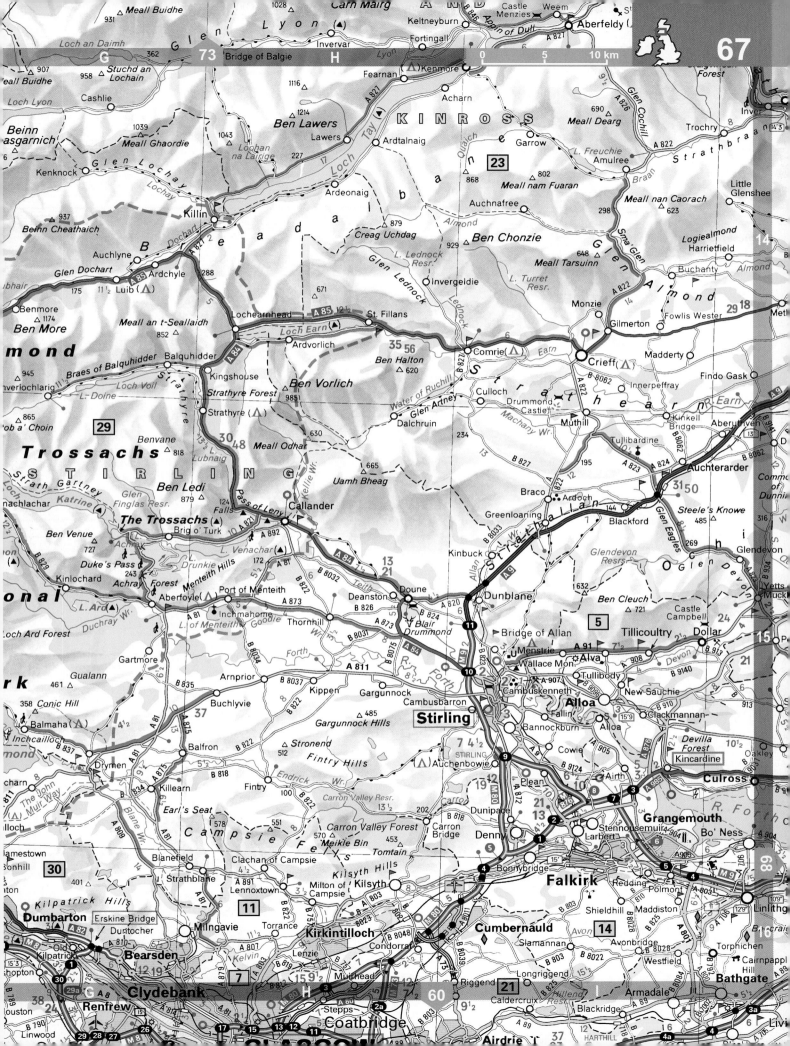

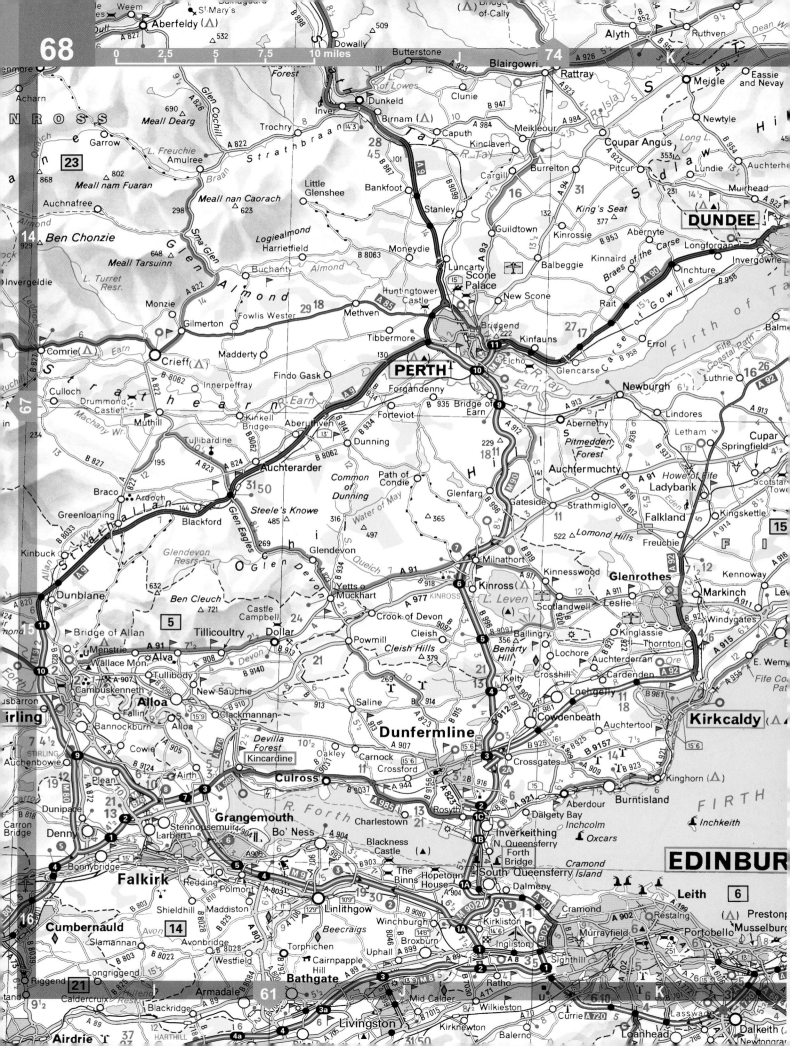

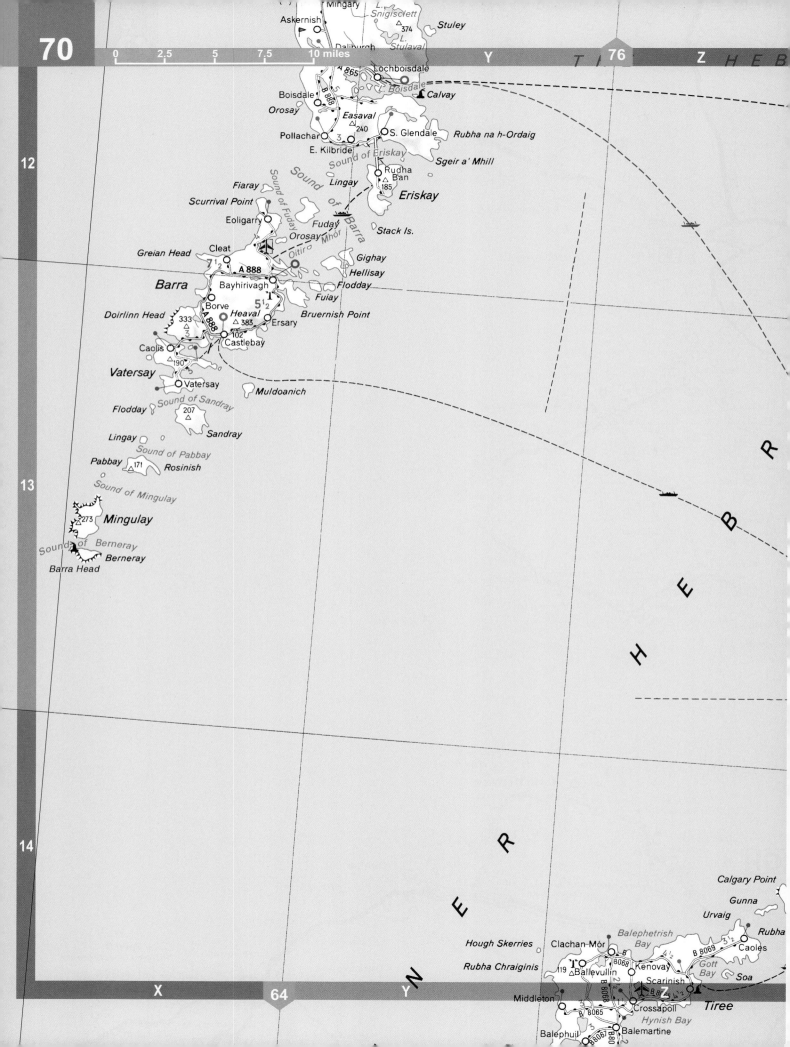

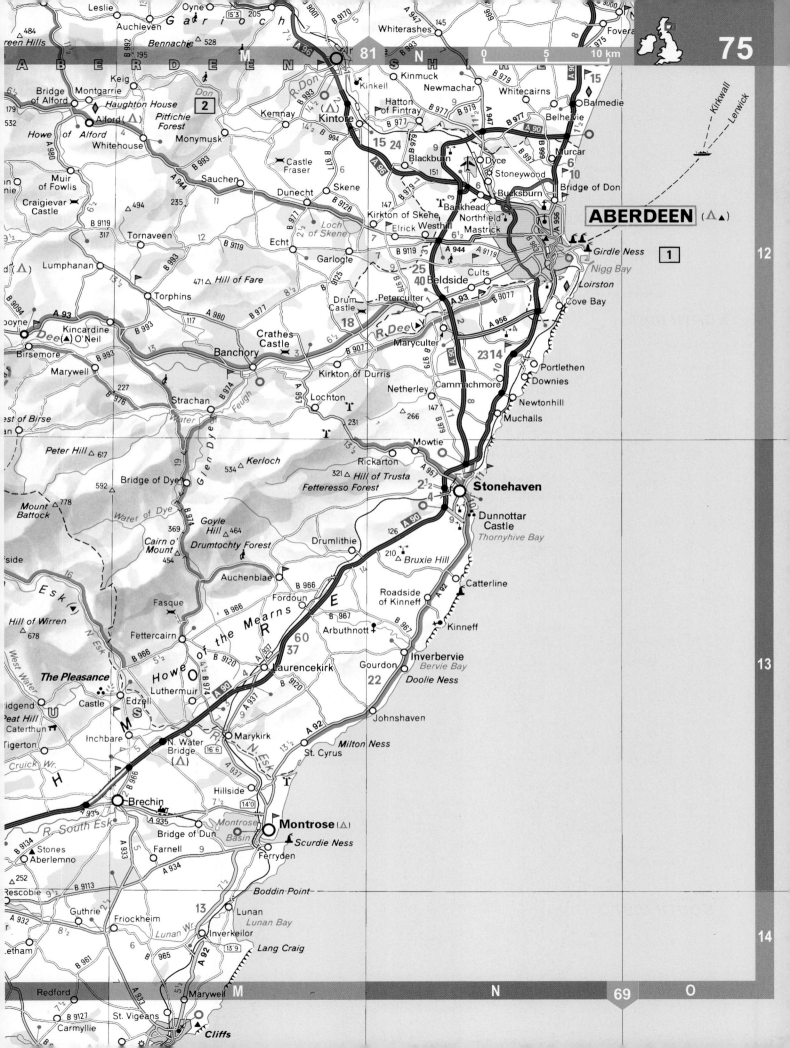

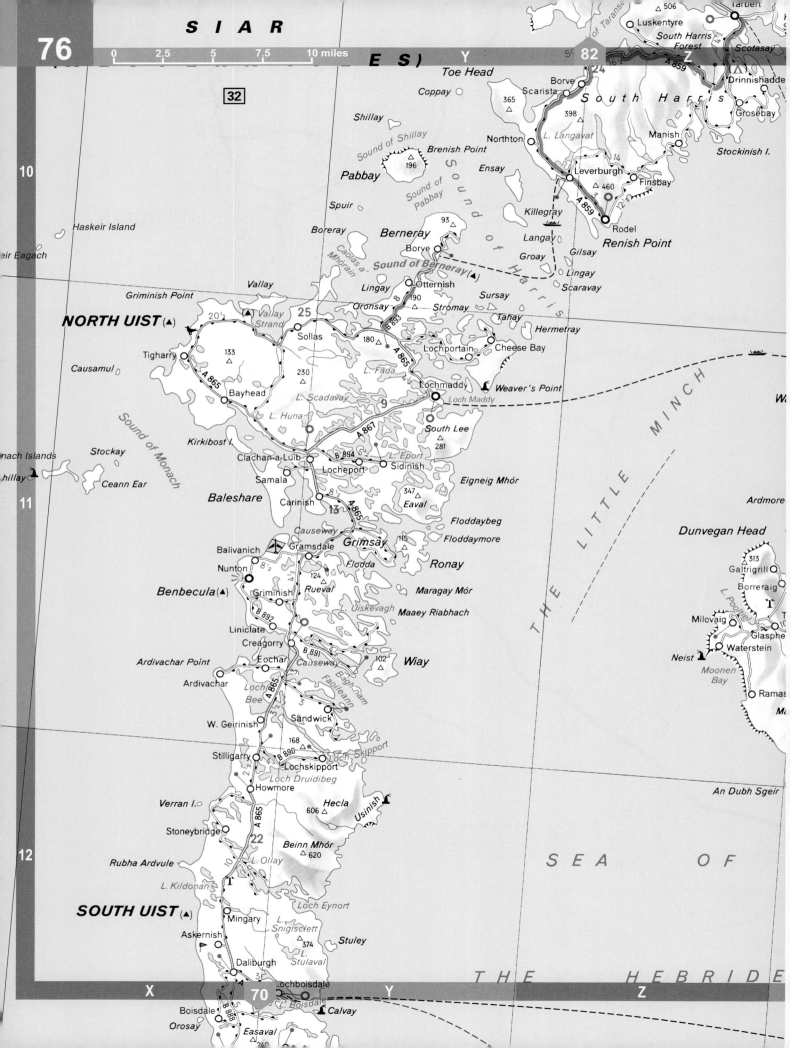

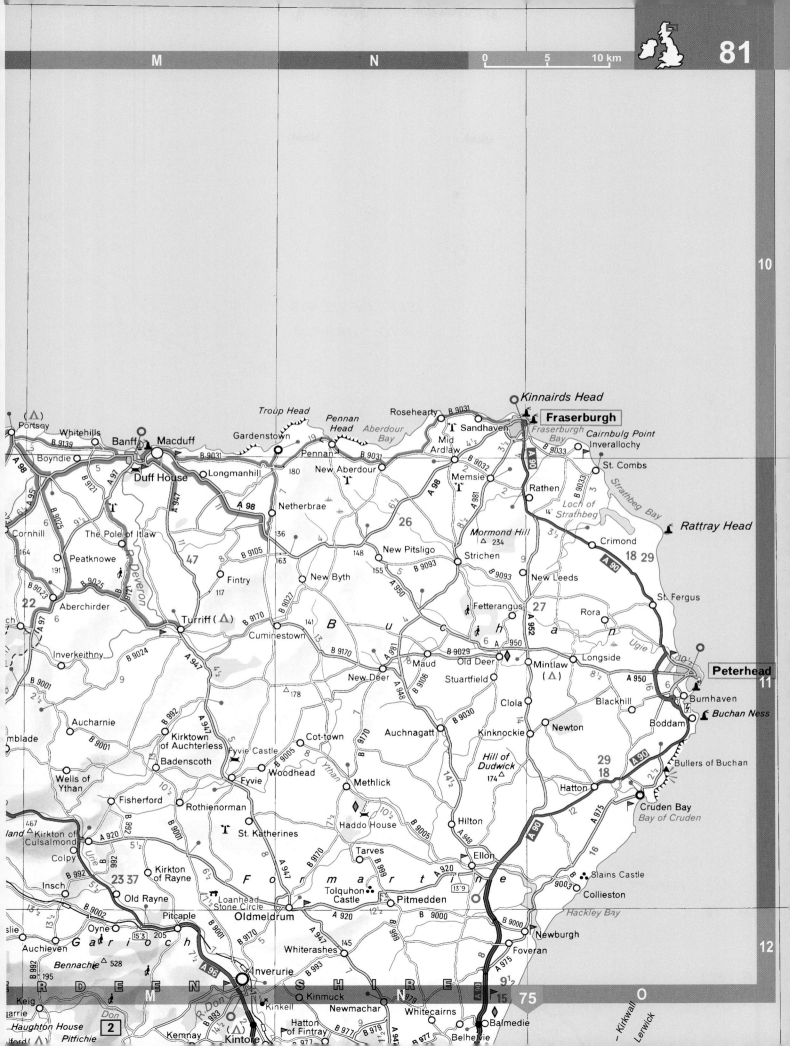

Butt of Lewis

Eoropie
Port of Ness
Habost
Skigersta
Cross
Dell
Ness

Loch Langavat

Cellar Head

△ 248
▲ *Muirneag*

Tolsta
Tolsta Head

Gress

Back

III

12 1/2

△

Tiumpan Head

Portnaguran

Broad Bay
(▲)

Melbost
12
Garrabost

Knock
Bayble

A 866

Eye Peninsula

Chicken Head

T H E   M I N C H

Point of Stoer

Culkein
Eilean Chrona
Clashnessie

Stoer

Clachtoll
Achmelvich
B 869
Baddidarach

Soyea Island

A' Chleit
Kirkaig Point

Rubha Còigeach

Eilean Mór

Enard Bay

Rubha Mór
Reiff
Brae of Achnahaird
△ 6

Eilean Mullagrach
Altandhu
L. Osgaig
Badnag

Isle Ristol
Polbain

Glas-leac Mór
L. Bad a' Gha

Tanera Beg
Tanera Mór
Achiltibuie

Badenscallie

Summer Is.

Horse I.

Eilean Dubh
Culnacr
Achduart

Priest Island
Bottle I.

Càrn nan Sgeir
Mart

Mhuire

ock Head

Eddrachill Bay

L. Cro

Inv

Lo

Annat Bay

Little Loch

Greenstone Point
Cailleach Head

Opinan
Rubha Beag

Gob a' Ghe
Mellon Udrigle
Stattic Point
Scoraig
Badluarach

Eilean Furadh Mór
Achgarve
Mungasdale

Rubha Réidh
Mellon
Charles
Laide
Badcaul

Cove
Gruinard
Bay

Gruinard
Island
△ 635
Beinn Ghob
Allt na
Badrallach

B 83

B   C

0   5   10 km

8

Butt of Lewis

Eoropie   Port of Ness
Habost
Skigersta
B 8015
Cross
Dell   *Ness*

Cellar Head

Loch Langavat

248
△
Muirneag   Tolsta
B 895   **Tolsta Head**

Gress

Back

Tiumpan Head

Portnaguran
Broad Bay
A 866
(▲)
Melbost 12 Garrabost
Knock Bayble *Eye Peninsula*
Chicken Head

T H E M I N C H

Eddrachill. Bay

Point of Stoer
Culkein
Eilean Chrona
Clashnessie
Stoer
Clachtoll
B 869
Achmelvich
9
Baddidara

Soyea Island

A' Chleit *Kirkaig Point*

Rubha Còigeach
Eilean Mór
Enard Bay
Rubha Mór
Reiff Brae of Achnahaird
6
Eilean Mullagrach Altandhu Badnag
Isle Ristol Polbain
Glas-leac Mór *L. Bad a' Gha*
Achiltibuie
Tanera Mór Badenscallie
Tanera Beg
Summer Is. *Horse I.* 84
Eilean Dubh Achduart
Priest Island *Bottle I.*
Càrn nan Sgeir 10

...ock Head

...hóraidh

...Mhuire

Greenstone Point *Cailleach Head* *Annat Bay*
Opinan *Rubha Beag*
Stattic Point Scoraig
Mellon Udrigle Badluarach *Little Loch B...*
B   C Gob a' Ghe... 77 D *Gruinard Island* Mungasdale *Beinn Ghob.*
Eilean Furadh Mór Achgarve Badrallach
△635
Rubha Réidh Mellon Charles Laide *Gruinard Bay* Badcaul
Cove B 832

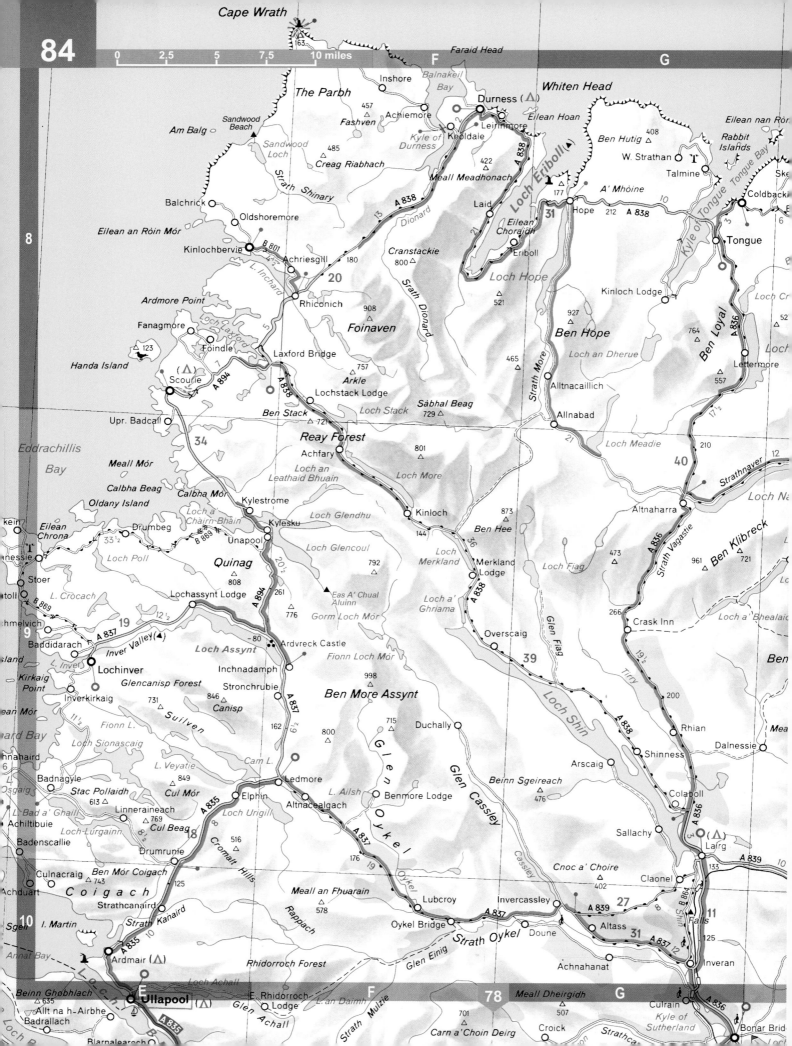

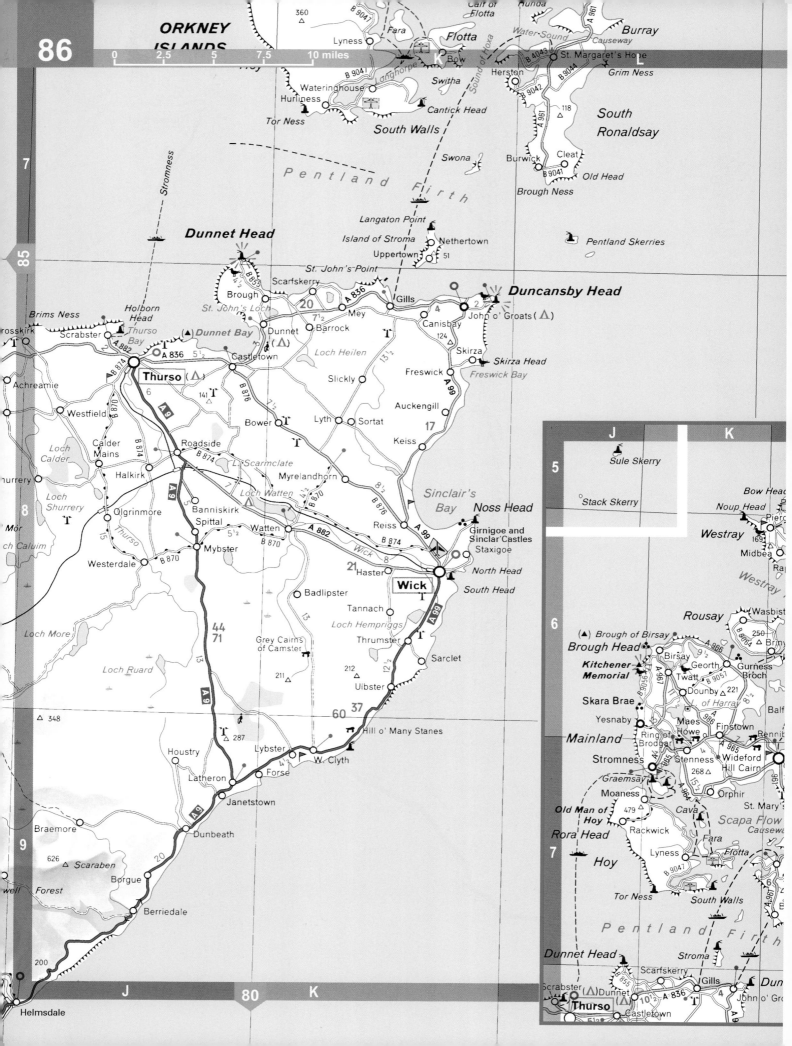

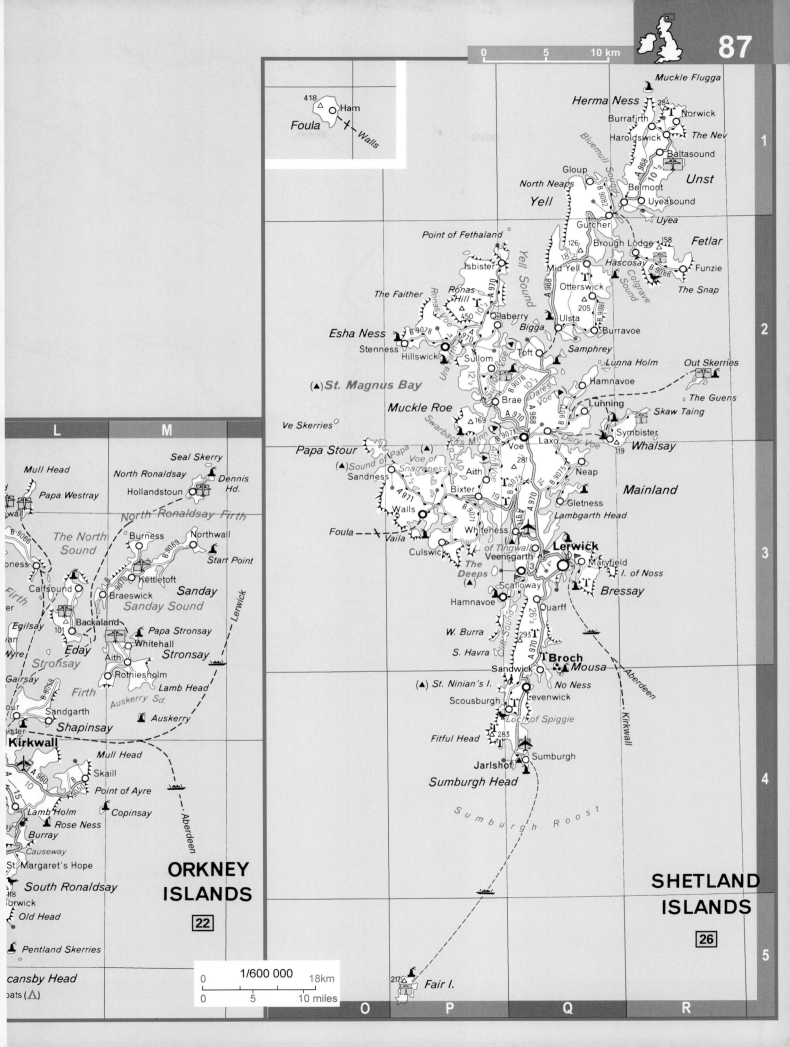

0   5   10 km

Foula
418 △ ● Ham
Walls

Muckle Flugga
Herma Ness   284 △
Burrafirth   ▲ Norwick
Haroldswick   *The Nev*
                 Baltasound
Gloup   Belmont   *Unst*
North Neaps   Uyeasound
Yell   Uyea
Gutcher
                 126 △ Brough Lodge   158 *Fetlar*
Point of Fethaland   Hascosay   Funzie
Isbister   Mid Yell   205 △   *The Snap*
The Faither   Otterswick
Ronas Hill △ 450   Ollaberry Ulsta
Esha Ness   Bigga   Burravoe
Stenness Hillswick Samphrey
                 Sullom   *Lunna Holm*   *Out Skerries*
(▲)*St. Magnus Bay*   Toft Hamnavoe   *The Guens*
                 Brae   *Lunning*   *Skaw Taing*
Muckle Roe 169 △   *Symbister* 119 *Whalsay*
Ve Skerries   Voe Laxo   *Dury Voe*
Papa Stour   (▲) Aith 281 △   Neap   *Mainland*
(▲)*Sound of Snarraness* Bixter Gletness
Sandness   Whiteness Lambgarth Head
                 L. of Tingwall
Walls   Culswick Veensgarth **Lerwick**
Foula   Vaila   *The Deeps* Scalloway Maryfield *I. of Noss*
                 (▲) Hamnavoe *Bressay*
                 Quarff
W. Burra
S. Havra   **Broch** *Mousa*
                 Sandwick *No Ness*
(▲)*St. Ninian's I.* Levenwick
Scousburgh   *Loch of Spiggie*
Fitful Head 283 △
Jarlshof   Sumburgh
Sumburgh Head

Sumburgh Roost

**SHETLAND
ISLANDS**
26

Mull Head
Seal Skerry
North Ronaldsay
Dennis Hd.
Hollandstoun
Papa Westray
North Ronaldsay Firth
The North Sound
Burness   Northwall
Sanday   Start Point
Calfsound Kettletoft
Braeswick *Sanday Sound*
Egilsay Backaland *Papa Stronsay*
Eday   Whitehall *Stronsay*
Aith Rothiesholm *Lamb Head*
Stronsay Firth *Auskerry Sd.* Auskerry
Sandgarth *Shapinsay*
Kirkwall
Mull Head
Skaill
Lamb Holm Point of Ayre Copinsay
Rose Ness
Burray
Causeway
St Margaret's Hope
South Ronaldsay
Old Head
Pentland Skerries

**ORKNEY
ISLANDS**
22

cansby Head
oats (△)

0   1/600 000   18km
0   5   10 miles

217 △ *Fair I.*

L   M
O   P   Q   R
1
2
3
4
5

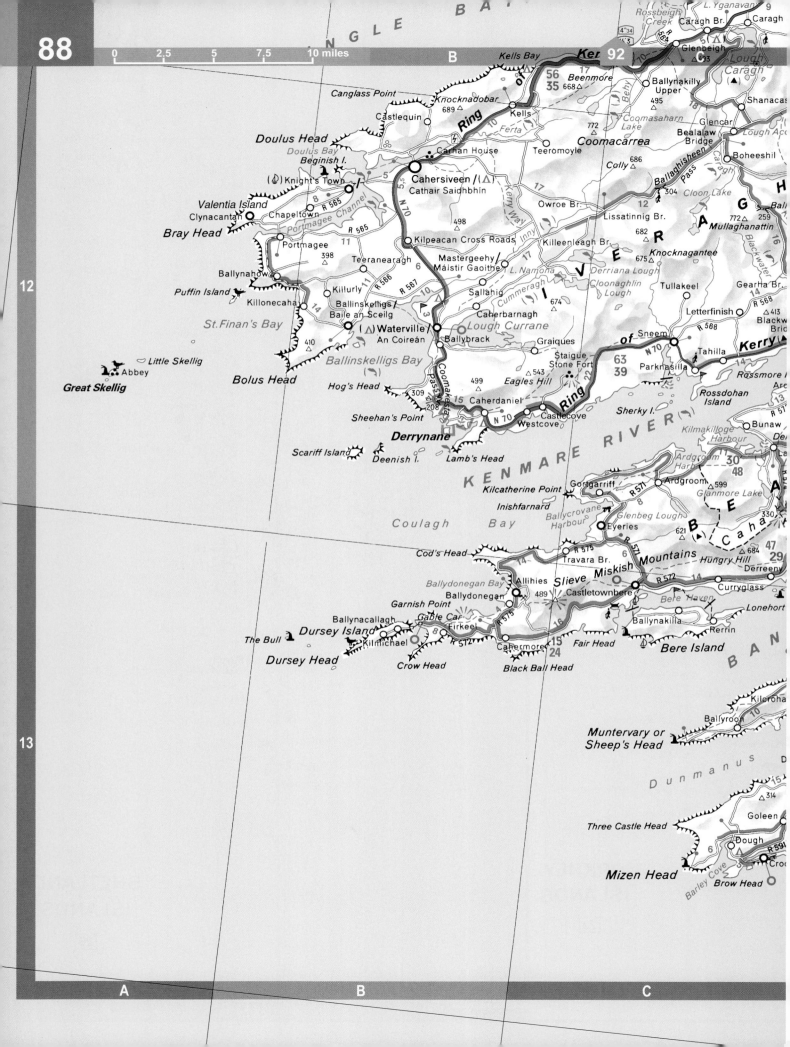

Feagarrid
aglogh
Ballyduff
Mt. Melleray Monastery
Ballynaguilkee
Ballynamult
Knockboy 725
Seefin
Mahon Bridge
Fews
Kilmacthomas
Newtow

W   A   T   E   R   F

95   J

0   5   10 km

R 688
14
R 669
Cappoquin/ Ceapach Choinn
R 671
22 36
Millstreet
25
Colligan
Boolatt

Lismore/ Lios Mór
N 72
9
Modelligo
484
Kilgobnet
The Pike
N 25
Lemybrien
40 25
Ballylaneen
20
R 675
2
Kill
Dunhill
Annestown
R 675
Fennor
Tramore Trá Mhór

24 39
Tallowbridge
Ballinaspick
River Bride
N 72
7½ 12
7
5
10
Stradbally
Bunmahon
Dunabrattin Head
Gt. Newtow Head

R 628
Tallow
R 672
2 3
R 675
Ballyvoyle Head

glass
R 627
R 634
Villierstown
8
Keereen
Dungarvan Dún Garbhán
Clonea Bay
Ballynacourty

The Pike
18
River Blackwater
Aglish
Drum
25 16
Hills
R 674
Ballynagaul
Helvick Head
Dungarvan Harbour

Boola
16
Cross
301
16 26
Ringville An Rinn
Muggort's Bay

Uniacke
angan
12
R 634
Tourig
Clashmore
Licky
N 25
9
Loskeran
15
Mine Head

Inch
Grange
R 673
7
Curragh

Killeagh
geely
N 25
10
Kinsalebeg
Moord
R 673
4
Youghal/ Eochaill
Ardmore/ Aird Mhór
58
Ram Head

Gortaroo
astlemartyr
Womanagh
R 633
11
Ballymadog
Whiting Bay
Youghal Bay

Kilcredan
Ballymacoda
Ballymacodoon Head

Garryvoe
Ballymakeagh
Knockadoon Head

Ballycotton Bay
cotton

0 2.5 5 7.5 10 miles

B

10

Loop Head (71)

MOU

THE

Dreenagh

Kerry Head 218

Glenderry 8

(△) Ballyh

Ballyheige Ba

The Seven Hogs or
Magharee Islands

Illauntannig

Rough Point

Brandon Point Fahamore

Kilshannig

Brandon Head

Brandon Bay

Tralee Bay

Barri
Harbou

Dingle Way

Brandon /
Cé Bhréanainn

Brandon Creek

Brandon
Mountain
△ 951

Tiduff

Ballydavid Head

Feohanagh

Smerwick
Harbour

Ballyquin (△) Lough Gill

Strand Killmey

Cloghane

Kilcummin

Stradbally

Castlegregory (△)

2 R560

Fer

Smerwick

Sybil Head

Murreagh

Ballydavid

Ballinloghig

Kilmalkedar

8

Ballyduff

Beenoskee
△ 825

Owenmore

12

Aughacasla

8

Camp

Derrymore I.

68

Ballyferriter /
Baile an Fheirtéaraigh

D I N G L E

(▲) L. Slat

825

Feohanagh

R 559

594

Gallarus Oratory
(△)

△ 623
456 △ 616

Connor Pass

Lougher N 86

Caherconree

Sliev

Clogher Head

Ballineanig

Ballynana

18

R 559

13

Owenascaul

50
31

17

Inishtooskert

Dunquin /
Dún Chaoin

Ventry

Milltown

Dingle /
Daingean Uí Chúis

Anascaul

Aughils R 561

Blasket Islands / (▲)
Na Blascaodaí

516 △ Mount
Eagle

R 559

Dingle
Harb.

N 86

18

Inch

R 561

Castlema
Harbour

Dunmore Head

Beehive
Huts

Lispole
Lios Póil

Doonmanagh

Inch

Great Blasket
Island

R 559

Ventry
Harbour

Castle

Tearaght I.

Slea Head

Parkmore Pt.

Bull's Head

Minard Head

Cromane

Knockaunnag

Illaunstookagh

Tullig

Inishnabro

L. Yganavan

Inishvickillane

D I N G L E   B A Y (▲)

Rossbeigh
Creek

Caragh Br.

Caragh

Behy △ 493

Lough
Caragh

9

Kells Bay

Kerry (▲)

Glenbeigh

(▲)

Canglass Point

of

56
35

17
Beenmore
668△

Ballynakilly
Upper

495

Shanacas

18

Knocknadobar
689 △

Ring

Kells

Coomasaharn
Lake

772
△

Glencar

Glenca

Lough Acc

Castlequin

Ferta

Coomacarrea

686

Bealalaw
Bridge

Boheeshil

Doulus Head

Teeromoyle

Colly

304

Cloon Lake

G
H

Doulus Bay

Carhan House

Kerry Way

Ballaghisheen Pass

Beginish I.

Caragh

(♨) Knight's Town

Cahersiveen / (△)
Cathair Saidhbhín

17

Owroe Br.

12

772 △ 259

Valentia Island

R 565

N 70

Lissatinnig Br.

CA

Mullaghanattin

Clynacantan

A

Cha

88

B 498

Bray Head

R 565

Killeenleagh Br.

682
△

675 △

Portmagee

11

Kilpeacan Cross Roads

Mastergeehy
Máistir Gaoithe

Knocknagantee

V
E
R

398

Teeranearagh

17

L. Namona

Derriana Lough

Ballynahow

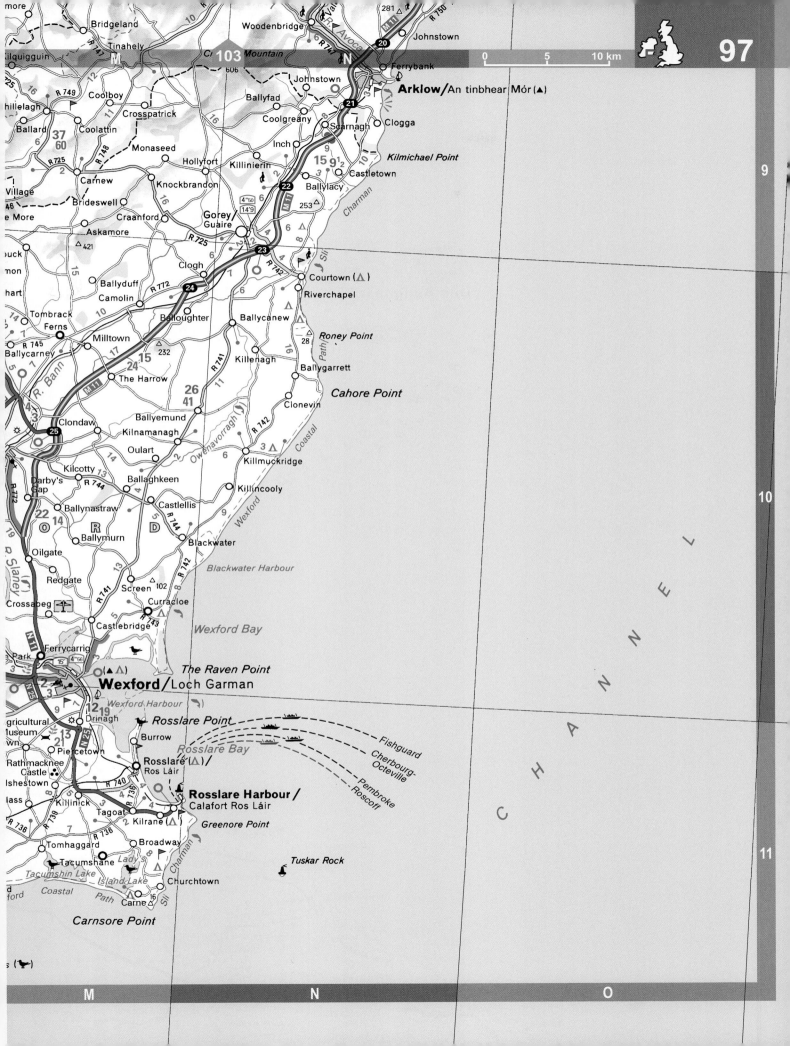

0   5   10 km

more
Bridgeland
Tinahely
Woodenbridge
R 750
M 11
281
R Avoca
20
Johnstown
Kilquigguin
M
103 Mountain
N
Ferrybank
606
Johnstown
21
Arklow/An tinbhear Mór (▲)
Ballyfad
Coolboy
R 749
Coolgreany
Scarnagh
Clogga
Ballard
Crosspatrick
Inch
Kilmichael Point
hillelagh
R 747
37
60
Coolattin
R 748
Monaseed
R 725
Hollyfort
Killinierin
15 9½
Charman
Castletown
Carnew
2
Knockbrandon
22
Ballylacy
Village
Craanford
M 11
4'50
14'9
253
9
Brideswell
R 725
Gorey
Guaire
e More
Askamore
△ 421
23
Clogh
R 742
Courtown (△)
46
buck
Ballyduff
R 772
24
Camolin
Riverchapel
mon
Balloughter
Ballycanew
Roney Point
hart
Tombrack
Ferns
Killenagh
Path
28
Ballygarrett
R 745
Ballycarney
232
R 741
Cahore Point
Milltown
24
15
The Harrow
26
41
Clonevin
R 742
R. Bann
Ballyemund
Clondaw
Kilnamanagh
Owenavorragh
R 742
Coastal
25
Oulart
Killmuckridge
Kilcotty
R 744
Ballaghkeen
Killincooly
Darby's
Gap
Ballynastraw
Castlellis
Wexford
22
14
R
D
R 744
9
Ballymurn
Blackwater
Oilgate
R. Slaney
Redgate
R 741
Screen
102
Blackwater Harbour
Crossabeg
Curracloe
R 743
N 11
Castlebridge
Wexford Bay
Park
Ferrycarrig
15
4'56
The Raven Point
Wexford/Loch Garman
Wexford Harbour
agricultural
Museum
wn
12 19
Drinagh
➤ **Rosslare Point**
Fishguard
Burrow
Rosslare Bay
13
Piercetown
Rathmacknee
Castle
Rosslare (△)
Ros Láir
Cherbourg-
Octeville
shestown
R 740
Rosslare Harbour /
Calafort Ros Láir
Pembroke
lass
Killinick
Tagoat
Greenore Point
Roscoff
R 738
Kilrane
Tomhaggard
R 736
Broadway
Charman
Tuskar Rock
Tacumshane
Lady
Churchtown
Tacumshin Lake
Island Lake
ford
Coastal
Carne
Path
16
Carnsore Point

M   N   O

9

10

11

C H A N N E L

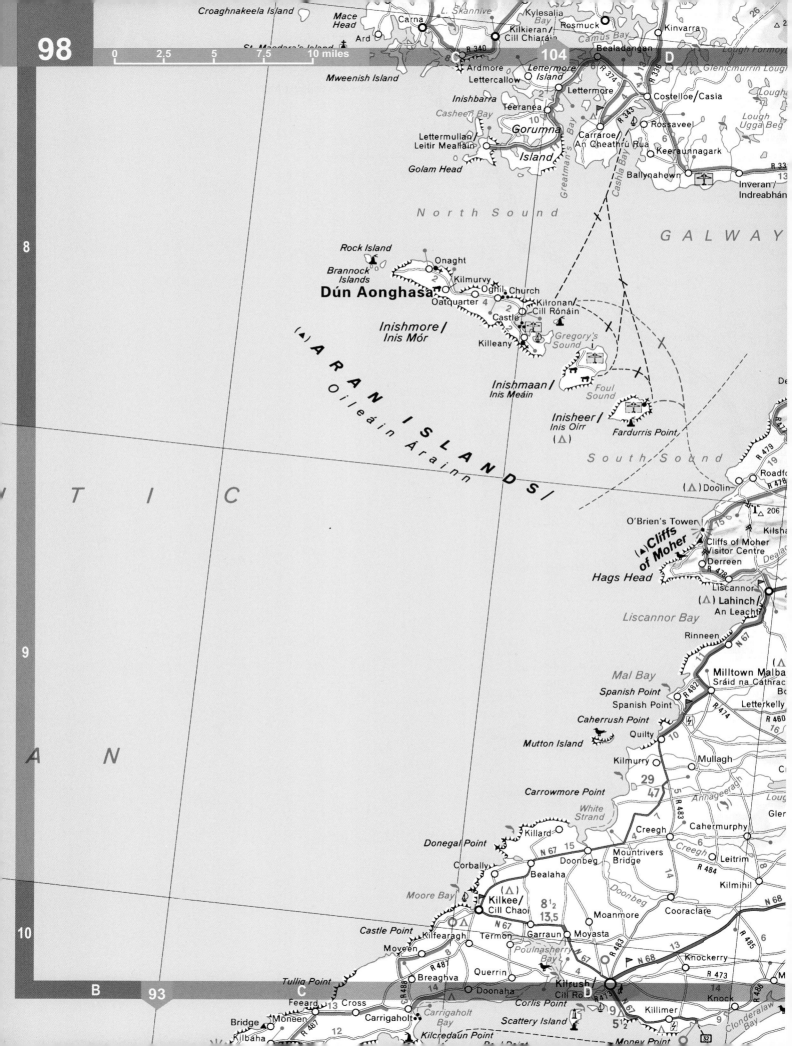

Croaghnakeela Island

Mace Head

L. Skannive

Kylesalia

Rosmuck

Kinvarra

Carna

26

Ard

Kilkieran/
Cill Chiaráin

Camus Bay

R 340

Bealadangan

Lough Formoyle

104

St. Maedara's Island

Mweenish Island

Ardmore

Lettercallow

Lettermore
Island

Lettermore

R 374

R 336

Glencmurrin Lough

Inishbarra

Teeranea

Casheen Bay

Costelloe/Casla

Lough
Ugga Beg

Gorumna

Carraroe/
An Cheathrú Rua

Rossaveel

Lettermullan/
Leitir Meallâin

Island

Keeraunnagark

R 33

Golam Head

Ballynahown

Inveran/
Indreabhán

13

North Sound

GALWAY

8

Rock Island

Onaght

Brannock
Islands

Kilmurvy

Dún Aonghasa

Oghil Church

Oatquarter 4

Kilronan/
Cill Rónáin

Castle

Gregory's
Sound

Inishmore/
Inis Mór

Killeany

Inishmaan/
Inis Meáin

Foul
Sound

ARAN ISLANDS/

Inisheer/
Inis Oírr

Fardurris Point

Oileáin Árainn

(△)

South Sound

TIC

De

R 479

Roadfo

19

R 478

(△) Doolin

O'Brien's Tower

△ 206

15

Kilsha

Cliffs
of Moher

(△) Cliffs
of Moher

Cliffs of Moher
Visitor Centre

Derreen

9

Hags Head

R 478

Liscannor

(△) Lahinch/
An Leacht

Dealagh

Liscannor Bay

AN

Rinneen

N 67

Mal Bay

Milltown Malba
Sráid na Cathrac

Bo

Spanish Point

R 482

Letterkelly

Spanish Point

R 474

R 460

16

Caherrush Point

Quilty

10

Mutton Island

Kilmurry

Mullagh

C

Carrowmore Point

29

47

Annageeragh

Loug

R 483

Gler

White
Strand

Creegh

Cahermurphy

Donegal Point

Killard

4

Mountrivers
Bridge

Creegh

6

Leitrim

Corbally

N 67 15

Doonbeg

R 484

Kilmihil

14

Bealaha

Doonbeg

Moore Bay

Kilkee/
Cill Chaoi

8½

Moanmore

Cooraclare

N 68

Castle Point

13,5

Garraun

Moyasta

R 485

6

Kilfearagh

Termon

N 67

R 483

13

Knockerry

Moveen

8

Poulnasherry
Bay

N 68

10

B

93

Tullia Point

Breaghva

Querrin

Kilrush
Cill Ro

R 473

Knock

C

Feeard

13 Cross

R 488

Doonaha

Corlis Point

D

9

Killimer

9

Clonderalaw

Bridge
Kilbaha

Moneen

Carrigaholt

Carrigaholt
Bay

R 487

Scattery Island

Kilcredaun Point

5½

32

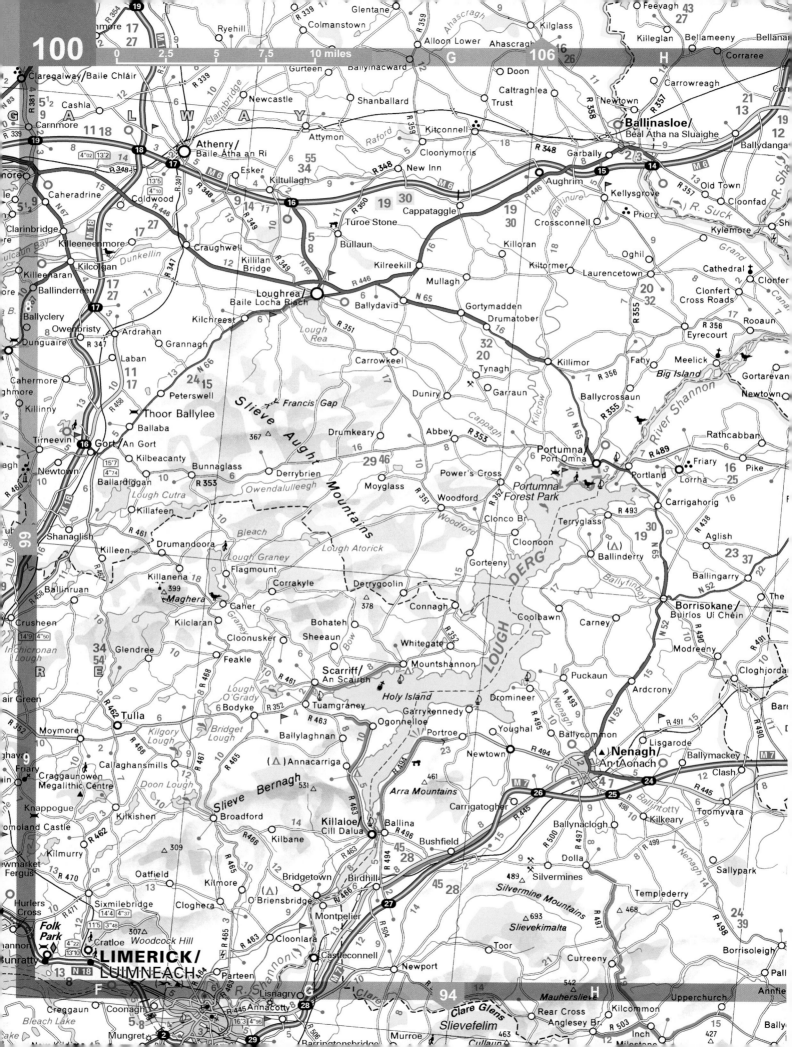

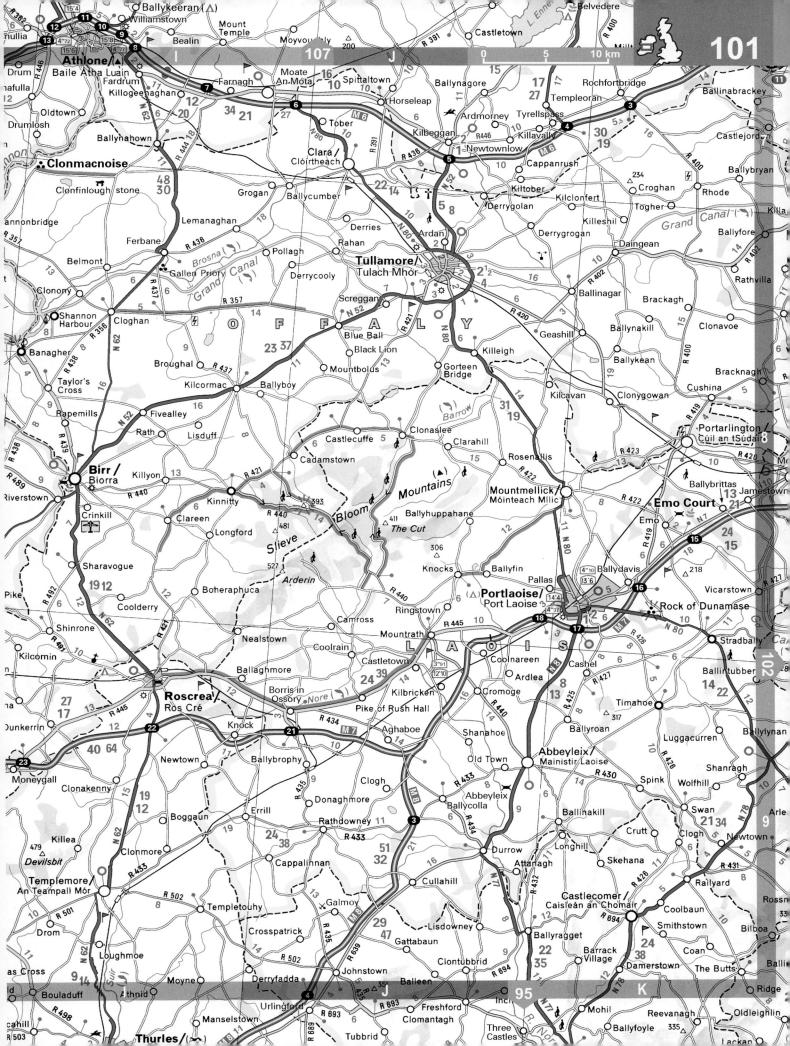

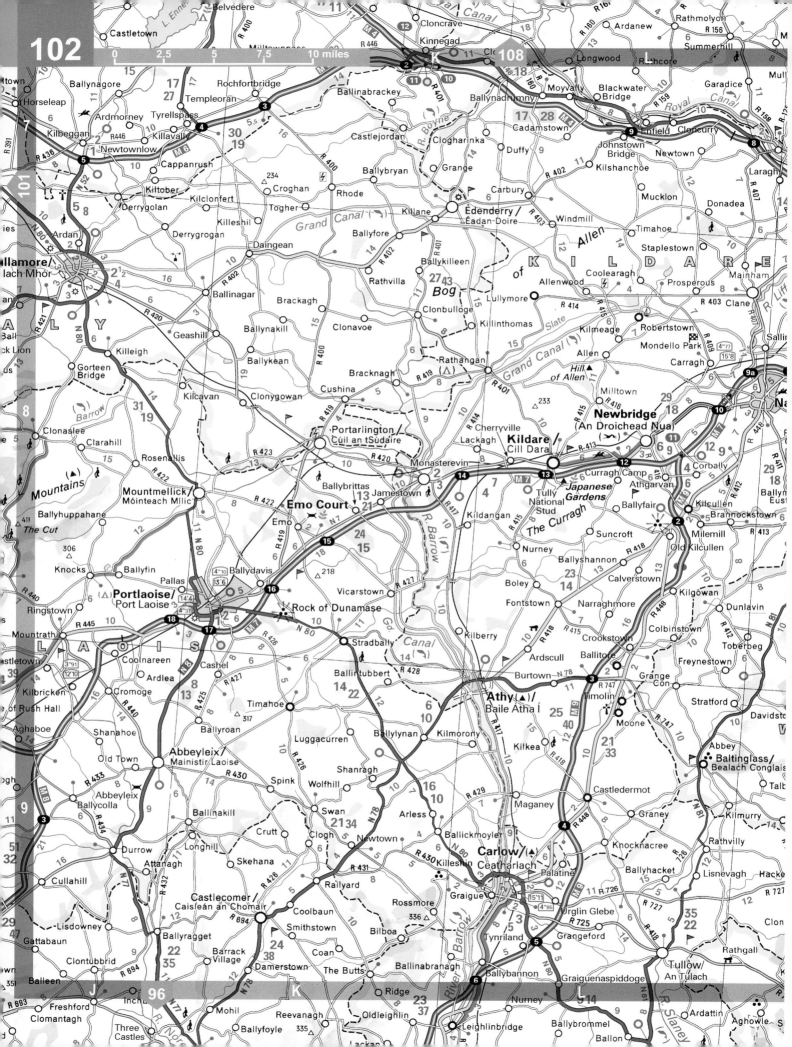

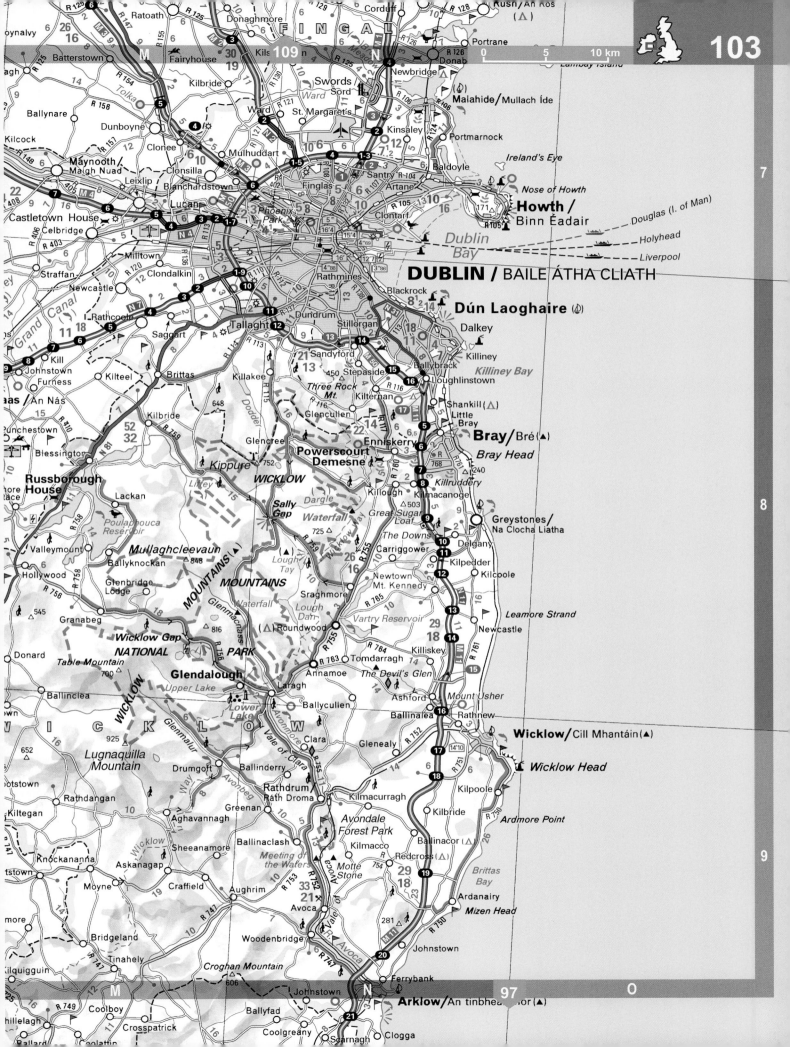

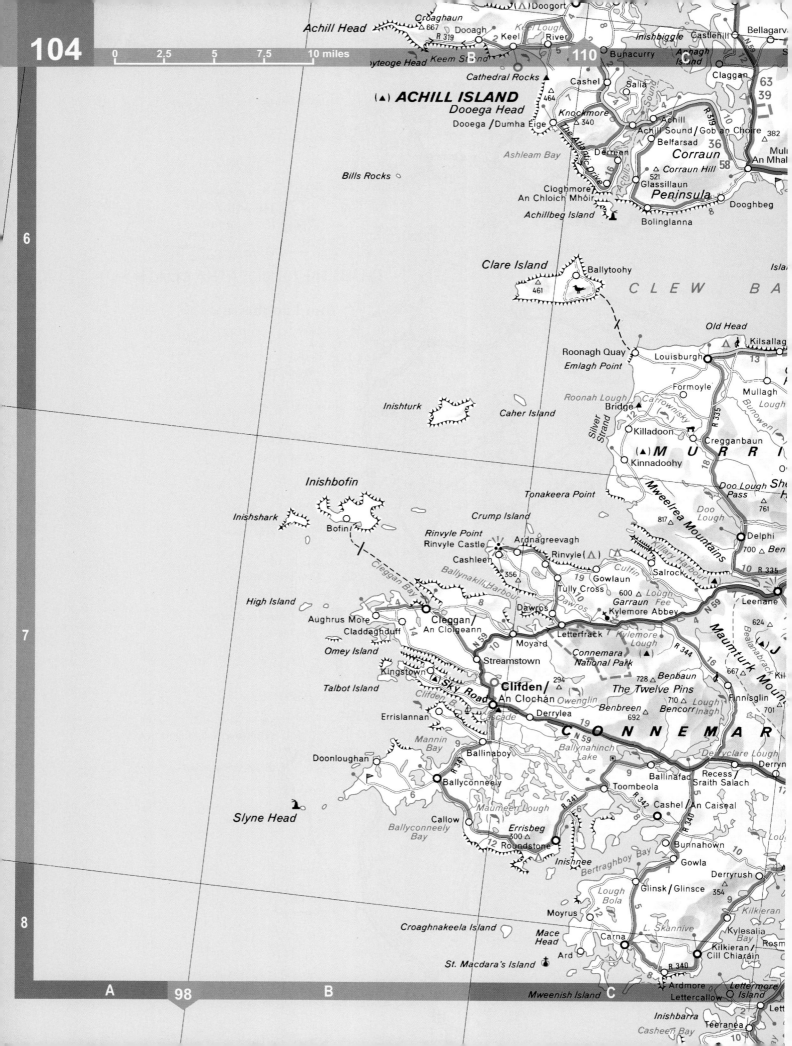

Achill Head
Croaghaun
△ 667 Dooagh
Keel
Keel Lough
River
Doogort
Inishbiggle Castlehill
Bellagarva
N 59
R 319
Bunacurry
Cashel
Achagh
Claggan
63
39
37
Keem Stand
byteoge Head

Cathedral Rocks ▲
Cashel
Salia
Achill Sound / Gob an Choire
Mulr
An Mhal

(▲) **ACHILL ISLAND**
Dooega Head
Dooega / Dumha Eige
Knockmore
△ 340
Achill
Belfarsad
△ 464
Corraun
521
△ Corraun Hill
Glassillaun
382
36
58
An Mhal

Ashleam Bay
Derreen
Peninsula
Dooghbeg

Bills Rocks ○
Cloghmore
An Chloich Mhóir
Achillbeg Island ⚓
Bolinglanna
8

Clare Island
Ballytoohy
C L E W   B A
Isla
△ 461

Roonagh Quay
Emlagh Point
Old Head
Kilsallag
△ ⚓ Kilsallag
Louisburgh
13
7

Formoyle
Mullagh
Lough
R 335

Roonah Lough
Bridge ▲ Carrownisky
Silver Strand
Killadoon
12
Cregganbaun
Bunowen

Inishturk
Caher Island
(▲) M U R R I
18
Kinnadoohy

Tonakeera Point
Doo Lough Pass
761
Mweelrea Mountains
817 △
Doo Lough
Delphi
700 △ Ben
R 335

Inishbofin
Crump Island
Rinvyle Point
Rinvyle Castle
Bofin
Cashleen
356 △
Ardnagreevagh
Rinvyle (△)
Culfin
Salrock
10 R 335

Inishshark
Ballynakill Harbour
Gowlaun
Tully Cross
Lough Fee
Leenane
19
Dawros
600 △ Garraun
692
Kylemore Abbey
N 59

High Island
Cleggan Bay
4
Dawros
Kylemore Lough
624 △
Aughrus More
Claddaghduff
Cleggan / An Cloigeann
14
Moyard
Letterfrack
Connemara National Park (▲)
R 344
16
667 △
J

Omey Island
Streamstown
N 59
10
294 △
728 △ Benbaun
The Twelve Pins
Benbreen
701

Kingstown
Talbot Island
Sky Road
Clifden / An Clochán
Owenglin
Benbreen
692
710 △ Lough Inagh
Finnisglin

Errislannan
Cascade
Derrylea
Bencorr
19
C O N N E M A R
N 59
Derryn

Mannin Bay
9
Ballynahinch Lake
Derryclare Lough
Ballinaboy
R 341

Doonloughan
Ballyconneely
6
Ballinafad
Recess Sraith Salach
17

Slyne Head
Callow
Errisbeg
300 △
Toombeola
R 341
6
Cashel / An Caiseal
R 342
R 340

Ballyconneely Bay
12 Roundstone
Bunnahown
10

Inishnee
Bertraghboy Bay
Gowla
Derryrush

Croaghnakeela Island
Mace Head
Lough Bola
Glinsk / Glinsce
354
Kilkieran

Moyrus
12
L. Skannive
Kylesalia

Ard
Carna
Kilkieran / Cill Chiaráin
Rosm

St. Macdara's Island ⚓
Ardmore
Lettermore Island
Letter

Mweenish Island
Inishbarra
Teeranea
Lett

Casheen Bay
10

0 2.5 5 7.5 10 miles

6

7

8

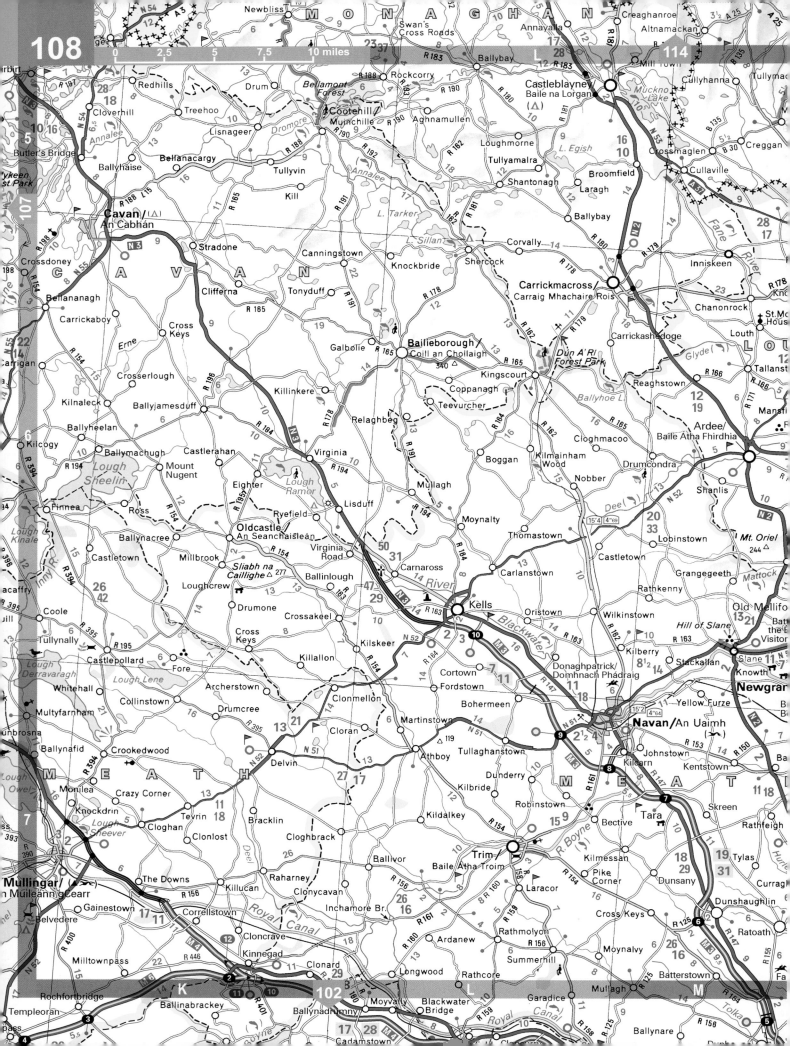

Belleek • Camlough 2
Lislea
Bernish Rock
Newry
Hilltown
Mayobridge
B 27
Newcastle (▲ △)
Tollymore Forest Park
Slieve Donard
Ulster Way

M
Slieve Gullion 573
Killevy Churches
Cloghoge
Narrow Water Castle
Donaghaguy
Rostrevor
Killowen
Spelga Dam
Mourne Mountains
708
626
Shannagh
Dunmore
Glasdrumman
Mullartown
Silent Valley
Attical
Lisnacree
40
25
Annalong

Silver Bridge
Forkill
Drumintee
Warrenpoint
Jonesborough
Omeath
Windy Gap 509
Ravensdale
Ballygowan
Castle
Greencastle
Kilkeel
Ballymartin
A2

Kilcurry
Dowdallshill
Proleek Dolmen
Carlingford Mt. 587
Carlingford
Greenore
Cranfield Point

Kilcurly
DUNDALK/ DUN DEALGAN
Grange
Ballagan Point
Giles Quay (△)
Rathcor
The Bush
Whites Town
Cooley Point

Blackrock
Dundalk Bay

Dromiskin
Castlebellingham
Annagassan
Kilsaran
Dunany Point
Drumcar
Togher
Dunany
Port
Dunleer
Grangebellew

Monasterboice
Clogher Head
Clogherhead
Ballymakenny
Termonfeckin

DROGHEDA/ DROICHEAD ÁTHA (▲)
Baltray
Mornington
Donacarney
Bettystown (△)
Julianstown
Laytown
Donore
Mosney (△)

Duleek
Bellewstown
Stamullin
Gormanston
Greenanstown
Balscaddan
Balbriggan/ Baile Brigin
Fourknocks
Ardcath
Clonalvy
Naul
Balrothery
Skerries/ Na Sceirí
Garristown
Damastown
Loughshinny

Ashbourne
Oldtown
Ballyboghil
Corduff
Lusk
Rush/ An Ros (△)
Rockabill

Donaghmore
Kilsallaghan
Portrane
Donabate
Lambay Island
FINGAL

Swords/ Sord
Newbridge
Malahide/ Mullach Íde
St. Margaret's

I R I
O P
S E A

0   2.5   5   7.5   10 miles

A T L A N T

Benwee Head

Kid Island

Erris Head

Broad Haven

Eagle Island

Aghadoon   *Rinroe Point*   C

138   11   △
Corclogh   6   Knocknalina   266

Annagh Head   Inver

R 313   ▶ Belmullet /
                        Béal an Mhuirthead   10   K

Inishglora   R 313   R 313   Barnatr
                   5   Barr na
Corraun Point   An Geata Mór   11   R 314

Mullet Peninsula   Drumreagh   *Trawmore*   Bunnahowen /
                                      Bay   Bun na hAbhna

                         11   *Elly Bay*   10   240
Inishkea North   12   △
                    R 313   *Doolough Point*   12
                                                 Srahmore   19
Inishkea South   Tristia   11

                   Aghleam   105   Dooyork
                            △
Black Rock   *Duvillaun More*   105   10 ▲Blacksod   Geesala /
                                          Point   Gaoth Saile
              Fallmore   *Duvillaun Beg*   *Blacksod*   10   6
                                                 Bay
                                          Doohooma   *Tullaghan*
                                                          Bay   Shranamann

                                                 Fahy Lough   Doona   N 59
Saddle Head   *Ridge Point*   Ballycroy

                   Slievemore   △671   Valley
                   (∧) Doogort
Croaghaun   N 59   Bellagarva
△667   Dooagh   *Keel Lough*   Castlehill
Achill Head   R 319   2 Keel   River   2   *Inishbiggle*   *Annagh*   N 59   12
                                      5   Bunacurry   *Island*
         Moyteoge Head   Keem Strand   63

Cathedral Rocks ▲   Cashel   Sala   C   Claggan   39

(▲) **ACHILL ISLAND**   △464   7   Knockmore   △340   Achill
              Dooega Head   Dooega / Dumha Éige

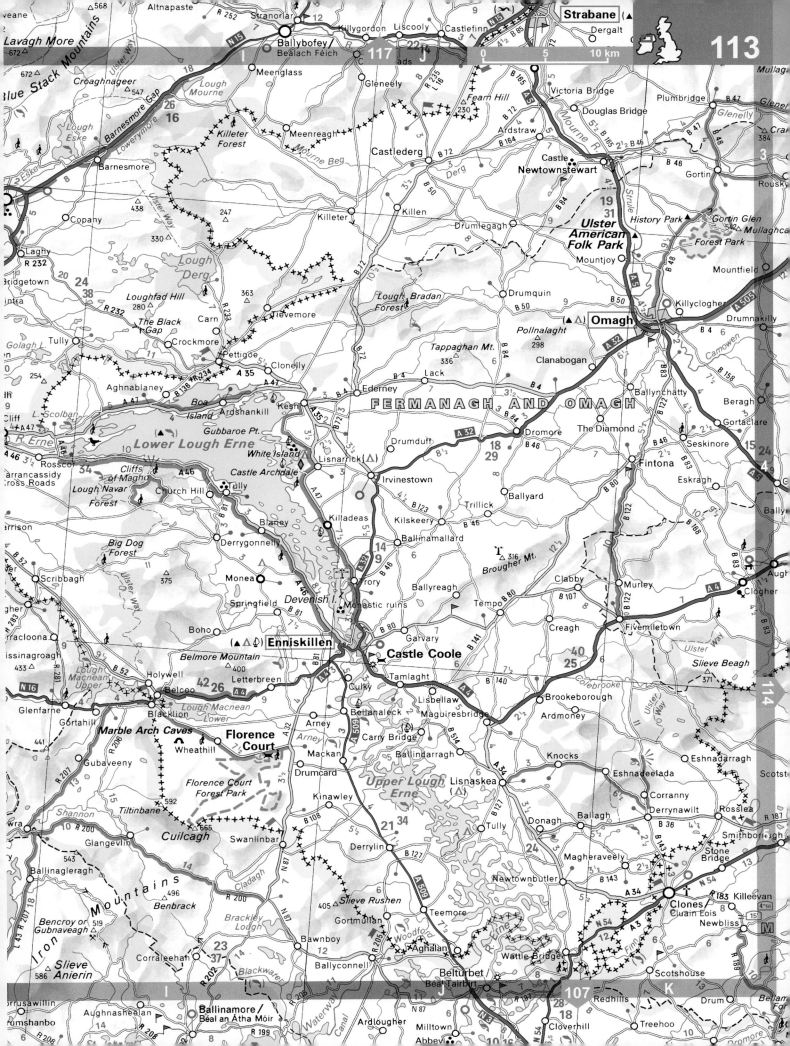

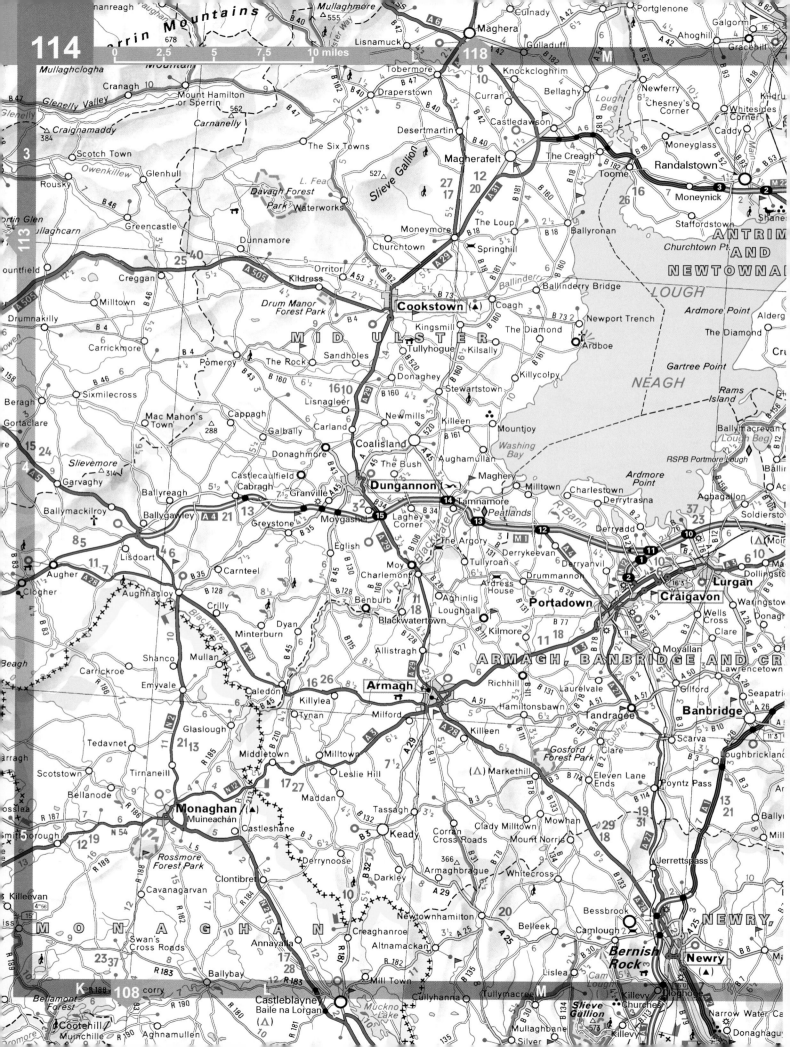

Arnicle
Glenbarr
Beinn

0   5   10 km

Bellochantuy
Saddell
Saddell Bay
Lussa Loch
Sgreadan Hill
397
Ugadale
Bay (▲)
Skeroblingarry
Drumadoon
Point
Black Bay (▲)
Blackwater
Kilchenzie
Drumadoon
A 83
9½
Peninver
Ardnacross Bay
Brown H
(▲) Machrihanish Bay
Campbeltown
Machrihanish
(▲)
Island Davaar
Campbeltown Loch
B 843
A 83
Drumlemble
Stewarton
Knocknaha
352
Beinn Ghuilean
Cnoc Moy
96
△ 446
9½
Feochaig
Rubha Dùin Bhàin
Conie Glen
B 842
Johnston's Point
S.
Carrine
Macharioch
Southend
Sanda Sound
Sheep Island

Bull
Point
Rathlin Island
(▲)
Church Quarter
Mull of Kintyre
Sanda Island
ck-a-rede
e Bridge
Rathlin Sound
Rue Point

B 15
Ballycastle
Bay
Benmore or Fair Head
nduff
Murlough
Bay
A
N
O
R
T
H

llycastle
A 2
Ulster Way
Torr Head
T
C
A 44
Ballyvoy
R
O
67
Carneatly
Glenshesk
379
△
I
A
Glentaisie
514
Ballypatrick
Forest
M
S
Knocklayd
Runabay Head
T
rmoy
9½
B 15
403
16
B 92
2
Crockaneel
Cushendun (△)
Ballyhoe
Bridge
Moyle Way
Glendun
6½
Knocknacarry
Glenaan
Slieveanorra
Glenann
Ossian's
Grave
Cushendall (△)
H
508
Red Bay
Loughguile
Trostan
Glenballyemon
Glenariff or Waterfoot
A 2
Corkey
550
B 14
6½
Glenariff
A 43
5½
Garron Point
ge
Glenariff
(▲)
mills
Glenariff
Waterfalls
Big
Trosk
Cargan
Forest
377
C
Newtown-
Cromelin
A 43
Park
Dungonnell
Dam
434
O
Clough
B 64
Collin Top
Carnlough (△)
A
Martinstown
Carnlough Bay
S
egor's
orner
Glenarm
Glencloy
The Sheddings
Carnageer
26
Glenarm
T
B 94
A 2
B 97
A 2
Quarrytown
381
△
Carnalbanagh
Sheddings
Feystown
A 42
12
Bucknan
B 148
M 2
Broughshane
437
Carncastle
Ballygalley Head
Slemish
Mountain
Carncastle
Ballygalley
11
Drains Bay
Ballymena
MID AND EAST ANTRIM
B 148
Larne (▲△)
10
13
A 26
Agnew's Hill
115
P
A
B 59
474
Mor fields
Shoptown 32
20
Kilwaughter
Millbrook
Isle
Portm
Kells
A 36
Glynn
A 8
Mullaghboy
Connor
Ballyboley
Forest
5½
Magheramorne
Milbay
B 98
Waterfall
Skilcoan
Islandmagee

A B C D E F G H I J K L M N O P Q R S T U V W X Y Z

Page number / Numéro de page / Seitenzahl
Paginanummer / Numero di pagina / Numéro de Página

Place / Localité / Ort
Plaatsen / Località / Localidad

Achmelvich 84 E 9

Grid coordinates / Coordonnées de carroyage
Koordinatenangabe / Verwijstekens ruitsysteem
Coordinate riferite alla quadrettatura
Coordenadas en los mapas

A

A Chill 71 A 12
A La Ronde 4 J 32
Abbas Combe 9 M 30
Abberley 27 M 27
Abbey 23 X 30
Abbey Dore 26 L 28
Abbey Town 54 K 19
Abbeydale 43 P 23
Abbeystead 48 L 22
Abbots Bromley 35 O 25
Abbots Langley 21 S 28
Abbots Leigh 18 M 29
Abbots Ripton 29 T 26
Abbotsbury 5 M 32
Abbotsford House 62 L 17
Abbotskerswell 4 J 32
Aber Banc 15 G 27
Aberaeron 24 H 27
Aberaman 17 J 28
Aberangell 33 I 25
Abercarn 18 K 29
Abercastle 14 E 28
Aberchirder 81 M 11
Abercynon 17 J 29
Aberdâr / Aberdare 17 J 28
Aberdare / Aberdâr 17 J 28
Aberdaron 32 F 25
Aberdaugleddau / Milford Haven 14 E 28
Aberdeen 75 N 12
Aberdour 68 K 15
Aberdour Bay 81 N 10
Aberdovey / Aberdyfi 33 H 26
Aberdyfi / Aberdovey 33 H 26
Aberedw 25 J 27
Abereiddy 14 E 28
Aberfeldy 73 I 14
Aberffraw 32 G 24
Aberford 43 P 22
Aberfoyle 67 G 15
Abergavenny / Y-Fenni 18 K 28
Abergele 41 J 23
Abergolech 15 H 28
Abergwaun / Fishguard 24 F 28
Abergwesyn 25 I 27
Abergwili 15 H 28
Abergwynfi 17 J 29
Abergwyngregyn 41 H 23
Abergynolwyn 33 I 26
Aberhonddu / Brecon 25 J 28
Aberkenfig 17 J 29
Aberlady 69 L 15
Aberlemno 75 L 13
Aberlour 80 K 11
Abermaw / Barmouth 33 H 25
Abermule 34 K 26
Abernethy 68 K 15
Abernyte 68 K 14
Aberpennar / Mountain Ash 17 J 28
Aberporth 15 G 27
Abersoch 32 G 25
Abersychan 18 K 28
Abertawe / Swansea 17 I 29
Aberteifi / Cardigan 15 G 27
Abertillery 18 K 28
Aberuthven 67 J 15
Aberystwyth 25 H 26
Abingdon 20 Q 28
Abinger Common 21 S 30
Abinger Hammer 21 S 30
Abingto *Cambs.* 30 U 27
Abington *South Lanarkshire* 61 I 17
Aboyne 75 L 12
Abriachan 79 G 11
Abridge 21 U 29
Accrington 42 M 22
Achahoish 65 D 16
Achallader 66 F 14
Achanalt 78 F 11
Achaphubuil 72 E 13
Acharacle 71 C 13
Achargary 85 H 8
Acharn 67 H 14
Achduart 83 E 10
Achgarve 78 D 10
Achiemore 84 F 8
Achiltibuie 83 D 9
Achintee 78 D 11
Achintraid 78 D 11
Achlean 73 I 12
Achleck 64 B 14
Achmelvich 84 E 9
Achmore 78 D 11
Achnahanat 84 G 10
Achnamara 65 D 15
Achnasellan 72 E 13
Achnasheen 78 E 11
Achnashellach Forest 78 E 11
Achosnich 71 B 13
Achranich 71 C 14
Achray (Loch) 67 G 15
Achreamie 85 I 8
Achriesgill 84 F 8
Achtalean 77 B 11
Achvaich 79 H 10
Acklington 63 P 18
Ackworth 44 P 23
Acle 39 Y 26
Acomb 55 N 19
Acrise Place 13 X 30
Acton Burnell 34 L 26
Acton Scott 26 L 26
Acton Turville 19 N 29
Adbaston 35 M 25
Adderbury 28 Q 27
Adderley 34 M 25
Adderstone 63 O 17
Addingham 49 O 22
Addlestone 21 S 29
Adfa 33 J 26
Adlington 42 M 23
Adlington Hall 43 N 24
Advie 80 J 11
Adwick-le-Street 44 Q 23
Ae (Forest of) 53 J 18
Ae Village 53 J 18
Afan Argoed 17 J 29
Affric (Glen) 78 F 12
Affric Lodge 78 E 12
Afon Dyfrdwy / Dee (River) 34 K 24
Afon Dyfrdwy (River) / Dee *Wales* 41 K 23
Afon-wen 41 K 23
Agneash 46 G 21
Aikton 54 K 19
Ailort (Loch) 72 C 13
Ailsa Craig 59 E 18
Ainderby Quernhow 50 P 21
Ainort (Loch) 77 B 12
Ainsdale 42 K 23
Air Uig 82 Y 9
Aird 65 D 15
Aird (The) 79 G 11
Aird of Sleat 71 C 12
Airdrie 61 I 16
Airigh na h-Airde (Loch) 82 Z 9
Airor 72 C 12
Airth 67 I 15
Airton 49 N 21
Aith *Orkney Is.* 87 M 6
Aith *Shetland Is.* 87 P 3
Aitnoch 80 I 11
Akeld 63 N 17
Albourne 11 T 31
Albrighton 35 N 26
Albyn or Mor (Glen) 73 F 12
Alcaig 79 G 11
Alcester 27 O 27
Alconbury 29 T 26
Aldborough 39 X 25
Aldbourne 19 P 29
Aldbrough 45 T 22
Aldbrough St. John 49 O 20
Aldbury 21 S 28
Alde (River) 31 Y 27
Aldeburgh 31 Y 27
Aldenham 21 S 28
Alderbury 9 O 30
Alderholt 9 O 31
Alderley Edge 43 N 24
Alderney *Channel I.* 5
Aldershot 20 R 30
Alderton 27 N 28
Aldford 34 L 24
Aldingbourne 11 R 31
Aldridge 35 O 26
Aldringham 31 Y 27
Aldsworth 19 O 28
Aldunie 80 K 12
Aldwick 11 R 31
Alexandria 66 G 16
Alfold Crossways 11 S 30
Alford *Aberdeenshire* 75 L 12
Alford *Lincs.* 45 U 24
Alfreton 36 P 24
Alfrick 27 M 27
Alfriston 12 U 31
Aline (Loch) 65 C 14
Alkborough 44 S 22
Alkham 13 X 30
All Stretton 34 L 26
Allanaquoich 74 J 12
Allanton *North Lanarkshire* 61 I 16
Allanton *Scottish Borders* 63 N 16
Allendale Town 55 N 19
Allenheads 55 N 19
Allensmore 26 L 27
Allerford 17 J 30
Allerston 51 S 21
Allestree 36 P 25
Allhallows 22 V 29
Alligin Shuas 78 D 11
Allington *Kennet* 19 O 29
Allington *Salisbury* 9 O 30
Allnabad 84 G 8
Alloa 67 I 15
Allonby 54 J 19
Alloway 60 G 17
Allt na h-Airbhe 78 E 10
Alltan Fhèarna (Loch an) 85 H 9
Alltnacaillich 84 G 8
Almond (Glen) 67 I 14
Almondbank 68 J 14
Almondsbury 18 M 29
Alness 79 H 10
Alnmouth 63 P 17
Alnwick 63 O 17
Alpheton 30 W 27
Alphington 4 J 31
Alpraham 34 M 24
Alresford 30 X 28
Alrewas 35 O 25
Alsager 35 N 24
Alsh (Loch) 78 D 12
Alston 55 M 19
Alstonefield 35 O 24
Alswear 7 I 31
Altadnduin 85 H 9
Altandhu 83 D 9
Altarnun 3 G 32
Altass 84 G 10
Alternative Technology Centre 33 I 26
Altham 42 M 22
Althorne 22 W 29
Althorpe 44 R 23
Altnabreac Station 85 I 8
Altnacealgach 84 F 9
Altnaharra 84 G 9
Alton *Hants.* 10 R 30
Alton *Staffs.* 35 O 25
Alton Pancras 9 M 31
Alton Priors 19 O 29
Alton Towers 35 O 25
Altrincham 42 M 23
Alum Bay 10 P 31
Alva 67 I 15
Alvaston 36 P 25
Alvechurch 27 O 26
Alvediston 9 N 30
Alves 80 J 11
Alvescot 19 P 28
Alvie 73 I 12
Alvingham 45 U 23
Alwinton 63 N 17
Alyth 74 K 14
Amberley 11 S 31
Amble 63 P 18
Amblecote 27 N 26
Ambleside 48 L 20
Ambrosden 28 Q 28
Amersham 21 S 29
Amesbury 9 O 30
Amhuinnsuidhe 82 Y 10
Amisfield 53 J 18
Amlwch 40 G 22
Ammanford / Rhydaman 15 I 28
Amotherby 50 R 21
Ampleforth 50 Q 21
Amport 20 P 30
Ampthill 29 S 27
Amroth 15 G 28
Amulree 67 I 14
An Riabhachan 78 E 11
An Socach 74 J 13
An Teallach 78 E 10
Anchor 26 K 26
Ancroft 63 O 16
Ancrum 62 M 17
Andover 20 P 30
Andoversford 27 O 28
Andreas 46 G 20
Angle 14 E 28
Anglesey (Isle of) 40
Anglesey Abbey 30 U 27
Angmering 11 S 31
Annan 54 K 19
Annan (River) 61 J 18
Annat 78 D 11
Annat Bay 83 E 10
Annbank 60 G 17
Annbank Station 60 G 17
Anne Hathaway's Cottage 27 O 27
Annesley-Woodhouse 36 Q 24
Annfield Plain 56 O 19
Ansley 28 P 26
Anstey 36 Q 25
Anston 44 Q 23
Anstruther 69 L 15
Anthorn 54 K 19
Antony House 3 H 32
Appin 72 E 14
Appleby *North Lincolnshire* 44 S 23
Appleby-in-Westmorland 55 M 20
Appleby Magna 36 P 25
Applecross 77 C 11
Appledore *Devon* 6 H 30
Appledore *Kent* 12 W 30
Appleford 20 Q 29
Appleton 20 P 28
Appleton Roebuck 44 Q 22
Appleton Wiske 50 P 20
Appletreewick 49 O 21
Aran Fawddwy 33 I 25
Arberth / Narberth 15 F 28
Arbigland 53 J 19
Arbirlot 69 M 14
Arbor Low 35 O 24
Arborfield 20 R 29
Arbroath 69 M 14
Arbury Hall 28 P 26
Arbuthnott 75 N 13
Archiestown 80 K 11
Ard (Loch) 67 G 15
Ardanaiseig 66 E 14
Ardarroch 78 D 11
Ardcharnich 78 E 10
Ardchiavaig 64 B 15
Ardchuilk 78 F 11
Ardchyle 67 G 14
Ardechive 72 E 13
Arden 66 G 15
Ardentallan 65 D 14
Ardeonaig 67 H 14
Ardersier 79 H 11
Ardery 72 C 13
Ardfern 65 D 15
Ardgartan 66 F 15
Ardgay 79 G 10
Ardgour 72 D 13
Ardhasaig 82 Z 10
Ardingly 11 T 30
Ardington 20 P 29
Ardivachar 76 X 11
Ardleigh 30 W 28
Ardley 28 Q 28
Ardlui 66 F 15
Ardlussa 65 C 15
Ardmair 84 E 10
Ardminish 58 C 16
Ardmore Point *Isle of Skye* 77 A 11
Ardnacross 71 C 14
Ardnamurchan 71 B 13
Ardnastang 72 D 13
Ardnave 64 A 16
Ardnave Point 64 B 16
Ardpatrick 59 D 16
Ardrishaig 65 D 15
Ardrossan 59 F 17
Ardshealach 71 C 13
Ardslignish 71 C 13
Ardtalla 58 B 16
Ardtalnaig 67 H 14
Ardtoe 71 C 13
Ardvasar 71 C 12
Ardverikie Forest 73 G 13
Ardvorlich 67 H 14
Ardwell 52 F 19
Argyll 65 D 15
Argyll Forest Park 66 F 15
Arichastlich 66 F 14
Arienas (Loch) 71 C 14
Arileod 71 A 14
Arinacrinachd 77 C 11
Arinagour 71 A 14
Arisaig 71 C 13
Arivruaich 82 Z 9
Arkaig (Loch) 72 E 13
Arkendale 50 P 21
Arkengarthdale 49 O 20
Arkholme 48 M 21
Arklet (Loch) 66 G 15
Arley 27 P 26
Arlingham 19 M 28
Arlington Court 7 I 30
Armadale *Highland* 85 H 8
Armadale *West Lothian* 61 I 16
Armadale Bay 71 C 12
Armitage 35 O 25
Armthorpe 44 Q 23
Arnabost 71 A 14
Arncliffe 49 N 21
Arncott 20 Q 28
Arncroach 69 L 15
Arne 9 N 31
Arnesby 28 Q 26
Arnicle 59 D 17
Arnisdale 72 D 12
Arnish 77 B 11
Arnol 82 A 8
Arnold 36 Q 25
Arnprior 67 H 15
Arnside 48 L 21
Aros 65 B 14
Arram 45 S 22
Arran (Isle of) 59 E 17
Arreton 10 Q 31
Arrochar 66 F 15
Arscaig 84 G 9
Arundel 11 S 31
Ascog 59 E 16
Ascot 21 R 29
Ascott House 29 R 28
Ascott-under-Wychwood 28 P 28
Ascrib Islands 77 A 11
Asfordby 36 R 25
Ash *Kent* 23 X 30
Ash *Surrey* 20 R 30
Ash Mill 7 I 31
Ashbourne 35 O 24
Ashburton 4 I 32
Ashbury 19 P 29
Ashby de la Zouch 36 P 25
Ashby Magna 28 Q 26
Ashcott 8 L 30
Ashdon 30 U 27
Ashford *Kent* 12 W 30
Ashford *Surrey* 21 S 29
Ashford-in-the-Water *Derbs.* 43 O 24
Ashie (Loch) 79 H 11
Ashill *Breckland* 38 W 26
Ashill *South Somerset* 8 L 31
Ashingdon 22 W 29
Ashington *Northumb* 56 P 18
Ashington *West Sussex* 11 S 31
Ashkirk 62 L 17
Ashleworth 27 N 28
Ashley *East Cambridgeshire* 30 V 27
Ashley *Newcastle-under-Lyme* 35 M 25
Ashley *Torridge* 7 I 31
Ashley Green 21 S 28
Ashmore 9 N 31
Ashover 36 P 24
Ashperton 26 M 27
Ashreigney 7 I 31
Ashtead 21 T 30
Ashton 34 L 24
Ashton-in-Makerfield 42 M 23
Ashton Keynes 19 O 29
Ashton-under-Lyne 43 N 23
Ashton-upon-Mersey 42 M 23
Ashurst 10 P 31
Ashwell *North Hertfordshire* 29 T 27
Ashwell *Rutland* 36 R 25
Ashwellthorpe 39 X 26
Askam in Furness 47 K 21
Askern 44 Q 23
Askernish 76 X 12
Askerswell 5 L 31
Askham 55 L 20
Askrigg 49 N 21
Askwith 49 O 22
Aslacton 31 X 26
Aslockton 36 R 25
Aspatria 54 K 19
Aspley Guise 29 S 27
Assynt (Loch) 84 E 9
Astley 34 L 25
Aston *Vale Royal* 44 Q 23
Aston *West Oxfordshire* 20 P 28
Aston Clinton 20 R 28
Aston Magna 27 O 27
Aston Rowant 20 R 28
Aston Tirrold 20 Q 29
Astwood Bank 27 O 27
Atcham 34 L 25
Athelhampton Hall 9 N 31
Athelney 8 L 30
Athelstaneford 69 L 16
Atherington 7 H 31
Athersley 43 P 23
Atherstone 36 P 26
Atherton 42 M 23
Atholl (Forest of) 73 H 13
Attadale 78 D 11
Attleborough *Breckland* 38 X 26
Attleborough *Nuneaton and Bedworth* 28 P 26
Attlebridge 39 X 25
Atwick 51 T 22
Atworth 19 N 29
Aucharnie 81 M 11
Auchavan 74 K 13
Auchenblae 75 M 13
Auchenbowie 67 I 15
Auchenbrack 61 I 18
Auchenbreck 65 E 16
Auchencairn 53 I 19
Auchencrosh 52 F 18
Auchencrow 63 N 16
Auchengray 61 J 16
Auchenmalg 52 F 19
Auchentiber 60 G 16

A
B
C
D
E
F
G
H
I
J
K
L
M
N
O
P
Q
R
S
T
U
V
W
X
Y
Z

Auchindrean ....78 E 10
Auchinleck ....60 H 17
Auchleven ....81 M 12
Auchlyne ....67 G 14
Auchnafree ....67 I 14
Auchnagallin ....80 J 11
Auchnagatt ....81 N 11
Aucholzie ....74 K 12
Auchronie ....74 L 13
Auchterarder ....67 I 15
Auchteraw ....73 F 12
Auchterderran ....68 K 15
Auchterhouse ....68 K 14
Auchtermuchty ....68 K 15
Auchtertyre ....78 D 12
Auckengill ....86 K 8
Auckley ....44 Q 23
Audenshaw ....43 N 23
Audlem ....34 M 25
Audley ....35 N 24
Audley End ....30 U 27
Aughton near Lancaster ....48 L 21
Aughton near Ormskirk ....42 L 23
Auldearn ....79 I 11
Auldgirth ....53 I 18
Auldhouse ....60 H 16
Ault a' Chruinn ....72 D 12
Aultbea ....78 D 10
Aust ....18 M 29
Austrey ....35 P 26
Austwick ....49 M 21
Avebury ....19 O 29
Aveley ....22 U 29
Avening ....19 N 28
Aveton Gifford ....4 I 33
Aviemore ....73 I 12
Avoch ....79 H 11
Avon (Glen) ....74 J 12
Avon (River) R. Severn ....28 Q 26
Avon (River) Wilts. ....9 O 31
Avonbridge ....67 I 16
Avonmouth ....18 L 29
Avonwick ....4 I 32
Awe (Loch) ....65 E 15
Awliscombe ....8 K 31
Awre ....19 M 28
Axbridge ....18 L 30
Axminster ....8 L 31
Axmouth ....5 K 31
Aylburton ....18 M 28
Aylesbury ....20 R 28
Aylesford ....22 V 30
Aylesham ....23 X 30
Aylsham ....39 X 25
Aylton ....26 M 27
Aymestrey ....26 L 27
Aynho ....28 Q 28
Ayr ....60 G 17
Aysgarth ....49 O 21
Ayside ....48 L 21
Ayton Scarborough ....51 S 21
Ayton Scottish Borders ....63 N 16

B

Bà (Loch) ....65 C 14
Babbacombe Bay ....4 J 32
Babcary ....8 M 30
Babell ....41 K 23
Babworth ....44 R 24
Back ....83 B 9
Backaland ....87 L 6
Backmuir of New Gilston ....69 L 15
Backwater Reservoir ....74 K 13
Backwell West Town ....18 L 29
Baconsthorpe ....39 X 25
Bacton Mid Suffolk ....30 X 27
Bacton North Norfolk ....39 Y 25
Bacup ....43 N 22
Bad a' Ghaill (Loch) ....84 E 9
Bad an Sgalaig (Loch) ....78 D 10
Badachro ....77 C 10
Badanloch (Loch) ....85 H 9
Badanloch Lodge ....85 H 9
Badcaul ....78 D 10
Baddesley Ensor ....35 P 26
Baddidarach ....84 E 9
Badenoch ....73 H 13
Badenscallie ....83 E 9
Badenyon ....74 K 12
Badlipster ....86 K 8
Badluarach ....78 D 10
Badminton ....19 N 29
Badrallach ....78 E 10
Bae Colwyn / Colwyn Bay ....41 I 23
Bagh nam Faoileann ....76 Y 11
Bagillt ....41 K 23
Bagley ....34 L 25

Bagshot ....21 R 29
Bagworth ....36 P 25
Bagwyllydiart ....26 L 28
Baile Mòr ....64 A 15
Bailiehill ....54 K 18
Bainbridge ....49 N 21
Bainton ....51 S 22
Bakewell ....35 O 24
Bala ....33 J 25
Balallan ....82 A 9
Balbeggie ....68 J 14
Balblair ....79 H 10
Balcary Point ....53 I 19
Balcombe ....11 T 30
Balderton ....36 R 24
Baldrine ....46 G 21
Baldwin ....46 G 21
Balemartine ....64 Z 14
Balephetrish Bay ....70 Z 14
Balephuil ....64 Z 14
Balephuil Bay ....64 Z 14
Balerno ....61 J 16
Baleshare ....76 X 11
Balevulin ....65 B 14
Balfour ....87 L 6
Balfron ....67 H 15
Balgray ....69 L 14
Balintore Angus ....74 K 13
Balintore Highland ....79 I 10
Balivanich ....76 X 11
Ballabeg ....46 F 21
Ballachulish ....72 E 13
Ballajora ....46 G 21
Ballamodha ....46 G 21
Ballasalla ....46 G 21
Ballater ....74 K 12
Ballaugh ....46 G 21
Ballevullin ....70 Z 14
Balliemore near Dunoon ....65 E 15
Balliemore near Oban ....65 D 14
Ballingry ....68 K 15
Ballinluig ....74 J 14
Ballochan ....75 L 12
Ballochroy ....59 D 16
Ballyhaugh ....71 A 14
Balmaclellan ....53 H 18
Balmaha ....67 G 15
Balmedie ....75 N 12
Balminnoch ....52 F 19
Balmoral Castle ....74 K 12
Balmullo ....69 L 14
Balnacra ....78 D 11
Balnafoich ....79 H 11
Balnaguard ....74 I 14
Balnahard ....64 B 14
Balnaknock ....77 B 11
Balnapaling ....79 H 10
Baltonsborough ....8 M 30
Balvicar ....65 D 15
Balvraid ....72 D 12
Bamburgh Castle ....63 O 17
Bamford ....43 O 23
Bampton Cumbria ....48 L 20
Bampton Devon ....7 J 31
Bampton Oxon. ....20 P 28
Banavie ....72 E 13
Banbury ....28 P 27
Banchory ....75 M 12
Bancyfelin ....15 G 28
Bandenscoth ....81 M 11
Banff ....81 M 10
Bangor ....40 H 23
Bankend ....53 J 18
Bankfoot ....68 J 14
Bankhead ....75 N 12
Banks ....42 L 22
Bankshill ....54 K 18
Banniskirk ....85 J 8
Bannockburn ....67 I 15
Banstead ....21 T 30
Banwell ....18 L 30
Bapchild ....22 W 30
Bar Hill ....29 U 27
Barbaraville ....79 H 10
Barbon ....48 M 21
Barcaldine ....65 E 14
Barcombe Cross ....11 U 31
Bardney ....45 T 24
Bardsea ....48 K 21
Bardsey ....43 P 22
Bardsey Island ....32 F 25

Barford ....39 X 26
Barford-St. Martin ....9 O 30
Barfreston ....23 X 30
Bargoed ....18 K 28
Bargrennan ....52 G 18
Barham ....23 X 30
Barking ....30 X 27
Barking and Dagenham
  London Borough ....21 U 29
Barkston ....37 S 25
Barkway ....29 U 28
Barlaston ....35 N 25
Barlborough ....44 Q 24
Barlestone ....36 P 26
Barley North Hertfordshire ....29 U 27
Barley Pendle ....42 N 22
Barlow ....43 P 24
Barmby on the Marsh ....44 R 22
Barming ....22 V 30
Barmouth / Abermaw ....33 H 25
Barmouth Bay ....33 H 25
Barmston ....51 T 21
Barnack ....37 S 26
Barnard Castle ....49 O 20
Barnby Dun ....44 Q 23
Barnby Moor
  East Riding of Yorks. ....50 R 22
Barnby Moor Notts. ....44 Q 23
Barnet London Borough ....21 T 29
Barnetby-le-Wold ....45 S 23
Barney ....38 W 25
Barnham ....30 W 26
Barnham Broom ....38 X 26
Barnhill ....80 J 11
Barnhills ....52 E 18
Barningham ....49 O 20
Barnoldswick ....49 N 22
Barnsley ....43 P 23
Barnstaple ....7 H 30
Barnston ....42 M 24
Barnwell ....29 S 26
Barr ....52 F 18
Barra ....70 X 13
Barra (Sound of) ....70 X 12
Barra Head ....70 X 13
Barregarrow ....46 G 21
Barrhead ....60 G 16
Barrhill ....52 F 18
Barri / Barry ....18 K 29
Barrington ....8 L 31
Barrisdale ....72 D 12
Barrisdale Bay ....72 D 12
Barmill ....60 G 16
Barrock ....86 K 8
Barrow ....30 V 27
Barrow Burn ....63 N 17
Barrow Gurney ....18 L 29
Barrow-in-Furness ....47 K 21
Barrow-upon-Humber ....45 S 22
Barrow-upon-Soar ....36 Q 25
Barrowby ....36 R 25
Barrowford ....43 N 22
Barry Angus ....69 L 14
Barry / Barri
  Vale of Glamorgan ....18 K 29
Barsham ....31 Y 26
Barston ....27 O 26
Bartestree ....26 M 27
Barton Eden ....49 P 20
Barton Lancs. ....42 L 22
Barton-le-Clay ....29 S 28
Barton le Willows ....50 R 21
Barton Mills ....30 V 26
Barton-on-Sea ....9 P 31
Barton-under-Needwood ....35 O 25
Barton-upon-Humber ....44 S 22
Barvas ....82 A 8
Barwell ....36 P 26
Barwick-in-Elmet ....43 P 22
Baschurch ....34 L 25
Bashall Eaves ....42 M 22
Basildon Berks. ....20 Q 29
Basildon Essex ....22 V 29
Basing ....20 Q 30
Basingstoke ....20 Q 30
Baslow ....43 P 24
Bass Rock ....69 M 15
Bassenthwaite ....54 K 19
Bassingham ....37 S 24
Baston ....37 S 25
Bastwick ....39 Y 25
Batcombe ....8 M 31
Bath ....19 M 29
Bathampton ....19 N 29
Batheaston ....19 N 29
Bathgate ....61 J 16
Batley ....43 P 22

Battle ....12 V 31
Baumber ....45 T 24
Bawburgh ....39 X 26
Bawdeswell ....38 X 25
Bawdsey ....31 Y 27
Bawtry ....44 Q 23
Bayble ....83 B 9
Baycliff ....48 K 21
Baydon ....19 P 29
Bayhead ....76 X 11
Bayston Hill ....34 L 25
Beachampton ....28 R 27
Beachy Head ....12 U 31
Beacon (The) ....2 E 33
Beacon End ....30 W 28
Beaconsfield ....21 S 29
Beadlam ....50 R 21
Beadnell Bay ....63 P 17
Beaford ....7 H 31
Beal ....63 O 16
Beaminster ....8 L 31
Beamish Hall ....56 P 19
Beamsley ....49 O 22
Bearsden ....67 G 16
Bearsted ....22 V 30
Beattock ....61 J 18
Beauchief ....43 P 24
Beaufort ....18 K 28
Beaulieu ....10 P 31
Beauly ....79 G 11
Beauly Firth ....79 G 11
Beaumaris ....40 H 23
Beaumont ....54 K 19
Beaupré Castle ....17 J 29
Bebington ....42 L 23
Beccles ....31 Y 26
Beckfoot ....54 J 19
Beckingham ....44 R 23
Beckington ....19 N 30
Beckley ....12 V 31
Beckton ....21 U 29
Bedale ....50 P 21
Beddau ....17 J 29
Beddgelert ....33 H 24
Beddingham ....11 U 31
Bedford ....29 S 27
Bedgebury Pinetum ....12 V 30
Bedlington ....56 P 18
Bedlinog ....17 K 28
Bedrule ....62 M 17
Bedwas ....18 K 29
Bedworth ....28 P 26
Bee (Loch) ....76 X 11
Beeston ....36 Q 25
Beeswing ....53 I 18
Begdbroke ....20 Q 28
Beguildy ....26 K 26
Beighton ....44 P 23
Beinn a' Ghlò ....74 I 13
Beinn a' Mheadhoin (Loch) ....78 F 12
Beinn Dearg Highland ....78 F 10
Beinn Dearg
  Perthshire and Kinross ....73 I 13
Beinn Heasgarnich ....67 G 14
Beinn Ime ....66 F 15
Beith ....60 G 16
Belbroughton ....27 N 26
Belchford ....45 T 24
Belford ....63 O 17
Belhelvie ....75 N 12
Bellabeg ....74 K 12
Bellanoch ....65 D 15
Bellingham ....55 N 18
Bellshill
  Berwick-upon-Tweed ....63 O 17
Bellshill North Lanarkshire ....60 H 16
Belmont ....87 R 1
Belnacraig ....74 K 12
Belnahua ....65 C 15
Belper ....36 P 24
Belsay ....56 O 18
Belstead ....31 X 27
Belstone ....4 I 31
Belton Lincs. ....37 S 25
Belton Norfolk ....39 Y 26
Belton North Lincs. ....44 R 23
Belton Rutland ....36 R 26
Belvoir ....36 R 25
Bembridge ....10 Q 31
Bempton ....51 T 21
Ben Alder ....73 G 13
Ben Armine Forest ....85 H 9
Ben Armine Lodge ....85 H 9
Ben Chonzie ....67 I 14
Ben Cruachan ....65 E 14
Ben-damph Forest ....78 D 11

Ben Hope ....84 G 8
Ben Klibreck ....84 G 9
Ben Lawers ....67 H 14
Ben Ledi ....67 H 15
Ben Lomond ....66 G 15
Ben Loyal ....84 G 8
Ben Macdui ....74 I 12
Ben More Argyll and Bute ....65 B 14
Ben More Stirling ....67 G 14
Ben More Assynt ....84 F 9
Ben Nevis ....72 E 13
Ben Starav ....66 E 14
Ben Vorlich ....67 H 14
Ben Wyvis ....79 G 10
Benbecula ....76 X 11
Benbuie ....60 H 18
Benderloch Argyll and Bute ....65 D 14
Benderloch Mountain ....65 E 14
Bendronaig Lodge ....78 E 11
Benenden ....12 V 30
Benfleet ....22 V 29
Benington ....37 U 25
Benllech ....40 H 23
Benmore Argyll and Bute ....65 D 14
Benmore Lodge ....84 F 9
Benson ....20 Q 29
Bentley Doncaster ....44 Q 23
Bentley East Hampshire ....20 R 30
Bentpath ....54 K 18
Bentworth ....10 Q 30
Benwick ....29 T 26
Beoraid (Loch) ....72 D 13
Bere Alston ....3 H 32
Bere Ferrers ....3 H 32
Bere Regis ....9 N 31
Berkeley ....18 M 28
Berkhamsted ....21 S 28
Berneray near Barra ....70 X 13
Berneray near North Uist ....76 Y 10
Bernice ....66 E 15
Bernisdale ....77 B 11
Berriew ....34 K 26
Berrington Hall ....26 L 27
Berrow ....18 K 30
Berry Head ....4 J 32
Berry Hill ....18 M 28
Berry Pomeroy ....4 J 32
Berrynarbor ....17 H 30
Bervie Bay ....75 N 13
Berwick-St. John ....9 N 31
Berwick-upon-Tweed ....63 O 16
Berwyn ....33 J 25
Bessacarr ....44 Q 23
Bethel ....33 H 24
Bethersden ....12 W 30
Bethesda ....33 H 24
Betley ....35 M 24
Bettiscombe ....8 L 31
Bettisfield ....34 L 25
Bettws Cedewain ....34 K 26
Bettws Evan ....15 G 27
Bettws Gwerfil Goch ....33 J 24
Bettyhill ....85 H 8
Betws-y-Coed ....33 I 24
Betws yn Rhos ....41 J 23
Beulah near Cardigan ....15 G 27
Beulah
  near Llandrindod-Wells ....25 J 27
Beverley ....45 S 22
Beverstone ....19 N 29
Bewaldeth ....54 K 19
Bewcastle ....55 L 18
Bewdley ....27 N 26
Bewholme ....51 T 22
Bexhill ....12 V 31
Bexley London Borough ....21 U 29
Beyton ....30 W 27
Bhaid-Luachraich (Loch) ....78 D 10
Bhealaich (Loch an) ....84 G 9
Bhraoin (Loch a') ....78 E 10
Bhrollum (Loch) ....82 A 10
Bibury ....19 O 28
Bicester ....28 Q 28
Bicker ....37 T 25
Bickington ....4 I 32
Bickleigh Mid Devon ....7 J 31
Bickleigh South Hams ....4 H 32
Bicton ....34 L 25
Bicton gardens ....5 K 31
Biddenden ....12 V 30
Biddenham ....29 S 27
Biddestone ....19 N 29
Biddulph ....35 N 24
Bidean nam Bian ....72 E 14
Bideford ....6 H 30
Bidford ....27 O 27
Bieldside ....75 N 12
Bierton ....20 R 28

Big Corlae ....60 H 18
Bigbury ....4 I 33
Bigbury-on-Sea ....4 I 33
Biggar Barrow-in-Furness ....47 K 21
Biggar South Lanarkshire ....61 J 17
Biggin Hill ....21 U 30
Biggleswade ....29 T 27
Bignor ....11 S 31
Bildeston ....30 W 27
Bildsgreen ....27 M 26
Bill of Portland ....8 M 32
Billericay ....22 V 29
Billesdon ....36 R 26
Billingborough ....37 S 25
Billinge ....42 L 23
Billingham ....57 Q 20
Billinghay ....37 T 24
Billingshurst ....11 S 30
Billingsley ....27 M 26
Billington ....42 M 22
Billockby ....39 Y 26
Billy Row ....56 O 19
Bilsborrow ....42 L 22
Bilsington ....12 W 30
Bilston ....35 N 26
Bilton ....45 T 22
Binbrook ....45 T 23
Binfield ....20 R 29
Bingham ....36 R 25
Bingley ....43 O 22
Binham ....38 W 25
Binns (The) ....68 J 16
Binsted ....10 R 30
Birchington ....23 X 29
Birdham ....10 R 31
Birdingbury ....28 P 27
Birdwell ....43 P 23
Birdworld ....10 R 30
Birgham ....62 N 17
Birkdale ....42 K 23
Birkenhead ....42 K 23
Birling Gap ....12 U 31
Birmingham ....27 O 26
Birsay ....86 K 6
Birsemore ....75 L 12
Birstall ....36 Q 25
Birtley Gateshead ....56 P 19
Birtley Tynedale ....55 N 18
Birtsmorton Court ....27 N 27
Bisham ....20 R 29
Bishop Auckland ....56 P 20
Bishop Burton ....44 S 22
Bishop Monkton ....50 P 21
Bishop Sutton ....18 M 29
Bishop Thornton ....50 P 21
Bishop Wilton ....50 R 22
Bishops Cannings ....19 O 29
Bishop's Castle ....26 L 26
Bishop's Caundle ....9 M 31
Bishop's Cleeve ....27 N 28
Bishop's Itchington ....28 P 27
Bishops Lydeard ....8 K 30
Bishops Nympton ....7 I 31
Bishop's Palace
  near St. David's ....14 E 28
Bishop's Palace near Tenby ....16 F 28
Bishop's Stortford ....30 U 28
Bishop's Tachbrook ....28 P 27
Bishop's Tawton ....7 H 30
Bishop's Waltham ....10 Q 31
Bishopsteignton ....4 J 32
Bishopstocke ....10 Q 31
Bishopston ....15 H 29
Bishopstone Salisbury ....9 O 30
Bishopstone Swindon ....19 P 29
Bishopthorpe ....50 Q 22
Bishopton Darlington ....56 P 20
Bishopton Renfrewshire ....67 G 16
Bishton ....18 L 29
Bisley ....19 N 28
Bispham ....42 K 22
Bix ....20 R 29
Bixter ....87 P 3
Blaby ....36 Q 26
Black Bay ....59 D 17
Black Corries ....72 F 13
Black Down Hills ....8 K 31
Black Isle ....79 G 11
Black Mount ....66 F 14
Black Mountain ....25 I 28
Black Mountains ....26 K 28
Black Notley ....30 V 28
Black Torrington ....6 H 31
Black Water Valley ....78 F 11
Blackawton ....4 I 32

A B C D E F G H I J K L M N O P Q R S T U V W X Y Z

Blackburn *Aberdeenshire* ...75 N 12
Blackburn *Lancs.* ......42 M 22
Blackburn *West Lothian* ...61 J 16
Blackfield ......10 P 31
Blackford *Cumbria* ......54 L 19
Blackford *Perthshire and Kinross* ...67 I 15
Blackhall ......57 Q 19
Blackhall Rocks ......57 Q 19
Blackhill *Aberdeenshire* ...81 O 11
Blackhill *Highland* ......77 A 11
Blacklunans ......74 J 13
Blackmoor Gate ......17 I 30
Blackmore ......22 U 28
Blackness Castle ......68 J 15
Blacko ......43 N 22
Blackpool ......42 K 22
Blackridge ......61 I 16
Blackthorn ......28 Q 28
Blacktoft ......44 R 22
Blackwater *Hart* ......20 R 30
Blackwater *Isle of Wight* ...10 Q 31
Blackwater (River) ......22 W 28
Blackwater Reservoir ...72 F 13
Blackwaterfoot ......59 D 17
Blackwell ......50 P 20
Blackwood ......18 K 29
Bladnoch ......52 G 19
Bladon ......20 P 28
Blaenannherch ......15 G 27
Blaenau Ffestiniog ......33 I 25
Blaenavon ......18 K 28
Blaengarw ......17 J 29
Blaengrwrach ......17 I 28
Blagdon ......18 L 30
Blaich ......72 E 13
Blaina ......18 K 28
Blair Atholl ......73 I 13
Blair Castle ......73 I 13
Blairgowrie ......68 J 14
Blairmore ......66 F 16
Blakeney *Glos.* ......18 M 28
Blakeney *Norfolk* ......38 X 25
Blakesley ......28 Q 27
Blamerino ......68 K 14
Blandford Forum ......9 N 31
Blanefield ......67 H 16
Blàr a Chaorainn ......72 E 13
Blarmachfoldach ......72 E 13
Blarnalearoch ......78 E 10
Blawith ......48 K 21
Blaxton ......44 R 23
Blaydon ......56 O 19
Bleadon ......18 L 30
Bleaklow Hill ......43 O 23
Blean ......23 X 30
Bleasby ......36 R 24
Blenheim Palace ......20 P 28
Bletchingdon ......20 Q 28
Bletchley ......28 R 27
Bletsoe ......29 S 27
Blewbury ......20 Q 29
Blickling ......39 X 25
Blickling Hall ......39 X 25
Blidworth ......36 Q 24
Blindley Heath ......21 T 30
Blisland ......3 F 32
Blisworth ......28 R 27
Blithe ......35 O 25
Blithfield Hall ......35 O 25
Blithfield Reservoir ......35 O 25
Blockley ......27 O 27
Blofield ......39 Y 26
Bloxham ......28 P 27
Blubberhouses ......49 O 22
Blue John Cavern ......43 O 23
Bluemull Sound ......87 Q 1
Blundellsands ......42 K 23
Blundeston ......39 Z 26
Blyth *Northumb.* ......56 P 18
Blyth *Notts.* ......44 Q 23
Blythburgh ......31 Y 27
Blythe Bridge ......35 N 25
Blyton ......44 R 23
Bo' Ness ......68 J 15
Boarhills ......69 L 15
Boat of Garten ......74 I 12
Boathvic ......79 G 10
Bocking Churchstreet ...30 V 28
Boddam ......81 O 11
Bodedern ......40 G 23
Bodelwyddan ......41 J 23
Bodenham ......26 L 27
Bodfari ......41 J 23
Bodfordd ......40 G 23
Bodham Street ......39 X 25
Bodiam Castle ......12 V 30

Bodicote ......28 Q 27
Bodmin ......3 F 32
Bodmin Moor ......3 G 32
Bodnant Garden ......41 I 23
Bognor Regis ......11 R 31
Bogue ......53 H 18
Boisdale ......70 X 12
Boisdale (Loch) ......70 Y 12
Boldon ......56 P 19
Bolham ......7 J 31
Bollington ......43 N 24
Bolney ......11 T 31
Bolnhurst ......29 S 27
Bolsover ......44 Q 24
Boltby ......50 Q 21
Bolton *Alnwick* ......63 O 17
Bolton *Bolton* ......42 M 23
Bolton Abbey ......49 O 22
Bolton-by-Bowland ......49 N 22
Bolton-le-Sands ......48 L 21
Bolton on Swale ......50 P 20
Bolton-upon-Dearne ...44 Q 23
Bomere Heath ......34 L 25
Bonar Bridge ......79 G 10
Bonawe Quarries ......65 E 14
Bonby ......44 S 23
Boncath ......15 G 27
Bonchester Bridge ......62 M 17
Bonhill ......66 G 16
Bonnybridge ......67 I 16
Bonnyrigg ......61 K 16
Bont-faen / Cowbridge ...17 J 29
Bontgoch Elerch ......25 I 26
Bontnewydd ......32 H 24
Boosbeck ......50 R 20
Boot ......47 K 20
Bootle *Cumbria* ......47 J 21
Bootle *Merseyside* ......42 K 23
Border Forest Park (The) ...55 M 18
Bordogan ......32 G 24
Boreham ......22 V 28
Boreham Street ......12 V 31
Borehamwood ......21 T 29
Boreland ......54 K 18
Borgue *Dumfries and Galloway* ...53 H 19
Borgue *Highland* ......85 J 9
Borness ......53 H 19
Borough Green ......22 U 30
Boroughbridge ......50 P 21
Borreraig ......77 Z 11
Borrobol Forest ......85 H 9
Borrowash ......36 P 25
Borth ......25 H 26
Borve *Barra Isle* ......70 X 13
Borve *Eilean Siar* ......70 X 13
Borve *Isle of Lewis* ......82 A 8
Borve *South Harris* ......76 Y 10
Borwick ......48 L 21
Bosbury ......26 M 27
Boscastle ......6 F 31
Boscombe ......9 O 31
Bosham ......10 R 31
Bosherston ......16 F 29
Bosley ......35 N 24
Boston ......37 T 25
Boston Spa ......50 P 22
Boswinger ......3 F 33
Botesdale ......30 W 26
Bothamsall ......44 R 24
Bothel ......54 K 19
Bothwell ......60 H 16
Botley ......10 Q 31
Botwnnog ......32 G 25
Boughton House ......29 R 26
Boughton Street ......22 W 30
Boulmer ......63 P 17
Boultham ......44 S 24
Bourn ......29 T 27
Bourne ......37 S 25
Bournemouth ......9 O 31
Bourton *North Dorset* ...9 N 30
Bourton *Vale of White Horse* ...19 P 29
Bourton-on-the-Water ...27 O 28
Bovey Tracey ......4 I 32
Bovingdon ......21 S 28
Bow ......7 I 31
Bow Street ......25 H 26
Bowden ......61 L 17
Bower *Highland* ......85 K 8

Bower *Tynedale* ......55 M 18
Bowerchalke ......9 O 30
Bowes ......49 N 20
Bowhill ......62 L 17
Bowland ......62 L 17
Bowland (Forest of) ......49 M 22
Bowmore ......58 B 16
Bowness ......48 L 20
Bowness-on-Solway ...54 K 19
Bowood House ......19 N 29
Box ......19 N 29
Box Hill ......21 T 30
Boxford *Babergh* ......30 W 27
Boxford *West Berkshire* ...20 P 29
Boxley ......22 V 30
Boxworth ......29 T 27
Boyton ......6 G 31
Bozeat ......29 R 27
Braaid ......46 G 21
Brabourne Lees ......12 W 30
Bracadale (Loch) ......77 A 12
Bracebridge Heath ......37 S 24
Brackley ......28 Q 27
Brackley Hatch ......28 Q 27
Bracknell ......20 R 29
Braco ......67 I 15
Bracora ......72 C 13
Bradan Resr (Loch) ......60 G 18
Bradfield *Sheffield* ......43 P 23
Bradfield *West Berkshire* ...20 Q 29
Bradford *Bradford* ......43 O 22
Bradford *Taunton Deane* ...8 K 31
Bradford Abbas ......8 M 31
Bradford-on-Avon ......19 N 29
Brading ......10 Q 31
Bradninch ......7 J 31
Bradpole ......5 L 31
Bradwell ......43 O 24
Bradwell-on-Sea ......22 W 28
Bradworthy ......6 G 31
Brae ......87 P 2
Brae of Achnahaird ......83 D 9
Brae Roy Lodge ......73 F 13
Braeantra ......79 G 10
Braedownie ......74 K 13
Braehead ......61 J 16
Braemar ......74 J 12
Braemore ......85 J 9
Braeriach ......74 I 12
Braeswick ......87 L 6
Brafferton Helperby ......50 Q 21
Bragar ......82 A 8
Braglenbeg ......65 D 15
Braich y Pwll ......32 F 25
Braidwood ......61 I 16
Bràigh Mòr ......82 Y 9
Brailes ......28 P 27
Brailsford ......35 P 25
Braintree ......30 V 28
Braishfield ......10 P 30
Braithwell ......44 Q 23
Bramcote ......36 Q 25
Bramfield ......31 Y 27
Bramford ......31 X 27
Bramhall ......43 N 23
Bramham ......43 P 22
Bramhope ......43 P 22
Bramley *Basingstoke and Deane* ...20 Q 30
Bramley *South Yorks.* ......44 Q 23
Bramley *Surrey* ......21 S 30
Brampton *Cambs.* ......29 T 27
Brampton *Cumbria* ......55 L 19
Brampton *Eden* ......55 M 20
Brampton *Rotherham.* ...43 P 23
Brampton *Suffolk* ......31 Y 26
Brampton Bryan ......26 L 26
Brancaster ......38 V 25
Branderburgh ......80 K 10
Brandesburton ......51 T 22
Brandon *Durham* ......56 P 19
Brandon *Suffolk* ......30 V 26
Brandsby ......50 Q 21
Branscombe ......5 K 31
Bransgore ......9 O 31
Branston ......37 S 24
Brassington ......35 P 24
Bratton ......19 N 30
Bratton Clovelly ......6 H 31
Bratton Fleming ......7 I 30
Braughing ......29 U 28
Braunston *Daventry* ......28 Q 27
Braunston *Rutland* ......36 R 26
Braunton ......6 H 30
Bray-on-Thames ......21 R 29

Bray Shop ......3 G 32
Braybrooke ......28 R 26
Brayford ......7 I 30
Brayton ......44 Q 22
Breaclete ......82 Z 9
Breadalbane ......67 G 14
Breage ......2 D 33
Bream ......18 M 28
Breamore House ......9 O 31
Brean ......18 K 30
Breasclete ......82 Z 9
Breaston ......36 Q 25
Brechin ......75 M 13
Breckland ......30 V 26
Brecon / Aberhonddu ...25 J 28
Brecon Beacons National Park ......25 J 28
Bredbury ......43 N 23
Brede ......12 V 31
Bredenbury ......26 M 27
Bredgar ......22 W 30
Bredon ......27 N 27
Bredwardine ......26 L 27
Bremhill ......19 N 29
Brenchley ......12 V 30
Brendon Hills ......7 J 30
Brenig Reservoir ......33 J 24
Brenish ......82 Y 9
Brent *London Borough* ...21 T 29
Brent Knoll ......18 L 30
Brent Pelham ......29 U 28
Brentwood ......22 U 29
Brenzett ......13 W 30
Brereton ......35 O 25
Bressay ......87 Q 3
Bretford ......28 P 26
Bretherton ......42 L 22
Brettenham ......30 W 26
Brewham ......9 M 30
Brewlands Bridge ......74 K 13
Brewood ......35 N 25
Bride ......46 G 20
Bridestowe ......4 H 31
Bridge ......23 X 30
Bridge of Alford ......75 L 12
Bridge of Allan ......67 I 15
Bridge of Avon ......80 J 11
Bridge of Balgie ......73 H 14
Bridge of Brown ......74 J 12
Bridge of Buchat ......74 L 12
Bridge of Craigisla ......74 K 13
Bridge of Dee ......53 I 19
Bridge of Don ......75 N 12
Bridge of Dun ......75 M 13
Bridge of Dye ......75 M 13
Bridge of Earn ......68 J 14
Bridge of Ericht ......73 G 13
Bridge of Gairn ......74 K 12
Bridge of Gaur ......73 G 13
Bridge of Orchy ......66 F 14
Bridge of Weir ......60 G 16
Bridgemary ......10 Q 31
Bridgend *Aberdeenshire* ...80 L 11
Bridgend *Angus* ......75 L 13
Bridgend *Argyll and Bute* ...65 D 15
Bridgend *Islay* ......58 B 16
Bridgend *Perthshire and Kinross* ...68 J 14
Bridgend / Pen-y-bont ...17 J 29
Bridgend of Lintrathen ...74 K 13
Bridgerule ......6 G 31
Bridgham ......30 W 26
Bridgnorth ......27 M 26
Bridgwater ......8 L 30
Bridlington ......51 T 21
Bridport ......5 L 31
Brierfield ......43 N 22
Brierley ......43 P 23
Brierley Hill ......27 N 26
Brigg ......44 S 23
Brigham ......54 J 20
Brighouse ......43 O 22
Brighstone ......10 P 32
Brighstone Forest ......10 P 32
Brightling ......12 V 31
Brightlingsea ......22 X 28
Brighton ......11 T 31
Brightwell ......20 Q 29
Brigstock ......29 S 26
Brill ......20 Q 28
Brimfield ......26 L 27
Brimham Rocks ......49 O 21
Brimington ......43 P 24
Brimpsfield ......19 N 28
Brimpton ......20 Q 29
Brington ......29 S 26
Brinkburn Priory ......63 O 18
Brinkley ......30 V 27

Brinklow ......28 P 26
Brinkworth ......19 O 29
Brinyan ......86 L 6
Brisley ......38 W 25
Brislington ......18 M 29
Bristol ......18 M 29
Briston ......38 X 25
Briton Ferry ......17 I 29
Brittle (Loch) ......71 B 12
Brittwell Salome ......20 Q 29
Brixham ......4 J 32
Brixton ......4 H 32
Brixworth ......28 R 27
Brize Norton ......20 P 28
Broad Bay ......83 B 9
Broad Blunsdon ......19 O 29
Broad Chalke ......9 O 30
Broad Haven ......14 E 28
Broad Hinton ......19 O 29
Broad Law ......61 J 17
Broad Oak ......12 V 31
Broadbridge Heath ......11 S 30
Broadclyst ......7 J 31
Broadford ......77 C 12
Broadlands ......10 P 31
Broadmayne ......9 M 31
Broadstairs ......23 Y 29
Broadstone ......9 O 31
Broadwas ......27 M 27
Broadway ......27 O 27
Broadwell Ho ......55 N 19
Broadwey ......8 M 32
Broadwindsor ......8 L 31
Broadwoodwidger ......6 H 31
Brochel ......77 B 11
Brockdish ......31 X 26
Brockenhurst ......10 P 31
Brockley ......18 L 29
Brockworth ......19 N 28
Brodick ......59 E 17
Brodick Bay ......59 E 17
Brodick Castle ......59 E 17
Brodie Castle ......79 I 11
Brodsworth ......44 Q 23
Brodsworth Hall ......44 Q 23
Brokenborough ......19 N 29
Brolass ......65 B 14
Bromborough ......42 L 24
Brome ......31 X 26
Bromfield ......26 L 26
Bromham *Bedford* ......29 S 27
Bromham *Kennet* ......19 N 29
Bromley *London Borough* ...21 U 29
Bromley *Kent* ......22 V 29
Brompton *near Northallerton* 50 P 20
Brompton-by-Sawdon ...51 S 21
Brompton on Swale ......49 O 20
Brompton Ralph ......7 K 30
Brompton Regis ......7 J 30
Bromsgrove ......27 N 26
Bromyard ......26 M 27
Bronllys ......26 K 27
Brook ......22 W 30
Brooke ......39 Y 26
Brookmans Park ......21 T 28
Broom (Loch) ......78 E 10
Broomfield *Chelmsford* ...22 V 28
Broomfield *Sedgemoor* ...8 K 30
Broomfleet ......44 S 22
Broomhaugh ......56 O 19
Brora ......85 I 9
Broseley ......34 M 26
Brotherton ......44 Q 22
Brotton ......57 R 20
Brough *East Riding of Yorkshire* ...44 S 22
Brough *Eden* ......49 N 20
Brough *Highland* ......86 J 8
Brough Head ......86 J 6
Brough Lodge ......87 R 2
Brough of Birsay ......86 J 6
Broughton *Cumbria* ......54 J 19
Broughton *Flintshire / Sir y Fflint* ...34 L 24
Broughton *Hants.* ......10 P 30
Broughton *Lancs.* ......42 L 22
Broughton *North Lincs.* ...44 S 23
Broughton *Northants.* ...28 R 26
Broughton *Oxon.* ......28 P 27
Broughton *Scottish Borders* .61 J 17
Broughton-in-Furness ...47 K 21
Broughton Mills ......47 K 21
Broughton Moor ......54 J 19
Broughton Poggs ......19 P 28
Broughty Ferry ......69 L 14
Brownhills ......35 O 26
Brownsea Island ......9 O 31

Broxbourne ......21 T 28
Broxburn ......68 J 16
Bruar Lodge ......73 I 13
Bruichladdich ......58 A 16
Brundall ......39 Y 26
Brushford ......7 J 30
Bruton ......8 M 30
Brydekirk ......54 K 18
Brymbo ......34 K 24
Bryn-Henllan ......24 F 27
Brynamman ......17 I 28
Brynbuga / Usk ......18 L 28
Bryncethin ......17 J 29
Bryneglwys ......34 K 24
Bryngwran ......40 G 23
Bryngwyn ......26 K 27
Brynhoffnant ......15 G 27
Brynmawr ......18 K 28
Brynsiencyn ......32 H 24
Brynteg ......40 H 23
Bualintur ......71 B 12
Bubwith ......44 R 22
Buccleuch ......61 K 17
Buchanty ......67 I 14
Buchlyvie ......67 H 15
Buckden *Cambs.* ......29 T 27
Buckden *North Yorks.* ...49 N 21
Buckfast ......4 I 32
Buckfast Abbey ......4 I 32
Buckfastleigh ......4 I 32
Buckhaven ......68 K 15
Buckhorn Weston ......9 M 30
Buckie ......80 L 10
Buckingham ......28 R 27
Buckland *Herts.* ......29 T 28
Buckland *Oxon.* ......20 P 28
Buckland Abbey ......4 H 32
Buckland Brewer ......6 H 31
Buckland Dinham ......19 M 30
Buckland in-the-Moor ...4 I 32
Buckland Newton ......8 M 31
Buckland St. Mary ......8 K 31
Bucklebury ......20 Q 29
Bucklers Hard ......10 P 31
Buckminster ......36 R 25
Bucknall ......37 T 24
Bucknell ......26 L 26
Bucks green ......11 S 30
Bucksburn ......75 N 12
Bude ......6 G 31
Budleigh Salterton ......5 K 32
Bugbrooke ......28 Q 27
Bugle ......3 F 32
Bugthorpe ......50 R 22
Buildwas Abbey ......34 M 26
Builth Wells / Llanfair-ym-Muallt ......25 J 27
Bulford ......19 O 30
Bulkeley ......34 L 24
Bulkington ......28 P 26
Bulwell ......36 Q 24
Bulwick ......37 S 26
Bunarkaig ......72 F 13
Bunessan ......64 B 15
Bungay ......31 Y 26
Bunnahabhainn ......64 B 16
Bunny ......36 Q 25
Buntingford ......29 T 28
Burbage *Leics.* ......28 P 26
Burbage *Wilts.* ......19 O 29
Bures ......30 W 28
Burford ......19 P 28
Burgess Hill ......11 T 31
Burgh-by-Sands ......54 K 19
Burgh Castle ......39 Y 26
Burgh Highland ......86 J 8
Burgh-le-Marsh ......38 U 24
Burgh-St. Peter ......39 Y 26
Burghead ......80 J 10
Burghfield ......20 Q 29
Burghill ......26 L 27
Burghley House ......37 S 26
Burham ......22 V 30
Burley ......9 O 31
Burley-in-Wharfedale ...49 O 22
Burlton ......34 L 25
Burneside ......48 L 20
Burneston ......50 P 21
Burnfoot ......62 L 17
Burnham ......21 S 29
Burnham Market ......38 W 25
Burnham-on-Crouch ...22 W 29
Burnham-on-Sea ......18 L 30
Burnhaven ......81 O 11
Burnhope ......56 O 19
Burniston ......51 S 21

Burnley ....43 N 22
Burntisland ....68 K 15
Burrafirth ....87 R 1
Burravoe ....87 Q 2
Burray ....87 L 7
Burrelton ....68 K 14
Burringham ....44 R 23
Burrington *North Devon* ....7 I 31
Burrington *North Somerset* ...18 L 30
Burrough Green ....30 V 27
Burrow Head ....53 G 19
Burry Port /Porth Tywyn ....15 H 28
Burscough ....42 L 23
Burscough Bridge ....42 L 23
Burshill ....51 S 22
Bursledon ....10 Q 31
Burslem ....35 N 24
Burstwick ....45 T 22
Burton *Christchurch* ....9 O 31
Burton *Ellesmere*
  Port and Neston ....48 L 21
Burton *South Lakeland* ....48 L 21
Burton *Wrecsam / Wrexham* ...34 L 24
Burton Agnes ....51 T 21
Burton Bradstock ....5 L 31
Burton Constable Hall ....45 T 22
Burton Fleming ....51 S 21
Burton in Lonsdale ....49 M 21
Burton Joyce ....36 Q 25
Burton Latimer ....29 R 26
Burton Leonard ....50 P 21
Burton Pidsea ....45 T 22
Burton-upon-Stather ....44 R 23
Burton-upon-Trent ....35 O 25
Burwarton ....26 M 26
Burwash ....12 V 31
Burwell *Cambs.* ....30 U 27
Burwell *Lincs.* ....45 U 24
Bury *Bury* ....42 N 23
Bury *Chichester* ....11 S 31
Bury St. Edmunds ....30 W 27
Busby ....60 H 16
Buscot ....19 P 28
Bushey ....21 S 29
Bute (Island of) ....59 E 16
Bute (Kyles of) ....59 E 16
Bute (Sound of) ....59 E 16
Butleigh ....8 L 30
Butley ....31 Y 27
Butt of Lewis ....83 B 8
Buttercrambe ....50 R 21
Buttermere ....47 K 20
Butterstone ....68 J 14
Buttington ....34 K 25
Buxted ....12 U 31
Buxton *Derbs.* ....43 O 24
Buxton *Norfolk* ....39 X 25
Bwcle / Buckley ....34 K 24
Bwlch ....26 K 28
Bwlch Oerddrws ....33 I 25
Bwlch y Ffridd ....33 J 26
Bwlch-y-Groes ....25 I 28
Bwlch-y-Sarnau ....25 J 26
Bwlchgwyn ....34 K 24
Bwlchllan ....25 H 27
Byfield ....28 Q 27
Byfleet ....21 S 30
Byland Abbey ....50 Q 21
Byrness ....62 M 18

C

Cabrach ....80 K 12
Cadair Idris ....33 I 25
Caddington ....29 S 28
Caddonfoot ....62 L 17
Cadhay ....5 K 31
Cadishead ....42 M 23
Cadnam ....10 P 31
Cadney ....44 S 23
Cadwell Park ....45 T 24
Caerau ....17 J 29
Caerdydd / Cardiff ....18 K 29
Caerffili / Caerphilly ....18 K 29
Caerfyrddin / Carmarthen ...15 H 28
Caergwrle ....34 K 24
Caergybi / Holyhead ....40 G 23
Caerlaverock Castle ....53 J 19
Caerleon ....18 L 29
Caernarfon ....32 H 24
Caernarfon Bay ....32 G 24
Caerphilly / Caerffili ....18 K 29
Caersws ....25 J 26
Caerwent ....18 L 29
Caerwys ....41 K 23
Cailliness Point ....52 F 19
Cairn Edward Forest ....53 H 18
Cairn Gorm ....74 J 12

Cairn Table ....60 H 17
Cairn Toul ....74 I 12
Cairnborrow ....80 L 11
Cairndow ....66 F 15
Cairngaan ....52 F 20
Cairngarroch ....52 E 19
Cairnie ....80 L 11
Cairnpapple Hill ....67 J 16
Cairnryan ....52 E 19
Cairnsmore of Carsphairn ..60 H 18
Cairnsmore of Fleet ....53 G 19
Cairraig Fhada ....58 B 17
Caister-on-Sea ....39 Z 26
Caistor ....45 T 23
Calbourne ....10 P 31
Caldbeck ....54 K 19
Caldecott ....36 R 26
Calder (Loch) ....85 J 8
Calder Bridge ....47 J 20
Calder Mains ....85 J 8
Caldercruix ....61 I 16
Calderdale ....43 N 22
Caldermill ....60 H 17
Caldey Island ....15 F 29
Caldicot ....18 L 29
Caldwell ....49 O 20
Calf of Man ....46 F 21
Calfsound ....87 L 6
Calgary ....71 B 14
Calgary Bay ....71 B 14
Caliach Point ....71 B 14
Calke Abbey ....36 P 25
Callander ....67 H 15
Callater (Glen) ....74 J 13
Callington ....3 H 32
Calne ....19 N 29
Calow ....43 P 24
Calstock ....3 H 32
Calthwaite ....55 L 19
Calvay ....70 Y 12
Calver ....43 P 24
Calverton ....36 Q 24
Calvine ....73 I 13
Cam ....29 U 27
Cam Loch ....84 E 9
Camas Chil Mhalieu ....72 D 14
Camas-luinie ....78 D 12
Camasnacroise ....72 D 14
Camastianavaig ....77 B 11
Camber ....12 W 31
Camberley ....20 R 30
Camblesforth ....44 Q 22
Cambo ....56 O 18
Cambois ....56 P 18
Camborne ....2 E 33
Cambrian Mountains ....25 I 27
Cambridge ....29 U 27
Cambusbarron ....67 I 15
Cambuskenneth ....67 I 15
Camden *London Borough* ....21 T 29
Camelford ....6 F 32
Cammachmore ....75 N 12
Campbeltown ....59 D 17
Campsie Fells ....67 H 15
Camptown ....62 M 17
Campville ....35 P 25
Camrose ....24 E 28
Camusnagaul ....78 E 10
Candlesby ....37 U 24
Canewdon ....22 W 29
Canisbay ....86 K 8
Canna ....71 A 12
Cannich ....78 F 11
Cannich (Glen) ....78 F 11
Cannington ....8 K 30
Cannock ....35 N 25
Canonbie ....54 L 18
Canons Ashby ....28 Q 27
Canterbury ....23 X 30
Cantley ....39 Y 26
Canvey Island ....22 V 29
Caol ....72 E 13
Caolas a' Mhòrain ....76 Y 10
Caoles ....70 Z 14
Caolis ....70 X 13
Caolisport (Loch) ....65 D 16
Cape Cornwall ....2 C 33
Cape Wrath ....84 E 8
Capel ....11 T 30
Capel Curig ....33 I 24
Capel Garmon ....33 I 24
Capel Le Ferne ....13 X 30
Capel St. Mary ....31 X 27
Capel-y-Ffin ....26 K 28
Capesthorne Hall ....43 N 24
Capheaton ....56 O 18
Cappercleuch ....61 K 17

Caputh ....68 J 14
Cara Island ....58 C 17
Carbis Bay ....2 D 33
Carbost *Minginish* ....77 A 12
Carbost *Trotternish* ....77 B 11
Cardenden ....68 K 15
Cardiff / Caerdydd ....18 K 29
Cardigan / Aberteifi ....15 G 27
Cardigan Bay ....24 G 26
Cardington ....34 L 26
Cardinham ....3 G 32
Cardrona ....61 K 17
Cardross ....66 G 16
Cardurnock ....54 K 19
Carew ....15 F 28
Carfraemill ....62 L 16
Cargill ....68 J 14
Carhampton ....7 J 30
Carie ....73 H 13
Carinish ....76 Y 11
Carisbrooke ....10 Q 31
Cark ....48 L 21
Carlbt ....37 S 25
Carleen ....2 D 33
Carleton ....49 N 22
Carlisle ....55 L 19
Carlops ....61 J 16
Carloway ....82 Z 9
Carlton *Bedford* ....29 S 27
Carlton *Hambleton* ....50 Q 20
Carlton
  Hinckley and Bosworth ...36 P 26
Carlton *North Yorks.* ....44 Q 22
Carlton *Notts.* ....36 Q 25
Carlton Colville ....31 Z 26
Carlton in Lindrick ....44 Q 23
Carlton-on-Trent ....36 R 24
Carluke ....61 I 16
Carmarthen / Caerfyrddin ...15 H 28
Carmel Head ....40 G 22
Carmunnock ....60 H 16
Carmyllie ....69 L 14
Carn Ban ....73 H 12
Carn Coire na h-Easgainn ..73 H 12
Carn Eige ....78 E 12
Carn Glas-choire ....79 I 11
Carn Mairg ....73 H 14
Carnaby ....51 T 21
Carnach ....78 E 12
Carnassarie Castle ....65 D 15
Carnedd Llewelyn ....33 I 24
Carnforth ....48 L 21
Carno ....33 J 26
Carnock ....68 J 15
Carnoustie ....69 L 14
Carnwath ....61 J 16
Carradale ....59 D 17
Carradale Bay ....59 D 17
Carrbridge ....79 I 12
Carrick ....66 F 15
Carrick Roads ....2 E 33
Carron ....80 K 11
Carron (Loch) ....77 C 11
Carron Bridge ....67 H 15
Carrshield ....55 N 19
Carrutherstown ....54 J 18
Carsaig ....65 C 15
Carse of Gowrie ....68 K 14
Carseriggan ....52 G 19
Carsethorn ....53 J 19
Carsluith ....53 G 19
Carsphairn ....53 H 18
Carstairs ....61 I 16
Carterton ....19 P 28
Carterway Heads ....56 O 19
Carthew ....3 F 32
Carthorpe ....50 P 21
Cartmel ....48 L 21
Carville ....56 P 19
Cas-Gwent / Chepstow ...18 M 29
Cashlie ....67 G 14
Casnewydd / Newport ...18 L 29
Cassington ....20 P 28
Cassley (Glen) ....84 F 9
Castell-Nedd / Neath ...17 I 29
Castell Newydd Emlyn /
  Newcastle Emlyn ....15 G 27
Castell-y-Rhingyll ....15 H 28
Castle Acre ....38 W 25
Castle Ashby ....28 R 27
Castle Bolton ....49 O 21
Castle Bytham ....37 S 25
Castle Campbell ....67 I 15
Castle Cary ....8 M 30
Castle Combe ....19 N 29
Castle Donington ....36 P 25
Castle Douglas ....53 I 19

Castle Drogo ....4 I 31
Castle Eaton ....19 O 29
Castle Fraser ....75 M 12
Castle frome ....26 M 27
Castle Hedingham ....30 V 28
Castle Howard ....50 R 21
Castle Kennedy ....52 F 19
Castle Lachlan ....65 E 15
Castle Loch ....52 F 19
Castle Rising ....38 V 25
Castlebay ....70 X 13
Castleford ....43 P 22
Castlemartin ....16 E 29
Castlerigg ....54 K 20
Castleton
  Casnewydd / Newport ......18 K 29
Castleton *Derbs.* ....43 O 23
Castleton *North Yorks.* ....50 R 20
Castletown *Highland* ....85 J 8
Castletown *Isle of Man* ...46 G 21
Caston ....38 W 26
Catacol ....59 E 16
Catacol Bay ....59 D 16
Caterham ....21 T 30
Catfield ....39 Y 25
Catlodge ....73 H 12
Catlowdy ....55 L 18
Caton ....48 L 21
Catrine ....60 H 17
Catterall ....42 L 22
Catterick ....50 P 20
Catterick Garrison ....49 O 20
Catterline ....75 N 13
Cattistock ....8 M 31
Catton *Broadland* ....39 X 26
Catton *Tynedale* ....55 N 19
Catworth ....29 S 26
Cauldcleuch Head ....62 L 18
Cauldon ....35 O 24
Caulkerbush ....53 I 19
Cautley ....49 M 20
Cava ....86 K 7
Cavendish ....30 V 27
Caversfield ....28 Q 28
Caversham ....20 R 29
Cawdor ....79 I 11
Cawood ....44 Q 22
Caxton ....29 T 27
Caynham ....26 M 26
Caythorpe ....37 S 24
Cayton ....51 S 21
Ceall (Loch nan) ....71 C 13
Cefn Bryn ....15 H 29
Cefn-Coed-y-cymmer ....17 J 28
Cefn-mawr ....34 K 25
Cefn-y-Pant ....15 G 28
Ceinewydd / New Quay ...24 G 27
Ceiriog (Vale of) ....34 K 25
Cemaes ....40 G 22
Cemaes Head ....15 F 27
Cemmaes ....33 I 26
Cemmaes road ....33 I 26
Cenarth ....15 G 27
Ceres ....69 L 15
Cerne Abbas ....8 M 31
Cerrigydrudion ....33 J 24
Chacewater ....2 E 33
Chacombe ....28 Q 27
Chadderton ....43 N 23
Chaddesden ....36 P 25
Chadlington ....28 P 28
Chadwell St. Mary ....22 V 29
Chagford ....4 I 31
Chailey ....11 T 31
Chàirn Bhain (Loch a') ...84 E 9
Chalfont St. Giles ....21 S 29
Chalfont St. Peter ....21 S 29
Chalford ....19 N 28
Chalgrove ....20 Q 29
Challacombe ....7 I 30
Challock ....52 G 19
Chalkerell ....5 M 32
Chambercombe Manor ....17 H 30
Chandler's Ford ....10 P 31
Channel Islands 5
Chapel Brampton ....28 R 27
Chapel-en-le-Frith ....43 O 24
Chapel Haddlesey ....44 Q 22
Chapel le Dale ....49 M 21
Chapel St. Leonards ....45 V 24
Chapel Stile ....48 K 20
Chapelhall ....61 I 16
Chapelknowe ....54 L 18
Chapelton ....60 H 16
Chapeltown *Moray* ....74 K 12
Chapeltown *Sheffield* ....43 P 23
Chapmanslade ....19 N 30
Chard ....8 L 31

Chardstock ....8 L 31
Charfield ....19 M 29
Charing ....22 W 30
Charlbury ....28 P 28
Charlecote *Park* ....27 P 27
Charleston *Manor* ....12 U 31
Charlestown *Highland* ...78 C 10
Charlestown *Restormel* ...3 F 33
Charlton ....19 N 29
Charlton Horethorne ....8 M 30
Charlton Kings ....27 N 28
Charlton Marshall ....9 N 31
Charlton Musgrove ....9 M 30
Charlton on Otmoor ....20 Q 28
Charlwood ....11 T 30
Charminster ....8 M 31
Charmouth ....5 L 31
Charney Basset ....20 P 29
Charsfield ....31 X 27
Chartham ....23 X 30
Chartridge ....21 S 28
Chartwell ....21 U 30
Chastleton ....27 P 28
Chatburn ....42 M 22
Chatham ....22 V 29
Chatsworth House ....43 P 24
Chatteris ....29 U 26
Chatto ....62 M 17
Chatton ....63 O 17
Chawleigh ....7 I 31
Cheadle *Gtr. Mches.* ....43 N 23
Cheadle *Staffs.* ....35 O 25
Checkendon ....20 Q 29
Cheddar ....18 L 30
Cheddar Gorge ....18 L 30
Cheddington ....21 S 28
Cheddleton ....35 N 24
Chedington ....8 L 31
Chedworth ....19 O 28
Chedzoy ....8 L 30
Cheese Bay ....76 Y 11
Chelford ....42 N 24
Chellaston ....36 P 25
Chelmarsh ....27 M 26
Chelmsford ....22 V 28
Cheltenham ....27 N 28
Chelveston ....29 S 27
Chelwood Gate ....11 U 30
Chepstow / Cas-Gwent ...18 L 29
Cherhill ....19 O 29
Cherington *Cotswold* ...19 N 28
Cherington
  Stratford-on-Avon ....27 P 27
Cheriton ....10 Q 30
Cheriton Bishop ....4 I 31
Cheriton Fitzpaine ....7 J 31
Cherry Burton ....44 S 22
Chertsey ....21 S 29
Cherwell (River) ....28 Q 28
Cheselbourne ....9 M 31
Chesham ....21 S 28
Chesham Bois ....21 S 28
Cheshunt ....21 T 28
Chesil Beach ....8 M 32
Cheslyn Hay ....35 N 26
Chester ....34 L 24
Chester-le-Street ....56 P 19
Chesterfield ....43 P 24
Chesters ....62 M 17
Chesters Fort ....55 N 18
Chesterton *Cambridge* ...29 U 27
Chesterton *Cherwell* ....28 Q 28
Cheswardine ....35 M 25
Cheswick ....63 O 16
Cheviot (The) ....63 N 17
Cheviot Hills (The) ....62 M 17
Chew Magna ....18 M 29
Chew Stoke ....18 M 29
Chewton Mendip ....18 M 30
Chicheley ....29 R 27
Chichester ....10 R 31
Chickerell ....5 M 32
Chicklade ....9 N 30
Chiddingfold ....11 S 30
Chiddingly ....12 U 31
Chiddingstone ....22 U 30
Chideock ....5 L 31
Chieveley ....20 Q 29
Chigwell ....21 U 29
Chilcompton ....18 M 30
Child Okeford ....9 N 31
Childrey ....20 P 29
Child's Ercall ....34 M 25
Chilham ....22 W 30
Chillingham ....63 O 17
Chilmark ....9 N 30
Chilton *Sedgefield* ....56 P 20

Chilton
  Vale of White Horse ...20 Q 29
Chilton Folia ....20 P 29
Chippenham
  North Wiltshire ....19 N 29
Chipping ....42 M 22
Chipping Campden ....27 O 27
Chipping Norton ....28 P 28
Chipping Ongar ....22 U 28
Chipping Sodbury ....19 M 29
Chipping Warden ....28 Q 27
Chirbury ....34 K 25
Chirk ....34 K 25
Chirk Castle ....34 K 25
Chirmorie ....52 F 18
Chirnside ....63 N 16
Chirton ....19 O 30
Chiseldon ....19 O 29
Chislet ....23 X 30
Chiswell Green ....21 S 28
Chitterne ....19 N 30
Chittlehamholt ....7 I 31
Chittlehampton ....7 I 30
Chobham ....21 S 29
Choire (Loch) ....84 H 9
Cholderton ....9 O 30
Cholesbury ....21 S 28
Chollerton ....55 N 18
Cholsey ....20 Q 29
Chon (Loch) ....67 G 15
Chopwell ....56 O 19
Chorley ....42 M 23
Chorleywood ....21 S 29
Christchurch *Christchurch* ...9 O 31
Christchurch *Fenland* ...38 U 26
Christian Malford ....19 N 29
Christleton ....34 L 24
Christmas Common ....20 R 29
Christow ....4 J 32
Chroisg (Loch a') ....78 E 11
Chudleigh ....4 J 32
Chulmleigh ....7 I 31
Church ....42 M 22
Church Crookham ....20 R 30
Church Eaton ....35 N 25
Church Enstone ....28 P 28
Church Fenton ....44 Q 22
Church Knowle ....9 N 32
Church Leigh ....35 O 25
Church Lench ....27 O 27
Church Minshull ....34 M 24
Church Stoke ....34 K 26
Church Stretton ....34 L 26
Churcham ....19 M 28
Churchdown ....27 N 28
Churchill *North Somerset* ...18 L 30
Churchill *Oxon.* ....27 P 28
Churchingford ....8 K 31
Churnet ....35 N 24
Churnsike Lodge ....55 M 18
Churston Ferrers ....4 J 32
Churt ....10 R 30
Chwilog ....32 H 25
Cifynydd ....17 K 29
Cilcain ....34 K 24
Cilcennin ....25 H 27
Cilgerran ....15 G 27
Cilmery ....25 J 27
Cilrhedyn ....15 G 28
Cilybebyll ....17 I 28
Cilycwn ....25 I 27
Cinderford ....18 M 28
Cirencester ....19 O 28
City of London
  London Borough ....21 T 29
Clachaig ....66 E 16
Clachan *Argyl* ....66 F 15
Clachan *Kintyre* ....59 D 16
Clachan Mòr ....70 Z 14
Clachan of Campsie ....67 H 16
Clachan of Glendaruel ...65 E 15
Clachtoll ....83 E 9
Clackavoid ....74 J 13
Clackmannan ....67 I 15
Clacton-on-Sea ....23 X 28
Claggain Bay ....58 B 16
Claggan ....71 C 14
Claidh (Loch) ....82 A 10
Claigan ....77 A 11
Clandon Park ....21 S 30
Clanfield ....10 Q 31
Claonel ....84 G 9
Clapham *Beds.* ....29 S 27
Clapham *North Yorks.* ...49 M 21
Clapton-in-Gordano ....18 L 29

A
B
C
D
E
F
G
H
I
J
K
L
M
N
O
P
Q
R
S
T
U
V
W
X
Y
Z

Clàr (Loch nan) ....85 H 9
Clarbeston Road ....24 F 28
Clare ....30 V 27
Clashindarroch ....80 L 11
Clashmore ....79 H 10
Clashnessie ....84 E 9
Clatt ....80 L 12
Clatteringshaws (Loch) ....53 H 18
Clavering ....29 U 28
Claverley ....27 N 26
Claverton Manor ....19 N 29
Clawdd-newydd ....33 J 24
Clawton ....6 G 31
Claxton Ryedale ....50 R 21
Claxton South Norfolk ....39 Y 26
Clay Cross ....36 P 24
Claydon ....31 X 27
Claydon House ....28 R 28
Claypole ....36 R 24
Clayton ....11 T 31
Clayton-le-Moors ....42 M 22
Clayton West ....43 P 23
Cleadale ....71 B 13
Cleadon ....57 P 19
Cleat ....70 X 12
Cleator Moor ....47 J 20
Cleckheaton ....43 O 22
Cleedownton ....26 M 26
Cleehill ....26 M 26
Cleethorpes ....45 T 23
Cleeve Abbey ....7 J 30
Cleeve Prior ....27 O 27
Clehonger ....26 L 27
Cleigh ....65 D 14
Clenchwarton ....38 V 25
Clent ....27 N 26
Cleobury Mortimer ....26 M 26
Cleobury North ....26 M 26
Clephanton ....79 I 11
Clevedon ....18 L 29
Clevedon-Court ....18 L 29
Cleveland Hills ....50 Q 20
Cleveleys ....42 K 22
Cley Next the Sea ....38 X 25
Cliburn ....55 M 20
Cliffe Edway ....22 V 29
Cliffe Selby ....44 R 22
Clifton
    City of Nottingham ....36 Q 25
Clifton Eden ....55 L 20
Clifton Rugby ....28 Q 26
Clifton Hampden ....20 Q 29
Clifton-upon-Teme ....27 M 27
Clipston ....28 R 26
Clisham ....82 Z 10
Clitheroe ....42 M 22
Clive ....34 L 25
Cliveden House ....21 R 29
Clocaenog ....33 J 24
Clocaenog Forest ....33 J 24
Clola ....81 O 11
Clophill ....29 S 27
Clopton ....29 S 26
Closeburn ....53 I 18
Clotton ....34 L 24
Clouds Hill ....9 N 31
Cloughton ....51 S 20
Clova ....74 K 13
Clova (Glen) ....74 K 13
Clove Lodge ....49 N 20
Clovelly ....6 G 31
Clovenfords ....62 L 17
Clovulin ....72 E 13
Clowne ....44 Q 24
Cluanie Loch ....72 E 12
Cluanie Lodge ....72 E 12
Clumber Park ....44 Q 24
Clun ....26 K 26
Clunbury ....26 L 26
Clunes Forest ....72 F 13
Clungunford ....26 L 26
Clunie ....68 J 14
Clutton ....18 M 30
Clwydian Range ....34 K 24
Clydach ....17 I 28
Clyde (Firth of) ....59 F 17
Clyde (River) ....61 J 17
Clydebank ....60 G 16
Clydesdale ....61 I 16
Clyffe Pypard ....19 O 29
Clynnog-Fawr ....32 G 24
Clyro ....26 K 27
Clyst Honiton ....4 J 31
Clyst Hydon ....7 J 31
Clytha ....18 L 28
Clywedog Resr. ....25 J 26

Coalburn ....61 I 17
Coaley ....19 N 28
Coalville ....36 P 25
Coast ....78 D 10
Coatbridge ....60 H 16
Coates ....19 N 28
Cobham ....21 S 30
Cock Bridge ....74 K 12
Cockayne ....50 Q 20
Cockburnspath ....69 M 16
Cockenzie and Port Seton ....69 L 16
Cockerham ....48 L 22
Cockermouth ....54 J 20
Cockfield Babergh ....30 W 27
Cockfield Teesdale ....56 O 20
Cocking ....10 R 31
Cockleford ....19 N 28
Cockshutt ....34 L 25
Coddenham ....36 R 24
Codford St. Mary ....9 N 30
Codicote ....21 T 28
Codnor ....36 P 24
Codsall ....35 N 26
Coe (Glen) ....72 F 14
Coed y Brenin Forest ....33 I 25
Coedpoeth ....34 K 24
Coggeshall ....30 W 28
Coigach ....84 E 10
Coignafearn ....73 H 12
Coignafearn Forest ....73 H 12
Coille Mhorgil ....72 E 12
Colaboll ....84 G 9
Colbost ....77 A 11
Colby Eden ....55 M 20
Colby Isle of Man ....46 F 21
Cold Ash ....20 Q 29
Cold Ashby ....28 Q 26
Cold Ashton ....19 M 29
Cold Fell ....55 M 19
Cold Norton ....22 W 28
Coldbackie ....84 G 8
Colden Common ....10 Q 31
Coldingham ....63 N 16
Coldstream ....63 N 17
Colebrooke ....7 I 31
Coleford Glos. ....18 M 28
Coleford Somerset ....18 M 30
Colemere ....34 L 25
Coleorton ....36 P 25
Coleshill
    North Warwickshire ....27 O 26
Coleshill
    Vale of White Horse ....19 P 29
Colgrave Sound ....87 R 2
Colkirk ....38 W 25
Coll Argyll and Bute ....71 A 14
Coll Eilean Siar ....83 B 9
Colliery Row ....56 P 19
Collieston ....81 O 11
Collin ....53 J 18
Collingbourne Ducis ....19 P 30
Collingbourne Kingston ....19 P 30
Collingham Notts. ....36 R 24
Collingham West Yorks. ....50 P 22
Collington ....26 M 27
Collyweston ....37 S 26
Colmonell ....52 F 18
Coln (River) ....19 O 28
Colnabaichin ....74 K 12
Colne ....43 N 22
Colne (River) ....22 X 28
Colonsay ....64 B 15
Colpy ....81 M 11
Colsterworth ....37 S 25
Coltishall ....39 Y 25
Colwall Stone ....27 M 27
Colwinston ....17 J 29
Colwyn Bay / Bae Colwyn ....41 I 23
Colyton ....5 K 31
Combe Florey ....8 K 30
Combe Martin ....17 H 30
Combe-St. Nicholas ....8 L 31
Combeinteignhead ....4 J 32
Comberton ....29 U 27
Combwich ....8 K 30
Come-to-Good ....2 E 33
Compton Berks. ....20 Q 29
Compton Guildford ....21 S 30
Compton West Sussex ....10 R 31
Compton Abdale ....19 O 28
Compton Basset ....19 O 29
Compton Castle ....4 J 32
Compton Dando ....18 M 29
Compton Wynyates ....28 P 27
Comrie ....67 I 14
Cona Glen ....72 D 13

Conchra ....65 E 15
Condicote ....27 O 28
Condover ....34 L 26
Congleton ....35 N 24
Congresbury ....18 L 29
Coningsby ....37 T 24
Conington ....29 T 26
Conisbrough ....44 Q 23
Conisholme ....45 U 23
Coniston ....48 K 20
Connah's Quay ....42 K 24
Connel ....65 D 14
Connel Park ....60 H 17
Conon Bridge ....79 G 11
Consett ....56 O 19
Constantine Bay ....2 E 32
Contin ....79 G 11
Convinth (Glen) ....79 G 11
Conway Falls ....33 I 24
Conwy ....41 I 23
Conwy (River) ....33 I 24
Conwy (Vale of) ....33 I 24
Cooden Beach ....12 V 31
Cookham ....21 R 29
Coolham ....11 S 31
Coombe Bissett ....9 O 30
Copdock ....31 X 27
Copford ....30 W 28
Copley ....56 O 20
Copmanthorpe ....50 Q 22
Copplestone ....7 I 31
Coppull ....42 M 23
Copthorne ....11 T 30
Coquet (River) ....63 N 17
Corbridge ....55 N 19
Corby ....28 R 26
Corby Glen ....37 S 25
Corfe Castle ....9 N 32
Corfe Mullen ....9 N 31
Corgarff Castle ....74 K 12
Corhampton ....10 Q 31
Cornforth ....56 P 19
Cornhill ....81 L 11
Cornhill-on-Tweed ....63 N 17
Cornwood ....4 I 32
Cornworthy ....4 J 32
Corpach ....72 E 13
Corpusty ....39 X 25
Corran ....72 E 13
Corrany ....46 G 21
Corrie ....59 E 17
Corrie Common ....54 K 18
Corrimony ....78 F 11
Corringham Thurrock ....22 V 29
Corringham West Lindsey ....44 R 23
Corris ....33 I 26
Corry ....77 C 12
Corryvreckan (Gulf of) ....65 C 15
Corscombe ....8 L 31
Corsham ....19 N 29
Corsham Court ....19 N 29
Corsley Heath ....19 N 30
Corsock ....53 I 18
Corstopitum ....55 N 19
Corton ....9 N 30
Corwen ....33 J 25
Cosby ....36 Q 26
Cosham ....10 Q 31
Cossessey ....39 X 26
Cot-town ....81 N 11
Cotehill ....55 L 19
Cotgrave ....36 Q 25
Cotham ....36 R 24
Cotherstone ....49 O 20
Cothi River ....25 H 28
Coton ....29 U 27
Cotswold Wildlife Park ....19 O 28
Cottenham ....29 U 27
Cottered ....29 T 28
Cottingham
    East Riding of Yorks. ....45 S 22
Cottingham Northants. ....28 R 26
Cottisford ....28 Q 28
Cottonshopeburn Foot ....62 M 18
Coulags ....78 D 11
Coulport ....66 F 15
Coulter ....61 J 17
Coundon ....56 P 20
Countesthorpe ....36 Q 26
Coupar Angus ....68 K 14
Coustoun ....66 E 16
Cove Argyll and Bute ....66 F 15
Cove Highland ....78 C 10
Cove Bay ....75 N 12
Coventry ....28 P 26
Coverack ....2 E 33
Cow Honeybourne ....27 O 27

Cowal ....65 E 15
Cowan Bridge ....48 M 21
Cowbit ....37 T 25
Cowbridge / Bont-faen ....17 J 29
Cowdenbeath ....68 J 15
Cowdray House ....10 R 31
Cowes Isle of Wight ....10 Q 31
Cowfold ....11 T 31
Cowie ....67 I 15
Cowling ....43 N 22
Cowplain ....10 Q 31
Coxheath ....22 V 30
Coxhoe ....56 P 19
Coxwold ....50 Q 21
Coylton ....60 G 17
Coylumbridge ....74 I 12
Crackington Haven ....6 G 31
Crafthole ....3 H 32
Craggan ....66 F 15
Cragside Gardens ....63 O 18
Crai ....25 J 28
Craig ....78 E 11
Craig Lodge ....65 E 16
Craig-y-nos ....17 I 28
Craigdarroch ....60 H 18
Craigellachie ....80 K 11
Craigencallie ....53 G 18
Craigendoran ....66 F 16
Craigens ....58 B 16
Craighead ....69 M 15
Craighouse ....58 C 16
Craigie ....60 G 17
Craigievar Castle ....75 L 12
Craigmalloch ....53 G 18
Craignish (Loch) ....65 D 15
Craignure ....65 C 14
Craigrothie ....69 L 15
Craigton ....74 K 14
Craik ....62 K 17
Crail ....69 M 15
Crailing ....62 M 17
Crailinghall ....62 M 17
Crakaig ....85 I 9
Cramlington ....56 P 18
Cramond ....68 K 16
Cranborne ....9 O 31
Cranbrook ....12 V 30
Crane Moor ....43 P 23
Cranford St. John ....29 S 26
Cranleigh ....11 S 30
Cranmore ....18 M 30
Cranshaws ....62 M 16
Cranstal ....46 G 20
Cranwell ....37 S 24
Cranworth ....38 W 26
Crask Inn ....84 G 9
Craster ....63 P 17
Crathes Castle ....75 M 12
Crathie ....74 K 12
Crathorne ....50 Q 20
Craven Arms ....26 L 26
Crawcrook ....56 O 19
Crawford ....61 J 17
Crawfordjohn ....61 I 17
Crawick ....61 I 17
Crawley Hants. ....10 P 30
Crawley West Sussex ....11 T 30
Crawley Down ....11 T 30
Creag Meagaidh ....73 G 13
Creagan ....65 E 14
Creagorry ....76 Y 11
Creake South ....38 W 25
Credenhill ....26 L 27
Crediton ....7 I 31
Creech St. Michael ....8 K 30
Creetown ....53 G 19
Creggans ....66 E 15
Creran (Loch) ....65 E 14
Cressage ....34 M 26
Cresswell Castle Morpeth ....56 P 18
Cresswell Pembrokeshire /
    Sir Benfro ....15 F 28
Creswell ....44 Q 24
Crewe ....35 M 24
Crewkerne ....8 L 31
Crianlarich ....66 G 14
Cribyn ....15 H 27
Criccieth ....33 H 25
Crich ....36 P 24
Crichton ....62 L 16
Crick ....28 Q 26
Crickadarn ....25 K 27
Cricket St. Thomas ....8 L 31
Crickhowell ....26 K 28
Cricklade ....19 O 29
Crickley Hill ....19 N 28
Crieff ....67 I 14

Crimond ....81 O 11
Crimplesham ....38 V 26
Crinan ....65 D 15
Crinan (Loch) ....65 D 15
Cringleford ....39 X 26
Croachy ....79 H 12
Crocketford ....53 I 18
Crockham Hill ....21 U 30
Croes-goch ....14 E 28
Croesyceiliog ....18 L 29
Croft Herefordshire ....26 L 27
Croft Richmondshire ....50 P 20
Croft-on-Tees ....50 P 20
Crofty ....15 H 29
Croggan ....65 C 14
Croglin ....55 M 19
Croick ....79 G 10
Croig ....71 B 14
Cromalt Hills ....84 E 9
Cromarty ....79 H 10
Cromarty Bay ....79 H 10
Cromarty Firth ....79 H 11
Cromdale ....80 J 11
Cromdale (Hills of) ....80 J 12
Cromer ....39 X 25
Cromford ....35 P 24
Cromore ....82 A 9
Cromra ....73 G 13
Crondall ....20 R 30
Cronk (The) ....46 G 21
Crook South Lakeland ....48 L 20
Crook Wear Valley ....56 O 19
Crook of Devon ....68 J 15
Crookham ....63 N 17
Crookham Village ....20 R 30
Crooklands ....48 L 21
Cropredy ....28 Q 27
Cropston ....36 Q 25
Cropwell Bishop ....36 R 25
Crosby Allerdale ....54 J 19
Crosby Isle of Man ....46 G 21
Crosby Sefton ....42 K 23
Crosby Ravensworth ....48 M 20
Croscombe ....18 M 30
Cross ....83 B 8
Cross Fell ....55 M 19
Cross Hands ....15 H 28
Cross Inn ....25 H 27
Crossaig ....59 D 16
Crossapol ....64 Z 14
Crossbost ....82 A 9
Crossford ....61 I 16
Crossgates ....68 J 15
Crossgill ....48 L 21
Crosshill Fife ....68 K 15
Crosshill South Ayrshire ....60 G 18
Crosshouse ....60 G 17
Crosskeys ....18 K 29
Crosskirk ....85 J 8
Crossmichael ....53 I 19
Crossraguel Abbey ....60 F 18
Crossways ....9 N 31
Croston ....42 L 23
Crouch (River) ....22 W 29
Croughton ....28 Q 28
Crow Hill ....26 M 28
Crowborough ....12 U 30
Crowcombe ....8 K 30
Crowhurst ....12 V 31
Crowland ....37 T 25
Crowle Doncaster ....44 R 23
Crowle Wychavon ....27 N 27
Crowlin Island ....77 C 11
Crowmarsh Gifford ....20 Q 29
Crowthorne ....20 R 29
Croxley Green ....21 S 29
Croxton ....30 W 26
Croxton Kerrial ....36 R 25
Croy ....79 H 11
Croyde ....6 H 30
Croydon London Borough ....21 T 29
Cruden Bay ....81 O 11
Crudgington ....34 M 25
Crudwell ....19 N 29
Crug-y-bar ....25 I 27
Crulivig ....82 Z 9
Crymmych ....15 G 28
Crynant ....17 I 28
Cuaig ....77 C 11
Cubbington ....28 P 27
Cubert ....2 E 32
Cuckfield ....11 T 30
Cuckney ....44 Q 24
Cuddington Aylesbury ....20 R 28
Cuddington Vale Royal ....42 M 24

Cudworth ....43 P 23
Cuffley ....21 T 28
Cuhxham ....20 Q 29
Cuilicudden ....79 H 11
Cuillin Sound ....71 B 12
Cuillin (The) ....77 B 12
Culbokie ....79 G 11
Culdrose ....2 E 33
Culgaith ....55 M 20
Culkein ....83 D 9
Cullen ....80 L 10
Cullen Bay ....80 L 10
Cullingworth ....43 O 22
Cullipool ....65 D 15
Culloch ....67 I 14
Cullompton ....7 J 31
Culmington ....26 L 26
Culmstock ....8 K 31
Culnacraig ....84 E 9
Culrain ....79 G 10
Culross ....68 J 15
Culshabbin ....52 G 19
Culswic ....87 P 3
Culter Fell ....61 J 17
Cults ....75 N 12
Culzean Castle ....59 F 17
Cumbernauld ....67 I 16
Cumbrian Moutains ....48 K 20
Cuminestown ....81 N 11
Cummersdale ....54 L 19
Cummertrees ....54 J 19
Cumnock ....60 H 17
Cumnor ....20 P 28
Cumwhitton ....55 L 19
Cunninghamhead ....60 G 17
Cupar ....69 K 15
Curbridge ....20 P 28
Curdridge ....10 Q 31
Currie ....61 K 16
Curry Rivel ....8 L 30
Cutcloy ....53 G 19
Cutnall green ....27 N 27
Cuxton ....22 V 29
Cwm ....18 K 28
Cwm Bychan ....33 H 25
Cwm Taf ....17 J 28
Cwmafan ....17 I 29
Cwmann ....17 I 28
Cwmbach Carmarthenshire /
    Sir Gaerfyrddin ....15 G 28
Cwmbach Powys / Powys ....25 J 27
Cwmbach Rhondda, Cynon, Taf /
    Rhondda, Cynon, Taff ....17 J 28
Cwmbrân ....18 L 29
Cwmcarn ....18 K 29
Cwmcoy ....15 G 27
Cwmllynfell ....17 I 28
Cwmystwyth ....25 I 26
Cwnduad ....15 G 28
Cwnfelin Boeth ....15 G 28
Cwrt-Newydd ....15 H 27
Cydweli / Kidwelly ....15 H 28
Cyffylliog ....33 J 24
Cymmer ....17 J 29
Cymyran Bay ....40 G 23
Cynwyl Elfed ....15 G 28

D

Dacre Eden ....55 L 20
Dacre Harrogate ....49 O 21
Daglingworth ....19 N 28
Dailly ....60 F 18
Daimh (Loch an) ....73 G 14
Dairsie or Osnaburgh ....69 L 14
Dalavich ....65 E 15
Dalbeattie ....53 I 19
Dalbeg ....73 H 12
Dalblair ....60 H 17
Dalby ....46 F 21
Dalchalloch ....73 H 13
Dalchruin ....67 H 15
Dale ....14 E 28
Dale Head ....48 L 20
Dalgonar ....60 H 18
Dalham ....30 V 27
Dalhavaig ....85 I 8
Daliburgh ....76 X 12
Dalkeith ....61 K 16
Dallas ....80 J 11
Dalleagles ....60 H 17
Dallington Northampton ....28 R 27
Dallington Rother ....12 V 31
Dalmally ....66 F 14
Dalmellington ....60 G 18
Dalmeny ....68 J 16
Dalmigavie ....73 H 12
Dalnabreck ....71 C 13

Dalnaspidal Lodge ....73 H 13
Dalnavaid ....74 J 13
Dalnavie ....79 H 10
Dalness ....72 F 14
Dalry
  Dumfries and Galloway ..53 H 18
Dalry *North Ayrshire* ..60 F 16
Dalrymple ....60 G 17
Dalston ....54 L 19
Dalswinton ....53 I 18
Dalton
  Dumfries and Galloway ..54 J 18
Dalton *North Yorks.* ..50 P 21
Dalton in Furness ..47 K 21
Damerham ....9 O 31
Damh (Loch) ....78 D 11
Dan-yr-Ogof ....17 I 28
Danbury ....22 V 28
Danby ....50 R 20
Dane ....35 N 24
Danehill ....11 U 30
Darenth ....22 U 29
Darfield ....43 P 23
Darlington ....50 P 20
Darowen ....33 I 26
Darras Hall ....56 O 18
Darrington ....44 Q 22
Darsham ....31 Y 27
Dartford ....22 U 29
Dartford Tunnel ....22 U 29
Dartington ....4 I 32
Dartmeet ....4 I 32
Dartmoor National Park ..4 I 32
Dartmouth ....4 J 32
Darton ....43 P 23
Darvel ....60 H 17
Darwen ....42 M 22
Datchet ....21 S 29
Datchworth ....29 T 28
Dava ....80 J 11
Daventry ....28 Q 27
Davidstow ....6 G 32
Davington ....61 K 18
Daviot ....79 H 11
Dawley ....34 M 26
Dawlish ....4 J 32
Deal ....23 Y 30
Dean ....54 J 20
Dean Forest Park ..18 M 28
Deanich Lodge ....78 F 10
Deanston ....67 H 15
Dearham ....54 J 19
Debden ....30 U 28
Deben (River) ....31 X 27
Debenham ....31 X 27
Deddington ....28 Q 28
Dedham ....30 W 28
Dee / Afon Dyfrdwy (River)
  Wales ....41 K 23
Dee (River) *Scotland* ..75 N 12
Dee (River) / Afon Dyfrdwy ..34 K 24
Deene ....29 S 26
Deepcut ....21 R 30
Deepdale ....49 M 21
Deeping-St. James ..37 T 25
Deeping St. Nicholas ..37 T 25
Deeps (The) ....87 P 3
Defford ....27 N 27
Deiniolen ....33 H 24
Delabole ....6 F 32
Delamere ....34 M 24
Delamere Forest ..42 L 24
Dell ....83 B 8
Dellifure ....80 J 11
Delnadamph Lodge ..74 K 12
Delph ....43 N 23
Denbigh / Dinbych ..33 J 24
Denby Dale ....43 P 23
Denchworth ....20 P 29
Denham ....21 S 29
Denholm ....62 L 17
Denmead ....10 Q 31
Dennington ....31 Y 27
Denny ....67 I 15
Dent ....49 M 21
Denton *South Kesteven* ..36 R 25
Denton *Stockport* ..43 N 23
Denver ....38 V 26
Derby ....36 P 25
Deri ....18 K 28
Dersingham ....38 V 25
Dervaig ....71 B 14
Derwent (River) *R. Ouse* ..44 R 22
Derwent (River) *R. Trent* ..36 P 24
Derwent (River) *R. Tyne* ..56 O 19
Derwent Dale ....43 O 23
Derwent Reservoir *Derbs.* ..43 O 23

Derwent Reservoir
  Northumb. ....56 N 19
Derwent Water ....54 K 20
Desborough ....28 R 26
Desford ....36 Q 26
Detling ....22 V 30
Devauden ....18 L 28
Deveron (River) ....81 M 11
Devil's Beef Tub ....61 J 17
Devil's Bridge / Pontarfynach 25 I 26
Devil's Elbow ....74 J 13
Devil's Punch Bowl ..10 R 30
Devizes ....19 O 29
Devonport ....3 H 32
Dewsbury ....43 P 22
Dherue (Loch an) ....84 G 8
Dial Post ....11 S 31
Dickleburgh ....31 X 26
Didcot ....20 Q 29
Diddlebury ....26 L 26
Digby ....37 S 24
Dilhorne ....35 N 25
Dilton Marsh ....19 N 30
Dilwyn ....26 L 27
Dinas ....24 F 27
Dinas Dinlle ....32 G 24
Dinas Head ....24 F 27
Dinas-Mawddwy ....33 I 25
Dinas Powys ....18 K 29
Dinbych / Denbigh ..33 J 24
Dinbych-y-pysgod / Tenby ..15 F 28
Dingwall ....79 G 11
Dinnet ....74 L 12
Dinnington
  Newcastle upon Tyne ..56 O 18
Dinnington *Rotherham* ..44 Q 23
Dinsdale ....50 P 20
Dinton ....9 O 30
Diptford ....4 I 32
Dirleton ....69 L 15
Dishforth ....50 P 21
Diss ....31 X 26
Disserth ....25 J 27
Distington ....53 J 20
Ditcheat ....8 M 30
Ditchingham ....31 Y 26
Ditchley Park ....28 P 28
Ditchling ....11 T 31
Ditton Priors ....26 M 26
Doc Penfro /
  Pembroke Dock ..16 F 28
Docherty (Glen) ....78 E 11
Dochgarroch ....79 H 11
Docking ....38 V 25
Dockray ....54 L 20
Dodburn ....62 L 17
Doddington *Cambs.* ..29 U 26
Doddington *Kent* ..22 W 30
Doddington *Lincs.* ..44 S 24
Doddington *Northumb.* ..63 O 17
Dodington ....19 M 29
Dodman Point ....3 F 33
Dodworth ....43 P 23
Doirlinn ....71 C 13
Dolanog ....33 J 25
Dolbenmaen ....33 H 25
Dolfor ....26 K 26
Dolgarrog ....33 I 24
Dolgellau ....33 I 25
Dolgoch Falls ....33 I 26
Dollar ....67 I 15
Dolphinholme ....48 L 22
Dolton ....7 H 31
Don (River) *R. Ouse* ..44 Q 23
Don (River) *R. Spey* ..74 K 12
Doncaster ....44 Q 23
Donhead-St. Andrew ..9 N 30
Donhead-St. Mary ..9 N 30
Donington ....37 T 25
Donington-on-Bain ..45 T 24
Donington Park Circuit ..36 P 25
Donisthorpe ....36 P 25
Donnington *Berks.* ..20 Q 29
Donnington *Salop* ..35 M 25
Donyatt ....8 L 31
Doon (Loch) ....60 G 18
Dorback Lodge ....74 J 12
Dorchester *Dorset* ..8 M 31
Dorchester *Oxon.* ..20 Q 29
Dordon ....35 P 26
Dore ....43 P 24
Dores ....79 H 11
Dorking ....21 T 30
Dormansland ....11 U 30
Dormanstown ....57 Q 20
Dornie ....78 D 12
Dornoch ....79 H 10

Dornoch Firth ....79 H 10
Dornock ....54 K 19
Dorrington ....34 L 26
Dorstone ....26 K 27
Dorusduain ....78 D 12
Douchary (Glen) ....78 F 10
Dougarie ....59 D 17
Douglas *Isle of Man* ..46 G 21
Douglas
  South Lanarkshire ..61 I 17
Douglastown ....74 L 14
Dounby ....86 K 6
Doune *Highland* ....84 G 10
Doune *Stirling* ....67 H 15
Dove (River) ....35 O 24
Dove Cottage ....48 K 20
Dove Holes ....43 O 24
Dovedale ....35 O 24
Dover ....13 X 30
Dovercourt ....31 X 28
Doveridge ....35 O 25
Dowally ....74 J 14
Dowdeswell ....27 N 28
Dowlish Wake ....8 L 31
Down Ampney ....19 O 28
Downderry ....3 G 32
Downham ....30 U 26
Downham Market ....38 V 26
Downies ....75 N 12
Downton ....9 O 31
Dowsby ....37 S 25
Doynton ....19 M 29
Drakes Broughton ..27 N 27
Draughton ....49 O 22
Drax ....44 R 22
Draycott ....36 P 25
Draycott-in-the-Clay ..35 O 25
Draycott-in-the-Moors ..35 N 25
Drayton *Norfolk* ..39 X 25
Drayton *Oxon.* ....20 Q 29
Drayton-St. Leonard ..20 Q 29
Drefach *near Carmarthen* ..15 H 28
Drefach
  near Newcastle-Emlyn ..15 G 27
Dreghorn ....60 G 17
Drem ....69 L 15
Drenewydd / Newtown ..26 K 26
Dreswick Point ....46 G 21
Driffield ....19 O 28
Drigg ....47 J 20
Drighlington ....43 P 22
Drimnin ....71 C 14
Drinnishadder ....76 Z 10
Drissaig ....65 E 15
Droitwich ....27 N 27
Dronfield ....43 P 24
Drongan ....60 G 17
Droxford ....10 Q 31
Druidibeg (Loch) ....76 Y 12
Druim a' Chliabhain (Loch) ..85 H 8
Druimindarroch ....71 C 13
Drum Castle ....75 M 12
Drumbeg ....84 E 9
Drumblade ....81 L 11
Drumburgh ....54 K 19
Drumchardine ....79 G 11
Drumclog ....60 H 17
Drumelzier ....61 J 17
Drumfearn ....71 C 12
Drumlanrig Castle ..61 I 18
Drumlemble ....58 C 17
Drumlithie ....75 M 13
Drummond Castle ..67 I 14
Drummore ....52 F 19
Drummossie Muir ....79 H 11
Drumnadrochit ....79 G 11
Drumrunie ....84 E 9
Drumsallie ....72 D 13
Drumtochty Forest ..75 M 13
Druridge Bay ....63 P 18
Drybrook ....18 M 28
Dryburgh Abbey ....62 M 17
Drygarn Fawr ....25 J 27
Drymen ....67 G 15
Drynoch ....77 B 12
Duachy ....84 F 9
Ducklington ....20 P 28
Duddington ....37 S 26
Duddo ....63 N 16
Dudley *Dudley* ....27 N 26
Dudley *North Tyneside* ..56 P 18
Duff House ....81 M 11
Dufftown ....80 K 11
Duffield ....36 P 25
Duffus ....80 J 10
Dufton ....55 M 20

Duggleby ....51 S 21
Duich (Loch) ....78 D 12
Duirinish ....77 C 12
Duke's Pass ....67 G 15
Dukinfield ....43 N 23
Dullingham ....30 V 27
Dulnain Bridge ....80 J 12
Duloe ....3 G 32
Dulverton ....7 J 30
Dumbarton ....67 G 16
Dumbleton ....27 O 27
Dumfries ....53 J 18
Dun Carloway Broch ..82 Z 9
Dunan ....66 F 16
Dunbar ....69 M 15
Dunbeath ....85 J 9
Dunblane ....67 I 15
Duncansby Head ....86 K 8
Dunchurch ....28 Q 26
Duncow ....53 J 18
Duncton ....11 S 31
Dundee ....69 K 14
Dundonald ....60 G 17
Dundrennan ....53 I 19
Dundry ....18 M 29
Dunecht ....75 M 12
Dunfermline ....68 J 15
Dungeness ....13 W 31
Dunholme ....44 S 24
Dunino ....69 L 15
Dunipace ....67 I 15
Dunkeld ....68 J 14
Dunkery Beacon ....7 J 30
Dunkeswell ....8 K 31
Dunkirk ....19 N 29
Dunley ....27 N 27
Dunlop ....60 G 16
Dunmaglass Lodge ..79 H 12
Dunnet ....85 J 8
Dunnet Bay ....85 J 8
Dunnet Head ....86 J 7
Dunning ....68 J 15
Dunnington ....50 R 22
Dunnockshaw ....42 N 22
Dunnottar Castle ....75 N 13
Dunoon ....66 F 16
Dunragit ....52 F 19
Dunrobin Castle ....85 I 10
Duns ....62 M 16
Duns Tew ....28 P 28
Dunscore ....53 I 18
Dunsfold ....11 S 30
Dunsford ....4 I 31
Dunsop Bridge ....49 M 22
Dunstable ....29 S 28
Dunstaffnage Castel ..65 D 14
Dunstanburgh Castle ..63 P 17
Dunster ....17 J 30
Dunston ....37 S 24
Dunstone ....4 I 32
Dunsyre ....61 J 16
Duntelchaig (Loch) ..79 H 11
Dunton bassett ....28 Q 26
Dunure ....59 F 17
Dunvegan ....77 A 11
Dunvegan (Loch) ....77 A 11
Dunvegan Castle ....77 A 11
Dunvegan Head ....76 Z 11
Dunwich ....31 Y 27
Durdle Door ....9 N 32
Durham ....56 P 19
Durisdeer ....61 I 18
Durlston Head ....9 O 32
Durness ....84 F 8
Durrington ....19 O 30
Dursley ....19 M 28
Dury Voe ....87 Q 2
Duston ....28 R 27
Duthil ....79 I 12
Duxford ....29 U 27
Dyce ....75 N 12
Dyfi / Dovey (River) ..33 I 26
Dyke ....80 I 11
Dykehead ....74 K 13
Dykends ....74 K 13
Dymchurch ....13 W 30
Dymock ....27 M 28
Dyrham ....19 M 29
Dyserth ....41 J 23

E

Eaglescliffe ....50 P 20
Eaglesfield ....54 K 18
Eaglesham ....60 H 16
Eakring ....36 R 24
Ealing *London Borough* ..21 T 29
Earba (Lochan na h-) ..73 G 13

Earby ....49 N 22
Eardisley ....26 K 27
Earl Shilton ....36 Q 26
Earl Soham ....31 X 27
Earl Stonham ....31 X 27
Earley Winnersh ....20 R 29
Earlish ....77 A 11
Earls Barton ....28 R 27
Earls Colne ....30 W 28
Earlsferry ....69 L 15
Earlston ....62 L 17
Earn (Loch) ....67 H 14
Earn (River) ....67 J 14
Earsdon ....56 P 18
Earsham ....31 Y 26
Eartham ....11 S 31
Easdale ....65 D 15
Easebourne ....10 R 31
Easington *Easington* ..57 P 19
Easington
  East Riding of Yorkshire ...45 U 23
Easington
  Redcar and Cleveland ..50 R 20
Easington Lane ....56 P 19
Easingwold ....50 Q 21
Eassie and Nevay ..68 K 14
East Aberthaw ....17 J 29
East Barkwith ....45 T 24
East Bergholt ....30 X 28
East Brent ....18 L 30
East Budleigh ....5 K 32
East Butterwick ....44 R 23
East-Challow ....20 P 29
East Chinnock ....8 L 31
East-Coker ....8 M 31
East Cowes ....10 Q 31
East Cowton ....50 P 20
East Dereham ....38 W 25
East Ferry ....44 R 23
East Glen (River) ....37 S 25
East Grafton ....19 P 29
East Grinstead ....11 T 30
East Hagbourne ....20 Q 29
East-Halton ....45 T 23
East Hanney ....20 P 29
East Hardwick ....44 Q 23
East Harling ....30 W 26
East Haven ....69 L 14
East Hendred ....20 P 29
East Hoathly ....12 U 31
East Horsley ....21 S 30
East Huntspill ....18 L 30
East Ilsley ....20 Q 29
East Keswick ....50 P 22
East Kilbride *Eilean Siar* ..70 X 12
East Kilbride
  South Lanarkshire ..60 H 16
East-Knoyle ....9 N 30
East Knoyle ....9 N 30
East Lambrook ....8 L 31
East Leake ....36 Q 25
East Linton ....69 M 16
East Loch Roag ....82 Z 9
East Loch Tarbet ....77 Z 10
East Looe ....3 G 32
East Lulworth ....9 N 32
East-Malling ....22 V 30
East Markham ....44 R 24
East Meon ....10 Q 31
East Mersea ....22 W 28
East Midlands Airport ..36 Q 25
East Moor ....35 P 24
East Norton ....36 R 26
East-Poringland ....39 Y 26
East Portlemouth ....4 I 33
East Rhidorroch Lodge ..78 F 10
East-Rudham ....38 W 25
East-Saltoun ....62 L 16
East Tisted ....10 R 30
East Wemyss ....68 K 15
East-Winch ....38 V 25
East Wittering ....10 R 31
East Witton ....49 O 21
East-Woodhay ....20 P 29
East-Wretham ....30 W 26
Eastbourne ....12 U 31
Eastchurch ....22 W 29
Eastdean ....12 U 31
Easter-Compton ....18 M 29
Easter Ross ....79 G 10
Eastergate ....11 S 31
Eastfield ....51 S 21
Eastgate ....55 N 19
Eastham ....42 L 24
Eastington ....19 N 28

Eastleach ....19 O 28
Eastleigh ....10 P 31
Easton *Carlisle* ....55 L 18
Eastoft ....44 R 23
Easton *Dorset* ....8 M 32
Easton *Norfolk* ....39 X 26
Easton-Grey ....19 N 29
Easton-in-Gordano ..18 L 29
Easton-Royal ....19 O 29
Eastriggs ....54 K 19
Eastrington ....44 R 22
Eastry ....23 X 30
Eastville ....37 U 24
Eastwood ....36 Q 24
Eaton ....34 M 24
Eaton Bray ....29 S 28
Eaton Socon ....29 T 27
Ebbw Vale / Glyn Ebwy ..18 K 28
Ebchester ....56 O 19
Ebrington ....27 O 27
Eccles ....62 M 17
Ecchinswell ....20 Q 29
Ecclefechan ....54 K 18
Eccles ....42 M 23
Eccleshall ....35 N 25
Echt ....75 M 12
Eckford ....62 M 17
Eckington *Derbs.* ..43 P 24
Eckington *Worc.* ..27 N 27
Edale ....43 O 23
Eday ....87 L 6
Eddelston ....61 K 16
Edderton ....79 H 10
Eddrachillis Bay ....84 E 9
Eden (River) ....55 M 19
Eden Project ....3 F 32
Edenbridge ....21 U 30
Edentaggart ....66 F 15
Edenthorpe ....44 Q 23
Edgefield ....39 X 25
Edgmond ....35 M 25
Edgton ....26 L 26
Edinbane ....77 A 11
Edinburgh ....68 K 16
Edington ....19 N 30
Edith Weston ....37 S 26
Edlesborough ....29 S 28
Edlingham ....63 O 17
Edmondsley ....56 P 19
Edmundbyers ....56 O 19
Edwalton ....36 Q 25
Edwinstowe ....36 Q 24
Edzell ....75 M 13
Efailnewydd ....32 G 25
Egerton ....22 W 30
Eggerness Point ....53 G 19
Eggleston ....56 N 20
Egham ....21 S 29
Egilsay ....87 L 6
Eglingham ....63 O 17
Egloskerry ....6 G 32
Eglwys Brewis ....17 J 29
Eglwysfach ....33 I 26
Eglwyswrw ....15 F 27
Egremont ....47 J 20
Egton ....50 R 20
Eigg ....71 B 13
Eigheach (Loch) ....73 G 13
Eight Ash Green ....30 W 28
Eil ....73 I 12
Eil (Loch) ....72 E 13
Eilde Mór (Loch) ....72 F 13
Eilean a' Chalmain ..64 A 15
Eilean Beag ....77 C 11
Eilean Chathastail ..71 B 13
Eilean Donan Castle ..78 D 12
Eilean Flodigarry ....77 B 10
Eilean Mhuire ....82 A 10
Eilean Mòr ....77 C 11
Eilean Mullagrach ..83 D 9
Eilean na Bà ....77 C 11
Eilean nan Each ....71 B 13
Eilean Trodday ....77 B 10
Eileanach Lodge ....79 G 10
Eilt (Loch) ....72 D 13
Eishken ....82 A 9
Eishort (Loch) ....71 C 12
Elan Valley ....25 J 27
Elan Village ....25 J 27
Elcho ....68 J 14
Elgin ....80 K 11
Elgol ....71 B 12
Elham ....23 X 30
Elie ....69 L 15
Elkesley ....44 R 24
Elkstone ....19 N 28

A B C D E F G H I J K L M N O P Q R S T U V W X Y Z

A
B
C
D
E
F
G
H
I
J
K
L
M
N
O
P
Q
R
S
T
U
V
W
X
Y
Z

Elland .... 43 O 22
Ellastone .... 35 O 25
Ellen's Green .... 11 S 30
Ellerbeck .... 50 P 20
Ellerton .... 44 R 22
Ellesmere .... 34 L 25
Ellesmere Port .... 42 L 24
Ellingham .... 31 Y 26
Ellington .... 56 P 18
Ellon .... 81 N 11
Elloughton .... 44 S 22
Elmdon .... 29 U 27
Elmley Castle .... 27 N 27
Elmore .... 19 N 28
Elmstead Market .... 30 W 28
Elmswell .... 30 W 27
Elphin .... 84 E 9
Elrick .... 75 N 12
Elrig .... 52 G 19
Elsdon .... 55 N 18
Elsenham .... 30 U 28
Elsham .... 45 S 23
Elsrickle .... 61 J 16
Elstead .... 21 R 30
Elstree .... 21 T 29
Elswick .... 42 L 22
Eltisley .... 29 T 27
Elton .... 37 S 26
Elveden .... 30 W 26
Elvington .... 50 R 22
Elwick .... 57 Q 19
Elworth .... 35 M 24
Ely .... 30 U 26
Emberton .... 28 R 27
Embleton Allerdale .... 54 K 20
Embleton Alnwick .... 63 P 17
Embo .... 79 I 10
Embsay .... 49 O 22
Emneth .... 37 U 26
Empingham .... 37 S 25
Emsworth .... 10 R 31
Enaclete .... 82 Z 9
Enard Bay .... 83 D 9
Enderby .... 36 Q 26
Endmoor .... 48 L 21
Endon .... 35 N 24
Enfield London Borough .... 21 T 29
Enford .... 19 O 30
Englefield Green .... 21 S 29
English Bicknor .... 18 M 28
Englishcombe .... 19 M 29
Enham Alamein .... 20 P 30
Enmore .... 8 K 30
Ensay .... 71 B 14
Enstone .... 28 P 28
Enterkinfoot .... 61 I 18
Enville .... 27 N 26
Eochar .... 76 X 11
Eoligarry .... 70 X 12
Eoropie .... 83 B 8
Eorsa .... 65 B 14
Eport (Loch) .... 76 Y 11
Epping .... 21 U 28
Epping Forest .... 21 U 29
Epsom .... 21 T 30
Epworth .... 44 R 23
Erddig .... 34 K 24
Eredine .... 65 E 15
Eredine Forest .... 65 D 15
Eriboll .... 84 F 8
Eriboll (Loch) .... 84 F 8
Ericht (Loch) .... 73 G 13
Ericstane .... 61 J 17
Eridge Green .... 12 U 30
Eriska .... 65 D 14
Eriskay .... 70 Y 12
Erisort (Loch) .... 82 A 9
Eriswell .... 30 V 26
Erlestoke .... 19 N 30
Ermington .... 4 I 32
Erpingham .... 39 X 25
Erraid .... 64 A 15
Errochty (Loch) .... 73 H 13
Errogie .... 79 G 12
Errol .... 68 K 14
Ersary .... 70 X 13
Erskine Bridge .... 67 G 16
Ervie .... 52 E 19
Erwood .... 25 K 27
Esh Winning .... 56 O 19
Esha Ness .... 87 P 2
Esher .... 21 S 29
Esk (Glen) .... 75 L 13
Esk (River) .... 54 K 19
Eskdale .... 54 K 18
Eskdalemuir .... 61 K 18
Essendon .... 21 T 28

Essich .... 79 H 11
Eston .... 57 Q 20
Etal .... 63 N 17
Etchilhampton .... 19 O 29
Etchingham .... 12 V 30
Etherow (River) .... 43 N 23
Etherow Park .... 43 N 23
Etive (Glen) .... 72 F 14
Etive (Loch) .... 65 E 14
Eton .... 21 S 29
Ettington .... 27 P 27
Ettrick .... 61 K 17
Ettrick Forest .... 62 K 17
Ettrick Pen .... 61 K 17
Etwall .... 35 P 25
Euston .... 30 W 26
Euxton .... 42 L 22
Evanton .... 79 G 11
Evelix .... 79 H 10
Evenlode .... 27 O 28
Evenwood .... 56 O 20
Everingham .... 44 R 22
Everleigh .... 19 O 30
Evershot .... 8 M 31
Eversley .... 20 R 29
Everton .... 44 R 23
Evesham .... 27 O 27
Evesham (Vale of) .... 27 O 27
Ewe (Isle of) .... 78 D 10
Ewell .... 21 T 29
Ewelme .... 20 Q 29
Ewenny .... 17 J 29
Ewes .... 54 L 18
Ewhurst .... 11 S 30
Exbourne .... 7 I 31
Exe (River) .... 7 J 31
Exebridge .... 7 J 30
Exeter .... 4 J 31
Exford .... 7 J 30
Exminster .... 4 J 31
Exmoor National Park .... 7 I 30
Exmouth .... 4 J 32
Exton .... 7 J 30
Eyam .... 43 O 24
Eye Cambs. .... 37 T 26
Eye Suffolk .... 31 X 27
Eye Peninsula .... 83 B 9
Eyemouth .... 63 N 16
Eynort .... 77 A 12
Eynort (Loch) Highland .... 77 A 12
Eynort (Loch) Western Isles .... 76 Y 12
Eynsford .... 22 U 29
Eynsham .... 20 P 28
Eyre Point .... 77 B 12
Eythorne .... 23 X 30

F

Fada (Loch) .... 76 Y 11
Failsworth .... 43 N 23
Fair Isle .... 87 P 5
Fair Oak .... 10 Q 31
Fairbourne .... 33 H 25
Fairburn .... 44 Q 22
Fairford .... 19 O 28
Fairlie .... 59 F 16
Fairlight .... 12 V 31
Fakenham .... 38 W 25
Fala .... 62 L 16
Faldingworth .... 45 S 23
Falfield .... 18 M 29
Falkirk .... 67 I 16
Falkland .... 68 K 15
Fallford .... 54 K 18
Fallin .... 67 I 15
Falmer .... 11 T 31
Falmouth .... 2 E 33
Falstone .... 55 M 18
Fanagmore .... 84 E 8
Fangfoss .... 50 R 22
Fannich (Loch) .... 78 E 11
Fannich Lodge .... 78 F 11
Fara .... 86 K 7
Fareham .... 10 Q 31
Faringdon .... 19 P 29
Farleigh-Hungerford .... 19 N 30
Farley .... 9 O 30
Farley Mount .... 10 P 30
Farlow .... 26 M 26
Farmborough .... 18 M 29
Farmers .... 25 I 27
Farmtown .... 80 L 11
Farnborough Hants. .... 20 R 30
Farnborough Warw. .... 28 P 27
Farnborough West Berkshire .... 20 P 29

Farndon Chester .... 34 L 24
Farndon Newark and Sherwood .... 36 R 24
Farne Islands .... 63 P 17
Farnell .... 75 M 13
Farnham Dorset .... 9 N 31
Farnham Surrey .... 20 R 30
Farnham Royal .... 21 S 29
Farningham .... 22 U 29
Farnley .... 49 O 22
Farnsfield .... 36 Q 24
Farnworth .... 42 M 23
Farr .... 85 H 8
Farrington Gurney .... 18 M 30
Farway .... 5 K 31
Fasnakyle .... 78 F 12
Fasnakyle Forest .... 78 F 11
Fasque .... 75 M 13
Fassfern .... 72 E 13
Fauldhouse .... 61 I 16
Faversham .... 22 W 30
Fawley .... 10 P 31
Fazeley .... 35 O 26
Fearby .... 49 O 21
Fearn Lodge .... 79 H 10
Fearnan .... 67 H 14
Fearnmore .... 77 C 11
Featherstone Staffs. .... 35 N 26
Featherstone West Yorks. .... 43 P 22
Feelindre .... 15 F 27
Feering .... 30 W 28
Feetham .... 49 N 20
Felbridge .... 11 T 30
Felindre Carmarthenshire / Sir Gaerfyrddin .... 25 I 28
Felindre Powys .... 26 K 26
Felinfach .... 25 K 28
Felinheli .... 33 H 24
Felixkirk .... 50 Q 21
Felixstowe .... 31 Y 28
Felling .... 56 P 19
Felmingham .... 39 Y 25
Felpham .... 11 S 31
Felsham .... 30 W 27
Felsted .... 30 V 28
Feltham .... 21 S 29
Felthorpe .... 39 X 25
Felton .... 63 O 18
Feltwell .... 30 V 26
Fence .... 42 N 22
Feniton .... 8 K 31
Fenny Bentley .... 35 O 24
Fenstanton .... 29 T 27
Fenton Stoke-on-Trent .... 35 N 25
Fenton West Lindsey .... 44 R 24
Fenwick Berwick-upon-Tweed .... 63 O 17
Fenwick East Ayrshire .... 60 G 17
Feochaig .... 59 D 17
Feochan (Loch) .... 65 D 14
Feock .... 2 E 33
Feolin Ferry .... 58 B 16
Fern .... 74 L 13
Ferndown .... 9 O 31
Ferness .... 79 I 11
Ferryden .... 75 M 13
Ferryhill .... 56 P 19
Ferryside .... 15 G 28
Fersit .... 73 F 13
Feshie (Glen) .... 73 I 12
Feshiebridge .... 73 I 12
Fetcham .... 21 S 30
Fetlar .... 87 R 2
Fetterangus .... 81 N 11
Fettercairn .... 75 M 13
Fewston .... 49 O 22
Ffestiniog .... 33 I 25
Ffestiniog (Vale of) .... 33 H 25
Fflint / Flint .... 42 K 24
Fforest Fawr .... 17 J 28
Ffostrasol .... 15 G 27
Fiaray .... 70 X 12
Fiddleton .... 62 L 18
Fifield .... 27 P 28
Filby .... 39 Y 26
Filey .... 51 T 21
Fillongley .... 27 P 26
Filton .... 18 M 29
Finchampstead .... 20 R 29
Finchingfield .... 30 V 28
Findern .... 80 J 11
Findhorn (River) .... 73 H 12
Findhorn Bay .... 80 J 11
Findo Gask .... 68 J 14
Findochty .... 80 L 10
Findon .... 11 S 31

Finedon .... 29 S 26
Fingest .... 20 R 29
Fingland .... 60 I 17
Finiskaig .... 72 D 13
Finmere .... 28 Q 28
Finniegill .... 61 K 18
Finningley .... 44 R 23
Finsbay .... 76 Z 10
Finstock .... 20 P 28
Finstown .... 86 K 6
Fintry Aberdeenshire .... 81 M 11
Fintry Stirling .... 67 H 15
Fionn Loch .... 78 D 10
Fionn Loch Mór .... 84 F 9
Fionnphort .... 64 A 15
Fishbourne Chichester .... 10 R 31
Fishbourne Isle of Wight .... 10 Q 31
Fishburn .... 56 P 19
Fisherfield Forest .... 78 D 10
Fisherford .... 81 M 11
Fishguard / Abergwaun .... 24 F 28
Fishnish Bay .... 65 B 14
Fishtoft .... 37 U 25
Fiskavaig .... 77 A 12
Fiskerton .... 44 S 24
Fittleworth .... 11 S 31
Fiunary .... 71 C 14
Fivehead .... 8 L 30
Flackwell Heath .... 21 R 29
Fladbury .... 27 N 27
Fladda-Chùain .... 77 A 10
Flagg .... 35 O 24
Flamborough .... 51 T 21
Flamborough Head .... 51 T 21
Flamingo Park .... 50 R 21
Flamstead .... 21 S 28
Flash .... 35 O 24
Flashader .... 77 A 11
Flatford Mill .... 30 X 28
Flax Bourton .... 18 L 29
Flaxton .... 50 R 21
Fleckney .... 36 Q 26
Fleet .... 20 R 30
Fleet (Islands of) .... 53 H 19
Fleet (Loch) .... 79 H 10
Fleet Hargate .... 37 U 25
Fleetwood .... 48 K 22
Flimby .... 53 J 19
Flint / Fflint .... 42 K 24
Flintham .... 36 R 24
Flitton .... 29 S 27
Flitwick .... 29 S 27
Flixton .... 31 Y 26
Flodday near Hellisay .... 70 X 13
Flodday near Sandray .... 70 X 13
Flodden Field .... 63 N 17
Flodigarry .... 77 B 11
Flookburgh .... 48 L 21
Floors Castle .... 62 M 17
Flotta .... 86 K 7
Flowerdale Forest .... 78 D 11
Flyford Flavell .... 27 N 27
Fochabers .... 80 K 11
Foggathorpe .... 44 R 22
Foinaven .... 84 F 8
Foindle .... 84 E 8
Folkestone .... 13 X 30
Folkingham .... 37 S 25
Folly Gate .... 7 H 31
Fontmell Magna .... 9 N 31
Ford Argyll and Bute .... 65 D 15
Ford Arun .... 11 S 31
Ford Berwick-upon-Tweed .... 63 N 17
Ford Buckinghamshire .... 20 R 28
Ford Cotswold .... 27 O 28
Ford Shrewsbury and Atcham .... 34 L 25
Forde Abbey .... 8 L 31
Forden .... 34 K 26
Fordham .... 30 V 27
Fordingbridge .... 9 O 31
Fordoun .... 75 M 13
Fordwich .... 23 X 30
Fordyce .... 80 L 11
Foreland .... 10 Q 31
Foreland Point .... 17 I 30
Foremark Reservoir .... 36 P 25
Forest Lodge .... 74 I 13
Forest Row .... 11 U 30
Forestburn Gate .... 63 O 18
Forfar .... 74 L 14
Forgandenny .... 68 J 14
Formby .... 42 K 23
Formby Point .... 42 K 23
Fornham All Saints .... 30 W 27

Forres .... 80 J 11
Forrest Lodge .... 53 H 18
Forse .... 85 K 9
Forsinard .... 85 I 8
Fort Augustus .... 73 F 12
Fort George .... 79 H 11
Fort Victoria .... 10 P 31
Fort William .... 72 E 13
Forter .... 74 K 13
Forteviot .... 68 J 14
Fortevot .... 61 I 16
Forth .... 61 I 16
Forth (Firth of) .... 68 K 15
Forth (River) .... 67 G 15
Forth Bridges .... 68 J 15
Fortingall .... 73 H 14
Forton .... 35 M 25
Fortrose .... 79 H 11
Fortuneswell .... 8 M 32
Fosdyke .... 37 T 25
Foss .... 73 I 13
Foston .... 36 R 25
Foston on the Wolds .... 51 T 22
Fotherby .... 45 T 23
Fotheringhay .... 29 S 26
Foulden .... 63 N 16
Foulness Point .... 22 W 29
Foulridge .... 43 N 22
Foulsham .... 38 X 25
Fountainhall .... 62 L 16
Fountains Abbey .... 50 P 21
Four Crosses .... 34 K 25
Four Elms .... 21 U 30
Four Marks .... 10 Q 30
Fovant .... 9 O 30
Foveran .... 81 N 12
Fowey .... 3 G 32
Fowlmere .... 29 U 27
Fownhope .... 26 M 27
Foxdale .... 46 G 21
Foxholes .... 51 S 21
Foxton .... 28 R 26
Foxup .... 49 N 21
Foyers .... 73 G 12
Fraddon .... 3 F 32
Framfield .... 12 U 31
Framingham .... 31 Y 27
Framlingham .... 31 Y 27
Frampton-on-Severn .... 19 M 28
Frant .... 12 U 30
Fraserburgh .... 81 O 10
Fraserburgh Bay .... 81 O 10
Freckenham .... 30 V 27
Freckleton .... 42 L 22
Freeland .... 20 P 28
Freethorpe .... 39 Y 26
Freevater Forest .... 79 F 10
Freiston .... 37 U 25
Fremington .... 7 H 30
Frensham .... 10 R 30
Freshwater .... 10 P 31
Freshwater Bay .... 10 P 31
Freshwater East .... 16 F 29
Freshwater West .... 14 E 29
Fressingfield .... 31 X 26
Freswick .... 86 K 8
Freuchie .... 68 K 15
Freuchie (Loch) .... 67 I 14
Friday Bridge .... 37 U 26
Fridaythorpe .... 51 S 21
Frimley .... 21 R 30
Frinton-on-Sea .... 31 X 28
Friockheim .... 75 M 14
Frisa (Loch) .... 71 B 14
Friskney .... 37 U 25
Frithville .... 37 T 24
Frittenden .... 12 V 30
Fritwell .... 28 Q 28
Frizington .... 47 J 20
Frocester .... 19 N 28
Frodsham .... 42 L 24
Froggatt .... 43 P 24
Frome .... 19 N 30
Frosterley .... 56 O 19
Froxfield .... 20 P 29
Fuday .... 70 X 12
Fuiay .... 70 X 13
Fulbourn .... 30 U 27
Fulking .... 11 T 31
Fuller Street .... 22 V 28
Fulwood .... 42 M 22
Funtington .... 10 R 31
Funzie .... 87 R 2
Furness Abbey .... 47 K 21
Furness Fells .... 48 K 20
Fyfield .... 22 U 28
Fyvie .... 81 M 11

G

Gaddesby .... 36 R 25
Gaick Lodge .... 73 H 13
Gainford .... 49 O 20
Gainsborough .... 44 R 23
Gairloch .... 78 C 10
Gairlochy .... 72 F 13
Gairsay .... 87 L 6
Gaitsgill .... 54 L 19
Galashiels .... 62 L 17
Galgate .... 48 L 22
Gallan Head .... 82 Y 9
Gallanach .... 65 D 14
Galloway Forest Park .... 52 G 18
Galltair .... 72 D 12
Galmisdale .... 71 B 13
Galmpton .... 4 J 32
Galson .... 82 A 8
Galston .... 60 G 17
Galtriggill .... 76 Z 11
Gamblesby .... 55 M 19
Gamlingay .... 29 T 27
Gamston .... 44 R 24
Ganavan .... 65 D 14
Ganton .... 51 S 21
Garboldisham .... 30 W 26
Gardenstown .... 81 N 10
Garelochhead .... 66 F 15
Garenin .... 82 Z 9
Garforth .... 43 P 22
Gargrave .... 49 N 22
Gargunnock .... 67 H 15
Garioch .... 81 M 12
Garlieston .... 53 G 19
Garlogte .... 75 M 12
Garmony .... 65 C 14
Garmouth .... 80 K 11
Garrabost .... 83 B 9
Garragie Lodge .... 73 G 12
Garraron .... 65 D 15
Garreg .... 33 H 25
Garrigill .... 55 M 19
Garrisdale Point .... 71 A 12
Garros .... 77 B 11
Garrow .... 67 I 14
Garry (Glen) Highland .... 72 E 12
Garry (Glen) Perthshire and Kinross .... 73 H 13
Garry (Loch) Highland .... 72 F 12
Garsington .... 20 Q 28
Garten (Loch) .... 74 I 12
Garth .... 25 J 27
Garthorpe .... 44 R 23
Gartmore .... 67 G 15
Gartocharn .... 67 G 15
Garton-on-The-Wolds .... 51 S 21
Garvald .... 69 M 16
Garvamore .... 73 G 12
Garve .... 79 F 11
Garvellachs .... 65 C 15
Garvestone .... 38 W 26
Garvock .... 66 F 16
Garway .... 26 L 28
Garynahine .... 82 Z 9
Gatehouse of Fleet .... 53 H 19
Gateshead .... 56 P 19
Gateside .... 68 K 15
Gatley .... 42 N 23
Gatwick Airport .... 11 T 30
Gaulden Manor .... 8 K 30
Gavard .... 64 B 15
Gaydon .... 28 P 27
Gayton King's Lynn and West Norfolk .... 38 V 25
Gayton Stafford .... 35 N 25
Gaywood .... 38 V 25
Geary .... 77 A 11
Geddington .... 29 R 26
Gedney Drove End .... 37 U 25
Gedney Hill .... 37 T 25
Gelligaer .... 18 K 29
Gelston .... 53 I 19
Georgeham .... 6 H 30
Georth .... 86 K 6
Gerrards Cross .... 21 S 29
Gestingthorpe .... 30 V 27
Gifford .... 62 L 16
Gigha (Sound of) .... 58 C 17
Gigha Island .... 58 C 16
Gighay .... 70 Y 12
Gilberdyke .... 44 R 22
Gilcrux .... 54 J 19
Gildersome .... 43 P 22
Gilfach Goch .... 17 J 29
Gillamour .... 50 R 21
Gilling East .... 50 Q 21

Gilling West	49 O 20	Gletness	87 Q 3
Gillingham *Dorset*	9 N 30	Glinton	37 T 26
Gillingham *Kent*	22 V 29	Glossop	43 O 23
Gillingham *South Norfolk*	31 Y 26	Gloucester	27 N 28
Gills	86 K 8	Gloup	87 Q 1
Gilmerton	67 I 14	Glusburn	49 O 22
Gilmorton	28 Q 26	Glutt Lodge	85 I 9
Gilston	62 L 16	Glympton	28 P 28
Gilwern	18 K 28	Glyn Ceiriog	34 K 25
Girthon	53 H 19	Glyn-Ebwy / Ebbw Vale	18 K 28
Girton	29 U 27	Glyn-neath	17 J 28
Girvan	59 F 18	Glyncorrwg	17 J 28
Gisburn	49 N 22	Glynde	11 U 31
Gisland	55 M 19	Glyndebourne	11 U 31
Gittisham	8 K 31	Glyndyfrdwy	34 K 25
Gladestry	26 K 27	Gnosall	35 N 25
Glaisdale	50 R 20	Goadby	36 R 26
Glamis	74 K 14	Goat Fell	59 E 17
Glamis Castle	74 L 14	Goathland	50 R 20
Glanaman	17 I 28	Gobowen	34 K 25
Glandwr	15 G 28	Godalming	21 S 30
Glanton	63 O 17	Godmanchester	29 T 27
Glas-allt-Shiel	74 K 13	Godmanstone	8 M 31
Glas-leac Mór	83 D 9	Godshill	10 Q 32
Glas Maol	74 J 13	Godstone	21 T 30
Glasbury	26 K 27	Goil (Loch)	66 F 15
Glascarnoch (Loch)	78 F 10	Golborne	42 M 23
Glascwm	26 K 27	Goldcliff	18 L 29
Glasdrum	72 E 14	Goldhanger	22 W 28
Glasgow	60 H 16	Goldthorpe	44 Q 23
Glasphein	76 Z 11	Golspie	85 I 10
Glaspwll	33 I 26	Gomersal	43 O 22
Glass (Loch)	79 G 10	Gometra	64 B 14
Glassburn	78 F 11	Gonerstone	38 V 26
Glasserton	52 G 19	Goodleigh	7 I 30
Glassford	60 H 16	Goodrich	26 M 28
Glasshouses	49 O 21	Goodrington	4 J 32
Glasson	48 L 22	Goodwick	24 F 27
Glassonby	55 M 19	Goodwood House	10 R 31
Glastonbury	8 L 30	Goole	44 R 22
Gleadless	43 P 23	Goonhavern	2 E 32
Gleann Beag	78 F 10	Goostrey	42 M 24
Gleann Mór	79 G 10	Gordon	62 M 16
Gleaston	48 K 21	Gordonbush	85 I 9
Glecknabae	59 E 16	Gordonstown	80 L 11
Glemsford	30 V 27	Gorebridge	61 K 16
Glen auldyn	46 G 21	Goring	20 Q 29
Glen Brittle Forest	77 B 12	Gorm Loch Mór	84 F 9
Glen Finglas Reservoir	67 G 15	Gorran Haven	3 F 33
Glen More Forest Park	74 I 12	Gorseinon	15 H 29
Glen Shee	74 J 13	Gorsleston-on-Sea	39 Z 26
Glen Trool Lodge	52 G 18	Gortantaoid	64 B 16
Glenbarr	59 C 17	Gosberton	37 T 25
Glenborrodale	71 C 13	Gosfield	30 V 28
Glenbranter	66 E 15	Gosforth *Cumbria*	47 J 20
Glenbrittle House	77 B 12	Gosforth	
Glenbuchat Castle	74 K 12	*Newcastle upon Tyne*	56 P 18
Glenbuck	60 I 17	Gosport	10 Q 31
Glencaple	53 J 18	Goswick	63 O 16
Glencarse	68 K 14	Gotham	36 Q 25
Glencoe	72 E 13	Gott Bay	70 Z 14
Glencoul (Loch)	84 F 9	Goudhurst	12 V 30
Glendoebeg	73 G 12	Gourdon	75 N 13
Glendurgan Garden	2 E 33	Gourock	66 F 16
Glenegedale	58 B 16	Gowerton	15 H 29
Glenelg	72 D 12	Goxhill	45 T 22
Glenelg Bay	72 D 12	Graemsay	86 K 7
Glenfarg	68 J 15	Grafton Underwood	29 S 26
Glenfeshie Lodge	73 I 12	Grain	22 W 29
Glenfiddich Lodge	80 K 11	Grainthorpe	45 U 23
Glenfield	36 Q 26	Granby	36 R 25
Glenfinnan	72 D 13	Grandtully	74 I 14
Glenforsa Airport	65 C 14	Grange-over-Sands	48 L 21
Glenfyne Lodge	66 F 15	Grangemouth	67 I 15
Glengorm	71 B 14	Grantchester	29 U 27
Glengoulandie	73 H 14	Grantham	37 S 25
Glengrasco	77 B 11	Grantown-on-Spey	80 J 12
Glenkens (The)	53 H 18	Grantshouse	62 N 16
Glenkin die	74 L 12	Grasby	45 S 23
Glenkirk	61 J 17	Grasmere	48 K 20
Glenlivet	80 J 11	Grassington	49 O 21
Glenluce	52 F 19	Grateley	9 P 30
Glenmassan	66 E 15	Graveley	29 T 27
Glenmaye	46 F 21	Gravesend	22 V 29
Glenmore	71 C 13	Gravir	82 A 9
Glenprosen Village	74 K 13	Grayrigg	48 M 20
Glenridding	48 L 20	Grays Thurrock	22 V 29
Glenrothes	68 K 15	Grayshott	10 R 30
Glenside	82 A 9	Grayswood	11 R 30
Glenstriven	66 E 16	Greasbrough	43 P 23
Glentham	44 S 23	Great Addington	29 S 26
Glentress	61 K 17	Great Altcar	42 K 23
Glentrool Village	52 G 18	Great Amwell	21 T 28
Glentworth	44 S 23	Great Asby	49 M 20
Glenuachdarach	77 B 11	Great Ayton	50 Q 20
Glenuig	71 C 13	Great Baddow	22 V 28
Great Bardfield	30 V 28	Greenhow Hill	49 O 21
Great Barford	29 S 27	Greenlaw	62 M 16
Great Barr	35 O 26	Greenloaning	67 I 15
Great Barrow	34 L 24	Greenock	66 F 16
Great Barugh	50 R 21	Greenodd	48 K 21
Great Bedwyn	19 P 29	Greens Norton	28 Q 27
Great Bentley	31 X 28	Greenside	56 O 19
Great Bernera	82 Z 9	Greenwich	
Great Bircham	38 V 25	*London Borough*	21 U 29
Great-Bollright	28 P 28	Grendon	28 R 27
Great Bookham	21 S 30	Grendon Underwood	28 Q 28
Great Bourton	28 Q 27	Gresford	34 L 24
Great Bowden	28 R 26	Greshornish	77 A 11
Great Brickhill	29 R 28	Greshornish (Loch)	77 A 11
Great Bridgeford	35 N 25	Gress	83 B 9
Great Bromley	30 X 28	Gretna	54 K 19
Great Broughton	50 Q 20	Gretton	37 R 26
Great-Budworth	42 M 24	Greys Court	20 R 29
Great Burdon	50 P 20	Greysouthen	54 J 20
Great Chalfield	19 N 29	Greystoke	55 L 19
Great Chesterford	30 U 27	Griffithstown	18 K 28
Great Chishill	29 U 27	Griminish	76 X 11
Great Clifton	53 J 20	Grimley	27 N 27
Great Coates	45 T 23	Grimoldby	45 U 23
Great-Comberton	27 N 27	Grimsay	76 Y 11
Great Cornard	30 W 27	Grimsby	45 T 23
Great Cubley	35 O 25	Gringley on the Hill	44 R 23
Great Cumbrae Island	59 F 16	Grinshill	34 L 25
Great-Dalby	36 R 25	Grinton	49 O 20
Great Doddington	28 R 27	Gristhorpe	51 T 21
Great Driffield	51 S 21	Grittleton	19 N 29
Great-Dunham	38 W 25	Groby	36 Q 26
Great Dunmow	30 V 28	Grogport	59 D 17
Great Easton *Essex*	30 U 28	Groombridge	12 U 30
Great Easton *Leics.*	28 R 26	Grosebay	76 Z 10
Great Eccleston	42 L 22	Grosmont *Monmouthshire /*	
Great Ellingham	38 W 26	*Sir Fynwy*	26 L 28
Great Finborough	30 W 27	Grosmont *Scarborough*	50 R 20
Great Glen	36 Q 26	Grove	20 P 29
Great Gonerby	37 S 25	Gruinard Bay	78 D 10
Great Gransden	29 T 27	Gruinard Island	78 D 10
Great Harrowden	28 R 27	Gruinart	58 B 16
Great Harwood	42 M 22	Gruinart (Loch)	64 B 16
Great Hockham	30 W 26	Grunavat (Loch)	82 Z 9
Great Horkesley	30 W 28	Grundisburgh	31 X 27
Great Horwood	28 R 28	Gualachulain	66 E 14
Great Houghton	43 P 23	Guardbridge	69 L 14
Great Langton	50 P 20	Guernsey *Channel I.*	5
Great-Limber	45 T 23	Guesting	12 V 31
Great Livermere	30 W 27	Guildford	21 S 30
Great Lumley	56 P 19	Guildtown	68 J 14
Great Malvern	27 N 27	Guilsborough	28 Q 26
Great Marton	42 K 22	Guisborough	50 Q 20
Great Massingham	38 W 25	Guiseley	43 O 22
Great Milton	20 Q 28	Guist	38 W 25
Great Missenden	21 R 28	Gullane	69 L 15
Great Mitton	42 M 22	Gunna	70 Z 14
Great Musgrave	49 M 20	Gunnerside	49 N 20
Great Oakley	31 X 28	Gunnerton	55 N 18
Great Ormes Head	41 I 22	Gunness	44 R 23
Great Orton	54 K 19	Gunnislake	3 H 32
Great Ouse (River)	38 V 25	Gunthorpe	36 R 25
Great Ouseburn	50 Q 21	Gurnard	10 Q 31
Great Ponton	37 S 25	Gurness Broch	86 K 6
Great Ryburgh	38 W 25	Gurnos	17 I 28
Great Salkeld	55 L 19	Gussage All Saints	9 O 31
Great Sampford	30 V 28	Gutcher	87 Q 1
Great Shefford	20 P 29	Guthrie	75 L 14
Great Shelford	29 U 27	Guyhirn	37 U 26
Great Smeaton	50 P 20	Gwalchmai	40 G 23
Great Somerford	19 N 29	Gwaun-Cae-Gurwen	17 I 28
Great Stainton	56 P 20	Gwbert-on-Sea	15 F 27
Great Strickland	55 L 20	Gweek	2 E 33
Great Torrington	6 H 31	Gwennap	2 E 33
Great Tosson	63 O 18	Gwithian	2 D 33
Great Totham	22 W 28	Gwyddelwern	33 J 24
Great Urswick	48 K 21	Gwyddgrug	15 H 28
Great Wakering	22 W 29	Gwydir Castle	33 I 24
Great Waltham	22 V 28	Gwytherin	33 I 24
Great Whernside	49 O 21		
Great Whittington	56 O 18	**H**	
Great Witley	27 M 27		
Great Wolford	27 P 27	Habost	83 B 8
Great Wyrley	35 N 26	Hackney *London Borough*	21 T 29
Great Yarmouth	39 Z 26	Haddenham *Bucks.*	20 R 28
Great Yeldham	30 V 27	Haddenham *Cambs.*	29 U 26
Greatford	37 S 25	Haddington	69 L 16
Greatham *Cleveland*	57 Q 20	Haddiscoe	39 Y 26
Greatham *Hants.*	10 R 30	Haddo House	81 N 11
Greatstone-on-Sea	12 W 31	Haddon Hall	35 P 24
Green Hammerton	50 Q 21	Hadfield	43 O 23
Greenfield		Hadleigh *Essex*	22 V 29
Flintshire / Sir y Fflint	41 K 23	Hadleigh *Suffolk*	30 W 27
Greenfield *Highland*	72 F 12	Hadley	34 M 25
Greenhaugh	55 N 18	Hadlow	22 V 30
Greenhead	55 M 19	Hadnall	34 L 25
Greenholm	60 H 17	Hadrian's Wall	55 M 18
		Haggbeck	55 L 18
Hagley	27 N 26	Harlosh	77 A 11
Hagworthingham	45 U 24	Harlow	21 U 28
Hailsham	12 U 31	Harlow Hill	56 O 18
Hainford	39 X 25	Harmston	37 S 24
Hainton	45 T 23	Haroldswick	87 R 1
Halam	36 R 24	Harpenden	21 S 28
Halberton	7 J 31	Harpley	38 V 25
Hale	42 M 23	Harport (Loch)	77 A 12
Hales	39 Y 26	Harray (Loch of)	86 K 6
Halesowen	27 N 26	Harrietfield	67 J 14
Halesworth	31 Y 26	Harrington *Allerdale*	53 J 20
Halford	27 P 27	Harrington *Kettering*	28 R 26
Halifax	43 O 22	Harringworth	37 S 26
Halkirk	85 J 8	Harris *Highland*	71 A 13
Hall	60 G 16	Harris *Western Isles*	82 Y 10
Hallaton	36 R 26	Harris (Sound of)	76 Y 10
Halling	22 V 29	Harrogate	50 P 22
Hallington	55 N 18	Harrow *London Borough*	21 S 29
Halloughton	36 R 24	Harston	29 U 27
Hallsands	4 J 33	Hartburn	56 O 18
Halsall	42 L 23	Hartest	30 W 27
Halsetown	2 D 33	Hartfield	11 U 30
Halstead	30 V 28	Harthill *North Lanarkshire*	61 I 16
Halstock	8 M 31	Harthill *Rotherham*	44 Q 24
Haltham	37 T 24	Harting	10 R 31
Halton *Aylesbury Vale*	20 R 28	Hartington	35 O 24
Halton *Lancaster*	48 L 21	Hartland	6 G 31
Halton Gill	49 N 21	Hartland Quay	6 G 31
Haltwhistle	55 M 19	Hartlebury	27 N 26
Halwill	4 I 32	Hartlepool	57 Q 19
Halwill Junction	6 H 31	Hartley	22 U 29
Hamble	10 Q 31	Hartley Wintney	20 R 30
Hambledon *Hants.*	10 Q 31	Hartpury	27 N 28
Hambledon *Surrey*	11 S 30	Hartshill	36 P 26
Hambleton *Lancs.*	42 L 22	Hartwell	20 R 28
Hambleton *North Yorks.*	44 Q 22	Hartwell	28 R 27
Hambleton Hills (The)	50 Q 21	Harvington	27 O 27
Hambridge	8 L 31	Harwell	20 Q 29
Hamilton	60 H 16	Harwich	31 X 28
Hammersmith and Fulham		Harwood Dale	51 S 20
London Borough	21 T 29	Harworth	44 Q 23
Hamnavoe *near Brae*	87 Q 2	Hascosay	87 R 2
Hamnavoe *near Scallway*	87 P 3	Haselbury Plucknett	8 L 31
Hampreston	9 O 31	Hasland	43 P 24
Hampstead Norris	20 Q 29	Haslemere	11 R 30
Hampsthwaite	50 P 21	Haslingden	42 N 22
Hampton Court	21 S 29	Haslingfield	29 U 27
Hampton in Arden	27 O 26	Haslington	35 M 24
Hamstead Marshall	20 P 29	Hassocks	11 T 31
Hamsterley	56 O 19	Haster	86 K 8
Hamstreet	12 W 30	Hastings	12 V 31
Hamworthy	9 N 31	Hatch Court	8 L 31
Handa Island	84 E 8	Hatfield	
Handbridge	34 L 24	*County of Herefordshire*	26 M 27
Handbury	27 N 27	Hatfield *Herts.*	21 T 28
Handcross	11 T 30	Hatfield *South Yorks.*	44 Q 23
Handforth	43 N 23	Hatfield Broad Oak	22 U 28
Handley	34 L 24	Hatfield Heath	22 U 28
Handsworth	43 P 23	Hatfield Peverel	22 V 28
Hanham	18 M 29	Hatfield Woodhouse	44 R 23
Hanley	35 N 24	Hatherleigh	7 H 31
Hanley Swan	27 N 27	Hathern	36 Q 25
Hanningfield	22 V 28	Hathersage	43 P 24
Hannington	19 O 29	Hatton *Aberdeenshire*	81 O 11
Hanslope	28 R 27	Hatton *Derbs.*	35 O 25
Happisburgh	39 Y 25	Hatton of Fintray	75 N 12
Hapton	42 N 22	Haugh of Urr	53 I 19
Harberton	4 I 32	Haughton	35 N 25
Harbertonford	4 I 32	Haunn	71 B 14
Harbledown	23 X 30	Havant	10 R 31
Harborough Magna	28 Q 26	Havering *London Borough*	22 U 29
Harbottle	63 N 17	Haverthwaite	48 K 21
Harbury	28 P 27	Hawarden	34 K 24
Harby	36 R 25	Hawes	49 N 21
Hardham	11 S 31	Hawick	62 L 17
Hardwick	44 Q 24	Hawkchurch	8 L 31
Hardwick Hall	36 Q 24	Hawkedon	30 V 27
Hardwicke	19 N 28	Hawkesbury Upton	19 M 29
Hardy Monument	5 M 31	Hawkhurst	12 V 30
Hardy's Cottage	9 M 31	Hawkridge	7 J 30
Hare Street	29 U 28	Hawkshead	48 L 20
Haresfield	19 N 28	Hawkwell	22 V 29
Harewood House	50 P 22	Hawley	20 R 30
Hargrave	29 S 27	Hawling	27 O 28
Hargrave Green	30 V 27	Haworth	43 O 22
Haringey *London Borough*	21 T 29	Hawsker	51 S 20
Harlaxton	36 R 25	Haxby	50 Q 21
Harlech	33 H 25	Haxey	44 R 23
Harlesden	21 T 29	Hay-on-Wye	26 K 27
Harleston	31 X 26	Haydock	42 M 23
Harlestone	28 R 27	Haydon Bridge	55 N 19
Harley	34 M 26	Haydon Wick	19 O 29
Harlington	29 S 27	Hayfield	43 O 23

Hayle ... 2 D 33
Hayling Island ... 10 R 31
Hayscastle ... 14 E 28
Hayton ... 50 R 22
Haywards Heath ... 11 T 31
Hazel Grove ... 43 N 23
Hazelbank ... 61 I 16
Hazelbury Bryan ... 9 M 31
Hazlemere ... 21 R 29
Heacham ... 38 V 25
Headcorn ... 22 V 30
Headington ... 20 Q 28
Headless Cross ... 27 O 27
Headley ... 10 R 30
Heads of Ayr ... 60 F 17
Healey ... 49 O 21
Healing ... 45 T 23
Heanor ... 36 P 24
Heast ... 71 C 12
Heath End ... 20 Q 29
Heath Hayes ... 35 O 25
Heather ... 36 P 25
Heathfield *Renfrewshire* ... 60 F 16
Heathfield *Wealden* ... 12 U 31
Heathrow Airport ... 21 S 29
Hebburn ... 56 P 19
Hebden Bridge ... 43 N 22
Hebrides (Sea of the) ... 76 Z 12
Heckfield ... 20 R 29
Heckington ... 37 T 25
Heddon on the Wall ... 56 O 19
Hedge End ... 10 Q 31
Hednesford ... 35 O 25
Hedon ... 45 T 22
Heighington *Durham* ... 56 P 20
Heighington *Lincs.* ... 44 S 24
Heights of Kinlochewe ... 78 E 11
Helensburgh ... 66 F 15
Helford ... 2 E 33
Hellifield ... 49 N 22
Hellingly ... 12 U 31
Hellisay ... 70 X 12
Hell's Mouth
  or Porth Neigwl ... 32 G 25
Helmdon ... 28 Q 27
Helmsdale ... 85 J 9
Helmsley ... 50 Q 21
Helpringham ... 37 T 25
Helpston ... 37 S 26
Helsby ... 42 L 24
Helston ... 2 E 33
Helton ... 55 L 20
Helvellyn ... 48 K 20
Hemel Hempstead ... 21 S 28
Hemingbrough ... 44 R 22
Hemingford Grey ... 29 T 27
Hemington ... 19 M 30
Hempnall ... 39 X 26
Hempton ... 38 W 25
Hemsby ... 39 Z 25
Hemswell ... 44 S 23
Hemsworth ... 43 P 23
Hemyock ... 8 K 31
Hendy ... 15 H 28
Henfield ... 11 T 31
Hengoed ... 18 K 29
Henham ... 30 U 28
Henley ... 27 O 27
Henley-on-Thames ... 20 R 29
Henllan ... 33 J 24
Henllys ... 18 K 29
Henlow ... 29 T 27
Hennock ... 4 J 32
Henshaw ... 55 M 19
Henstead ... 31 Y 26
Henstridge ... 9 M 31
Heol Senni ... 25 J 28
Hepple ... 63 N 18
Heptonstall ... 43 N 22
Herbrandston ... 14 E 28
Hereford ... 26 L 27
Heriot ... 62 L 16
Herm *Channel I.* ... 5
Herma Ness ... 87 R 1
Hermitage ... 20 Q 29
Hermitage Castle ... 62 L 18
Herne Bay ... 23 X 29
Herriard ... 20 Q 30
Herrington ... 56 P 19
Herstmonceux ... 12 U 31
Hertford ... 21 T 28
Hesket Newmarket ... 54 K 19
Hesketh Bank ... 42 L 22
Hesleden ... 57 Q 19
Hessenford ... 3 G 32
Hessle ... 45 S 22
Hest Bank ... 48 L 21

Heswall ... 42 K 24
Hethersgill ... 55 L 19
Hethpool ... 63 N 17
Hetton-le-Hole ... 56 P 19
Heveningham ... 31 Y 27
Hever ... 21 U 30
Heversham ... 48 L 21
Hevingham ... 39 X 25
Hewelsfield ... 18 M 28
Hexham ... 55 N 19
Heybridge ... 22 W 28
Heysham ... 48 L 21
Heyshott ... 11 R 31
Heytesbury ... 9 N 30
Heythrop ... 28 P 28
Heywood ... 43 N 23
Hibaldstow ... 44 S 23
Hickling ... 36 R 25
Hickling Green ... 39 Y 25
Hidcote Manor Garden ... 27 O 27
High Bentham ... 49 M 21
High Bickington ... 7 I 31
High Birkwith ... 49 N 21
High Easter ... 22 V 28
High Ercall ... 34 M 25
High Etherley ... 56 O 20
High Halden ... 12 W 30
High Halstow ... 22 V 29
High Ham ... 8 L 30
High Hesket ... 55 L 19
High Newton *Alnwick* ... 63 P 17
High Newton
  South Lakeland ... 48 L 21
High Offley ... 35 N 25
High Ongar ... 22 U 28
High Peak ... 43 O 23
High Willhays ... 4 I 31
High Wycombe ... 20 R 29
Higham *Kent* ... 22 V 29
Higham *Lancs.* ... 42 N 22
Higham
  North East Derbyshire ... 36 P 24
Higham *Suffolk* ... 30 V 27
Higham Ferrers ... 29 S 27
Higham on the Hill ... 36 P 26
Highbridge ... 18 L 30
Highclere ... 20 P 29
Highcliffe ... 9 O 31
Higher Penwortham ... 42 L 22
Highland Wildlife Park ... 73 I 12
Highley ... 27 M 26
Highmoor Cross ... 20 R 29
Highnam ... 27 N 28
Hightown *Congleton* ... 35 N 24
Hightown *Sefton* ... 42 K 23
Highworth ... 19 O 29
Hilborough ... 38 W 26
Hildenborough ... 22 U 30
Hilderstone ... 35 N 25
Hilgay ... 38 V 26
Hill ... 18 M 29
Hill of Fearn ... 79 I 10
Hill of Tarvit ... 69 L 15
Hillhead ... 52 G 19
Hillingdon
  London Borough ... 21 S 29
Hillington ... 38 V 25
Hillside ... 75 M 13
Hillswick ... 87 P 2
Hilmarton ... 19 O 29
Hilperton ... 19 N 30
Hilpsford Point ... 47 K 21
Hilton *Aberdeenshire* ... 81 N 11
Hilton *Eden* ... 55 M 20
Hilton *Huntingdonshire* ... 29 T 27
Hilton *North Dorset* ... 9 N 31
Hilton *South Derbyshire* ... 35 P 25
Hilton of Cadboll ... 79 I 10
Himbleton ... 27 N 27
Himley ... 35 N 26
Hinchingbrooke House ... 29 T 27
Hinckley ... 36 P 26
Hinderwell ... 50 R 20
Hindhead ... 10 R 30
Hindley ... 42 M 23
Hindolveston ... 38 X 25
Hindon ... 9 N 30
Hingham ... 38 W 26
Hinstock ... 34 M 25
Hintlesham ... 31 X 27
Hinton-Blewett ... 18 M 30
Hirst Courtney ... 44 Q 22
Hirwaun ... 17 J 28
Histon ... 29 U 27
Hitcham ... 30 W 27
Hitchin ... 29 T 28

Hockering ... 38 X 25
Hockerton ... 36 R 24
Hockley ... 22 V 29
Hockley Heath ... 27 O 26
Hockliffe ... 29 S 28
Hoddesdon ... 21 T 28
Hodnet ... 34 M 25
Hodthorpe ... 44 Q 24
Hogsthorpe ... 45 U 24
Holbeach ... 37 U 25
Holbeach-St. Johns ... 37 T 25
Holbeach-St. Matthew ... 37 U 25
Holbeck ... 44 Q 24
Holbrook ... 31 X 28
Holbury ... 10 P 31
Holcombe ... 18 M 30
Holcombe Rogus ... 7 J 31
Holdenby ... 28 R 27
Holford ... 8 K 30
Holkam Hall ... 38 W 25
Hollesley ... 31 Y 27
Hollesley Bay ... 31 Y 27
Hollingbourne ... 22 V 30
Hollingworth ... 43 O 23
Hollybush ... 60 G 17
Hollym ... 45 U 22
Holmbridge ... 43 O 23
Holme *Huntingdonshire* ... 29 T 26
Holme *South Lakeland* ... 48 L 21
Holme-next-the-Sea ... 38 V 25
Holme
  upon Spalding-Moor ... 44 R 22
Holmer Green ... 21 R 29
Holmes Chapel ... 35 M 24
Holmesfield ... 43 P 24
Holmfirth ... 43 O 23
Holmhead ... 60 H 17
Holmpton ... 45 U 22
Holnest ... 8 M 31
Holsworthy ... 6 G 31
Holt *Dorset* ... 9 O 31
Holt *Norfolk* ... 38 X 25
Holt *Wilts.* ... 19 N 29
Holt *Wrexham* ... 34 L 24
Holt Heath ... 27 N 27
Holton *Lincs.* ... 45 T 24
Holton *Norfolk* ... 31 Y 26
Holton *South Somerset* ... 8 M 30
Holton Heath ... 9 N 31
Holton-le-Clay ... 45 T 23
Holwick ... 55 N 20
Holy Island *Anglesey* ... 40 F 23
Holy Island *North Ayrshire* ... 59 E 17
Holy Island *Northumb.* ... 63 O 17
Holybourne ... 10 R 30
Holyhead / Caergybi ... 40 G 23
Holystone ... 63 N 18
Holywell ... 2 E 32
Holywell / Treffynnon ... 41 K 23
Holywell Bay ... 2 E 32
Holywood ... 53 J 18
Honing ... 39 Y 25
Honiton ... 8 K 31
Hoo St. Werburgh ... 22 V 29
Hook
  Basingstoke and Deane ... 20 R 30
Hook
  East Riding of Yorkshire ... 44 R 22
Hook Norton ... 28 P 28
Hooke ... 8 M 31
Hope *Derbs.* ... 43 O 23
Hope *Flintshire* ... 34 K 24
Hope *Highland* ... 84 G 8
Hope *South Shropshire* ... 34 L 26
Hope (Loch) ... 84 G 8
Hope Bowdler ... 26 L 26
Hope under Dinmore ... 26 L 27
Hopeman ... 80 J 10
Hopetoun House ... 68 J 16
Hopton ... 39 Z 26
Horam ... 12 U 31
Horbury ... 43 P 23
Horden ... 57 Q 19
Hordley ... 34 L 25
Horeb ... 15 G 27
Horley ... 21 T 30
Hornby ... 48 M 21
Horncastle ... 45 T 24
Hornchurch ... 22 U 29
Horncliffe ... 63 N 16
Horning ... 39 Y 25
Horninglow ... 35 P 25
Horn's Cross ... 6 H 31
Hornsea ... 51 T 22
Hornton ... 28 P 27
Horrabridge ... 4 H 32

Horseheath ... 30 V 27
Horsehouse ... 49 O 21
Horsell ... 21 S 30
Horsford ... 39 X 25
Horsforth ... 43 P 22
Horsham ... 11 T 30
Horsham St. Faith ... 39 X 25
Horsington *East Lindsey* ... 37 T 24
Horsington
  South Somerset ... 9 M 30
Horsley *Stroud* ... 19 N 28
Horsley *Tynedale* ... 56 O 19
Horsmonden ... 12 V 30
Horstead ... 39 Y 25
Horsted Keynes ... 11 T 30
Horton *Abertawe /*
  Swansea ... 15 H 29
Horton *East Dorset* ... 9 O 31
Horton *South Somerset* ... 8 L 31
Horton Court ... 19 M 29
Horton-in-Ribblesdale ... 49 N 21
Horwich ... 42 M 23
Hoton ... 36 Q 25
Hott ... 55 M 18
Houghton ... 10 P 30
Houghton Hall ... 38 V 25
Houghton House ... 29 S 27
Houghton-le-Spring ... 56 P 19
Houghton-on-the-Hill ... 36 R 26
Hougton ... 55 L 19
Hounslow
  London Borough ... 21 S 29
Hourn (Loch) ... 72 D 12
Housesteads Fort ... 55 N 18
Houston ... 60 G 16
Houstry ... 85 J 9
Hove ... 11 T 31
Hoveton ... 39 Y 25
Hovingham ... 50 R 21
How Caple ... 26 M 28
Howden ... 44 R 22
Howe of the Mearns ... 75 M 13
Howick ... 63 P 17
Howmore ... 76 X 12
Hownam ... 62 M 17
Howwood ... 60 G 16
Hoxa (Sound of) ... 86 K 7
Hoxne ... 31 X 26
Hoy ... 86 J 7
Hoylake ... 41 K 22
Hoyland Nether ... 43 P 23
Huby ... 50 Q 21
Hucknall ... 36 Q 24
Huddersfield ... 43 O 23
Huggate ... 51 S 22
Hugh Town *I. of Scilly* ... 2
Hughenden ... 20 R 29
Hughley ... 34 M 26
Huish Champflower ... 7 J 30
Huish Episcopi ... 8 L 30
Hull (River) ... 45 S 22
Hulland ... 35 P 24
Hullavington ... 19 N 29
Hullbridge ... 22 V 29
Humber (River) ... 45 T 23
Humber Bridge ... 44 S 22
Humberston ... 45 T 23
Humbleton ... 45 T 22
Hume Castle ... 62 M 17
Humshaugh ... 55 N 18
Hundleton ... 16 F 28
Hundred House ... 26 K 27
Hungerford ... 20 P 29
Hunmanby ... 51 T 21
Hunstanton ... 38 V 25
Hunter's Inn ... 17 I 30
Hunter's Quay ... 66 F 16
Huntingdon ... 29 T 26
Huntingtower Castle ... 68 J 14
Huntly ... 80 L 11
Hunton ... 49 O 21
Huntspill ... 18 L 30
Hunwick ... 56 O 19
Hurlford ... 60 G 17
Hurn ... 9 O 31
Hursley ... 10 P 30
Hurst Green ... 12 V 30
Hurstbourne Priors ... 20 P 30
Hurstbourne Tarrant ... 20 P 30
Hurstpierpoint ... 11 T 31
Hurworth-on-Tees ... 50 P 20
Hury ... 55 N 20
Husbands Bosworth ... 28 Q 26
Huthwaite ... 36 Q 24
Hutton *Scottish Borders* ... 63 N 16

Hutton *South Ribble* ... 42 L 22
Hutton Cranswick ... 51 S 22
Hutton Rudby ... 50 Q 20
Huxley ... 34 L 24
Huyton ... 42 L 23
Hwlffordd / Haverfordwest ... 16 F 28
Hyde ... 43 N 23
Hynish ... 64 Z 14
Hynish Bay ... 64 Z 14
Hythe *Hants.* ... 10 P 31
Hythe *Kent* ... 13 X 30

I

Ibsley ... 9 O 31
Ibstock ... 36 P 25
Ickleford ... 29 T 28
Icklingham ... 30 V 27
Ickworth House ... 30 V 27
Iddesleigh ... 7 H 31
Ideford ... 4 J 32
Iden ... 12 W 31
Iden Green ... 12 V 30
Idmiston ... 9 O 30
Idrigill Point ... 77 A 12
Ightham ... 22 U 30
Ightham Mote ... 22 U 30
Ilchester ... 8 L 30
Ilderton ... 63 O 17
Ilfracombe ... 17 H 30
Ilkeston ... 36 Q 25
Ilkley ... 49 O 22
Illogan ... 2 E 33
Ilmington ... 27 O 27
Ilminster ... 8 L 31
Ilsington ... 4 I 32
Ilton ... 8 L 31
Immingham ... 45 T 23
Immingham Dock ... 45 T 23
Ince Blundell ... 42 K 23
Ince-in-Makerfield ... 42 M 23
Inch Kenneth ... 64 B 14
Inchard (Loch) ... 84 E 8
Inchbare ... 75 M 13
Inchgrundle ... 74 L 13
Inchkeith ... 68 K 15
Inchlaggan ... 72 E 12
Inchmarnock ... 59 E 16
Inchnadamph ... 84 F 9
Inchture ... 68 K 14
Indaal (Loch) ... 58 A 16
Inerval ... 58 B 17
Ingatestone ... 22 V 28
Ingbirchworth ... 43 P 23
Ingham ... 30 W 27
Ingleby Barwick ... 50 Q 20
Ingleton *Durham* ... 56 O 20
Ingleton *North Yorks.* ... 49 M 21
Inglewood Forest ... 55 L 19
Ingliston ... 68 J 16
Ingoldmells ... 38 V 24
Ingoldsby ... 37 S 25
Ingram ... 63 O 17
Ings ... 48 L 20
Inkpen ... 20 P 29
Innellan ... 59 F 16
Inner Hebrides ... 70 Y 14
Inner Sound ... 77 C 11
Innerleithen ... 61 K 17
Innerpeffray ... 67 I 14
Innerwick ... 69 M 16
Insch ... 81 M 11
Inshore ... 84 F 8
Instow ... 6 H 30
Inver *Highland* ... 79 I 10
Inver *Perth and Kinross* ... 68 J 14
Inver (Loch) ... 84 E 9
Inver Bay ... 79 I 10
Inver Mallie ... 72 E 13
Inver Valley ... 84 E 9
Inveralligin ... 78 D 11
Inverallochy ... 81 O 10
Inveran ... 84 G 10
Inveraray ... 66 E 15
Inverarity ... 69 L 14
Inverarnan ... 66 F 15
Inverbeg ... 66 G 15
Inverbervie ... 75 N 13
Invercassley ... 84 G 10
Invercauld House ... 74 J 12
Inverchapel ... 66 F 15
Invercreran ... 72 E 14
Inverdruie ... 73 I 12
Inverewe Gardens ... 78 C 10
Inverey ... 74 J 13
Inverfarigaig ... 79 G 12

Invergarry ... 72 F 12
Invergeldie ... 67 H 14
Invergordon ... 79 H 10
Invergowrie ... 68 K 14
Inverie ... 72 C 12
Inverinan ... 65 E 15
Inverinate ... 78 D 12
Inverkeithing ... 68 J 15
Inverkeithny ... 81 M 11
Inverkip ... 66 F 16
Inverkirkaig ... 84 E 9
Inverliever Forest ... 65 D 15
Inverlochlarig ... 67 G 15
Invermoriston ... 73 G 12
Inverness ... 79 H 11
Inversanda ... 72 D 13
Inversnaid Hotel ... 66 F 15
Inveruglas ... 66 F 15
Inverurie ... 81 M 12
Invervar ... 73 H 14
Inwardleigh ... 7 H 31
Iona ... 64 A 15
Ipplepen ... 4 J 32
Ipstones ... 35 O 24
Ipswich ... 31 X 27
Irby *East Lindsey* ... 37 U 24
Irby *Wirral* ... 42 K 23
Irchester ... 29 S 27
Ireby ... 54 K 19
Ireleth ... 47 K 21
Irlam ... 42 M 23
Iron Acton ... 18 M 29
Ironbridge ... 34 M 26
Irthington ... 55 L 19
Irthlingborough ... 29 S 27
Irvine ... 60 F 17
Irwell (River) ... 42 N 23
Isbyty Ystwyth ... 25 I 27
Isla (Glen) ... 74 K 13
Islay (Sound of) ... 64 B 16
Isle of Whithorn ... 53 G 19
Isleham ... 30 V 26
Isleornsay ... 71 C 12
Isleworth ... 21 S 29
Islington *London Borough* ... 21 T 29
Islip ... 20 Q 28
Islivig ... 82 Y 9
Itchingfield ... 11 S 30
Ithon (River) ... 25 K 27
Itteringham ... 39 X 25
Iver ... 21 S 29
Iver Heath ... 21 S 29
Ivinghoe ... 21 S 28
Ivybridge ... 4 I 32
Ivychurch ... 12 W 30
Iwade ... 22 W 29
Iwerne Minster ... 9 N 31
Ixworth ... 30 W 27

J

Jacobstow ... 6 G 31
Jacobstowe ... 7 H 31
Jameston ... 15 F 29
Jamestown
  Dumfries and Galloway ... 61 K 18
Jamestown
  West Dunbartonshire ... 66 G 16
Janetstown ... 85 J 9
Jarrow ... 56 P 19
Jaywick ... 23 X 28
Jedburgh ... 62 M 17
Jedburgh Abbey ... 62 M 17
Jeffreyston ... 15 F 28
Jemimaville ... 79 H 10
Jersey *Channel I.* ... 5
Jevington ... 12 U 31
John Muir ... 69 M 15
John o' Groats ... 86 K 8
Johnshaven ... 75 N 13
Johnston ... 16 F 28
Johnstone ... 60 G 16
Johnstonebridge ... 54 J 18
Jura (Isle of) ... 58 B 16
Jura (Sound of) ... 65 C 16
Jura Forest ... 65 B 16
Jura Ho. ... 58 B 16
Jurby West ... 46 G 20

K

Kainakill ... 77 C 11
Kames ... 65 E 16
Katrine (Loch) ... 67 G 15
Kea ... 2 E 33
Keal ... 37 U 24
Keal (Loch na) ... 65 B 14
Kearsley ... 42 M 23
Keasden ... 49 M 21

Kebock Head ....82 A 9
Kedington ....30 V 27
Kedleston Hall ....36 P 25
Keelby ....45 T 23
Keevil ....19 N 30
Kegworth ....36 Q 25
Keig ....75 M 12
Keighley ....43 O 22
Keillmore ....65 C 16
Keinton Mandeville ....8 M 30
Keir Mill ....53 I 18
Keiss ....86 K 8
Keith ....80 L 11
Keld ....49 N 20
Kellas Angus ....69 L 14
Kellas Moray ....80 J 11
Kelleth ....49 M 20
Kellie Castle ....69 L 15
Kellington ....44 Q 22
Kelloe ....56 P 19
Kelly Bray ....3 H 32
Kelmarsh ....28 R 26
Kelsall ....34 L 24
Kelso ....62 M 17
Kelston ....19 M 29
Keltneyburn ....73 H 14
Kelty ....68 J 15
Kelvedon ....30 W 28
Kelvedon Hatch ....22 U 29
Kemble ....19 N 28
Kemnay ....75 M 12
Kempley ....26 M 28
Kempsey ....27 N 27
Kempsford ....19 O 28
Kempston ....29 S 27
Kemsing ....22 U 30
Kendal ....48 L 21
Kenfig ....17 I 29
Kenilworth ....27 P 26
Kenknock ....67 G 14
Kenmore Highland ....77 C 11
Kenmore
  Perthshire and Kinross ....67 I 14
Kenn ....18 L 29
Kennet (River) ....19 O 29
Kennethmont ....80 L 11
Kenninghall ....30 X 26
Kennington Kent ....22 W 30
Kennington Oxon. ....20 Q 28
Kennoway ....68 K 15
Kenovay ....70 Z 14
Kensaleyre ....77 B 11
Kentallen ....72 E 13
Kentford ....30 V 27
Kentisbeare ....7 K 31
Kentmere ....48 L 20
Kenton ....4 J 32
Kents Bank ....48 L 21
Keoldale ....84 F 8
Keresley ....28 P 26
Kerrera ....65 D 14
Kerry ....26 K 26
Kersey ....30 W 27
Kershader ....82 A 9
Kershopefoot ....55 L 18
Kesgrave ....31 X 27
Kessingland ....31 Z 26
Keswick ....54 K 20
Kettering ....28 R 26
Kettleness ....50 R 20
Kettleshulme ....43 N 24
Kettletoft ....87 M 6
Kettlewell ....49 N 21
Ketton ....37 S 26
Kew ....21 T 29
Kewstoke ....18 L 29
Kexbrough ....43 P 23
Kexby ....44 R 23
Keyingham ....45 T 22
Keymer ....11 T 31
Keynsham ....18 M 29
Keyworth ....36 Q 25
Kibworth Harcourt ....36 R 26
Kidderminster ....27 N 26
Kidermorie Lodge ....79 G 10
Kidlington ....20 Q 28
Kidsgrove ....35 N 24
Kidstones ....49 N 21
Kidwelly / Cydweli ....15 H 28
Kielder ....55 M 18
Kielder Forest ....55 M 18
Kielder Reservoir ....55 M 18
Kiiphedir ....85 I 9
Kilamarsh ....44 Q 24
Kilbarchan ....60 G 16
Kilbirnie ....60 F 16
Kilbrannan Sound ....59 D 17

Kilbride ....65 D 14
Kilburn Amber Valley ......36 P 24
Kilburn Hambleton ....50 Q 21
Kilchattan ....59 E 16
Kilchenzie ....59 C 17
Kilcheran ....65 D 14
Kilchiaran ....58 A 16
Kilchoan ....71 B 13
Kilchoman ....58 A 16
Kilconquhar ....69 L 15
Kilcreggan ....66 F 16
Kildale ....50 Q 20
Kildary ....79 H 10
Kildavanan ....59 E 16
Kildonan ....59 E 17
Kildonan Lodge ....85 I 9
Kildrummy ....74 L 12
Kildrummy Castle ....74 L 12
Kilfinnan ....72 F 12
Kilgetti ....15 F 28
Kilham
  Berwick-upon-Tweed ....63 N 17
Kilham
  East Riding of Yorkshire ...51 S 21
Kilkhampton ....6 G 31
Killay ....15 H 29
Killean ....59 D 17
Killearn ....67 G 15
Killerton ....7 J 31
Killiechronan ....65 C 14
Killilan ....78 D 12
Killin ....67 H 14
Killinghall ....50 P 21
Killundine ....71 C 14
Kilmacolm ....60 G 16
Kilmaluag ....77 B 10
Kilmany ....69 L 14
Kilmarie ....71 B 12
Kilmarnock ....60 G 17
Kilmartin ....65 D 15
Kilmaurs ....60 G 17
Kilmelford ....65 D 15
Kilmersdon ....19 M 30
Kilmington East Devon ....8 K 31
Kilmington Salisbury ......9 N 30
Kilmorack ....79 G 11
Kilmore ....71 C 12
Kilmory Ardnamurchan ...71 B 13
Kilmory Argyll and Bute ...65 C 16
Kilmory I. Rhum ....71 A 12
Kilmory North Ayrshire ...59 E 17
Kilmuir ....77 A 11
Kilmun ....66 F 16
Kilncadzow ....61 I 16
Kilninver ....65 D 14
Kilnsey ....49 N 21
Kiloran ....64 B 15
Kilpeck ....26 L 28
Kilrenny ....69 L 15
Kilsyth ....67 H 16
Kilt Rock ....77 B 11
Kiltarlity ....79 G 11
Kilvaxter ....77 A 11
Kilwinning ....60 F 17
Kimberley Broxtowe ....36 Q 25
Kimberley South Norfolk ..38 X 26
Kimble ....20 R 28
Kimbolton ....29 S 27
Kimmeridge ....9 N 32
Kimpton ....21 T 28
Kinbrace ....85 I 9
Kinbuck ....67 I 15
Kincardine Fife ....67 I 15
Kincardine Highland ......79 G 10
Kincardine O' Neil ....75 L 12
Kinclaven ....68 J 14
Kincraig ....73 I 12
Kineton ....28 P 27
Kinfauns ....68 J 14
Kingairloch ....72 D 14
Kingarth ....59 E 16
Kinghorn ....68 K 15
Kinglassie ....68 K 15
King's Bromley ....35 O 25
King's Cliffe ....37 S 26
Kings Langley ....21 S 28
King's Lynn ....38 V 25
King's Meaburn ....55 M 20
King's Somborne ....10 P 30
King's Sutton ....28 Q 27
King's Walden ....29 T 28
Kings Worthy ....10 Q 30
Kingsbarns ....69 M 15
Kingsbridge ....4 I 33
Kingsburgh ....77 A 11

Kingsbury Episcopi ....8 L 31
Kingsclere ....20 Q 30
Kingscote ....19 N 29
Kingsdon ....8 L 30
Kingsdown ....23 Y 30
Kingsgate ....23 Y 29
Kingshouse Highland ......72 F 14
Kingshouse Stirling ....67 H 14
Kingskerswell ....4 J 32
Kingskettle ....68 K 15
Kingsland ....26 L 27
Kingsley East Hampshire ..10 R 30
Kingsley
  Staffordshire Moorlands ...35 O 24
Kingsmuir ....74 L 14
Kingsnorth ....12 W 30
Kingsteignton ....4 J 32
Kingsthorpe ....28 R 27
Kingston Devon ....4 I 33
Kingston East Hampshire ..69 L 15
Kingston Moray ....80 K 10
Kingston
  South Cambridgeshire ....29 T 27
Kingston Bagpuize ....20 P 28
Kingston Deverill ....9 N 30
Kingston Lacy ....9 N 31
Kingston Lisle ....20 P 29
Kingston Seymour ....18 L 29
Kingston-St. Mary ....8 K 30
Kingston-upon-Hull ....45 S 22
Kingston-upon-Thames
  London Borough ....21 T 29
Kingstone ....26 L 27
Kingswear ....4 J 32
Kingswinford ....27 N 26
Kingswood ....19 M 29
Kingswood Powys ....34 K 26
Kingswood South Glos. ..18 M 29
Kington ....26 K 27
Kington Langley ....19 N 29
Kington-St. Michael ......19 N 29
Kingussie ....73 H 12
Kinkell Bridge ....67 I 15
Kinknockie ....81 O 11
Kinlet ....27 M 26
Kinloch ....71 B 12
Kinloch Hourn ....72 D 12
Kinloch Lodge ....84 G 8
Kinloch Rannoch ....73 H 13
Kinlochard ....67 G 15
Kinlochbervie ....84 E 8
Kinlocheil ....72 E 13
Kinlochewe ....78 E 11
Kinlochleven ....72 F 13
Kinlochmoidart ....71 C 13
Kinloss ....80 J 11
Kinmuck ....75 M 12
Kinnaird ....68 K 14
Kinneff ....75 M 13
Kinnelhead ....61 J 18
Kinnerley ....34 L 25
Kinnersley ....26 L 27
Kinnesswood ....68 K 15
Kinninvie ....56 O 20
Kinoulton ....36 R 25
Kinross ....68 J 15
Kinrossie ....68 K 14
Kintbury ....20 P 29
Kintessack ....80 I 11
Kintore ....75 M 12
Kintra ....58 B 17
Kintyre (Peninsula) ....59 D 17
Kinver ....27 N 26
Kippax ....43 P 22
Kippen ....67 H 15
Kippford ....53 I 19
Kirby Bellars ....36 R 25
Kirby Cross ....31 X 28
Kirby Hall ....29 S 26
Kirby Misperton ....50 R 21
Kirby Muxloe ....36 Q 26
Kirby Underwood ....37 S 25
Kirdford ....11 S 30
Kirk Ella ....45 S 22
Kirk Ireton ....35 P 24
Kirk Merrington ....56 P 19
Kirk Michael ....46 G 21
Kirk Yetholm ....63 N 17
Kirkbampton ....54 K 19
Kirkbean ....53 J 19
Kirkbride ....54 K 19
Kirkburn ....51 S 22
Kirkburton ....43 O 23
Kirkby ....42 L 23
Kirkby Fleetham ....50 P 20

Kirkby-in-Ashfield ....36 Q 24
Kirkby-la-Thorpe ....37 S 25
Kirkby Lonsdale ....48 M 21
Kirkby Malham ....49 N 21
Kirkby Mallory ....36 Q 26
Kirkby Malzeard ....49 P 21
Kirkby Overblow ....50 P 22
Kirkby Stephen ....49 M 20
Kirkby Thore ....55 M 20
Kirkbymoorside ....50 R 21
Kirkcaldy ....68 K 15
Kirkcolm ....52 E 19
Kirkconnel ....60 I 17
Kirkcowan ....52 F 19
Kirkcudbright ....53 I 18
Kirkcudbright Bay ....53 H 19
Kirkfieldbank ....61 I 16
Kirkgunzeon ....53 I 19
Kirkham ....42 L 22
Kirkheaton ....56 O 19
Kirkhill ....79 G 11
Kirkhope ....61 J 18
Kirkinner ....52 G 19
Kirkintilloch ....67 H 16
Kirkland
  Dumfries and Galloway ..53 I 18
Kirkland Eden ....55 M 19
Kirklees ....43 O 23
Kirklevington ....50 P 20
Kirklington
  North Yorkshire ....50 P 21
Kirklington
  Nottinghamshire ....36 R 24
Kirkliston ....68 J 16
Kirkmaiden ....52 F 19
Kirkmichael
  Perthshire and Kinross ..74 J 13
Kirkmichael
  South Ayrshire ....60 G 17
Kirkmuirhill ....61 I 17
Kirknewton
  Berwick-upon-Tweed ....63 N 17
Kirknewton
  West Lothian ....61 J 16
Kirkoswald ....59 F 18
Kirkpatrick Durham ....53 I 18
Kirkpatrick-Fleming ......54 K 18
Kirkstone Pass ....48 L 20
Kirkton
  Dumfries and Galloway ..53 J 18
Kirkton Scottish Borders ..62 L 17
Kirkton Manor ....61 K 17
Kirkton of Culsalmond ..81 M 11
Kirkton of Durris ....75 M 12
Kirkton of Glenisla ....74 K 13
Kirkton of Kingoldrum ....74 K 13
Kirkton of Largo ....69 L 15
Kirkton of Skene ....75 N 12
Kirkton of Strathmartine ..69 K 14
Kirktown of Auchterless ..81 M 11
Kirktown of Deskford ....80 L 11
Kirkwall ....86 L 7
Kirkwhelpington ....56 O 19
Kirmington ....45 T 23
Kirn ....66 F 16
Kirriemuir ....74 K 13
Kirtlebridge ....54 K 18
Kirtlington ....28 Q 28
Kirtomy ....85 H 8
Kirton Boston ....37 T 25
Kirton Suffolk Coastal ....31 X 27
Kirton End ....37 T 25
Kirton-in-Lindsey ....44 S 23
Kishorn (Loch) ....78 D 11
Kislingbury ....28 R 27
Kitchener Memorial ....86 J 6
Kiveton ....44 Q 23
Knaresborough ....50 P 21
Knarsdale ....55 M 19
Knebworth ....29 T 28
Kneesall ....36 R 24
Kneesworth ....29 T 27
Knighton / Trefyclawdd ..26 K 26
Knightshayes Court ....7 J 31
Kniveton ....35 O 24
Knock Argyll and Bute ..65 C 14
Knock Moray ....80 L 11
Knock Western Isles ......83 B 9
Knockandhu ....80 K 12
Knockbrex ....53 H 19
Knockie Lodge ....73 G 12
Knockin ....34 L 25
Knocknaha ....59 D 17
Knocksharry ....46 G 21
Knockvennie Smithy ......53 I 18
Knole ....22 U 30
Knossington ....36 R 25

Knottingley ....44 Q 22
Knowe ....52 G 18
Knowehead ....53 H 18
Knowesgate ....55 N 18
Knowle ....27 O 26
Knowsley ....42 L 23
Knoydart ....72 D 12
Knutsford ....42 M 24
Kyle Forest ....60 G 17
Kyle of Durness ....84 F 8
Kyle of Lochalsh ....77 C 12
Kyle of Sutherland ....79 G 10
Kyle of Tongue ....84 G 8
Kyleakin ....77 C 12
Kylerhea ....72 C 12
Kyles Scalpay ....82 Z 10
Kylestrome ....84 E 9
Kynance Cove ....2 E 34
Kyre park ....26 M 27

L

La Rocque Jersey I. 5
Laceby ....45 T 23
Lacey Green ....20 R 28
Lache ....34 L 24
Lacock ....19 N 29
Ladder Hills ....74 K 12
Ladock ....3 F 33
Ladybank ....68 K 15
Ladybower Reservoir ....43 O 23
Ladyhill ....55 N 18
Lagg ....65 C 16
Laggan Argyll and Bute ..58 B 16
Laggan near Invergarry ..72 F 12
Laggan
  near Newtonmore ....73 H 12
Laggan (Loch) ....73 G 13
Laggan Point ....58 B 16
Lagganulva ....64 B 14
Laide ....78 D 10
Lair ....78 E 11
Lairg ....84 G 9
Lake District National Park .48 K 20
Lakenheath ....30 V 26
Lamanva ....2 E 33
Lamberhurst ....12 V 30
Lambeth London Borough ..21 T 29
Lambley Gedling ....36 Q 24
Lambley Tynedale ....55 M 19
Lambourn ....20 P 29
Lamerton ....3 H 32
Lamington ....61 J 17
Lamlash ....59 E 17
Lamlash Bay ....59 E 17
Lammermuir Hills ....62 L 16
Lampeter /
  Llanbedr Pont Steffan ..15 H 27
Lamplugh ....54 J 20
Lamport ....28 R 26
Lanark ....61 I 16
Lancaster ....48 L 21
Lanchester ....56 O 19
Lancing ....11 T 31
Landmark Visitor Centre ..79 I 12
Landrake ....3 H 32
Land's End ....2 C 33
Landulph ....3 H 32
Lane End ....20 R 29
Laneast ....6 G 32
Lanercost ....55 L 19
Langar ....36 R 25
Langavat (Loch) Lewis ..82 Z 9
Langavat (Loch)
  South Harris ....76 Z 10
Langbank ....66 G 16
Langcliffe ....49 N 21
Langdale End ....51 S 21
Langdale Valley ....48 K 20
Langdon Beck ....55 N 19
Langenhoe ....30 W 28
Langford
  Mid Bedfordshire ....29 T 27
Langford
  West Oxfordshire ....19 P 28
Langford Budville ....8 K 31
Langham ....36 R 25
Langholm ....54 L 18
Langleeford ....63 N 17
Langley ....21 S 29
Langley Park ....56 O 19
Langold ....44 Q 23
Langport ....8 L 30
Langrick ....37 T 24
Langrish ....10 Q 30
Langsett ....43 O 23
Langshaw ....62 L 17
Langstrothdale Chase ..49 N 21

Langthwaite ....49 O 20
Langtoft ....51 S 21
Langton ....50 R 21
Langton Matravers ....9 O 32
Langwathby ....55 L 19
Lanhydrock ....3 F 32
Lanivet ....3 F 32
Lanlivery ....3 F 32
Lanreath ....3 G 32
Lansallos ....3 G 32
Lanton ....62 M 17
Lapford ....7 I 31
Larachbeg ....71 C 14
Larbert ....67 I 15
Largs ....59 F 16
Larkhall ....61 I 16
Larkhill ....19 O 30
Larling ....30 W 26
Lastingham ....50 R 21
Latchingdon ....22 W 28
Latton ....19 O 29
Lauder ....62 L 16
Lauderdale ....62 L 16
Laugharne ....15 G 28
Laughton Wealden ....12 U 31
Laughton West Lindsey ..44 R 23
Launcells ....6 G 31
Launceston ....6 G 32
Launton ....28 Q 28
Laurencekirk ....75 M 13
Laurieston ....53 H 19
Lauriston Castle ....68 K 16
Lavendon ....29 S 27
Lavenham ....30 W 27
Laverstock ....9 O 30
Laverstoke ....20 Q 30
Lawford ....30 X 28
Lawrenny ....16 F 28
Lawshall ....30 W 27
Laxay ....82 A 9
Laxey ....46 G 21
Laxey Bay ....46 G 21
Laxfield ....31 Y 27
Laxford (Loch) ....84 E 8
Laxford Bridge ....84 E 8
Laxo ....87 Q 2
Laxton
  East Riding of Yorkshire ..44 R 22
Laxton
  Newark and Sherwood ....36 R 24
Layer-de-la-Haye ....30 W 28
Layer Marney ....22 W 28
Laytham ....44 R 22
Layton ....42 K 22
Lazonby ....55 L 19
Lea Herefordshire ....26 M 28
Lea North Wiltshire ....19 N 29
Lea West Lindsey ....44 R 23
Leaden Roding ....22 U 28
Leadenham ....37 S 24
Leadgate Derwentside ..56 O 19
Leadgate Eden ....55 M 19
Leadhills ....61 I 17
Leaflied ....20 P 28
Leagrave ....29 S 28
Lealholm ....50 R 20
Lealt ....65 C 15
Leargybreck ....65 C 16
Leasingham ....37 S 24
Leathaid Bhuain (Loch an) .84 F 9
Leatherhead ....21 T 30
Leathley ....49 P 22
Leavening ....50 R 21
Lebberston ....51 S 21
Lechlade ....19 O 28
Lecht Road ....74 K 12
Leckmelm ....78 E 10
Leconfield ....44 S 22
Ledbury ....27 M 27
Ledmore ....84 F 9
Ledsham ....44 Q 22
Lee ....16 H 30
Lee-on-the-Solent ....10 Q 31
Leebotwood ....34 L 26
Leeds Kent ....22 V 30
Leeds West Yorks. ....43 P 22
Leedstown ....2 D 33
Leek ....35 N 24
Leek Wootton ....27 P 27
Leeming Bar ....50 P 21
Leeswood ....34 K 24
Legbourne ....45 U 23
Legerwood ....62 M 16
Leicester ....36 Q 26
Leicester Forest East ....36 Q 26
Leigh ....42 M 23

Leigh *Mole Valley* ....21 T 30
Leigh *North Wiltshire* ....19 O 29
Leigh *Sevenoaks* ....22 U 30
Leigh *West Dorset* ....8 M 31
Leigh-on-Sea ....22 V 29
Leigh Sinton ....27 N 27
Leighterton ....19 N 29
Leighton Buzzard ....29 S 28
Leim ....58 C 17
Leintwardine ....26 L 26
Leirinmore ....84 F 8
Leiston ....31 Y 27
Leith ....68 K 16
Leitholm ....62 M 16
Lemreway ....82 A 9
Lendalfoot ....52 F 18
Lenham ....22 W 30
Lennoxtown ....67 H 16
Leominster ....26 L 27
Leonard Stanley ....19 N 28
Lepe ....10 P 31
Lephinmore ....65 E 15
Lerwick ....87 Q 3
Lesbury ....63 P 17
Leslie *Aberdeenshire* ....81 L 12
Leslie *Fife* ....68 K 15
Lesmahagow ....61 I 17
Leswalt ....52 E 19
Letchworth ....29 T 28
Letham *Angus* ....75 L 14
Letham *Fife* ....68 K 15
Letheringsett ....38 X 25
Letterewe Forest ....78 D 10
Letterfearn ....78 D 12
Lettermore ....84 G 8
Letters ....78 E 10
Letterston ....24 F 28
Leuchars ....69 L 14
Leurbost ....82 A 9
Leven
  East Riding of Yorks. ......51 T 22
Leven *Fife* ....69 K 15
Leven (Loch) ....72 E 13
Leven (River) ....72 F 13
Levens ....48 L 21
Levens Hall ....48 L 21
Levenwick ....87 Q 4
Leverington ....37 U 25
Leverton
  with Habblesthorpe ....44 R 24
Levington ....31 X 27
Levisham ....50 R 21
Lewannick ....3 G 32
Lewdown ....6 H 32
Lewes ....11 U 31
Lewis (Isle of) ....82 Z 9
Lewis and Harris (Isle of) ..82 Z 8
Lewisham
  London Borough ....21 T 29
Lewknor ....20 R 28
Leyburn ....49 O 21
Leyland ....42 L 22
Leysdown-on-Sea ....22 W 29
Lezant ....3 G 32
Lhanbryde ....80 K 11
Lhen (The) ....46 G 20
Liathach ....78 D 11
Libberton ....61 J 16
Lichfield ....35 O 25
Liddesdale ....55 L 18
Lidgate ....30 V 27
Lifton ....6 H 32
Ligger or Perran Bay ....2 E 32
Lilbourne ....28 Q 26
Lilleshall ....35 M 25
Lilliesleaf ....62 L 17
Limerhaugh ....60 H 17
Limpsfield ....21 U 30
Linchmere ....10 R 30
Lincoln ....44 S 24
Lincolnshire Wolds ....45 T 23
Lindfield ....11 T 30
Lindores ....68 K 14
Lingague ....46 F 21
Lingay *near Eriskay* ....70 X 12
Lingay *near Pabbay* ....70 X 13
Lingen ....26 L 27
Lingfield ....21 T 30
Liniclate ....76 X 11
Linlithgow ....67 J 16
Linn of Dee ....74 J 13
Linn of Tummel ....74 I 13
Linnerineach ....84 E 9
Linney Head ....14 E 29
Linnhe (Loch) ....72 D 14
Linslade ....29 R 28
Lintmill ....80 L 10

Linton *Craven* ....49 N 21
Linton *Herefordshire* ....26 M 28
Linton *Scottish Borders* ....62 M 17
Linton
  South Cambridgeshire ......30 U 27
Linton *South Derbyshire* ....35 P 25
Linton-on-Ouse ....50 Q 21
Lintrathen (Loch of) ....74 K 13
Linwood *Renfrewshire* ....60 G 16
Linwood *West Lindsey* ....45 T 23
Liphook ....10 R 30
Liskeard ....3 G 32
Lismore ....65 D 14
Liss ....10 R 30
Lisset ....51 T 21
Lisvane ....18 K 29
Litcham ....38 W 25
Litchborough ....28 Q 27
Litchfield ....20 P 30
Litherland ....42 L 23
Litlington ....40 H 23
Little-Baddow ....22 V 28
Little-Barningham ....39 X 25
Little Berkhamsted ....21 T 28
Little Budworth ....34 M 24
Little Bytham ....37 S 25
Little Chalfont ....21 S 28
Little Clacton ....31 X 28
Little Colonsay ....64 B 14
Little-Coxwell ....19 P 29
Little Cumbrae Island ....59 F 16
Little Dewchurch ....26 L 28
Little Galdenoch ....52 E 19
Little Glenshee ....67 J 14
Little Hadham ....29 U 28
Little Hallingbury ....22 U 28
Little Harrowden ....28 R 27
Little Houghton ....28 R 27
Little Loch Broom ....78 D 10
Little Loch Roag ....82 Z 9
Little Mill ....18 L 28
Little-Milton ....20 Q 28
Little Minch (The) ....76 Z 11
Little Moreton Hall ....35 N 24
Little Ouse (River) ....30 V 26
Little Ouseburn ....50 Q 21
Little-Raveley ....29 T 26
Little Snoring ....38 W 25
Little-Stretton ....26 L 26
Little-Stukeley ....29 T 26
Little Torrington ....6 H 31
Little Urswick ....48 K 21
Little Walsingham ....38 W 25
Little Waltham ....22 V 28
Little Wenlock ....34 M 26
Littleborough ....43 N 23
Littlebourne ....23 X 30
Littlebury ....30 U 27
Littlecote House ....20 P 29
Littleferry ....79 H 10
Littleham ....4 J 32
Littlehampton ....11 S 31
Littlemill ....79 I 11
Littleport ....30 U 26
Littlestone-on-Sea ....12 W 31
Littleton ....10 P 30
Littleworth ....20 P 28
Litton Cheney ....5 M 31
Liverpool ....42 L 23
Liverton ....50 R 20
Livet (Glen) ....80 K 12
Livingston ....61 J 16
Lizard ....2 E 34
Lizard Peninsula ....2 E 33
Llam ....35 O 24
Llan ....33 J 26
Llan-non ....15 H 28
Llan-y-Bri ....15 G 28
Llanarmon-yn-Ial ....34 K 24
Llanarthne ....24 H 28
Llanarthney ....15 H 28
Llanasa ....41 J 23
Llanbabadarn Fawr ....25 H 26
Llanbedr ....33 H 25
Llanbedr Pont Steffan /
  Lampeter ....15 H 27
Llanbedrog ....32 G 25
Llanberis ....33 H 24
Llanberis (Pass of) ....33 H 24
Llanbister ....26 K 26
Llanboidy ....15 G 28
Llanbradach ....18 K 29
Llanbrynmair ....33 J 25
Llanddarog ....15 H 28
Llanddeiniol ....25 H 27
Llandderfel ....33 J 25
Llanddeusant ....40 G 22

Llanddewi Brefi ....25 I 27
Llanddewi Ystradenni ....26 K 27
Llanddona ....40 H 23
Llanddowror ....15 G 28
Llanddulas ....41 J 23
Llandegla ....34 K 24
Llandeilo ....15 I 28
Llandenny ....18 L 28
Llandinam ....25 J 26
Llandissilio ....15 F 28
Llandogo ....18 L 28
Llandovery / Llanymddyfri ..25 I 28
Llandrindod Wells ....25 J 27
Llandrinio ....34 K 25
Llandudno ....41 I 23
Llandudno Junction ....41 I 23
Llandwrog ....32 H 24
Llandybie ....15 H 28
Llandyfaelog ....15 H 28
Llandygai ....40 H 23
Llandysul ....15 H 27
Llanegryn ....33 H 26
Llanelidan ....34 K 24
Llanellen ....18 K 28
Llanelli ....15 H 28
Llanelltyd ....33 I 25
Llanengan ....32 G 25
Llanerchymedd ....40 G 23
Llanerfyl ....33 J 25
Llanfachraeth ....40 G 23
Llanfaethlu ....40 G 22
Llanfair ....33 H 25
Llanfair-Caereinion ....34 K 26
Llanfair-Pwllgwyngyll ..40 H 23
Llanfair-ym-Muallt /
  Builth Wells ....25 J 27
Llanfair-yn-Neubwll ....40 G 23
Llanfairfechan ....41 I 23
Llanfairynghornwy ....40 G 22
Llanfechell ....40 G 22
Llanferres ....34 K 24
Llanfihangel-ar-arth ....15 H 27
Llanfihangel Glyn Myfyr ...33 J 24
Llanfihangel Nant Bran ...25 J 28
Llanfihangel Rhyditon ......26 K 27
Llanfihangel-y-Creuddyn ..25 I 26
Llanfilo ....26 K 28
Llanfoist ....18 K 28
Llanfrynach ....25 J 28
Llanfwrog ....40 G 23
Llanfyllin ....34 K 25
Llanfynydd *Carmarthenshire* /
  Sir Gaerfyrddin ....15 H 28
Llanfynydd *Flintshire* /
  Sir y Fflint ....34 K 24
Llanfyrnach ....15 G 28
Llangadfan ....33 J 25
Llangadog ....25 I 28
Llangain ....15 G 28
Llangammarch Wells ....25 J 27
Llangarron ....26 L 28
Llangathen ....15 H 28
Llangedwyn ....34 K 25
Llangefni ....40 H 23
Llangeinor ....17 J 29
Llangeitho ....25 H 27
Llangeler ....15 G 27
Llangenith ....15 H 29
Llangennech ....15 H 28
Llangernyw ....33 I 24
Llangoed ....40 H 23
Llangollen ....34 K 25
Llangorse ....26 K 28
Llangorwen ....25 H 26
Llangrannog ....15 G 27
Llangunllo ....26 K 27
Llangunnor ....15 H 28
Llangurig ....25 J 26
Llangwm ....33 J 25
Llangwn *Monmouthshire* /
  Sir Fynwy ....18 L 28
Llangwn *Pembrokeshire* /
  Sir Benfro ....16 F 28
Llangwnnadl ....32 F 25
Llangwyryfon ....25 H 27
Llangybi ....15 H 27
Llangyndeyrn ....15 H 28
Llangynidr ....26 K 28
Llangynog *Carmarthenshire* /
  Sir Gaerfyrddin ....15 G 28
Llangynog *Powys* ....33 J 25
Llangynwyd ....17 J 29
Llangywer ....33 J 25
Llanharan ....17 J 29
Llanharry ....17 J 29
Llanhilleth ....18 K 28
Llanidloes ....25 J 26

Llanilar ....25 H 26
Llanishen ....18 L 28
Llanllwchaiarn ....26 K 26
Llanllyfni ....32 H 24
Llanmadoc ....15 H 29
Llannefydd ....41 J 23
Llanon ....25 H 27
Llanpumsaint ....15 H 28
Llanrhaeadr ....33 J 24
Llanrhaeadr-ym-
  Mochnant ....34 K 25
Llanrhidian ....15 H 29
Llanrhystud ....25 H 27
Llanrug ....33 H 24
Llanrwst ....33 I 24
Llansannffraid Glan Conwy ..41 I 23
Llansannan ....33 J 24
Llansantffraid ....25 H 27
Llansantffraid-ym-Mechain ..34 K 25
Llansawel ....15 H 27
Llansilin ....34 K 25
Llansoy ....18 L 28
Llansteffan ....15 G 28
Llanthony ....26 K 28
Llanthony Priory ....26 K 28
Llantilio Crossenny ....18 L 28
Llantrisant ....17 J 29
Llantwit Major ....17 J 29
Llanuwchllyn ....33 I 25
Llanvetherine ....18 L 28
Llanwddyn ....33 J 25
Llanwenog ....15 H 27
Llanwnda ....32 H 24
Llanwnen ....15 H 27
Llanwnog ....25 J 26
Llanwrda ....25 I 28
Llanwrin ....33 I 26
Llanwrtyd Wells ....25 J 27
Llanwyddelan ....33 J 26
Llanybydder ....15 H 27
Llanychaer ....24 F 28
Llanymawddwy ....33 J 25
Llanymddyfri / Llandovery ..25 I 28
Llanymynech ....34 K 25
Llanynghenedl ....40 G 23
Llanystumdwy ....32 H 25
Llawhaden ....15 F 28
Llechryd ....15 G 27
Lledrod ....25 I 27
Lleyn Peninsula ....32 G 25
Llithfaen ....32 G 25
Llowes ....26 K 27
Llston ....15 H 29
Llwyndafydd ....24 G 27
Llwyngwril ....33 H 25
Llwynmawr ....34 K 25
Llyfnant Valley ....33 I 26
Llyn Brianne ....25 I 27
Llyn Celyn ....33 I 25
Llyn Tegid or Bala Lake ......33 I 25
Llyswen ....26 K 27
Llysworney ....17 J 29
Llywel ....25 J 28
Loanhead ....61 K 16
Lochailort ....72 D 13
Lochaline ....65 C 14
Lochans ....52 E 19
Lochanbriggs ....53 J 18
Lochassynt Lodge ....84 E 9
Lochawe ....66 E 14
Lochay (Glen) ....67 G 14
Lochboisdale ....70 Y 12
Lochbuie ....65 C 14
Lochcarron ....78 D 11
Lochdonhead ....65 C 14
Lochdrum ....78 F 10
Lochearnhead ....67 H 14
Locheport ....76 Y 11
Locherben ....61 J 18
Lochfoot ....53 I 18
Lochgair ....65 D 15
Lochgarthside ....73 G 12
Lochgelly ....68 K 15
Lochgilphead ....65 D 15
Lochgoilhead ....66 F 15
Lochinver ....84 E 9
Lochluichart ....78 F 11
Lochmaben ....54 J 18
Lochmaddy ....76 Y 11
Lochore ....68 K 15
Lochportain ....76 Y 11
Lochranza ....59 E 16
Lochsie (Glen) ....74 J 13
Lochstack ....84 F 8
Lochton *Aberdeenshire* ....75 M 12
Lochton *South Ayrshire* ....52 F 18
Lochtyn / Ynys ....15 G 27

Lochuisge ....72 D 14
Lochwinnoch ....60 G 16
Lochy (Loch) ....72 F 13
Lockerbie ....54 J 18
Lockerley ....9 P 30
Locking ....18 L 30
Loddington ....28 R 26
Loddon ....39 Y 26
Lode ....30 U 27
Lodsworth ....11 R 31
Lofthouse ....49 O 21
Loftus ....50 R 20
Logan Gardens ....52 F 19
Loggerheads ....35 M 25
Logie Coldstone ....74 L 12
Logiealmond ....67 I 14
Login ....15 F 28
Lomond (Loch) ....66 G 15
Londesborough ....51 R 22
London ....21 T 29
London Colney ....21 T 28
Long (Loch) *Angus* ....68 K 14
Long (Loch)
  Argyll and Bute ....66 F 15
Long Ashton ....18 M 29
Long Bennington ....36 R 25
Long Bredy ....5 M 31
Long Buckby ....28 Q 27
Long Clawson ....36 R 25
Long Crendon ....20 R 28
Long Eaton ....36 Q 25
Long Hanborough ....20 P 28
Long Itchington ....28 P 27
Long Lawford ....28 Q 26
Long Man (The) ....12 U 31
Long Marston ....50 Q 22
Long Marton ....55 M 20
Long Melford ....30 W 27
Long Mountain ....34 K 26
Long Mynd (The) ....26 L 26
Long Preston ....49 N 21
Long Stratton ....31 X 26
Long Sutton *Lincs.* ....37 U 25
Long Sutton *Somerset* ....8 L 30
Long Wittenham ....20 Q 29
Longay ....77 C 12
Longbenton ....56 P 18
Longborough ....27 O 28
Longbridge Deverill ....9 N 30
Longburton ....8 M 31
Longcot ....19 P 29
Longdon ....35 O 25
Longfield ....22 U 29
Longford
  Derbyshire Dales ....35 O 25
Longford *Tewkesbury* ....27 N 28
Longforgan ....68 K 14
Longformacus ....62 M 16
Longham ....38 W 25
Longhirst ....56 P 18
Longhorsley ....56 O 18
Longhoughton ....63 P 17
Longleat House ....19 N 30
Longmanhil ....81 M 11
Longnewton ....50 P 20
Longney ....19 M 28
Longniddry ....69 L 16
Longnor ....35 O 24
Longridge *Ribble Valley* ..42 M 22
Longridge
  South Staffordshire ......35 N 25
Longridge *West Lothian* ..61 I 16
Longside ....81 O 11
Longstanton ....29 U 27
Longton *South Ribble* ....42 L 22
Longton *Stoke-on-Trent* ...35 N 25
Longtown *Carlisle* ....54 L 18
Longtown *Herefordshire* ...26 L 28
Longwick ....20 R 28
Longworth ....20 P 28
Lonmore ....77 A 11
Looe ....3 G 32
Loose ....22 V 30
Loppington ....34 L 25
Lorn ....65 E 14
Lorn (Firth of) ....65 D 14
Lossiemouth ....80 K 10
Lostwithiel ....3 G 32
Lothbeg ....85 I 9
Lothersdale ....49 N 22
Lothmore ....85 I 9
Loudwater ....21 S 29
Loughborough ....36 Q 25
Loughor (River) ....17 H 29
Loughton ....21 U 29
Louth ....45 U 23
Lovington ....8 M 30

Low Bradley ....49 O 22
Low Crosby ....55 L 19
Low Row *Carlisle* ....55 M 19
Low Row *Richmondshire* ...49 N 20
Low Street ....39 Y 25
Lowca ....53 J 20
Lowdham ....36 Q 24
Lower Beeding ....11 T 30
Lower Bentham ....49 M 21
Lower Boddington ....28 Q 27
Lower Broadheath ....27 N 27
Lower Cam ....19 M 28
Lower Diabaig ....78 C 11
Lower Dounreay ....85 I 8
Lower Dunsforth ....50 Q 21
Lower Halstow ....22 W 29
Lower Hardres ....23 X 30
Lower Heyford ....28 Q 28
Lower Killeyan ....58 B 17
Lower Largo ....69 L 15
Lower Mayland ....22 W 28
Lower Peover ....42 M 24
Lower Upham ....10 Q 31
Lower-Whitley ....42 M 24
Lowestoft ....31 Z 26
Lowgill ....49 M 21
Lowick
  Berwick-upon-Tweed ....63 O 17
Lowick
  East Northamptonshire ...29 S 26
Lowick Bridge ....48 K 21
Lowther ....55 L 20
Lowther Hills ....61 J 18
Loxwood ....11 S 30
Loyal (Loch) ....84 G 8
Loyne (Loch) ....72 E 12
Lùb Score ....77 A 10
Lubcroy ....84 F 10
Lubenham ....28 R 26
Lubnaig (Loch) ....67 H 15
Luccombe ....17 J 30
Luce Bay ....52 F 19
Lucker ....63 O 17
Luddesdown ....22 V 29
Ludford *East Lindsey* ....45 T 23
Ludford *South Shropshire* ...26 L 26
Ludgershall *Bucks.* ....20 Q 28
Ludgershall *Wilts.* ....19 P 30
Ludgvan ....2 D 33
Ludham ....39 Y 25
Ludlow ....26 L 26
Luffincott ....60 G 16
Luib *Highland* ....77 B 12
Luib *Stirling* ....67 G 14
Luichart (Loch) ....78 F 11
Luing ....65 D 15
Lullington ....35 P 25
Lulsgate Bottom ....18 L 29
Lulworth Cove ....9 N 32
Lumphanan ....75 L 12
Lumsden ....80 L 12
Lunan ....75 M 14
Lunanhead ....74 L 14
Luncarty ....68 J 14
Lund ....51 S 22
Lundie ....68 K 14
Lundie (Loch) ....78 C 11
Lundin Links ....69 L 15
Lundy ....16 G 30
Lunning ....87 Q 2
Lurgainn (Loch) ....84 E 9
Lurgashall ....11 S 30
Luskentyre ....82 Z 10
Luss ....66 G 15
Lusta ....77 A 11
Lustleigh ....4 I 32
Luston ....26 L 27
Luthermuir ....75 M 13
Luthrie ....68 K 14
Luton ....29 S 28
Luton Hoo ....21 S 28
Lutterworth ....28 Q 26
Lutton ....37 U 25
Luxborough ....7 J 30
Lybster ....86 K 9
Lydbury North ....26 L 26
Lydd ....12 W 31
Lydd-on-Sea ....12 W 31
Lydden ....23 X 30
Lydeard-St. Lawrence ....8 K 30
Lydford *Mendip* ....8 M 30
Lydford *West Devon* ....4 H 32
Lydham ....26 L 26
Lydiard Millicent ....19 O 29
Lydiard Park ....19 O 29
Lydiate ....42 L 23
Lydlinch ....9 M 31

Great Britain 131

Lydney 18 M 28
Lydstep 15 F 29
Lyme Bay 5 L 32
Lyme Park 43 N 23
Lyme Regis 5 L 31
Lyminge 13 X 30
Lymington 10 P 31
Lymm 42 M 23
Lympne 13 X 30
Lympstone 4 J 32
Lyndhurst 10 P 31
Lyne 61 K 17
Lyneham *North Wiltshire* 19 O 29
Lyneham
West Oxfordshire 27 P 28
Lynemouth 56 P 18
Lyness 86 K 7
Lynmouth 17 I 30
Lynton 17 I 30
Lyon (Glen) 73 H 14
Lyonshall 26 L 27
Lytchett Matravers 9 N 31
Lytchett Minster 9 N 31
Lytes Cary 8 L 30
Lyth 86 K 8
Lytham 42 L 22
Lytham St. Anne's 42 K 22
Lythe 51 R 20

M

Maaruig 82 Z 10
Mabie 53 J 18
Mablethorpe 45 U 23
Macaskin (Island) 65 D 15
Macclesfield 43 N 24
Macduff 81 M 10
Machars (The) 52 G 19
Machen 18 K 29
Machir Bay 58 A 16
Machrihanish 58 C 17
Machrihanish Bay 58 C 17
Machynlleth 33 I 26
Madderty 67 I 14
Maddiston 67 I 16
Maddy (Loch) 76 Y 11
Madeley *Staffs* 35 M 24
Madeley
Telford and Wrekin 35 M 26
Madingley 29 U 27
Madron 2 D 33
Maenclochog 15 F 28
Maentwrog 33 I 25
Maerdy *Conwy* 33 J 25
Maerdy
Rhondda, Cynon, Taf 17 J 28
Maes Howe 86 K 7
Maesbrook 34 K 25
Maesteg 17 J 29
Maghull 42 L 23
Magor 18 L 29
Maiden Bradley 9 N 30
Maiden Castle 8 M 31
Maiden Newton 8 M 31
Maidenhead 20 R 29
Maidens 59 F 17
Maidford 28 Q 27
Maids Morelon 28 R 27
Maidstone 22 V 30
Maidwell 28 R 26
Mainland *Orkney Islands* 86 J 6
Mainland *Shetland Islands* 87 R 3
Mainstone 26 K 26
Maisemore 27 N 28
Malborough 4 I 33
Maldon 22 W 28
Malham 49 N 21
Mallaig 71 C 12
Mallory Park Circuit 36 P 26
Mallwyd 33 I 25
Malmesbury 19 N 29
Malpas 34 L 24
Maltby 44 Q 23
Maltby-le-Marsh 45 U 24
Malton 50 R 21
Malvern Wells 27 N 27
Mamble 26 M 26
Mamore Forest 72 F 13
Man (Isle of) 46 G 21
Manaccan 2 E 33
Manaton 4 I 32
Manchester 43 N 23
Manderston 62 N 16
Manea 29 U 26
Mangersta 82 Y 9
Mangotsfield 18 M 29
Manish 76 Z 10
Manningford Bruce 19 O 30
Mannings Heath 11 T 30
Manningtree 31 X 28
Manorbier 15 F 29
Mansfield 36 Q 24
Mansfield Woodhouse 36 Q 24
Manstone 9 N 31
Manton 36 R 26
Manuden 30 U 28
Maplebeck 36 R 24
Mapledurham 20 Q 29
Mappleton 45 T 22
Mappowder 9 M 31
Mar (Forest of) 74 J 12
Marazion 2 D 33
March 37 U 26
Marcham 20 P 29
Marchington 35 O 25
Marchwood 10 P 31
Marden 22 V 30
Maree (Loch) 78 D 10
Mareham-le-Fen 37 T 24
Maresfield 11 U 31
Margam 17 I 29
Margaretting 22 V 28
Margate 23 Y 29
Margnaheglish 59 E 17
Marham 38 V 26
Marhamchurch 6 G 31
Marholm 37 T 26
Marian-Glas 40 H 22
Marishader 77 B 11
Mark *Sedgemoor* 18 L 30
Mark *South Ayrshire* 52 E 18
Market Bosworth 36 P 26
Market Deeping 37 T 25
Market Drayton 34 M 25
Market Harborough 28 R 26
Market Lavington 19 O 30
Market Overton 36 R 25
Market Rasen 45 T 23
Market Weighton 44 S 22
Markfield 36 Q 25
Markinch 68 K 15
Marks Tey 30 W 28
Marksbury 18 M 29
Markyate 21 S 28
Marlborough 19 O 29
Marldon 4 J 32
Marlesford 31 Y 27
Marloes 14 E 28
Marlow 20 R 29
Marnhull 9 N 31
Marple 43 N 23
Marros 15 G 28
Marsden 43 O 23
Marsett 49 N 21
Marsh Gibbon 28 Q 28
Marsham 39 X 25
Marshaw 48 M 22
Marshchapel 45 U 23
Marshfield
Casnewydd / Newport 18 K 29
Marshfield
South Gloucestershire 19 N 29
Marshwood 8 L 31
Marske 49 O 20
Marske-by-the-Sea 57 Q 20
Marstch 20 Q 28
Marston 37 R 25
Marston Magna 8 M 31
Marston Moretaine 29 S 27
Martham 39 Y 25
Martin *New Forest* 9 O 31
Martin *North Kesteven* 37 T 24
Martin (Isle) 84 E 10
Martin Mill 23 Y 30
Martindale 48 L 20
Martinstown 5 M 31
Martlesham 31 X 27
Martletwy 15 F 28
Martley 27 M 27
Martock 8 L 31
Marton *Harrogate* 50 P 21
Marton *Macclesfield* 35 N 24
Marvig 82 A 9
Marwell Zoological Park 10 Q 31
Mary Arden's House 27 O 27
Mary Tavy 4 H 32
Marybank 79 G 11
Maryburgh 79 G 11
Maryculter 75 N 12
Maryfield 87 Q 3
Marykirk 75 M 13
Marypark 80 J 11
Maryport *Allerdale* 53 J 19
Maryport
Dumfries and Galloway 52 F 19
Marywell *Aberdeenshire* 75 L 12
Marywell *Angus* 69 M 14
Masham 49 P 21
Matching Green 22 U 28
Mathry 14 E 28
Matlock 36 P 24
Matlock Bath 35 P 24
Mattersey 44 R 23
Mattingley 20 R 30
Mattishall 38 X 26
Mauchline 60 G 17
Maud 81 N 11
Maughold 46 H 21
Maughold Head 46 H 21
Mawbray 54 J 19
Mawnan 2 E 33
Maxstoke 27 P 26
Maxton 62 M 17
Maybole 60 F 17
Mayfield *East Sussex* 12 U 30
Mayfield *Staffs* 35 O 24
Mc Arthur's Head 58 B 16
Meadie (Loch) 84 G 9
Meal Bank 48 L 20
Mealsgate 54 K 19
Meare 8 L 30
Measach (Falls of) 78 E 10
Measham 36 P 25
Meavaig 82 Z 10
Meavy 4 H 32
Medbourne 28 R 26
Medmenham 20 R 29
Medstead 10 Q 30
Medway (River) 22 W 29
Meidrim 15 G 28
Meifod 34 K 25
Meigle 68 K 14
Meikleour 68 J 14
Melbost 83 B 9
Melbourn 29 U 27
Melbourne
East Riding of Yorkshire 44 R 22
Melbourne
South Derbyshire 36 P 25
Melbury Osmond 8 M 31
Meldon 56 O 18
Melfort 65 D 15
Melgarve 73 G 12
Melksham 19 N 29
Melldalloch 65 E 16
Mellerstain 62 M 17
Melling 48 M 21
Mellon Charles 78 D 10
Mellon Udrigle 78 D 10
Mells 19 M 30
Melmerby *Eden* 55 M 19
Melmerby *Harrogate* 50 P 21
Melrose 62 L 17
Meltham 43 O 23
Melton 31 X 27
Melton Mowbray 36 R 25
Melvaig 77 C 10
Melvich 85 I 8
Memsie 81 N 11
Menai Bridge /
Porthaethwy 40 H 23
Menai Strait 33 H 24
Mendip Hills 18 L 30
Mendlesham 31 X 27
Menheniot 3 G 32
Mennock 61 I 17
Menston 43 O 22
Menstrie 67 I 15
Menteith Hills 67 H 15
Mentmore 29 R 28
Meonstoke 10 Q 31
Meopham 22 V 29
Mepal 29 U 26
Mere *Cheshire* 42 M 24
Mere *Wilts* 9 N 30
Mereworth 22 V 30
Meriden 27 P 26
Merkland Lodge 84 F 9
Mermaid Inn 32 H 24
Merrick 52 G 18
Merriott 8 L 31
Merrylaw 62 K 18
Mersey (River) 42 M 23
Merthyr Cynog 25 J 27
Merthyr Tydfil 17 J 28
Merton *Cherwell* 20 Q 28
Merton *Devon* 7 H 31
Merton *London Borough* 21 T 29
Meshaw 7 I 31
Messing 30 W 28
Messingham 44 S 23
Metfield 31 Y 26
Metheringham 37 S 24
Methil 69 K 15
Methlick 81 N 11
Methven 68 J 14
Methwold 38 V 26
Mevagissey 3 F 33
Mexborough 44 Q 23
Mhór (Loch) 73 G 12
Miavaig 82 Z 9
Michaelchurch Escley 26 L 27
Michaelstow 3 F 32
Micheldever 10 Q 30
Michelham Priory 12 U 31
Micklefield 44 Q 22
Mickleover 36 P 25
Mickleton *Cotswold* 27 O 27
Mickleton *Teesdale* 55 N 20
Mid Ardlaw 81 N 10
Mid Calder 61 J 16
Mid Lavant 10 R 31
Mid Sannox 59 E 17
Mid Yell 87 Q 2
Midbea 86 L 6
Middle Barton 28 P 28
Middle Rasen 45 S 23
Middle Tysoe 28 P 27
Middle Wallop 9 P 30
Middle Woodford 9 O 30
Middlebie 54 K 18
Middleham 49 O 21
Middlesbrough 57 Q 20
Middlestown 43 P 23
Middleton *Argyll and Bute* 64 Z 14
Middleton
Berwick-upon-Tweed 63 O 17
Middleton *Bradford* 49 O 22
Middleton *Gtr. Mches* 43 N 23
Middleton Cheney 28 Q 27
Middleton-in-Teesdale 55 N 20
Middleton-on-Sea 11 S 31
Middleton on the Wolds 51 S 22
Middleton St. George 50 P 20
Middleton Tyas 49 P 20
Middletown *Powys* 34 K 25
Middlewich 35 M 24
Midgeholme 55 M 19
Midhurst 10 R 31
Midlem 62 L 17
Midsomer Norton 18 M 30
Midtown 78 C 10
Miefield 53 H 19
Migdale (Loch) 79 H 10
Milborne Port 8 M 31
Milborne St. Andrew 9 N 31
Milbourne 56 O 18
Milburn 55 M 20
Mildenhall *Forest Heath* 30 V 26
Mildenhall *Kennet* 19 O 29
Mile End 30 W 28
Milfield 63 N 17
Milford 11 S 30
Milford Haven /
Aberdaugleddau 14 E 28
Milford-on-Sea 9 P 31
Milland 10 R 30
Millbrook 3 H 32
Millhouse 59 E 16
Millmeece 35 N 25
Millom 47 K 21
Millport 59 F 16
Milltown
Dumfries and Galloway 54 K 18
Milltown *Highland* 78 F 11
Milltown *Moray* 80 L 11
Milnathort 68 J 15
Milngavie 67 H 16
Milnrow 43 N 23
Milnthorpe 48 L 21
Milovaig 76 Z 11
Milton 79 H 10
Milton *Cambs* 29 U 27
Milton *Carlisle* 55 L 19
Milton *Dumfries* 53 I 18
Milton *Highland* 79 G 11
Milton *Stranraer* 52 F 19
Milton Abbas 9 N 31
Milton Abbot 3 H 32
Milton Bryan 29 S 28
Milton Ernest 29 S 27
Milton Keynes 28 R 27
Milton Libourne 19 O 29
Milton of Campsie 67 H 16
Milton of Cushnie 75 L 12
Milton-on-Stour 9 N 30
Miltonduff 80 J 11
Miltown of Edinvillie 80 K 11
Milverton 8 K 30
Milwich 35 N 25
Minard 65 E 15
Minch (The) 83 C 9
Minehead 17 J 30
Minety 19 O 29
Mingary 76 X 12
Minginish 77 B 12
Mingulay 70 X 13
Minnigaff 52 G 19
Minster *near Sheerness* 22 W 29
Minster *near Ramsgate* 23 X 29
Minsterley 34 L 26
Minsterworth 19 N 28
Minterne Magna 8 M 31
Minting 45 T 24
Mintlaw 81 O 11
Minto 62 L 17
Mirfield 43 O 22
Miserden 19 N 28
Misson 44 R 23
Misterton *Notts* 44 R 23
Misterton *Somerset* 8 L 31
Mistley 31 X 28
Mitcheldean 26 M 28
Mitchell 2 E 32
Mitford 56 O 18
Mithcham 21 T 29
Mithian 2 E 33
Moaness 86 K 7
Mochdre 41 I 23
Mochrum 52 G 19
Modbury 4 I 32
Moelfre 40 H 22
Moffat 61 J 17
Moidart 72 C 13
Moira 36 P 25
Mol-Chlach 71 B 12
Mold / Yr Wyddgrug 34 K 24
Molland 7 I 30
Monach Islands 76 W 11
Monadhliath Mountains 73 H 12
Monar (Loch) 78 E 11
Monar Lodge 78 F 11
Monaughty Forest 80 J 11
Moneydie 68 J 14
Moniaive 53 I 18
Monifieth 69 L 14
Monikie 69 L 14
Monk Fryston 44 Q 22
Monkland 26 L 27
Monkokehampton 7 H 31
Monks Eleigh 30 W 27
Monksilver 7 K 30
Monkton 60 G 17
Monmouth / Trefynwy 18 L 28
Monreith 52 G 19
Montacute 8 L 31
Montgarrie 75 L 12
Montgomery / Trefaldwyn 34 K 26
Montrose 75 M 13
Monyash 35 O 24
Monymusk 75 M 12
Monzie 67 I 14
Moonen Bay 76 Z 11
Moor Monkton 50 Q 21
Moorends 44 R 23
Moorfoot Hills 61 K 16
Moors (The) 52 F 19
Moortown 45 S 23
Morar 71 C 13
Moray Firth 79 H 11
Morchard Bishop 7 I 31
Morcott 37 S 26
Morden 9 N 31
Mordiford 26 M 27
More (Glen) 65 C 14
More (Loch) *near Kinloch* 84 F 9
More (Loch)
near Westerdale 85 J 8
Morebath 7 J 30
Morebattle 62 M 17
Morecambe 48 L 21
Morecambe Bay 48 L 21
Moresby 53 J 20
Moreton *Epping Forest* 22 U 28
Moreton *Purbeck* 9 N 31
Moreton-in-Marsh 27 O 28
Moreton-on-lugg 26 L 27
Moreton Say 34 M 25
Moretonhampstead 4 I 32
Morfa Nefyn 32 G 25
Moricambe Bay 54 K 19
Morie (Loch) 79 G 10
Moriston (Glen) 72 F 12
Morland 55 M 20
Morley 43 P 22
Morlich (Loch) 74 I 12
Morpeth 56 O 18
Morriston 17 I 29
Morte Bay 6 H 30
Mortehoe 16 H 30
Mortimer 20 Q 29
Morton *near Bourne* 37 S 25
Morton
near Gainsborough 44 R 23
Morton
North East Derbyshire 36 P 24
Morton on Swale 50 P 21
Morval 3 G 32
Morven 85 I 9
Morvern 71 C 14
Morvich 72 D 12
Morville 34 M 26
Morwelham 3 H 32
Morwenstow 6 G 31
Mosborough 43 P 24
Moss Bank 42 L 23
Mossdale 53 H 18
Mossend 60 H 16
Mossley 43 N 23
Mosstodloch 80 K 11
Mostyn 41 K 23
Motherwell 61 I 16
Moulin 74 I 13
Moulton *Forest Heath* 30 V 27
Moulton *Lincs* 37 T 25
Moulton *Northants* 28 R 27
Moulton Chapel 37 T 25
Mount Pleasant 9 P 31
Mountain Ash /
Aberpennar 17 J 28
Mount's Bay 2 D 33
Mountsorrel 36 Q 25
Mousa 87 Q 4
Mousehole 2 D 33
Mouswald 54 J 18
Mow Cop 35 N 24
Mowtie 75 N 13
Moy 79 H 11
Muasdale 59 C 17
Much Dewchurch 26 L 28
Much Hadham 29 U 28
Much Hoole 42 L 22
Much Marcle 26 M 28
Much Wenlock 34 M 26
Muchalls 75 N 12
Muchelney 8 L 30
Muchrachd 78 F 11
Muck 71 B 13
Muckle Roe 87 P 2
Mucklestone 35 M 25
Muddiford 7 H 30
Mudford 8 M 31
Mugeary 77 B 11
Muick (Loch) 74 K 13
Muie 85 H 9
Muir of Fowlis 75 L 12
Muir of Ord 79 G 11
Muirdrum 69 L 14
Muirhead 60 H 16
Muirkirk 60 H 17
Muirshearlich 72 E 13
Muker 49 N 20
Mulbarton 39 X 26
Mulben 80 K 11
Muldoanich 70 X 13
Mull (Isle of) 64 B 14
Mull (Sound of) 71 C 14
Mull of Galloway 52 F 20
Mull of Oa 58 A 17
Mullardoch (Loch) 78 E 12
Mullardoch House 78 F 11
Mullion 2 E 33
Mumbles (The) 15 H 29
Mumby 45 U 24
Mundesley 39 Y 25
Mundford 30 V 26
Mundham 10 R 31
Munlochy 79 H 11
Munlochy Bay 79 H 11
Munslow 26 L 26
Murlaggan 72 E 13
Murrayfield 68 K 16
Mursley 28 R 28
Murton *Easington* 57 P 19
Murton *Eden* 55 M 20
Musbury 5 K 31
Musselburgh 68 K 16
Muston 51 T 21
Muthill 67 I 15
Mwnt 15 G 27
Mybster 85 J 8
Myddfai 25 I 28
Myddle 34 L 25

A B C D E F G H I J K L M N O P Q R S T U V W X Y Z

A B C D E F G H I J K L M N O P Q R S T U V W X Y Z

Mydroilyn .... 15 H 27
Mynach Falls .... 25 I 26
Mynachlog-ddu .... 15 F 28
Mynydd Eppynt .... 25 J 27
Mynydd Mawr .... 32 F 25
Mynydd Preseli .... 15 F 28
Myrelandhorn .... 86 K 8
Mytchett .... 21 R 30
Mytholmroyd .... 43 O 22

N

Na Cùiltean .... 58 C 16
Naburn .... 50 Q 22
Nacton .... 31 X 27
Nafferton .... 51 S 21
Nailsea .... 18 L 29
Nailstone .... 36 P 26
Nailsworth .... 19 N 28
Nairn .... 79 I 11
Nant (Loch) .... 65 E 14
Nant-y-Moch Reservoir .. 25 I 26
Nant-y-moel .... 17 J 29
Nantgwynant Valley ...... 33 H 24
Nantwich .... 34 M 24
Nantyglo .... 18 K 28
Napton .... 28 Q 27
Narberth / Arberth .... 15 F 28
Narborough Blaby .... 36 Q 26
Narborough Breckland .. 38 V 25
Naseby .... 28 R 26
Nash Point .... 17 J 29
Nassington .... 37 S 26
Nateby .... 49 M 20
National Exhibition Centre .. 27 O 26
National Motor Museum .. 10 P 31
Naunton .... 27 O 28
Navenby .... 37 S 24
Naver (Loch) .... 84 G 9
Nayland .... 30 W 28
Naze (The) .... 31 X 28
Neap .... 87 Q 3
Neath / Castell-nedd .... 17 I 29
Neath (River) .... 17 I 28
Nebo .... 33 I 24
Necton .... 38 W 26
Needham Market .... 31 X 27
Needingworth .... 29 T 27
Needles (The) .... 10 P 32
Nefyn .... 32 G 25
Neidpath Castle .... 61 K 17
Neilston .... 60 G 16
Neist Point .... 76 Z 11
Nelson
  Caerffili / Caerphilly .. 18 K 29
Nelson Pendle .... 43 N 22
Nene (River) .... 37 T 26
Nenthead .... 55 M 19
Nercwys .... 34 K 24
Nereabolls .... 58 A 16
Ness .... 83 B 8
Ness (Loch) .... 73 G 12
Nesscliffe .... 34 L 25
Nestley Marsh .... 10 P 31
Neston .... 42 K 24
Nether Broughton .... 36 R 25
Nether Kellet .... 48 L 21
Nether Langwith .... 44 Q 24
Nether Stowey .... 8 K 30
Nether Wasdale .... 47 J 20
Nether Whitecleuch .... 61 I 17
Netheravon .... 19 O 30
Netherbrae .... 81 M 11
Netherbury .... 8 L 31
Netherend .... 18 M 28
Netherhampton .... 9 O 30
Nethermill .... 54 J 18
Netherthong .... 43 O 23
Netherton .... 63 N 17
Nethertown .... 86 K 7
Netherwitton .... 56 O 18
Nethy Bridge .... 74 J 12
Netley .... 10 P 31
Nettlebed .... 20 R 29
Nettleham .... 44 S 24
Nettleton .... 45 T 23
Nevern .... 15 F 27
Nevis (Glen) .... 72 E 13
Nevis (Loch) .... 72 C 12
New Abbey .... 53 J 19
New Aberdour .... 81 N 11
New Alresford .... 10 Q 30
New Buckenham .... 31 X 26
New Byth .... 81 N 11
New Clipstone .... 36 Q 24
New Cumnock .... 60 H 17
New Deer .... 81 N 11
New Edlington .... 44 Q 23

New Forest National Park .. 9 P 31
New Galloway .... 53 H 18
New Holland .... 45 S 22
New Hythe .... 22 V 30
New Leeds .... 81 N 11
New Luce .... 52 F 19
New Marske .... 57 Q 20
New Mills .... 43 O 23
New Mills Powys .... 33 K 26
New Milton .... 9 P 31
New Pitsligo .... 81 N 11
New Quay / Ceinewydd .. 24 G 27
New Rackheath .... 39 Y 26
New Radnor .... 26 K 27
New Romney .... 12 W 31
New Rossington .... 44 Q 23
New Sauchie .... 67 I 15
New Scone .... 68 J 14
New Silksworth .... 57 P 19
New Tredegar .... 18 K 28
New Waltham .... 45 T 23
Newark-on-Trent .... 36 R 24
Newbiggin Eden .... 55 L 19
Newbiggin Teesdale ..... 55 N 20
Newbiggin-by-the-Sea ... 56 P 18
Newbigging Angus .... 69 L 14
Newbigging
  South Lanarkshire ..... 61 J 16
Newbold Verdon .... 36 P 26
Newborough
  East Staffordshire .... 35 O 25
Newborough
  Isle of Anglesey .... 32 G 24
Newbridge Caerffili /
  Caerphilly .... 18 K 29
Newbridge Isle of Wight .. 10 P 31
Newbridge-on-Wye ...... 25 J 27
Newbrough .... 55 N 18
Newburgh Aberdeenshire .. 81 N 12
Newburgh Fife .... 68 K 14
Newburgh Lancashire ... 42 L 23
Newburn .... 56 O 19
Newbury .... 20 Q 29
Newby Bridge .... 48 L 21
Newby Hall .... 50 P 21
Newcastle Monmouthshire /
  Sir Fynwy .... 18 L 28
Newcastle
  South Shropshire ...... 26 K 26
Newcastle Emlyn /
  Castell Newydd Emlyn .. 15 G 27
Newcastle-under-Lyme .. 35 N 24
Newcastle-upon-Tyne ... 56 P 19
Newcastle-upon-Tyne
  Airport .... 56 O 18
Newcastleton .... 55 L 18
Newchapel .... 15 G 27
Newchurch Carmarthenshire /
  Sir Gaerfyrddin .... 15 G 28
Newchurch Isle of Wight .. 10 Q 32
Newchurch Powys .... 26 K 27
Newchurch Shepway ... 12 W 30
Newdigate .... 11 T 30
Newent .... 27 M 28
Newgale .... 14 E 28
Newhall .... 34 M 24
Newham Isle of Wight .. 63 O 17
Newham London Borough .. 21 U 29
Newhaven .... 11 U 31
Newick .... 11 U 31
Newington .... 22 V 29
Newland .... 18 M 28
Newlyn .... 2 D 33
Newmachar .... 75 N 12
Newmains .... 61 I 16
Newmarket Isle of Lewis .. 82 A 9
Newmarket Suffolk ..... 30 V 27
Newmill Moray .... 80 L 11
Newmill Scottish Borders .. 62 L 17
Newmilns .... 60 G 17
Newnham Daventry ..... 28 Q 27
Newnham Glos. .... 18 M 28
Newnham Kent .... 22 W 30
Newnham Bridge .... 26 M 27
Newport Essex .... 30 U 28
Newport I.O.W. .... 10 Q 31
Newport Pembrokes. ... 15 F 27
Newport Stroud .... 19 M 28
Newport
  Telford and Wrekin ... 35 M 25
Newport /
  Casnewydd Newport .. 18 L 29
Newport-on-Tay .... 69 L 14
Newport Pagnell .... 28 R 27
Newquay .... 2 E 32
Newsham .... 49 O 20
Newstead .... 36 Q 24

Newstead Abbey .... 36 Q 24
Newton Aberdeenshire .. 81 O 11
Newton Argyll and Bute .. 65 E 15
Newton Babergh .... 30 W 27
Newton Moray .... 80 J 11
Newton Ribble Valley ... 49 M 22
Newton Rushcliffe .... 36 R 25
Newton Abbot .... 4 J 32
Newton Arlosh .... 54 K 19
Newton-Aycliffe .... 56 P 20
Newton Ferrers .... 4 H 33
Newton Flotman .... 39 X 26
Newton-le-Willows ...... 42 M 23
Newton Longville .... 28 R 28
Newton Mearns .... 60 H 16
Newton-on-Rawcliffe ... 50 R 20
Newton-on-Trent .... 44 R 24
Newton Poppleford ..... 5 K 31
Newton Reigny .... 55 L 19
Newton St. Cyres .... 7 J 31
Newton Stewart .... 52 G 19
Newton Tracey .... 7 H 30
Newton Wamphray ...... 54 J 18
Newtongrange .... 61 K 16
Newtonhill .... 75 N 12
Newtonmore .... 73 H 12
Newtown Cheshire ...... 43 N 23
Newtown Heref. .... 26 M 27
Newtown Highland ...... 73 F 12
Newtown Isle of Man ... 46 G 21
Newtown /
  Drenewydd Powys .... 26 K 26
Newtown Linford .... 36 Q 25
Newtown St. Boswells .. 62 L 17
Newtyle .... 68 K 14
Neyland .... 16 F 28
Nicholaston .... 15 H 29
Nigg .... 79 H 10
Nigg Bay .... 79 H 10
Nine Ladies .... 35 P 24
Ninebanks .... 55 M 19
Ninfield .... 12 V 31
Nisbet .... 62 M 17
Nith (River) .... 53 J 19
Niths .... 61 I 18
Niton .... 10 Q 32
Nocton .... 37 S 24
Nolton .... 14 E 28
Nordelph .... 38 U 26
Norfolk Broads .... 39 Y 25
Norham .... 63 N 16
Normanby .... 50 R 21
Normandy .... 21 S 30
Normanton .... 43 P 22
Normanton-on-the-Wolds .. 36 Q 25
North Baddesley .... 10 P 31
North Ballachulish ...... 72 E 13
North Berwick .... 69 L 15
North Bovey .... 4 I 32
North Bradley .... 19 N 30
North Brentor .... 4 H 32
North Cadbury .... 8 M 30
North Cave .... 44 S 22
North-Cerney .... 19 O 28
North-Charlton .... 63 O 17
North Cliffe .... 44 R 22
North Cowton .... 50 P 20
North Crawley .... 29 S 27
North Creake .... 38 W 25
North Curry .... 8 L 30
North Dalton .... 51 S 22
North Deighton .... 50 P 22
North Erradale .... 77 C 10
North Esk (Riv.) .... 75 L 13
North Fearns .... 77 B 11
North Foreland .... 23 Y 29
North Frodingham .... 51 T 22
North Grimston .... 51 R 21
North Harris .... 82 Z 10
North Hill .... 3 G 32
North Hinksey .... 20 Q 28
North Holmwood .... 21 T 30
North Hykeham .... 37 S 24
North Kelsey .... 45 S 23
North Kessock .... 79 H 11
North Kyme .... 37 T 24
North Leigh .... 20 P 28
North-Molton .... 7 I 30
North Morar .... 72 C 13
North Newbald .... 44 S 22
North Nibley .... 19 M 29
North Otterington .... 50 P 21
North Petherton .... 8 K 30
North Petherwin .... 6 G 31
North Rigton .... 50 P 22
North Ronaldsay .... 87 M 5
North-Scarle .... 36 R 24

North-Shian .... 65 D 14
North Shields .... 56 P 18
North Shore .... 42 K 22
North Somercotes ...... 45 U 23
North Sound (The) ..... 87 L 6
North Stainley .... 50 P 21
North Stainmore .... 49 N 20
North Sunderland ...... 63 P 17
North Tamerton .... 6 G 31
North Tawton .... 7 I 31
North Thoresby .... 45 T 23
North Tidworth .... 19 P 30
North Uist .... 76 X 11
North Walsham .... 39 Y 25
North Warnborough .... 20 R 30
North Water Bridge .... 75 M 13
North Weald Bassett ... 22 U 28
North Wootton .... 38 V 25
North York Moors
  National Park .... 50 R 20
Northallerton .... 50 P 20
Northam .... 6 H 30
Northampton .... 28 R 27
Northaw .... 21 T 28
Northchapel .... 11 S 30
Northchurch .... 21 S 28
Northfleet .... 22 V 29
Northiam .... 12 V 31
Northleach .... 19 O 28
Northleigh .... 5 K 31
Northlew .... 7 H 31
Northop .... 34 K 24
Northrepps .... 39 Y 25
Northstowe .... 29 U 27
Northton .... 76 Y 10
Northumberland
  National Park .... 63 N 18
Northwich .... 42 M 24
Northwold .... 38 V 26
Northwood .... 34 L 25
Norton Daventry .... 28 Q 27
Norton Doncaster .... 44 Q 23
Norton Ryedale .... 50 R 21
Norton Tewkesbury ..... 27 N 28
Norton Disney .... 36 R 24
Norton Fitzwarren .... 8 K 30
Norton in Hales .... 35 M 25
Norton St. Philip .... 19 N 30
Norwich .... 39 X 26
Norwick .... 87 R 1
Noss (Isle of) .... 87 Q 3
Noss Head .... 86 K 8
Nottingham .... 36 Q 25
Nuffield .... 20 Q 29
Nunburnholme .... 51 R 22
Nuneaton .... 28 P 26
Nuneham Courtenay ... 20 Q 28
Nunney .... 19 M 30
Nunthorpe .... 50 Q 20
Nunton .... 76 X 11
Nutley .... 11 U 30
Nympsfield .... 19 N 28

O

Oa (The) .... 58 B 17
Oadby .... 36 Q 26
Oakamoor .... 35 O 24
Oakdale .... 18 K 28
Oakengates .... 35 M 25
Oakford .... 7 J 31
Oakham .... 36 R 25
Oakhill .... 18 M 30
Oakington .... 29 U 27
Oakley Aylesbury Vale .. 20 Q 28
Oakley Bedfordshire ... 29 S 27
Oakley Fife .... 68 J 15
Oaksey .... 19 N 29
Oakworth .... 43 O 22
Oare Kennet .... 19 O 29
Oare Swale .... 22 W 30
Oare West Somerset ... 17 I 30
Oathlaw .... 74 L 13
Oban .... 65 D 14
Occold .... 31 X 27
Ochil Hills .... 68 I 15
Ochiltree .... 60 G 17
Ockbrook .... 36 P 25
Ockle .... 71 C 13
Ockley .... 11 S 30
Odiham .... 20 R 30
Odland .... 18 M 29
Odstock .... 9 O 30
Offa's Dyke Path .... 26 K 26
Offord Cluny .... 29 T 27
Ogbourne St. Andrew .. 19 O 29
Ogbourne St. George .. 19 O 29
Ogil .... 74 L 13

Ogle .... 56 O 18
Ogmore-by-Sea .... 17 J 29
Ogmore Vale .... 17 J 29
Oich (Loch) .... 73 F 12
Oidhche (Loch na h-) .. 78 D 11
Oigh-Sgeir .... 71 Z 13
Okeford Fitzpaine .... 9 N 31
Okehampton .... 4 H 31
Old Alresford .... 10 Q 30
Old Bolingbroke .... 37 U 24
Old Burghclere .... 20 Q 30
Old Castleton .... 55 L 18
Old Colwyn .... 41 I 23
Old Dailly .... 59 F 18
Old Deer .... 81 N 11
Old Fletton .... 37 T 26
Old Harry Rocks .... 9 O 32
Old Head .... 87 L 7
Old Hurst .... 29 T 26
Old Hutton .... 48 L 21
Old Kilpatrick .... 67 G 16
Old Knebworth .... 29 T 28
Old Leake .... 37 U 24
Old Man of Hoy .... 86 J 7
Old Man of Storr .... 77 B 11
Old Radnor .... 26 K 27
Old Rayne .... 81 M 11
Old' Sarum .... 9 O 30
Old Sodbury .... 19 M 29
Old Somerby .... 37 S 25
Old Warden .... 29 S 27
Old Windsor .... 21 S 29
Oldany Island .... 84 E 9
Oldbury .... 27 N 26
Oldbury on Severn ...... 18 M 29
Oldcotes .... 44 Q 23
Oldham .... 43 N 23
Oldhamstocks .... 69 M 16
Oldmeldrum .... 81 N 11
Oldshoremore .... 84 E 8
Olgrinmore .... 85 J 8
Ollaberry .... 87 P 2
Ollach .... 77 B 11
Ollay (Loch) .... 76 X 12
Ollerton Macclesfield ... 42 M 24
Ollerton
  Newark and Sherwood .. 36 Q 24
Olney .... 28 R 27
Olveston .... 18 M 29
Ombersley .... 27 N 27
Once Brewed .... 55 M 19
Onchan .... 46 G 21
Onecote .... 35 O 24
Onich .... 72 E 13
Onllwyn .... 17 I 28
Opinan .... 83 D 10
Orchy (Glen) .... 66 F 14
Ord .... 71 C 12
Ordie .... 74 L 12
Orford .... 31 Y 27
Orford Ness .... 31 Y 27
Orkney Islands 87
Orleton .... 26 L 27
Ormesby .... 50 Q 20
Ormesby St. Margaret .. 39 Z 25
Ormiston .... 62 L 16
Ormskirk .... 42 L 23
Oronsay .... 64 B 15
Orosay near Fuday ..... 70 X 12
Orosay near Lochboisdale .. 70 X 12
Orphir .... 86 K 7
Orrin (Glen) .... 78 F 11
Orrin Reservoir .... 78 F 11
Orsay .... 58 A 16
Orsett .... 22 V 29
Orston .... 36 R 25
Orton .... 48 M 20
Orwell .... 29 T 27
Orwell (River) .... 31 X 28
Osborne House .... 10 Q 31
Osdale .... 77 A 11
Osgaig (Loch) .... 83 E 9
Osgodby .... 45 S 23
Oskaig .... 77 B 11
Osmington .... 9 M 32
Ossett .... 43 P 22
Ossington .... 36 R 24
Oswaldtwistle .... 42 M 22
Oswestry .... 34 K 25
Otford .... 22 U 30
Othery .... 8 L 30
Otley Suffolk .... 31 X 27
Otley West Yorks. .... 49 O 22
Otterbourne .... 10 P 30
Otterburn .... 55 N 18
Otternish .... 76 Y 10
Otterswick .... 87 Q 2

Otterton .... 5 K 32
Ottery St. Mary .... 5 K 31
Ottringham .... 45 T 22
Oulton Broad .... 39 Z 26
Oulton Park Circuit ..... 34 M 24
Oundle .... 29 S 26
Ouse (River)
  English Channel .... 11 T 30
Ouse (River) North Sea .. 50 Q 21
Out-Rawcliffe .... 42 L 22
Out Skerries .... 87 R 2
Outer Hebrides .... 82 Y 9
Outhgill .... 49 M 20
Outwell .... 38 U 26
Over .... 29 U 27
Over Compton .... 8 M 31
Overseal .... 35 P 25
Overstrand .... 39 Y 25
Overton Hants. .... 20 Q 30
Overton Lancs. .... 48 L 21
Overton Wrexham .... 34 L 25
Overtown .... 61 I 16
Ower .... 10 P 31
Owermoigne .... 9 N 32
Owlswick .... 20 R 28
Owslebury .... 10 Q 30
Owston .... 36 R 26
Owston Ferry .... 44 R 23
Oxburgh Hall .... 38 V 26
Oxen Park .... 48 K 21
Oxenhope .... 43 O 22
Oxford .... 20 Q 28
Oxnam .... 62 M 17
Oxted .... 21 T 30
Oxton
  Newark and Sherwood .. 36 Q 24
Oxton Scottish Borders .. 62 L 16
Oxwich .... 15 H 29
Oxwich Bay .... 15 H 29
Oykel (Glen) .... 84 F 9
Oykel Bridge .... 84 F 10
Oyne .... 81 M 12

P

Pabay near Harris .... 77 C 12
Pabbay near Harris ..... 76 Y 10
Pabbay near Mingulay .. 70 X 13
Pabbay (Sound of) ..... 76 Y 10
Packington .... 36 P 25
Padbury .... 28 R 28
Paddock Wood .... 22 V 30
Paddockhole .... 54 K 18
Padiham .... 42 N 22
Padstow .... 3 F 32
Pagham .... 10 R 31
Paignton .... 4 J 32
Pailton .... 28 Q 26
Painscastle .... 26 K 27
Painswick .... 19 N 28
Paisley .... 60 G 16
Pakefield .... 31 Z 26
Palnackie .... 53 I 19
Pamber End .... 20 Q 30
Pandy
  Monmouthshire / Sir Fynwy .. 26 L 28
Pandy Powys .... 33 J 26
Pangbourne .... 20 Q 29
Pant .... 34 K 25
Pantymenyn .... 15 F 28
Papa Stour .... 87 O 3
Papa Westray .... 87 L 5
Papplewick .... 36 Q 24
Paps of Jura .... 65 B 16
Papworth Everard ...... 29 T 27
Parbh (The) .... 84 F 8
Parbold .... 42 L 23
Parc Cefn Onn .... 18 K 29
Parham House .... 11 S 31
Park Gate .... 10 Q 31
Park of Pairc .... 82 A 9
Parkeston .... 31 X 28
Parkgate .... 53 J 18
Parkhurst .... 10 Q 31
Parnham House .... 8 L 31
Parracombe .... 17 I 30
Parrett (River) .... 8 K 30
Parson Drove .... 37 U 26
Partney .... 37 U 24
Parton
  Dumfries and Galloway .. 53 H 18
Partridge Green .... 11 T 31
Parwich .... 35 O 24
Patchway .... 18 M 29
Pateley Bridge .... 49 O 21
Path of Condie .... 68 J 15
Pathhead .... 62 L 16

Patna .... 60 G 17
Patrick .... 46 F 21
Patrington .... 45 T 22
Patrixbourne .... 23 X 30
Patterdale .... 48 L 20
Pattingham .... 35 N 26
Pattishall .... 28 Q 27
Paulerspury .... 28 R 27
Paull .... 45 T 22
Paulton .... 18 M 30
Paxton .... 63 N 16
Peacehaven .... 11 T 31
Peak District
    National Park .... 43 O 23
Pearsie .... 74 K 13
Peasedown St. John .... 19 M 30
Peasemore .... 20 P 29
Peasenhall .... 31 Y 27
Peaslake .... 21 S 30
Peasmarsh .... 12 W 31
Peat Inn .... 69 L 15
Peatknowe .... 81 M 11
Pebmarsh .... 30 W 28
Pebworth .... 27 O 27
Peebles .... 61 K 17
Peel .... 46 F 21
Peel Fell .... 62 M 18
Pegswood .... 56 P 18
Pegwell Bay .... 23 Y 30
Peinchorran .... 77 B 12
Peldon .... 22 W 28
Pelton .... 56 P 19
Pelynt .... 3 G 32
Pembrey .... 15 H 28
Pembridge .... 26 L 27
Pembroke / Penfro .... 16 F 28
Pembroke Dock /
    Doc Penfro .... 16 F 28
Pembrokeshire Coast
    National Park .... 15 F 29
Pembury .... 12 V 30
Pen-y-bont / Bridgend .... 17 J 29
Pen-y-groes .... 32 H 24
Penalun .... 15 F 29
Penarth .... 18 K 29
Pencader .... 15 H 27
Pencaitland .... 62 L 16
Pencarrow .... 3 F 32
Penclawdd .... 15 H 29
Pencombe .... 26 M 27
Penderyn .... 17 J 28
Pendine .... 15 G 28
Pendine Sands .... 15 G 28
Pendlebury .... 42 N 23
Pendoylan .... 17 J 29
Penelewey .... 2 E 33
Penfro / Pembroke .... 16 F 28
Pengethley .... 26 M 28
Penhow .... 18 L 29
Penicuik .... 61 K 16
Penifiler .... 77 B 11
Peninver .... 59 D 17
Penistone .... 43 P 23
Penketh .... 42 L 23
Penkridge .... 35 N 25
Penley .... 34 L 25
Penmaen .... 15 H 29
Penmaenmawr .... 41 I 23
Penmaenpool .... 33 I 25
Penmark .... 17 J 29
Penmon .... 40 H 23
Pennal .... 33 I 26
Pennant .... 33 J 26
Pennerley .... 34 L 26
Pennines (The) .... 49 N 20
Pennyghael .... 65 B 14
Penpont .... 53 I 18
Penrhiwpal .... 15 G 27
Penrhyn .... 40 H 23
Penrhyn Bay .... 41 I 23
Penrhyndeudraeth .... 33 H 25
Penrith .... 55 L 19
Penruddock .... 55 L 20
Penryn .... 2 E 33
Pensarn .... 41 J 23
Penshaw .... 56 P 19
Penshurst .... 22 U 30
Pensilva .... 3 G 32
Pentewan .... 3 F 33
Pentire Point .... 3 F 32
Pentland Firth .... 86 K 7
Pentland Hills .... 61 J 16
Pentland Skerries .... 87 L 7
Pentraeth .... 40 H 23
Pentre-Berw .... 40 H 23
Pentre-Celyn .... 34 K 24
Pentrebeirdd .... 34 K 25

Penwith .... 2 D 33
Penybont .... 26 K 27
Penysarn .... 40 H 22
Penzance .... 2 D 33
Pernrhyn-Coch .... 25 I 26
Perranarworthal .... 2 E 33
Perranporth .... 2 E 32
Perranzabuloe .... 2 E 33
Pershore .... 27 N 27
Pertenhall .... 29 S 27
Perth .... 68 J 14
Peterborough .... 37 T 26
Peterculter .... 75 N 12
Peterhead .... 81 O 11
Peterlee .... 57 P 19
Petersfield .... 10 R 30
Peterstone Wentlooge .... 18 K 29
Peterstow .... 26 M 28
Petham .... 23 X 30
Petrockstowe .... 7 H 31
Pett .... 12 V 31
Pettaugh .... 31 X 27
Petworth .... 11 S 31
Pevensey Bay .... 12 V 31
Pewsey .... 19 O 29
Pickering .... 50 R 21
Picklescott .... 34 L 26
Picton Castle .... 16 F 28
Piddlehinton .... 9 M 31
Piddletrenthide .... 9 M 31
Piercebridge .... 49 O 20
Pierowall .... 86 L 6
Pilgrims Hatch .... 22 U 29
Pilleron Hersey .... 28 P 27
Pillerton Priors .... 27 P 27
Pilley .... 43 P 23
Pilling .... 48 L 22
Pilning .... 18 M 29
Pilton .... 8 M 30
Pinchbeck .... 37 T 25
Pinchbeck-West .... 37 T 25
Pinhoe .... 4 J 31
Pinmore Mains .... 52 F 18
Pinner .... 21 S 29
Pinvin .... 27 N 27
Pinwherry .... 52 F 18
Pinxton .... 36 Q 24
Pirbright .... 21 S 30
Pirnmill .... 59 D 17
Pirton .... 29 T 28
Pishill .... 20 R 29
Pitcaple .... 81 M 12
Pitcombe .... 8 M 30
Pitlochry .... 74 I 13
Pitmedden .... 81 N 11
Pitminster .... 8 K 31
Pitscottie .... 69 L 15
Pitsford .... 28 R 27
Pittentrail .... 85 H 10
Pittenween .... 69 L 15
Pladda .... 59 E 17
Plaistow .... 11 S 30
Plas Newydd Anglesey .... 33 H 24
Plas Newydd
    Denbighshire .... 34 K 25
Plean .... 67 I 15
Pleasington .... 42 M 22
Pleasley .... 36 Q 24
Plenmeller .... 55 M 19
Plockton .... 78 D 11
Pluckley .... 22 W 30
Plumbland .... 54 K 19
Plumpton .... 11 T 31
Plymouth .... 4 H 32
Plympton .... 4 H 32
Plymstock .... 4 H 32
Plymtree .... 7 J 31
Plynlimon
    (Pumlumon Fawr) .... 25 I 26
Pocklington .... 50 R 22
Point Lynas .... 40 H 22
Point of Ayr Flintshire .... 41 K 22
Point of Ayre Isle of Man ..... 46 G 20
Polbain .... 83 D 9
Pole of Itlaw (The) .... 81 M 11
Polebrook .... 29 S 26
Polegate .... 12 U 31
Polesden Lacey .... 21 S 30
Polesworth .... 35 P 26
Polkerris .... 3 F 32
Polloch .... 72 D 13
Pollock House .... 60 H 16
Polmont .... 67 I 16
Polperro .... 3 G 33
Polruan .... 3 G 33
Polwarth .... 62 M 16

Pondersbridge .... 29 T 26
Pont-ar-Gothi .... 15 H 28
Pontardawe .... 17 I 28
Pontarddulais .... 15 H 28
Pontarfynach /
    Devil's Bridge .... 25 I 26
Pontargothi .... 15 H 28
Pontarsais .... 15 H 28
Pontefract .... 44 Q 22
Ponteland .... 56 O 18
Ponterwyd .... 25 I 26
Pontesbury .... 34 L 26
Pontlottyn .... 18 K 28
Pontlyfni .... 32 G 24
Pontneddfechan .... 17 J 28
Pontrhydfendigaid .... 25 I 27
Pontrhydygroes .... 25 I 26
Pontrilas .... 26 L 28
Pontsticill .... 17 J 28
Pontyates .... 15 H 28
Pontyberem .... 15 H 28
Pontyclun .... 17 J 29
Pontycymer .... 17 J 29
Pontypool / Pontypwl .... 18 K 28
Pontypridd .... 17 J 29
Pontypwl / Pontypool .... 18 K 28
Poole .... 9 O 31
Poole Bay .... 9 O 31
Poolewe .... 78 D 10
Pooley Bridge .... 55 L 20
Pooltiel (Loch) .... 76 Z 11
Porlock .... 17 J 30
Port Appin .... 65 D 14
Port Askaig .... 58 B 16
Port Bannatyne .... 59 E 16
Port Carlisle .... 54 K 19
Port Charlotte .... 58 A 16
Port Driseach .... 65 E 16
Port Ellen .... 58 B 17
Port Erin .... 46 F 21
Port-Eynon .... 15 H 29
Port-Eynon Point .... 15 H 29
Port Gaverne .... 3 F 32
Port Glasgow .... 66 F 16
Port Henderson .... 77 C 10
Port Isaac .... 3 F 32
Port Lamont .... 59 E 16
Port Logan .... 52 F 19
Port Mór .... 71 B 13
Port of Menteith .... 67 H 15
Port of Ness .... 83 B 8
Port Ramsay .... 65 D 14
Port St. Mary .... 46 F 21
Port Talbot .... 17 I 29
Port William .... 52 G 19
Portavadie .... 59 E 16
Portchester .... 10 Q 31
Portencross .... 59 F 16
Portesham .... 5 M 31
Portgordon .... 80 K 11
Portgower .... 85 I 9
Porth .... 17 J 29
Porth Neigwl
    or Hell's Mouth .... 32 G 25
Porth Tywyn /Burry Port .... 15 H 28
Porthaethwy /
    Menai Bridge .... 40 H 23
Porthcawl .... 17 I 29
Porthcothan .... 2 E 32
Porthcurno .... 2 D 33
Porthgwarra .... 2 C 33
Porthkerry .... 17 K 29
Porthleven .... 2 E 33
Porthmadog .... 33 H 25
Porthtowan .... 2 E 33
Porthyrhyd .... 15 H 28
Portinnisherrich .... 65 E 15
Portishead .... 18 L 29
Portknockie .... 80 L 10
Portland (Isle of) .... 8 M 32
Portlethen .... 75 N 12
Portmahomack .... 79 I 10
Portmeirion .... 33 H 25
Portnacroish .... 72 D 14
Portnaguran .... 83 B 9
Portnahaven .... 58 A 16
Portnalong .... 77 A 12
Portobello .... 68 K 16
Portpatrick .... 2 E 33
Portree .... 77 B 11
Portscatho .... 3 F 33
Portskerra .... 85 I 8
Portskewett .... 18 L 29
Portslade .... 11 T 31
Portsmouth .... 10 Q 31
Portsoy .... 81 L 10

Portuairk .... 71 B 13
Postbridge .... 4 I 32
Potten End .... 21 S 28
Potter Heigham .... 39 Y 25
Potter Street .... 21 U 28
Potterhanworth .... 37 S 24
Potterne .... 19 N 30
Potters Bar .... 21 T 28
Potton .... 29 T 27
Poughill .... 6 G 31
Poulshot .... 19 N 29
Poulton .... 19 O 28
Poulton-le-Fylde .... 42 L 22
Poundstock .... 6 G 31
Powburn .... 63 O 17
Powerstock .... 8 L 31
Powick .... 27 N 27
Powis .... 34 K 26
Powmill .... 68 J 15
Poynings .... 11 T 31
Poynton .... 43 N 23
Praa Sands .... 2 D 33
Prawle Point .... 4 I 33
Praze-an-Beeble .... 2 E 33
Prees .... 34 M 25
Preesall .... 48 L 22
Prendwick .... 63 O 17
Prescot .... 42 L 23
Prestatyn .... 41 J 22
Prestbury Cheltenham .... 27 N 28
Prestbury Macclesfield .... 43 N 24
Presteigne .... 26 K 27
Preston
    East Riding of Yorks. ...... 45 T 22
Preston Kent .... 23 X 30
Preston Lancs. .... 42 L 22
Preston Rutland .... 36 R 26
Preston West Sussex .... 11 S 31
Preston Candover .... 10 Q 30
Preston Capes .... 28 Q 27
Prestonpans .... 69 L 16
Prestwich .... 42 N 23
Prestwick .... 60 G 17
Prestwood .... 20 R 28
Prickwillow .... 30 V 26
Priest Island .... 83 D 10
Priest Weston .... 34 K 26
Princes Risborough .... 20 R 28
Princethorpe .... 28 P 26
Princetown .... 4 I 32
Priors Marston .... 28 Q 27
Probus .... 3 F 33
Prosen (Glen) .... 74 K 13
Prudhoe .... 56 O 19
Puckeridge .... 29 U 28
Pucklechurch .... 19 M 29
Pucks Gutter .... 23 X 30
Puddletown .... 9 M 31
Pudsey .... 43 P 22
Pulborough .... 11 S 31
Pulford .... 34 L 24
Pulham .... 9 M 31
Pulham Market .... 31 X 26
Puncheston .... 24 F 28
Punchardon .... 7 H 30
Purbeck (Isle of) .... 9 N 32
Purbrook .... 10 Q 31
Puriton .... 8 L 30
Purleigh .... 22 V 28
Purley .... 20 Q 29
Purse Caundle Manor .... 9 M 31
Purston Jaglin .... 43 P 22
Purton .... 19 O 29
Putsborough .... 6 H 30
Puttenham .... 21 S 30
Pwllheli .... 32 G 25
Pyecombe .... 11 T 31
Pyle .... 17 I 29
Pylle .... 8 M 30

Quainton .... 28 R 28
Quantock Hills .... 8 K 30
Quarff .... 87 Q 3
Quarr .... 10 Q 31
Quatt .... 27 M 26
Quedgeley .... 19 N 28
Queen Camel .... 8 M 30
Queen Elizabeth
    Forest Park .... 67 G 15
Queenborough .... 22 W 29
Queensbury .... 43 O 22
Queensferry .... 34 K 24
Quendon .... 30 U 28
Quenington .... 19 O 28
Quinag .... 84 E 9
Quines's Hill .... 46 G 21
Quinish Point .... 71 B 14

Quiraing .... 77 B 11
Quoich (Loch) .... 72 E 12
Quorndon .... 36 Q 25
Quothquan .... 61 J 17

R

Raasay (Island of) .... 77 B 11
Raasay (Sound of) .... 77 B 11
Raasay Ho .... 77 B 11
Rachub .... 33 H 24
Radcliffe .... 42 N 23
Radcliffe-on-Trent .... 36 Q 25
Radlett .... 21 T 28
Radley .... 20 Q 28
Radnor Forest .... 26 K 27
Radstock .... 18 M 30
Radyr .... 18 K 29
Rafford .... 80 J 11
Raglan .... 18 L 28
Ragley Hall .... 27 O 27
Rainford .... 42 L 23
Rainham .... 22 V 29
Rainworth .... 36 Q 24
Rait .... 68 K 14
Ramasaig .... 76 Z 11
Rampisham .... 8 M 31
Rampside .... 47 K 21
Rampton .... 44 R 24
Ramsbottom .... 42 N 23
Ramsbury .... 19 P 29
Ramsey Cambs. .... 29 T 26
Ramsey Isle of Man .... 46 G 21
Ramsey Bay .... 46 G 21
Ramsey Island .... 14 D 28
Ramsey St. Mary's .... 29 T 26
Ramsgate .... 23 Y 29
Ramsgill-in-Nidderdale .... 49 O 21
Ranby .... 44 Q 24
Rangeworthy .... 18 M 29
Ranish .... 82 A 9
Rankinston .... 60 G 17
Rannoch (Loch) .... 73 H 13
Rannoch Moor .... 73 F 14
Rannoch Sta. .... 73 G 13
Ranskill .... 44 Q 23
Ranton .... 35 N 25
Ranworth .... 39 Y 25
Rapness .... 87 L 6
Rappach .... 84 F 10
Ratby .... 36 Q 26
Rathen .... 81 O 11
Rathmell .... 49 N 21
Ratho .... 68 J 16
Ratlinghope .... 34 L 26
Rattlesden .... 30 W 27
Rattray .... 68 K 14
Rattray Head .... 81 O 11
Raunds .... 29 S 26
Ravenglass .... 47 J 20
Ravenscar .... 51 S 20
Ravensthorpe .... 28 Q 27
Ravenstone .... 36 P 25
Ravenstonedale .... 49 M 20
Ravensworth .... 49 O 20
Rawcliffe .... 44 R 22
Rawmarsh .... 44 P 23
Rawtenstall .... 42 N 22
Rayleigh .... 22 V 29
Rayne .... 30 V 28
Read .... 42 M 22
Reading .... 20 R 29
Rearsby .... 36 Q 25
Reay .... 85 I 8
Reay Forest .... 84 F 9
Red Wharf Bay .... 40 H 23
Redbourn .... 21 S 28
Redbourne .... 44 S 23
Redbridge
    London Borough .... 21 U 29
Redcar .... 57 Q 20
Redcliff Bay .... 18 L 29
Reddding .... 67 I 16
Redditch .... 27 O 27
Redesmouth .... 55 N 18
Redford .... 69 L 14
Redhill North Somerset .... 18 L 29
Redhill
    Reigate and Banstead .... 21 T 30
Redisham .... 31 Y 26
Redmarley d'Abitot .... 27 M 28
Redmarshall .... 57 P 20
Redmire .... 49 O 21
Redpoint .... 77 C 11

Redruth .... 2 E 33
Redwick .... 18 L 29
Reedham .... 39 Y 26
Reekie Linn .... 74 K 13
Reepham .... 45 S 24
Reeth .... 49 O 20
Regarby .... 46 G 20
Reiff .... 83 D 9
Reigate .... 21 T 30
Reighton .... 51 T 21
Reiss .... 86 K 8
Relubbus .... 2 D 33
Rempstone .... 36 Q 25
Rendcomb .... 19 O 28
Rendham .... 31 Y 27
Renfrew .... 60 G 16
Renish Point .... 76 Z 10
Renishaw .... 44 P 24
Rennington .... 63 O 17
Renton .... 66 G 16
Renwick .... 55 M 19
Repton .... 36 P 25
Rescobie .... 75 L 14
Resipole .... 72 C 13
Resolven .... 17 I 28
Resort (Loch) .... 82 Z 9
Restalrig .... 68 K 16
Reston .... 63 N 16
Restormel Castle .... 3 G 32
Retford .... 44 R 24
Rettendon .... 22 V 29
Reynoldston .... 15 H 29
Rhaeadr / Rhayader .... 25 J 27
Rhaeadr Ddu .... 33 I 25
Rhandirmwyn .... 25 I 27
Rhayader / Rhaeadr .... 25 J 27
Rheidol (Vale of) .... 25 I 26
Rhenigidale .... 82 Z 10
Rhian .... 84 G 9
Rhiconich .... 84 F 8
Rhigos .... 17 J 29
Rhilochan .... 85 H 9
Rhondda .... 17 J 29
Rhoose .... 17 J 29
Rhos .... 17 I 28
Rhoscolyn .... 40 G 23
Rhoscrowther .... 14 E 28
Rhosllanerchrugog .... 34 K 24
Rhosmaen .... 25 I 28
Rhosneigr .... 40 G 23
Rhossili .... 15 H 29
Rhostyllen .... 34 K 24
Rhosybol .... 40 G 22
Rhu .... 66 F 15
Rhuddlan .... 41 J 23
Rhum .... 71 A 13
Rhuthun / Ruthin .... 34 K 24
Rhyd-Ddu .... 33 H 24
Rhydaman /
    Ammanford .... 15 I 28
Rhydcymerau .... 15 H 27
Rhydd .... 27 N 27
Rhyddhywel .... 25 J 26
Rhydowen .... 15 H 27
Rhyl .... 41 J 23
Rhymmi / Rhymney .... 18 K 28
Rhymney / Rhymmi .... 18 K 28
Rhynie .... 80 L 12
Ribble (River) .... 49 N 21
Ribblesdale .... 49 N 21
Ribchester .... 42 M 22
Riber Castle .... 36 P 24
Riccall .... 44 Q 22
Riccarton .... 60 G 17
Richards Castle .... 26 L 27
Richborough .... 23 X 30
Richmond .... 49 O 20
Richmond-upon-Thames
    London Borough .... 21 T 29
Rickarton .... 75 N 13
Rickmansworth .... 21 S 29
Ridgeway Cross .... 27 M 27
Ridgeway Path (The) .... 20 P 29
Ridsdale .... 55 N 18
Rievaulx Abbey .... 50 Q 21
Rigg .... 77 B 11
Rigside .... 61 I 17
Rillington .... 51 R 21
Rimington .... 49 N 22
Rimsdale (Loch) .... 85 H 9
Ringford .... 53 H 19
Ringmer .... 11 U 31
Ringshall .... 30 W 27
Ringstead
    East Northamptonshire .... 29 S 26

A B C D E F G H I J K L M N O P Q R S T U V W X Y Z

Ringstead *King's Lynn and West Norfolk* .....38 V 25
Ringwood .....9 O 31
Ringwould .....23 Y 30
Rinnes (Glen) .....80 K 11
Rinns of Islay .....58 A 16
Rinns Point .....58 A 16
Ripe .....12 U 31
Ripley *Derbs.* .....36 P 24
Ripley *North Yorks.* .....50 P 21
Ripley *Surrey* .....21 S 30
Riplingham .....44 S 22
Ripon .....50 P 21
Rippingale .....37 S 25
Ripponden .....43 O 22
Risabus .....58 B 17
Risby .....30 V 27
Risca .....18 K 29
Risegate .....37 T 25
Riseley .....29 S 27
Rishton .....42 M 22
Risplith .....50 P 21
Ristol (Isle) .....83 D 9
Roadside of Kinneff .....75 N 13
Roag .....77 A 11
Roag (Loch) .....82 Z 9
Roan of Graigoch .....60 F 18
Roberton
  Dumfries and Galloway ....61 I 17
Roberton
  Scottish Borders .....62 L 17
Robertsbridge .....12 V 31
Robin Hood's Bay .....51 S 20
Roby .....42 L 23
Rocester .....35 O 25
Rochdale .....43 N 23
Roche .....3 F 32
Rochester .....22 V 29
Rochester
  Northumberland .....63 N 18
Rochford .....22 W 29
Rock .....3 F 32
Rockcliffe *Cumbria* .....54 K 19
Rockcliffe
  Dumfries and Galloway ....53 I 19
Rockfield .....18 L 28
Rockingham .....28 R 26
Rode .....19 N 30
Rode Heath .....35 N 24
Rodel .....76 Z 10
Rodmel .....11 U 31
Rodney Stoke .....18 L 30
Rogart .....85 H 9
Rogerstone .....18 K 29
Rogiet .....18 L 29
Rokeby Hall .....49 O 20
Rolleston *Notts.* .....36 R 24
Rolleston-on-Dove *Staffs.* ...35 P 25
Rolvenden .....12 V 30
Romannobridge .....61 J 16
Romiley .....43 N 23
Romney Marsh .....12 W 30
Romsey .....10 P 31
Romsley .....27 N 26
Rona (Island of) .....77 C 11
Ronaldsway .....46 G 21
Ronas Voe .....87 P 2
Ronay .....76 Y 11
Rookhope .....55 N 19
Roos .....45 T 22
Rootpark .....61 I 16
Ropley .....10 Q 30
Ropsley .....37 S 25
Rora .....81 O 11
Rora Head .....86 J 7
Rosedale Abbey .....50 R 20
Rosehearty .....81 N 10
Rosemarket .....16 F 28
Rosemarkie .....79 H 11
Rosewell .....61 K 16
Rosgill .....48 L 20
Roshven .....71 C 13
Rosley .....54 K 19
Roslin .....61 K 16
Rosliston .....35 P 25
Rosneath .....66 F 15
Ross
  Berwick-upon-Tweed ....63 O 17
Ross
  Dumfries and Galloway ....53 I 19
Ross of Mull .....64 B 15
Rossall Point .....48 K 22
Rossett .....34 L 24
Rosudgeon .....2 D 33
Rosyth .....68 J 15
Rothbury .....63 O 18

Rothbury Forest .....63 O 18
Rotherfield .....12 U 30
Rotherham .....43 P 23
Rothersthorpe .....28 R 27
Rothes .....80 K 11
Rothesay .....59 E 16
Rothienorman .....81 M 11
Rothiesholm .....87 M 6
Rothwell *Leeds.* .....43 P 22
Rothwell *Northamp.* .....28 R 26
Rotterspury .....28 R 27
Rottingdean .....11 T 31
Roughburn .....73 F 13
Roughsike .....55 L 18
Roughton .....39 X 25
Rounton .....50 P 20
Rousay .....86 K 6
Rousdon .....5 L 31
Routh .....45 S 22
Rowardennan Lodge .....66 G 15
Rowington .....27 O 27
Rowland's Castle .....10 R 31
Rowland's Gill .....56 O 19
Rownhams .....10 P 31
Rowsley .....35 P 24
Roxburgh .....62 M 17
Roxwell .....22 V 28
Roy (Glen) .....72 F 13
Royal Leamington Spa .....28 P 27
Royal Military Academy .....20 R 29
Royal Tunbridge Wells .....12 U 30
Roybridge .....72 F 13
Roydon *Essex* .....21 U 28
Roydon *Norfolk* .....31 X 26
Royston *Herts.* .....29 T 27
Royston *South Yorks.* .....43 P 23
Royton .....43 N 23
Ruabon .....34 K 25
Ruan High Lanes .....3 F 33
Ruan Minor .....2 E 34
Ruardean .....18 M 28
Rubbha na Faing .....58 A 16
Rubha a' Mhail .....64 B 16
Rubha Còigeach .....83 D 9
Rubha Dubh .....70 Z 14
Rubha Hunish .....77 A 10
Rubha na
  h-Easgainne .....71 B 12
Rubha Réidh .....77 C 10
Rubha Suisnish .....71 B 12
Rubh'an Dùnain .....71 A 12
Rubha na .....
Rudbaxton .....24 F 28
Ruddington .....36 Q 25
Rudgeway .....18 M 29
Rudgwick .....11 S 30
Rudha Ban .....70 Y 12
Rudston .....51 T 21
Rudyard .....35 N 24
Rufford Old Hall .....42 L 23
Rufforth .....50 Q 22
Rugby .....28 Q 26
Rugeley .....35 O 25
Rumburgh .....31 Y 26
Rumney .....18 K 29
Runcorn .....42 L 23
Runswick Bay .....50 R 20
Runtaleave .....74 K 13
Runwell .....22 V 29
Rushall .....19 O 30
Rushden .....29 S 27
Ruskington .....37 S 24
Rusland .....48 K 21
Rusper .....11 T 30
Ruspidge .....18 M 28
Rustington .....11 S 31
Ruswarp .....51 S 20
Rutherglen .....60 H 16
Ruthin / Rhuthun .....34 K 24
Ruthven *Aberdeenshire* .....80 L 11
Ruthven *Angus* .....74 K 14
Ruthven *Highland* .....79 I 11
Ruthven (Loch) .....79 H 12
Ruthven Barracks .....73 H 12
Ruthwell .....54 J 19
Rutland Water .....37 S 26
Ruyton
  of the Eleven Towns .....34 L 25
Ryal .....56 O 18
Ryan (Loch) .....52 E 19
Rycote .....20 Q 28
Rydal .....48 L 20
Ryde .....10 Q 31
Rye .....12 W 31
Ryhall .....37 S 25
Ryhill .....43 P 23
Ryhope .....57 P 19
Ryton .....56 O 19

S

Sabden .....42 M 22
Sacriston .....56 P 19
Sadberge .....50 P 20
Saddell .....59 D 17
Saddell Bay .....59 D 17
Sadgill .....48 L 20
Saffron Walden .....30 U 27
Saham Toney .....38 W 26
St. Abbs .....63 N 16
St. Abb's Head .....63 N 16
St. Agnes .....2 E 33
St. Albans .....21 T 28
St. Aldhelm's Head .....9 N 32
St. Andrews .....69 L 14
St. Ann's .....54 J 18
St. Ann's Head .....14 E 28
St. Arvans .....18 L 29
St. Asaph .....41 J 23
St. Athan .....17 J 29
St. Austell .....3 F 32
St. Bees .....47 J 20
St. Bees Head .....47 J 20
St. Blazey .....3 F 32
St. Boswells .....62 M 17
St. Breock .....3 F 32
St. Breward .....3 F 32
St. Briavels .....18 M 28
St. Brides .....14 E 28
St. Bride's Bay .....14 E 28
St. Brides Major .....17 J 29
St. Brides-Super-Ely .....17 K 29
St. Bride-Wentlooge .....18 K 29
St. Buryan .....2 D 33
St. Catherine's Point .....10 Q 32
St. Clears / Sanclêr .....15 G 28
St. Cleer .....3 G 32
St. Columb Major .....3 F 32
St. Combs .....81 O 11
St. Cyrus .....75 M 13
St. David's / Tyddewi .....14 E 28
St. David's Head .....14 D 28
St. Day .....2 E 33
St. Dennis .....3 F 32
St. Dogmaels .....15 F 27
St. Dominick .....3 H 32
St. Donats .....17 J 29
St. Endellion .....3 F 32
St. Erth .....2 D 33
St. Ewe .....3 F 33
St. Fagans .....18 K 29
St. Fergus .....81 O 11
St. Fillans .....67 H 14
St. Florence .....15 F 28
St. Gennys .....6 G 31
St. Germans .....3 H 32
St. Giles .....7 H 31
St. Giles-on-the-Heath .....6 H 31
St. Govan's Head .....16 F 29
St. Harmon .....25 J 26
St. Helen Auckland .....56 O 20
St. Helens *I.O.W.* .....10 Q 31
St. Helens *Merseyside* .....42 L 23
St. Helier *Jersey* 5
St. Ishmael's .....14 E 28
St. Issey .....3 F 32
St. Ive .....3 G 32
St. Ives *Cambs.* .....29 T 27
St. Ives *Cornwall* .....2 D 33
St. John's .....46 G 21
St. John's Chapel .....55 N 19
St. John's Loch .....86 J 8
St. Jude .....46 G 20
St. Just .....2 C 33
St. Just in Roseland .....2 F 33
St. Keverne .....2 E 33
St. Kew .....3 F 32
St. Leonards *Dorset* .....9 O 31
St. Leonards *East Sussex* ...12 V 31
St. Mabyn .....3 F 32
St. Magnus Bay .....87 P 2
St. Margaret's at Cliffe .....23 Y 30
St. Margaret's Bay .....23 Y 30
St. Margaret's Hope .....87 L 7
St. Mark's .....46 G 21
St. Martin's .....34 K 25
St. Mary in the Marsh .....12 W 30
St. Mary's *Orkney Islands* ..86 L 7
St. Mary's
  Perth and Kinross .....73 I 14
St. Mary's-Bay .....13 W 30
St. Mary's-Hoo .....22 V 29
St. Mary's Loch .....61 K 17
St. Mawes .....2 E 33
St. Mawgan .....3 F 32
St. Mellion .....3 H 32

St. Mellons .....18 K 29
St. Merryn .....3 F 32
St. Michael Penkevil .....2 E 33
St. Michael's Mount .....2 D 33
St. Michaels-on-Wyre .....42 L 22
St. Minver .....3 F 32
St. Monans .....69 L 15
St. Neot .....3 G 32
St. Neots .....29 T 27
St. Nicholas *Pembrokes* .....14 E 28
St. Nicholas
  Vale of Glamorgan .....17 K 29
St. Nicholas-at-Wade .....23 X 29
St. Ninian's Isle .....87 P 4
St. Osyth .....23 X 28
St. Patrick's Isle .....46 F 21
St. Paul's Walden .....29 T 28
St. Peter Port *Guernsey* 5
St. Peter's .....23 Y 29
St. Pool .....4 I 33
St. Stephen .....3 F 32
St. Teath .....3 F 32
St. Tudwal's Islands .....32 G 25
St. Tudy .....3 F 32
St. Vigeans .....69 M 14
St. Wenn .....3 F 32
St. Weonards .....26 L 28
Salcombe .....4 I 33
Salcombe Regis .....5 K 31
Sale .....42 N 23
Salehurst .....12 V 31
Salen *Argyll and Bute* .....65 C 14
Salen *Highland* .....71 C 13
Salford .....42 N 23
Salfords .....21 T 30
Salhouse .....39 Y 25
Saline .....68 J 15
Salisbury .....9 O 30
Salisbury Plain .....19 O 30
Sallachy
  Ben More Assynt .....84 G 9
Sallachy
  near Kyle of Lochalsh .....78 D 12
Saltash .....3 H 32
Saltburn .....79 H 10
Saltburn-by-the-Sea .....57 R 20
Saltcoats .....59 F 17
Salter .....48 M 21
Saltfleet .....45 U 23
Saltford .....18 M 29
Salthouse .....38 X 25
Saltney .....34 L 24
Salton .....50 R 21
Samala .....76 X 11
Samlesbury Old Hall .....42 M 22
Sampford Courtenay .....7 I 31
Sampford Peverell .....7 J 31
Sanaigmore .....58 A 16
Sancler / St. Clears .....15 G 28
Sancreed .....2 D 33
Sancton .....44 S 22
Sand Side .....47 K 21
Sanda Island .....59 D 18
Sanday *Highland* .....71 A 12
Sanday *Orkney Islands* .....87 M 6
Sandbach .....35 M 24
Sandbank .....66 F 16
Sandbanks .....9 O 31
Sandend .....80 L 10
Sandford *Eden* .....49 M 20
Sandford *Mid Devon* .....7 J 31
Sandford *North Somerset* ...18 L 30
Sandford
  South Lanarkshire .....60 H 17
Sandford Orcas .....8 M 31
Sandgate .....13 X 30
Sandgreen .....53 H 19
Sandhaven .....81 N 10
Sandhead .....52 F 19
Sandhurst *Berks.* .....20 R 29
Sandhurst *Kent* .....12 V 30
Sandleigh .....20 Q 28
Sandlins .....31 Y 27
Sandness .....87 P 3
Sandon
  North Hertfordshire .....29 T 28
Sandon *Stafford* .....35 N 25
Sandown .....10 Q 32
Sandray .....70 X 13
Sandridge .....21 T 28
Sandringham House .....38 V 25
Sandsend .....51 R 20
Sandwell .....27 O 26
Sandwich .....23 Y 30
Sandwick *Eden* .....48 L 20
Sandwick *Eilean Siar* .....76 Y 11
Sandwick *Shetland Islands* ..87 Q 4

Sandwood Loch .....84 E 8
Sandy .....29 T 27
Sandygate .....46 G 20
Sandyhills .....53 I 19
Sanna .....71 B 13
Sanquhar .....61 I 17
Santon Downham .....30 W 26
Santon Head .....46 G 21
Sapperton .....19 N 28
Saracen's Head .....37 T 25
Sarclet .....86 K 8
Sarisbury .....10 Q 31
Sark *Channel I.* 5
Sarn Meyllteyrn .....32 G 25
Sarre .....23 X 29
Satley .....56 O 19
Satterthwaite .....48 K 21
Sauchen .....75 M 12
Saughall .....42 L 24
Saughtree .....62 L 18
Saundersfoot .....15 F 28
Saunderton .....20 R 28
Sawbridgeworth .....21 U 28
Sawrey .....48 L 20
Sawston .....29 U 27
Sawtry .....29 T 26
Saxby .....36 R 25
Saxilby .....44 S 24
Saxlingham Nethergate .....39 X 26
Saxmundham .....31 Y 27
Saxtead Green .....31 X 27
Scadavay (Loch) .....76 Y 11
Scaddle (Glen) .....72 D 13
Scafell Pikes .....47 K 20
Scagglethorpe .....50 R 21
Scalasaig .....64 B 15
Scalby .....51 S 21
Scaleby .....55 L 19
Scalford .....36 R 25
Scalloway .....87 Q 3
Scalpay *Highland* .....77 C 12
Scalpay *Western Isles* .....77 A 10
Scambleby .....45 T 24
Scampton .....44 S 24
Scaniport .....79 H 11
Scapa Flow .....86 K 7
Scarba .....65 C 15
Scarborough .....51 S 21
Scarcliffe .....44 Q 24
Scardroy .....78 F 11
Scarfskerry .....86 K 8
Scarisbrick .....42 L 23
Scarista .....76 Y 10
Scarp .....82 Y 9
Scavaig (Loch) .....71 B 12
Scawby .....44 S 23
Schiehallion .....73 H 13
Scilly (Isles of) .....2 B 34
Scone Palace .....68 J 14
Scopwick .....37 S 24
Scoraig .....83 D 10
Scorton .....50 P 20
Scotby .....55 L 19
Scotch-Corner .....49 P 20
Scothern .....45 S 24
Scotlandwell .....68 K 15
Scotney .....12 V 30
Scotstown .....72 D 13
Scotter .....44 S 23
Scotton *Harrogate* .....50 P 21
Scotton *Richmondshire* .....49 O 20
Scottow .....39 Y 25
Scourie .....84 E 8
Scousburgh .....87 Q 4
Scrabster .....85 J 8
Scraptoft .....36 Q 26
Scredington .....37 S 25
Scridain (Loch) .....64 B 14
Scruton .....50 P 21
Sculthorpe .....38 W 25
Scunthorpe .....44 S 23
Sea Palling .....39 Y 25
Seaford .....12 U 31
Seaforth (Loch) .....82 Z 10
Seaforth Head .....82 A 9
Seagrave .....36 Q 25
Seaham .....57 P 19
Seahouses .....63 O 17
Seal .....22 U 30
Seale .....21 R 30
Sealga (Loch na) .....78 D 10
Seamer *Hambleton* .....50 Q 20
Seamer *Scarborough* .....51 S 21
Seamill .....59 F 16
Seasalter .....23 X 29
Seascale .....47 J 20
Seaton *Allerdale* .....53 J 20
Seaton *East Devon* .....5 K 31
Seaton Carew .....57 Q 20

Seaton Delaval .....56 P 18
Seaton Delaval Hall .....56 P 18
Seaton Ross .....44 R 22
Seaton Sluice .....56 P 18
Seave Green .....50 Q 20
Seaview .....10 Q 31
Sebergham .....54 L 19
Sedbergh .....49 M 21
Sedgebrook .....36 R 25
Sedgley .....27 N 26
Sedlescombe .....12 V 31
Seend .....19 N 29
Seething .....39 Y 26
Seighford .....35 N 25
Seil (Isle of) .....65 D 15
Seilich (Loch an t-) .....73 H 13
Selattyn .....34 K 25
Selborne .....10 R 30
Selby .....44 Q 22
Selker Bay .....47 J 21
Selkirk .....62 L 17
Sellindge .....13 W 30
Selmeston .....12 U 31
Selsey .....10 R 31
Selston .....36 Q 24
Selworthy .....17 J 30
Semley .....9 N 30
Senghenydd .....18 K 29
Sennen .....2 C 33
Sennybridge .....25 J 28
Sessay .....50 Q 21
Settle .....49 N 21
Seven Sisters
  East Sussex .....12 U 31
Seven Sisters
  Neath and Port Talbot .....17 I 28
Sevenhampton .....27 O 28
Sevenoaks .....22 U 30
Severn (River) .....27 M 28
Severn Bridge .....18 M 29
Severn Stoke .....27 N 27
Sgibacleit (Loch) .....82 A 9
Sgiwen .....17 I 29
Sgurr Mòr .....78 E 10
Shader .....82 A 8
Shaftesbury .....9 N 30
Shalbourne .....20 P 29
Shaldon .....4 J 32
Shalfleet .....10 P 31
Shalford .....21 S 30
Shandon .....66 F 15
Shanklin .....10 Q 32
Shap .....48 L 20
Shapinsay .....87 L 6
Shapwick .....8 L 30
Shardlow .....36 P 25
Sharlston .....43 P 23
Sharnbrook .....29 S 27
Sharnford .....28 Q 26
Sharperton .....63 N 18
Sharpness .....18 M 28
Shavington .....34 M 24
Shaw *Gtr. Mches.* .....43 N 23
Shaw *West Berkshire* .....20 Q 29
Shaw *Wilts.* .....19 N 29
Shawbost .....82 Z 9
Shawbury .....34 M 25
Shawford .....10 Q 30
Shawhead .....53 I 18
Shawell .....6 H 31
Shebbear .....6 H 31
Shebster .....85 I 8
Sheepwash .....6 H 31
Sheepy Magna .....36 P 26
Sheering .....22 U 28
Sheerness .....22 W 29
Sheffield .....43 P 23
Sheffield Park .....11 T 31
Shefford .....29 S 27
Sheldon .....19 N 29
Sheldon Manor .....19 N 29
Sheldwich .....22 W 30
Shell or Sealg (Loch) .....82 A 9
Shelley .....43 O 23
Shellingford .....20 P 29
Shelsley Beauchamp .....27 M 27
Shelton *Rushcliffe* .....36 R 25
Shelton *South Norfolk* .....31 X 26
Shelton Lock .....36 P 25
Shelve .....34 L 26
Shenley Church End .....28 R 27
Shenstone .....27 O 26
Shenval .....80 K 11
Shepley .....43 O 23
Sheppey (Isle of) .....22 W 29
Shepreth .....29 U 27
Shepshed .....36 Q 25
Shepton Mallet .....18 M 30

Sherborne *Cotswold* ....19 O 28
Sherborne *West Dorset* ....8 M 31
Sherborne St. John ....20 Q 30
Sherburn *Durham* ....56 P 19
Sherburn *Ryedale* ....51 S 21
Sherburn-in-Elmet ....44 Q 22
Shere ....21 S 30
Sherfield English ....9 P 31
Sheriff Hutton ....50 Q 21
Sheriffhales ....35 M 25
Sheringham ....39 X 25
Sherington ....28 R 27
Shernborne ....38 V 25
Sherston ....19 N 29
Sherwood Forest ....36 Q 24
Shetland Islands 87
Shevington ....42 L 23
Shiant (Sound of) ....82 A 10
Shiant Island ....82 A 10
Shiel (Glen) ....72 D 12
Shiel (Loch) ....72 D 13
Shieldaig *Loch Gairloch* ....78 C 10
Shieldaig *Loch Torridon* ....78 D 11
Shieldaig (Loch) ....78 C 11
Shieldhill ....67 I 16
Shifnal ....35 M 25
Shilbottle ....63 O 17
Shildon ....56 P 20
Shillay ....76 W 11
Shillingford ....7 J 30
Shillingstone ....9 N 31
Shillington ....29 S 28
Shilton *Rugby* ....28 P 26
Shilton *West Oxfordshire* ....19 P 28
Shimpling ....31 X 26
Shin (Loch) ....84 G 9
Shiney Row ....56 P 19
Shinfield ....20 R 29
Shipdham ....38 W 26
Shiplake ....20 R 29
Shipley *Salop* ....35 N 26
Shipley *West Yorks.* ....43 O 22
Shipston-on-Stour ....27 P 27
Shipton *Bridgnorth* ....26 M 26
Shipton *Cotswold* ....27 O 28
Shipton *Hambleton* ....50 Q 21
Shipton Moyne ....19 N 29
Shipton-under-Wychwood ....19 P 28
Shiptonthorpe ....44 R 22
Shira (Lochan) ....66 F 14
Shirebrook ....36 Q 24
Shiremoor ....56 P 18
Shirenewton ....18 L 29
Shirley *Derbyshire* ....35 O 25
Shirley *Solihull* ....27 O 26
Shoadoxhurst ....12 W 30
Shobdon ....26 L 27
Shoeburyness ....22 W 29
Shoreham ....11 T 31
Shorne ....22 V 29
Shotesham ....39 X 26
Shotley Bridge ....56 O 19
Shotley Gate ....31 X 28
Shottenden ....22 W 30
Shottermill ....10 R 30
Shotton Colliery ....57 P 19
Shotts ....61 I 16
Shouldham ....38 V 26
Shrewsbury ....34 L 25
Shrewton ....19 O 30
Shrivenham ....19 P 29
Shuna Sound ....65 D 15
Shurdington ....27 N 28
Shurrery ....85 J 8
Sibbertoft ....28 Q 26
Sibford Ferris ....28 P 27
Sible Hedingham ....30 V 28
Sibsey ....37 U 24
Sidbury ....5 K 31
Siddington ....19 O 28
Siddlington ....43 N 24
Sidford ....5 K 31
Sidinish ....76 Y 11
Sidlaw Hills ....68 K 14
Sidlesham ....10 R 31
Sidmouth ....5 K 31
Sighthill ....68 K 16
Sileby ....36 Q 25
Silecroft ....47 K 21
Silkstone ....43 P 23
Silloth ....54 J 19
Silsden ....49 O 22
Silver End ....30 V 28
Silverdale *Lancaster* ....48 L 21
Silverdale *Newcastle-under-Lyme* ....35 N 24
Silverstone ....28 Q 27

Silverstone Circuit ....28 Q 27
Silverton ....7 J 31
Simonburn ....55 N 18
Simonsbath ....7 I 30
Sinclair's Bay ....86 K 8
Sinclairston ....60 G 17
Singleton *Chichester* ....10 R 31
Singleton *Fylde* ....42 L 22
Sionascaig (Loch) ....84 E 9
Sissinghurst ....12 V 30
Sithney ....2 E 33
Sittingbourne ....22 W 29
Sixpenny Handley ....9 N 31
Skara Brae ....86 J 6
Skares ....60 H 17
Skeabost ....77 B 11
Skegness ....38 V 24
Skellingthorpe ....44 S 24
Skelmanthorpe ....43 P 23
Skelmersdale ....42 L 23
Skelmorlie ....59 F 16
Skelpick ....85 H 8
Skelton *Cleveland* ....50 R 20
Skelton *Cumbria* ....55 L 19
Skelwith Bridge ....48 K 20
Skene ....75 M 12
Skene (Loch of) ....75 M 12
Skenfrith ....26 L 28
Skeroblingarry ....59 D 17
Skerray ....85 H 8
Skervuile Lighthouse ....65 C 16
Skidby ....44 S 22
Skiddaw ....54 K 20
Skigersta ....83 B 8
Skilgate ....7 J 30
Skillington ....37 S 25
Skipsea ....51 T 22
Skipport (Loch) ....76 Y 12
Skipton ....49 N 22
Skipton-on-Swale ....50 P 21
Skipwith ....44 R 22
Skirlaugh ....45 T 22
Skirling ....61 J 17
Skirwith ....55 M 19
Skirza ....86 K 8
Skokholm Island ....14 E 28
Skomer Island ....14 E 28
Skye (Isle of) ....77 B 12
Slaggyford ....55 M 19
Slaidburn ....49 M 22
Slaithwaite ....43 O 23
Slamannan ....67 I 16
Slapin (Loch) ....71 B 12
Slapton ....4 J 33
Sleaford ....37 S 25
Sleagill ....48 M 20
Sleat (Sound of) ....71 C 12
Sledmere ....51 S 21
Sleekburn ....56 P 18
Sleights ....51 S 20
Slickly ....86 K 8
Sligachan ....77 B 12
Sligachan (Loch) ....77 B 12
Slimbridge ....19 M 28
Slindon ....11 S 31
Slingsby ....50 R 21
Slochd ....79 I 12
Slockavullin ....65 D 15
Slough ....21 S 29
Sloy (Loch) ....66 F 15
Slumbay ....78 D 11
Slyne ....48 L 21
Smailholm ....62 M 17
Smailholm Tower ....62 M 17
Small Dole ....11 T 31
Small Hythe ....12 W 30
Smallfield ....11 T 30
Smarden ....12 W 30
Smart'Hill ....12 U 30
Smedmore ....9 N 32
Smithfield ....55 L 19
Snaefell ....46 G 21
Snainton ....51 S 21
Snaith ....44 Q 22
Snape ....31 Y 27
Snetterton Circuit ....30 W 26
Snettisham ....38 V 25
Snitterfield ....27 O 27
Snizort (Loch) ....77 A 11
Snodland ....22 V 30
Snowdon / Yr Wyddfa ....33 H 24
Snowdonia National Park ....33 I 24
Snowshill ....27 O 27
Soa ....70 Z 14
Soa Island ....64 A 15

Soar (River) ....36 Q 25
Soay ....71 B 12
Soay Sound ....71 B 12
Soham ....30 V 26
Solent (The) ....10 Q 31
Solihull ....27 O 26
Sollas ....76 X 11
Solva ....14 E 28
Solway Firth ....53 J 19
Somerby ....36 R 25
Somercotes ....36 P 24
Somerford Keynes ....19 O 29
Somersham *Huntingdonshire* ....29 U 26
Somersham *Mid Suffolk* ....31 X 27
Somerton *Norfolk* ....39 Y 25
Somerton *Oxon.* ....28 Q 28
Somerton *Somerset* ....8 L 30
Sompting ....11 S 31
Sonning Common ....20 R 29
Sopley ....9 O 31
Sorbie ....52 G 19
Sorisdale ....71 A 13
Sorn ....60 H 17
Sortat ....86 K 8
Soulby ....49 M 20
Sound (The) ....4 H 32
Sourhope ....63 N 17
South-Alloa ....67 I 15
South Balloch ....60 G 18
South Brent ....4 I 32
South Cairn ....52 E 19
South Carrine ....59 C 18
South Cave ....44 S 22
South Cerney ....19 O 28
South Charlton ....63 O 17
South Croxton ....36 R 25
South Downs ....11 R 31
South Elmsall ....44 Q 23
South Esk (River) ....75 L 13
South Ferriby ....44 S 22
South Foreland ....23 Y 30
South Glendale ....70 Y 12
South Hanningfield ....22 V 29
South Harris ....76 Z 10
South Harris Forest ....82 Z 10
South Hayling ....10 R 31
South-Heighton ....11 U 31
South Hetton ....56 P 19
South Kelsey ....45 S 23
South Killingholme ....45 T 23
South Kirkby ....44 Q 23
South Kyme ....37 T 24
South Lancing ....11 T 31
South Leverton ....44 R 24
South Lopham ....30 X 26
South-Marston ....19 O 29
South Mary Bourne ....20 P 30
South Mimms ....21 T 28
South Molton ....7 I 30
South Morar ....72 C 13
South Moreton ....20 Q 29
South Newington ....28 P 28
South-Newton ....9 O 30
South Normanton ....36 P 24
South Ockendon ....22 U 29
South Otterington ....50 P 21
South Oxhey ....21 S 29
South Petherton ....8 L 31
South Petherwin ....3 G 32
South Queensferry ....68 J 16
South Rauceby ....37 S 25
South Raynham ....38 W 25
South Ronaldsay ....87 L 7
South Shields ....56 P 19
South Shore ....42 K 22
South Stack ....40 F 23
South Stainley ....50 P 21
South Tawton ....4 I 31
South Thoresby ....45 U 24
South Uist ....70 X 12
South Walls ....86 K 7
South Warnborough ....20 R 30
South Witham ....37 S 25
South Woodham Ferrers ....22 V 29
South Wootton ....38 V 25
South Wraxall ....19 N 29
South Zeal ....4 I 31
Southam *Stratford-on-Avon* ....28 P 27
Southam *Tewkesbury* ....27 N 28
Southampton ....10 P 31
Southborough ....12 U 30
Southbourne *Dorset* ....9 O 31
Southbourne *West Sussex* ....10 R 31
Southend ....59 D 18
Southend-on-Sea ....22 W 29

Southerness ....53 J 19
Southery ....38 V 26
Southill ....29 T 27
Southminster ....22 W 29
Southport ....42 K 23
Southsea ....10 Q 31
Southrop ....19 O 28
Southwaite ....55 L 19
Southwater ....11 S 30
Southwell ....36 R 24
Southwick *East Northamptonshire* ....29 S 26
Southwick *Sunderland* ....56 P 19
Southwick *West Sussex* ....11 T 31
Southwick *Wilts.* ....19 N 30
Southwick Widley ....10 Q 31
Southwold ....31 Z 27
Sowerby Bridge ....43 O 22
Spalding ....37 T 25
Spaldwick ....29 S 26
Spanish Head ....46 F 21
Sparkford ....8 M 30
Spaxton ....8 K 30
Spean (Glen) ....73 F 13
Spean Bridge ....72 F 13
Speeton ....51 T 21
Speldhurst ....12 U 30
Spelsbury ....28 P 28
Spelve (Loch) ....65 C 14
Spennymoor ....56 P 19
Spey (River) ....73 G 12
Spey Bay ....80 K 10
Speymouth Forest ....80 K 11
Spilsby ....37 U 24
Spinningdale ....79 H 10
Spital *Dumfries and Galloway* ....52 G 19
Spittal *Highland* ....85 J 8
Spittal *Northumb.* ....63 O 16
Spittal *Pembrokeshire / Sir Benfro* ....24 F 28
Spittal of Glenshee ....74 J 13
Spixworth ....39 X 25
Spofforth ....50 P 22
Spondon ....36 P 25
Spooner Row ....39 X 26
Spott ....69 M 16
Spreyton ....7 I 31
Spridlington ....44 S 23
Springfield ....68 K 15
Springholm ....53 I 18
Sproatley ....45 T 22
Sprotbrough ....44 Q 23
Sproughton ....31 X 27
Sprouston ....62 M 17
Sprowston ....39 X 26
Spurn Head ....45 U 23
Sronlairig Lodge ....73 G 12
Sronphadruig Lodge ....73 H 13
Stack (Loch) ....84 F 8
Stack Island ....70 Y 12
Stack Rocks ....16 E 29
Staffa ....64 A 14
Staffin Bay ....77 B 11
Stafford ....35 N 25
Stagsden ....29 S 27
Staincross ....43 P 23
Staindrop ....56 O 20
Staines-upon-Thames ....21 S 29
Stainforth *North Yorks.* ....49 N 21
Stainforth *South Yorks.* ....44 Q 23
Stainton ....55 L 20
Stainton-le-Vale ....45 T 23
Staintondale ....51 S 20
Stair *Allerdale* ....54 K 20
Stair *South Ayrshire* ....60 G 17
Staithes ....50 R 20
Stakeford ....56 P 18
Stalbridge ....9 M 31
Stalham ....39 Y 25
Stalisfield ....22 W 30
Stalling Busk ....49 N 21
Stallingborough ....45 T 23
Stalmine ....48 L 22
Stalybridge ....43 N 23
Stamford ....37 S 26
Stamford Bridge ....50 R 22
Stamfordham ....56 O 18
Stanbridge ....29 S 28
Standford-in-the-Vale ....20 P 29
Standing Stones ....82 Z 9
Standish ....42 M 23
Standlake ....20 P 28
Standon ....29 U 28
Stane ....61 I 16
Stanford ....13 X 30

Stanford-le-Hope ....22 V 29
Stanford-on-Avon ....28 Q 26
Stanghow ....50 R 20
Stanhoe ....38 W 25
Stanhope ....55 N 19
Stanion ....29 S 26
Stanley *Durham* ....56 O 19
Stanley *Perthshire and Kinross* ....68 J 14
Stanley *Wakefield.* ....43 P 22
Stanmer Park ....11 T 31
Stannington ....43 P 23
Stansted Abbotts ....21 U 28
Stansted Mountfitchet ....30 U 28
Stanton ....30 W 27
Stanton Harcourt ....20 P 28
Stanton Long ....26 M 26
Stanton-upon-Hine-Heath ....34 M 25
Stanway ....27 O 28
Stanwell ....21 S 29
Stanwick ....29 S 27
Staple Fitzpaine ....8 K 31
Stapleford *Melton* ....36 R 25
Stapleford *Notts.* ....36 Q 25
Stapleford *Wilts.* ....9 O 30
Staplehurst ....22 V 30
Starcross ....4 J 32
Start Point ....4 J 33
Startforth ....49 O 20
Stathern ....36 R 25
Staughton Highway ....29 S 27
Staunton *Forest of Dean* ....27 N 28
Staunton *Monmouthshire / Sir Fynwy* ....18 M 28
Staveley *Cumbria* ....48 L 20
Staveley *Derbs.* ....43 P 24
Staxigoe ....86 K 8
Staxton ....51 S 21
Staylittle ....25 J 26
Stean ....49 O 21
Stebbing ....30 V 28
Stedham ....10 R 31
Steel ....18 K 30
Steele ....30 V 28
Steeple ....22 W 28
Steeple Ashton ....19 N 30
Steeple Aston ....28 Q 28
Steeple Barton ....28 P 28
Steeple Bumpstead ....30 V 27
Steeple Claydon ....28 R 28
Steeple Langford ....9 O 30
Steeple Morden ....29 T 27
Steeton ....49 O 22
Stelling Minnis ....23 X 30
Stenhousemuir ....67 I 15
Stenness *Orkney Islands* ....86 K 7
Stenness *Shetland Islands* ....87 P 2
Stenton ....69 M 16
Steppingley ....29 S 27
Stevenage ....29 T 28
Stevenston ....60 F 17
Steventon ....20 Q 29
Stewartby ....29 S 27
Stewarton ....60 G 16
Stewkley ....28 R 28
Steyning ....11 T 31
Steynton ....16 E 28
Stichill ....62 M 17
Sticker ....3 F 33
Sticklepath ....4 I 31
Stickney ....37 U 24
Stiffkey ....38 W 25
Stilligarry ....76 X 12
Stillingfleet ....44 Q 22
Stillington *Hambleton* ....50 Q 21
Stillington *Stockton-on-Tees* ....56 P 20
Stilton ....29 T 26
Stirling ....67 I 15
Stithians ....2 E 33
Stob Choire Claurigh ....72 F 13
Stobo ....61 K 17
Stobs Castle ....62 L 17
Stock ....22 V 29
Stockbridge ....10 P 30
Stocke Talmage ....20 Q 28
Stockland ....8 K 31
Stockland Bristol ....18 K 30
Stockport ....43 N 23
Stocksbridge ....43 P 23
Stocksfield ....56 O 19
Stockton Heath ....42 M 23
Stockton-on-Tees ....50 P 20
Stockton-on-Teme ....27 M 27
Stockton on the Forest ....50 R 22
Stoer ....83 D 9
Stogumber ....7 K 30
Stogursey ....18 K 30

Stoke ....22 V 29
Stoke Albany ....28 R 26
Stoke Ash ....31 X 27
Stoke-by-Nayland ....30 W 28
Stoke Climsland ....3 H 32
Stoke Fleming ....4 J 33
Stoke Gabriel ....4 J 32
Stoke Goldington ....28 R 27
Stoke Hammond ....28 R 28
Stoke Lacy ....26 M 27
Stoke Lyne ....28 Q 28
Stoke Mandeville ....20 R 28
Stoke-on-Trent ....35 N 24
Stoke Orchard ....27 N 28
Stoke Poges ....21 S 29
Stoke-St. Mary ....8 K 31
Stoke-St. Michael ....18 M 30
Stoke St. Milborough ....26 M 26
Stoke sub Hamdon ....8 L 31
Stokeham ....44 R 24
Stokenchurch ....20 R 29
Stokenham ....4 I 33
Stokesay ....26 L 26
Stokesley ....50 Q 20
Stone *Bucks.* ....20 R 28
Stone *Staffs.* ....35 N 25
Stone Edge ....36 P 24
Stonehaugh ....55 N 18
Stonehaven ....75 N 13
Stonehenge ....9 O 30
Stonehouse *Glos.* ....19 N 28
Stonehouse *South Lanarkshire* ....61 I 16
Stoneleigh ....28 P 26
Stonesfield ....20 P 28
Stoney Cross ....9 P 31
Stoney Stanton ....36 Q 26
Stoneybridge ....76 X 12
Stoneykirk ....52 F 19
Stoneywood ....75 N 12
Stony Stratford ....28 R 27
Stornoway ....82 A 9
Storr (The) ....77 B 11
Storrington ....11 S 31
Stort (River) ....29 U 28
Stotfold ....29 T 27
Stottesdon ....26 M 26
Stoughton ....10 R 31
Stoul ....72 C 13
Stoulton ....27 N 27
Stour (River) *English Channel* ....9 N 31
Stour (River) *North Sea* ....30 V 27
Stour (River) *R. Severn* ....27 N 26
Stourbridge ....27 N 26
Stourhead House ....9 N 30
Stourport-on-Severn ....27 N 26
Stourton Caundle ....9 M 31
Stow ....62 L 16
Stow-on-the-Wold ....27 O 28
Stowbridge ....38 V 26
Stowe-by-Chartley ....35 O 25
Stowe School ....28 Q 27
Stowmarket ....30 W 27
Stowupland ....30 X 27
Straad ....59 E 16
Strachan ....75 M 12
Strachur ....66 E 15
Stradbroke ....31 X 27
Stradishall ....30 V 27
Stradsett ....38 V 26
Straiton ....60 G 18
Straloch ....74 J 13
Stranraer ....52 E 19
Strata Florida Abbey ....25 I 27
Stratfield Saye ....20 Q 29
Stratford St. Mary ....30 W 28
Stratford-upon-Avon ....27 O 27
Strath Brora ....85 H 9
Strath Dearn ....79 I 11
Strath Halladale ....85 I 8
Strath Isla ....80 K 11
Strath More ....78 E 10
Strath Mulzie ....78 F 10
Strath of Kildonan ....85 I 9
Strath Oykel ....84 F 10
Strath Skinsdale ....85 H 9
Strath Tay ....68 J 14
Strathallan ....67 I 15
Strathan ....72 E 13
Strathardle ....74 J 13
Strathaven ....60 H 16
Strathbeg (Loch of) ....81 O 11
Strathblane ....67 H 16
Strathbogie ....80 L 11
Strathbraan ....67 I 14
Strathcanaird ....84 E 10

A
B
C
D
E
F
G
H
I
J
K
L
M
N
O
P
Q
R
S
T
U
V
W
X
Y
Z

A B C D E F G H I J K L M N O P Q R S T U V W X Y Z

Strathcarron ....78 D 11
Strathcoil ....65 C 14
Strathconon ....78 F 11
Strathconon Forest ....78 F 11
Strathearn ....67 I 14
Stratherrick ....73 G 12
Strathkinness ....69 L 14
Strathmashie ....73 H 13
Strathmiglo ....68 K 15
Strathmore ....75 M 13
Strathnairn ....79 H 11
Strathnaver ....85 H 8
Strathpeffer ....79 G 11
Strathrannoch ....79 F 10
Strathspey ....80 J 11
Strathvaich Lodge .....78 F 10
Strathy ....85 I 8
Strathy Point ....85 H 8
Strathyre ....67 H 15
Stratton *Cornwall* ......6 G 31
Stratton *Glos.* ....19 O 28
Stratton *West Dorset* ...5 M 31
Stratton Audley ....28 Q 28
Stratton-on-the-Fosse ..18 M 30
Stratton-St. Margaret ...19 O 29
Streatley ....20 Q 29
Street ....8 L 30
Strensall ....50 Q 21
Stretford ....42 N 23
Stretham ....30 U 26
Stretton *Cheshire* ....42 M 23
Stretton *Staffs.* ....35 N 25
Stretton-on-Dunsmore ..28 P 26
Strichen ....81 N 11
Striven (Loch) ....66 E 16
Stroma (Island of) .....86 K 7
Stromeferry ....78 D 11
Stromemore ....78 D 11
Stromness ....86 K 7
Stronachlachar ....66 G 15
Stronchreggan ....72 E 13
Stronchrubie ....84 F 9
Strone ....66 F 16
Stronmilchan ....66 F 14
Stronsay ....87 M 6
Stronsay Firth ....87 L 6
Strontian ....72 D 13
Stroud ....19 N 28
Strumble Head ....14 E 27
Stuart Castel ....79 H 11
Stuartfield ....81 N 11
Stubbington ....10 Q 31
Studland ....9 O 32
Studley *Warw.* ....27 O 27
Studley *Wilts.* ....19 N 29
Studley Royal Gardens ..50 P 21
Stuley ....76 Y 12
Sturminster Marshall ....9 N 31
Sturminster Newton ....9 N 31
Sturry ....23 X 30
Sturton-le-Steeple .....44 R 23
Suainaval (Loch) ....82 Z 9
Sudbourne ....31 Y 27
Sudbury *Derbs.* ......35 O 25
Sudbury *Suffolk* ......30 W 27
Sudbury Hall ....35 O 25
Sudeley Castle ....27 O 28
Süil Ghorm ....71 A 13
Sulby ....46 G 21
Sulgrave ....28 Q 27
Sulhamstead ....20 Q 29
Sullom ....87 P 2
Sullom Voe ....87 P 2
Sully ....18 K 29
Sumburgh ....87 Q 4
Sumburgh Roost ....87 P 4
Summer Island ....83 D 9
Summerbridge ....49 O 21
Summercourt ....3 F 32
Sunart ....72 D 13
Sunart (Loch) ....71 C 13
Sunbury-on-Thames ...21 S 29
Sunderland ....57 P 19
Sunderland Bridge .....56 P 19
Sunk Island ....45 T 23
Sunningdale ....21 S 29
Sunninghill ....21 S 29
Surfleet ....37 T 25
Surlingham ....39 Y 26
Sutterton ....37 T 25
Sutton *Bassetlaw* ....44 R 23
Sutton *Cambs.* ....29 U 26
Sutton *Guildford* .....21 S 30
Sutton *London Borough* ..21 T 29
Sutton *Shrops.* ....34 M 25
Sutton Bank ....50 Q 21
Sutton Benger ....19 N 29

Sutton Bonington ......36 Q 25
Sutton Bridge ....37 U 25
Sutton Cheney ....36 P 26
Sutton Coldfield ....35 O 26
Sutton Courtenay ......20 Q 29
Sutton-in-Ashfield .....36 Q 24
Sutton-on-Hull ....45 T 22
Sutton-on-Sea ....45 U 24
Sutton-on-the-Forest ..50 Q 21
Sutton-on-the-Hill .....35 P 25
Sutton-on-Trent ....36 R 24
Sutton Scotney ....10 P 30
Sutton St. Edmund .....37 U 25
Sutton St. James ....37 U 25
Sutton-St. Nicholas ....26 L 27
Sutton
  under Whitestonecliffe ..50 Q 21
Sutton Valence ....22 V 30
Sutton Veny ....9 N 30
Swadlincote ....36 P 25
Swaffham ....38 W 26
Swaffham Bulbeck .....30 U 27
Swainby ....50 Q 20
Swainswick ....19 M 29
Swainshead ....19 M 29
Swalcliffe ....28 P 27
Swale (River) ....50 P 21
Swale (The) ....22 W 29
Swale Dale ....49 O 20
Swallow ....45 T 23
Swallow Falls ....33 I 24
Swallowcliffe ....9 N 30
Swallowfield ....20 R 29
Swanage ....9 O 32
Swanbridge ....18 K 29
Swanland ....44 S 22
Swanley ....22 U 29
Swannery ....5 M 32
Swanscombe ....22 U 29
Swansea / Abertawe ..17 I 29
Swanton Abbot ....39 Y 25
Swanton Morley ....38 W 25
Swanwick ....36 P 24
Swarbacks Minn ....87 P 2
Swavesey ....29 T 27
Sway ....9 P 31
Swaythling ....10 P 31
Swimbridge ....7 I 30
Swinbrook ....19 P 28
Swinderby ....36 R 24
Swindon *Cheltenham* ..27 N 28
Swindon *Swindon* ....19 O 29
Swinefleet ....44 R 22
Swineshead ....37 T 25
Swinford ....28 Q 26
Swinithwaite ....23 X 30
Swinton *Rotherham.* ..44 Q 23
Swynnerton ....35 N 25
Swyre ....5 M 31
Sydenham ....20 R 28
Syderstone ....38 W 25
Sydling St. Nicholas ....8 M 31
Sykehouse ....44 Q 23
Symbister ....87 Q 2
Symington *South Ayrshire* ..60 G 17
Symington
  South Lanarkshire ..61 J 17
Symonds Yat ....18 M 28
Symonds Yat Rock .....18 M 28
Symondsbury ....5 L 31
Syresham ....28 Q 27
Syston ....36 Q 25
Sywell ....28 R 27

T

Tackley ....28 Q 28
Tadcaster ....44 Q 22
Taddington ....43 O 24
Tadley ....20 Q 29
Tadmarton ....28 P 27
Tadworth ....21 T 30
Taff (River) ....18 K 29
Taibach ....17 I 29
Tain ....79 H 10
Takeley ....30 U 28
Tal-y-bont *Dyfed* ....25 I 26
Tal-y-Bont *Gwynedd* ..33 H 25
Tal-y-Cafn ....41 I 23
Tal-y-Llyn Lake ....33 I 25
Talacre ....41 K 22
Talaton ....7 K 31
Talgarreg ....15 H 27
Talgarth ....26 K 28
Talke ....35 N 24
Tall-y-llyn ....33 I 26
Talladale ....78 D 10
Tallaminnock ....60 G 18
Talley ....25 I 28

Talsarnau ....33 H 25
Talwrn ....40 H 23
Talybont-on-Usk *Powys* ..26 K 28
Talywern ....33 I 26
Tamanavay (Loch) ......82 Y 9
Tamar (River) ....6 G 31
Tamerton Foliot ....4 H 32
Tamworth ....35 O 26
Tan Hill ....49 N 20
Tan-y-pistill ....33 J 25
Tanera Beg ....83 D 9
Tanera Mór ....83 D 9
Tangley ....20 P 30
Tangmere ....11 R 31
Tannach ....86 K 8
Tannadice ....74 L 13
Tantallon Castle ....69 M 15
Taransay ....82 Y 10
Taransay (Sound of) ...82 Z 10
Tarbat Ness ....79 I 10
Tarbert *Argyll and Bute* ..59 D 16
Tarbert *Gigha Island* ..65 C 16
Tarbert *Western Isles* ..82 Z 10
Tarbert (Loch) ....65 C 16
Tarbet *Argyll and Bute* ..66 F 15
Tarbet *Highland* ....72 D 13
Tarbolton ....60 G 17
Tardy Gate ....42 L 22
Tarfside ....74 L 13
Tarland ....74 L 12
Tarleton ....42 L 22
Tarn (The) ....48 L 20
Tarporley ....34 M 24
Tarrant Gunville ....9 N 31
Tarrant Hinton ....9 N 31
Tarrant Keyneston ....9 N 31
Tarskavaig ....71 C 12
Tarskavaig Point ....71 B 12
Tarves ....81 N 11
Tarvin ....34 L 24
Tathwell ....45 T 24
Tattersett ....38 W 25
Tattershall ....37 T 24
Tatton Hall ....42 M 24
Taunton ....8 K 30
Taunton Deane ....7 K 30
Taverham ....39 X 25
Tavernspite ....15 G 28
Tavistock ....4 H 32
Taw (River) ....7 I 31
Tay (Firth of) ....68 K 14
Tay (Loch) ....67 H 14
Tay Road Bridge ....69 L 14
Taynton ....27 M 28
Taynuilt ....65 E 14
Tayport ....69 L 14
Tayvallich ....65 D 15
Teacuis (Loch) ....71 C 14
Tealby ....45 T 23
Teangue ....71 C 12
Tebay ....48 M 20
Tedburn St. Mary ....4 I 31
Teddington ....27 N 28
Tees (River) ....50 P 20
Teesdale ....55 N 20
Teifi (River) ....15 G 27
Teignmouth ....4 J 32
Telford ....34 M 25
Teme (River) ....27 M 27
Templand ....54 J 18
Temple ....61 K 16
Temple Ewell ....23 X 30
Temple Grafton ....27 O 27
Temple Sowerby ....55 M 20
Templeton ....15 F 28
Tempsford ....29 T 27
Tenbury Wells ....26 M 27
Tenby / Dinbych-y-pysgod ..15 F 28
Tendring ....31 X 28
Tenterden ....12 W 30
Terling ....22 V 28
Tern Hill ....34 M 25
Terrington St. Clement ..38 U 25
Test (River) ....20 P 30
Tetbury ....19 N 29
Tetford ....45 T 24
Tetney ....45 T 23
Tetsworth ....20 Q 28
Tettenhall ....35 N 26
Tewin ....21 T 28
Tewkesbury ....27 N 28
Texa ....58 B 17
Teynham ....22 W 30
Thakeham ....11 S 31
Thame ....20 R 28
Thame (River) ....20 R 28

Thames (River) ....20 Q 29
Thanet (Isle of) ....23 Y 29
Thankerton ....61 J 17
Thatcham ....20 Q 29
Thaxted ....30 V 28
Theale *Berks.* ....20 Q 29
Theale *Somerset* .....18 L 30
Theddlethorpe St. Helen ..45 U 23
Thetford ....30 W 26
Theviothead ....62 L 17
Theydon Bois ....21 U 28
Thirlestane ....62 L 16
Thirlspot ....48 K 20
Thirsk ....50 P 21
Thistleton ....37 S 25
Thixendale ....51 R 21
Thompson ....38 W 26
Thornbill ....80 K 11
Thoralby ....49 N 21
Thoresway ....45 T 23
Thorganby ....44 R 22
Thornaby-on-Tees ......50 Q 20
Thornborough ....28 R 28
Thornbury *Heref.* .....26 M 27
Thornbury *South Glos.* ..18 M 29
Thornbury *Torridge* ....6 H 31
Thornby ....28 Q 26
Thorncombe ....8 L 31
Thorne ....44 R 23
Thorner ....43 P 22
Thorney ....37 T 26
Thornford ....8 M 31
Thornham ....38 V 25
Thornhill
  Dumfries and Galloway ..61 I 18
Thornhill *Stirling* .....67 H 15
Thornton *Fife* ....68 K 15
Thornton *Lancs.* ......42 K 22
Thornton Curtis ....45 S 23
Thornton-in-Craven ....49 N 22
Thornton-le-Dale ....51 R 21
Thorntonloch ....69 M 16
Thornyhive Bay ....75 N 13
Thorpe *Derbs.* ....35 O 24
Thorpe *Essex* ....22 W 29
Thorpe-le-Soken ....31 X 28
Thorpe-on-the-Hill .....37 S 24
Thorpe Thewles ....57 P 20
Thorpeness ....31 Y 27
Thorrington ....31 X 28
Thorverton ....7 J 31
Thrapston ....29 S 26
Threapwood ....34 L 24
Three Cocks ....26 K 27
Three Crosses ....15 H 29
Threekingham ....37 S 25
Threlkeld ....54 K 20
Thringstone ....36 P 25
Throckley ....56 O 19
Thropton ....63 O 18
Throwleigh ....4 I 31
Thrumster ....86 K 8
Thruxton Circuit ....20 P 30
Thrybergn ....44 Q 23
Thundersley ....22 V 29
Thurcroft ....44 Q 23
Thurgarton ....36 R 24
Thurgoland ....43 P 23
Thurlby ....37 S 25
Thurlestone ....4 I 33
Thurlow ....30 V 27
Thurlton ....39 Y 26
Thurmaston ....36 Q 25
Thurne ....39 Y 25
Thurnham ....22 V 30
Thurnscoe ....44 Q 23
Thursby ....54 K 19
Thurso ....85 J 8
Thurstaston ....42 K 23
Thurston ....39 Y 26
Thwaite ....49 N 20
Tibbermore ....68 J 14
Tibberton *Glos.* ....27 M 28
Tibberton *Salop* ......34 M 25
Tibberton *Wychavon* ..27 N 27
Tibshelf ....36 P 24
Ticehurst ....12 V 30
Tickhill ....44 Q 23
Ticknall ....36 P 25
Tiddington ....20 Q 28
Tidenham ....18 M 29
Tideswell ....43 O 24
Tigerton ....75 L 13
Tigharry ....76 X 11
Tighnabruaich ....65 E 16
Tilbury ....22 V 29

Tillathrowie ....80 L 11
Tillicoultry ....67 I 15
Tillington ....11 S 31
Tilney St. Lawrence ...38 U 25
Tilshead ....19 O 30
Tilstock ....34 L 25
Tilton-on-the-Hill ......36 R 26
Timberscombe ....7 J 30
Timsbury ....18 M 30
Timsgarry ....82 Y 9
Timsgearraidh
  London Borough ....21 T 29
Tingewick ....28 Q 28
Tingwall (Loch) ....87 P 3
Tintagel ....6 F 32
Tintern Abbey ....18 L 28
Tintinhull ....8 L 31
Tintwistle ....43 O 23
Tinwald ....53 J 18
Tipton ....27 N 26
Tipton-St. john ....5 K 31
Tiptree ....22 W 28
Tirabad ....25 J 27
Tiree ....64 Z 14
Tirga Mór ....82 Z 10
Tirley ....27 N 28
Tiroran ....65 B 14
Tisbury ....9 N 30
Titchfield ....10 Q 31
Titchmarsh ....29 S 26
Tiumpan Head ....83 B 9
Tiverton *Chester* .....34 L 24
Tiverton *Mid Devon* ...7 J 31
Tobermory ....71 B 14
Toberonochy ....65 D 15
Tobson ....82 Z 9
Tockwith ....50 Q 22
Todber ....9 N 31
Toddington ....29 S 28
Todenham ....27 P 27
Todmorden ....43 N 22
Toe Head ....76 Y 10
Togston ....63 P 18
Tokavaig ....71 C 12
Toll of Birness ....81 O 11
Toller Porcorum ....8 M 31
Tollerton ....50 Q 21
Tollesbury ....22 W 28
Tolleshunt d'Arcy ......22 W 28
Tolpuddle ....9 N 31
Tolquhon Castle ....81 N 11
Tolsta ....83 B 8
Tolsta Chaolais ....82 Z 9
Tolsta Head ....83 B 8
Tomatin ....79 I 11
Tombreck ....79 H 11
Tomcrasky ....72 F 12
Tomdoun ....72 E 12
Tomich ....78 F 12
Tomintoul ....74 J 12
Tomnavoulin ....80 K 12
Tomsléibhe ....65 C 14
Tondu ....17 J 29
Tong ....82 A 9
Tongham ....20 R 30
Tongland ....53 H 19
Tongue ....84 G 8
Tongwynlais ....18 K 29
Tonna ....17 I 28
Tonypandy ....17 J 29
Tonyrefail ....17 J 29
Topcliffe ....50 P 21
Topsham ....4 J 31
Tor Ness ....86 K 7
Torbay ....4 J 32
Torcross ....4 J 33
Torksey ....44 R 24
Torlundy ....72 E 13
Tormarton ....19 N 29
Tornapress ....78 D 11
Tornaveen ....75 M 12
Torness ....79 G 12
Torphichen ....67 J 16
Torphins ....75 M 12
Torpoint ....3 H 32
Torquay ....4 J 32
Torquhan ....62 L 16
Torridon (Loch) ....77 C 11
Torrin ....71 B 12
Torrisdale Bay ....85 H 8
Torthorwald ....53 J 18
Tortworth ....19 M 29
Torver ....48 K 20
Toscaig ....77 C 11
Totaig *Loch Alsh* .....78 D 12
Totaig *Loch Dunvegan* ..77 A 11
Totland ....10 P 31

Totley ....43 P 24
Totnes ....4 I 32
Toton ....36 Q 25
Totscore ....77 A 11
Tottenhoe ....29 S 28
Totton ....10 P 31
Tournaig ....78 D 10
Tow Law ....56 O 19
Towcester ....28 R 27
Tower Hamlets
  London Borough ....21 T 29
Towie ....74 L 12
Town Yetholm ....62 N 17
Towneley Hall ....43 N 22
Townhead ....53 H 19
Townhead of Greenlaw ..53 I 19
Tradespark ....79 I 11
Trallwng / Welshpool ..34 K 26
Tranent ....69 L 16
Trapp ....25 I 28
Traquair House ....61 K 17
Trawden ....43 N 22
Trawsfynydd ....33 I 25
Trealaval (Loch) ....82 A 9
Trearddur Bay ....40 G 23
Trecastle ....25 J 28
Trecwn ....24 F 28
Tredington ....27 P 27
Treen ....2 D 33
Trefaldwyn / Montgomery ..34 K 26
Trefeglwys ....25 J 26
Treffynnon / Holywell ..41 K 23
Trefil ....18 K 28
Trefin ....24 E 28
Trefnant ....41 J 23
Trefonen ....34 K 25
Trefor ....40 G 23
Trefriw ....33 H 24
Trefyclawdd / Knighton ..26 K 26
Trefynwy / Monmouth ..18 L 28
Tregaron ....25 I 27
Tregony ....3 F 33
Tregurrian ....2 E 32
Tregynon ....33 J 26
Treharris ....18 K 29
Treherbert ....17 J 29
Treig (Loch) ....73 F 13
Trelawnyd ....41 J 23
Trelech ....15 G 28
Trelech a'r Betws ......15 G 28
Trelissick Gardens ......2 E 33
Trellech ....18 L 28
Tremadog ....33 H 25
Tremadog Bay ....32 H 25
Trenance ....2 E 32
Trengwainton Garden ...2 D 33
Trent ....8 M 31
Trent (River) ....36 R 24
Trentham ....35 N 25
Treorchy ....17 J 29
Trerice ....2 E 32
Treshnish Isles ....64 A 14
Treshnish Point ....71 A 14
Tressait ....73 I 13
Tretower ....26 K 28
Treuddyn ....34 K 24
Trevine ....14 E 28
Trevone ....3 F 32
Trevor ....32 G 25
Trevose Head ....2 E 32
Trewithen ....3 F 33
Trimdon ....56 P 19
Trimley Heath ....31 X 28
Trimsaran ....15 H 28
Tring ....21 S 28
Trispen ....2 E 33
Trochry ....67 J 14
Troedyrhiw ....17 J 28
Trollamarig (Loch) .....82 Z 10
Tromie (Glen) ....73 H 12
Troon ....60 G 17
Trossachs (The) ....67 G 15
Trotternish ....77 B 11
Troutbeck *Eden* ....54 L 20
Troutbeck *South Lakeland* ..48 L 20
Trowbridge ....19 N 30
Trudoxhill ....19 M 30
Truim (Glen) ....73 H 13
Trull ....8 K 31
Trumpington ....29 U 27
Trunch ....39 Y 25
Truro ....2 E 33
Trusthorpe ....45 U 24
Trwyn Cilan ....32 G 25
Tuath (Loch) ....64 B 14
Tuddenham *Forest Heath* ..30 V 27
Tuddenham
  Suffolk Coastal ....31 X 27
Tudhoe ....56 P 19

Tudweiliog ...... 32 G 25
Tugford ...... 26 M 26
Tulla (Loch) ...... 66 F 14
Tullibardine ...... 67 I 15
Tullibody ...... 67 I 15
Tullymurdoch ...... 74 K 14
Tumble ...... 15 H 28
Tummel (Loch) ...... 73 I 13
Tunstall
   East Riding of Yorkshire ...45 T 22
Tunstall *Staffs.* ...... 35 N 24
Tunstall *Suffolk* ...... 31 Y 27
Tur Langton ...... 36 R 26
Turnberry ...... 59 F 18
Turnditch ...... 35 P 24
Turret
   (Loch and Reservoir) ...67 I 14
Turriff ...... 81 M 11
Turvey ...... 29 S 27
Tusker Rock ...... 17 I 29
Tutbury ...... 35 O 25
Tuxford ...... 44 R 24
Twatt ...... 86 K 6
Tweed (River) ...... 61 J 17
Tweeddale ...... 61 J 17
Tweedmouth ...... 63 N 16
Tweedsmuir Hills ...... 61 J 17
Twemlow Green ...... 35 N 24
Twickenham ...... 21 S 29
Two Dales ...... 35 P 24
Twyford *Berks.* ...... 20 R 29
Twyford *Hants.* ...... 10 Q 30
Twyford *Leics.* ...... 36 R 25
Twynholm ...... 53 H 19
Twynllanan ...... 25 I 28
Tydd-St. Giles ...... 37 U 25
Tydd St. Mary ...... 37 U 25
Tyddewi / St. David's ...... 14 E 28
Tyldesley ...... 42 M 23
Tylorstown ...... 17 J 29
Tyne (River) ...... 56 P 19
Tynehead ...... 62 L 16
Tynemouth ...... 56 P 18
Tynewydd ...... 17 J 28
Tynron ...... 53 I 18
Tythegston ...... 17 J 29
Tytherington ...... 18 M 29
Tywardreath ...... 3 F 32
Tywi (River) ...... 25 I 27
Tywyn ...... 33 H 26

U

Ubiey ...... 18 L 30
Uckfield ...... 11 U 31
Uddingston ...... 60 H 16
Udimore ...... 12 V 31
Uffculme ...... 7 K 31
Uffington ...... 37 S 26
Ufford ...... 31 Y 27
Ugadale Bay ...... 59 D 17
Ugborough ...... 4 I 32
Ugbrooke House ...... 4 J 32
Ugthorpe ...... 50 R 20
Uig *Highland* ...... 77 A 11
Uig *Western Isles* ...... 82 Y 9
Uisg (Loch) ...... 65 C 14
Uiskevagh (Loch) ...... 76 Y 11
Ulbster ...... 86 K 8
Ulceby *East Lindsey* ...... 45 U 24
Ulceby *North Lincolnshire* ...45 T 23
Ulcombe ...... 22 V 30
Uldale ...... 54 K 19
Uley ...... 19 N 28
Ulgham ...... 56 P 18
Ullapool ...... 78 E 10
Ulleskelf ...... 44 Q 22
Ullesthorpe ...... 28 Q 26
Ullinish ...... 77 A 11
Ullock ...... 54 J 20
Ullswater ...... 48 L 20
Ulpha ...... 47 K 21
Ulsta ...... 87 Q 2
Ulva ...... 64 B 14
Ulverston ...... 48 K 21
Unapool ...... 84 E 9
Union Mills ...... 46 G 21
Unst ...... 87 R 1
Upavon ...... 19 O 30
Upchurch ...... 22 V 29
Uphall ...... 68 J 16
Uphill ...... 18 L 30
Upleadon ...... 27 M 28
Uplyme ...... 5 L 31
Upottery ...... 8 K 31
Upper Arley ...... 27 M 26
Upper Badcall ...... 84 E 9
Upper Beeding ...... 11 T 31

Upper Bighouse ...... 85 I 8
Upper Broughton ...... 36 R 25
Upper Chapel ...... 25 J 27
Upper Chute ...... 20 P 30
Upper Dicker ...... 12 U 31
Upper Hale ...... 20 R 30
Upper Heyford ...... 28 Q 28
Upper Hindhope ...... 62 M 17
Upper Knockando ...... 80 J 11
Upper Loch Torridon ...78 D 11
Upper Poppleton ...... 50 Q 22
Upper Sandaig ...... 72 D 12
Upper Tean ...... 35 O 25
Uppertown ...... 86 K 7
Uppingham ...... 36 R 26
Upton *Dorset* ...... 9 N 31
Upton *Notts.* ...... 36 R 24
Upton *Vale of White Horse* ..20 Q 29
Upton *Wakefield* ...... 44 Q 23
Upton *West Somerset* ...... 7 J 30
Upton Grey ...... 20 Q 30
Upton House ...... 28 P 27
Upton Magna ...... 34 M 25
Upton Noble ...... 9 M 30
Upton Scudamore ...... 19 N 30
Upton-upon-Severn ...... 27 N 27
Upwell ...... 38 U 26
Upwood ...... 29 T 26
Urchfont ...... 19 O 30
Ure (River) ...... 50 Q 21
Urigill (Loch) ...... 84 F 9
Urmston ...... 42 M 23
Urquhart ...... 80 K 11
Urquhart (Glen) ...... 79 G 11
Urquhart Castle ...... 79 G 12
Urrahag (Loch) ...... 82 A 8
Ushaw Moor ...... 56 P 19
Usk / Brynbuga ...... 18 L 28
Usk (River) ...... 18 K 28
Uttoxeter ...... 35 O 25
Uyea ...... 87 R 2
Uyeasound ...... 87 R 1

V

Vallay Strand ...... 76 X 11
Valle Crucis ...... 34 K 25
Valley ...... 40 G 23
Valtos ...... 82 Z 9
Vatersay ...... 70 X 13
Vatten ...... 77 A 11
Ve Skerries ...... 87 O 2
Venachar (Loch) ...... 67 H 15
Ventnor ...... 10 Q 32
Verham Dean ...... 20 P 30
Verulamium ...... 21 S 28
Verwood ...... 9 O 31
Veryan ...... 3 F 33
Veyatie (Loch) ...... 84 E 9
Vindolanda ...... 55 M 19
Voe ...... 87 Q 2
Voil (Loch) ...... 67 G 14
Vowchurch ...... 26 L 27
Vyrnwy (Lake) ...... 33 J 25

W

Waddesdon ...... 20 R 28
Waddingham ...... 44 S 23
Waddington *Lancs.* ...... 42 M 22
Waddington *Lincs.* ...... 37 S 24
Wadebridge ...... 3 F 32
Wadhurst ...... 12 U 30
Wag ...... 85 I 9
Wainfleet All Saints ...... 38 U 24
Wainstalls ...... 43 O 22
Wakefield ...... 43 P 22
Wakerley ...... 37 S 26
Wakes Colne ...... 30 W 28
Walberswick ...... 31 Y 27
Walcott ...... 37 T 24
Walden Head ...... 49 N 21
Walderslade ...... 22 V 29
Waldringfield ...... 31 X 27
Waldron ...... 12 U 31
Walesby ...... 44 R 24
Walford ...... 34 L 25
Walgherton ...... 34 M 24
Walgrave ...... 28 R 26
Walkden ...... 42 M 23
Walkeringham ...... 44 R 23
Walkern ...... 29 T 28
Wall ...... 35 O 26
Wallace Monument ...... 67 I 15
Wallasey ...... 42 K 23
Wallend ...... 22 W 29
Wallingford ...... 20 Q 29
Wallington House ...... 56 O 18
Walls ...... 87 P 3

Wallsend ...... 56 P 18
Wallyford ...... 69 K 16
Walney (Isle of) ...... 47 K 21
Walpole ...... 31 Y 27
Walpole St. Andrew ...... 38 U 25
Walpole St. Peter ...... 38 U 25
Walsall ...... 35 O 26
Walsden ...... 43 N 22
Walsham le Willows ...... 30 W 27
Walshford ...... 50 P 22
Walston ...... 61 J 16
Waltham *Kent* ...... 23 X 30
Waltham *North East Lincs.* ...45 T 23
Waltham Abbey ...... 21 U 28
Waltham Forest
   London Borough ...... 21 T 29
Waltham-on-the-Wolds ...36 R 25
Walton *Carlisle* ...... 55 L 19
Walton *Leeds* ...... 50 Q 22
Walton *Powys* ...... 26 K 27
Walton-East ...... 24 F 28
Walton-in-Gordano ...... 18 L 29
Walton-le-Dale ...... 42 M 22
Walton-on-Thames ...... 21 S 29
Walton-on-the-Naze ...... 31 X 28
Walton-Upon-Trent ...... 35 O 25
Walworth ...... 49 P 20
Wanborough ...... 19 O 29
Wandsworth
   London Borough ...... 21 T 29
Wangford ...... 31 Y 26
Wanlockhead ...... 61 I 17
Wansford
   East Riding of Yorkshire ...51 S 22
Wansford *Peterborough* ...37 S 26
Wanstrow ...... 9 M 30
Wantage ...... 20 P 29
Wappenham ...... 28 Q 27
Warboys ...... 29 T 26
Warbstow ...... 6 G 31
Warcop ...... 49 M 20
Wardington ...... 28 Q 27
Wardour Castle ...... 9 N 30
Ware ...... 21 T 28
Wareham ...... 9 N 31
Wargrave ...... 20 R 29
Wark *near Coldstream* ...63 N 17
Wark *near Hexham* ...... 55 N 18
Wark Forest ...... 55 M 18
Warkworth ...... 63 P 17
Warley ...... 27 O 26
Warlingham ...... 21 T 30
Warmington
   East Northamptonshire ...29 S 26
Warmington
   Stratford-on-Avon ...... 28 P 27
Warminster ...... 19 N 30
Warmsworth ...... 44 Q 23
Warmwell ...... 9 M 31
Warnborough ...... 20 R 30
Warnford ...... 10 Q 30
Warnham ...... 11 S 30
Warren ...... 43 N 24
Warren (The) ...... 13 X 30
Warrington ...... 42 M 23
Warsash ...... 10 Q 31
Warslow ...... 35 O 24
Warsop ...... 36 Q 24
Warter ...... 51 R 22
Warton *Alnwick* ...... 63 O 18
Warton *near Morecambe* ...48 L 21
Warton *near Preston* ...42 L 22
Warwick ...... 27 P 27
Warwick Bridge ...... 55 L 19
Wasbister ...... 86 K 6
Wasdale Head ...... 47 K 20
Wash (The) ...... 38 U 25
Washington
   Tyne and Wear ...... 56 P 19
Washington *West Sussex* ...11 S 31
Wast Water ...... 47 K 20
Watchet ...... 17 K 30
Watchfield ...... 19 P 29
Watchgate ...... 48 L 20
Water Orton ...... 27 O 26
Waterbeach ...... 30 U 27
Waterbeck ...... 54 K 18
Watergate Bay ...... 2 E 32
Waterhead ...... 74 L 13
Waterhouses ...... 35 O 24
Wateringbury ...... 22 V 30
Waterlooville ...... 10 Q 31
Waternish Point ...... 77 A 11
Waters Upton ...... 34 M 25
Waterside ...... 60 G 17
Waterstein ...... 76 Z 11
Watford *Daventry* ...28 Q 27

Watford *Watford* ...... 21 S 29
Wath ...... 50 P 21
Wath-upon-Dearne ...44 P 23
Watlington ...... 20 Q 29
Watten ...... 85 K 8
Watton *Breckland* ...38 W 26
Watton
   East Riding of Yorkshire ...51 S 22
Watton at Stone ...... 29 T 28
Waunfawr ...... 33 H 24
Waveney (River) ...... 31 Y 26
Waverton *Allerdale* ...54 K 19
Waverton *Chester* ...34 L 24
Wawne ...... 45 S 22
Wear (River) ...... 56 O 20
Weardale ...... 55 N 19
Weasenham St. Peter ...38 W 25
Weaver (River) ...... 34 M 24
Weaverthorpe ...... 51 S 21
Wedmore ...... 18 L 30
Wednesbury ...... 35 N 26
Wednesfield ...... 35 N 26
Weedon-Bec ...... 28 Q 27
Week St. Mary ...... 6 G 31
Weeley ...... 31 X 28
Weem ...... 73 I 14
Weeting ...... 30 V 26
Weeton ...... 42 L 22
Welborn ...... 50 R 21
Welby ...... 37 S 25
Welcombe ...... 6 G 31
Welford *Daventry* ...28 Q 26
Welford *Stratford-on-Avon* ...27 O 27
Welford *West Berkshire* ...20 P 29
Welham Green ...... 21 T 28
Well ...... 50 P 21
Welland ...... 27 N 27
Welland (River) ...... 37 T 25
Wellesbourne ...... 27 P 27
Wellingborough ...... 29 R 27
Wellington
   Herefordshire ...... 26 L 27
Wellington *Salop* ...34 M 25
Wellington *Somerset* ...8 K 31
Wellow
   Bath and North East ...19 M 30
Wellow
   Newark and Sherwood ...36 R 24
Wells ...... 18 M 30
Wells-next-the-Sea ...38 W 25
Wells of Ythan ...... 81 M 11
Welney ...... 38 U 26
Welsh Newton ...... 26 L 28
Welshampton ...... 34 L 25
Welshpool / Trallwng ...34 K 26
Welton *Allerdale* ...54 K 19
Welton *Daventry* ...28 Q 27
Welton *West Lindsey* ...44 S 24
Welton-le-Wold ...... 45 T 23
Welwyn ...... 21 T 28
Welwyn Garden City ...21 T 28
Wem ...... 34 L 25
Wembdon ...... 8 K 30
Wembley ...... 21 T 29
Wembury ...... 4 H 33
Wembworthy ...... 7 I 31
Wemyss Bay ...... 59 F 16
Wendens Ambo ...... 30 U 27
Wendlebury ...... 28 Q 28
Wendover ...... 20 R 28
Wendron ...... 2 E 33
Wenlock Edge ...... 26 L 26
Wennington ...... 48 M 21
Wensley ...... 49 O 21
Wensleydale ...... 49 O 21
Wentbridge ...... 44 Q 23
Wentnor ...... 26 L 26
Wentworth ...... 43 P 23
Wenvoe ...... 18 K 29
Weobley
   Hereford and Worcester ...26 L 27
Wereham ...... 38 V 26
Werrington ...... 6 G 32
West Alvington ...... 4 I 33
West Auckland ...... 56 O 20
West-Barns ...... 69 M 16
West Bay ...... 8 M 32
West Bergholt ...... 30 W 28
West-Bradenham ...38 W 26
West Bridgford ...... 36 Q 25
West Bromwich ...... 27 O 26
West-Buckland
   North Devon ...... 7 I 30
West-Buckland
   Taunton Deane ...8 K 31
West Butterwick ...44 R 23
West Calder ...... 61 J 16

West Camel ...... 8 M 30
West Charleton ...... 4 I 33
West Chevington ...... 63 P 18
West Chiltington ...... 11 S 31
West-Chinnock ...... 8 L 31
West Coker ...... 8 L 31
West Dean ...... 9 P 30
West-Dereham ...... 38 V 26
West Down ...... 7 H 30
West End ...... 10 Q 31
West Farleigh ...... 22 V 30
West-Felton ...... 34 L 25
West-Firle ...... 11 U 31
West Geirinish ...... 76 X 11
West-Grinstead ...... 11 T 31
West Hanningfield ...22 V 28
West Harptree ...... 18 M 30
West Heath ...... 20 R 30
West Heslerton ...... 51 S 21
West-Hill ...... 5 K 31
West Hoathly ...... 11 T 30
West-Huntspill ...... 18 L 30
West Kilbride ...... 59 F 16
West Kingsdown ...22 U 29
West Kirby ...... 41 K 22
West Langwell ...85 H 9
West Lavington ...19 O 30
West Linton ...... 61 J 16
West Loch Roag ...82 Z 9
West Loch Tarbert
   Argyll and Bute ...59 D 16
West Loch Tarbert
   Western Isles ...82 Z 10
West Looe ...... 3 G 32
West Lulworth ...... 9 N 32
West Lutton ...... 51 S 21
West Malling ...... 22 V 30
West Malvern ...... 27 M 27
West Meon ...... 10 Q 30
West Mersea ...22 W 28
West Moors ...... 9 O 31
West-Overton ...... 19 O 29
West Putford ...... 6 G 31
West-Quantoxhead ...8 K 30
West Rainton ...... 56 P 19
West Runton ...... 39 X 25
West-Stafford ...... 9 M 31
West Strathan ...84 G 8
West Tanfield ...... 50 P 21
West-Tarbert ...... 59 D 16
West Thorney ...... 10 R 31
West Town ...... 18 L 29
West-Tytherley ...... 9 P 30
West Walton ...... 37 U 25
West Wellow ...... 9 P 31
West Wickam ...... 21 T 29
West Winch ...... 38 V 25
West Wittering ...... 10 R 31
West Woodburn ...55 N 18
West Wycombe ...... 20 R 29
Westbourne ...... 10 R 31
Westbury *Cheshire* ...34 L 25
West Coomb ...... 61 K 17
Westbury *Wilts.* ...... 19 N 30
Westbury-on-Severn ...19 M 28
Westcliff ...... 22 W 29
Westcott ...... 21 S 30
Westenhanger ...... 13 X 30
Wester Ross ...... 78 D 11
Westerdale *Highland* ...85 J 8
Westerdale *Scarborough* ...50 R 20
Westerfield ...... 31 X 27
Westerleigh ...... 19 M 29
Western Cleddau ...24 E 28
Westfield *Highland* ...85 J 8
Westfield *Rother* ...12 V 31
Westfield *West Lothian* ...67 I 16
Westgate-on-Sea ...23 Y 29
Westham ...... 12 U 31
Westhoughton ...42 M 23
Westleton ...... 31 Y 27
Westleton ...... 11 T 31
Westmill ...... 29 T 28
Westnewton ...54 J 19
Weston *Devon* ...8 K 31
Weston
   North Hertfordshire ...29 T 28
Weston *South Holland* ...37 T 25
Weston
   South Northamptonshire ..28 Q 27
Weston *Staffs.* ...35 N 25
Weston-by-Welland ...28 R 26
Weston Favell ...... 28 R 27
Weston-on-the-Green ...28 Q 28
Weston-on-Trent ...36 P 25
Weston Rhyn ...... 34 K 25
Weston-super-Mare ...18 L 29

Weston Turville ...... 20 R 28
Weston-under-Lizard ...35 N 25
Weston-under-Penyard ...26 M 28
Westonbirt ...... 19 N 29
Westonzoyland ...... 8 L 30
Westray ...... 86 K 6
Westruther ...... 62 M 16
Westward ...... 54 K 19
Westward Ho ...... 6 H 30
Westwood ...... 19 N 30
Wetheral ...... 55 L 19
Wetherby ...... 50 P 22
Wetheringsett ...... 31 X 27
Wethersfield ...... 30 V 28
Wetwang ...... 51 S 21
Wey (River) ...... 10 R 30
Weybourne ...... 39 X 25
Weybridge ...... 21 S 29
Weyhill ...... 20 P 30
Weymouth ...... 8 M 32
Whaddon ...... 28 R 28
Whaley Bridge ...... 43 O 24
Whalley ...... 42 M 22
Whalsay ...... 87 R 2
Whalton ...... 56 O 18
Whaplode ...... 37 T 25
Whaplode Drove ...37 T 25
Wharfe (River) ...44 Q 22
Wharfedale ...... 49 O 22
Whatlington ...... 12 V 31
Whatsandwell ...... 36 P 24
Whauphill ...... 52 G 19
Whaw ...... 49 N 20
Wheathampstead ...21 T 28
Wheatley *Notts.* ...44 R 23
Wheatley *Oxon.* ...20 Q 28
Wheatley Hill ...56 P 19
Wheaton Aston ...35 N 25
Wheldrake ...... 50 R 22
Whepstead ...... 30 W 27
Whernside ...... 49 M 21
Wherwell ...... 10 P 30
Whickham ...... 56 O 19
Whimple ...... 7 J 31
Whipsnade ...... 21 S 28
Whissendine ...... 36 R 25
Whissonsett ...38 W 25
Whitburn *South Tyneside* ...57 P 19
Whitburn *West Lothian* ...61 I 16
Whitby ...... 51 S 20
Whitchurch
   Basingstoke and Deane ...20 P 30
Whitchurch
   Bath and N.E. Somerset ..18 M 29
Whitchurch *Bucks.* ...28 R 28
Whitchurch
   Caerdydd / Cardiff ...18 K 29
Whitchurch *Devon* ...4 H 32
Whitchurch
   Heref. and Worc. ...18 M 28
Whitchurch *Oxon.* ...20 Q 29
Whitchurch *Salop* ...34 L 25
White Coomb ...61 K 17
White Horse Hill ...20 P 29
White Scarcaves ...49 M 21
White Waltham ...20 R 29
Whitebridge ...... 73 G 12
Whitecairns ...... 75 N 12
Whitchurch Canonicorum ...5 L 31
Whitefield ...... 42 N 23
Whitehall ...... 87 M 6
Whitehaven ...... 47 J 20
Whitehill ...... 10 R 30
Whitehills ...... 81 M 10
Whitehouse
   Aberdeenshire ...75 M 12
Whitehouse
   Argyll and Bute ...59 D 16
Whitekirk ...... 69 M 15
Whiten Head ...... 84 G 8
Whiteness Sands ...79 I 10
Whiteparish ...... 9 P 30
Whiterashes ...... 81 N 12
Whitermire ...... 79 I 11
Whitesand Bay *Cornwall* ...2 C 33
Whitesand Bay
   Pembrokes ...14 E 28
Whiteshill ...... 19 N 28
Whiteside ...... 55 M 18
Whitewell ...... 49 M 22
Whitewreath ...... 80 K 11
Whitfield *Dover* ...23 X 30
Whitfield
   South Northamptonshire ...28 Q 27
Whitfield *Tynedale* ...55 M 19
Whitgift ...... 44 R 22
Whithorn ...... 52 G 19

A B C D E F G H I J K L M N O P Q R S T U V W X Y Z

A

Aasleagh ....105 D 7
Abbert ....106 F 7
Abbey ....100 G 8
Abbeydorney ....93 C 10
Abbeyfeale ....93 E 10
Abbeylara ....107 J 6
Abbeyleix /
    Mainistir Laoise ....101 J 9
Abbeyshrule ....107 J 7
Abington ....94 G 10
Achill ....104 C 6
Achill Head ....110 B 6
Achill Island ....104 B 6
Achill Sound ....104 C 6
Achillbeg Island ....104 C 6
Achonry ....112 G 5
Aclare ....112 F 5
Acoose (Lough) ....89 C 11
Adamstown ....96 L 10
Adare ....94 F 10
Adrigole ....89 C 12
Aghaboe ....101 J 9
Aghabullogue ....90 F 12
Aghada ....90 H 12
Aghadiffin ....106 F 6
Aghadoe ....89 D 11
Aghadoon ....110 B 5
Aghadowey ....118 M 2
Aghagallon ....114 N 4
Aghagower ....105 D 6
Aghalane ....113 J 5
Aghalee ....114 N 4
Aghamore *Leitrim* ....107 I 6
Aghamore *Mayo* ....105 F 6
Aghamuck ....106 H 6
Aghavannagh ....103 M 9
Aghavas ....107 I 6
Aghaville ....89 D 13
Aghinlig ....114 M 4
Aghla Mountain ....116 H 3
Aghleam ....110 B 5
Aghnablaney ....113 I 4
Aghnacliff ....107 J 6
Aghnamullen ....108 L 5
Aghowle ....96 M 9
Agivey ....118 M 2
Aglish *Tipperary* ....100 H 8
Aglish *Waterford* ....91 I 11
Agnew's Hill ....115 O 3
Ahakista ....89 D 13
Ahalia (Loughs) ....105 D 7
Ahascragh ....106 G 7
Ahenny ....95 J 10
Aherla ....90 F 12
Aherlow ....94 H 10
Aherlow (Glen of) ....95 H 10
Ahoghill ....118 M 3
Aillwee Cave ....99 E 8
Ailt an Chorráin /
    Burtonport ....116 G 3
Aird Mhór / Ardmore ....91 I 12
Akeragh Lough ....93 C 10
Aldergrove ....115 N 4
Allaghaun ....93 E 10
Allen ....102 L 8
Allen (Bog of) ....102 K 8
Allen (Lough) ....112 H 5
Allenwood ....102 L 8
Allihies ....88 B 13
Allistragh ....114 L 4
Alloon Lower ....106 G 7
Allow ....94 F 11
Allua (Lough) ....89 E 12
Altagowlan ....112 H 5
Altan Lough ....117 H 2
Altnamackan ....114 M 5
Altnapaste ....117 I 3
An Blascaod Mór /
    Blasket Islands ....92 A 11
An Bun Beag / Bunbeg ....116 H 2
An Caisleán Nua /
    Newcastle West ....93 E 10
An Caisleán Riabhach /
    Castlerea ....106 G 6
An Chathair / Caher ....95 I 10
An Cheathrú Rua /
    Carraroe ....98 C 8
An Chloich Mhóir /
    Cloghmore ....104 C 6
An Clochán / Clifden ....104 B 7
An Clochán / Cloghan
    Donegal ....117 I 3
An Clochán Liath /
    Dungloe ....116 G 3
An Cloigeann / Cleegan ....104 B 7

An Cóbh / Cobh ....90 H 12
An Coimín / Commeen ....117 I 3
An Coireán / Waterville ....88 B 12
An Corrán / Currane ....104 C 6
An Creagán /
    Mount Bellew ....106 G 7
An Daingean / Dingle ....92 B 11
An Dúchoraidh /
    Doocharry ....116 H 3
An Fhairche / Clonbur ....105 D 7
An Fál Carrach /
    Falcarragh ....117 H 2
An Gleann Garbh /
    Glengarriff ....89 C 12
An Gort / Gort ....99 F 8
An Gort Mór / Gortmore ....105 D 7
An Leacht / Lahinch ....99 D 9
An Longfort / Longford ....107 I 6
An Mám / Maam Cross ....105 D 7
An Mhala Raithní /
    Mulrany ....104 C 6
An Móta / Moate ....101 I 7
An Muileann gCearr /
    Mullingar ....107 J 7
An Nás / Naas ....102 M 8
An Ráth / Charleville ....94 F 10
An Ros / Rush ....109 N 7
An Sciobairín / Skibbereen ....89 E 13
An Seanchaisleán /
    Oldcastle ....108 K 6
An Spidéal / Spiddal ....99 E 8
An tAonach / Nenagh ....100 H 9
An Teampall Mór /
    Templemore ....101 I 9
An Tearmann / Termon ....117 I 2
An tInbhear Mór / Arklow ......97 N 9
An Tulach / Tullow ....102 L 9
An Uaimh / Navan ....108 L 7
Anascaul ....92 B 11
Anayalla ....114 L 5
Anglesborough ....94 H 10
Anglesey Bridge ....95 H 11
Annacarriga ....99 G 9
Annacarty ....95 H 10
Annaclone ....115 N 5
Annacloy ....115 O 4
Annacotty ....94 G 9
Annadorn ....115 O 5
Annagary ....116 H 2
Annagassan ....109 M 6
Annageeragh (River) ....98 D 9
Annagh Head ....110 B 5
Annagh Island ....110 C 6
Annaghdown ....105 E 7
Annaghmore Lough ....106 H 6
Annahilt ....115 N 4
Annalee ....107 J 5
Annalong ....109 O 5
Annamoe ....103 N 8
Annes Grove Gardens ....94 G 11
Annestown ....91 K 11
Annfield ....95 I 9
Annie Brady Bridge ....111 C 5
Annsborough ....115 O 5
Antrim ....115 N 3
Antrim (Glens of) ....119 N 2
Antrim Coast ....119 O 2
Antrim Mountains ....119 N 2
Anure (Lough) ....116 H 3
Araglin ....95 H 11
Árainn Mhór /
    Aran or Aranmore Island ...116 G 2
Aran Islands /
    Oileáin Árainn ....98 C 8
Archdale (Castle) ....113 I 4
Archerstown ....108 K 7
Ard ....104 C 8
Ardagh *Donegal* ....117 J 3
Ardagh *Limerick* ....93 E 10
Ardan ....101 J 8
Ardanairy ....103 N 9
Ardanew ....108 L 7
Ardara ....116 G 3
Ardattin ....96 L 9
Ardboe ....114 M 4
Ardcath ....109 M 7
Ardcloon ....105 F 7
Ardcrony ....100 H 9
Ardea ....89 C 12
Arderin ....101 J 8
Ardfert ....93 C 10
Ardfield ....89 F 13
Ardfinnan ....95 I 11
Ardgehane ....90 F 13
Ardglass ....115 P 5
Ardglass ....90 H 12

Ardgroom ....88 C 12
Ardgroom Harbour ....88 C 12
Ardkeen ....115 P 4
Ardlea ....101 J 9
Ardlougher ....107 J 5
Ardmillan ....115 O 4
Ardmoney ....113 J 5
Ardmore *Derry* ....117 K 3
Ardmore *Galway* ....104 C 8
Ardmore Point *Antrim* ....114 N 4
Ardmore Point *Craigavon* .....114 M 4
Ardmore Point
    Dunganstown East ....103 N 9
Ardmorney ....101 J 7
Ardmoy ....106 G 6
Ardnagreevagh ....104 B 7
Ardnasodan ....105 F 7
Ardpatrick ....94 G 10
Ardrahan ....99 F 8
Ardress House ....118 M 2
Ards Forest Park ....117 I 2
Ards Peninsula ....115 P 4
Ardscull ....102 L 8
Ardshankill ....113 I 4
Ardstraw ....113 J 3
Argideen ....89 F 13
Argory (The) ....114 M 4
Arigna ....112 H 5
Arinagh ....112 F 5
Arless ....102 K 9
Armagh ....114 M 4
Armaghbrague ....114 M 5
Armoy ....118 N 2
Arney ....113 I 5
Arra Mountains ....100 G 9
Arrow (Lough) ....106 H 5
Arryheernabin ....117 J 2
Artane ....103 N 7
Arthurstown ....96 L 11
Articlave ....118 L 2
Artigarvan ....117 J 3
Arvagh ....107 J 6
Asdee ....93 D 10
Ashbourne ....109 M 7
Ashford *Gleneely* ....103 N 8
Ashford *Limerick* ....93 E 10
Ashford Castle ....105 E 7
Ashleam Bay ....104 B 6
Ashton ....90 F 12
Askamore ....97 M 9
Askanagap ....103 M 9
Askeaton ....94 F 10
Askill ....112 H 4
Atedaun (Lough) ....99 E 9
Áth Cinn / Headford ....105 E 7
Athassel Abbey ....95 I 10
Athboy ....108 L 7
Athea ....93 E 10
Athgarvan ....102 L 8
Athlacca ....94 G 10
Athleague ....106 H 7
Athnid ....95 I 9
Athy / Baile Átha Í ....102 L 9
Atlantic Drive (The) ....104 C 6
Atorick (Lough) ....99 G 8
Attanagh ....101 J 9
Attavally ....111 C 5
Attical ....109 N 5
Attymass ....111 E 5
Attymon ....99 G 8
Aucloggen ....105 F 7
Audley's Castle ....115 P 4
Aughacasla ....92 C 11
Aughagault ....117 I 3
Aughamullan ....114 M 4
Augher ....114 K 4
Aughils ....92 C 11
Aughinish ....99 E 8
Aughinish Island ....93 E 10
Aughkeely ....117 I 3
Aughnacleagh ....118 M 3
Aughnacloy ....114 L 4
Aughnanure Castle ....105 E 7
Aughnasheelan ....107 I 5
Aughrim *Galway* ....100 H 8
Aughrim *Wicklow* ....103 N 9
Aughris ....112 F 5
Aughris Head ....112 F 5
Aughrus More ....104 B 7
Avoca ....103 N 9
Avoca (River) ....103 N 9
Avoca (Vale of) ....103 N 9
Avonbeg ....103 M 9
Avonmore (River) ....103 N 9
Awbeg ....94 G 11

B

Baginbun Head ....96 L 11
Baile an Fheirtéaraigh /
    Ballyferriter ....92 A 11
Baile an Mhóta /
    Ballymote ....112 G 5
Baile an Róba /
    Ballinrobe ....105 E 7
Baile an Sceilg /
    Ballinskelligs ....88 B 12
Baile Átha an Rí / Athenry ....99 F 8
Baile Átha Cliath / Dublin ....103 N 8
Baile Átha Fhirdhia / Ardee ...108 M 6
Baile Átha Luain / Athlone ....107 I 7
Baile Átha Troim / Trim ....108 L 7
Baile Brigín / Balbriggan .....109 N 7
Baile Chláir / Claregalway ....99 F 7
Baile Locha Riach /
    Loughrea ....99 G 8
Baile Mhic Andáin /
    Thomastown ....96 K 10
Baile Mhistéala /
    Mitchelstown ....94 H 11
Baile na Finne / Fintown ......117 H 3
Baile na Lorgan /
    Castleblayney ....108 L 5
Baile Uí Fhiacháin /
    Newport ....105 D 6
Baile Uí Mhatháin /
    Ballymahon ....107 I 7
Baileysmill ....115 O 4
Baldoyle ....103 N 7
Balla ....105 E 6
Ballaba ....99 F 8
Ballagan Point ....109 N 5
Ballagh *Fermanagh* ....113 I 5
Ballagh *Galway* ....106 F 7
Ballagh *Limerick* ....93 E 10
Ballagh *near Curraghroe* .....107 H 6
Ballagh *near Nahara* ....106 H 7
Ballagh *Tipperary* ....95 I 10
Ballagh (Neck of the) ....112 G 3
Ballaghaderreen /
    Bealach an Doirín ....106 G 6
Ballaghbeama Gap ....89 C 12
Ballaghbehy ....93 E 10
Ballaghisheen Pass ....88 C 12
Ballaghkeen ....97 M 10
Ballaghmore ....101 I 9
Ballaghnatrillick ....112 G 4
Ballard ....97 M 9
Ballardiggan ....99 F 8
Balleen ....101 J 9
Ballickmoyler ....102 K 9
Balliggan ....115 P 4
Ballina ....99 G 9
Ballina / Béal an Átha ....111 E 5
Ballinaboy ....104 B 7
Ballinabrackey ....102 K 7
Ballinabranagh ....102 L 9
Ballinaclash ....103 N 9
Ballinacor ....103 N 9
Ballinadee ....90 G 12
Ballinafad *Aghanagh* ....106 G 5
Ballinafad *Galway* ....104 C 7
Ballinagar ....101 J 8
Ballinageragh ....93 D 10
Ballinakill ....101 K 9
Ballinalack ....107 J 7
Ballinalea ....103 N 8
Ballinalee ....107 J 6
Ballinamallard ....113 J 4
Ballinamara ....95 J 9
Ballinameen ....106 H 6
Ballinamore Bridge ....106 G 7
Ballinamuck ....107 I 6
Ballinascarty ....90 F 12
Ballinaspick ....91 I 11
Ballinclashet ....90 G 12
Ballinclea ....103 M 9
Ballincloher ....93 C 10
Ballincollig ....90 G 12
Ballincrea ....96 K 11
Ballincurrig ....90 H 12
Ballindaggan ....96 L 10
Ballindarragh ....113 J 5
Ballinderreen ....99 F 8
Ballinderry *Cookstown* ....114 M 4
Ballinderry *Terryglass* ......100 H 8
Ballinderry *Wicklow* ....103 N 9
Ballinderry Bridge ....114 M 4
Ballindine ....105 F 7
Ballindrait ....117 J 3
Ballineanig ....92 A 11
Ballineen ....89 F 12
Ballingarrane ....94 F 10

Ballingarry *Galway* ....100 H 8
Ballingarry *Limerick* ....94 F 10
Ballingarry *Tipperary* ....95 J 10
Ballingeary / Béal Átha
    an Ghaorthaidh ....89 E 12
Ballingurteen ....89 E 12
Ballinhassig ....90 G 12
Ballinkillin ....96 L 10
Ballinlea ....118 M 2
Ballinleeny ....94 F 10
Ballinloghig ....92 B 11
Ballinlough *Meath* ....108 K 6
Ballinlough *Roscommon* ....106 G 6
Ballinluska ....90 H 12
Ballinruan ....99 F 9
Ballinskelligs Bay ....88 B 12
Ballinspittle ....90 G 12
Ballintober ....106 G 6
Ballintogher ....112 G 5
Ballintotty ....100 H 9
Ballintoy ....118 M 2
Ballintra *Donegal* ....112 H 4
Ballintra *near Leabgarrow* ...116 G 3
Ballintubber ....105 E 6
Ballintubber ....105 E 6
Ballinunty ....95 I 10
Ballinure (River) ....100 H 8
Ballinvarry ....96 L 10
Ballitore ....102 L 8
Ballivor ....108 L 7
Ballon ....96 L 9
Balloo Cross Roads ....115 O 4
Balloor ....112 G 4
Ballough ....97 M 10
Ballure ....112 H 4
Ballvengland ....94 F 10
Ballyagran ....94 F 10
Ballyallinan ....94 F 10
Ballyalton ....115 P 5
Ballybannon ....102 L 9
Ballybay
    near Carrickmacross .....108 L 5
Ballybay
    near Castleblayney ......108 L 5
Ballybeg ....95 I 11
Ballyboghil ....109 N 7
Ballybogy ....118 M 2
Ballyboy ....101 I 8
Ballybrack *Dublin* ....103 N 8
Ballybrack *Kerry* ....88 B 12
Ballybrittas ....101 K 8
Ballybrommel ....96 L 9
Ballybrood ....94 G 10
Ballybrophy ....101 J 9
Ballybryan ....101 K 7
Ballybunnion ....93 D 10
Ballycahill ....95 I 9
Ballycallan ....95 J 10
Ballycanew ....97 N 10
Ballycarney ....97 M 10
Ballycarry ....115 O 3
Ballycastle *Mayo* ....111 D 5
Ballycastle *Moyle* ....119 N 2
Ballycastle Bay ....119 N 2
Ballyclare *Newtonabbey* ......115 N 3
Ballyclare *Roscommon* ....107 I 6
Ballyclerahan ....95 I 10
Ballyclery ....99 F 8
Ballyclogh ....94 F 11
Ballycolla ....101 J 9
Ballycommon ....100 H 9
Ballyconneely ....104 B 7
Ballyconneely Bay ....104 B 7
Ballyconnell *Cavan* ....113 J 5
Ballyconnell *Sligo* ....112 G 4
Ballycorick ....99 E 9
Ballycotton ....91 H 12
Ballycotton Bay ....91 H 12
Ballycrossaun ....100 H 8
Ballycrovane Harbour ....88 C 12
Ballycroy ....110 C 5
Ballycuirke Lough ....99 E 8
Ballycullane ....96 L 11
Ballycullen ....103 N 8
Ballycumber ....101 I 8
Ballydangan ....100 H 7
Ballydavid *Galway* ....100 G 8
Ballydavid *Kilmalkedar* ......92 A 11
Ballydavid Head ....92 A 11
Ballydavis ....101 K 8
Ballydehob ....89 D 13
Ballydesmond ....93 E 11
Ballydonegan ....88 B 13
Ballydonegan Bay ....88 B 13
Ballyduff *Dingle* ....92 B 11

Ballyduff *Kerry* ....93 D 10
Ballyduff *Waterford* ....91 H 11
Ballyduff *Wexford* ....97 M 10
Ballyeaston ....115 O 3
Ballyfad ....97 N 9
Ballyfarnagh ....105 F 6
Ballyfarnan ....106 H 5
Ballyfasy ....96 K 10
Ballyfeard ....90 G 12
Ballyferis Point ....115 P 4
Ballyfin ....101 J 8
Ballyfinboy ....100 H 8
Ballyforan ....106 H 7
Ballyfore ....102 K 8
Ballyfoyle ....96 K 9
Ballygalley ....119 O 3
Ballygalley Head ....119 O 3
Ballygar ....106 H 7
Ballygarrett ....97 N 10
Ballygawley *Dungannon* ....114 K 4
Ballygawley *Sligo* ....112 G 5
Ballyglass
    near Cornanagh ....105 E 6
Ballyglass *near
    Kilmovee* ....106 G 6
Ballygorman ....117 K 1
Ballygowan *Ards* ....115 O 4
Ballygowan
    Newry-Mourne ....109 N 5
Ballygriffin ....95 I 10
Ballyhack ....96 L 11
Ballyhacket ....102 L 9
Ballyhahill ....94 G 10
Ballyhaght ....93 E 10
Ballyhaise ....107 K 5
Ballyhalbert ....115 P 4
Ballyhale *Galway* ....105 E 7
Ballyhale *Kilkenny* ....96 K 10
Ballyhar ....93 D 11
Ballyhaunis /
    Béal Átha hAmhnais ....106 F 6
Ballyhean ....105 E 6
Ballyheelan ....107 J 6
Ballyheerin ....117 I 2
Ballyheige ....93 C 10
Ballyheige Bay ....93 C 10
Ballyhillin ....117 J 1
Ballyhoe Bridge ....118 N 2
Ballyhoe Lough ....108 L 6
Ballyhooly ....94 G 11
Ballyhoura Mountains ....94 G 11
Ballyhuppahane ....101 J 8
Ballyjamesduff ....107 K 6
Ballykean ....101 K 8
Ballykeefe ....95 J 10
Ballykeel ....115 N 4
Ballykeeran ....107 I 7
Ballykelly ....118 K 2
Ballykilleen ....102 K 8
Ballykinler ....115 O 5
Ballyknockan ....103 M 8
Ballylacy ....97 N 10
Ballylaghnan ....99 G 9
Ballylanders ....94 G 10
Ballylaneen ....91 J 11
Ballylesson ....115 O 4
Ballylickey ....89 D 12
Ballyliffin ....117 J 2
Ballyline ....95 J 10
Ballylintagh ....118 L 2
Ballylongford ....93 D 10
Ballylongford Bay ....93 D 10
Ballylooby ....95 I 11
Ballyloughbeg ....118 M 2
Ballylynan ....102 K 9
Ballymacarbry ....95 I 11
Ballymacaw ....96 K 11
Ballymachugh ....107 K 6
Ballymack ....96 K 10
Ballymackey ....100 H 9
Ballymackilroy ....114 K 4
Ballymacoda ....91 I 12
Ballymacrevan ....115 N 4
Ballymacurly ....106 H 6
Ballymacward ....106 G 7
Ballymadog ....91 I 12
Ballymagan ....117 J 2
Ballymagaraghy ....118 K 2
Ballymagorry ....117 J 3
Ballymakeagh ....91 I 12

A B C D E F G H I J K L M N O P Q R S T U V W X Y Z

Ballymakeery /
  Baile Mhic Íre ....89 E 12
Ballymakenny .... 109 M 6
Ballymartin .... 109 O 5
Ballymartle ....90 G 12
Ballymena .... 119 N 3
Ballymoe .... 106 G 6
Ballymoney *Ballymoney* ..118 N 4
Ballymoney *Limavady* ......118 K 3
Ballymore *Donegal* ....117 I 2
Ballymore *Westmeath* .... 107 I 7
Ballymore Eustace .... 103 M 8
Ballymore Lough .... 111 E 5
Ballymurphy ....96 L 10
Ballymurragh ....93 E 10
Ballymurray .... 106 H 7
Ballynabola ....96 L 10
Ballynacallagh ....88 B 13
Ballynacally ....99 E 9
Ballynacarrick ....116 H 3
Ballynacarriga ....89 E 12
Ballynacarrigy .... 107 J 7
Ballynacarrow ....112 G 5
Ballynaclogh .... 100 H 9
Ballynacorra ....90 H 12
Ballynacourty ....91 J 11
Ballynadrumny .... 102 L 7
Ballynafid .... 107 J 7
Ballynagaul ....91 J 11
Ballynagoraher .... 105 D 6
Ballynagore .... 101 J 7
Ballynagree ....90 F 12
Ballynaguilkee ....95 I 11
Ballynahinch .... 115 O 4
Ballynahinch Lake .... 104 C 7
Ballynahow ....88 A 12
Ballynahown *Kilcummin* ..98 D 8
Ballynahown
  Westmeath .... 101 I 7
Ballynakill *Carlow* ....96 L 9
Ballynakill *Offaly* ....101 K 8
Ballynakill *Westmeath* ..... 107 I 7
Ballynakill Harbour .... 104 B 7
Ballynakilla ....88 C 13
Ballynakilly Upper .... 88 C 11
Ballynamallaght ....117 K 3
Ballynamona ....90 G 11
Ballynamult ....95 I 11
Ballynana ....92 A 11
Ballynare .... 103 M 7
Ballynashannagh ....117 J 2
Ballynaskeagh ....114 N 5
Ballynaskreena ....93 C 10
Ballynastangford .... 105 E 6
Ballynastraw ....97 M 10
Ballynchatty ....113 K 4
Ballyneaner ....118 K 3
Ballyneety ....94 G 10
Ballyneill ....95 J 10
Ballynoe *Cork* ....90 H 11
Ballynoe *Down* ....115 O 5
Ballynure .... 115 O 3
Ballyorgan ....94 G 11
Ballypatrick ....95 J 10
Ballypatrick Forest ......119 N 2
Ballyporeen ....95 H 11
Ballyquin ....92 B 11
Ballyquintin Point ......115 P 5
Ballyragget .... 101 J 9
Ballyrashane ....118 M 2
Ballyreagh *Dungannon* ......114 L 4
Ballyreagh *Fermanagh* ......113 J 4
Ballyroan ....101 K 9
Ballyroddy .... 106 H 6
Ballyroebuck ....97 M 10
Ballyronan .... 114 M 3
Ballyroney ....115 N 5
Ballyroon ....88 C 13
Ballysadare ....112 G 5
Ballysadare Bay .... 112 G 5
Ballyshannon *Donegal* ....112 H 4
Ballyshannon *Kildare* ..... 102 L 8
Ballysloe ....95 J 10
Ballysteen ....94 F 10
Ballyteige Bay ....96 L 11
Ballytoohy .... 104 C 6
Ballyvaughan ....99 E 8
Ballyvaughan Bay .... 99 E 8
Ballyvester ....115 P 4
Ballyvoge /
  Baile Uí Bhuaigh ....89 E 12
Ballyvoneen .... 106 G 7
Ballyvourney /
  Baile Bhuirne ....89 E 12
Ballyvoy .... 119 N 2
Ballyvoyle Head ....91 J 11
Ballywalter .... 115 P 4

Ballyward .... 115 N 5
Ballywilliam ....96 L 10
Balnamore .... 118 M 2
Balrath .... 108 M 7
Balrothery .... 109 N 7
Balscaddan .... 109 N 7
Baltimore ....89 D 13
Baltray .... 109 N 6
Banada .... 106 F 5
Banagher .... 101 I 8
Banagher Forest ......118 L 3
Banbridge ....114 N 4
Bandon River ....89 F 12
Bangor *Mayo* .... 111 C 5
Bangor *North-Down* ......115 O 4
Bangor Trail .... 111 C 5
Bann (River)
  Lough Neagh ....115 N 5
Bann (River) *River Slaney* ....97 M 10
Banna ....93 C 10
Banna Strand ....93 C 11
Bannow ....96 L 11
Bannow Bay ....96 L 11
Bansha ....95 H 10
Banteer ....94 F 11
Bantry / Beanntraí ....89 D 12
Bantry Bay ....89 C 13
Barefield ....99 F 9
Barley Cove ....88 C 13
Barna *Limerick* ....94 H 10
Barna *Offaly* .... 101 I 9
Barnacahoge .... 105 F 6
Barnaderg .... 106 F 7
Barnesmore .... 113 H 3
Barnesmore Gap ......113 I 3
Barnmeen .... 115 N 5
Barnycarroll .... 105 F 6
Baronscourt Forest ......113 J 3
Barr na Trá / Barnatra ......110 C 5
Barra (Lough) ....117 H 3
Barrack Village .... 101 K 9
Barraduff ....89 D 11
Barrigone ....93 E 10
Barringtonsbridge ....94 G 10
Barrow (River) .... 102 K 8
Barrow Harbour ....93 C 11
Barry .... 107 I 7
Barry's Point ....90 F 13
Batterstown .... 108 M 7
Baunskeha ....96 K 10
Bauntlieve ....99 E 9
Baurtregaum ....93 C 11
Bawn Cross Roads ......94 F 11
Bawnboy .... 113 I 5
Beagh *Galway* .... 105 F 7
Beagh *Roscommon* ......112 H 5
Beagh (Lough) ....117 I 2
Beagh (Slieve) ....113 K 4
Beal ....93 D 10
Béal an Átha / Ballina ...... 111 E 5
Béal an Átha Mhóir /
  Ballinamore .... 107 I 5
Béal an Mhuirthead /
  Belmullet .... 110 C 5
Béal Átha an Ghaorthaidh /
  Ballingeary ....89 E 12
Béal Átha na Muice /
  Swinford .... 105 F 6
Béal Átha na Sluaighe /
  Ballinasloe .... 100 H 8
Béal Átha Seanaidh /
  Ballyshannon ....112 H 4
Béal Deirg / Belderrig ......111 D 5
Beal Point ....93 D 10
Binn Éadair / Howth ...... 103 N 7
Béal Tairbirt / Belturbet ..... 107 J 5
Bealach Conglais /
  Baltinglass .... 102 L 9
Bealach Féich /
  Ballybofey ....117 I 3
Bishops Court ....115 P 5
Bealaclugga / New Quay ....99 E 8
Bealad Cross Roads ......89 F 13
Bealadangan .... 105 D 8
Bealaha ....98 D 9
Bealalaw Bridge ....88 C 12
Bealanabrack .... 104 C 7
Bealin .... 107 I 7
Bealnablath ....90 F 12
Beara ....89 C 12
Bearna / Barna ....99 E 8
Beaufort ....89 D 11
Bective .... 108 L 7
Beehive Huts ....92 A 11
Beenmore ....88 B 11
Beennaskehy ....90 G 11
Beenoskee ....92 B 11
Beg (Lough) *Antrim* ......114 N 4
Beg (Lough) *River Bann* ......114 M 3

Beginish Island ....88 B 12
Behy ....88 C 11
Bekan .... 105 F 6
Belcarra .... 105 E 6
Belclare .... 105 F 7
Belcoo .... 113 I 5
Belderg Harbour .... 111 D 5
Belfarsad .... 104 C 6
Belfast .... 115 O 4
Belfast Lough .... 115 O 3
Belgooly ....90 G 12
Belhavel Lough ....112 H 5
Bellacorick .... 111 D 5
Belladrihid ....112 G 5
Bellaghy .... 114 M 3
Bellahy .... 106 F 6
Bellameeny .... 106 H 7
Bellamont Forest .... 108 K 5
Bellanaboy Bridge .... 111 C 5
Bellanagare .... 106 G 6
Bellanagraugh Bridge ..112 F 5
Bellanaleck .... 113 J 5
Bellanamore ....117 H 3
Bellanamullia .... 107 H 7
Bellananagh .... 107 J 6
Bellanode .... 114 K 5
Bellarena .... 118 L 2
Bellavary .... 105 E 6
Belleek .... 114 M 5
Belleek .... 113 H 4
Bellewstown .... 109 M 7
Belmont .... 101 I 8
Belmore Mountain .... 113 I 5
Beltra *Croaghmoyle* ...... 105 D 6
Beltra *Sligo* ....112 G 5
Beltra Lough .... 105 D 6
Belvelly ....90 H 12
Belview Port ....96 K 11
Belville .... 111 D 5
Ben Gorm .... 104 C 7
Benbane Head ....118 M 2
Benbaun .... 104 C 7
Benbo .... 112 H 5
Benbrack .... 113 I 5
Benbreen .... 104 C 7
Benbulben ....112 G 4
Benburb .... 114 L 4
Bencroy or
  Gubnaveagh ....113 I 5
Bendooragh ....118 M 2
Benettsbridge ....96 K 10
Benmore .... 111 D 5
Benmore or Fair Head ......119 N 2
Bennacunneen .... 105 D 7
Benwee Head .... 111 C 4
Beragh .... 114 K 4
Bere Haven ....88 C 13
Bere Island ....88 C 13
Bernish Rock ....114 M 5
Berrings ....90 F 12
Bertraghboy Bay .... 104 C 7
Bessbrook .... 114 M 5
Bettystown .... 109 N 6
Big Dog Forest ....113 I 4
Big Island .... 100 H 8
Big Trosk .... 119 N 2
Bilboa .... 102 K 9
Bilboa (River) ....95 H 10
Bills Bridge .... 108 K 6
Bills Rocks .... 104 B 6
Binevenagh ....118 L 2
Binn Éadair / Howth ...... 103 N 7
Biorra / Birr .... 101 I 8
Birdhill ....99 G 9
Birreencorragh .... 105 D 6
Bishops Court ....115 P 5
Black *Galway* .... 105 E 7
Black (River) *Longford* ......107 I 6
Black Ball Head ....88 B 13
Black Bull .... 103 M 7
Black Gap (The) ....113 I 4
Black Head *Clare* ....99 E 8
Black Head *Larne* ....115 O 3
Black Lion .... 101 J 8
Black Rock .... 110 B 5
Blacklion .... 113 I 5
Blackpool ....94 G 10
Blackrock *Cork* ....90 G 12
Blackrock *Louth* .... 109 M 6
Blackrock *Rathdown* ...... 103 N 8
Blackskull ....88 B 11
Blacksod Bay .... 110 B 5
Blacksod Point .... 110 B 5
Blackstairs Mountains ......96 L 10
Blackwater ....97 M 10

Blackwater (River) *Cork* ......89 F 11
Blackwater (River)
  Lough Neagh ....114 L 4
Blackwater (River)
  River Boyne .... 108 L 6
Blackwater Bridge
  Innfield .... 102 L 7
Blackwater Bridge *Tahilla* ..88 C 12
Blackwater Harbour ....97 N 10
Blackwatertown ....114 L 4
Blanchardstown .... 103 M 7
Blane Bridge ....93 E 10
Blaney .... 113 I 4
Blarney ....90 G 12
Blasket Sound ....92 A 11
Bleach ....99 G 8
Bleach Lake ....94 F 10
Blennerville ....93 C 11
Blessington .... 103 M 8
Bloody Foreland ....116 H 2
Blue Ball .... 101 J 8
Blue Stack Mountains ......113 H 3
Blueford ....93 E 11
Boa Island .... 113 I 4
Boardmills .... 115 O 4
Boderg (Lough) .... 107 I 6
Bodyke ....99 G 9
Bofeenaun .... 105 E 6
Bofin .... 104 B 7
Bofin (Lough) *Galway* ......105 D 7
Bofin (Lough)
  Roscommon .... 107 I 6
Bogay ....117 J 3
Boggan *Meath* .... 108 L 6
Boggan *Tipperary* ......95 J 9
Boggaun .... 101 I 8
Boggeragh Mountains ......89 F 11
Bohateh ....99 G 9
Bohaun .... 105 D 6
Boheeshil ....88 C 12
Boher ....94 G 10
Boheraphuca .... 101 I 8
Boherbue ....93 E 11
Bohereen ....94 G 10
Boherlahan ....95 I 10
Bohermeen .... 108 L 7
Boherquill .... 107 J 6
Boho .... 113 I 4
Bohola .... 105 E 6
Bola (Lough) .... 104 C 7
Bolea .... 118 L 2
Boleran .... 118 L 2
Boley .... 102 L 8
Bolinglanna .... 104 C 6
Boliska Lough ....99 E 8
Bolton's Cross Roads ......93 D 10
Bolus Head ....88 A 12
Bonet .... 112 H 5
Boola ....91 I 11
Boolakennedy ....95 H 10
Boolattin ....93 C 11
Boolteens ....93 C 11
Boolyduff ....99 E 9
Boolyglass ....96 K 10
Borris ....96 L 10
Borris in Ossory .... 101 J 9
Borrisoleigh .... 100 I 9
Boston ....99 F 8
Bottlehill ....90 G 11
Bouladuff ....95 I 9
Boviel .... 118 L 3
Bow ....99 G 9
Boyerstown .... 108 L 7
Boyle (River) .... 106 H 6
Boyne (River) .... 102 K 7
Brackagh .... 101 K 9
Brackley Lough ....113 I 5
Bracklin .... 108 K 7
Brackloon *Mayo* .... 106 G 6
Brackloon *Roscommon* ......106 G 6
Bracknagh *Offaly* .... 102 K 8
Bracknagh *Roscommon* ......107 H 7
Brackwanshagh .... 111 E 5
Brandon Bay ....92 B 11
Brandon Head ....92 B 11
Brandon Hill ....96 L 10
Brannock Islands ....98 C 8
Brannockstown .... 102 L 8
Bray Head *Kerry* ....88 A 12
Bray Head *Wicklow* ...... 103 N 8
Bré / Bray .... 103 N 8
Breaghva ....98 C 10
Breaghwy .... 105 E 6
Bree ....96 M 10
Breenagh .... 117 I 3
Brickeens .... 105 F 6
Bricklieve Mountains ......106 G 5

Blackwater (River) *Cork* ......89 F 12
Bride *Cork* .... 89 F 12
Bride *River Blackwater* ......91 I 11
Bridebridge ....90 H 11
Brideswell *Ballyellis* ......97 M 9
Brideswell *Ballynamona* ..106 H 7
Bridge End .... 117 J 2
Bridgeland .... 103 M 9
Bridgetown
  Cannock Chase ....96 M 11
Bridgetown *Clare* ....99 G 9
Bridgetown *Donegal* ......112 H 4
Briensbridge ....99 G 9
Brittas *Limerick* ....94 G 10
Brittas *Saggart* .... 103 M 8
Brittas Bay .... 103 N 9
Britway ....90 H 11
Broad Haven .... 110 C 5
Broad Meadow .... 109 N 7
Broadford *Clare* ....99 G 9
Broadford *Limerick* ......94 F 10
Broadway ....97 M 11
Brookeborough ....113 J 5
Broomfield .... 108 L 5
Brosna ....93 E 11
Brosna (River) .... 101 I 8
Broughal .... 101 I 8
Broughane Cross Roads ......93 D 11
Brougher Mount ....113 J 4
Broughshane .... 119 N 3
Brow Head ....88 C 13
Brown Flesk ....93 D 11
Brownstown ....96 K 11
Brownstown Head ....96 K 11
Bruckless .... 112 G 4
Bruff ....94 G 10
Bruree ....94 G 10
Bryansford .... 115 O 5
Buckode .... 112 H 4
Buiriós Uí Chéin /
  Borrisokane .... 100 H 9
Bulgaden ....94 G 10
Bull (The) ....88 B 13
Bull Point .... 119 N 2
Bullaba .... 117 I 3
Bullaun ....99 G 8
Bull's Head ....92 B 11
Bun Cranncha /
  Buncrana .... 117 J 2
Bun Dobhráin / Bundoran ..112 H 4
Bun na hAbhna /
  Bunnahowen .... 110 C 5
Bun na Leaca /
  Brinlack ....116 H 2
Bunaclugga Bay ....93 D 10
Bunacurry .... 110 C 6
Bunatrahir Bay .... 111 D 5
Bunaveela Lough .... 111 D 5
Bunaw ....88 C 12
Bunbrosna .... 107 J 7
Bunclody ....96 M 10
Buncrana .... 117 J 2
Bunmahon ....91 J 11
Bunnafollistran .... 105 E 7
Bunnaglass ....99 F 8
Bunnahown .... 104 C 7
Bunnanaddan ....112 G 5
Bunny (Lough) ....99 F 8
Bunnyconnellan .... 111 E 5
Bunowen .... 105 C 6
Bunratty ....99 F 9
Burnchurch ....96 K 10
Burncourt ....95 H 11
Burnfoot *Birdstown* ....117 J 2
Burnfoot *Limavady* ......118 L 3
Burnfort ....90 G 11
Burr Point .... 115 P 4
Burren *Clare* ....99 E 8
Burren *Cork* ....90 F 12
Burren *Mayo* .... 105 E 6
Burren (The) ....99 E 8
Burren Centre Kifenora ......99 E 8
Burrenfadda ....99 E 9
Burrishoole Abbey .... 105 D 6
Burrow ....97 M 11
Burtown .... 102 L 9
Bush .... 118 M 2
Bush (The) *Dungannon* ......114 L 4
Bush (The) *Rathcor* ...... 109 N 6
Bushfield .... 118 M 2
Bushmills .... 118 M 2
Butler's Bridge .... 107 J 5
Butlerstown ....96 F 13
Buttevant ....94 F 11
Butts (The) .... 101 K 9
Bweeng ....90 F 11

C

Cabragh .... 114 L 4
Cadamstown *Kildare* ...... 102 L 7
Cadamstown *Offaly* ...... 101 J 8
Caddy .... 114 N 3
Caggan .... 105 D 7
Caha Mountains ....89 C 12
Caha pass ....89 D 12
Caher *Clare* ....99 G 9
Caher *Mayo* .... 105 E 7
Caher Island .... 104 B 6
Caher Roe's Den ....96 L 10
Caheradrine ....99 F 8
Caheragh ....89 E 13
Caherbarnagh
  Corcaigh / Cork ....89 E 11
Caherbarnagh *Kerry* ......88 B 12
Caherconlish ....94 G 10
Caherconnel ....99 E 8
Caherconree ....92 C 11
Caherdaniel ....88 B 12
Caherea ....99 E 9
Caherlistrane .... 105 E 7
Cahermore *Cork* ....88 B 13
Cahermore *Galway* ....99 F 8
Cahermurphy ....98 D 9
Cahernahallia ....95 H 10
Cahore Point ....97 N 10
Caiseal / Cashel ....95 I 10
Caisleán an Bharraigh /
  Castlebar .... 105 E 6
Caisleán an Chomair /
  Castlecomer .... 101 K 9
Calafort Ros Láir /
  Rosslare Harbour ......97 M 11
Caledon .... 114 L 4
Calf Islands ....89 D 13
Callaghansmills ....99 F 9
Callainn / Callan ....95 J 10
Callow *Galway* .... 104 B 7
Callow *Mayo* .... 105 E 6
Callow *Roscommon* ...... 106 G 6
Caltra .... 106 G 7
Caltraghlea .... 100 H 7
Calverstown .... 102 L 8
Cam Forest .... 118 L 2
Camlin (River) .... 107 I 6
Camlough .... 114 M 5
Camoge ....94 G 10
Camolin ....97 M 10
Camowen .... 113 K 4
Camp ....92 C 11
Campile ....96 L 11
Campsey .... 118 K 2
Camross .... 101 J 8
Camus Bay .... 105 D 8
Canglass Point ....88 B 12
Canningstown .... 108 K 6
Canon Island ....99 E 9
Cappagh *Dungannon* ......114 L 4
Cappagh *Limerick* ....94 F 10
Cappagh *River* .... 100 G 8
Cappagh White ....95 H 10
Cappaghmore ....99 F 8
Cappalinnan .... 101 J 9
Cappamore ....94 G 10
Cappanacreha .... 105 D 7
Cappanrush .... 101 J 7
Cappataggle .... 100 G 8
Cappeen ....89 F 12
Car (Slieve) .... 111 D 5
Caragh (Lough) ....88 C 12
Caragh (River) ....89 C 12
Caragh Bridge ....92 C 11
Caragh Lake ....92 C 11
Carbery's Hundred Isles ......89 D 13
Carbury .... 102 L 7
Cardy .... 115 P 4
Cargan .... 119 N 3
Carhan House ....88 B 12
Cark .... 117 I 3
Cark Mountain .... 117 I 3
Carland .... 114 L 4
Carlanstown .... 108 L 6
Carlingford .... 109 N 5
Carlingford Lough .... 109 N 5
Carn .... 113 I 4
Carna .... 104 C 8
Carnagh .... 119 O 3
Carnageer .... 119 O 3
Carnaghan .... 117 J 2
Carnalbanagh Sheddings ..119 N 3
Carnanelly .... 114 L 3
Carnanreagh .... 118 K 3
Carnaross .... 108 L 6
Carnaween .... 112 H 3
Carncastle .... 119 O 3

Carndonagh / Carn Domhnach ....118 K 2
Carnduff ....119 N 2
Carne ....97 M 11
Carneatly ....119 N 2
Carnew ....97 M 9
Carney Sligo ....112 G 4
Carney Tipperary ....100 H 9
Carnlough ....119 O 3
Carnlough Bay ....119 O 3
Carnmore ....99 F 8
Carnoneen ....105 F 7
Carnowen ....117 J 3
Carnsore Point ....97 M 11
Carnteel ....114 L 4
Carntogher ....118 L 3
Carra (Lough) ....105 E 6
Carracastle ....106 F 6
Carragh ....102 L 8
Carraholly ....105 D 6
Carraig Airt / Carrigart ....117 I 2
Carraig Mhachaire Rois / Carrickmacross ....108 L 6
Carraig na Siúire / Carrick-on-Suir ....95 J 10
Carran ....99 E 8
Carrantuohill ....89 C 11
Carrick Wexford ....96 L 11
Carrick / An Charraig Donegal ....112 G 4
Carrick-a-Rede Rope Bridge ....118 M 2
Carrick-on-Shannon / Cora Droma Rúisc ....107 H 6
Carrickaboy ....107 K 6
Carrickashedoge ....108 L 6
Carrickboy ....107 I 7
Carrickfergus ....115 O 3
Carrickhugh ....118 K 2
Carrickmore ....114 K 4
Carrickroe ....114 K 4
Carrig ....94 G 11
Carrig Island ....93 D 10
Carrigadrohid ....90 F 12
Carrigafoyle Castle ....93 D 10
Carrigagulla ....90 F 11
Carrigaholt ....93 C 10
Carrigaholt Bay ....93 C 10
Carrigahorig ....100 H 8
Carrigaline ....90 G 12
Carrigallen ....107 J 6
Carrigan ....107 J 6
Carrigan Head ....112 F 4
Carriganimmy ....89 E 12
Carrigans ....117 J 3
Carrigatogher ....100 H 9
Carrigfadda ....89 E 13
Carrigglass Manor ....107 I 6
Carriggower ....103 N 8
Carrigkerry ....93 E 10
Carrignavar ....90 G 12
Carrigrohane ....90 G 12
Carrigtohill ....90 H 12
Carrowbehy ....106 G 6
Carrowdore ....115 P 4
Carrowkeel Donegal ....117 J 2
Carrowkeel Galway ....99 G 8
Carrowkennedy ....105 D 6
Carrowmore Galway ....99 F 8
Carrowmore Kilmacowen ..112 G 5
Carrowmore near Cloonacool ....112 F 5
Carrowmore near Crossboyne ....105 E 6
Carrowmore near Killasser ....105 F 6
Carrowmore near Killogeary ....111 E 5
Carrowmore Lake ....110 C 5
Carrowmore Point ....98 D 9
Carrowmoreknock ....105 E 7
Carrownacon ....105 E 6
Carrowneden ....112 F 5
Carrownisky ....104 C 6
Carrowntanlis ....105 F 7
Carrowreagh Roscommon ....100 H 7
Carrowreagh Sligo ....112 F 5
Carrowrory ....107 I 7
Carry Bridge ....113 J 5
Carrybeg ....95 J 10
Carryduff ....115 O 4
Casheen bay ....98 C 8
Cashel Donegal ....117 I 2
Cashel Mayo ....104 C 6
Cashel near Glennamaddy ....106 G 7

Cashel / An Caiseal Galway ....104 C 7
Cashel (Rock of) ....95 I 10
Cashelgarran ....112 G 4
Cashelmore ....117 I 2
Cashen River ....93 D 10
Cashla ....99 F 8
Cashla Bay ....98 D 8
Cashleen ....104 B 7
Casla / Costelloe ....98 D 8
Casltepollard ....107 K 6
Castle Carry ....118 K 2
Castle Coole ....113 J 4
Castle Gardens ....90 F 13
Castle Haven ....89 E 13
Castle Island ....89 D 13
Castle Point ....98 C 10
Castlebaldwin ....112 G 5
Castlebar (River) ....105 E 6
Castlebellingham ....109 M 6
Castleblakeney ....106 G 7
Castlebridge ....97 M 10
Castlecaulfield ....114 L 4
Castleconnell ....99 G 9
Castleconor ....111 E 5
Castlecor ....94 F 11
Castlecove ....88 B 12
Castlecuffe ....101 J 8
Castledawson ....114 M 3
Castlederg ....113 J 3
Castledermot ....102 L 9
Castlefinn ....117 J 3
Castlefreke ....89 F 13
Castlegal ....112 G 4
Castlegar ....99 E 8
Castlegregory ....92 B 11
Castlehill near Rake Street ....111 D 5
Castlehill Ballycroy South ..110 C 6
Castlejordan ....102 K 7
Castleknock ....103 M 7
Castlellis ....97 M 10
Castlelyons ....90 H 11
Castlemaine ....93 C 11
Castlemaine Harbour ....92 C 11
Castlemartyr ....90 H 12
Castleplunket ....106 G 6
Castlequin ....88 B 12
Castlerahan ....108 K 6
Castlerock ....118 L 2
Castleroe ....118 M 2
Castleshane ....114 L 5
Castletown Clare ....99 E 8
Castletown Cork ....89 F 12
Castletown Laois ....101 J 9
Castletown Limerick ....94 F 10
Castletown Meath ....108 L 6
Castletown near Finnea ....107 K 6
Castletown Westmeath ....107 J 7
Castletown Wexford ....97 N 9
Castletown House ....103 M 7
Castletownbere ....88 C 13
Castletownroche ....94 G 11
Castletownshend ....89 E 13
Castleville ....105 E 7
Castleward House ....115 P 4
Castlewarren ....96 K 9
Castlewellan ....115 O 5
Castlewellan Forest Park ..115 O 5
Cathair na Mart / Westport ....105 D 6
Cathair Saidhbhín / Cahersiveen ....88 B 12
Cathedral Rocks ....104 B 6
Causeway ....93 C 10
Causeway Head ....118 M 2
Cavan / An Cabhán ....107 J 6
Cavanagarvan ....114 L 4
Cavangarden ....112 H 4
Cé Bhréanainn / Brandon ..92 B 11
Ceanannas / Ceanannus Mór (Kells) ....108 L 6
Ceann Toirc / Kanturk ....94 F 11
Ceapach Choinn / Cappoquin ....91 I 11
Ceatharlach / Carlow ....102 L 9
Ceathrú Thaidhg / Carrowteige ....111 C 5
Cecilstown ....94 F 11
Celbridge ....103 M 7
Chanonrock ....108 M 6
Chapeltown Down ....115 P 5
Chapeltown near Portmagee ....88 A 12
Chapeltown near Tralee ....93 C 11
Charlemont ....114 L 4

Charlestown Craigavon .....114 M 4
Charlestown Mayo ....106 F 6
Cheekpoint ....96 K 11
Chesney's Corner ....114 M 3
Cherryville ....102 L 8
Church Ballee ....115 P 5
Church Cross ....89 D 13
Church Hill Donegal ....117 I 3
Church Hill Fermanagh .....113 I 4
Church Quarter ....119 N 2
Church Town ....117 J 3
Church Village ....105 E 6
Churchstreet ....106 G 6
Churchtown Cookstown ....114 L 3
Churchtown Cork ....90 H 12
Churchtown Down ....115 P 4
Churchtown Wexford ....96 L 11
Churchtown Point ....114 M 3
Cill Airne / Killarney ....89 D 11
Cill Chainnigh / Kilkenny ...96 K 10
Cill Chaoi / Kilkee ....98 D 9
Cill Dalua / Killaloe ....99 G 9
Cill Dara / Kildare ....102 L 8
Cill Mhantáin / Wicklow ...103 N 9
Cill Mocheallóg / Kilmallock ....94 G 10
Cill Orglan / Killorglin ....93 C 11
Cill Rois / Kilrush ....93 D 10
Cill Rónáin / Kilronan ....98 C 8
Cionn tSáile / Kinsale ....90 G 12
City Walls ....96 K 11
Clabby ....113 J 4
Cladagh ....113 I 5
Claddagh ....106 F 7
Claddaghduff ....104 B 7
Clady Antrim ....115 N 4
Clady Magherafelt ....118 M 3
Clady Strabane ....117 J 3
Clady (River) ....116 H 2
Clady Milltown ....114 M 5
Claggan Donegal ....117 J 2
Claggan Mayo ....104 C 6
Clamper Cross ....93 E 11
Clanabogan ....113 J 4
Clane ....102 L 8
Clár Chlainne Mhuiris / Claremorris ....105 F 6
Clara ....103 N 9
Clara (Valle of) ....103 N 9
Clarahill ....101 J 8
Clare Armagh ....114 M 5
Clare Craigavon ....114 N 4
Clare (River) ....105 F 7
Clare Island ....104 B 6
Clarecastle ....99 F 9
Clareen ....101 I 8
Clarina ....94 F 10
Clarinbridge ....99 F 8
Clark's Cross Roads ....107 J 7
Clash ....100 H 9
Clash North ....93 E 10
Clashmore ....91 I 11
Claudy ....118 K 3
Cleggan / An Cloigeann ...104 B 7
Cleggan Bay ....104 B 7
Cléire (Oileán) / Clear Island ....89 D 13
Cleristown ....96 M 11
Clew Bay ....104 C 6
Clifden Bay ....104 B 7
Cliff ....112 H 4
Clifferna ....108 K 6
Cliffony ....112 G 4
Clogga Kilkenny ....96 K 11
Clogga Wicklow ....97 N 9
Clough Ballymena ....119 N 3
Clogh Kilkenny ....101 K 9
Clogh Laois ....101 J 9
Clogh Wexford ....97 M 10
Cloghan Offaly ....101 I 8
Cloghan Westmeath ....107 K 7
Cloghane ....92 B 11
Cloghaneely ....117 H 2
Clogharinka ....102 K 7
Cloghaun ....105 F 7
Cloghboley ....112 G 4
Cloghbrack Cloonbur ....105 D 7
Cloghbrack Meath ....108 K 7
Clogheen ....95 I 11
Clogher Dungannon ....113 K 4
Clogher Kerry ....93 D 11
Clogher near Carrownacon .....105 E 6
Clogher near Westport .....105 D 6
Clogher Roscommon ....107 H 6
Clogher Head Kerry ....92 A 11

Clogher Head Louth / Lú .. 109 N 6
Cloghera ....99 G 9
Clogherhead ....109 N 6
Cloghjordan ....100 H 9
Cloghmacoo ....108 L 6
Cloghoge ....109 M 5
Cloghroe Cork ....90 G 12
Cloghroe Donegal ....117 I 3
Cloghy ....115 P 4
Cloghy Bay ....115 P 4
Clohamon ....96 M 10
Clohernagh ....96 K 11
Cloich na Coillte / Clonakilty ....89 F 13
Clóirtheach / Clara ....101 J 7
Clomantagh ....95 J 9
Clonakenny ....101 I 9
Clonakilty Bay ....90 F 13
Clonalis House ....106 G 6
Clonalvy ....109 M 7
Clonard ....108 K 7
Clonaslee ....101 J 8
Clonavoe ....101 K 8
Clonbern ....106 G 7
Clonbulloge ....102 K 8
Cloncagh ....94 F 10
Clonco Bridge ....100 G 8
Cloncrave ....108 K 7
Cloncullen ....107 I 7
Cloncurry ....102 L 7
Clondalkin ....103 M 8
Clondaw ....97 M 10
Clonderalaw Bay ....93 E 10
Clondulane ....90 H 11
Clonea ....95 J 11
Clonea Bay ....91 J 11
Clonee ....103 M 7
Cloneen ....95 J 10
Clonegall ....96 M 9
Clonelly ....113 I 4
Clonevin ....97 N 10
Clonfert ....100 H 8
Clonfert Cross Roads ....100 H 8
Clonkeevy ....112 G 5
Clonleigh ....117 J 3
Clonlost ....107 K 7
Clonmacnoise ....101 I 8
Clonmany ....117 J 2
Clonmellon ....108 K 7
Clonmore Carlow ....103 M 9
Clonmore Tipperary ....101 I 9
Clonmult ....90 H 12
Clonony ....101 I 8
Clonoulty ....95 I 10
Clonroche ....96 L 10
Clonsilla ....103 M 7
Clontarf ....103 N 7
Clontibret ....114 L 5
Clontubbrid ....101 J 9
Clonycavan ....108 L 7
Clonygowan ....101 K 8
Cloon Lake ....88 C 12
Cloonacleigha Lake ....112 G 5
Cloonacool ....112 F 5
Cloonagh Lough ....106 F 6
Cloonaghlin Lough ....88 C 12
Cloonaghmore ....111 D 5
Cloonboo ....105 E 7
Cloondaff ....105 D 6
Cloondara ....107 I 6
Cloone ....107 I 6
Cloone Grange ....107 I 6
Cloonee Loughs ....89 C 12
Clooneen ....107 J 6
Clooney ....116 G 3
Cloonfad Kiltullagh ....106 F 6
Cloonfad near Old Town ...100 H 8
Cloonfallagh ....105 F 6
Cloonfinish ....105 F 6
Cloonfower ....106 G 6
Cloonfree Lough ....106 H 6
Cloonkeen Kerry ....89 E 12
Cloonkeen Mayo ....105 D 6
Cloonkeen Roscommon ....106 G 6
Cloonlara ....99 G 9
Cloonloogh ....106 G 6
Cloonlusk ....94 H 10
Cloonmore ....106 F 6
Cloonoon ....100 H 8
Cloontia ....106 G 6
Cloonusker ....99 G 9
Cloonymorris ....100 G 8
Cloonyquin ....106 H 6
Cloran ....108 L 7
Clough ....115 O 5
Cloughmills ....118 N 3

Cloverhill Cavan ....107 J 5
Cloverhill Galway ....105 E 7
Cloyfin ....118 M 2
Cloyne ....90 H 12
Cluain Eois / Clones ....113 K 5
Cluain Meala / Clonmel .....95 I 10
Cluainín / Manorhamilton ..112 H 5
Clydagh ....105 E 6
Clynacantan ....88 A 12
Coachford ....90 F 12
Coagh ....114 M 4
Coalbrook ....95 J 10
Coalisland ....114 L 4
Coan ....101 K 9
Cod's Head ....88 B 13
Coill an Chollaigh / Bailieborough ....108 L 6
Colbinstown ....102 L 8
Coldwood ....99 F 8
Colebrooke ....113 J 5
Colehill ....107 I 7
Coleraine ....118 L 2
Colgagh ....112 G 5
Colgagh Lough ....112 G 5
Colligan (River) ....95 I 11
Collin Top ....119 N 3
Collinstown ....107 K 7
Collon ....109 M 6
Collooney ....112 G 5
Colly ....88 C 12
Colmanstown ....106 G 7
Comber ....115 O 4
Comeragh Mountains ....95 J 11
Commeen ....117 H 3
Commons ....95 J 10
Conay Island ....112 G 5
Cong / Conga ....105 E 7
Conlig ....115 O 4
Conn (Lough) ....111 E 5
Conna ....90 H 11
Connagh ....100 G 9
Connemara ....104 C 7
Connemara National Park ....104 C 7
Connolly ....99 E 9
Connonagh ....89 E 13
Connor ....115 N 3
Connor Pass ....92 B 11
Convoy ....117 I 3
Coogue ....105 F 6
Cookstown ....114 L 4
Coola ....112 G 5
Coolagarry ....106 H 7
Coolaney ....112 G 5
Coolattin ....97 M 9
Coolbaun ....101 K 9
Coolbawn ....105 D 6
Coolboy ....97 M 9
Coolcull ....96 L 11
Coolderry ....101 I 8
Coole (Castle) ....113 J 4
Coole Abbey ....90 H 11
Coolea / Cúil Aodha ....89 E 12
Cooleragh ....102 L 8
Cooley Point ....109 N 6
Coolgrange ....96 K 10
Coolgreany ....97 N 9
Coolkeeragh ....117 K 2
Coolkellure ....89 E 12
Coolmeen ....93 E 10
Coolmore ....112 H 4
Coolnareen ....101 J 9
Coolrain ....101 J 9
Coolroebeg ....96 K 10
Coolshaghtena ....107 H 6
Coolteige ....106 H 6
Coomacarrea ....88 B 12
Coomakesta Pass ....88 B 12
Coomasaharn Lake ....88 C 12
Coomhola ....89 D 12
Coomhola Bridge ....89 D 12
Coonagh ....94 F 10
Cooraclare ....98 D 9
Coorleagh ....96 K 9
Coornagillagh ....89 C 12
Cootehall ....106 H 6
Copany ....113 H 4
Copeland Island ....115 P 3
Coppanagh ....108 L 6
Cora Droma Rúisc / Carrick-on-Shannon ....107 H 6
Corbally Castleconor West ....111 E 5
Corbally Clare ....98 D 9
Corbally Kildare ....102 L 8
Corbay Upper ....107 I 6
Corbet Milltown ....115 N 4

Corcaigh / Cork ....90 G 12
Corclogh ....110 B 5
Corcomroe Abbey ....99 E 8
Cordal ....93 D 11
Cordarragh ....105 D 6
Corduff ....109 N 7
Cork Harbour ....90 H 12
Corkey ....119 N 2
Corkscrew Hill ....99 E 8
Corlea ....107 I 7
Corlee ....105 E 5
Corlis Point ....93 D 10
Corn Hill ....107 I 6
Cornafulla ....101 H 7
Cornagillagh ....117 I 3
Cornamona ....105 D 7
Cornanagh ....105 E 6
Corracloona ....113 H 4
Corrakyle ....99 G 9
Corraleehan ....113 I 5
Corran Cross Roads ....114 M 5
Corrandulla ....105 F 7
Corranny ....113 K 5
Corraree ....106 H 7
Corraun Hill ....104 C 6
Corraun Peninsula ....104 C 6
Corraun Point ....110 B 5
Corrawaleen ....107 I 5
Correllstown ....107 K 7
Corrib (Lough) ....105 E 7
Corries ....96 L 10
Corriga ....107 I 6
Corrigeenroe ....106 H 5
Corrofin ....99 E 9
Corronoher ....94 F 10
Corroy ....111 E 5
Corry ....112 H 5
Corstown ....95 J 10
Cortowm ....108 L 6
Corvally ....108 L 6
Corvoley ....111 D 5
Cottoners ....89 C 11
Coulagh Bay ....88 B 12
Coumfea ....95 J 11
Courtmacsherry ....90 F 13
Courtmacsherry Bay ....90 G 13
Courtown ....97 N 10
Cousane Gap ....89 E 12
Craffield ....103 M 9
Crag Cave ....93 D 11
Cragganowen Megalithic Centre ....99 F 9
Craig ....118 K 3
Craigantlet ....115 O 4
Craigavad ....115 O 4
Craigavon ....114 M 4
Craignamaddy ....114 K 3
Craigs ....118 M 3
Cranagh ....117 J 2
Cranagh ....114 K 3
Cranfield Point ....109 N 5
Cranford ....117 I 2
Crannogeboy ....116 G 3
Cranny ....99 E 9
Cratloe ....99 F 9
Craughwell ....99 F 8
Crawfordsburn ....115 O 4
Crazy Corner ....107 K 7
Creagh ....113 J 4
Creagh (The) ....114 M 3
Creaghanroe ....114 L 5
Crean's Cross Roads ....90 F 12
Crecora ....94 F 10
Creegh ....98 D 9
Creeslough ....117 I 2
Creevagh ....111 D 5
Creevagh Head ....111 E 5
Creeves ....93 E 10
Creevykeel ....112 G 4
Cregg Clare ....99 E 8
Cregg Cork ....89 E 13
Cregg Galway ....105 E 7
Cregg Sligo ....112 G 5
Creggan Armagh ....108 M 5
Creggan Dungannon ....114 K 4
Cregganbaun ....104 C 6
Creggaun ....94 F 10
Creggs ....106 G 7
Crilly ....114 L 4
Crindle ....118 L 2
Crinkill ....101 I 8
Croagh Donegal ....112 G 3
Croagh Limerick ....94 F 10
Croagh Patrick ....105 C 6
Croaghaun ....110 B 6
Croaghmoyle ....105 D 6

A
B
C
D
E
F
G
H
I
J
K
L
M
N
O
P
Q
R
S
T
U
V
W
X
Y
Z

A B C D E F G H I J K L M N O P Q R S T U V W X Y Z

Croaghnageer 113 I3
Croaghnakeela Island 104 C8
Croaghrimbeg 105 D6
Croan (Lough) 106 H7
Croangar (Lough) 116 H3
Crockaneel 119 N2
Crockets Town 111 E5
Crockmore 113 I4
Crocknasmug 118 L2
Croghan Offaly 101 K7
Croghan Roscommon 106 H6
Croghan Mountain 103 N9
Crohane 89 D12
Crohy Head 116 G3
Crois Mhaoiliona /
   Crossmolina 111 E5
Croithlí / Crolly 116 H2
Cromane 92 C11
Cromoge 101 J9
Croob (Slieve) 115 N4
Crookedwood 107 K7
Crookhaven 88 C13
Crookstown Kildare 102 L8
Crookstown Moviddy 90 F12
Croom 94 F10
Croos 106 H7
Cross Cong 105 E7
Cross Waterford 91 I11
Cross (River) 105 D7
Cross Barry 90 G12
Cross Keys Cavan 107 K6
Cross Keys Meath 108 K6
Cross Keys Meath 108 M7
Cross Roads 117 I3
Crossabeg 97 M10
Crossakeel 108 K6
Crossboyne 105 E6
Crossconnell 100 H8
Crossdoney 107 J6
Crossea 107 J7
Crosserlough 107 K6
Crossgar 115 O4
Crossgare 118 L2
Crosshaven 90 H12
Crossmaglen 108 M5
Crossna 106 H5
Crossooha 99 F8
Crosspatrick Kilkenny ..101 J9
Crosspatrick Wicklow ..97 M9
Crosswell 106 G7
Crove 112 G3
Crow Head 88 B13
Crownarad 112 G4
Cruit Island 116 G2
Crumlin Antrim 115 N4
Crumlin Cong 105 D7
Crusheen 99 F9
Crutt 101 K9
Cúil an tSúdaire /
   Portarlington 101 K8
Cuilcagh 113 I5
Cuilkillew 111 E5
Cuilmore 105 F6
Culdaff 118 K2
Culdaff Bay 118 K2
Culfadda 106 G5
Culfin 104 C7
Culky 113 J5
Cullahill 101 J9
Cullane 94 G10
Cullaun 94 H10
Cullaville 108 M5
Culleens 111 F5
Cullen Cork 94 H10
Cullen Tipperary 93 E11
Cullenagh (River) 99 E9
Cullenstown
   near Duncormick ..96 L11
Cullenstown
   near Newbawn 96 L10
Cullin 105 E6
Cullin (Lough) 105 E6
Cullybackey 118 M3
Cullyhanna 108 M5
Culmore 117 K2
Culnady 118 M3
Cummeragh 88 B12
Cunningburn 115 P4
Curlew Mountains 106 G6
Curracloe 97 M10
Curragh 91 I12
Curragh (The) 102 L8
Curragh Camp 102 L8
Curragh West 106 G7
Curragha 109 M7
Curraghbonaun 106 F6
Curraghboy 106 H7

Curraghmore Gardens 95 J11
Curraghroe 107 H6
Curraglass 91 H11
Currahchase Forest Park ...94 F10
Curran 114 M3
Currane (Lough) 88 B12
Currans 93 D11
Curraun 105 D7
Curreel (Lough) 104 C7
Curreeny 100 H9
Currow 93 D11
Curry 105 E6
Curryglass 88 C12
Curryskeskin 118 M2
Cushendall 119 N2
Cushendun 119 N2
Cusher 114 M5
Cushina 101 K8
Cut (The) 101 J8
Cutra (Lough) 99 F8

D

Dahybaun (Lough) 111 D5
Daingean 101 K8
Dalgar 105 F7
Dalkey 103 N8
Damastown 109 N7
Damerstown 101 K9
Damhead 118 M2
Dan (Lough) 103 N8
Danesfort Kilkenny ...96 K10
Danesfort Longford ...107 I6
Dangan Cork 91 H12
Dangan Waterford 96 K11
Darby's Gap 97 M10
Dargle 103 N8
Dark Hedges (The) ...118 M2
Darkley 114 L5
Darragh 99 E9
Dartry Mountains 112 G4
Davagh Forest Park ..114 L3
Davidstown 103 M9
Dawros 104 C7
Dawros Head 116 G3
Dead 94 H10
Dealagh 98 D9
Dee 108 L6
Deel Limerick 94 F10
Deel Mayo 111 D5
Deel Westmeath 108 K7
Deel Bridge 111 D5
Deele (River) 117 I3
Deelish 89 E12
Deenish Island 88 B12
Delamont 115 O4
Delgany 103 N8
Delphi 104 C7
Delvin 108 K7
Delvin (River) 109 N7
Dennet (Burn) 117 J3
Derg (Lough)
   near Donegal 113 I4
Derg (Lough)
   near Nenagh 100 H9
Dergalt 117 J3
Dernagree 93 E11
Derravaragh (Lough) .107 J7
Derreen
   near Ballynagoraher ..105 D6
Derreen near Cloghmore ..104 C6
Derreen near Formoyle ...99 E8
Derreen near Lahinch 98 D9
Derreen Gardens 89 C12
Derreendarragh 89 C12
Derreeny 88 C12
Derreeny Bridge 89 E13
Derriana Lough 88 C12
Derries 101 J8
Derry 112 G5
Derryadd 114 M4
Derryanvil 114 M4
Derrybeg 116 H2
Derryboye 115 O4
Derrybrien 99 G8
Derryclare Lough 104 C7
Derrycooly 101 I8
Derrycraff 105 D6
Derrydruel 116 G3
Derryerglinna 105 D7
Derryfadda 101 J8
Derrygolan 101 J8
Derrygonnelly 113 I4
Derrygoolin 100 G9
Derrygrogan 101 J8
Derrykeevan 114 M4
Derrykeighan 118 M2

Derrylea 104 C7
Derrylin 113 J5
Derrylough 116 G3
Derrymore 93 C11
Derrymore Island 93 C11
Derrynane 88 B12
Derrynane House 88 B12
Derrynasaggart Mountains .89 E11
Derrynawilt 113 K5
Derryneen 104 C7
Derrynoose 114 L5
Derryrush 104 C7
Derrytrasna 114 M4
Derryveagh Mountains .117 H3
Derryvohy 105 E6
Derrywode 106 G6
Dervock 118 M2
Desertmartin 114 L3
Devenish Island 113 J4
Devilsbit 101 I9
Devilsmother 105 D7
Diamond (The) Antrim ..114 N4
Diamond (The)
   Cookstown 114 M4
Diamond (The) Omagh ..113 J4
Dingle / Daingean Uí Chúis 92 B11
Dingle Bay 92 B11
Dingle Harbour 92 B11
Divis 115 N4
Doagh Newtownabbey ..115 N3
Doagh Rosguill 117 I2
Doagh Beg /
   Dumhaigh Bhig ...117 J2
Doagh Isle 117 J2
Dodder 103 M8
Doe Castle 117 I2
Dolla 100 H9
Dollingstown 114 N4
Domhnach Phádraig /
   Donaghpatrick ...108 L6
Donabate 109 N7
Donacarney 109 N6
Donadea 102 L7
Donagh 113 J5
Donaghadee 115 P4
Donaghaguy 109 N5
Donaghcloney 114 N4
Donaghey 114 L4
Donaghmore 114 L4
Donaghmore Meath ...109 M7
Donard Wexford 96 L10
Donard Wicklow 103 M8
Donard (Slieve) 115 O5
Donaskeagh 95 H10
Donegal / Dún na nGall ..113 H4
Donegal Airport 116 G2
Donegal Bay 112 G5
Donegal Point 98 D9
Doneraile 94 G11
Donohill 95 H10
Donore 109 M6
Donoughmore 90 F12
Doo (Lough) 99 E9
Doo Lough 104 C7
Doo Lough Pass 104 C7
Dooagh 110 B6
Doobehy 111 D5
Doocastle 106 G5
Dooega Head 104 B6
Dooey Point 116 G3
Doogary 107 J5
Dooghbeg 104 C6
Doogort 110 B5
Doohooma 110 C5
Dooish Mount 117 J3
Doolough Point 110 C5
Doon Galway 100 G7
Doon Limerick 94 H10
Doon Lough 99 F9
Doona 110 C5
Doonaha 93 D10
Doonbeg 98 D9
Doonloughan 104 B7
Doonmanagh 92 B11
Doorin Point 112 H4
Dooyork 110 C5
Dore 88 C13
Dorrusawillin 107 H5
Dough 88 C13
Douglas 90 G12
Douglas Bridge ...113 J3
Doulus Bay 88 A12
Doulus Head 88 A12
Dowdallshill 109 M5
Dowling 96 K10
Downhill 118 L2
Downpatrick 115 O5

Downpatrick Head 111 D5
Downs (The) 107 K7
Dowra 113 H5
Dowth 109 M6
Drains Bay 119 O3
Drangan 95 J10
Draperstown 114 L3
Dreen 118 K3
Dreenagh 92 C10
Drimoleague 89 E13
Drinagh Cork 89 E13
Drinagh Wexford 97 M11
Drinaghan 111 E5
Dring 107 J6
Dripsey 90 F12
Dripsey (River) 90 F11
Drishaghaun 105 D7
Drishane Bridge 89 D13
Droichead Átha /
   Drogheda 109 M6
Droichead na Bandan /
   Bandon 90 F12
Drom 101 I9
Dromahair 112 H5
Dromara 115 N4
Dromcolliher 94 F10
Dromin Limerick ...94 G10
Dromin Louth 109 M6
Dromina 94 F11
Dromineer 100 H9
Dromiskin 109 M6
Dromkeen 94 G10
Drommahane 90 F11
Dromod 107 I6
Dromoland Castle ..99 F9
Dromore Banbridge ..115 N4
Dromore Omagh 113 J4
Dromore Lake 94 F10
Dromore West 112 F5
Dromtrasna 93 E10
Drones (The) 118 M2
Drowes 112 H4
Drum Monaghan 108 K5
Drum Roscommon ...101 H7
Drum Sligo 112 G5
Drum Manor
   Forest Park 114 L4
Drumandoora 99 F8
Drumaness 115 O4
Drumanoo Head 112 G4
Drumatober 100 G8
Drumbane 95 I10
Drumbeg Feddyglass ..117 J3
Drumbeg Lisburn ...115 O4
Drumbo 115 O4
Drumbologe 117 I3
Drumcar 109 M6
Drumcard 113 I5
Drumcliff 112 G5
Drumcliff Bay 112 G5
Drumcondra 108 M6
Drumcong 107 I5
Drumcree 108 K7
Drumcullen 114 M3
Drumduff 113 J4
Drumena Cashel ...115 O5
Drumfea 96 L10
Drumfin 112 G5
Drumfree 117 J2
Drumgoft 103 M9
Drumintee 109 M5
Drumkeary 99 G8
Drumkeen 117 I3
Drumkeeran 112 H5
Drumlaheen Lough ..107 I5
Drumlea 107 I5
Drumlegagh 113 J4
Drumlish 107 I6
Drumlosh 101 I7
Drummannon 114 M4
Drummin 96 L10
Drummullin 106 H6
Drumnakilly 114 K4
Drumone 108 K6
Drumquin 113 J4
Drumraney 107 I7
Drumreagh 110 B5
Drumshanbo 107 H5
Drumsna 107 H6
Drumsurn 118 L3
Duagh 93 D10
Dually 95 I10
Dublin Bay 103 N7
Duff 112 H4
Duffy 102 L7

Duleek 109 M7
Dumha Éige / Dooega ..104 B6
Dún Aengus 98 C8
Dún A'Rí Forest Park ..108 L6
Dún Chaoin / Dunquin ..92 A11
Dún Dealgan / Dundalk ..109 M5
Dún Garbhán /Dungarvan ..91 J11
Dún Laoghaire 103 N8
Dún Mánmhaí /
   Dunmanway 89 E12
Dún Mór / Dunmore ..106 F7
Dún na nGall / Donegal ..113 H4
Dunabrattin Head 91 K11
Dunadry 115 N3
Dunaff 117 J2
Dunaff Head 117 J2
Dunaghy 118 M2
Dunagree Point 118 L2
Dunamase (Rock of) ..101 K8
Dunamon 106 H7
Dunany 109 N6
Dunany Point 109 N6
Dunbel 96 K10
Dunboyne 103 M7
Dunbrody Abbey ...96 L11
Dunbulcaun Bay 99 F8
Duncannon 96 L11
Duncormick 96 L11
Dundalk Bay 109 N6
Dunderrow 90 G12
Dunderry 108 L7
Dundonald 115 O4
Dundrod 115 N4
Dundrum Down 115 O5
Dundrum Dublin 103 N8
Dundrum Tipperary ..95 H10
Dundrum Bay 115 O5
Dunfanaghy 117 I2
Dungannon 114 L4
Dunganstown 96 L10
Dungarvan Harbour ..91 J11
Dungiven /
   ....118 L3
Dungloe /
   An Clochán Liath ..116 G3
Dungonnell Dam 119 N3
Dungourney 90 H12
Dunguaire Castle ...99 F8
Dunhill 91 K11
Duniry 100 G8
Dunkellin 99 F8
Dunkerrin 101 I9
Dunkineely 112 G4
Dunkitt 96 K11
Dunlavin 102 L8
Dunleer 109 M6
Dunlewy 117 H2
Dunloe (Gap of) ...89 D11
Dunloy 118 M2
Dunluce Castle 118 M2
Dunmanus 89 D13
Dunmanus Bay 88 C13
Dunmore 109 O5
Dunmore Cave 96 K9
Dunmore East 96 L11
Dunmore Head
   near Culdaff 118 K2
Dunmore Head
   near Portnoo 116 G3
Dunmurry 115 N4
Dunnamaggan 96 K10
Dunnamanagh 117 K3
Dunnamore 114 L3
Dunnycove Bay 89 F13
Dunowen Head 89 F13
Dunree Head 117 J2
Dunsany 108 M7
Dunshaughlin 108 M7
Dunworly Bay 90 F13
Durlas / Thurles ...95 I9
Durrow 101 J9
Durrus 89 D13
Dursey Head 88 B13
Dursey Island 88 B13
Duvillaun Beg 110 B5
Duvillaun More ...110 B5
Dyan 114 L4
Dysart 107 J7
Dysert O'Dea 99 E9

E

Éadan Doire / Édenderry .102 K7
Eagle (Mount) 92 A11
Eagle Island 110 B5
Eagles Hill 88 B12
Eany 112 H3
Eanymore 112 H3

Easky 111 F5
Easky Lough 112 F5
East Ferry 90 H12
East Town 116 H2
Eddy Island 99 F8
Eden 115 O3
Ederny 113 J4
Edgeworthstown ..107 J6
Edgeworthstown /
   Meathas Troim ..107 J6
Egish (Lough) 108 L5
Eglinton 118 K2
Eglish 114 L4
Eighter 108 K6
Eleven Lane Ends ..114 M5
Ellistrin 117 I3
Elly Bay 110 B5
Elphin 106 H6
Elton 94 G10
Elva (Slieve) 99 E8
Emlagh Point 104 C6
Emly 94 G10
Emmoo 106 H7
Emo 101 K8
Emo Court 101 K8
Emyvale 114 L4
Ennel (Lough) 107 J7
Ennis / Inis 99 F9
Enniscorthy /
   Inis Córthaidh ..97 M10
Enniskean 89 F12
Enniskerry 103 N8
Enniskillen 113 J4
Ennistimon /
   Inis Díomáin ...99 E9
Eochaill / Youghal ..91 I12
Erne (Lower Lough) ..113 I4
Erne (River) 107 J6
Erne (Upper Lough) ..113 J5
Erra 107 I6
Errew Abbey 111 E5
Erriff (River) 105 D7
Errigal Mountain ..117 H2
Erril 101 I9
Erris Head 110 B5
Errisbeg 104 C7
Errislannan 104 B7
Errit Lough 106 F6
Ervey Cross Roads ..118 K3
Eshnadarragh ...113 K5
Eshnadeelada ...113 K5
Eske 113 H3
Eske (Lough) ...113 H3
Esker 99 F8
Esker South ...107 I6
Eskeragh 111 D5
Eskragh 113 K4
Eyeries 88 C12
Eyrecourt 100 H8

F

Faha 91 J11
Fahamore 92 B11
Fahan 117 J2
Fahy 100 H8
Fahy Lough 110 C5
Fair Green 99 F9
Fair Head 88 C13
Fairyhouse 108 M7
Fairymount 106 G6
Fallmore 110 B5
Fanad 117 I2
Fanad Head 117 J2
Fane River 108 M5
Fanore 99 E8
Farahy 94 G11
Fardrum 101 I7
Fardurris Point ..98 D8
Farmer's Bridge ..93 C11
Farnagh 101 I7
Farnaght 107 I6
Farnanes Cross Roads ..90 F12
Farnoge 96 K10
Farran 90 F12
Farran Forest Park ..90 F12
Farrancassidy
   Cross Roads ...112 H4
Farranfore 93 D11
Fastnet Rock ...89 D13
Faughan 118 K3
Fawney 117 K3
Fea (Lough) ...114 L3
Feagarrid 95 I11
Feakle 99 G9
Feale (River) ..93 D10
Fearn Hill 113 J3
Fedamore 94 G10

Fee (Lough) 104 C7
Feeagh (Lough) 105 D6
Feeard 93 C10
Feenagh 94 F10
Feeny 118 K3
Feevagh 106 H7
Fenagh 107 I5
Fenit 92 C11
Fennagh 96 L9
Fennor 91 K11
Feohanagh *Kerry* 92 A11
Feohanagh *Limerick* 94 F10
Feohanagh (River) 92 B11
Ferbane 101 I8
Fergus (River) 99 E9
Fern (Lough) 117 I2
Ferns 97 M10
Ferry Bridge 94 F10
Ferrybank 97 N9
Ferrycarrig 97 M10
Ferta 88 B12
Fethard 96 L11
Fews 95 J11
Feystown 119 O3
Fiddown 96 K10
Fieries 93 D11
Finavarra 99 E8
Finglas 103 N7
Finglass 89 C11
Finn (Lough) 117 H3
Finn (River) 117 J3
Finnea 107 J6
Finnisglin 104 C7
Fintona 113 K4
Fintragh Bay 112 G4
Finuge 93 D10
Finvoy 118 M2
Fiodh Ard / Fethard 95 I10
Fionnaithe / Finny 105 D7
Firkeel 88 B13
Fisherhill 105 E6
Five Corners 115 N3
Fivealley 101 I8
Fivemilebridge 90 G12
Fivemiletown 113 K4
Flagmount *Corlea* 99 G9
Flagmount *Kilkenny* 96 K10
Flat Head 90 G12
Flesk 89 D11
Florence Court 113 I5
Florence Court
   Forest Park 113 I5
Foaty Island/Fota Island 90 H12
Foilycleara 95 H10
Folk Park 99 F9
Fontstown 102 L8
Forbes (Lough) 107 I6
Fordstown 108 L6
Fore 107 K6
Forkill 109 M5
Forlorn Point 96 M11
Formoyle *Lonford* 107 I7
Formoyle *Mayo* 104 C6
Formoyle
   near Ballivaghan 99 E8
Formoyle near Inagh 99 E9
Formoyle (Lough) 105 D7
Fort Stewart 117 J2
Forthill 107 I7
Fota Island 90 H12
Foul Sound 98 D8
Foulksmills 96 L11
Fountain Cross 99 E9
Four Mile House 106 H6
Four Roads 106 H7
Fourknocks 109 N7
Foxford 105 E6
Foxhall 105 E7
Foyle (Lough) 118 K2
Foynes 93 E10
Foynes Island 93 E10
Francis' Gap 99 G8
Freemount 94 F11
Frenchpark 106 G6
Freshford 95 J9
Freynestown 102 L8
Frosses 112 H3
Frower Point 90 G12
Fuerty 106 H7
Funshin More 99 F8
Funshinagh (Lough) 106 H7
Funshion 94 G11
Furbogh 99 E8
Furnace 105 D7
Furnace Lough 105 D6
Furness 103 M8
Fyagh (Slieve) 111 D5

G
Gabriel (Mount) 89 D13
Gaddagh 89 C11
Gaillimh / Galway 99 E8
Gainestown 107 K7
Galbally *Dungannon* 114 L4
Galbally *Limerick* 94 H10
Galbally *Wexford* 96 M10
Galbolie 108 K6
Galey 93 D10
Galgorm 118 N3
Gallarus Oratory 92 A11
Galley Head 89 F13
Gallion (Slieve) 114 L3
Galmoy 101 J9
Galty Mountains 95 H10
Galtymore Mountain 95 H10
Galway Bay 98 D8
Galways Bridge 89 D12
Gaoth Dobhair /
   Gweedore 116 H2
Gaoth Sáile / Geesala 110 C5
Gap (The) 95 I11
Gara (Lough) 106 G6
Garadice 102 L7
Garadice Lough 107 I5
Garbally 100 H8
Garinish Island 88 C12
Garnavilla 95 I10
Garnish Point 88 B13
Garrane 89 E12
Garranlahan 106 G6
Garraun *Clare* 98 D9
Garraun *Galway* 100 G8
Garraun (Mount) 104 C7
Garries Bridge 89 D12
Garrison 112 H4
Garristown 109 M7
Garron Point 119 O2
Garrycloonagh 111 E5
Garrycullen 96 L11
Garryduff 118 M2
Garryfine 94 F10
Garrykennedy 100 G9
Garryspillane 94 G10
Garryvoe 91 H12
Gartan Lough 117 I3
Gartree Point 114 N4
Garty Lough 107 J6
Garvagh *Coleraine* 118 L3
Garvagh *Rowan* 107 I6
Garvaghy 114 K4
Garvary 113 J4
Gattabaun 101 J9
Gearagh (The) 90 F12
Gearha Bridge 88 C12
Geashill 101 K8
Geevagh 112 H5
George (Lough) 99 F9
Gerahies 89 D13
Giant's Causeway 118 M2
Giles Quay 109 N6
Gilford 114 M4
Gill (Lough) *near Sligo* 112 G5
Gill (Lough) *nearTralee* 92 B11
Glanaruddery Mountains 93 D11
Glandore 89 E13
Glandore Harbour 89 E13
Glangevlin 113 I5
Glanmire 90 G12
Glanmore Lake 89 C12
Glanoe 93 D10
Glantane 90 F11
Glanworth 94 G11
Glarryford 118 M3
Glasdrumman 109 O5
Glaslough 114 L5
Glasmullan 117 J2
Glassan 107 I7
Glasshouse Lake 107 J5
Glassillaun 104 C6
Glastry 115 P4
Gleann Cholm Cille /
   Glencolumbkille 112 F3
Gleann Domhain /
   Glendowan 117 I3
Gleann na Muaidhe /
   Glenamoy 111 C5
Gort an Choirce /
   Gortahork 117 H2
Glen 117 I2
Glen (River) *Cork* 90 F11
Glen (River) *Donegal* 112 G3
Glen Head 112 F3
Glen Lough *Donegal* 117 I2
Glen Lough
   Westmeath 107 J7

Glenaan 119 N2
Glenade 112 H4
Glenade Lough 112 H4
Glenamoy (River) 111 D5
Glenariff 119 N2
Glenariff Forest Park 119 N2
Glenariff or Waterfoot 119 N2
Glenarm 119 O3
Glenavy 115 N4
Glenballyemon 119 N2
Glenbeg Lough 88 C12
Glenbeigh 92 C11
Glenboy 112 H5
Glenbridge Lodge 103 M8
Glenbrohane 94 G10
Glenbrook 90 G12
Glencar 88 C12
Glencar Lough 112 G4
Glencloy 119 O3
Glencolmcille Folk Village 112 F3
Glencree 103 N8
Glencullen 103 N8
Glendalough *Brockagh* 103 M8
Glendalough *Waterford* 95 J10
Glenderry 92 C10
Glendorragha 116 G3
Glendovan Mountains 117 H3
Glendree 99 F9
Glendum 119 N2
Glenealy 103 N8
Gleneely *near Ballybofey* 113 I3
Gleneely
   near Cardonagh 118 K2
Glenelly 114 K3
Glenelly Valley 114 K3
Glenfarne 113 I5
Glenflesk 89 D11
Glengad Head 118 K1
Glengarriff (River) 89 D12
Glengarriff Harbour 89 D12
Glengesh Pass 112 G3
Glengormley 115 O3
Glenhead 118 K2
Glenhull 114 K3
Glenicmurrin Lough 98 D8
Glenmacnass 103 M8
Glenmalur 103 M9
Glenmore *Clare* 99 E9
Glenmore *Kilkenny* 96 K10
Glennagevlagh 105 D7
Glennamaddy 106 G7
Glennascaul 99 F8
Glenoe 115 O3
Glenshane Pass 118 L3
Glenshesk 119 N2
Glentaisie 119 N2
Glentane 106 G7
Glenties 116 H3
Glentogher 118 K2
Glentrasna 105 D7
Glenvale 118 M3
Glenvar / Gleann Bhairr 117 J2
Glenveagh National Park 117 I2
Glenville 90 G11
Glin 93 E10
Glin Castle 93 E10
Glinsce / Glinsk 104 C7
Glinsk *Donegal* 117 I2
Glinsk *Mayo* 111 D5
Glounthaune 90 G12
Glyde (River) 108 M6
Glynn *Carlow* 96 L10
Glynn *Larne* 115 O3
Gneevgullia 93 E11
Gob an Choire /
   Achill Sound 104 C6
Gobbins (The) 115 O3
Gokane Point 89 E13
Gola Island / Gabhla 116 G2
Golagh Lough 113 H4
Golam Head 98 C8
Golden 95 I10
Golden Vale 95 H10
Goleen 88 C13
Good's Cross 95 I10
Goresbridge 96 K10
Gorey / Guaire 97 N9
Gormanston 109 N7
Gort an Choirce /
   Gortahork 117 H2
Gortaclare 113 K4
Gortahill 113 I5
Gortaleam 106 F7
Gortarevan 100 H8
Gortaroo 91 I12
Gortaway 117 J2
Gorteen 106 G6

Gorteen Bridge 101 J8
Gorteeny 100 G8
Gortgarriff 88 C12
Gortgarrigan 112 H5
Gortin 113 K3
Gortin Glen Forest Park 113 K3
Gortletteragh 107 I6
Gortmore *near*
   Ballycastle 111 D5
Gortmore *near Bangor* 111 C5
Gortmullan 113 J5
Gortnadeeve 106 G7
Gortnahoo 95 J9
Gortnasillagh 106 G6
Gortree 117 J3
Gortymadden 100 G8
Gorumna Island 98 C8
Gosford Forest Park 114 M5
Gougane Barra
   Forest Park 89 D12
Gougane Barra Lake 89 E12
Gouladoo 89 C13
Gowla 104 C7
Gowlaun 104 C7
Gowlin 96 L10
Gowna (Lough) 107 J6
Gowran 96 K10
Gracehill 118 N3
Gráig na Manach /
   Graiguenamanagh 96 L10
Graigue 102 L9
Graigue Hill 96 L9
Graigue More 96 M10
Graigues 88 B12
Granabeg 103 M8
Gránard / Granard 107 J6
Grand Canal 101 I8
Graney 102 L9
Graney (Lough) 99 F9
Graney (River) 99 G9
Grange *Kildare* 102 K7
Grange *Kilkenny* 96 K10
Grange *Louth* 109 N5
Grange *Sligo* 112 G4
Grange *Waterford* 91 I12
Grange (River) 106 F7
Grange Con 102 L9
Grangebellew 109 M6
Grangeford 102 L9
Grangegeeth 108 M6
Granias Gap 117 K2
Grannagh 99 F8
Gransha 115 O3
Granville 114 L4
Greagh 107 I6
Great Blasket Island 92 A11
Great Island 90 H12
Great Newtown Head 96 K11
Great Skellig 88 A12
Great Sugar Loaf 103 N8
Greatman's Bay 98 D8
Greenan 103 N9
Greenanstown 109 N7
Greencastle *Donegal* 118 L2
Greencastle
   Newry-Mourne 109 N5
Greencastle *Omagh* 114 K3
Greenfield 105 E7
Greenisland 115 O3
Greenore 109 N5
Greenore Point 97 N11
Gregans Castle 99 E8
Gregory's Sound 98 D8
Grenagh 90 G11
Grey Abbey 115 P4
Grey Point 115 O3
Greysteel 118 K2
Greystone 114 L4
Grianán of Aileach 117 J2
Grogan 101 I8
Groomsport 115 P3
Gubaveeny 113 I5
Gubbaroe Point 113 I4
Gulladoo Lough 107 J6
Gulladuff 118 M3
Gullion (Slieve) 109 M5
Gur (Lough) 94 G10
Gurteen *Cappalusk* 99 G7
Gurteen *Leitrim* 112 H5
Gusserane 96 L11
Gwebarra Bridge 116 H3
Gweebarra 116 H3
Gweebarra Bay 116 G3
Gweestin 105 E6
Gweestion 105 E6
Gyleen 90 H12

H
Hacketstown 103 M9
Hags Head 98 D9
Hamiltonsbawn 114 M4
Hand Cross Roads (The) 99 E9
Hannahstown 115 N4
Hare Island 89 D13
Harristown 96 K10
Harrow (The) 97 M10
Healy Pass 89 C12
Helen's Bay 115 O3
Helvick Head 91 J11
Herbertstown 94 G10
High Island 104 B7
Highwood 112 H5
Hill Street 107 H6
Hillsborough 115 N4
Hilltown *Harristown* 96 L11
Hilltown
   Newry and Mourne 115 N5
Hind 106 H7
Hog's Head 88 B12
Holeopen Bay West 90 G13
Hollyford 95 H10
Hollyfort 97 M9
Hollymount 105 E7
Hollywood 103 M8
Holy Cross 95 I10
Holy Island 99 G9
Holycross 94 G10
Holywell 113 I5
Holywell Hill 117 J2
Holywood 115 O4
Hook Head 96 L11
Hore Abbey 95 I10
Horn Head 117 I2
Horse and Jockey 95 I10
Horse Island 89 D13
Horseleap 101 J7
Hospital 94 G10
Hugginstown 96 K10
Hungry Hill 88 C12
Hurlers Cross 99 F9
Hurley 109 M7
Hyne (Lough) 89 E13

I
Ilen 89 E13
Illaunstookagh 92 C11
Illauntannig 92 B11
Illies 117 J2
Illnacullin 89 D12
Inagh 99 E9
Inagh (Lough) 104 C7
Inch *Donegal* 117 J2
Inch *near Whitegate* 90 H12
Inch *near Youghal* 91 I12
Inch *Tipperary* 95 H9
Inch *Wexford* 97 N9
Inch Abbey 115 O4
Inch Island 117 J2
Inchagoill 105 E7
Inchamore Bridge 108 L9
Inchbeg 96 J9
Inchcleraun 107 H7
Inchee Bridge 89 D12
Inchicronan Lough 99 F9
Inchigeelagh 89 E12
Inchiquin 105 E7
Inchiquin Lough *Clare* 99 E9
Inchiquin Lough *Kerry* 89 D12
Inchmore 107 I7
Inchnamuck 95 H11
Inchydoney Island 90 F13
Indreabhán / Inveran 98 D8
Inis / Ennis 99 F9
Inis Bó Finne / Inishbofin 117 I1
Inis Meáin / Inishmaan 98 D8
Inis Mór / Inishmore 98 D8
Inis Oírr / Inisheer 98 D8
Inishannon 90 G12
Inishbarra 98 C8
Inishbiggle 110 C6
Inishbofin 104 B7
Inishcarra 90 G12
Inishcarra Reservoir 90 F12
Inishcrone 111 E5
Inishdoorus 105 D7
Inishfarnard 88 B12
Inishfree Bay 116 G2
Inishfree Upper 116 G3
Inishglora 110 B5
Inishkea North 110 B5
Inishkea South 110 B5
Inishmaine Island 105 E7

Inishmicatreer 105 E7
Inishmurray 112 G4
Inishnabro 92 A11
Inishnee 104 C7
Inishowen 117 J2
Inishowen Head 118 L2
Inishshark 104 B7
Inishtooskert 92 A11
Inishtrahull 118 K1
Inishtrahull Sound 118 K1
Inishturk 104 B6
Inishvickillane 92 A11
Inistioge 96 K10
Innfield 102 L7
Innisfree 112 G5
Inniskeen 108 M5
Inny (River) 107 J6
Inver *Donegal* 112 H4
Inver *Mayo* 110 C5
Inver Bay 112 H4
Inver's Eye 103 N7
Irish Agricultural
   Museum 97 M11
Irishtown 105 E7
Iron (Lough) 107 J7
Iron Mountains 113 I5
Irvinestown 113 J4
Island Lake 106 F6
Island Reavy (Lough) 115 N5
Islandmagee 115 O3
Islandmore 115 P4
Iveragh 88 B12

J
J. F. Kennedy Park 96 L11
Jamestown *Cloonteem* 107 H6
Jamestown *Laois* 101 K8
Japanese Gardens 102 L8
Jerpoint Abbey 96 K10
Jerrettspass 114 M5
Johnstown *Kildare* 103 M8
Johnstown *Kilkenny* 101 J9
Johnstown *Meath* 108 M7
Johnstown *near Arklow* 103 N9
Johnstown
   near Coolgreany 97 N9
Johnstown Bridge 107 I6
Johnstownbridge 102 L7
Jonesborough 109 M5
Joyce 105 D7
Julianstown 109 N6

K
Kanturk Castle 94 F11
Katesbridge 115 N5
Keadew 107 H5
Keady 114 L5
Keady Mountain 118 L2
Kealduff 89 C12
Kealkill 89 D12
Kearney 115 P4
Kearney Point 115 P4
Keeagh 99 E8
Keel 110 B6
Keel (Lough) 117 I2
Keel Lough 110 B6
Keeloges 106 G7
Keem Strand 110 B6
Keenagh *Longford* 107 I7
Keenagh *Mayo* 111 D5
Keeraunnagark 98 C8
Keereen 91 I11
Keimaneigh (The pass of) 89 E12
Kells *Ballymena* 115 N3
Kells *Kerry* 88 B12
Kells *Kilkenny* 96 K10
Kells (Ceanannus Mor) /
   Ceanannas *Meath* 108 L6
Kells Bay 88 B11
Kells Priory 96 K10
Kellysgrove 100 H8
Kenmare River 88 B12
Kentstown 108 M7
Kerry (Ring of) 88 B12
Kerry Head 92 C10
Kesh *Fermanagh* 113 I4
Kesh *Toomour* 106 G5
Keshcarrigan 107 I5
Key (Lough) 106 H5
Kid Island 110 C5
Kilbaha 93 C10
Kilbaha Bay 93 C10
Kilbane 99 G9
Kilbarry 89 E12
Kilbeacanty 99 F8
Kilbeggan 101 J7
Kilbeheny 94 H11

A B C D E F G H I J K L M N O P Q R S T U V W X Y Z

A B C D E F G H I J K L M N O P Q R S T U V W X Y Z

Kilbennan ... 105 F7
Kilberry *Bert* ... 108 L6
Kilbreedy ... 94 F10
Kilbrickan ... 105 D7
Kilbricken ... 101 J9
Kilbride *near Blessington* ... 103 M8
Kilbride *near Ratoah* ... 103 M7
Kilbride *near Trim* ... 108 L7
Kilbride *near Wicklow* ... 103 N9
Kilbrien ... 95 J11
Kilbrin ... 94 F11
Kilbrittain ... 90 F12
Kilcaimin ... 99 F8
Kilcar ... 112 G4
Kilcarn ... 108 L7
Kilcatherine Point ... 88 B12
Kilcavan ... 101 J8
Kilchreest ... 99 G8
Kilclaran ... 99 G9
Kilclief ... 115 P5
Kilcolier ... 93 C10
Kilclonfert ... 101 J8
Kilclooney ... 116 G3
Kilcock ... 102 L7
Kilcogy ... 107 J6
Kilcolgan ... 99 F8
Kilcolman *Cashel* ... 90 F12
Kilcolman
  Dunmoylan East ... 93 E10
Kilcoltrim ... 96 L10
Kilcomin ... 101 I9
Kilcommon *near Caher* ... 95 I10
Kilcommon *near Milestone* ... 95 H9
Kilcon ... 111 E5
Kilconly *Galway* ... 105 F7
Kilconly *Kerry* ... 93 D10
Kilcoo ... 115 N5
Kilcoole ... 103 N8
Kilcormac ... 101 I8
Kilcornan ... 94 F10
Kilcotty ... 97 M10
Kilcredan ... 91 I12
Kilcredaun Point ... 93 C10
Kilcrohane ... 89 C13
Kilcrow ... 100 H8
Kilcullen ... 102 L8
Kilcummin *Kerry* ... 92 B11
Kilcummin *Mayo* ... 111 E5
Kilcummin Farmhill ... 93 D11
Kilcurly ... 109 M5
Kilcurry ... 109 M5
Kildalkey ... 108 L7
Kildangan ... 102 K8
Kildavin ... 96 L9
Kilderry ... 96 K9
Kildoney Point ... 112 H4
Kildorrery ... 94 G11
Kildress ... 114 L4
Kildrum ... 115 N3
Kilfeakle ... 95 H10
Kilfearagh ... 98 D10
Kilfenora ... 99 E9
Kilfinnane ... 94 G10
Kilfinny ... 94 F10
Kilflyn ... 93 D10
Kilgarvan ... 89 D12
Kilglass *Galway* ... 106 G7
Kilglass *Sligo* ... 111 E5
Kilglass Lough ... 107 H6
Kilgobnet *Kerry* ... 89 C11
Kilgobnet *Waterford* ... 91 J11
Kilgory Lough ... 99 F9
Kilgowan ... 102 L8
Kiljames ... 96 K10
Kilkea ... 102 L9
Kilkeary ... 100 H9
Kilkeasy ... 96 K10
Kilkeel ... 109 N5
Kilkeeran High Crosses ... 95 J10
Kilkenny West ... 107 I7
Kilkerrin ... 106 G7
Kilkieran / Cill Chiaráin ... 104 C8
Kilkieran Bay ... 104 C7
Kilkieran ... 96 K9
Kilkinamurry ... 115 N5
Kilkinlea ... 93 E10
Kilkishen ... 99 F9
Kill *Cavan* ... 108 K5
Kill *Waterford* ... 91 J11
Killabunane ... 89 D12
Killaclug ... 94 H11
Killacolla ... 94 F11
Killadangan ... 105 D6
Killadeas ... 113 I4
Killadoon ... 104 C6
Killadysert ... 99 E9

Killafeen ... 99 F8
Killag ... 96 M11
Killagan Bridge ... 118 M2
Killaghteen ... 93 E10
Killahy ... 95 J9
Killakee ... 103 N8
Killala ... 111 E5
Killala Bay ... 111 E5
Killallon ... 108 K6
Killaloo ... 118 K3
Killamery ... 95 J10
Killane ... 102 K8
Killanena ... 99 F9
Killann ... 96 L10
Killard ... 98 D9
Killard Point ... 115 P5
Killarga ... 112 H5
Killarney National Park ... 89 D11
Killarone ... 105 E7
Killary Harbour ... 104 C7
Killashandra ... 107 J5
Killashee ... 107 I6
Killasser ... 105 F6
Killavally *Mayo* ... 105 D6
Killavally *Westmeath* ... 101 J7
Killavil ... 106 G5
Killavullen ... 94 G11
Killea *Donegal* ... 117 J3
Killea *Tipperary* ... 101 I9
Killeagh ... 91 H12
Killealy ... 115 N3
Killeany ... 98 D8
Killedmond ... 96 L10
Killeedy ... 93 E10
Killeen *Ardamullivan* ... 99 F9
Killeen *Armagh* ... 114 M5
Killeen *Dungannon* ... 114 M4
Killeenaran ... 99 F8
Killeenenmore ... 99 F8
Killeenleagh Bridge ... 88 B12
Killeevan ... 113 K5
Killeglan ... 106 H7
Killeigh ... 101 J8
Killen ... 113 J3
Killenaule ... 95 I10
Killeshil ... 101 K8
Killeshin ... 102 K9
Killeter ... 113 I3
Killeter Forest ... 113 I3
Killilan Bridge ... 99 G8
Killimer ... 93 D10
Killimor ... 100 H8
Killinaboy ... 99 E9
Killinaspick ... 96 K10
Killinchy ... 115 O4
Killiney *Dublin* ... 103 N8
Killiney *Kerry* ... 92 B11
Killiney Bay ... 103 N8
Killinick ... 97 M11
Killinierin ... 97 N9
Killinkere ... 108 K6
Killinny ... 99 F8
Killinthomas ... 102 L7
Killinure Lough ... 107 I7
Killiskey ... 103 N8
Killkelly ... 105 F6
Killmuckbridge ... 97 N10
Killogeary ... 111 E5
Killogeenaghan ... 101 I7
Killonecaha ... 88 B12
Killoran ... 100 G8
Killoscobe ... 106 G7
Killough ... 115 P5
Killowen ... 109 N5
Killucan ... 108 K7
Killukin ... 107 H6
Killurin ... 96 M10
Killurly ... 88 B12
Killusty ... 95 J10
Killwaughter ... 115 O3
Killyclogher ... 113 K4
Killyclug ... 105 F7
Killycolpy ... 114 M4
Killygar ... 107 J5
Killygordon ... 117 I3
Killykeen Forest Park ... 107 J5
Killylea ... 114 L4
Killyleagh ... 115 P4
Killyon ... 101 I8
Kilmacanoge ... 103 N8
Kilmacduagh Monastery ... 99 F8
Kilmacoo ... 103 N9

Kilmacow ... 96 K11
Kilmacrenan ... 117 I2
Kilmacteige ... 111 F5
Kilmacthomas ... 95 J11
Kilmactranny ... 106 H5
Kilmacurragh ... 103 N9
Kilmaganny ... 96 K10
Kilmaine ... 105 E7
Kilmainham Wood ... 108 L6
Kilmakilloge Harbour ... 88 C12
Kilmaley ... 99 E9
Kilmalkedar ... 92 B11
Kilmanagh ... 95 J10
Kilmeadan ... 96 K11
Kilmeage ... 102 L8
Kilmeedy ... 94 F10
Kilmeelickin ... 105 D7
Kilmeena ... 105 D6
Kilmessan ... 108 M7
Kilmichael
  near Castletownbere ... 88 B13
Kilmichael *near Macroom* ... 89 E12
Kilmichael Point ... 97 N9
Kilmihil ... 98 E9
Kilmona ... 90 G12
Kilmoon ... 89 D13
Kilmore *Armagh* ... 114 M4
Kilmore *Clare* ... 99 G9
Kilmore *Down* ... 115 O4
Kilmore *Mayo* ... 105 E6
Kilmore *Roscommon* ... 107 H6
Kilmore *Wexford* ... 96 M11
Kilmore Quay ... 96 M11
Kilmorna ... 93 D10
Kilmorony ... 102 L9
Kilmovee ... 106 F6
Kilmurry *Cork* ... 90 F12
Kilmurry *Limerick* ... 94 G10
Kilmurry *near Kilkishen* ... 99 F9
Kilmurry *near Milltown* ... 98 D9
Kilmurry *Wicklow* ... 102 L9
Kilmurry Mac Mahon ... 93 E10
Kilmurvy ... 98 C8
Kilmyshall ... 96 M10
Kilnagross ... 107 I6
Kilnalag ... 106 G6
Kilnaleck ... 107 K6
Kilnamanagh ... 97 M10
Kilnamona ... 99 E9
Kilntown ... 115 N4
Kilpatrick ... 90 F12
Kilpeacan
  Cross Roads ... 88 B12
Kilpedder ... 103 N8
Kilquigguin ... 97 M9
Kilraghts ... 118 M2
Kilrane ... 97 M11
Kilrea ... 118 M3
Kilrean ... 116 H3
Kilreekill ... 100 G8
Kilross *Donegal* ... 117 I3
Kilross *Tipperary* ... 94 H10
Kilruddery ... 103 N8
Kilsallagh *Galway* ... 106 G7
Kilsallagh *Mayo* ... 104 C6
Kilsallaghan ... 103 N7
Kilsally ... 114 M4
Kilsaran ... 109 M6
Kilshanchoe ... 102 L7
Kilshannig ... 92 B11
Kilshanny ... 99 E9
Kilsheelan ... 95 J10
Kilskeer ... 108 L6
Kilskeery ... 113 J4
Kiltealy ... 96 L10
Kilteel ... 103 M8
Kilteely ... 94 G10
Kiltegan ... 103 M9
Kilternan ... 103 N8
Kiltimagh ... 105 E6
Kiltober ... 101 J7
Kiltoom ... 107 H7
Kiltormer ... 100 H8
Kiltullagh ... 99 G8
Kiltyclogher ... 113 H4
Kilvine ... 105 F7
Kilworth ... 94 H11
Kilworth Mountains ... 94 H11
Kinale (Lough) ... 107 J6
Kinard ... 93 E10
Kinawley ... 113 J5
Kincasslagh ... 116 G2
Kindrohid ... 117 J2
Kindrum ... 117 I2
Kingarrow ... 117 H3
Kings River ... 95 J10

Kingscourt ... 108 L6
Kingsland ... 106 G6
Kingsmill ... 114 M4
Kingstown ... 104 B7
Kinlough ... 112 H4
Kinnadoohy ... 104 C6
Kinnagoe Bay ... 118 K2
Kinnegad ... 108 K7
Kinnitty ... 101 I8
Kinsale (Old Head of) ... 90 G13
Kinsale Harbour ... 90 G12
Kinsalebeg ... 91 I12
Kinsaley ... 103 N7
Kinvarra
  near Camus Bay ... 105 D7
Kinvarra
  near Kinvarra Bay ... 99 F8
Kinvarra Bay ... 99 F8
Kippure ... 103 N8
Kircubbin ... 115 P4
Kirkhills ... 118 M2
Kirkistown ... 115 P4
Kishkeam ... 93 E11
Kitconnell ... 100 G8
Knappagh ... 105 D6
Knappogue Castle ... 99 F9
Knight's Town ... 88 B12
Knock *Clare* ... 93 E10
Knock *Mayo* ... 105 E6
Knock *Tipperary* ... 101 I9
Knockaderry ... 94 F10
Knockadoon Head ... 91 I12
Knockainy ... 94 G10
Knockalla Mount ... 117 J2
Knockalongy ... 112 F5
Knockalough ... 99 E9
Knockananna ... 103 M9
Knockanefune ... 93 E11
Knockanevin ... 94 G11
Knockanillaun ... 111 E5
Knockanimpaha ... 93 E10
Knockanure ... 93 D10
Knockaunalour ... 90 G11
Knockaunavoher ... 94 G10
Knockaunnaglashy ... 92 C11
Knockboy
  near Dungarvan ... 95 I11
Knockboy
  near Waterford ... 96 K11
Knockboy (Mount) ... 89 D12
Knockbrack ... 117 I3
Knockbrandon ... 97 M9
Knockbride ... 108 L6
Knockbridge ... 109 M6
Knockbrit ... 95 I10
Knockcloghrim ... 114 M3
Knockcroghery ... 106 H7
Knockdrin ... 107 K7
Knockerry ... 98 D10
Knockferry ... 105 E7
Knocklayd ... 119 N2
Knocklofty ... 95 I10
Knocklomena ... 89 C12
Knocklong ... 94 G10
Knockmealdown ... 95 I11
Knockmealdown
  Mountains ... 95 H11
Knockmore ... 104 B6
Knockmore (Mount) ... 104 C6
Knockmourne ... 90 H11
Knockmoy Abbey ... 106 F7
Knocknaboul Cross ... 93 E11
Knocknacarry ... 119 N2
Knocknacree ... 102 L9
Knocknadobar ... 88 B12
Knocknagantee ... 88 C12
Knocknagashel ... 93 D11
Knocknagree ... 93 E11
Knocknahilan ... 90 F12
Knocknalina ... 110 C5
Knocknalower ... 110 C5
Knockowen ... 89 C12
Knockranny ... 90 G12
Knocks *Cork* ... 89 F12
Knocks *Fermanagh* ... 113 J5
Knocks *Laois* ... 101 J8
Knockshanahullion ... 95 H11
Knockskagh ... 89 F12
Knocktopher ... 96 K10
Knocktown ... 96 M11
Knockundervaul ... 93 D10
Knockvicar ... 106 H5
Knowth ... 108 M6
Kylemore ... 100 H8
Kylemore Abbey ... 104 C7
Kylemore Lough ... 104 C7

L

Laban ... 99 F8
Labasheeda ... 93 E10
Lack ... 113 J4
Lackagh ... 102 K8
Lackan *Carlow* ... 96 K9
Lackan *Wicklow* ... 103 M8
Lackan bay ... 111 E5
Lackareagh ... 89 F12
Laconnell ... 116 G3
Ladies View ... 89 D12
Lady's Island Lake ... 97 M11
Ladysbridge ... 90 H12
Ladywell ... 96 K10
Laffansbridge ... 95 I10
Lag ... 117 K2
Lagan (River) ... 115 N4
Lagan Valley ... 115 O4
Lagavara ... 118 M2
Lagganstown ... 95 I10
Laghey Corner ... 114 L4
Laghtnafrankee ... 95 J11
Laghy ... 113 H4
Lahardaun ... 111 E5
Lakyle ... 93 E10
Lambay Island ... 109 N7
Lamberg ... 115 N4
Lamb's Head ... 88 B12
Lanesborough ... 107 I6
Laney (River) ... 89 F12
Laracor ... 108 L7
Laragh *Kildare* ... 102 L7
Laragh *Monaghan* ... 108 L5
Laragh *Wicklow* ... 103 N8
Largan *Mayo* ... 111 D5
Largan *Sligo* ... 111 F5
Largy ... 112 G4
Largydonnell ... 112 H4
Larne ... 115 O3
Larne Lough ... 115 O3
Lattin ... 94 H10
Laune (River) ... 93 C11
Lauragh ... 88 C12
Laurelvale ... 114 M4
Laurencetown ... 100 H8
Lavagh ... 112 F5
Lavagh More ... 117 H3
Lawrencetown ... 114 N4
Leabgarrow ... 116 G3
Leamaneh Castle ... 99 E9
Leamlara ... 90 H12
Leamore Strand ... 103 N8
Leane (Lough) ... 89 D11
Leannan (River) ... 117 I2
Leap ... 89 E13
Leap (The)
  near Enniscorthy ... 96 M10
Leap (The) *near New Ross* ... 96 L10
Lecale Peninsula ... 115 O5
Lecarrow *Leitrim* ... 112 H5
Lecarrow *Roscommon* ... 107 H7
Leckanarainey ... 112 H4
Leckanvy ... 105 C6
Leckaun ... 112 H5
Leckavrea Mountain ... 105 D7
Leckemy ... 118 K2
Lee (River) ... 90 G12
Lee Reservoir ... 90 F12
Leek Point ... 93 C10
Leenane ... 104 C7
Legan or Lenamore ... 107 J7
Leganammy Dolmen ... 115 N5
Leggah ... 107 J6
Legoniel ... 115 O4
Lehardan ... 117 J2
Leighlinbridge ... 96 L9
Leinster (Mount) ... 96 L10
Leitir Meallàin /
  Lettermullan ... 98 C8
Leitir Mhic an Bhaird /
  Lettermacaward ... 116 H3
Leitrim *Banbridge* ... 115 O5
Leitrim *Creegh* ... 98 D9
Leitrim *Leitrim* ... 107 H6
Leixlip ... 103 M7
Lemanaghan ... 101 I8
Lemybrien ... 91 J11
Lenadoon Point ... 111 E5
Lenan Head ... 117 J2
Lene (Lough) ... 107 K7
Lerrig ... 93 C10
Leslie Hill ... 114 L5
Letterbarra ... 112 H3

Letterbreen ... 113 I5
Lettercallow ... 98 C8
Lettercraffroe Lough ... 105 D7
Letterfinish ... 88 C12
Letterfrack ... 104 C7
Letterkelly / ... 99 E9
Letterkenny /
  Leitir Ceanainn ... 117 I3
Letterleague ... 117 I3
Lettermore ... 98 D8
Lettermore Island ... 98 C8
Levally ... 106 F7
Levally Lough ... 105 E6
Licketstown ... 96 K11
Liffey (River) ... 102 M8
Lifford ... 117 J3
Light House Island ... 115 P3
Limavady ... 118 L2
Limerick / Luimneach ... 94 G10
Limerick Junction ... 95 H10
Lios Dúin Bhearna /
  Lisdoonvarna ... 99 E8
Lios Mór / Lismore ... 91 I11
Lios Póil / Lispole ... 92 B11
Lios Tuathail / Listowel ... 93 D10
Lisacul ... 106 G6
Lisbane ... 115 O4
Lisbellaw ... 113 J5
Lisburn ... 115 N4
Liscannor ... 98 D9
Liscannor Bay ... 98 D9
Liscarney ... 105 D6
Liscarroll ... 94 F11
Liscolman ... 118 M2
Liscooly ... 117 J3
Lisdoart ... 114 K4
Lisdowney ... 101 J9
Lisduff *Cavan* ... 108 K6
Lisduff *Leitrim* ... 107 I6
Lisduff *Offaly* ... 101 I8
Lisgarode ... 100 H9
Lisgoold ... 90 H12
Lislea *Magherafelt* ... 118 M3
Lislea *Newry-Mourne* ... 114 M5
Lismacaffry ... 107 J6
Lismoghry ... 117 J3
Lismoyle ... 106 H7
Lisnacree ... 109 N5
Lisnageer ... 108 K5
Lisnagleer ... 114 L4
Lisnagry ... 94 G9
Lisnagunogue ... 118 M2
Lisnamuck ... 118 L3
Lisnarrick ... 113 I4
Lisnaskea ... 113 J5
Lisnavagh ... 102 L9
Lispatrick ... 90 G13
Lisroe ... 99 E9
Lisronagh ... 95 I10
Lisryan ... 107 J6
Lissadell House ... 112 G4
Lissalway ... 106 G6
Lissamona ... 89 D13
Lissatinnig Bridge ... 88 C12
Lissavaird ... 89 F13
Lisselton ... 93 D10
Lissinagroagh ... 112 H5
Lissiniska ... 112 H4
Lissycasey ... 99 E9
Listellick ... 93 C11
Listerlin ... 96 K10
Listooder ... 115 O4
Lisvarrinane ... 94 H10
Little Bray ... 103 N8
Little Island ... 90 G12
Little Skellig ... 88 A12
Littleton ... 95 I10
Lixnaw ... 93 D10
Loanends ... 115 N4
Lobinstown ... 108 M6
Loch Garman / Wexford ... 97 M10
Loghill ... 93 E10
Lombardstown ... 94 F11
Londonderry ... 117 K3
Lonehort Point ... 88 C13
Long Island ... 89 D13
Longford ... 101 I8
Longhill ... 101 K9
Longwood ... 108 L7
Loo Bridge ... 89 D12
Loobagh ... 94 G10
Loop Head ... 92 C10
Loskeran ... 91 J11
Losset *Cavan* ... 107 J6
Losset *Donegal* ... 117 I2
Lough Bradan Forest ... 113 J4

Lough Gowna .... 107 J 6
Lough Key Forest Park .... 106 H 6
Lough Navar Forest .... 113 I 4
Loughanavally .... 107 J 7
Loughanillaunmore .... 98 D 8
Loughanure .... 116 H 2
Loughbrickland .... 114 N 5
Lougher .... 92 C 11
Loughermore .... 118 K 3
Loughfad Hill .... 113 I 4
Loughgall .... 114 M 4
Loughglinn .... 106 G 6
Loughguile .... 119 N 2
Loughinisland .... 115 O 4
Loughlinstown .... 103 N 8
Loughmoe .... 101 I 9
Loughmorne .... 108 L 5
Loughros More Bay .... 116 G 3
Loughros Point .... 116 G 3
Loughsalt Mount .... 117 I 2
Loughshinny .... 109 N 7
Louisburgh .... 104 C 6
Loup (The) .... 114 M 3
Louth .... 108 M 6
Lower Ballinderry .... 114 N 4
Lower Lake .... 103 N 8
Lowertown .... 89 D 13
Lowerymore .... 113 I 3
Lowtown .... 115 N 5
Lucan .... 103 M 7
Luggacurren .... 101 K 9
Lugnaquillia Mountain .... 103 M 9
Luimneach / Limerick ..... 94 G 10
Lukeswell .... 96 K 10
Lullymore .... 102 L 8
Lurgan Craigavon .... 114 N 4
Lurgan Frenchpark .... 106 G 6
Lurganboy Donegal .... 117 J 2
Lurganboy Leitrim .... 112 H 5
Lusk .... 109 N 7
Lyle .... 115 N 3
Lyracrumpane .... 93 D 10
Lyre .... 90 F 11
Lyrenaglogh .... 95 H 11

M
Maas .... 116 G 3
Mac Gregor's Corner ...... 119 N 3
Mac Laughlins Corner ..... 118 M 3
Mac Mahon's Town .... 114 K 4
Mac Swyne's Bay .... 112 G 4
Mace .... 103 D 6
Mace Head .... 104 C 8
Macgillycuddy's Reeks .... 89 C 12
Machugh (Lough) .... 116 G 3
Mackan .... 113 J 5
Macnean Lower (Lough) .. 113 I 5
Macnean Upper (Lough) .. 113 I 5
Macosquin .... 118 L 2
Macroom/
  Maigh Chromtha .... 89 F 12
Maddan .... 114 L 5
Maddockstown .... 96 K 10
Maganey .... 102 L 9
Maghaberry .... 115 N 4
Maghanlawaun .... 89 C 12
Maghera Clare .... 99 F 9
Maghera Donegal .... 116 G 3
Maghera Down .... 115 O 5
Maghera Magherafelt ..... 118 L 3
Magherabane .... 117 J 2
Magherafelt .... 114 M 3
Magheragall .... 114 N 4
Magheralin .... 114 N 4
Magheramason .... 117 J 3
Magheramorne .... 115 O 3
Magheraveely .... 113 K 5
Maghery near Dungannon .114 M 4
Maghery near Dunglow .... 118 L 2
Magilligan .... 118 L 2
Magilligan Point .... 118 L 2
Magilligan Strand .... 118 L 2
Maguiresbridge .... 113 J 5
Mahee Island .... 115 P 4
Mahon .... 95 J 11
Mahon (Lough) .... 90 G 12
Mahoonagh .... 93 E 10
Maigh Chromtha /
  Macroom .... 89 F 12
Maigh Cuilinn /
  Moycullen .... 105 E 7
Maigh Nuad / Maynooth .. 103 M 7
Maigue (River) .... 94 F 10
Main .... 118 N 3
Maine (River) .... 93 C 11
Mainham .... 102 L 8
Mainistir Fhear Maí /

Fermoy .... 90 H 11
Mainistir na Búille /
  Boyle .... 106 H 6
Mainistir na Corann /
  Midleton .... 90 H 12
Máistir Gaoithe /
  Mastergeehy .... 88 B 12
Mal Bay .... 98 D 9
Mala / Mallow .... 94 G 11
Málainn Bhig / Malin Beg .. 112 F 3
Malin .... 118 K 2
Malin Bay .... 112 F 3
Malin Head .... 117 J 1
Malin More .... 112 F 3
Mallusk .... 115 N 3
Mamore (Gap of) .... 117 J 2
Manger .... 112 H 4
Mangerton Mountain ...... 89 D 12
Mannin Bay .... 104 B 7
Mannin Lake .... 105 F 6
Manorcunningham .... 117 J 3
Manselstown .... 95 I 9
Mansfieldstown .... 109 M 6
Mantua .... 106 H 6
Manulla .... 105 E 6
Manulla (River) .... 105 E 6
Maothail / Mohill .... 107 I 6
Marble Arch Caves .... 113 I 5
Marble Hill .... 117 I 2
Mardyke .... 95 J 10
Markethill .... 114 M 5
Marshalstown .... 96 M 10
Martin .... 90 G 12
Martinstown Emlygrennan ..94 G 10
Martinstown
  Grennanstown .... 108 L 7
Martinstown
  South Somerset .... 119 N 3
Mask (Lough) .... 105 D 7
Massford .... 115 N 4
Masshill .... 112 F 5
Masterstown .... 95 I 10
Matehy .... 90 G 12
Matrix (Castle) .... 94 F 10
Mattock (River) .... 108 M 6
Mauherslieve .... 95 H 9
Maum .... 105 D 7
Maumakeogh .... 111 D 5
Maumeen Lough .... 104 B 7
Maumtrasna .... 105 D 7
Maumturk Mountains ...... 104 C 7
Mauricesmills .... 99 F 9
Mayo .... 105 E 6
Mayo (Plains of) .... 105 E 6
Mazetown .... 115 N 4
Mealagh .... 89 D 12
Meanus .... 94 G 10
Meathas Troim /
  Edgeworthstown .... 107 J 6
Meela (Lough) .... 116 G 3
Meelick .... 100 H 8
Meelin .... 93 E 11
Meenaclady .... 116 H 2
Meenacross .... 116 G 3
Meenanarwa .... 117 H 3
Meenaneary /
  Min na Aoire .... 112 G 3
Meenatotan .... 116 H 3
Meenavean .... 112 F 3
Meencorwick .... 116 H 3
Meenglass .... 113 I 3
Meenlaragh .... 117 H 2
Meenreagh .... 113 I 3
Meentullynagarn .... 112 G 3
Meenybraddan .... 112 H 3
Meeting of the Waters .... 103 N 9
Mellifont Abbey .... 109 M 6
Melmore Head .... 117 I 2
Melvin (Lough) .... 112 H 4
Mew Island .... 115 P 3
Michelstown Caves .... 95 H 11
Middledown .... 116 H 2
Middletown Armagh .... 114 L 5
Midfield .... 105 F 6
Mile .... 117 J 2
Milebush .... 115 O 3
Milehouse .... 96 M 10
Milemill .... 102 L 8
Milestone .... 95 H 9
Milford Armagh .... 114 L 5
Milford Cork .... 94 F 10
Mill Town .... 114 L 5
Millbay .... 115 O 3
Millbrook Derry .... 118 K 3
Millbrook Larne .... 115 O 3

Millbrook Oldcastle .... 108 K 6
Milleen .... 93 E 11
Millford .... 117 I 2
Millisle .... 115 P 4
Millroad .... 96 M 11
Millstreet Cork .... 89 E 11
Millstreet Waterford .... 91 I 11
Milltown Armagh .... 114 L 5
Milltown Ballymoney ...... 118 M 2
Milltown Banbridge .... 114 N 5
Milltown Cavan .... 107 J 5
Milltown Craigavon .... 114 M 4
Milltown Dublin .... 103 M 8
Milltown Kildare .... 102 L 8
Milltown near Dingle ...... 92 B 11
Milltown
  near Mount Bellew ...... 106 G 7
Milltown near Tralee ...... 93 C 11
Milltown near Tuam .... 105 F 7
Milltown Omagh .... 114 K 4
Milltown Wexford .... 97 M 10
Miltownpass .... 107 K 7
Minane Bridge .... 90 G 12
Minard Head .... 92 B 11
Mine Head .... 91 J 12
Minerstown .... 115 O 5
Minterburn .... 114 L 4
Mizen Head .... 88 C 13
Moanmore .... 98 D 9
Modelligo .... 91 I 11
Modreeny .... 100 H 9
Mogeely .... 90 H 12
Moglass .... 95 I 10
Moher (Cliffs of) .... 98 D 9
Moher Lough .... 105 D 6
Mohil .... 96 K 9
Móinteach Milic /
  Mountmellick .... 101 K 8
Moira .... 115 N 4
Moll's Gap .... 89 D 12
Monard .... 95 H 10
Monaseed .... 97 M 9
Monaster .... 94 G 10
Monasteraden .... 106 G 6
Monasteranenagh Abbey ...94 G 10
Monasterboice .... 109 M 6
Monasterevin .... 102 K 8
Monavullagh Mountains ...95 J 11
Mondello Park .... 102 L 8
Monea .... 113 I 4
Moneen Clare .... 93 C 10
Moneen Galway .... 105 F 7
Money Point .... 93 D 10
Moneydig .... 118 M 2
Moneygall .... 101 I 9
Moneyglass .... 114 M 3
Moneygold .... 112 G 4
Moneylahan .... 112 G 4
Moneymore .... 114 L 3
Moneyneany .... 118 L 3
Moneyreagh .... 115 O 4
Monilea .... 107 K 7
Monivea .... 106 F 7
Monkstown Cork .... 90 G 12
Monkstown
  Newtownabbey .... 115 O 3
Monroe .... 107 J 7
Montpelier .... 99 G 9
Mooncoin .... 96 K 11
Moone .... 102 L 9
Moord .... 91 I 12
Moore Bay .... 98 C 9
Moorfields .... 115 N 3
More (Island) .... 105 D 6
Morenane .... 94 F 10
Morley's Bridge .... 89 D 12
Morningstar .... 94 G 10
Mornington .... 109 N 6
Mosney .... 109 N 7
Moss-Side .... 118 M 2
Mossley .... 115 O 3
Mothel .... 95 J 11
Motte Stone .... 103 N 9
Mount Falcon .... 111 E 5
Mount Garret .... 96 L 10
Mount Hamilton or Sperrin 114 K 3
Mount Melleray Monastery .95 I 11
Mount Norris .... 114 M 5
Mount Nugent .... 107 K 6
Mount Stewart Gardens ... 115 P 4
Mount Talbot .... 106 H 7
Mount Temple .... 107 I 7
Mount Uniacke .... 91 H 12
Mount Usher Gardens ... 103 N 8
Mountbolus .... 101 J 8
Mountcastle .... 117 J 3
Mountcharles .... 112 H 4

Mountcollins .... 93 E 11
Mountfield .... 114 K 4
Mounthenry .... 105 E 7
Mountjoy Dungannon ...... 114 M 4
Mountjoy Omagh .... 113 J 4
Mountrath .... 101 J 8
Mountrivers Bridge .... 98 D 9
Mountshannon .... 100 G 9
Mourne (Lough)
  near Ballybofey .... 113 I 3
Mourne (Lough)
  near Carrickfergus .... 115 O 3
Mourne Beg .... 113 I 3
Mourne Mountains .... 109 N 5
Mourne River .... 113 J 3
Moveen .... 98 C 10
Moville / Bun an Phobail ... 118 K 2
Mowhan .... 114 M 5
Moy .... 114 L 4
Moy (River) .... 111 E 5
Moyagh .... 117 J 3
Moyallan .... 114 M 4
Moyard .... 104 B 7
Moyarget .... 118 N 2
Moyasta .... 98 D 9
Moydow .... 107 I 7
Moygashel .... 114 L 4
Moyglass .... 99 G 8
Moylough Galway .... 106 G 7
Moylough Sligo .... 106 F 5
Moynalty .... 108 L 6
Moynalvy .... 108 L 7
Moyne Roscommon .... 106 G 6
Moyne Tipperary .... 107 J 6
Moyne Wicklow .... 103 M 9
Moyne Abbey .... 111 E 5
Moyrus .... 104 C 7
Moyteoge Head .... 110 B 6
Moyvally .... 102 L 7
Moyvore .... 107 J 7
Moyvoughly .... 107 I 7
Muck (Isle of) .... 115 O 3
Muckamore .... 115 N 3
Muckanagh Lough .... 99 F 9
Muckish Mountain .... 117 H 2
Mucklon .... 102 L 7
Muckno Lake .... 108 L 5
Muckros Head .... 112 G 4
Muckross .... 89 D 11
Muff .... 117 K 2
Muggort's Bay .... 91 J 11
Muinchille / Cootehill ..... 108 K 5
Muine Bheag /
  Bagenalstown .... 96 L 9
Muineachán / Monaghan .. 114 L 5
Muing .... 111 D 5
Muingnabo .... 111 C 5
Mulhuddart .... 103 M 7
Mulkear .... 94 G 10
Mullach Íde / Malahide ... 103 N 7
Mullagh Cavan .... 108 L 6
Mullagh Galway .... 100 G 8
Mullagh Mayo .... 104 C 7
Mullagh Meath .... 103 M 7
Mullaghanattin .... 88 C 12
Mullaghanish .... 89 E 12
Mullaghareirk Mountains .. 93 E 10
Mullaghash .... 118 K 3
Mullaghbane .... 109 M 5
Mullaghboy .... 115 O 3
Mullaghcarn .... 113 K 3
Mullaghcleevaun .... 103 M 8
Mullaghclogha .... 113 K 3
Mullaghmore
  Cliffony North .... 112 G 4
Mullaghmore Magherafelt ..118 L 3
Mullaghmore Head .... 112 G 4
Mullaghroe .... 106 G 6
Mullan Coleraine .... 118 L 2
Mullan Figullar .... 114 L 4
Mullan'sCross .... 111 F 5
Mullartown .... 109 O 5
Mullen .... 106 G 6
Mullenbeg .... 96 K 10
Mullet Peninsula .... 110 B 5
Mullinahone .... 95 J 10
Mullinasole .... 112 H 4
Mullinavat .... 96 K 10
Mulroy Bay .... 117 I 2
Multeen .... 95 H 10
Multyfarnham .... 107 J 7
Mungret .... 94 F 10
Muntervary
  or Sheep's Head .... 88 C 13
Murley .... 113 K 4
Murlough Bay .... 119 N 2
Murntown .... 97 M 11

Murreagh .... 92 A 11
Murrisk .... 105 D 6
Murroe .... 94 G 10
Murroogh .... 99 E 8
Musheramore .... 89 F 11
Mussenden Temple .... 118 L 2
Mutton Island .... 98 D 9
Mweelrea Mountains ...... 104 C 7
Mweenish Island .... 104 C 8
Myshall .... 96 L 9

N
Na Cealla Beaga /
  Killybegs .... 112 G 4
Na Clocha Liatha /
  Greystones .... 103 N 8
Na Dúnaibh / Downies ..... 117 I 2
Na Sceirí / Skerries .... 109 N 7
Nacorra (Lough) .... 105 D 6
Nacung (Lough) .... 117 H 2
Nad .... 90 F 11
Nafooey (Lough) .... 105 D 7
Nagles Mountains .... 90 G 11
Nalughraman (Lough) ...... 116 G 3
Namanfin (Lough) .... 117 J 2
Namona (Lough) .... 88 B 12
Nanny .... 108 M 7
Narin .... 116 G 3
Narraghmore .... 102 L 8
Narrow Water Castle .... 109 N 5
Naul .... 109 N 7
Neagh (Lough) .... 114 M 4
Neale .... 105 E 7
Nealstown .... 101 I 9
Neidín / Kenmare .... 89 D 12
Nenagh .... 100 H 9
Nephin .... 111 D 5
Nephin (Glen) .... 105 D 6
Nephin Beg .... 111 D 5
Nephin Beg Range .... 111 C 5
New Birmingham .... 95 J 10
New Buildings .... 117 J 3
New Inn Cavan .... 108 K 6
New Inn Galway .... 100 G 8
New Kildimo .... 94 F 10
New Quay / Bealaclugga .. 99 E 8
New Twopothouse Village ..94 G 11
Newbawn .... 96 L 10
Newbliss .... 113 K 5
Newbridge
  near Tuomard .... 106 G 7
Newbridge /
  An Droichead Nua .... 102 L 8
Newcastle Down .... 115 O 5
Newcastle Dublin .... 103 M 8
Newcastle Galway .... 99 F 7
Newcastle Tipperary .... 95 I 11
Newcastle Wicklow .... 103 N 8
Newcestown .... 90 F 12
Newchapel .... 95 I 10
Newferry .... 114 M 3
Newgrange .... 109 M 6
Newinn .... 95 I 10
Newmarket Cork .... 93 F 11
Newmarket Kilkenny .... 96 K 10
Newmarket on Fergus ..... 99 F 9
Newmills Donegal .... 117 I 3
Newmills Dungannon ...... 114 L 4
Newport Tipperary .... 100 G 9
Newport Bay .... 105 C 6
Newport Trench .... 114 M 4
Newry .... 114 M 5
Newtown Galway .... 99 F 8
Newtown Kildare .... 102 L 7
Newtown Laois .... 101 K 9
Newtown Limerick .... 94 G 10
Newtown near Knock ...... 101 I 9
Newtown near Nenagh ... 100 H 9
Newtown Offaly .... 100 H 8
Newtown Roscommon ..... 100 H 7
Newtown Tipperary .... 95 H 10
Newtown Waterford .... 95 J 11
Newtown Wexford .... 96 M 11
Newtown Cashel .... 107 I 7
Newtown Cloghans .... 111 E 5
Newtown Cunningham ... 117 J 3
Newtown Forbes .... 107 I 6
Newtown Gore .... 107 I 5
Newtown
  Mount Kennedy .... 103 N 8
Newtown Sandes .... 93 D 10
Newtownabbey .... 115 O 4
Newtownards .... 115 O 4

Newtownbreda .... 115 O 4
Newtownbutler .... 113 J 5
Newtownhamilton .... 114 M 5
Newtownlow .... 101 J 7
Newtownlynch .... 99 E 8
Newtownshandrum .... 94 F 10
Newtownstewart .... 113 J 3
Nier .... 95 J 11
Ninemilehouse .... 95 J 10
Nobber .... 108 L 6
Nohaval .... 90 G 12
Nore .... 101 J 9
Nore (River) .... 96 K 10
North Channel .... 119 O 2
North Ring .... 90 F 13
North Sound .... 98 C 8
Nose of Howth .... 103 N 7
Noughaval Doora .... 99 F 9
Noughaval Noughaval ...... 99 E 8
Nowen Hill .... 89 E 12
Nuns Quarter .... 115 O 4
Nurney Carlow .... 96 L 9
Nurney Kildare .... 102 L 8
Nutt's Corner .... 115 N 4

O
Oaghley .... 93 D 10
Oatfield .... 99 F 9
Oatquarter .... 98 C 8
O'Brien's Tower .... 98 D 9
O'Flynn (Lough) .... 106 G 6
Oghil Clare .... 100 H 8
Oghil Galway .... 98 C 8
Ogonnelloe .... 99 G 9
O'Grady (Lough) .... 99 G 9
Oileán Ciarraí /
  Castleisland .... 93 D 11
Oilgate .... 97 M 10
Oily .... 112 G 4
Old Court .... 89 E 13
Old Head Ballymackean .. 90 G 13
Old Head Louisburgh ...... 104 C 6
Old Kilcullen .... 102 L 8
Old Kildimo .... 94 F 10
Old Ross .... 96 L 10
Old Town Donegal .... 117 I 3
Old Town Laois .... 101 J 9
Old Town Roscommon ... 100 H 8
Old Town Wexford .... 96 L 10
Old Twopothouse .... 94 G 11
Oldleighlin .... 96 K 9
Oldmill Bridge .... 93 E 10
Oldtown Dublin .... 109 N 7
Oldtown Roscommon ... 101 I 7
Omagh .... 113 K 4
Omeath .... 109 N 5
Omey Island .... 104 B 7
Onaght .... 98 C 8
Oola .... 94 H 10
Oorid Lough .... 105 D 7
Oranmore .... 99 F 8
Oriel (Mount) .... 108 M 6
Oristown .... 108 L 6
Oritor .... 114 L 4
Ossian's Grave .... 119 N 2
Ougther (Lough) .... 107 J 6
Oulart .... 97 M 10
Ovens .... 90 G 12
Owel (Lough) .... 107 J 7
Owenascaul .... 92 B 11
Owenator .... 116 H 3
Owenavorragh .... 97 M 10
Owenbeagh .... 117 H 3
Owenbeg .... 111 F 5
Owenbeg (River) .... 112 G 5
Owenboliska .... 99 E 8
Owenboy .... 90 G 12
Owenbristy .... 99 F 8
Owencarrow .... 117 I 2
Owendalulleegh .... 99 G 8
Owenea .... 116 G 3
Owengarve Clew Bay ...... 105 D 6
Owengarve River Moy ..... 106 F 5
Owenglin .... 104 C 7
Oweniny .... 111 D 5
Owenkillew Glenelly .... 114 K 3
Owenkillew Lough Swilly .117 J 2
Owenmore Bridge .... 105 D 6
Owennacurra .... 90 H 12
Owenreagh Hill .... 117 J 3
Owenriff .... 105 D 7
Owentaraglin .... 93 E 11
Owentocker .... 116 H 3
Owenur (River) .... 106 H 6
Ower .... 105 E 7
Owning .... 95 J 10
Owroe Bridge .... 88 B 12

A B C D E F G H I J K L M N O P Q R S T U V W X Y Z

A B C D E F G H I J K L M N O P Q R S T U V W X Y Z

Owvane .... 89 D 12
Oysterhaven .... 90 G 12

P
Palace .... 96 L 10
Palatine .... 102 L 9
Pallas .... 101 J 8
Pallas Cross .... 100 I 9
Pallas Green .... 94 G 10
Pallaskenry .... 94 F 10
Paps (The) .... 89 E 11
Park *Bellavary* .... 105 E 6
Park *Derry* .... 118 K 3
Parke's Castle .... 112 H 5
Parkgate .... 115 N 3
Parkmore .... 99 F 8
Parkmore Point .... 92 A 11
Parknasilla .... 88 C 12
Parteen .... 99 G 9
Partry .... 105 E 6
Partry Mountains .... 105 D 7
Passage .... 106 H 7
Passage East .... 96 L 11
Passage West .... 90 G 12
Patrickswell .... 94 F 10
Patterson's Spade Mill .... 115 N 3
Paulstown .... 96 K 9
Peake .... 90 F 12
Peatlands .... 114 M 4
Peterswell .... 99 F 8
Pettigoe .... 113 I 4
Phoenix Park .... 103 M 7
Piercetown .... 97 M 11
Pigeons (The) .... 107 I 7
Pike .... 100 H 8
Pike (The) *near Boola* .... 91 I 11
Pike (The) *near Lamybrien* .... 91 J 11
Pike (The) *Tipperary* .... 100 H 8
Pike Corner .... 108 L 7
Pike of Rush Hall .... 101 J 9
Piltown .... 95 K 10
Pluck .... 117 J 3
Plumbridge .... 113 K 3
Pollagh .... 101 I 8
Pollan Bay .... 117 J 2
Pollatomish .... 111 C 5
Pollnalaght .... 113 J 4
Pollshask .... 106 G 7
Pomeroy .... 114 L 4
Pontoon .... 105 E 6
Port .... 116 F 3
Port Ballintrae .... 118 M 2
Port Durlainne / Porturlin .... 111 C 5
Port Láirge / Waterford .... 96 K 11
Port Laoise / Portlaoise .... 101 K 8
Port Omna / Portumna .... 100 H 8
Portacloy .... 111 C 5
Portadown .... 114 M 4
Portaferry .... 115 P 4
Portaleen .... 118 K 2
Portavogie .... 115 P 4
Portbradden .... 118 M 2
Portglenone .... 118 M 3
Portland .... 100 H 8
Portlaw .... 96 K 11
Portmagee .... 88 A 12
Portmagee Channel .... 88 A 12
Portmarnock .... 103 N 7
Portmuck .... 115 O 3
Portnablagh .... 117 I 2
Portnoo .... 116 G 3
Portrane .... 109 N 7
Portroe .... 100 G 9
Portrush .... 118 M 2
Portsalon .... 117 J 2
Portstewart .... 118 L 2
Poulaphouca Reservoir .... 103 M 8
Poulnamucky .... 95 I 10
Poulnasherry Bay .... 98 D 10
Power Head .... 90 H 12
Power's Cross .... 100 H 8
Powerscourt Demesne .... 103 N 8
Powerstown .... 96 K 10
Poyntz Pass .... 114 M 5
Priesthaggard .... 96 L 11
Prosperous .... 102 L 8
Puckaun .... 100 H 9
Puffin Island .... 88 A 12
Punchestown .... 103 M 8

Q
Quarrytown .... 119 N 3
Querrin .... 93 D 10
Quigley's Point .... 118 K 2
Quilty .... 98 D 9
Quin .... 99 F 9
Quoile .... 115 O 4

R
Rabbit Islands .... 89 E 13
Race End .... 117 I 2
Raffrey .... 115 O 4
Raghly .... 112 G 5
Raghtin More .... 117 I 2
Rahan .... 101 J 8
Rahanagh .... 93 E 10
Rahara .... 106 H 7
Raharney .... 108 K 7
Raheen .... 96 L 10
Raigh .... 105 D 7
Railyard .... 101 K 9
Rake Street .... 111 D 5
Ram Head .... 91 I 12
Ramor (Lough) .... 108 K 6
Ramore Head .... 118 M 2
Rams Island .... 114 N 4
Ramsgrange .... 96 L 11
Randalstown .... 114 N 3
Rapemills .... 101 I 8
Raphoe .... 117 J 3
Rasharkin .... 118 M 3
Rashedoge .... 117 I 3
Rath .... 101 I 8
Ráth Caola / Rathkeale .... 94 F 10
Ráth Droma / Rathdrum .... 103 N 9
Rathangan .... 102 L 8
Rathaspick .... 107 J 7
Rathbrit .... 95 I 10
Rathcabban .... 100 H 8
Rathconrath .... 107 J 7
Rathcool .... 89 F 11
Rathcoole .... 103 M 8
Rathcor .... 109 N 6
Rathcore .... 102 L 7
Rathcormack *near Fermoy* .... 90 H 11
Rathcormack *near Sligo* .... 112 G 5
Rathcroghan .... 106 H 6
Rathdangan .... 103 M 9
Rathdowney .... 101 J 9
Rathduff .... 90 G 11
Rathedan .... 96 L 9
Rathfeigh .... 108 M 7
Rathfriland .... 115 N 5
Rathfylane .... 96 L 10
Rathgarogue .... 96 L 10
Rathgormuck .... 95 J 11
Rathkeevin .... 95 I 10
Rathkenny .... 108 M 6
Rathlackan .... 111 E 5
Rathlee .... 111 E 5
Rathlin Island .... 119 N 2
Rathlin O'Birne Island .... 112 F 4
Rathlin Sound .... 119 N 2
Rathmelton .... 117 J 2
Rathmines .... 103 N 8
Rathmolyon .... 108 L 7
Rathmore .... 89 E 11
Rathmullan .... 117 J 2
Rathnew .... 103 N 9
Rathnure .... 96 L 10
Rathowen .... 107 J 7
Rathvilla .... 101 K 8
Rathvilly .... 102 L 9
Ratoath .... 108 M 7
Raven Point (The) .... 97 M 10
Ravensdale .... 109 M 5
Ray *near Dunfanaghy* .... 117 H 2
Ray *near Rathmillan* .... 117 J 2
Ray (River) .... 99 G 8
Rea (Lough) .... 99 G 8
Reagh Island .... 115 P 4
Reananagowan Cross Roads .... 93 D 11
Reananeree /
Rae na nDoiri .... 89 E 12
Reanascreena .... 89 E 13
Rear Cross .... 95 H 9
Red Bay .... 119 N 2
Redcastle .... 118 K 2
Redcross .... 103 N 9
Redgate .... 97 M 10
Redhills .... 107 K 5
Ree (Lough) .... 107 I 7
Reelan .... 117 H 3
Reen .... 89 D 12
Reens .... 94 F 10
Reevanagh .... 96 K 9
Relaghbeg .... 108 L 6
Rerrin .... 88 C 13
Rhode .... 101 K 7
Richhill .... 114 M 4
Ridge .... 96 K 9
Ridge Point .... 110 C 5
Rine (River) .... 99 F 9

Rineanna Point .... 99 F 9
Ringabella Bay .... 90 H 12
Ringarogy Island .... 89 D 13
Ringaskiddy .... 90 H 12
Ringboy .... 115 P 4
Ringfad Point .... 115 P 5
Ringsend .... 118 L 2
Ringstown .... 101 J 8
Ringville / An Rinn .... 91 J 11
Rinmore Point .... 117 I 2
Rinn (River) .... 107 I 6
Rinn Lough .... 107 I 6
Rinneen *Clare* .... 98 D 9
Rinneen *Cork* .... 89 E 13
Rinroe Point .... 110 C 5
Rinville .... 99 F 8
Rinvyle .... 104 C 7
Rinvyle Castle .... 104 B 7
Rinvyle Point .... 104 B 7
River .... 110 B 6
Riverchapel .... 97 N 10
Riverstick .... 90 G 12
Riverstown *Cork* .... 90 G 12
Riverstown *Sligo* .... 112 G 5
Riverstown *Tipperary* .... 101 I 8
Riverville .... 93 D 11
Roadford .... 98 D 8
Roaninish .... 116 G 3
Roaringwater Bay .... 89 D 13
Robe .... 105 E 6
Robert's Head .... 90 H 12
Robertstown .... 102 L 8
Robinstown .... 108 L 7
Roche's Point .... 90 H 12
Rochestown .... 96 K 11
Rochfortbridge .... 101 K 7
Rock (The) .... 114 L 4
Rock Island .... 98 C 8
Rockabill .... 109 N 7
Rockchapel .... 93 E 11
Rockcorry .... 108 K 5
Rockhill .... 94 F 10
Rockmills .... 94 G 11
Rodeen .... 107 H 6
Roe .... 118 L 3
Roe Valley .... 118 L 2
Roney Point .... 97 N 10
Rooaun .... 100 H 8
Roonagh Quay .... 104 C 6
Roonah Lough .... 104 C 6
Roosky *Leitrim* .... 112 H 4
Roosky *Mayo* .... 106 F 6
Roosky *Roscommon* .... 107 I 6
Ropefield .... 112 G 5
Ros an Mhil / Rossaveel .... 98 D 8
Ros Comáin /
Roscommon .... 106 H 7
Ros Cré / Roscrea .... 101 I 9
Ros Láir / Rosslare .... 97 M 11
Ros Mhic Thriúin /
New Ross .... 96 L 10
Rosapenna .... 117 I 2
Rosbercon .... 96 L 10
Rosegreen .... 95 I 10
Rosenallis .... 101 J 8
Rosguill .... 117 I 2
Roskeeragh Point .... 112 F 4
Rosmuck .... 105 D 7
Rosmuck .... 95 I 9
Rosnakill .... 117 I 2
Ross *Lough Leane* .... 89 D 11
Ross *Lough Sheelin* .... 107 K 6
Ross Abbey .... 105 E 7
Ross Lake .... 105 E 7
Ross Port .... 111 C 5
Ross West .... 105 E 6
Rossan Point .... 112 F 3
Rossbeg .... 116 G 3
Rossbeigh Creek .... 92 C 11
Rossbrin .... 89 D 13
Rosscahill .... 105 E 7
Rosscarbery .... 89 E 13
Rosscarbery Bay .... 89 E 13
Rosscor .... 113 H 4
Rossdohan Island .... 88 C 12
Rosserk Abbey .... 111 E 5
Rosses (The) .... 116 G 2
Rosses Bay .... 116 G 2
Rosses Point .... 112 G 5
Rossglass .... 115 O 5
Rossgeir .... 117 J 3
Rossinver .... 112 H 4
Rosslare Bay .... 97 M 11
Rosslare Point .... 97 M 11
Rosslea .... 113 K 5
Rossmore *Cork* .... 89 F 12
Rossmore *Laois* .... 102 K 9

Rossmore Forest Park .... 114 L 5
Rossmore Island .... 88 C 12
Rossnowlagh .... 112 H 4
Rostellan .... 90 H 12
Rostrevor .... 109 N 5
Rosturk .... 105 C 6
Rough Point .... 92 B 11
Roughty .... 89 D 12
Roundfort .... 105 E 7
Roundstone .... 104 C 7
Roundwood .... 103 N 8
Roury .... 89 E 13
Rousky .... 114 K 3
Rowallane Gardens .... 115 O 4
Rower (The) .... 96 L 10
Royal Canal .... 107 I 7
Royaloak .... 96 L 9
Ruan .... 99 F 9
Rubane .... 115 P 4
Rue Point .... 119 N 2
Runabay Head .... 119 N 2
Runnabackan .... 106 H 6
Rushen (Slieve) .... 113 J 5
Russborough House .... 103 M 8
Rutland Island .... 116 G 3
Ryefield .... 108 K 6
Ryehill .... 106 F 7
Rylane Cross .... 90 F 12

S
Saddle Head .... 110 B 5
Saggart .... 103 M 8
St. Finan's Bay .... 88 A 12
St. John's Lough .... 107 I 5
St. John's Point .... 115 P 5
St. John's Point .... 112 G 4
St. Johnstown .... 117 J 3
St. Macdara's Island .... 104 C 8
St. Margaret's .... 103 N 7
St. Mochta's House .... 108 M 6
St. Mullin's .... 96 L 10
Saintfield .... 115 O 4
Saleen *Cork* .... 90 H 12
Saleen *Kerry* .... 93 D 10
Salia .... 104 C 6
Sallahig .... 88 B 12
Sallins .... 102 M 8
Sally Gap .... 103 N 8
Sallybrook .... 90 G 12
Sallypark .... 100 H 9
Salrock .... 104 C 7
Saltee Islands .... 96 M 11
Salthill .... 99 E 8
Saltsea .... 101 K 9
Sandholes .... 114 L 4
Sandyford .... 103 N 8
Santry .... 103 N 7
Saul .... 115 O 4
Sawel Mountain .... 118 K 3
Scalp Mountain .... 117 J 2
Scardaun *Mayo* .... 105 E 7
Scardaun *Roscommon* .... 106 H 7
Scarnagh .... 97 N 9
Scarriff / An Scairbh .... 99 G 9
Scarriff Island .... 88 B 12
Scartaglin .... 93 D 11
Scarva .... 114 M 5
Scattery Island .... 93 D 10
Schull / Skull .... 89 D 13
Scolban (Lough) .... 113 H 4
Scotch Town .... 114 K 3
Scotshouse .... 113 K 5
Scotstown .... 114 K 5
Scrabo Hill .... 115 O 4
Scramoge .... 107 H 6
Screeb Cross .... 105 D 7
Screen .... 97 M 10
Screggan .... 101 J 8
Scribbagh .... 113 H 4
Scullogue Gap .... 96 L 10
Scur (Lough) .... 107 I 5
Seaforde .... 115 O 5
Seapatrick .... 114 N 4
Seefin .... 95 J 11
Seskinore .... 113 K 4
Seskinryan .... 96 L 9
Seven Heads .... 90 F 13
Seven Hogs or
Magharee Islands (The) .... 92 B 11
Shalwy .... 112 G 4
Shanacashel .... 88 C 11
Shanagarry .... 90 H 12
Shanaglish .... 99 F 8
Shanagolden .... 93 E 10
Shanahoe .... 101 J 9
Shanballard .... 99 G 7
Shanbally *Cork* .... 90 G 12
Shanbally *Galway* .... 106 G 7

Shanballymore .... 94 G 11
Shanco .... 114 L 4
Shanes Castle .... 114 N 3
Shankill .... 103 N 8
Shanlaragh .... 89 E 12
Shanlis .... 108 M 6
Shannagh (Lough) .... 115 N 5
Shannakea .... 93 E 10
Shannawona .... 105 D 7
Shannon .... 99 F 9
Shannon (River) .... 100 H 8
Shannon Airport .... 99 F 9
Shannon Harbour .... 101 I 8
Shannonbridge .... 100 H 8
Shanragh .... 101 K 9
Shantonagh .... 108 L 5
Sharavogue .... 101 I 8
Sheddings (The) .... 119 N 3
Sheeanamore .... 103 M 9
Sheeaun .... 99 G 9
Sheeffry Hills .... 105 C 6
Sheehan's Point .... 88 B 12
Sheelin (Lough) .... 107 K 6
Sheep Haven .... 117 I 2
Sheever (Lough) .... 107 K 7
Shehy Mountains .... 89 D 12
Shercock .... 108 L 6
Sherkin Island .... 89 D 13
Sherky Island .... 88 C 12
Sheskin .... 111 D 5
Sheskinapoll .... 117 J 3
Shillelagh .... 97 M 9
Shinrone .... 101 I 9
Shiven .... 106 G 7
Shoptown .... 115 N 3
Shot Head .... 89 C 13
Shranamanragh Bridge .... 110 C 5
Shrule .... 105 E 7
Silent Valley .... 109 O 5
Sillan (Lough) .... 108 L 5
Silver Bridge .... 108 M 5
Silver Strand .... 104 C 6
Silvermine Mountains .... 100 H 9
Silvermines .... 100 H 9
Sinking .... 106 F 7
Sion Mills .... 113 J 3
Six Crosses .... 93 D 10
Six Road Ends .... 115 P 4
Six Towns (The) .... 114 L 3
Sixmilebridge .... 99 F 9
Sixmilecross .... 114 K 4
Skannive (Lough) .... 104 C 8
Skeagh .... 107 J 7
Skehana .... 101 K 9
Skehanagh .... 106 G 7
Skerries (The) .... 118 M 2
Skreen *Meath* .... 108 M 7
Skreen *Sligo* .... 112 F 5
Sky Road .... 104 B 7
Slade .... 96 L 11
Slane .... 108 M 6
Slane (Hill of) .... 108 M 6
Slaney (River) .... 97 M 10
Slat (Lough) .... 92 B 11
Slate (River) .... 102 L 8
Slea Head .... 92 A 11
Slemish Mountain .... 119 N 3
Sliabh na Caillighe .... 108 K 6
Slieve Anierin .... 113 I 5
Slieve Aught Mountains .... 99 G 9
Slieve Bernagh .... 99 G 9
Slieve Bloom Mountains .... 101 J 8
Slieve Gamph
or the Ox Mountains .... 111 F 5
Slieve Mish Mountains .... 93 C 11
Slieve Miskish Mountains .... 88 C 13
Slieveanorra .... 119 N 2
Slievecallan .... 99 E 9
Slievefelim Mountains .... 94 H 9
Slievekimalta .... 100 H 9
Slievekirk .... 117 K 3
Slievemore *Dungannon* .... 114 K 4
Slievemore *Mayo* .... 110 B 5
Slievemurry .... 106 G 7
Slievenamon .... 95 J 10
Slieveroe .... 96 K 11
Slievetooey .... 116 G 3
Sligeach / Sligo .... 112 G 5
Sligo Bay .... 112 F 5
Sliveardagh Hills .... 95 J 10
Slyne Head .... 104 B 7
Smerwick .... 92 A 11
Smerwick Harbour .... 92 A 11
Smithborough .... 114 K 5
Smithstown .... 101 K 9
Snaght (Slieve)
Derryveagh Mts. .... 117 H 3

Snaght (Slieve) *Inishowen* .... 117 J 2
Snave .... 89 D 12
Sneem .... 88 C 12
Soldierstown .... 115 N 4
Sord / Swords .... 103 N 7
South Sound .... 98 D 8
Spa .... 93 C 11
Spa (The) .... 115 O 4
Spanish Point *Locality* .... 98 D 9
Spanish Point *Mal Bay* .... 98 D 9
Speenoge .... 117 J 2
Spelga Dam .... 115 N 5
Sperrin Mountains .... 118 K 3
Spink .... 101 K 9
Spittaltown .... 101 J 7
Springfield .... 113 I 4
Springhill .... 114 M 3
Springwell Forest .... 118 L 2
Squires Hill .... 115 O 4
Sraghmore .... 103 N 8
Srah / An tSraith .... 105 E 6
Sráid na Cathrach /
Milltown Malbay .... 98 D 9
Stabannan .... 109 M 6
Stackallan .... 108 M 6
Stack's Mountains .... 93 D 11
Staffordstown .... 114 M 3
Stags (The) .... 89 E 13
Stags of Broad Haven .... 111 C 4
Staigue Stone Fort .... 88 B 12
Stamullin .... 109 N 7
Staplestown .... 102 L 8
Stepaside .... 103 N 8
Stewartstown .... 114 L 4
Stickstown .... 90 F 12
Stillorgan .... 103 N 8
Stone Bridge .... 113 K 5
Stonyford *Kilkenny* .... 96 K 10
Stonyford *Lisburn* .... 115 N 4
Stormont .... 115 O 4
Strabane .... 117 J 3
Stracashel .... 117 H 3
Stradbally *Kerry* .... 92 B 11
Stradbally *Laois* .... 101 K 8
Stradbally *Waterford* .... 91 J 11
Strade .... 105 E 6
Stradone .... 107 K 6
Stradreagh .... 118 L 2
Straffan .... 103 M 8
Stragar .... 112 G 3
Strahart .... 96 M 10
Straid *Donegal* .... 117 J 2
Straid *Larne* .... 115 O 3
Straid *Moyle* .... 118 M 2
Straith Salach / Recess .... 104 C 7
Strand .... 93 E 10
Strandhill .... 112 G 5
Strangford .... 115 P 4
Strangford Lough .... 115 P 4
Stranocum .... 118 M 2
Stranorlar .... 117 I 3
Stratford .... 102 L 9
Stravally .... 112 G 3
Streamstown .... 104 B 7
Streedagh Point .... 112 G 4
Streek Head .... 89 C 13
Street .... 107 J 6
Strokestown .... 106 H 6
Stroove .... 118 L 2
Struell Wells .... 115 O 5
Struic .... 113 J 3
Sturrakeen .... 95 H 10
Suck (River) .... 106 G 6
Suir (River) .... 101 I 9
Summercove .... 90 G 12
Summerhill .... 108 L 7
Suncroft .... 102 L 8
Sunderlin (Lough) .... 107 I 7
Swan .... 101 K 9
Swanlinbar .... 113 I 5
Swan's Cross Roads .... 114 K 5
Swatragh .... 118 L 3
Sweep (The) .... 95 J 10
Swilly (Lough) .... 117 J 2
Swilly (River) .... 117 J 2
Sybil Head .... 92 A 11

T
Table Mountain .... 103 M 8
Tacumshane .... 97 M 11
Tacumshin Lake .... 97 M 11
Taghmon .... 96 M 11
Taghshinny .... 107 I 7

Tagoat ....97 M 11
Tahilla ....88 C 12
Talbot Island ....104 B 7
Talbotstown ....102 M 9
Tallaght ....103 M 8
Tallanstown ....108 M 6
Tallow ....91 H 11
Tallowbridge ....91 H 11
Talt (Lough) ....111 F 5
Tamlaght *Fermanagh* ....113 J 5
Tamlaght *Magherafelt* ....118 M 3
Tamnamore ....114 M 4
Tandragee ....114 M 4
Tang ....107 I 7
Tangaveane ....116 H 3
Tappaghan Mount ....113 J 4
Tara (Hill of) ....108 M 7
Tarbert ....93 D 10
Tardree Forest ....115 N 3
Tarker (Lough) ....108 L 5
Tarmon ....112 H 5
Tarsaghaunmore ....111 C 5
Tassagh ....114 L 5
Taughblane ....115 N 4
Taur ....93 E 11
Tawin ....99 E 8
Tawin Island ....99 E 8
Tawny ....117 I 2
Tawnyinah ....106 F 6
Tawnylea ....112 H 5
Tay ....95 J 11
Tay (Lough) ....103 N 8
Taylor's Cross ....101 I 8
Tearaght Island ....92 A 11
Tedavnet ....114 K 5
Teelin ....112 G 4
Teemore ....113 J 5
Teeranea ....98 D 8
Teeranearagh ....88 B 12
Teerelton ....89 F 12
Teermaclane ....99 E 9
Teernakill ....105 D 7
Teeromoyle ....88 B 12
Teevurcher ....108 L 6
Temple ....115 O 4
Temple of the Winds ....115 P 4
Templeboy ....112 F 5
Templederry ....100 H 9
Templeglentan ....93 E 10
Templehouse Lake ....112 G 5
Templemartin ....90 F 12
Templenoe ....89 C 12
Templeoran ....101 J 7
Templepatrick ....115 N 3

Templeshanbo ....96 L 10
Templetouhy ....101 I 9
Templetown ....96 L 11
Tempo ....113 J 4
Terenure ....103 N 8
Termon ....98 D 10
Termonbarry ....107 I 6
Termonfeckin ....109 N 6
Terryglass ....100 H 8
Tevrin ....107 K 7
Thomas Street ....106 H 7
Thomastown *Meath* ....108 L 6
Thomastown *Tipperrary* ....95 H 10
Thoor Ballylee ....99 F 8
Three Castle Head ....88 C 13
Three Castles ....96 J 9
Three Rock ....103 N 8
Tiduff ....92 B 11
Tievealehid ....116 H 2
Tievemore ....113 I 4
Tillyvoos ....112 H 4
Tiltinbane ....113 I 5
Timahoe ....102 L 8
Timoleague ....90 F 13
Timolin ....102 L 9
Tinahely ....103 M 9
Tinnahinch ....96 L 10
Tinriland ....102 L 9
Tiobraid Árann /
   Tipperary ....95 H 10
Tirnaneill ....114 L 5
Tirneevin ....99 F 8
Toames ....89 F 12
Tobar an Choire /
   Tubbercurry ....112 F 5
Tober ....101 J 7
Toberbeg ....102 M 8
Toberdoney ....118 M 2
Tobermore ....114 L 3
Tobernadarry ....105 E 7
Toberscanavan ....112 G 5
Toe Head ....89 E 13
Toem ....95 H 10
Togher *Cork* ....89 E 12
Togher *Louth* ....109 N 6
Togher *Offaly* ....101 K 8
Tolka ....103 M 7
Tollymore Forest Park ....115 O 5
Tombrack ....97 M 10
Tomdarragh ....103 N 8
Tomhaggard ....97 M 11
Tonabrocky ....99 E 8
Tonakeera Point ....104 C 7
Tonyduff ....108 K 6

Toomaghera ....99 E 8
Toomard ....106 G 7
Toombeola ....104 C 7
Toome ....114 M 3
Toomyvara ....100 H 9
Toor ....100 H 9
Tooraree ....93 E 10
Tooreencahill ....93 E 11
Toorlestraun ....112 F 5
Toormore ....89 D 13
Toormore Bay ....89 D 13
Toornafulla ....93 E 10
Toraigh /
   Tory Island ....116 H 2
Torc Waterfall ....89 D 11
Torneady Point ....116 G 2
Torr Head ....119 N 2
Tory Sound ....117 H 2
Tourig (River) ....91 I 11
Tower ....90 G 12
Trá Lí / Tralee ....93 C 11
Trá Mhór /
   Tramore ....96 K 11
Trabane Strand ....112 F 4
Tracton ....90 G 12
Trafrask ....89 D 12
Tragumna ....89 E 13
Tralee Bay ....92 C 11
Tramore Bay ....96 K 11
Tranarossan Bay ....117 I 2
Travara Bridge ....88 C 12
Trawbreaga Bay ....117 K 2
Trawenagh Bay ....116 G 3
Trawmore Bay ....110 C 5
Trean ....105 D 7
Treantagh ....117 I 2
Treehoo ....107 K 5
Trien ....106 G 6
Trillick ....113 J 4
Tristia ....110 C 5
Trory ....113 J 4
Trostan ....119 N 2
Truskmore ....112 G 4
Trust ....100 G 7
Tuaim / Tuam ....105 F 7
Tuamgraney ....99 G 9
Tuar Mhic Éadaigh /
   Tourmakeady ....105 D 7
Tubber ....99 F 8
Tubbrid *Kilkenny* ....95 J 9
Tubbrid *Tipperary* ....95 I 11
Tulach Mhór /
   Tullamore ....101 J 8
Tulla *near Ennis* ....99 F 9

Tulla *near Gort* ....99 F 8
Tullagh Point ....117 J 2
Tullaghan ....112 G 4
Tullaghan Bay ....110 C 5
Tullaghanstown ....108 L 7
Tullagher ....96 K 10
Tullaghobegly ....117 H 2
Tullaherin ....96 K 10
Tullahought ....95 J 10
Tullakeel ....88 C 12
Tullamore ....93 D 10
Tullaroan ....95 J 10
Tullig ....92 C 11
Tullig Point ....93 C 10
Tullokyne ....105 E 7
Tully
   Lower Lough Erne ....113 I 4
Tully *near Ballyshannon* ....113 H 4
Tully *Upper Lough Erne* ....113 J 5
Tully Cross ....104 C 7
Tully National Stud ....102 L 8
Tullyallen ....109 M 6
Tullyamalra ....108 L 5
Tullycanna ....96 L 11
Tullydush ....117 J 2
Tullyhogue ....114 L 4
Tullylease ....94 F 11
Tullymacreeve ....109 M 5
Tullynaha ....112 H 3
Tullynally Castle ....107 J 6
Tullyroan ....114 M 4
Tullyvin ....108 K 5
Tulrohaun ....105 F 6
Tulsk ....106 H 6
Turlough ....105 E 6
Turloughmore ....105 F 7
Turner's Rock Tunnel ....89 D 12
Turreen ....107 I 7
Tuskar Rock ....97 N 11
Twelve Pins (The) ....104 C 7
Twomileborris ....95 I 9
Tylas ....108 M 7
Tynagh ....100 G 8
Tynan ....114 L 5
Tyrella ....115 O 5
Tyrrellspass ....101 J 7

U

Uachtar Ard /
   Oughterard ....105 E 7
Uaigh / Owey Island ....116 G 2
Ugga Beg (Lough) ....98 D 8
Ulster American
   Folk Park ....113 J 4

Ulster Folk
   Museum (The) ....115 O 4
Union Hall ....89 E 13
Unshin ....112 G 5
Upper Ballinderry ....115 N 4
Upper Lake ....103 M 8
Upperchurch ....95 H 9
Upperlands ....118 M 3
Urbalreagh ....117 K 1
Urglin Glebe ....102 L 9
Urlaur ....106 F 6
Urlaur Lough ....106 F 6
Urlingford ....95 J 9

V

Valencia Island ....88 A 12
Valley ....110 C 5
Valleymount ....103 M 8
Vartry Reservoir ....103 N 8
Ventry ....92 A 11
Ventry Harbour ....92 A 11
Vicarstown ....102 K 8
Victoria Bridge ....113 J 3
Villierstown ....91 I 11
Virginia ....108 K 6
Virginia Road ....108 K 6
Vow ....118 M 3

W

Waddingtown ....96 M 11
Walshestown ....97 M 11
Walshtown ....90 H 12
Ward ....103 N 7
Ward (River) ....103 N 7
Waringsford ....115 N 4
Waringstown ....114 N 4
Warrenpoint ....109 N 5
Washing Bay ....114 M 4
Watch Ho.-Village ....96 M 9
Waterfall ....90 G 12
Waterfoot or Glenariff ....119 N 2
Waterford Harbour ....96 L 11
Watergrasshill ....90 G 11
Waterworks ....114 L 3
Wattle Bridge ....113 J 5
Welchtown ....117 I 3
Wellington Bridge ....96 L 11
Wells Cross ....114 M 4
Wesport Bay ....105 C 6
West Town ....116 H 2
Westcove ....88 B 12
Westport House ....105 D 6
Westport Quay ....105 D 6
Wexford Bay ....97 N 10

Wexford Harbour ....97 M 10
Whale Head ....117 J 2
Wheathill ....113 I 5
Whiddy Island ....89 D 12
White *Limerick* ....93 E 10
White *Louth* ....109 M 6
White Castle ....118 K 2
White Hall ....89 D 13
White Island ....113 I 4
White Park Bay ....118 M 2
White Strand ....98 D 9
Whiteabbey ....115 O 3
Whitechurch *Cork* ....90 G 12
Whitechurch *Waterford* ....91 I 11
Whitecross ....114 M 5
Whitegate ....90 H 12
Whitehall *Roscommon* ....107 I 6
Whitehall *Westmeath* ....107 K 7
Whitehead ....115 O 3
Whites Town ....109 N 6
White'sCross ....90 G 12
Whitesides Corner ....114 M 3
Wicklow Gap ....103 M 8
Wicklow Mountains ....103 N 8
Wicklow Way ....103 N 8
Wildfowl
   and Wetlands Trust ....115 O 4
Wilkinstown ....108 L 6
Willbrook ....99 E 9
Williamstown *Galway* ....106 G 6
Williamstown
   Westmeath ....107 I 7
Windgap ....95 J 10
Windmill ....102 L 7
Windy Gap *Kerry* ....89 D 12
Windy Gap *Louth* ....109 N 5
Windy Gap *Mayo* ....105 E 6
Wolfhill ....101 K 9
Womanagh ....91 I 12
Woodburn ....115 O 3
Woodcock Hill ....99 F 9
Woodenbridge ....103 N 9
Woodford (River) ....99 G 8
Woodstown ....96 L 11

Y

Yellow Furze ....108 M 6
Yganavan (Lough) ....92 C 11
Youghal ....100 H 9
Youghal Bay ....91 I 12

A B C D E F G H I J K L M N O P Q R S **T** **U** **V** **W** **X** **Y** **Z**

Town plans

Sights
Place of interest - Tower
Interesting place of worship
Roads
Motorway - Dual carriageway
Numbered junctions: complete, limited
Major thoroughfare
Tunnel
Pedestrian street
Tramway
Car park - Park and Ride
Station and railway
Funicular
Cable-car
Various signs
Place of worship
Tower - Ruins
Windmill
Garden, park, wood
Cemetery
Stadium
Golf course - Racecourse
Outdoor or indoor swimming pool
View - Panorama
Monument - Fountain
Beach - Zoo
Pleasure boat harbour - Lighthouse
Tourist Information Centre
Airport
Underground station - Coach station
Ferry services:
passengers and cars - passengers only
Main post office with poste restante - Hospital
Covered market
Police - Town Hall
Suggested stroll

Plans

Curiosités
Bâtiment intéressant - Tour
Édifice religieux intéressant
Voirie
Autoroute - Double chaussée de type autoroutier
Échangeurs numérotés : complet - partiels
Grande voie de circulation
Tunnel
Rue piétonne
Tramway
Parking - Parking Relais
Gare et voie ferrée
Funiculaire, voie à crémaillère
Téléphérique, télécabine
Signes divers
Édifice religieux
Tour - Ruines
Moulin à vent
Jardin, parc, bois
Cimetière
Stade
Golf - Hippodrome
Piscine de plein air, couverte
Vue - Panorama
Monument - Fontaine
Plage - Zoo
Port de plaisance - Phare
Information touristique
Aéroport
Station de métro - Gare routière
Transport par bateau :
passagers et voitures, passagers seulement
Bureau principal de poste restante - Hôpital
Marché couvert
Police - Hôtel de ville
Suggestion de promenade

Stadtpläne

Sehenswürdigkeiten
Sehenswertes Gebäude - Turm
Sehenswerter Sakralbau
Straßen
Autobahn - Schnellstraße
Nummerierte Voll- bzw. Teilanschlussstellen
Hauptverkehrsstraße
Tunnel
Fußgängerzone
Straßenbahn
Parkplatz - Park-and-Ride-Plätze
Bahnhof und Bahnlinie
Standseilbahn
Seilschwebebahn
Sonstige Zeichen
Sakralbau
Turm - Ruine
Windmühle
Garten, Park, Wäldchen
Friedhof
Stadion
Golfplatz - Pferderennbahn
Freibad - Hallenbad
Aussicht - Rundblick
Denkmal - Brunnen
Badestrand/ Strand - Zoo
Yachthafen- Leuchtturm
Informationsstelle
Flughafen
U-Bahnstation - Autobusbahnhof
Schiffsverbindungen:
Autofähre, Personenfähre
Hauptpostamt (postlagernde Sendungen) - Krankenhaus
Markthalle
Polizei - Rathaus
Vorschlag für einen Spaziergang

Plattegronden

Bezienswaardigheden
Interessant gebouw - Toren
Interessant kerkelijk gebouw
Wegen
Autosnelweg - Weg met gescheiden rijbanen
Knooppunt / aansluiting: volledig, gedeeltelijk
Hoofdverkeersweg
Tunnel
Voetgangersgebied
Tramlijn
Parkeerplaats - P & R
Station, spoorweg
Kabelspoor
Tandradbaan
Overige tekens
Kerkelijk gebouw
Toren - Ruïne
Windmolen
Tuin, park, bos
Begraafplaats
Stadion
Golfterrein - Renbaan
Zwembad: openlucht, overdekt
Uitzicht - Panorama
Gedenkteken, standbeeld - Fontein
Strand - Zoo
Jachthaven - Vuurtoren
Informatie voor toeristen
Luchthaven
Metrostation - Busstation
Vervoer per boot:
Passagiers en auto's - uitsluitend passagiers
Hoofdkantoor voor poste-restante - Ziekenhuis
Overdekte markt
Politie - Stadhuis
Aanbevolen wandeling

Piante

Curiosità
Edificio interessante - Torre
Costruzione religiosa interessante
Viabilità
Autostrada - Doppia carreggiata tipo autostrada
Svincoli numerati: completo, parziale
Grande via di circolazione
Galleria
Via pedonale
Tranvia
Parcheggio - Parcheggio Ristoro
Stazione e ferrovia
Funicolare
Funivia, cabinovia
Simboli vari
Costruzione religiosa
Torre - Ruderi
Mulino a vento
Giardino, parco, bosco
Cimitero
Stadio
Golf - Ippodromo
Piscina: all'aperto, coperta
Vista - Panorama
Monumento - Fontana
Spiaggia- Zoo
Porto turistico - Faro
Ufficio informazioni turistiche
Aeroporto
Stazione della metropolitana - Autostazione
Trasporto con traghetto:
passeggeri ed autovetture - solo passeggeri
Ufficio centrale di fermo posta - Ospedale
Mercato coperto
Polizia - Municipio
Passeggiata consigliata

Planos

Curiosidades
Edificio interesante - Torre
Edificio religioso interesante
Vías de circulación
Autopista - Autovía
Enlaces numerados: completo, parciales
Via importante de circulacíon
Túnel
Calle peatonal
Tranvía
Aparcamiento - Aparcamientos «P+R»
Estación y línea férrea
Funicular, línea de cremallera
Teleférico, telecabina
Signos diversos
Edificio religioso
Torre - Ruinas
Molino de viento
Jardín, parque, madera
Cementerio
Estadio
Golf - Hipódromo
Piscina al aire libre, cubierta
Vista parcial - Vista panorámica
Monumento - Fuente
Playa - Zoo
Puerto deportivo - Faro
Oficina de Información de Turismo
Aeropuerto
Estación de metro - Estación de autobuses
Transporte por barco:
pasajeros y vehículos, pasajeros solamente
Oficina de correos - Hospital
Mercado cubierto
Policía - Ayuntamiento
Propuesta de paseo

Plans de ville
Town plans / Stadtpläne / Stadsplattegronden
Piante di città / Planos de ciudades

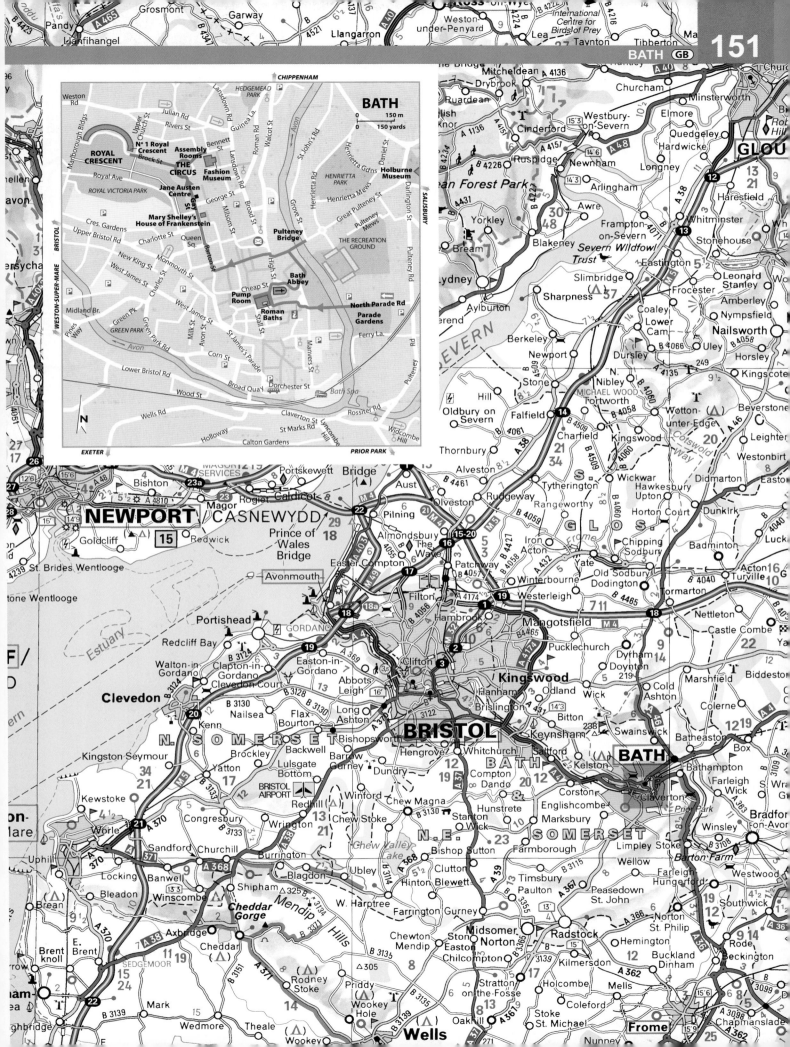

BATH

150 m
150 yards

CHIPPENHAM

HEDGEMEAD PARK

Weston Rd
Julian Rd
Rivers St
Upper Church St
Guinea La.
Walcot St
Roman Rd
St John's Rd
Avon

ROYAL CRESCENT
N° 1 Royal Crescent
Brock St
THE CIRCUS
Bennett St
Assembly Rooms
Fashion Museum
Lansdown Rd

Royal Ave
ROYAL VICTORIA PARK
Upper Bristol Rd
Cres. Gardens

Jane Austen Centre
Gay St
George St
Milsom St
Broad St
Queen Sq.
Mary Shelley's House of Frankenstein

BRISTOL
WESTON-SUPER-MARE
Midland Br.
Pines Way
New King St
West James St
Charlotte St
Monmouth St
Charles St
West James St
Mill St
GREEN PARK
Green Pk
Green Park Rd
St James's Parade
Corn St
Avon St
Manvers St
Pump Room
Cheap St
Roman Baths
Stall St
High St
Bath Abbey

Barton St

Henrietta Rd
HENRIETTA PARK
Henrietta Gdns
Henrietta Mews
Holburne Museum
Great Pulteney St
Pulteney Mews
Daniel St
Darlington St
SALISBURY

Pulteney Bridge
Grove St
Pulteney Rd

THE RECREATION GROUND

North Parade Rd
Parade Gardens
Ferry La.

Lower Bristol Rd
Wood St
Wells Rd
Broad Quay
Dorchester St
Bath Spa
Claverton St
Lyncombe Hill
St Marks Rd
Rossiter Rd
Widcombe Hill
Calton Gardens
Holloway

N
EXETER
PRIOR PARK

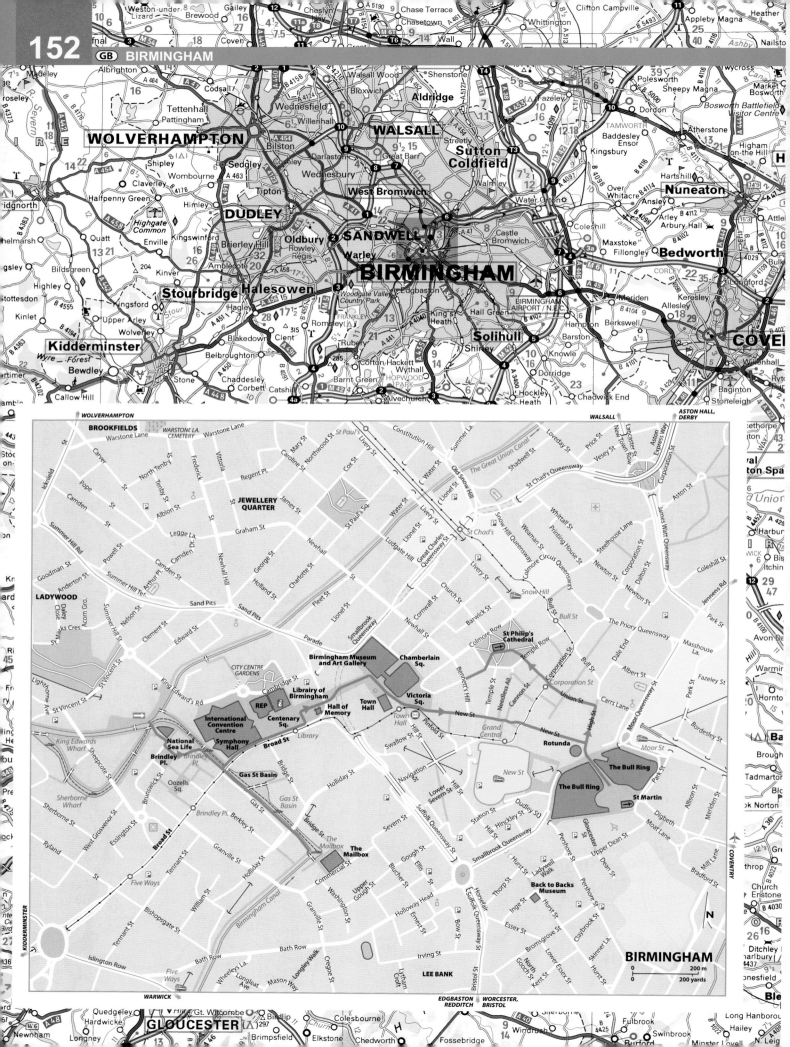

BRISTOL

AEROSPACE BRISTOL, YATE, SWINDON

0   200 m

N

WESTBURY PARK

COTHAM

Bristol Zoological Gardens

All Saints Church

St Peter and St Paul's Cathedral

Clifton Suspension Br.

Bridge Visitor Center

Clifton Village

Brandon Hill

Hope Chapel Hill

Bristol Museum and Art Gallery

Berkeley Sq.

Georgian House Museum

Lord Mayor's Chapel

Cathedral

Aquarium

We The Curious

Millenium Sq.

Pero's Bridge

St Stephen's Church

Corn St

St John the Baptist's Church

St Nicholas Market

Merchant Seamen's Almshouses

Brunel Statues

Bristol Old Vic

King St

Queen Sq.

Arnolfini Arts Center

Castle Park

Newgate

Brunel's SS Great Britain

Maritime Heritage Center

Spike Island

Floating Harbour

M Shed

Redcliffe Parade W

St Mary Redcliffe

ASHTON PARK

Avon

Cumberland Rd

Coronation Rd

Commercial Rd

Clarence Rd

ASTON GATE STADIUM

BEDMINSTER

Bedminster

KEYNSHAM, BATH

CLEVEDON COURT

WESTON-SUPER-MARE, BRIDGEWATER

NEWPORT, GLOUCESTER

Goldcliff

Redwick

Prince of Wales Bridge

The Wave

Almondsbury

Chipping Sodbury

Iron Acton

Badminton

St. Brides Wentlooge

Avonmouth

Easter Compton

Patchway

Winterbourne

Old Sodbury Dodington

Acton Turville

stone Wentlooge

Filton

Westerleigh

Portishead

Hambrook

Mangotsfield

GORDANO

Redcliff Bay

Clevedon

Walton-in-Gordano

Clapton-in-Gordano

Easton-in-Gordano

Abbots Leigh

Clifton

Pucklechurch

Dyrham Doynton

Nettleton

Castle Combe

Clevedon Court

Long Ashton

Kingswood

Hanham

Odland

Wick

Cold Ashton

Marshfield

Colerne

Kingston Seymour

Nailsea

Flax Bourton

Bishopsworth

Brislington

Bitton

Swainswick

N. SOMERSET

Backwell

Barrow Gurney

BRISTOL

Hengrove

Whitchurch

Keynsham

Kelston

Batheaston

BATH

Box

Kingston Seymour

Brockley

Lulsgate Bottom

Dundry

Compton Dando

Corston

Bathampton

BRISTOL AIRPORT

Redhill

Winford

Chew Magna

Stanton Wick

Englishcombe

Marksbury

Farleigh Wick

Worle

Congresbury

Wrington

Chew Stoke

N.E. SOMERSET

Hunstrete

Priston

Winsley

Kewstoke

Churchill

Chew Valley Lake

Bishop Sutton

Farmborough

Wellow

Peasedown

Banwell

Blagdon

Shipham

Ubley

Clutton

Timsbury

Paulton

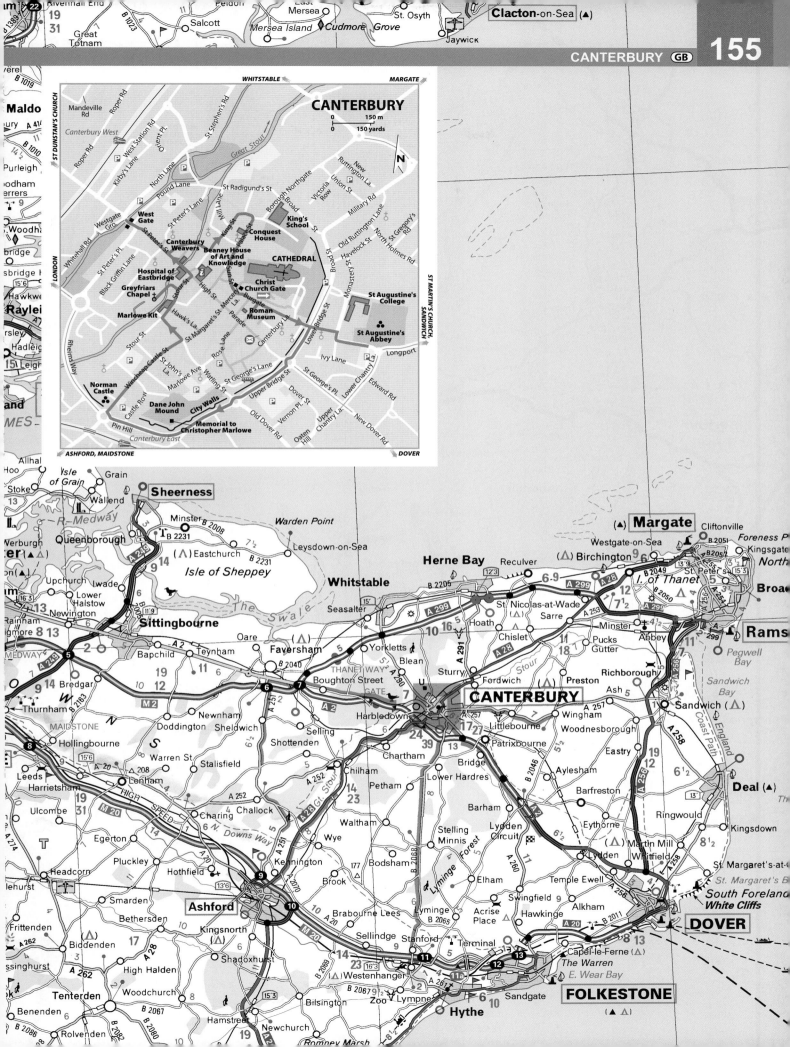

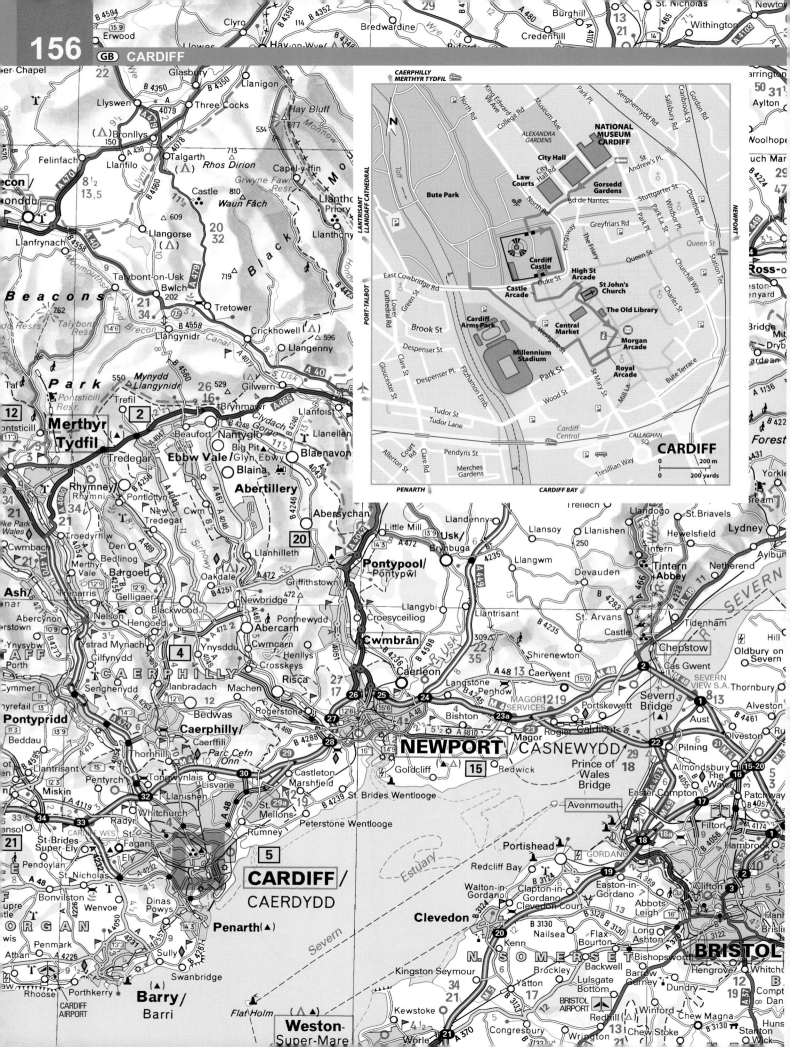

CHESTER (inset map)

HOYLAKE ELLESMERE PORT MANCHESTER, LIVERPOOL

Garden Lane Bouverie St Walpole St Walter St Cornwall St Station Rd
Louise St Chichester St Victoria Rd Gloucester St Trafford St St Anne St Brook St Hoole Way
Whipcord La. Wharf View Delamere St St Oswalds Way Francis St Egerton St Crewe St City Rd
Raymond St Canal St George St Milton St Leadworks La. Queen's Ave
Tower Rd ST MARTIN'S King St Northgate King Charles' Tower Union Ter St Oswalds Way Russell St
GATE St Martin's Way Kaleyard's Gate York St The Bars
The Walls Town Hall Chester Cathedral St Werburgh St The Dee Lane
City Walls Rd Stanley St Hamilton Pl. Eastgate Foregate St Love St Bath St
New Crane St Eastgate St THE ROWS Queen St Union St
WATERGATE Stanley Palace Watergate St Dewa Roman Experience Newgate Grosvenor Park
Grey Friars Three Old Arches Grosvenor Shopping Centre St John's
Black Friars Nicholas St Park St The Groves
The Roodee Grosvenor Museum Dee
Castle St Duke St
Grosvenor Rd Nun's Rd Bridgegate Old Dee Bridge QUEEN'S PARK
Castle Drive Victoria Crescent Lower Park Rd
Queen's Park Rd Northern Pathway

CHESTER
0 150 m
0 150 yards

WREXHAM, CONWY

N

Regional map

SOUTHPORT Mere Brow Rufford Wildfowl Trust Rufford
Birkdale Scarisbrick Burscough Bridge
Ainsdale Halsall Burscough
Formby Ormskirk Skelm
Gt. Altcar Aughton
Formby Point Ince Blundell Lydiate
Hightown Maghull
Blundellsands Aintree Kirkby
Crosby Litherland ST. H
Bootle Knowsley
New Brighton
Wallasey LIVERPOOL Roby
Moreton Huy
BIRKENHEAD Woolton
West Kirby Irby Port Sunlight Hough Green
Thurstaston Pensby Bebington Wid
Heswall Bromborough Speke
Thornton Hough LIVERPOOL JOHN LENNON AIRPORT
Parkgate Eastham River Mersey
Neston Whitby Ellesmere Port
Willaston Backford Cross Elton R
Puddington Stoak
Flint / Fflint Bridge T
Greenfield Connah's Quay Saughall
Bagillt Queensferry Sealand Upton Great Barrow
Halkyn Ewloe CHESTER
Northop Hawarden Lache Christle
Point of Ayr Northop Hall Saltney CHESHIRE W
Talacre Mold Buckley Broughton Handbridge
Prestatyn Yr Wyddgrug Bwlch Penyffordd AND
Rhyl Llanasa Hope Pulford CHESTE
Kinmel Bay Trelawnyd Mostyn Holywell Treffynnon Waun y llyn Burton Aldford
Bay Dyserth Babell Nercwys Caergwrle Handley
Pensarn Castle Caerwys Leeswood Rossett
Abergele Rhuallt Afon-wen Treuddyn Gresford
Bodelwyddan Tremeirchion Llanfynydd Brymbo Holt
St. Asaph Bodfari Llanarmon yn-Ial Bwlchgwyn Farndon
Llannefydd Nannerch Coedpoeth Broxton
Trefnant FLINTS Rhostyllen
Henllan Cilcain WREXHAM / Wrecsam
Bylchau Denbigh / Dinbych Loggerheads Erddig Marchwiel
Llansannan Llandyrnog Moel Fammau Worthenbury Malpa
Llanrhaeadr DENBIGHSHIRE Tilston
Cyffylliog Ruthin / Rhuthun Range Llanfynydd
Clocaenog Llanelidan
Clocaenog Forest Brenig Resr. Offa's Dyke
Llanfihangel Glyn Myfyr Clawdd newydd
Bettws Gwerfil Goch Bryneglwys

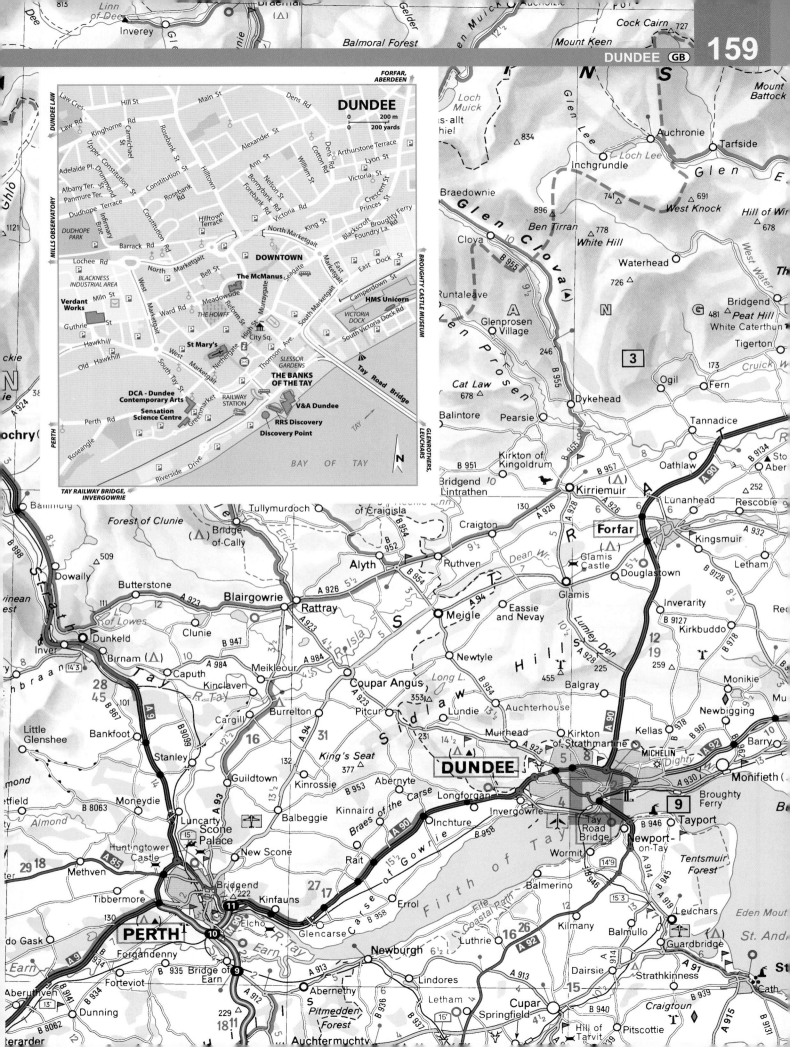

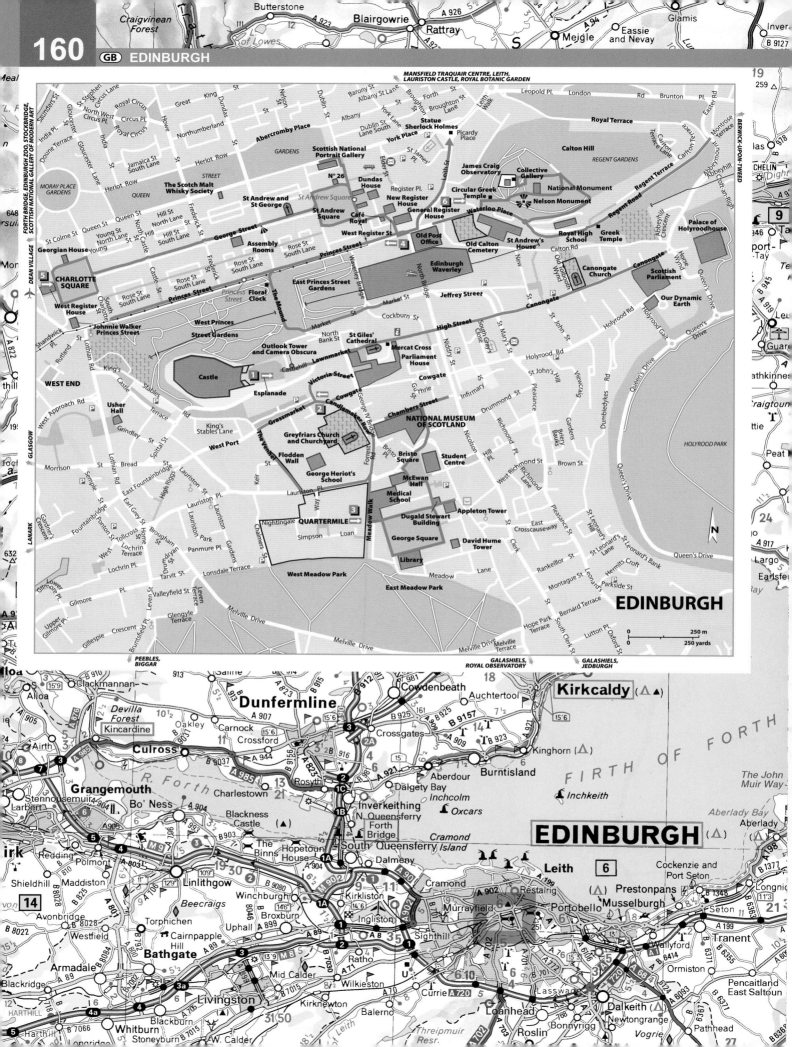

MANSFIELD TRAQUAIR CENTRE, LEITH,
LAURISTON CASTLE, ROYAL BOTANIC GARDEN

FORTH BRIDGE, EDINBURGH ZOO, STOCKBRIDGE,
SCOTTISH NATIONAL GALLERY OF MODERN ART

EDINBURGH

PEEBLES,
BIGGAR

GALASHIELS,
ROYAL OBSERVATORY

GALASHIELS,
JEDBURGH

FIRTH OF FORTH

EDINBURGH (△)

EXETER

Hele Rd
New North Rd
St David's Hill
Richmond Rd
Richmond Ct
Queen St
Elm Grove Rd
New North Rd
Blackall Rd
Howell Rd
Longbrook St
Longbrook Ter.
New North Rd
Sidwell St
Cheeke St
High St
Paris St
Dix's Field
Exeter Central
Dinham Crescent
Dinham Mount
Lower North St
Northernhay St
Bonhay Rd
Eye St
Paul St
Gandy St
Royal Albert Memorial Museum
Guildhall
High St
St Martin's Church
Mol's Coffee House
Cathedral
Cathedral Close
Western Way
Archibald Rd
Athelstan Rd
Barnfield Rd
Barnfield Rd
Denmark Rd
SOUTHERNHAY PARK
Southernhay Gdns
Magdalen Rd
BULLMEADOW
Wonford Rd
Fairpark Rd
Temple Rd
Roberts Rd
Radford Rd
Cedars Rd
Barnardo's Rd
Topsham Rd
Tudor St
Bonhay Rd
Bear St
North St
Fore St
George St
Smythen St
Market St
King St
Preston St
South St
St Nicholas Priory
Palace Gate
New Br. St
Frog St
Western Way
Bull Meadow Rd
Holloway St
Lucky Lane
Colleton Crescent
Alphington St
Edmund St
Commercial Rd
Custom House Visitor Centre
HISTORC QUAYSIDE
St Thomas
The Quay
Haven Banks
Haven Rd
Haven Rd

N

0 150 m
0 150 yards

BRISTOL
HONITON

BARNSTAPLE

OKEHAMPTON, PLYMOUTH
EXEMOUTH

Main map

DEVON

Brushford
Morebath
Exebridge
Shillingford
Ash Mill
B 3227
Oakford
Bampton
283
Rackenford
R. Exe
A 396
286
Knightshayes Court
Little Dart
Witheridge
Bolham
A 361
Halberton
Tiverton
B 3042
B 3137
B 3137
Morchard Bishop
Creedy
Cheriton Fitzpaine
Bickleigh
Cullompton
Coplestone
Sandford
A 3072
Bradninch
Thorverton
Silverton
Killerton
B 3181
Crediton
Yeo
Newton St. Cyres
A 377
Stoke Canon
Broadclyst
Tedburn St. Mary
Pinhoe
Clyst Honiton
EXETER AIRPORT
EXETER
Cheriton Bishop
A 30
Ide
Alphington
Topsham
Clyst St Mary
Dunsford
B 3212
Kennford
Exminster
Exton
Lympstone
Doddiscombsleigh
Christow
Trusham
Kenton
Starcross
Becky Falls
Hennock
Chudleigh
Ideford
Dawlish
Bovey Tracey
Bishopsteignton
Ilsington
Kingsteignton
Teignmouth
Shaldon
Newton Abbot
Combeinteignhead
Ashburton
Abbotskerswell
Maidencombe
Buckfast
Kingskerswell
Babbacombe Bay
Buckfastleigh
Ipplepen
Compton
TORQUAY
Staverton
Marldon
Babbacombe
Dartington
Cockington
TORBAY
Castle
Tor Bay
Berry Pomeroy
PAIGNTON
Totnes
Goodrington
Harberton
Stoke Gabriel
Churston Fer6rs
Ashprington
Galmpton
Berry Head
Diptford
Cornworthy
Brixham
Avonwick
Harbertonford
Dittisham

Okehampton
Sticklepath
S. Tawton
Spreyton
Bratton Clovelly
Belstone
S. Zeal
Whiddon Down
Drewsteignton
Spinster's Rock
High Willhays
Throwleigh
Sandy Park
Castle Drogo
Fingle Bridge
Sourton
Scorhill
Easton
Bridestowe
Chagford
A 382
Lydford
Dartmoor Forest
Shovel Down
Moretonhampstead
N. Bovey
Lydford gorge
Cut Hill
Grey Wethers
Manaton
Lustleigh
N. Brentor
Brent Tor
Wistman's Wood
Postbridge
Widecombe-in-the-Moor
Haytor Rocks
Mary Tavy
Great Mis Tor
Dartmoor
Two Bridges
Buckland-in-the-Moor
Bickington
Tavistock
Dartmoor Prison
Princetown
Dartmeet
Whitchurch
National
River Dart
Horrabridge
Ryder's Hill
Holne
Park
Buckland Abbey
Meavy
Buckfast
Buckfastleigh
Yelverton
Bere Ferrers
Bickleigh
Cornwood
S. Brent
PLYMOUTH
Plympton
Saltram
Ivybridge
Avonwick
Ugborough
Ermington

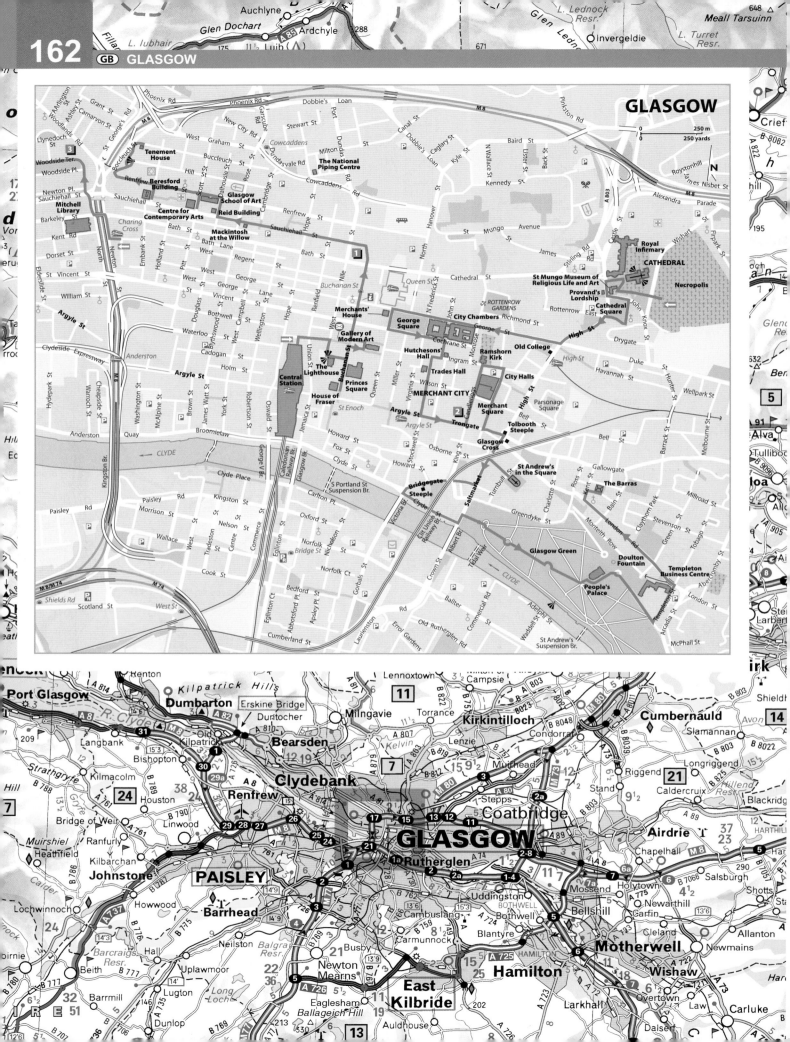

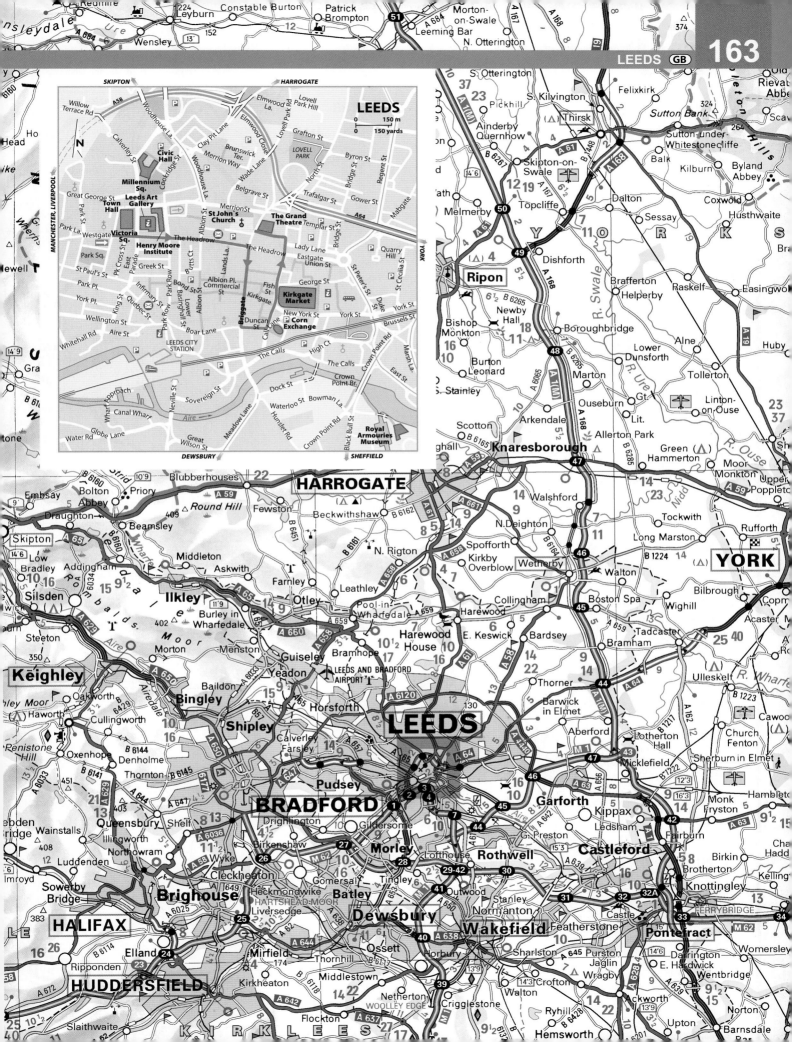

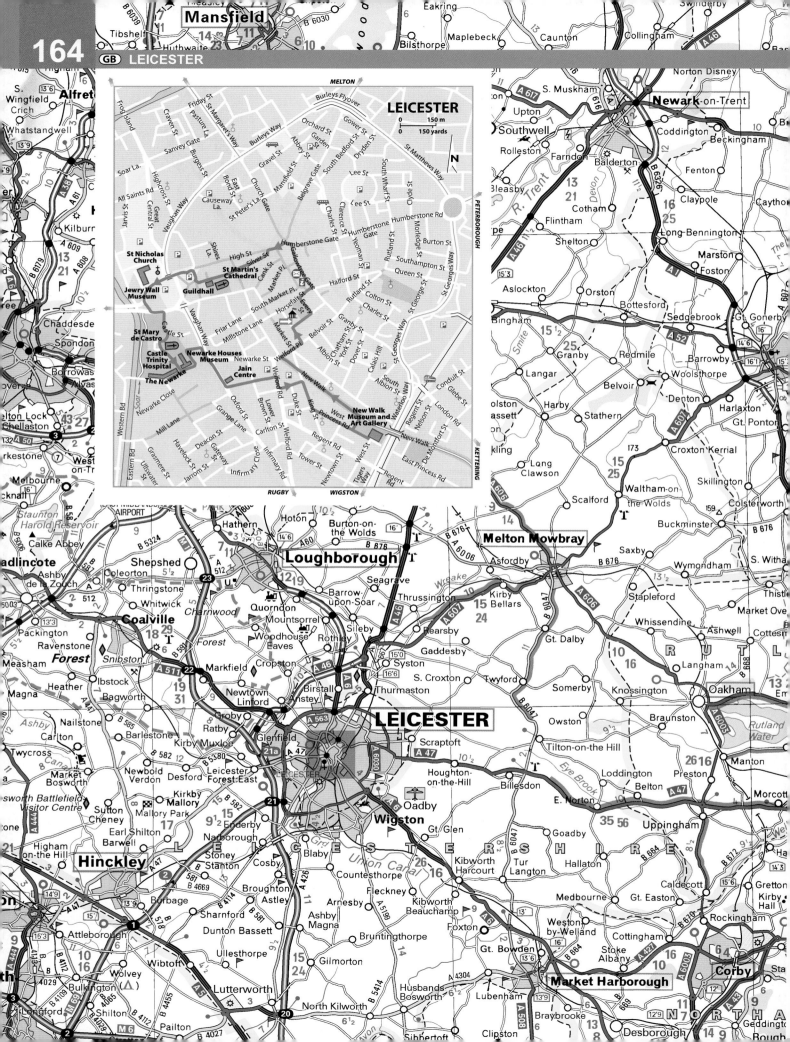

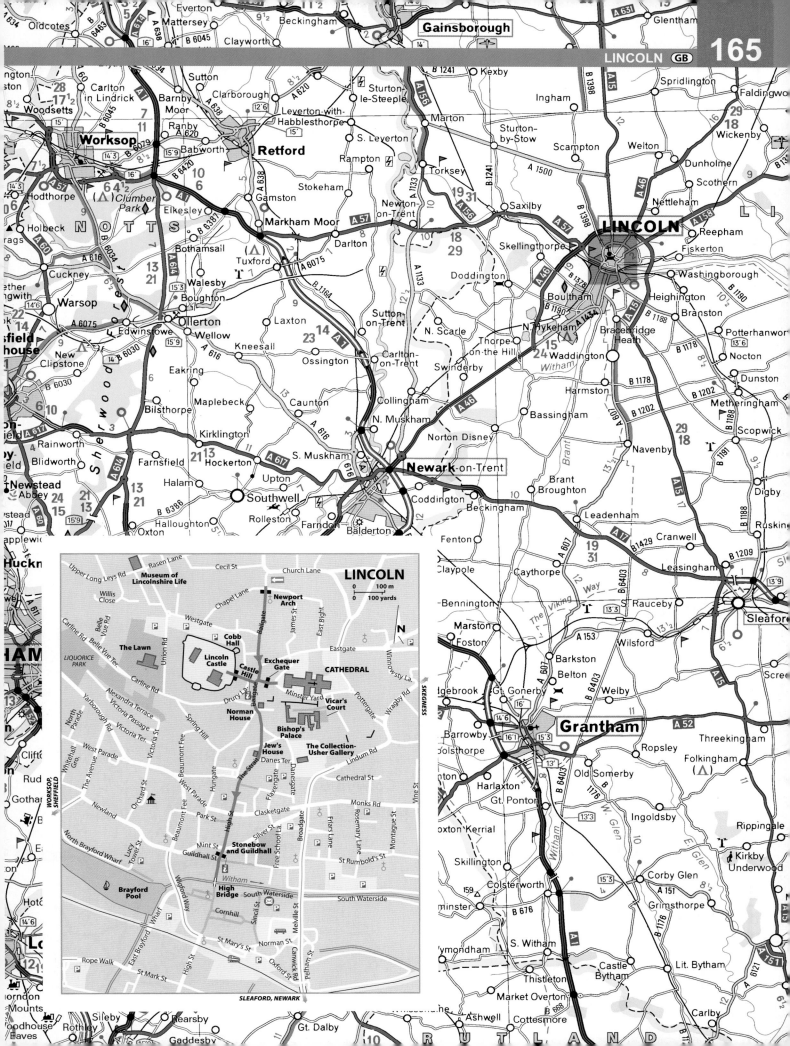

CROSBY   PRESTON   MANCHESTER

Waterloo Rd
Paisley St
Roberts St
King Edward St
Gibraltar Row
Bath St
Princes Parade
William Jessop Way
New Quay
Old Hall St

Eaton St
Gascoyne St
Pall Mall
Oriel St
Vauxhall Rd
Naylor St
Leeds St

Scotland Rd
Byrom St
Hunter St

Midghall St
Marlborough St
Highfield St
Great Crosshall St
Lace St

St Josephs Cres
Christian St
St Anne St
Soho St
Bidder St
John St
Shaw St
Langsdale St
North College St
Low Hill
Canterbury St
Salisbury St
Brunswick Rd
Phythian St
Walker Rd

Old Leeds St
East St
Pall Mall
Cheapside
Cunliffe St
Vernon St
Moorfields
Dale St
Hatton Garden
Trueman St
North St
Fontenoy St

New Islington
Devon St
Craven St
Stafford St
Kempston St
Moss St
Epworth St
Prescot St

World Museum
Walker Art Gallery
Central Library
St John's Garden
St George's Hall
Lime St
London Rd
Bridport St
Lord Nelson St
Norton St
Fraser St
Seymour St
Hart St
Pembroke Pl
West Derby St
Ashton St
Crown St

Western Approaches Museum
Temple St
Princes St
Victoria St
Statue of Eleanor Rigby
Whitechapel
Crosshall St

Copperas Hill
Bolton St
Russell St
Gill St
Great Newton St
Brownlow St
Dansie St
Dover St
Brownlow Hill
Minshull St
Smithdown La
WARRINGTON

Royal Liver Building
British Music Experience
Cunard Building
PIER HEAD
Port of Liverpool Building
SEACOMBE
Queensway Tunnel
BIRKENHEAD
WOODSIDE
Museum of Liverpool

Castle St
Cook St
Lower Castle St
Fenwick St
James St
Red Cross St
Lord St
North John St
Williamson St
Tarleton St
Church St
Basnett St
Parker St
Ranelagh St
Bluecoat Art Centre
School La
Liverpool One
Hanover St
Central
Ranelagh Pl
Hawke St
Brownlow Hill
Pleasant St
Mount Pleasant
Wood St
Bold St
Renshaw St
Oldham St
Rodney St
Metropolitan Cathedral of Christ the King
Peach St
Oxford St
Grove St

Open Eye Gallery
Strand St
Canning Pl
CHAVASSE PARK
Paradise St
Duke St
Slater St
Wood St
Colquitt St
Seel St
Hope St
Arrad St
Mulberry St
Cambridge St
Melville Pl

Merseyside Maritime Museum
Salthouse Quay
ROYAL ALBERT DOCK
Tate Liverpool
Beatles Story
Gower St
Strand St
Wapping
Park Lane
Gilbert St
Campbell Henry St
Back Seel St
Parr St
Kent St
Upper Frederick St
Berry St
Duke St
Hardman St
Rodney St
Hardman St
The Hardman's House
Caledonia St
Myrtle St
Chatham St
Myrtle St
Falkner St

MERSEY
Kings Parade
Queens Wharf
Keel Wharf
Kings Dock St
BALTIC TRIANGLE QUARTER
Jamaica St
Blundell St
Kitchen St
Bridgewater St
Watkinson St
Norfolk St
Brick St
Jordan St
New Bird St
Greenland St
Shaws Alley
Tabley St
St James St
Chinese Arch
CHINATOWN
Great George St
Upper Pitt St
Upper Frederick St
St James St
Liverpool Anglican Cathedral
Back Canning St
Little St Bedford St
Canning St
Grove St
Little Canning St
Huskisson St
Egerton St
Lowther St
Percy St
Upper Parliament St
Upper Hampton St
Selborne St

Chaloner St
Halftide Wharf
Queens Wharf
Parliament St
St James Rd
Hope St
Upper Parliament St
Hampton St
Upper Stanhope St
Windsor St
Upper Stanhope St
Bluefields St
Emerson St
Carter St
Gibson St
Princes Ave
Rosebery St
Selborne St
Mulgrave St
Princes Rd
WIDNES

LIVERPOOL
N
0 — 300 m
0 — 300 yards

LARK LANE, PALM HOUSE

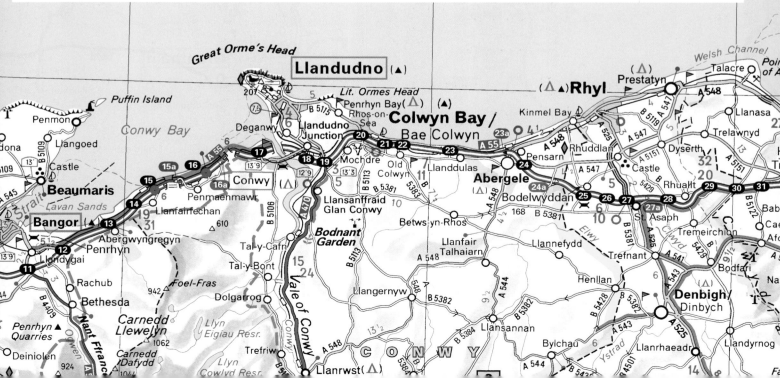

Great Orme's Head
Llandudno (▲)
Lit. Ormes Head
Penrhyn Bay (△)
Rhos-on-Sea
Colwyn Bay / Bae Colwyn
Kinmel Bay
Welsh Channel
Talacre
Prestatyn
Rhyl
Llanasa
Trelawnyd

Puffin Island
Penmon
Llangoed
Castle
dona
Conwy Bay
Deganwy
Llandudno Junction
Mochdre
Old Colwyn
Llanddulas
Pensarn
Abergele
Rhuddlan
Castle
Rhualt
Dyserth
Bodelwyddan
St Asaph

Beaumaris
Lavan Sands
Conwy
Penmaenmawr
Llanfairfechan
Llansanffraid Glan Conwy
Betws-yn-Rhos
Llanfair Talhaiarn
Henllan
Trefnant
Bodfari

Bangor
Abergwyngregyn
Penrhyn
Llandygai
Rachub
Bethesda
Tal-y-Cafn
Tal-y-Bont
Vale of Conwy
Llangernyw
Llannefydd
Denbigh / Dinbych
Llandyrnog

Penrhyn Quarries
Deiniolen
Carnedd Llewelyn
Carnedd Dafydd
Foel-Fras
Dolgarrog
Llyn Eigiau Resr.
Trefriw
Llanrwst
Bodnant Garden
Llansannan
Bylchau
Llanrhaeadr
Ystrad
CONWY

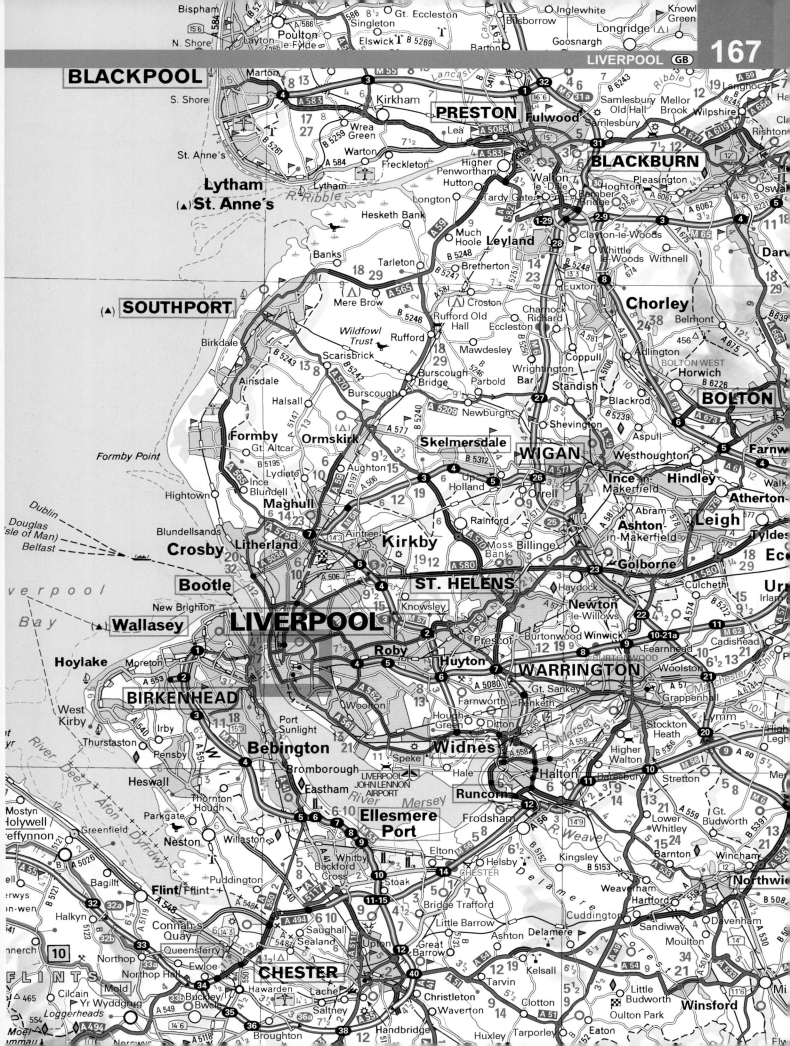

Chesham · Amersham · Beaconsfield · Slough · Eton · Windsor · Ascot · Woking · Guildford · Watford · Bushey · Rickmansworth · Chorleywood · Gerrards Cross · Harrow · Wembley · Ealing · Uxbridge · Hillingdon · Hayes · Southall · Heston · Staines-upon-Thames · Egham · Chertsey · Weybridge · Esher · Addlestone · Chobham · Potters Bar · Barnet · Edgware · Mill Hill · Hendon · Finchley · Borehamwood · Elstree · Stanmore · Pinner · Wealdstone · Kingsbury · Greenhill · Hampstead · Highgate · Camden · Kensington · Hammersmith · Chelsea · Fulham · Westminster · Chiswick · Brentford · Isleworth · Hounslow · Twickenham · Richmond upon Thames · Teddington · Kingston upon Thames · Surbiton · Wimbledon · Wandsworth · Putney · Merton · Mitcham · Morden · Malden · Sutton · Cheam · Ewell · Epsom · Banstead · Carshalton · Wallington · Purley · Leatherhead · Ashtead · Tadworth · Kingswood · Redhill · Reigate · Dorking · Caterham

Heathrow Airport · Windsor Great Park · Richmond Park · Hampton Court · Thorpe Park · Virginia Water · Legoland · Bushy Park · Osterley Park · Box Hill · Trent Park · R.A.F. Museum

LEEDS, BIRMINGHAM · AYLESBURY · ST. ALBANS · LUTON, BEDFORD · GRANTHAM · OXFORD · HIGH WYCOMBE · MAIDENHEAD/READING · BRISTOL · BASINGSTOKE/READING · SOUTHAMPTON · FARNHAM, SOUTHAMPTON · PORTSMOUTH · WORTHING · GATWICK AIRPORT, CRAWLEY, BRIGHTON · BRIGHTON

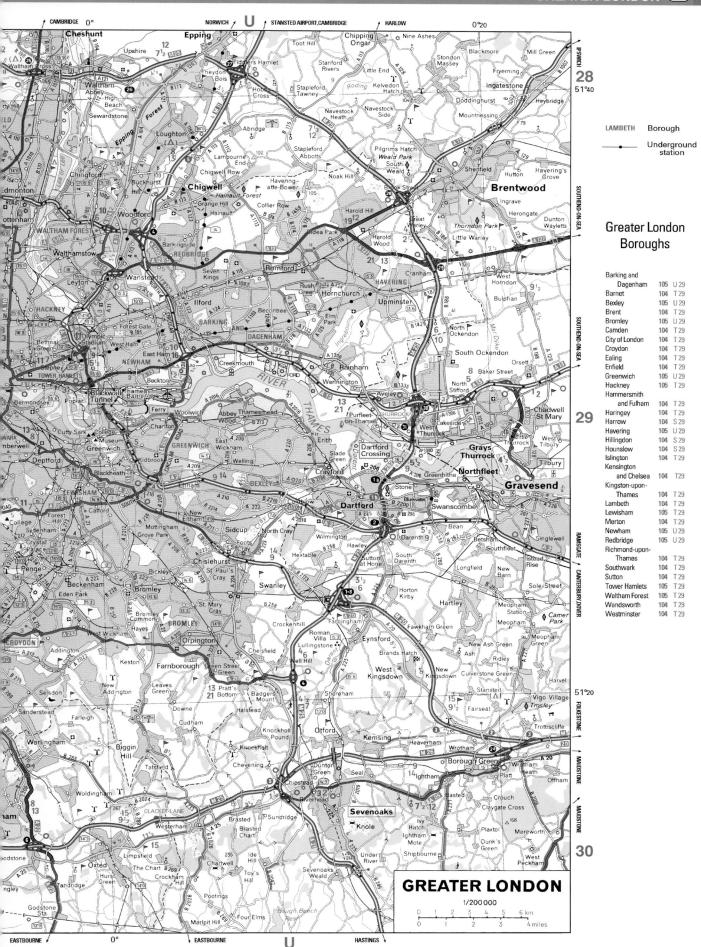

LAMBETH Borough

Underground station

Greater London Boroughs

Barking and		
Dagenham	105	U 29
Barnet	104	T 29
Bexley	105	U 29
Brent	104	T 29
Bromley	105	U 29
Camden	104	T 29
City of London	104	T 29
Croydon	104	T 29
Ealing	104	T 29
Enfield	104	T 29
Greenwich	105	U 29
Hackney	105	T 29
Hammersmith		
and Fulham	104	T 29
Haringey	104	T 29
Harrow	104	S 29
Havering	105	U 29
Hillingdon	104	S 29
Hounslow	104	S 29
Islington	104	T 29
Kensington		
and Chelsea	104	T 29
Kingston-upon-		
Thames	104	T 29
Lambeth	104	T 29
Lewisham	105	T 29
Merton	104	T 29
Newham	105	U 29
Redbridge	105	U 29
Richmond-upon-		
Thames	104	T 29
Southwark	104	T 29
Sutton	104	T 29
Tower Hamlets	104	T 29
Waltham Forest	105	T 29
Wandsworth	104	T 29
Westminster	104	T 29

GREATER LONDON

1/200 000

0 1 2 3 4 5 6 km
0   1   2   3   4 miles

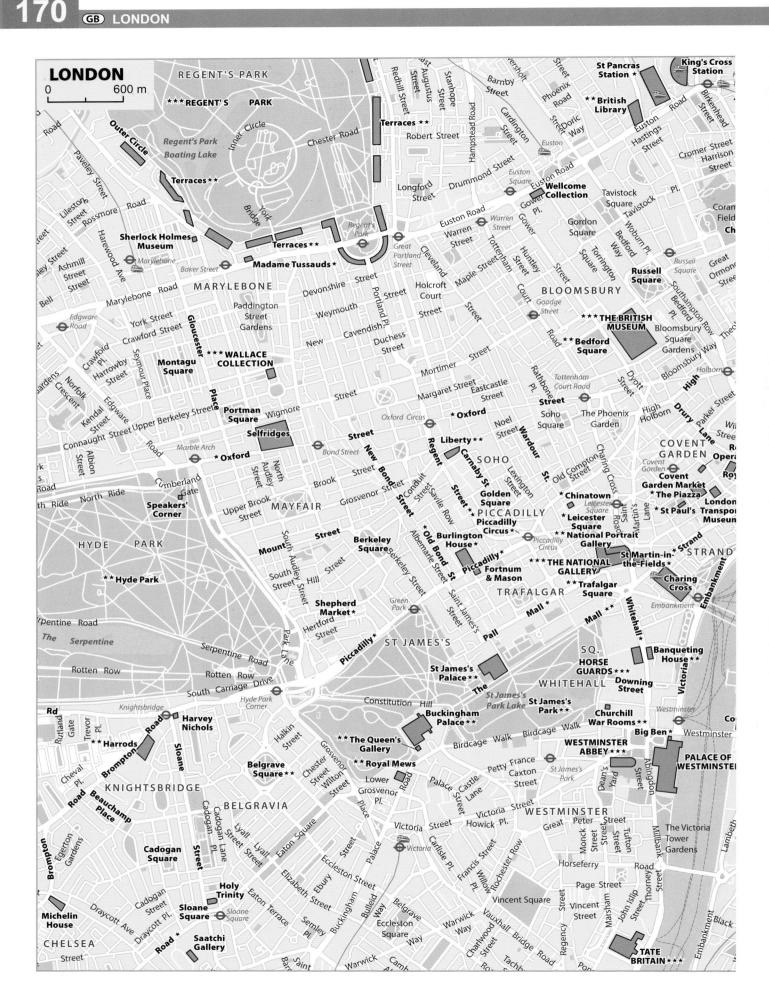

LONDON

0   600 m

REGENT'S PARK

***REGENT'S PARK

Outer Circle

Regent's Park Boating Lake

Inner Circle

York Bridge

Chester Road

Terraces ★★

Terraces ★★

Sherlock Holmes Museum

Marylebone

Baker Street

Terraces ★★

Madame Tussauds ★

MARYLEBONE

Paddington Street Gardens

Marylebone Road

Edgware Road

York Street

Crawford Street

Montagu Square

★★★WALLACE COLLECTION

Portman Square

Selfridges

Marble Arch

★ Oxford

North Audley Street

Oxford Circus

★ Oxford Street

Bond Street

Liberty ★★

Carnaby St.

SOHO

Golden Square

Regent Street

New Bond Street

BLOOMSBURY

Russell Square

***THE BRITISH MUSEUM

★★ Bedford Square

Bloomsbury Square Gardens

High Holborn

Drury Lane

COVENT GARDEN

Covent Garden Market

★ The Piazza

St Paul's

London Transport Museum

Chinatown

Leicester Square

★ Leicester Square

Piccadilly Circus

National Portrait Gallery

***THE NATIONAL GALLERY

St Martin-in-the-Fields ★

STRAND

Charing Cross

Speakers' Corner

MAYFAIR

HYDE PARK

★★ Hyde Park

Mount Street

Berkeley Square

Shepherd Market ★

Piccadilly ★

ST JAMES'S

The Serpentine

Serpentine Road

Rotten Row

South Carriage Drive

Hyde Park Corner

Knightsbridge

Harvey Nichols

★★ Harrods

Brompton Road

Sloane

KNIGHTSBRIDGE

Beauchamp Place

Belgrave Square ★★

BELGRAVIA

Cadogan Square

Holy Trinity

Michelin House

Sloane Square

CHELSEA

Saatchi Gallery

Old Bond St.

Burlington House ★

Piccadilly

Fortnum & Mason

TRAFALGAR

★ Trafalgar Square

Mall

Pall Mall

St James's Palace ★★

Buckingham Palace ★★

★★The Queen's Gallery

★★ Royal Mews

Constitution Hill

St James's Park Lake

St James's Park ★★

Birdcage Walk

WHITEHALL

HORSE GUARDS ★★★

Downing Street

Banqueting House ★★

Churchill War Rooms ★★

Big Ben ★

WESTMINSTER ABBEY ★★★

WESTMINSTER

PALACE OF WESTMINSTER

The Victoria Tower Gardens

TATE BRITAIN ★★★

St Pancras Station ★

King's Cross Station

★★ British Library

Wellcome Collection

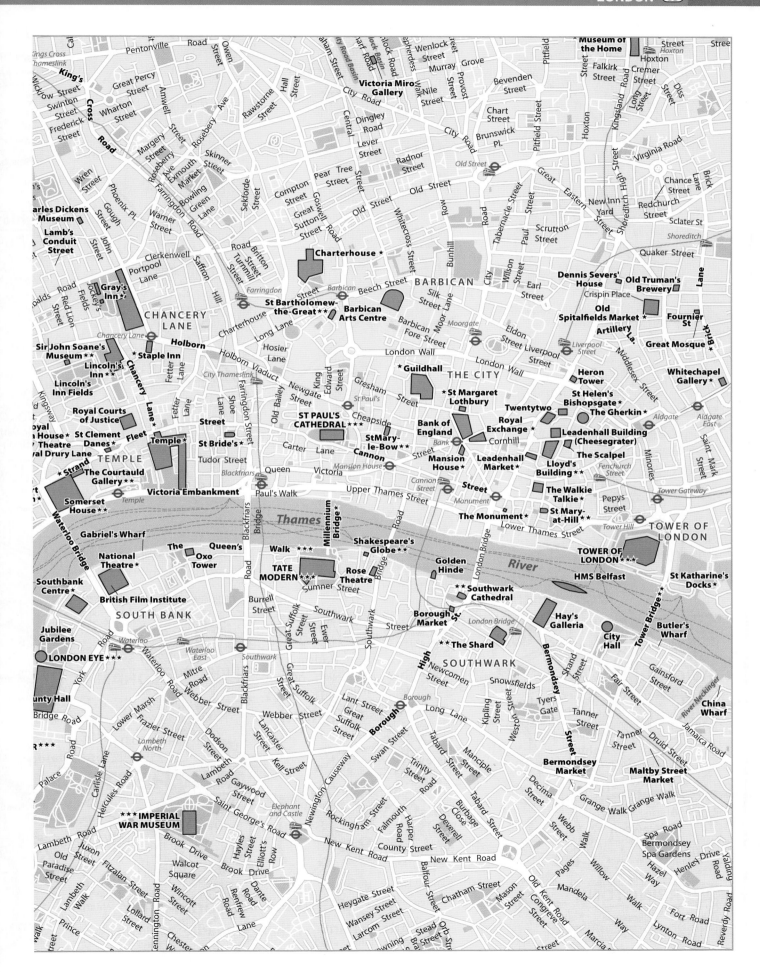

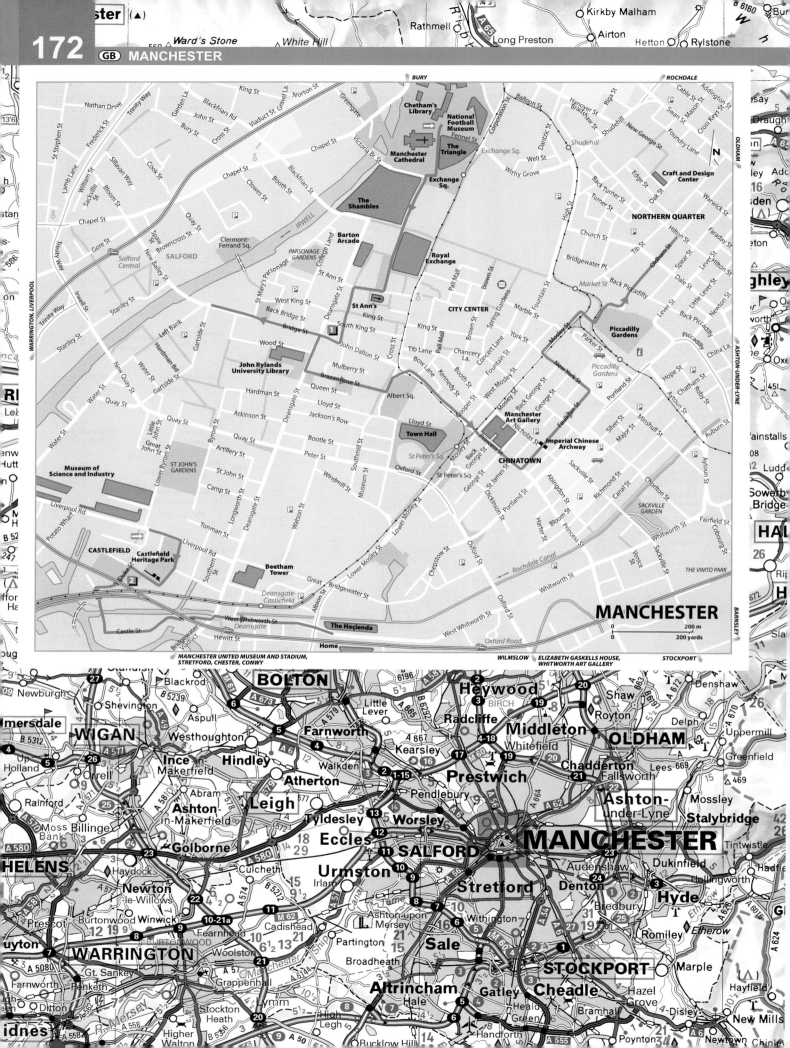

Whalton

Riessey Woods

A1

Stannington

Ogle

Belsay

124

Blyth

Seaton Delaval Hall

Milbourne

Seaton Burn

Dudley

Seaton Delava

Earsdon

Whitley Bay

Ponteland

Wide Open

Dinnington

Shiremoor

Stamfordham

Darras Hall

NEWCASTLE UPON-TYNE

Longbenton
Gosforth

TYNEMOUTH

Priory

Wallsend

N. Shields

Harlow Hill

Throckley

A167

SOUTH SHIELDS

Heddon-on-the-W

Newburn

A193
A186

Tyne-Tunnel

A1058

Amsterdam

Horsley

Wylam

Ryton

Crawcrock

Jarrow
Hebburn

A1300

Cleadon

Whitburn

Prudhoe

Stocksfield

Greenside

Blaydon

Whickham

A1

Felling

GATESHEAD

Wrekenton

A184

A194

Boldon

Southwick

A183

SUNDERLAND

N O R

Whittonstall

Chopwell

Rowland's Gill

Birtley

65

Washington

A1231

A1290

A183

Burnopfield

Beamish Hall

14

63 64

Chester-le-Street

Penshaw

Herrington

Shiney Row

New Silksworth

Ryhope

Stanley

Pelton

WASHINGTON

A182

A193

Houghton-le-Spring

Murton

Seaham

Leadgate

Annfield

A1052

A19

A690

S. Hetton

Easington

Great North Museum : Hancock

Horden

Shotton Colliery

Thornley

Wheatley Hill

Peterlee

Blackhall

Blackhall Rocks

B1281

Wingate

Hesleden

Hart

A1086

HARTLEPOOL

Trimdon

Fishburn

Elwick

Sedgefield

Seaton Carew

Tees Bay

A689

Greatham

Thorpe Thewles

Wolviston

Billingham

Bishopton

Redmarshall

Stockton-on-Tees

Longnewton

Eaglescliffe

MIDDLESBROUGH

Thornaby-on-Tees

Ormesby

Ingleby Barwick

Yarm

Nunthorpe

A174

A171

TEESSIDE INTERNATIONAL AIRPORT

Kirklevington

Seamer

Stokesley

Crathorne

Appleton Wiske

Hutton Rudby

Gt. Ayton

Gt. Broughton

Inglet

Carlton

Moulton

N. Cowton

NEWCASTLE-UPON-TYNE

EXHIBITION PARK

0 150 m
0 150 yards

N

A167

Brandling Park

Jesmond

Park Terrace

Windsor Ter.

Jesmond Rd

Great North Rd

Claremont Rd

West Jesmond Rd

Osborne Ter.

Sandyford Rd

Richardson Rd

Queen Victoria Rd

King's Rd

Sandyford Rd

Dyke St

Byron St

Haymarket

St Mary's Pl.

College St

Camden St

Falconar St

LEAZES PARK

St Thomas St

John Dobson St

Ellison Pl.

A167

ST JAMES PARK

Terrace Pl.

Leazes Pk Rd

Percy St

Northumberland St

Seville Row

Laing Art Gallery and Museum

Barrack Rd

Strawberry Pl.

Gallowgate

Blackett St

Grey's Monument

Market St

New Br. St

Manors

Trafalgar St

Argyle St

Pitt St

Herber St

St James' Bd

St Andrew's St

Newgate St

Clayton St

The Gate

Groat Market

Melbourne St

Tower St

City Rd

Blackfriars

Wellington St

St James' Rd

Bath Lane

Westgate Rd

Grey St

Pilgrim St

All Saints

Neville St

Collingwood St

Black Gate

Bessie Surtees' House

Quayside

Waterloo St

West Clayton St

Westgate Rd

Mosley St

Discovery Museum

Life Science Centre

Central Station

Newcastle Castle

Guildhall

Tyne Bridge

Swing Bridge

Sage Gateshead

Forth St

South St

Hanover St

Forth Banks

Pottery La.

Pipewellgate

Close

TYNE

High Level Bridge

GATESHEAD MILLENNIUM BRIDGE, BALTIC CENTRE

CONSETT, DURHAM

SUNDERLAND

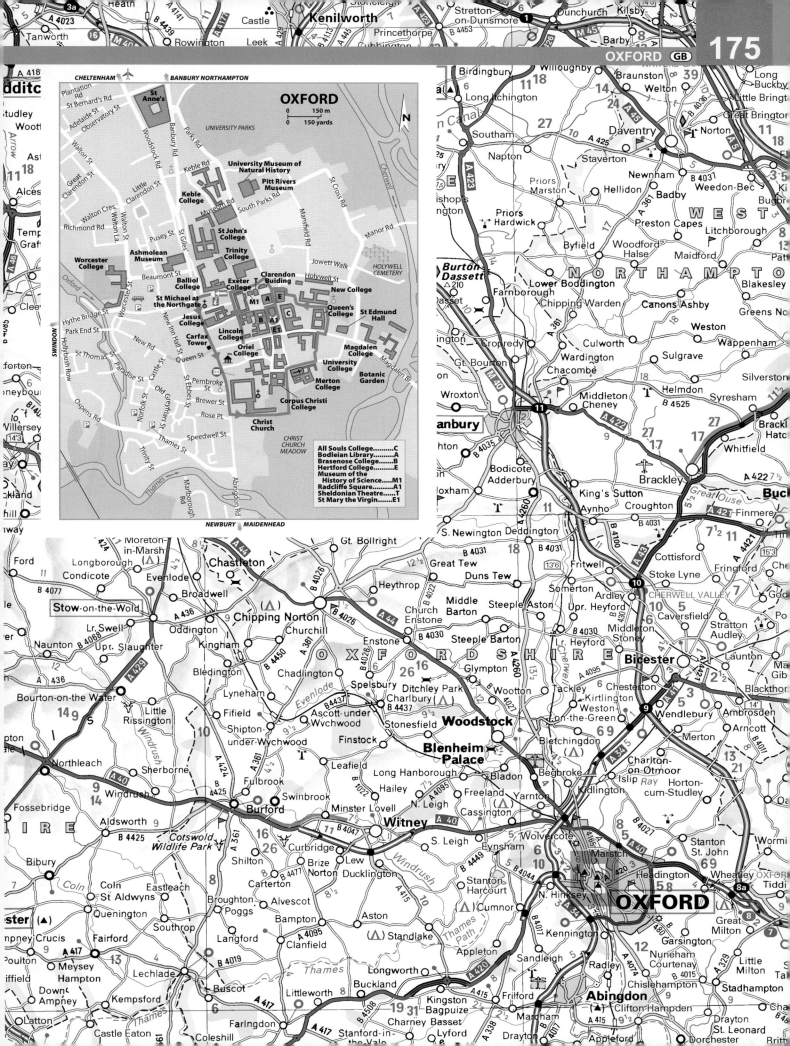

PERTH

0 100 m
0 100 yards
N

The Black Watch Castle and Museum

INVERNESS, CAITHNESS GLASS
CRIANLARICH, CRIEFF

BELL'S SPORTS CENTRE

North Inch

TAY

Isla Rd
Main St
Lochie Brae

Hay St
Balhousie Ave.
Dunkeld Rd
Barrack St
Melville St
Barossa Pl.
Old Perth Academy
Rose Terrace
Georgian Terraces

Atholl St
Charlotte St
Perth Bridge

Atholl Crescent
Blackfriars St
North Methven St
Caledonian Rd
Town's Lode
Longcauseway

Fair Maid's House and Visitor Centre
Perth Museum and Art Gallery
Perth Concert Hall

STIRLING, GLASGOW, CHERRY BANK

Lower City Mills
Murray St
Mill St
George St
Tay St
East Bank

High St
South Methven St
Skinnergate
High St

City Hall
St John's Kirk
St John's Shopping Centre
King Edward St
St John's Pl.
Bishops Palace

Milne St
York Pl.
Country Pl.
Hospital St
South St
Sheriff Court
Queen's Bridge

Caledonian Rd
Alexandra St
Exchange La.
Leonard St
King St
James St
Scott St
Charles St
Canal St
Salutation Hotel
Speygate

King James VI Hospital

St Andrew's St
Cross St
Pomarium St
Victoria St
Princes St
GREYFRIARS
RODNEY GARDENS
Riverside
Gowrie St

RAILWAY STATION
South William St
Marshall Place
St Leonard's Bank
St Leonard's-in-the-Fields
Water Works Building and Fergusson Gallery

SOUTH INCH
Edinburgh Rd
Shore Rd
Perth Railway Bridge

BELLWOOD RIVERSIDE PARK

DUNDEE
BRANKLYN GARDEN, FRIARTON BRIDGE

FORTH ROAD BRIDGE, EDINBURGH

Loch Muick
Glas-allt
Loch Lee
Inchgrundle
Glen
Braedownie
Glen Clova
West Knock
Ben Tirran
White Hill
Clova
Waterhead
Runtaleave
Glenprosen Village
Glen Prosen
Glenisla Forest
Backwater Resr.
Cat Law
Ogil
Fern
Dykehead
Balintore
Pearsie
Dykends
Kirkton of Kingoldrum
Kirriemuir
Oathlaw
Bridgend of Lintrathen
L. of Lintrathen
Craigisla
Reekie Linn
Craigton
Lunanhead
Kingsmuir
Forfar
Ruthven
Glamis Castle
Douglastown
Glamis
Meigle
Eassie and Nevay
Inverarity
Kirkbuddo
Dunkeld
Inver
Birnam
Clunie
Meikleour
R. Isla
Coupar Angus
Newtyle
Sidlaw Hills
Balgray
Auchterhouse
Trochry
Strathbraan
Caputh
Kinclaven
Burrelton
Pitcur
Lundie
Muirhead
Kirkton of Strathmartine
MICHELIN
Little Glenshee
Bankfoot
Cargill
King's Seat
Balbeggie
Kinnaird
DUNDEE
Longforgan
Broughty Ferry
Caorach
Stanley
Guildtown
Kinrossie
Abernyte
Braes of the Carse
Invergowrie
Tayport
Logiealmond
Harrietfield
Moneydie
King's Seat
Balbeggie
Rait
Inchture
Tay Road Bridge
Newport-on-Tay
Buchanty
Almond
Luncarty
Scone Palace
New Scone
Wormit
Tentsmuir Forest
Methven
Huntingtower Castle
Bridgend
Kinfauns
Errol
Balmerino
Tibbermore
PERTH
Elcho
Glencarse
Carse of Gowrie
Firth of Tay
Findo Gask
Forgandenny
R. Earn
Glencarse
Newburgh
Luthrie
Kilmany
Balmullo
Guardbridge
Aberuthven
Forteviot
Bridge of Earn
Abernethy
Lindores
Dairsie
Strathkinness
Dunning
R. Earn
Pitmedden Forest
Letham
Springfield
Cupar
Craigtoun
Pitscottie
Auchterarder
Common of Dunning
Path of Condie
Auchtermuchty
Howe of Fife
Ladybank
Hill of Tarvit
Scotstarvit Tower
Ceres
Peat Inn
Steele's Knowe
Glenfarg
Gateside
Strathmiglo
Falkland
Kingskettle
Backmuir of New Gilston
Largoward
Water of May
Lomond Hills
Freuchie

N. Petherwin
Werrington Broadwoodwidger 15
Ottery 24 15
A 386
tagel 308 △ N. Brentor Lydford gorge Dartmoor
Davidstow 26 Yeolmbridge Lifton Lydford gorge 604 △ Cut Hill
Laneast Chillaton Brent Tor Wistma's
Delabole Launceston Milton Abbot Mary Tavy Wood
Camelford Altarnun A 30 S. Petherwin 539 △ Great Mis
(△) Lewannick B 3362 Lamerton Tor Dartmoor
St. Teath Brown Lezant A 386 Tavistock (△) Two
B 3267 420 △ Willy North Hill B 3254 35 Stoke Gulworthy Whitchurch Dartmoor P
Michaelstow Bolventor 301 Kilmar 22 Climsland (△) Gunnislake 13 B 3357 Princetow
Kew St. Breward Tor 390 The Cheesewring Bray Morwellham
St. Tudy 34 Shop B 3257 Calstock A 386 B 3212 Nation
B 3266 Blisland 21 The Hurlers Kelly Bray A 390 Cotehele House Horrabridge Meavy
Helland Caradon 369 Callington St. Dominick Calstock Yelverton
row CORNWALL Hill Pensilva (△) St. Mellion Bere Buckland 492 △
Cardinham St. Cleer St. Ive 18 162 Alston Abbey
Bodmin Dobwalls St. Neot A 390 8½ St. Mellion △ 162 Bere Ferrers Plym
12 19 Liskeard Menheniot Pillaton Landulph Tamerton Foliot Bickleigh
A 38 A 390 Landrake PLYMOUTH Cornw
Lanhydrock E. Taphouse 27 Landrake (△) Plympton
Restormel 18 B 3359 17 St. Germans Saltash 27
Castle 29 Duloe Widegates Antony House 17
Lostwithiel B 3359 Hessenford Torpoint Saltram
Lanlivery Lanreath Morval Crafthole Antony Devonport Plymstock Brixton
Eden Pelynt (△) Downderry Cremyll The Plympton Dunstone
Project St. Blazey Golant Mt. Edgcumbe Sound Wembury
Fowey E. Cornwall Coast Path Millbrook Cawsand Newton Holbeton
Polkerris Lansallos Talland-by-Looe Whitsand Ferrers
Charlestown Polruan W. Looe (△) Bay Rame Head Noss Mayo S. Devon Stoke
St. Austell Polperro (△) Santander Wembury Point Bigbury
Bay Gribbin Head Roscoff Bay

LISKEARD,
TAVISTOCK

Penrose St. The Box
Cobourg St. Gibbon La. Camden St.
Hastings Ter. Drake Circus Regent St. Lipson Rd Greenbank Ave
Cornwall St. Charles St. North St. Tothill Ave
Armada Way New George St. Ebrington Gasking St. Beaumont Rd Tothill Rd
Western Approach Royal Parade St. Breton Side Exeter St.
St. Andrew's Vauxhall Exeter St.
Prysten House St. KINGSBRIDGE
House Merchant's Sutton Rd
Princess St. House Musem SUTTON
Notte St. HARBOUR
St. James' Pl. The Barbican Eddystone Rocks
Citadel Rd BARBICAN National Marine
FERRY TERMINAL Naval War Elizabethan Aquarium
Memorial House Teats Hill Rd
Drake Armada Mayflower
Statue Memorial Museum Mayflower S H
The Promenade Stone
THE HOE Royal
Cliff Rd Citadel
Grand Parade Smeaton's
Pier St. Hoe Rd Tower
St Katherine

PLYMOUTH

N

0   200 m
0   200 yards

THE SOUND

FOOT FERRY,   MOUNT BATTEN FERRY
ROSCOFF, SANTANDER

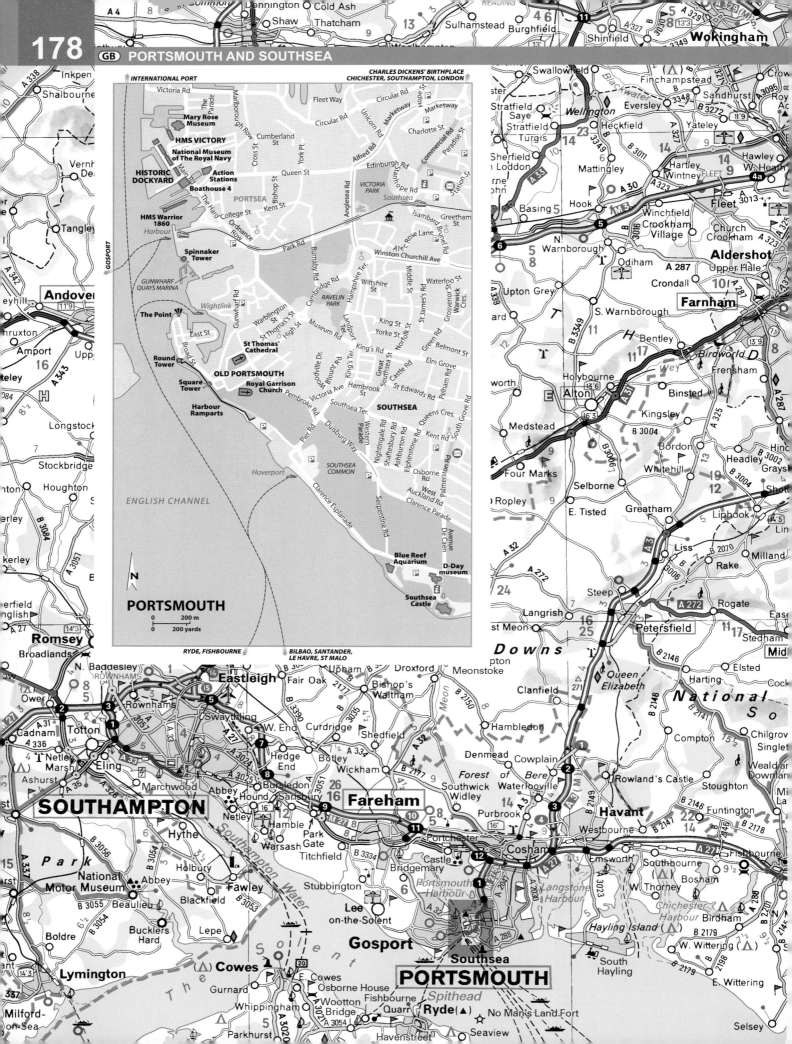

PORTSMOUTH

INTERNATIONAL PORT

CHARLES DICKENS' BIRTHPLACE
CHICHESTER, SOUTHAMPTON, LONDON

Victoria Rd
Mary Rose Museum
HMS VICTORY
National Museum of The Royal Navy
HISTORIC DOCKYARD
Action Stations
Boathouse 4
HMS Warrior 1860
Harbour
Spinnaker Tower
GUNWHARF QUAYS MARINA
Wightlink
The Point
East St
Round Tower
Square Tower
Broad St
St Thomas' Cathedral
OLD PORTSMOUTH
Royal Garrison Church
Harbour Ramparts
Hoverport

PORTSEA
Fleet Way
Circular Rd
Marketway
Marketway
Cumberland St
Charlotte St
Commercial Rd
Alfred Rd
Queen St
Edinburgh Rd
Paradise St
Station St
VICTORIA PARK
Southsea
Isambard Brunel Rd
Greetham St
Winston Churchill Ave
RAVELIN PARK
King St
Yorke St
Norfolk St
King's Rd
Elm Grove
SOUTHSEA
St Edwards Rd
Pembroke Rd
Southsea Ter
Pier Rd
Duisburg Way
Western Parade
SOUTHSEA COMMON
Nightingale Rd
Shaftesbury Rd
Ashburton Rd
Osborne Rd
West Auckland Rd
Clarence Parade
Palmerston Rd
Clarence Esplanade
Serpentine Rd
Avenue De Caen
Blue Reef Aquarium
D-Day museum
Southsea Castle

ENGLISH CHANNEL

N

200 m
200 yards

RYDE, FISHBOURNE

BILBAO, SANTANDER, LE HAVRE, ST MALO

Andover
Romsey
Broadlands
SOUTHAMPTON
Eastleigh
Fareham
PORTSMOUTH
Southsea
Gosport
Cowes
Lymington
Farnham
Aldershot
Alton
Petersfield
Havant
Cosham

Southampton city centre (inset map)

WINCHESTER

Henstead Rd · Morris Rd · Devonshire Rd · Bedford Pl · London Rd · Kings Park Rd · Dorset St · Bullar St · Graham Rd · Clovelly Rd · Oxford Ave · Charlotte Pl · St Mary's Rd · Argyle Rd · Northbrook Rd · Brintons Rd · Derby Rd

Park Lane · Cumberland Pl · WATTS PARK · ANDREWS PARK · Commercial Rd · West Park Rd · Comercial Rd · **City Art Gallery** · Guidhall Sq. · East Park Walk · St Andrews Rd · New Rd · Northam Rd · A3024

Seacity Museum · Civic Centre Rd · Above Bar St · PALMERSTON PARK · Palmerston Rd · North Front · PORTSMOUTH

Pirelli St · Ogle Rd · Sussex Rd · Winton St · Cossack Grn · Johnson St · South Front · Kingsway · St Mary St

Portland errace · Pound Tree Rd · Vincents Walk · HOUNDWELL PARK · HOGLANDS PARK · James St · Coleman St

Harbour Parade · Portland errace · **Arundel Tower** · Hanover Buildings · **Bargate** · Houndwell Pl. · Chapel Rd

Catchcold Tower · **Western Esplanade** · High St · East St · Queensway · East St · Lime St · Marsh Lane · Whitestar Pl. · FAREHAM

West Quay Rd · Castle Way · Eastgate St · Back of the Walls · Canal Walk · Queensway · Threefield Lane · Richmond St · Central Bridge

Tudor House · **St Michael's Church** · French St · High St · St Bernard St · College St · Terminus Terrace

West Gate · Herbert Walker Ave · **Merchant's Hall** · Bugle St · **Wool House** · Briton St · Oxford St · Latimer St · John St

MAYFLOWER PARK · **Mayflower Memorial** · Town Quay · Lower Canal Walk · Queen's Terrace · QUEEN'S PARK

God's House · **God's House Gate** · **God's House Tower** · Platform Rd

N

SOUTHAMPTON

0   100 m
0   100 yards

COWES

Regional map

Sutton Benger · Christian Malford · Lyneham · Chiseldon · Lambourn · Peasemore · Baydon · B 4005

Kington Langley · Clyffe Pypard · Barbury Castle · A 346 · A 4361 · M 4 · A 338 · A 34

Sheldon · Lacoc · Welford · Boxford · Snelsmore Common · CHIEVELEY · Hermitage · Bradfield · Bucklebury

Newbury · Woolhampton · Aldermaston · Brimpton · Padw

Hungerford · Little Bedwyn · Kintbury · Inkpen · Hamstead Marshall · Highclere · Burghclere · Ecchinswell · Heath End · Tadley

Shalbourne · Walbury Hill 297 · E. Woodhay · Old Burghclere · Kingsclere · Pamber End

Vernham Dean · Hurstbourne Tarrant · Enham-Alamein · St. Mary Bourne · **Basingstoke** · Overton · Oakley

Tangley · Thruxton · Weyhill · **Andover** · Hurstbourne Priors · Whitchurch · Laverstoke · N. Waltham

Amport · Upper Clatford · Wherwell · Barton Stacey · Sutton Scotney · Micheldever · Preston Candover

Longstock · Crawley · A 30 · A 34 · Kings Worthy · New Alresford · Old Alres

Stockbridge · Houghton · King's Somborne · Littleton · **WINCHESTER** · Cheriton · Bramdea

Farley Mount · Sparsholt · Braishfield · Hursley · Ampfield · Otterbourne · Shawford · Owslebury · Warnford

Romsey · Broadlands · N. Baddesley · Chandler's Ford · Colden Common · Marwell Zoological Park

ROWNHAMS · Rownhams · Bishopstoke · Lower Upham · Droxford

Owe · Cadnam · Totton · **Eastleigh** · Fair Oak · Bishop's Waltham

Stoney Cross · Netley Marsh · Eling · Swaythling · W. End · Curdridge · Shedfield

SOUTHAMPTON · Marchwood · Hound · Botley · Wickham

Fordingbridge · **FORES T** · Lyndhurst · Hythe · Bursledon · Sarisbu · **Fareham**

Wimborne St. Giles · Alderholt · Ibsley · Ringwood · NATIONAL PARK · Netley · Hamble · Park Gate · Titchfield

Gussage All Saints · Woodlands · Verwood · Burley · Brockenhurst · Warsash · Lee on-the-Solent

Witchampton · Holt · W. Moors · St. Leonards · National Motor Museum · Abbey · Holbury · Blackfield · Gosport

Wimborne Minster · Ferndown · Sopley · Sway · Beaulieu · Fawley · Stubbington

Kingston Lacy · Hampreston · Hurn · Bransgore · Boldre · Bucklers Hard · Lepe · Portsmo

Corfe Mullen · Broadstone · New Milton · Mount Pleasant · **Lymington** · **Cowes** · Gurnard · E. Cowes · Osborne House

Lytchett Matravers · Upton · Burton · Highcliffe · Milford-on-Sea · **PORT** · Whippingham · Wootton Bridge · Quarr · Ryde

Lytchett Minster · Boscombe · **Christchurch** · Mudeford · Barton-on-Sea · Totland · Yarmouth · Parkhurst · **Newport** · Robin Hill · Havenstreet

Poole · Poole Harbour · Brownsea Island · Southbourne · Hengistbury Head · Fort Victoria · Freshwater · Shalfleet · Carisbrooke · Brading · Alverstone

BOURNEMOUTH · Sandbanks · Christchurch Bay · Fort Victoria · Newbridge · Calbourne · Blackwater · Arreton · Newchurch

Wareham · Arne · Poole Bay · The Needles · Freshwater Bay · Tennyson Down & Monument (NT) · Brighstone Forest · Brighstone · Shorwell · Godshill · San

Corfe Castle · Studland · **Old Harry Rocks** · Alum Bay · Whitwell · Wroxall · Shank

Swanage · Durlston Head · **ISLE OF WIGHT** · St Catherine's Oratory · Chale · Bonchurch · **Ventnor**

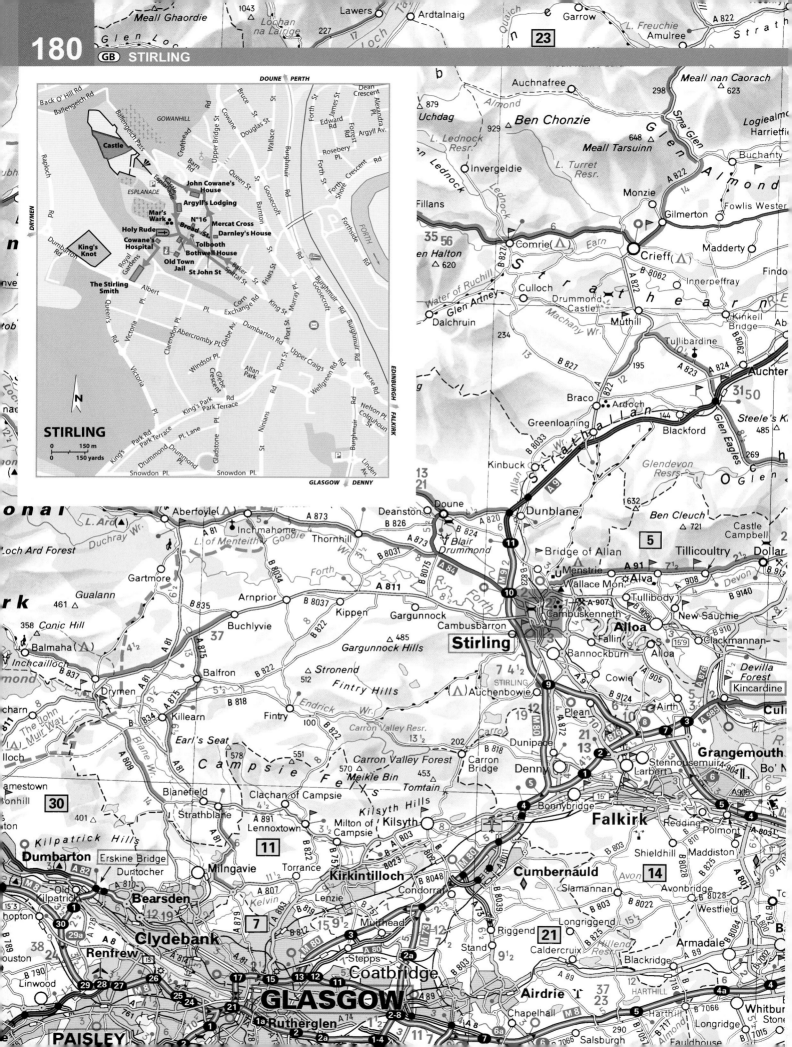

STIRLING

Castle

GOWANHILL

Back O' Hill Rd
Ballengeich Rd
Ballengeich Pass
Crofthead
Esplanade
Castle
John Cowane's House
Argyll's Lodging
Mar's Wark
N°16
Holy Rude
Broad St
Mercat Cross
Darnley's House
Cowane's Hospital
Tolbooth
Bothwell House
Old Town Jail
St John St
The Stirling Smith

King's Knot
Royal Gardens
Dumbarton Rd
Raploch

DRYMEN

DOUNE PERTH

Bruce St
Cowane St
Upper Bridge St
Barn Rd
Queen St
Douglas St
Wallace St
Barnton St
Goosecroft
Dean Crescent
Forth St
James St
Edward Rd
Forrest Rd
Argyll Av.
Alexandra Pl.
Rosebery Pl.
Forth Crescent Rd
Forth Pl.

FORTH

Burghmuir Rd
Forthside Rd

Albert Pl.
Clarendon Pl.
Victoria
Windsor Pl.
Abercromby Pl.
Glebe Av.
Dumbarton Rd
Corn Exchange Rd
Baker St
Spittal St
Friars St
Port St
Murray Pl.
King St
Upper Craigs
Goosecroft Rd
Burghmuir Rd

Glebe Crescent
Allan Park
King's Park Rd
Park Terrace
Wellgreen Rd
Kerse Rd

Queen's Rd
Victoria Rd
King's Park Rd
Park Terrace
Pl. Lane
Drummond Pl.
Gladstone Pl.
Ninians Rd
Snowdon Pl.
Snowdon Pl.
Nelson Pl.
Colquhoun St
Linden Av.

EDINBURGH FALKIRK

N

STIRLING

0 ——— 150 m
0 ——— 150 yards

GLASGOW DENNY

BIRMINGHAM
SANDWELL
West Bromwich
Nuneaton
Bedworth
COVENTRY
Solihull
Stourbridge
Halesowen
Bromsgrove
Redditch
Droitwich
Kenilworth
Warwick
Royal Leamington Spa
WORCESTER
STRATFORD UPON-AVON
Evesham
CHELTENHAM
GLOUCESTER
Tewkesbury
WORCESTERSHIRE
WARWICKSHIRE
GLOUCESTERSHIRE
BIRMINGHAM AIRPORT / N.E.C.
Alcester
Broadway
Winchcombe
Sudeley Castle
Witney
Burford
STRATFORD-UPON-AVON
BIRMINGHAM
WARWICK
WORCESTER
EVESHAM
BANBURY
OXFORD
Shakespeare's Birthplace
Garrick Inn
Shakespeare's New Place
Guild Chapel
Hall's Croft
Royal Shakespeare Theatre
Holy Trinity Church
THE BANCROFT
Clopton Bridge
Bridge St
High St
Henley St
Wood St
Sheep St
Chapel Lane
Church St
Old Town
Southern Lane
Waterside
Avon
0 100 m
0 100 yards

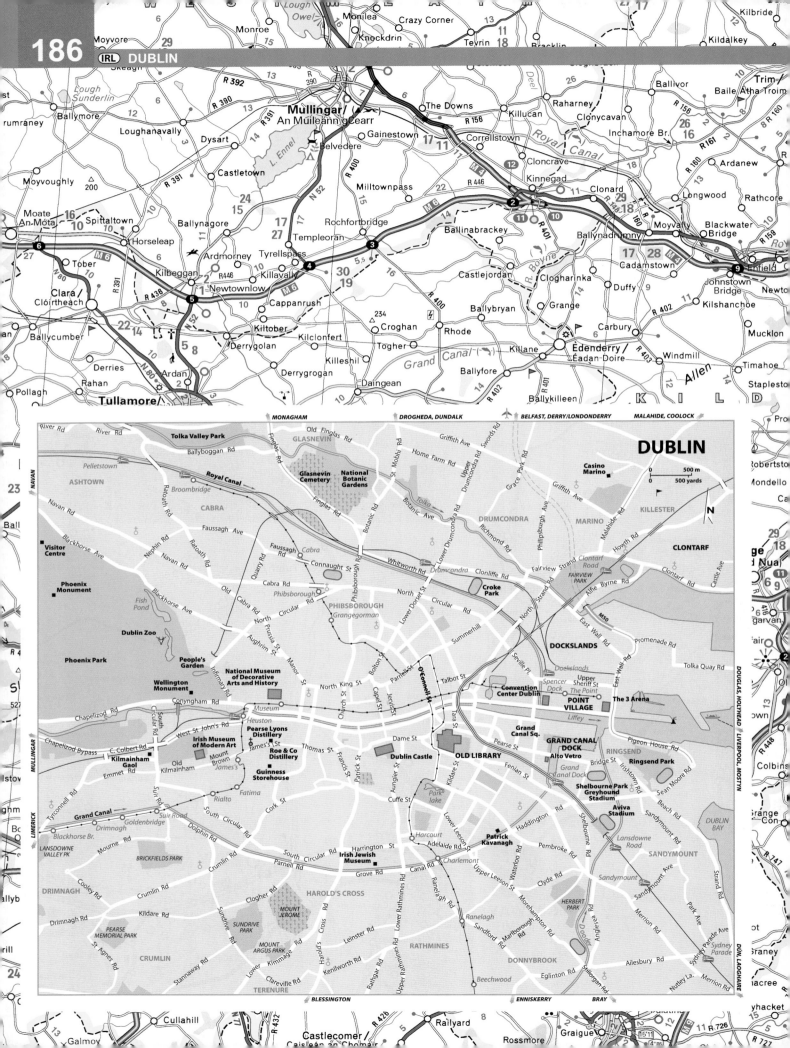

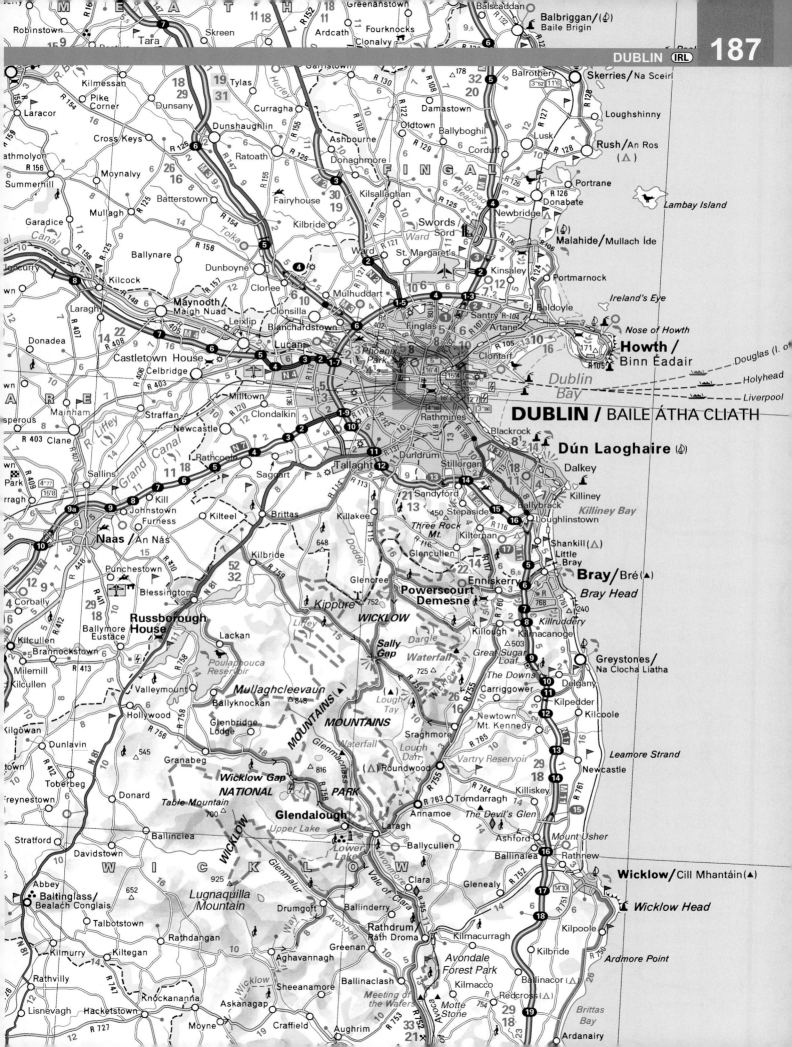

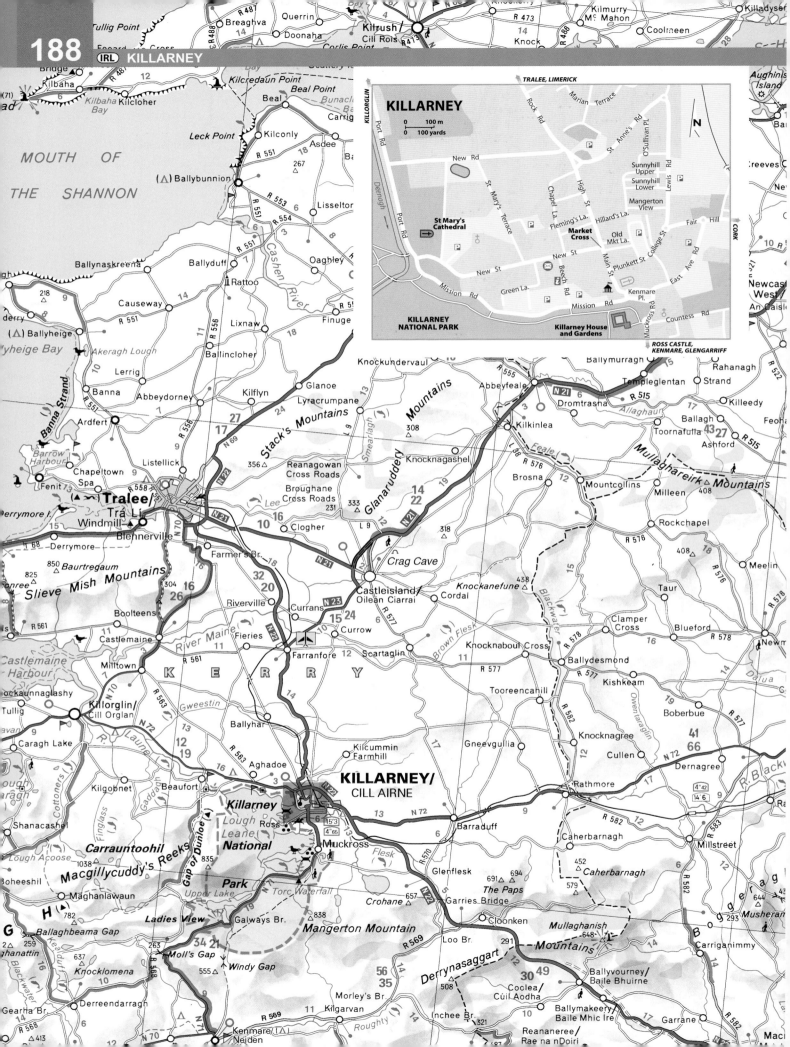

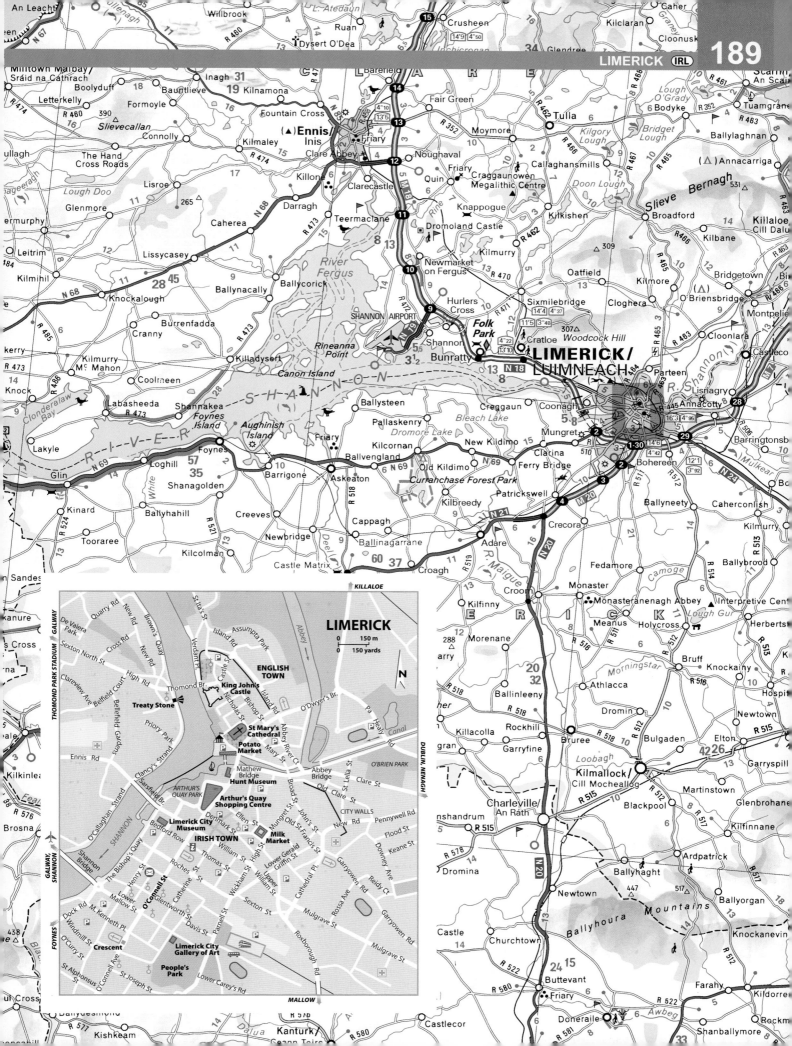

Eochair

Bóithre
Mótarbhealach - Limistéar seirbhíse
Carrbhealach dúbailte le saintréithe mótarbhealaigh
Acomhail mótarbhealaigh: iomlán - teoranta
Vimhreacha ceangail
Líonra idirnáisiúnta agus náisiúnta bóithre
Bóthar idir-réigiúnach nach bhfuil chomh plódaithe
Bóthar nuadheisithe - gan réitiú
Cosán - Conair mharcáilte / Cosán marcaíochta
Mótarbhealach, bóthar á dhéanamh
(an dáta oscailte sceidealta, mas eol)

Leithead bóithre
Carrshlí dhéach
4 lána - 2 leathanlána
2 lána - 2 chunglána

Fad bóthar
(iomlán agus meánfhad)
Bhóithre dola ar an mótarbhealach
Saor ó dhola ar an mótarbhealach
i mílte - i gciliméadair
ar an mbóthar

Aicmiú oifigiúil bóithre
Mótarshl - GB: Priomhbhealach
(Primary route)
IRL: Bóithre eile ,
(National primary and secondary route)
Priomhbóithre agus fobhóithre náisiúnta
Ceann scríbe ar ghréasán bóithre priomha

Constaicí
Timpeall - Bearnas agus a airde os cionn leibhéal na mara (i méadair)
Fána ghéar
(suas treo an gha)
IRL: Bealach deacair nó baolach
Bóthar cúng le hionaid phasála
(in Albain)
Crosaire comhréidh: iarnród ag dul, faoi bhóthar, os cionn bóthair
Bóthar toirmeasctha - Bóthar faoi theorannú
Bacainn dola - Bóthar aonslí
Teorainneacha airde
(faoi 15'6" IRL, faoi 16'6" GB)
Teorann Mheáchain
(faoi 16t)

Iompar
Leithead caighdeánach - Staisiún paisinéirí
Aerfort - Aerpháirc
Longsheirbhísí :
(Seirbhísí séasúracha: dearg)
Bád
Fartha (uas - ulach : tonnaí méadracha)
Coisithe agus lucht rothar

Lóistín - Riarachán
Teorainneacha riaracháin
Teorainn na hAlban agus teorainn na Breataine Bige
Teorainn idirnáisiúnta - Custam

Áiseanna Spóirt agus Súgartha
Machaire Gailf - Ráschúrsa
Timpeall rásaíochta - Cuan bád aeraíochta
Láthair champa , láthair charbhán
Conair mharcáilte - Páirc thuaithe
Zú - Tearmannéan mara
IRL: Lascaireacht - Ráschúrsa con Larnród thraein ghaile
Traein cábla
Carr cábla , cathaoir cábla

Amhairc
Príomhradharcanna:
féach AN EOLAÍ UAINE
Bailte nó áiteanna inspéise, baill lóistín
Foirgneamh Eaglasta - Caisleán
Fothrach - Leacht meigiliteach - Pluais
Páirc, Gáirdíní - Ionaid eile spéisiúla
IRL: Dunfort - Cros Cheilteach - Cloigtheach
Lánléargas - Cothrom Radhairc
Bealach Aoibhinn

Comharthaí Eile
Cáblashlí thionsclaíoch
Crann teileachumarsáide - Teach solais
Stáisiún Giniúna - Cairéal
Mianach - Tionsclaíocht
Scaglann - Aill
Páirc Fhoraoise Naisiúnta - Páirc Naisiúnta

Allwedd

Ffyrdd
Traffordd - Mannau gwasanaeth
Ffordd ddeuol â nodweddion traffordd
Cyfnewidfeyd: wedi'i chwblhau - cyfyngedig
Rhifau'r cyffyrdd
Ffordd ar rwydwaith rhyngwladol a chenedlaethol
Ffordd rhyngranbarthol a llai prysur
Ffordd ac wyneb iddi - heb wyneb
Llwybr troed - Llwybr troed ag arwyddion / Llwybr ceffyl
Traffordd - ffordd yn cael ei hadeiladu
(Os cyfodi yr achos: dyddiad agor disgwyliedig)

Ffyrdd
ffordd ddeuol
4 lôn - 2 lôn lydan
2 lôn - 2 lôn gul

Pellter
(cyfanswm a'r rhyng-bellter)
Tollffyrdd ar y draffordd
Rhan di-doll ar y draffordd
mewn miltiroedd - mewn kilometrau
ar y ffordd

Dosbarthiad ffyrdd swyddogol
Traffordd - GB : Prif ffordd
(Primary route)
IRL: Prif ffordd genedlaethol a ffordd eilradd
(National primary and secondary route)
Ffyrdd eraill
Cylchfan ar rwydwaith y prif ffyrdd

Rhwystrau
Cylchfan - Bwlch a'i uchder uwchlaw lefel y môr (mewn metrau)
Rhiw serth
(esgyn gyda'r saeth)
IRL: Darn anodd neu beryglus o ffordd
Yn yr Alban :
ffordd gul â mannau pasio
Croesfan rheilffordd: croesfan rheilffordd, o dan y ffordd, dros y ffordd
Ffordd waharddedig - Ffordd a chyfyngiadau arni
Rhwystr Toll - Unffordd
Terfyn uchder
(llai na 15'6" IRL, 16'6" GB)
Terfyn pwysau
(llai na 16t)

Cludiant
Lled safonol - Gorsaf deithwyr
Maes awyr - Maes glanio
Llongau ceir :
(Gwasanaethau tymhorol: mewn coch)
llong
Fferi (llwyth uchaf: mewn tunelli metrig)
Teithwyr ar droed neu feic yn unig

Lletly - Gweinyddiaeth
Ffiniau gweinyddol
Ffin Cymru, ffin yr Alban
Ffin ryngwladol - Tollau

Cyfleusterau Chwaraeon a Hamdden
Cwrs golff - Rasio Ceffylau
Rasio Cerbydau - Harbwr cychod pleser
Leoedd i wersylla
Llwybr troed ag arwyddion - Parc gwlad
Parc saffari, sw - Gwarchodfa natur
IRL: Pysgota - Maes rasio milgwn
Trên twristiaid
Rhaffordd, car cêbl, cadair esgyn

Golygfeydd
Gweler Llyfr Michelin
Trefi new fannau o ddiddordeb, mannau i aros
Adeilag eglwysig - Castell
Adfeilion - Heneb fegalithig - Ogof
Gerddi, parc - Mannau eraill o ddiddordeb
IRL: Caer - Cros Geltaidd - twr crwn
Panorama - Golygfan
Ffordd dygfeydd

Symbolau eraill
Lein gêbl ddiwydiannol
Mast telathrebu - Goleudy
Gorsaf bwer - Chwarel
Mwyngloddio - Gweithgarwch diwydiannol
Purfa - Clogwyn
Parc Coedwig Cenedlaethol - Parc Cenedlaethol

Comnarthaí ar phleanna bailte

Ionaid inspéise
Ionad inspéise agus
Ionad inspéise adhartha

Bóithre
Mótarbhealach, carrbhealach dúbailte le saintréithe mótar
Acomhail mótarbhealaigh : iomlán - teoranta
Priomh-thrébhealach
Sráid: coisithe
Carrchlós

Comhtharthaí Éagsúla
Aerfort
Leithead caighdeánach - Staisiún paisinéirí
Ionad eolais turasóireachta - Ospidéal
Gairdín, páirc, coill
Reilig
Staidiam
Galfchúrsa
Zú
Teach Solais
Stáisiún traenach faoi thalamh
Lánléargas
Príomhoifi g phoist le poste restante
Póitíní (ceanncheathrú)

Symbolau ar gynlluniau'r trefi

Golygfeydd
Man diddorol
Lle diddorol o addoliad

Ffyrdd
Traffordd, ffordd ddeuol
Cyfnewidfeyd : wedi'i chwblhau - cyfyngedig
Prif ffordd drwodd
Stryd: Cerddwr
Parc ceir

Arwyddion amrywiol
Maes awyr
Lled safonol - Gorsaf deithwyr
Canolfan croeso - Ysbyty
Gardd, parc, coedwig
Mynwent
Stadiwm
Cwrs golff
Sŵ
Goleudy
Gorsaf danddaearol
Panorama
Prif swyddfa bost gyda poste restante
Yr Heddlu (pencadlys)

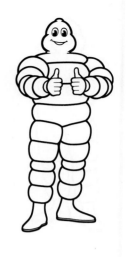

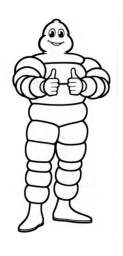